Why Do You Need This New Edition?

If you're wondering why you need to buy this new edition of *Perspectives on Personality*, here are 6 good reasons!

1. The text has been tightened and streamlined overall, resulting in a volume that is more manageable and more focused.
2. Two chapters were removed. In two other cases, pairs of chapters were integrated into one.
3. The "perspectives" organizational theme has been refocused and simplified, with more emphasis on the nature of thematic diversity among viewpoints.
4. Chapters 6 and 7 have both undergone major updates, reflecting the rapid advances in work on genetics, temperament, neurotransmitters, and other biological processes and how they relate to personality. New topics include the "new" behavioral genetics (genes correlating with and interacting with environments) and epigenetic influences on gene expression.
5. New content and reorganization in the chapters on the cognitive and self-regulation perspectives.
6. More than 200 new citations.

Perspectives on Personality

SEVENTH
EDITION

Perspectives on Personality

Charles S. Carver
University of Miami

Michael F. Scheier
Carnegie Mellon University

PEARSON

Boston • Columbus • Indianapolis • New York • San Francisco • Upper Saddle River
Amsterdam • Cape Town • Dubai • London • Madrid • Milan • Munich • Paris • Montreal • Toronto
Delhi • Mexico City • Sao Paulo • Sydney • Hong Kong • Seoul • Singapore • Taipei • Tokyo

Executive Acquisitions Editor: Susan Hartman
Editorial Assistant: Alexandra Mitton
Marketing Manager: Nicole Kunzmann
Marketing Assistant: Jessica Warren
Production Editor: Patrick Cash-Peterson
Manufacturing Buyer: Linda Cox
Art Director: Leslie Osher
Editorial Production and Composition Service: Element LLC
Cover Designer: Ilze Lemesis

Library of Congress Cataloging-in-Publication Data
Carver, Charles S.
  Perspectives on personality / Charles S. Carver, Michael F. Scheier. — 7th ed.
    p. cm.
  Includes bibliographical references and index.
  ISBN 978-0-205-15136-3
  1. Personality. I. Scheier, Michael F. II. Title.
  BF698.C22 2012
  155.2—dc22   2011014739

10 9 8 7 6 5 4 3 2 1 EB

ISBN-10: 0-205-15136-1
ISBN-13: 978-0-205-15136-3

To Youngmee Kim
CSC

To Karen Matthews
MFS

Brief Contents

Contents

Preface

PERSPECTIVES ON PERSONALITY, Seventh Edition, examines one of the most engaging topics in all of life: human personality. As the title of the book implies, there are many perspectives on personality, many ways to think about human nature. This book describes a range of viewpoints that are held by personality psychologists today.

WHAT'S THE SAME IN THIS EDITION?

As in earlier editions, the content of this book reflects two of our strongly held beliefs. The first is that *ideas* are the most important part of a first course on personality. For this reason, we stress concepts throughout the book. Our first priority has been to present as clearly as we can the ideas that form each theoretical viewpoint.

The second belief is that *research* is important in personality psychology. Ideas and intuitions are valuable, but an idea shouldn't lie around too long before someone checks to see whether it actually works. For this reason, each theory is accompanied by discussion of research that bears on the theory. This emphasis on the role of research stresses the fact that personality psychology is a living, dynamic process of ongoing scientific exploration.

As in previous editions, we focus on the idea that each viewpoint discussed in the book represents a *perspective* on personality. By that, we mean a particular orienting viewpoint, an angle from which the theorists proceeded. Each perspective reflects fundamental assumptions about human nature. As in previous editions, each perspective chapter includes discussion of personality assessment from that perspective and some discussion of how behavior problems can arise and be treated from that perspective. Each chapter concludes with a discussion of current problems within that theoretical viewpoint and our own guess about its future prospects.

The perspectives are presented in an order that makes sense to us, but the chapters can easily be read in other orders. Each theoretical section of the book is intended to stand more or less on its own. When one chapter is linked to a previous chapter, it is generally easy to see the point without having read the prior chapter. There are a few exceptions to this, however. We refer back to the trait perspective relatively often, so it's probably best to read that chapter (Chapter 4) early on. It also makes historical sense to place the psychoanalytic perspective before the psychosocial perspective, because the latter grew in part from the former.

As in the previous editions, the final chapter takes up the question of how the different viewpoints relate to each other. The main goal of this chapter is to tie together ideas from theories discussed separately in earlier chapters. A secondary goal is to consider the usefulness of blending theoretical viewpoints, treating theories as complementary, rather than competing.

In this revision, we've continued to try very hard to make the content accessible. We use an informal, conversational style to try to draw readers into the ideas. We've also used examples of how the ideas can apply to one's own life. We hope these qualities make the book engaging and enjoyable, as well as informative.

What's Different about This Edition?

This edition also incorporates several rather major changes.

In two cases, we combined material that previously formed pairs of chapters into a single chapter. This decision was made partly because these topics (the psychoanalytic perspective and the learning perspective) had received greater attention than other perspectives in previous editions, and we wanted to rebalance things.

Two other chapters were omitted from this edition (ego psychology and personal construct psychology), although the topics are the subjects of boxes in chapters that remain. These chapters were omitted because, frankly, contemporary personality psychology has left them behind. With all the activity that's taking place in other areas of the field, we felt it was no longer sensible to spend that much space on these subjects.

The result of these changes is a book that's tighter and far more streamlined than the previous edition. Even the chapters that resulted from compressing two into one are reasonable in length. Indeed, we made it a priority to keep this edition as lean as we could make it.

The sense of *perspective* on personality has also been refocused in this edition. Now, we focus more explicitly on the idea that any theoretical position provides a vantage point, not necessarily a complete explanation of personality. Each provides an orientation to human nature, a window on the human experience. And each substantive chapter provides a description of what can be seen (thus far) through that window.

As usual, all of the substantive chapters have received updates in this edition. (More than 200 new citations have been added.) Enhancements to existing topics include the "new" behavioral genetics (genes correlating with and interacting with environments) and epigenetic influences on gene expression. Despite adding a great deal of new information, we've also been able to shorten the book's longer chapters.

For more information on *Perspectives on Personality*, Seventh Edition, consult its webpage: www.abacon.com/carver.

Supplements

Pearson Education is pleased to offer the following supplements to qualified adopters.

Instructor's Manual and Test Bank (0205155863).   Prepared by Steve Graham, the instructor's manual is a wonderful tool for classroom preparation and management. Corresponding to the chapters in the text, each of the manual's 14 chapters contains a brief overview of the chapter with suggestions on how to present the material, sample lecture outlines, classroom activities and discussion topics, ideas for in-class and out-of-class projects, recommended outside readings and related films and videos.

The test bank contains over 1,400 multiple choice, short answer and essay questions, each referencing the relevant page in the text.

PowerPoint Presentation (0205155413).   Also prepared by Steve Graham, the PowerPoint Presentation is an exciting interactive tool for use in the classroom. Each chapter pairs key concepts with images from the textbook to reinforce student learning.

Pearson MyTest Computerized Test Bank (0205228542).   The Seventh Edition Test Bank comes with Pearson MyTest, a powerful assessment-generation program that helps instructors easily create and print quizzes and exams. You can do this online, allowing flexibility and the ability to efficiently manage assessments at any time. You can easily access existing questions and edit, create, and store questions using the simple drag-and-drop and Wordlike controls. Each question comes with information on its level of difficulty and related page number in the text. For more information, go to **www.PearsonMyTest.com**.

MySearchLab (0205699421)
MySearchLab is the easiest way to master a writing or research project. Features include round-the-clock access to reliable content for Internet research from a variety of databases, Pearson SourceCheck™, and Autocite. Learning resources such as step-by-step tutorials and an exclusive online grammar and usage handbook guide students through the research and writing process. **www.pearsonhighered.com**

Acknowledgments

W E WISH TO ACKNOWLEDGE SEVERAL people who have been helpful and important to us, in one way or another over the past several years. First, our thanks to Brent Roberts and Oliver Schultheiss for the suggestions they offered for improvements from the sixth edition to the seventh. Second, our thanks, yet again, to those who mentored us in various ways many years ago (alphabetically): Mark Bickhard, Arnie Buss, Kenneth Craik, David Glass, Lew Goldberg, Al Riley, and Bob Wicklund. We owe them a great debt of gratitude.

We would also like to thank the reviewers: Michelle Anderson, Loyola Marymount University; Joelle LeMoult, University of Miami; Chris Logan, Southern Methodist University; Matthew Scullin, University of Texas at El Paso; Frances Shen, University of Illinois Springfield; and Jefferson Singer, Connecticut College.

Each of us also would like to make individual acknowledgments:

• From Coral Gables, my thanks to those who have been part of my life during the past four years, particularly Youngmee Kim, Linda Cahan, Sheri Johnson, Jutta Joormann, André Perwin, Rod Gillis, Mike Antoni, Jean-Philippe Laurenceau, and Rod Wellens. I am unceasingly grateful to my family: Jeff, Allysen, Alexandra, and Julia; Nancy Lorey; all the Sherricks; and Mike, Karen, Meredith, and Jeremy. My thanks to Nancy Quartin, who worked very hard to help bring this revision to fruition. Finally, a sad note: My shag terrier Calvin, who had been with me for 15 years (www.psy.miami.edu/faculty/ccarver/CCdog.html), crossed over the Rainbow Bridge in August 2010 and is now chasing birds in doggie heaven. We miss him.

• From Pittsburgh, thanks go to Karen Matthews, my partner in life, and to our two children, Jeremy and Meredith. Thanks also to the following group of friends and colleagues: Chuck Carver, Sheldon Cohen, Ed Gerrard, David Klahr, Ken Kotovsky, Rich Schulz, and Jim Staszewski. Collectively, they make my life more than interesting. I'd also like to express my gratitude to Ginger Placone, my administrative assistant, for her help in keeping my professional life organized (better than anyone else might) and me on task. Finally, I'd like to thank Jamie Armstrong for her help with some of the literature reviews for the revised edition.

About the Authors

Charles S. Carver and Michael F. Scheier met in graduate school at the University of Texas at Austin, where they both earned doctoral degrees in personality psychology. After graduation, they took jobs at the University of Miami and Carnegie Mellon University, respectively, where they have remained throughout their careers. They've collaborated for over three and a half decades in work that spans personality, social, motivational, clinical, and health psychology. In 1998, they received awards for Outstanding Scientific Contribution (Senior Level) from the Division of Health Psychology of the American Psychological Association. In 2007, they received the Donald T. Campbell Award for Distinguished Contributions to Social Psychology from APA's Division of Personality and Social Psychology. Mike was the 2003–2004 President of APA's Division of Health Psychology and currently serves as Department Head at CMU. Along with seven editions of *Perspectives on Personality*, the authors have published two books on self-regulation (the more recent titled *On the Self-Regulation of Behavior*, in 1998) and more than 320 articles and chapters. Mike is an avid outdoorsman, hunter, and fisherman. Chuck keeps intending to take up painting but getting distracted by things that need fixing.

www.psy.miami.edu/faculty/ccarver
www.psy.cmu.edu/~scheier/mscheier/html

Perspectives on Personality

What Is Personality Psychology?

Sue met Rick in a philosophy class when both were sophomores. They started to go out, and their relationship gradually deepened. Now, two years later, they're talking seriously of marriage. Sue describes Rick this way: "He's good looking and smart. He knows how to do lots of things you don't expect a guy to know, like cooking. But the best part, I don't even know how to describe, except to say he has a really great personality."

Personality produces consistencies in behavior across different contexts. Although this woman finds herself in different situations, her warm and caring nature comes through in all of them.

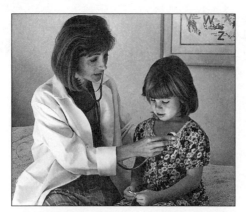

Every now and then, someone surveys the qualities people value in a potential husband or wife. Most people want to see a sense of humor, good looks, and a streak of romance. Almost always, though, a high priority is placed on the person's personality. Most people want someone who has a "good personality." What does that mean? If you were to describe a friend of yours who *does* have a good personality, what would you say? "Rick has a really wonderful personality . . ." But then what?

Describing someone's personality means trying to portray the essence of who that person is. It means crystallizing something from the things you know about the person. It means taking a large pile of information and reducing it to a smaller set of qualities. Personality is reflected in what people say and do and also in *how* they do what they do—the style that puts a unique stamp on their actions.

Defining Personality

Trying to describe someone's personality is an exercise in being a psychologist. We all play the role of psychologist part of the time, because we all spend part of our lives trying to understand what other people are like. When you think about how to describe someone and what reveals those qualities to you, you're doing informally what personality psychologists do more formally.

There's a little difference in focus between what you do in daily life and what personality psychologists do. Use of the word *personality* in everyday speech tends to focus on the specific personalities of specific persons (Rick, for instance). Psychologists are more likely to focus on personality as an abstraction. When psychologists use the word *personality*, they usually are referring to a conception of what everyone's personality consists of.

What *is* personality, viewed that way? Psychologists have argued for a long time about exactly how to define personality. Many definitions have been offered, but none is universally accepted. Personality is, in fact, something of an elusive concept.

WHY USE PERSONALITY AS A CONCEPT?

In trying to define personality as a concept, we might start by thinking about why the word is used. Understanding why it's used should help us decide what it means. When *you* use the word *personality,* why do you use it? Why that word instead of another one?

One reason people use the word *personality* is to convey a sense of *consistency* or *continuity* about a person. There are several kinds of consistency. All of them evoke the concept of personality. There is consistency across time (talked a lot when you first met her, and years later, she still dominates conversations). There is consistency across similar situations (André is very polite to waiters in restaurants and has been that way every time you've had dinner with him). You sometimes even see consistency across situations that are quite different from each other (Victoria tends to order people around—in stores, at work, even at *parties*). In each of these cases, there's the sense that it's undeniably the same person from one instance to another, because the person acts (or talks, or thinks, or feels) in consistent ways from time to time and from setting to setting. One reason for using the word *personality* is to capture this consistency or continuity within the person.

A second reason people use the word *personality* is to convey the sense that whatever the person is doing (or thinking or feeling) *originates from within.* The idea that behavior comes from inside the person may seem so obvious that it hardly deserves mention, but not everyone sees it that way. Nonetheless, the term *personality* conveys the sense of a causal force *within* the person, influencing how the person acts. There is, in fact, good reason to assert that personality has very important behavioral consequences (Ozer & Benet-Martínez, 2006; Roberts, Kuncel, Shiner, Caspi, & Goldberg, 2007).

These two reasons for using the term *personality* combine when you try to predict and understand people's behavior (even your own). It can be important to predict behavior. When you choose a roommate for next year, you're predicting that you'll get along well. When you tell a chronically tardy friend that the movie starts at 8:00, but it really starts at 8:30, you're predicting that this will get her to arrive more or less on time. An important contributor to these predictions is your view of the other person's personality.

The term *personality* is also used for another reason. It often conveys the sense that a few qualities can summarize what a person is like, because they're so prominent in that person's behavior. Saying that Karen has a sociable personality implies that sociability stands out in her actions. Saying that Tanya has a hostile personality implies that hostility is a key quality in her. Taking note of the most prominent characteristics of a person brings

Individual differences in behavior and reactions are an important part of personality.

to mind the concept of personality, because those characteristics seem to capture what the person is like.

This patchwork of reasons for using the term *personality* moves us closer to defining it. That is, the word *personality* conveys a sense of consistency, internal causality, and distinctiveness. As it happens, these elements are included in almost all definitions of personality.

A Working Definition

Here's one definition. We're not saying it's the "right" one, but we think it comes close. We've adapted it slightly from one written decades ago by Gordon Allport (1961): ***Personality** is a dynamic organization, inside the person, of psychophysical systems that create the person's characteristic patterns of behavior, thoughts, and feelings.*

This definition makes several points:

- Personality isn't just an accumulation of bits and pieces; it has *organization*.
- Personality doesn't just lie there; it has *processes* of some sort.
- Personality is a *psychological* concept, but it's inextricably tied to the *physical* body.
- Personality is a *causal force* that helps determine how the person relates to the world.
- Personality shows up in individualized *patterns*—recurrences and consistencies.
- Personality is displayed not just one way but *many ways*—in behaviors, thoughts, and feelings.

This definition covers a lot. It points to several elements that should be part of any conceptualization of personality. As good as it is, though, it isn't perfect. Even this careful definition seems to let something about the concept slip through your fingers. This elusiveness is something that personality psychologists have struggled with for many years.

Two Fundamental Themes in Personality Psychology

Two themes stand out in thinking about personality. One is the existence of **individual differences.** Each person who ever lived is different from everyone else. No two personalities are quite alike—not even those of identical twins. Some people are generally happy, some are sad. Some people are sociable, some are shy. As we said earlier, one reason to use the word *personality* in the first place is to capture central features of a person. This couldn't happen if the features didn't differ from one person to another. Thus, the notion of individual differences is key to everyday use of the term *personality*.

Individual differences are also important to theorists who try to understand personality. To be useful, any approach to personality has to have something to say about these differences. A really complete account of personality should address where the differences come from. A complete account should also consider why the differences matter.

The other theme concerns what we'll call **intrapersonal functioning**. By this phrase, we mean the processes within the person that Allport (1961) called a "dynamic organization" of systems. The idea here is that personality isn't like a rubber stamp that you pound onto each situation you enter. Instead, there are processes that go on inside you, leading you to act the way you do. The processes create a sense of continuity within the person, even if the person acts differently in different circumstances. That is, the same processes are engaged, even if the results differ across situations.

Here's an example. Some theorists believe that behavior is a product of motives. Motive tendencies rise and fall as time passes and situations change. Which motive is strongest at any given time determines what the person does at that time. A person may work in isolation for four hours, then spend a couple of hours socializing, then go eat dinner, and then do some reading. The behaviors differ, but they all stem from motives within the person that vary in strength over the course of the day. This view of personality treats the motives as key variables. The processes by which motives vary in strength are some of the processes of intrapersonal functioning, in this view.

This is just one example of an intrapersonal process. It's not the only kind of process that has been argued for. Regardless of what processes are assumed, though, the idea of *process* is important. A complete account of personality should say something about processes underlying personality and how and why they work.

Various approaches to personality emphasize these two themes to varying degrees. Some approaches emphasize process and consist largely of a view of intrapersonal functioning. Other approaches treat individual uniqueness as the most important aspect of personality and are more vague about the processes underlying the uniqueness. These differing emphases contribute to the diversity among personality theories.

Why spend so many words on what personality psychology is about? We've put you in the role of a theorist here. Theorists have to keep in mind what aspects of human experience they want to understand. To understand the theories, you'll have to do that too.

Theory in Personality Psychology

Much of this book is a series of statements of theoretical principles. Because theories are so important, let's spend a little time on what they are, what they do, and how to evaluate them.

WHAT DO THEORIES DO?

What *is* a theory? A **theory** is a summary statement, a general principle or set of principles about a class of events. Put differently, a theory is a set of ideas about how to think about that class of events. A theory can apply to a very specific class of events, or it can be broader. Some theories in psychology are about processes in a single nerve cell. Others concern complex behaviors, such as maintaining close relationships, playing chess, and living a full life.

Theories are used for two purposes (no matter what they are about). The first purpose is to *explain* the phenomena it addresses. A theory always provides a way to explain some things that are known to be true. For example, some biological personality theories hold that heredity influences personality. This idea provides a way to explain why children act like their parents in certain ways (things we know to be true).

Every theory about personality provides an account of at least some phenomena. This first purpose of the theory—explanation—is fundamental. Without giving an explanation for at least some of what's already known, a theory would be useless.

Theories also have a second purpose, though. A theory should suggest possibilities you don't yet know for sure are true. Put differently, a theory should allow you to *predict new information*. A theory of personality should let you predict things you haven't thought to look for yet—maybe things *nobody* has thought to look for yet. For the psychologist, this is where much of the excitement lies.

Psychologists generally want to make predictions about large numbers of people, but the same principle holds when you make predictions in your own life. It's exciting to take an idea about personality and use it to predict how your roommate will react to a situation you haven't seen her in before. It's particularly exciting when your prediction turns out to be right!

The predictive aspect of theories is more subtle and more difficult than the explanatory aspect. The difficulty lies partly in the fact that most theories have a little ambiguity. This often makes it unclear exactly what the prediction should be. In fact, the broader the theory (the more things it has to account for), the more likely it will be ambiguous. As you've seen, personality is a very broad concept. This forces theories of personality to be broad and complex. As a result, it's sometimes hard to use them to make very specific predictions.

EVALUATING THEORIES: THE ROLE OF RESEARCH

How do psychologists decide whether a theory is any good? In describing the predictive function of theories, we've revealed a bias held by most of today's personality psychologists: Theories should be *testable*, and they should be *tested*. It's important to find out whether a theory makes predictions that receive support.

We want to be quite clear about what we're saying here. Personality is so important in life that lots of people besides psychologists think about it. Theologians, philosophers, artists, poets, novelists, and songwriters have all written about personality, and many of them have had good insights about it. We don't mean to diminish the value of these insights. But are they enough?

People have different opinions on this question. Some believe that insight stands on its own. Even some personality theorists believed this. Sigmund Freud, who's often viewed as the father of personality psychology, wasn't much interested in whether his ideas were supported in research by others. He saw the insights as sufficient in themselves.

The view that dominates today's psychology, however, is that ideas—even brilliant ideas—have to be tested before they can be trusted. Too often, things that *seem* true turn out not to be true after all. Unfortunately, until you test them, you never know which ideas are brilliant and right and which are brilliant but wrong. Because of this, today's personality psychology is a scientific field, in which research counts for a lot. Studies of personality provide information about how accurate or useful a theory is. The studies either confirm or disconfirm predictions and thereby support or undermine the theory.

When theories are used to generate predictions for research, a continuous interplay arises (see Figure 1.1). If a theory makes predictions, the result is research—scientific studies—to test the predictions. Results often support the predictions. Sometimes, however, the result either fails to support the theory or supports it only partly. This may suggest a limit on the theory—perhaps it predicts under some conditions but not others. Such a finding leads to revision of the theory.

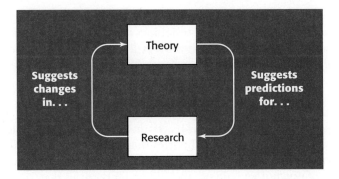

FIGURE 1.1

In a scientific approach to personality psychology, there is a continuous cycling between theory and research. Theory suggests predictions to be tested, and the results of studies suggest the need for new or modified theory.

Once it's been revised, the theory must be tested again, because it's no longer quite the same theory as before. Its new elements must be examined for other predictions they might make. The cycle of prediction, testing, revision or refinement, and additional prediction and testing can be virtually never ending.

WHAT ELSE MAKES A THEORY GOOD?

An important basis for deciding whether a theory is good is whether it does what a theory's supposed to do: explain and predict. But that's not the only way people evaluate theories. There are several more criteria for why one theory may be preferable to another.

One criterion is the breadth of the information behind the theory. Some theories are criticized because they're based heavily on the theorists' experience conducting therapy. Other theories are criticized because they're based on studies of laboratory animals in highly artificial situations. Others are criticized because they rest largely on information from long sets of rating scales. None of these sources of information is bad in itself. But to base a theory on just one source of information weakens the theory.

A theory should also have the quality of **parsimony**. That is, it should include as few assumptions (or concepts) as possible. Put differently, it should be as simple as possible. This

Like a good work of art, a good theory should evoke some sort of reaction, either good or bad, but not indifferent.

criterion is important, but there's a danger in applying it too rigidly. Knowledge is far from complete. A theory that looks parsimonious today may not be able to account for something that will be discovered tomorrow. A theory that looks too complex today may be the *only* one that can handle tomorrow's discovery. Nevertheless, excess theoretical "baggage" is a cause for concern.

Another basis for evaluating theories is highly subjective. Some theories just "feel" better than others. Some theories will fit your personal worldview better than others. You're not the only one who reacts this way. So do psychologists. There's even evidence that scientists prefer theories that fit their images of *themselves* (J. A. Johnson, Germer, Efran, & Overton, 1988). William James, an important figure in the early years of psychology, said people will prefer theories that "are most interesting, . . . appeal most urgently to our æsthetic, emotional, and active needs" (James, 1890, p. 312). Which theories feel best to you, then, depends partly on how you see the world.

Perspectives on Personality

Next, let's preview the views of personality you will be reading about. The chapters all describe viewpoints that are influential today and will likely continue to be influential for some time to come. The theories range considerably in their starting points, which can make matters a little confusing. The starting point, in some sense, is always a view of human nature—of what aspect of human experience is the key to understanding people.

In explaining why someone did something, people often say "It's just human nature." But what *is* human nature? *In what terms* should we think about people? Different theorists have provided very different answers.

PERSPECTIVES TO BE EXAMINED HERE

Each theoretical orientation discussed in this book has a somewhat different angle on human nature. Thus, each represents a different *perspective* on what are the central elements of the human experience. Here are brief overviews of the perspectives you'll be reading about.

The *trait perspective* begins with the intuitive idea that people have fairly stable qualities (traits) that are displayed across many settings but are deeply embedded in the person. This way of thinking about personality originated in ancient times, but it remains very important today. From this point of view, the big issues are what (and how many) traits are the important ones in personality and how trait differences are expressed in behavior.

The *motive perspective* begins with the idea that the key element in human experience is the motive forces that underlie behavior. Theorists have posited many different motives and have examined how some of them wax and wane under different circumstances. People also differ in their patterns of underlying strengths of different motives. These differences in the balance of motives are seen as the core of personality from this perspective.

The *inheritance and evolution perspective* emphasizes the fact that humans are creatures that evolved across millennia and that human nature (whatever it is) is deeply rooted in our genes. In this view, personality is genetically based. Dispositions are inherited. Indeed, some theorists take this idea a step further to suggest that many qualities of human behavior (and thus personality) exist precisely because long ago they had evolutionary benefits.

Another biological view, the *biological process perspective,* stems from the idea that personality reflects the workings of the body we inhabit and the brain that runs the body. This biological perspective focuses on how the nervous system and hormones influence people's behavior and how differences in those functions influence the kind of person you are.

The *psychoanalytic perspective*, taken up next, takes a very different view of human nature. It's based on the idea that personality is a set of internal forces that compete and conflict with one another. The focus of this perspective is on the dynamics of these forces (and the way they influence behavior). Human nature, from this viewpoint, involves a set of pressures inside the person that sometimes work with each other and sometimes are at war with each other. One specific theory dominates the perspective—the theory of Sigmund Freud.

We've termed the next perspective *psychosocial.* The theories in this perspective start from the assumption that the most important aspect of human nature is our formation of relationships with other people and the ways in which these relationships play out. The psychosocial theories have historical links to psychoanalytic theory (they sometimes are called *neoanalytic*), but they really represent a very different worldview.

The *social learning perspective* begins with a view of human nature in which change, rather than constancy, is paramount. That is, from this perspective, the key quality of human nature is that behavior changes systematically as a result of experiences. Because there are several views of how learning takes place, several theories link learning to personality. This perspective assumes that a person's personality is the integrated sum of what the person has learned up till now.

The *self-actualization and self-determination perspective,* also sometimes referred to as an *organismic perspective*, has its roots in the idea that every person has the potential to grow and develop into a valuable human being if permitted to do so. In this view, people naturally tend toward self-perfection. People can move themselves more fully in that direction by exercising their free will to do so and by having environments that support that effort. The sense of self-determination is central to this view of human nature. Personality, in this view, is partly a matter of the uniqueness hidden within and partly a matter of what the person chooses to make of that uniqueness.

The *cognitive perspective* takes as its starting point the idea that human nature involves deriving meaning from experiences. The mind imposes organization and form on experience, and those mental organizations influence how people act. An understanding of personality from this viewpoint means thinking about those processes of construing the world and how they are used to determine one's actions in and reactions to the surrounding world.

The *self-regulation perspective* starts from the idea that people are complex psychological systems, in the same sense that homeostatic processes reflect complex physiological systems and weather reflects complex atmospheric systems. There are recurrent processes that form organized actions that attain specific endpoints. Thus, there is an assumption of organization, coherence, and patterning. Self-regulating psychologically means (in part) synthesizing goals and moving toward those goals.

PERSPECTIVES RECONSIDERED

As we said, each perspective takes a different starting point to think about personality. We should also say one more thing about them: Most of them weren't really intended to be full models of personality, and it can be a little misleading to present them (and judge them) as though they were.

There was a time when personality psychologists created grand theories aimed at the total complexity of personality (Freud's theory is the best example). However, this is less common now. More common are theories that deal with some *aspect* of personality or some set of issues in personality. The fact that a theory isn't grand in scale doesn't mean it has nothing important to say about personality. It does mean, though, that it won't say *everything* about personality. It gives us a particular viewing angle on personality. This viewing angle may be special and may yield insights you can't find from other angles. But it yields only part of the picture. This limitation is important to keep in mind as you think about the various theories and what each has to say.

Will personality return in the future to grand-scale theories? Several contemporary personality psychologists hope so (e.g., McAdams & Olson, 2010; McAdams & Pals, 2006; Roberts & Wood, 2006). They argue that a full understanding of personality requires much more than is generally addressed by "perspective" theories. This movement is partly a reaction to the concern that personality psychology has lost its focus on individuality.

What should be included in the full picture, though, is a matter of opinion (see Table 1.1). Most who write on this topic say the genetic design of the human should be included, along with traits. Some include motives, values, abilities, and skills as part of personality. Some include adaptations to the world, such as beliefs and attitudes. Most now include integrative narratives—stories that people develop about themselves to provide coherence and meaning to their self-understanding. In some accounts, culture is part of the personality picture; in others, it is seen as a force outside personality that can affect personality.

It's very hard to present a picture of personality that incorporates all of these topics at once. In some respects, the emerging broader accounts actually aren't really grand-scale theories but a putting-together of several perspective views. We'll touch on most of the ideas that go into these broader accounts at one point or another, but we'll do so one perspective at a time.

Table 1.1 Topics that some now argue should be included for a full understanding of personality

Topic	Level of Consensus
Genetic design of the human	High
Dispositional traits	High
Motives and values	Moderate
Abilities (skills)	Moderate
Adaptations (e.g., beliefs)	Moderate
Integrative narratives	High
Culture	Low

Source: Based on discussions by McAdams and Pals (2006), McCrae (2010), and Roberts and Wood (2006).

Organization within Chapters

We should also say a little bit about how chapters are organized. Most of the content of each perspective chapter is a description of the basic elements and processes of personality, as viewed from that perspective. Each chapter thus tells you about individual differences and intrapersonal functioning, as seen by that theoretical viewpoint.

Each chapter also addresses two more subjects. One is the process of measuring personality, called *assessment*. The other is the potential for problems to arise in human experience, and the processes by which behavior is changed for the better through therapy. Here's a brief preview of what these sections will be like.

ASSESSMENT

Personality psychologists give considerable attention to the process of measuring personality, for at least three reasons. First, they want to be able to portray the personalities of specific persons, just as you characterize the personalities of people you know. To be confident these pictures are accurate, psychologists need good ways to measure personality.

A second reason concerns the research enterprise. To study qualities of personality, psychologists have to measure those qualities. Without ways to assess individual differences or intrapersonal functioning, it's impossible to study them. Good assessment, then, lies at the heart of personality research.

A third reason to measure personality strays a bit from the main focus of this book. Assessing people's personality is an important part of applied psychology. For example, organizational psychologists use personality to help make hiring decisions (e.g., you might want to hire someone with a desired pattern of motives). Clinical psychologists also use personality assessment to help diagnose problems.

Assessment is important throughout personality psychology. Some issues in assessment are the same for all viewpoints (these are addressed in Chapter 3), but aspects of assessment are viewed somewhat differently from different perspectives. As a result, perspectives often differ in the techniques they emphasize. In discussing assessment in each later chapter, we focus on how assessment from that viewpoint has its own special character.

Personality does not always function smoothly. Each perspective on personality has its own view about why problems occur.

PROBLEMS IN BEHAVIOR, AND BEHAVIOR CHANGE

The other topic included in each theory chapter concerns the fact that people's lives don't always go smoothly. Each view of normal personality also suggests a way to think about problems. Indeed, it can be argued that a theory of personality gains credibility from saying useful things about problems. To clarify how each approach to personality views problems, we briefly take up this issue in each chapter from that chapter's viewpoint. As with assessment, our emphasis is on that theoretical orientation's special contribution to thinking about problems.

Finally, we describe how the theoretical orientation under discussion contributes to understanding therapeutic management of problems. If each view has a way of thinking about normal processes and about how things can go wrong, each view also has a way to think about how to make things better. Each suggests ways to turn problematic functioning back into effective and satisfying functioning.

· SUMMARY ·

Personality is a hard concept to define. Thinking about how people use the concept, however, suggests three reasons for its use. People use it to convey a sense of consistency or continuity within a person, to convey the sense that the person is the origin of behavior, and to convey the sense that the essence of a person can be summarized or captured in a few salient qualities.

The field of personality addresses two fundamental themes. One is the existence of differences among people. The other is how best to conceptualize intrapersonal functioning—the processes that take place within all persons, giving form and continuity to behavior.

Much of this book deals with theories. Theories are summary statements, sets of principles that pertain to certain classes of events. Theories have two purposes: to explain things that are known and to predict possibilities that haven't yet been examined. One way to evaluate the worth of a theory is to ask whether research supports its predictions. Scientific psychology has a continuing cycle between theory and research, as theories are tested, modified on the basis of results, and tested again.

Theories can be evaluated on grounds other than research. For example, a theory shouldn't be based on a single kind of information. Theories benefit from being parsimonious—having relatively few assumptions (or concepts). People also tend to favor theories that fit well with their intuitions.

The theories described in this book derive from several perspectives, or viewpoints, on human nature. Each theory chapter focuses on assumptions about the nature of personality within a particular theoretical framework. Also included are a discussion of assessment from the viewpoint of the theory under discussion, and a discussion of problems in behavior and how they can be remedied.

· GLOSSARY ·

Individual differences   Differences in personality from one person to another.

Intrapersonal functioning   Psychological processes that take place within the person.

Parsimony   The quality of requiring few assumptions; simplicity.

Personality   A dynamic organization, inside the person, of psychophysical systems that create the person's characteristic patterns of behavior, thoughts, and feelings.

Theory   A summary statement, a principle or set of principles about a class of events.

Methods in the Study of Personality

Sam and Dave are taking a break from studying. Sam says, "My roommate's girl at home broke up with him. Chicks here better watch out, 'cause he's gonna be looking for some serious partying to help forget her."

"What makes you think so?"

"What kind of question is that? It's obvious. That's what *I'd* do."

"Huh. I know guys whose hometown girls dumped them, and *none* of them did that. It was exactly the opposite. They laid around moping. I think you're wrong about how people react to this kind of thing."

W HEN PEOPLE try to understand personality, where do they start? Where do theories come from? How are they tested? How do psychologists decide what to believe? These are all questions about the methods of science. They can be asked in all areas of science, from astronomy to zoology. They are particularly challenging, though, when applied to personality.

Gathering Information

SOURCES: OBSERVE YOURSELF AND OBSERVE OTHERS

One way to gather information about personality is to look to your own experience—a process called *introspection*. This technique (used by Sam in the opening example) is open to everyone. Try it. You have a personality. If you want to understand personality, take a look at yours. Sit back and think about events in your life. Think about what you did and how you felt, and pull from those recollections a thread of continuity. From this might come the start of a theory—a set of principles to explain your thoughts, feelings, and actions.

Examining your own experience is an easy beginning, but it has a problem. Specifically, your own consciousness has a special relationship to your memories because they're yours. It's hard to be sure this special relationship doesn't distort what you're seeing. For instance, you can misrecall something you experienced, yet feel sure your memory is correct.

This problem lessens when you look at someone else instead of yourself (Dave in the opening example). That's the second method of gathering information: observe someone else. This method also has a problem, though—the opposite of introspection's problem. Specifically, it's impossible to be "inside another person's head," to really know what that person is thinking and feeling. This difference in perspective can create vast differences in understanding. It can lead to misinterpretation.

Which starting point is better? Each has a place in the search for truth. Neither is perfect, but they sometimes can be used to complement one another.

SEEKING DEPTH: CASE STUDIES

These starting points lead in several directions. Personality psychologists sometimes seek explicitly to understand an entire person at once, rather than just part of the person. Henry Murray (1938), who emphasized the need to study the person as a coherent entity, coined the term **personology** to refer to that effort.

This view promotes a technique called the **case study**. A case study is in-depth study of one person. It usually entails a long period of observation and typically includes unstructured interviews. Sometimes, it involves spending a day or two being around the person to see how he or she interacts with others. Repeated observations let the observer confirm initial impressions or correct wrong impressions. Confirming or disconfirming an impression doesn't happen if you make only one observation. The depth of probing that's possible in a case study can reveal detail that otherwise wouldn't be apparent. This, in turn, can yield insights.

Case studies are rich in detail and can create vivid descriptions of the people under study. Particularly compelling incidents or examples may illustrate broader themes in the person's life. Because case studies examine the person in his or her life situation instead of settings created by the researcher, the information pertains to normal life. Because they're open ended, the observer can follow whatever leads seem interesting, not just ask questions chosen ahead of time.

DEPTH FROM EXPERIENCE SAMPLING

Another kind of depth is provided by what are called **experience sampling** studies, or diary studies (Kamarck, Shiffman, & Wethington, 2011; Laurenceau & Bolger, 2005). These studies are also conducted across extended periods of time, like case studies. Instead of using an external observer, though, this procedure involves repeatedly prompting the person under study to stop and report on some aspect of his or her current experience. The prompt often is in the form of a signal from a pager. Sometimes these studies are very intensive, with reports made several times a day. Sometimes they are less intensive (e.g., morning and evening).

An important advantage of experience sampling methods is that they don't require the person to think back very far in time (maybe a half-day, maybe only an hour or so, maybe not at all). This allows less opportunity for distortion in recalling what the experiences actually were. Unfortunately, there is evidence that people don't do a very good job of remembering details of an event many hours later (Kamarck, Muldoon, Shiffman, & Sutton-Tyrrell, 2007; Stone, Kennedy-Moore, & Neale, 1995). Experience sampling methods let you get the events more "on line" than do other methods.

Experience sampling studies share with case studies the fact that a lot of information is obtained about each person being studied. In both cases, it's possible to search within this information for patterns of behavior within a given person across many situations. This is referred to an **idiographic** method (Conner, Tennen, Fleeson, & Barrett, 2009; Molenaar & Campbell, 2009), because the focus is on the individual. (The word *idiographic* has the same source as *idiosyncratic*.)

SEEKING GENERALITY: STUDIES OF MANY PEOPLE

Case studies can provide insights into the human experience. They provide useful information for researchers and often serve as an important source of ideas. But single case studies aren't the main source of information about personality today. In large part, this is because a case study, no matter how good, is deficient in an important way: It deals with just one person. When you're forming theories or drawing conclusions from observations, you want them to apply to many people—if possible, to *all* people.

How widely a conclusion can be applied is called its **generality** or its **generalizability.** For a conclusion to be generalizable, it must be based on many people, not one or two. The more people examined, the more convinced you can

The generality of a conclusion can be established only by studying a mix of people from different backgrounds.

be that what you see is true of people in general, instead of only a few people. In most research on personality, researchers look at tens—even hundreds—of people to increase the generality of their conclusions.

To truly ensure generality, researchers should study people of many ages and from all walks of life—indeed, from all cultures. For various reasons, this isn't always done, though it is becoming more common. As a matter of convenience, a lot of research on personality examines college students. Do college students provide a good picture of processes that are important in personality? Maybe yes, maybe no. College students differ from older people in several ways. For one, they have a less fully formulated sense of self. This may affect the research findings. How different college students are from everyone else is unclear. It does seem clear, though, that we should be cautious in assuming that conclusions drawn from research on college students always apply to "people in general."

Similarly, most observations on personality come from research done in the United States and western Europe. Most of the research has been done with middle- to upper-middle-class people. Some of it has used only one sex. We must be cautious in assuming that conclusions apply to people from other cultures, other socioeconomic groups, and (sometimes) both sexes.

Generalizability, then, is a kind of continuum. Rarely does any study range broadly enough to ensure total generalizability. Some are better than others. How broadly a conclusion can be generalized is an issue that must always be kept in mind in evaluating research results.

The desire for generality and the desire for in-depth understanding of a person are competing pressures. They force a trade-off. That is, given the same investment of time and energy, you can know a great deal about the life of one person (or a very few people), or you can know a little bit about the lives of a much larger number of people. It's nearly impossible to do both at once. As a result, researchers tend to choose one path or the other, according to which pressure they find more important.

Establishing Relationships among Variables

Insights from introspection or observation can suggest relationships between variables. A **variable** is a dimension along which variations exist. There must be at least two values or levels on that dimension, though some variables have an infinite number of values. For example, *sex* is a variable with values of *male* and *female*. *Self-esteem* is a variable that has a virtually limitless number of values (from *very low* to *very high*) as you make finer discriminations among people.

It's important to distinguish between a variable and its values, because conclusions about relationships involve the whole dimension, not just one end of it. Thus, researchers always study at least two levels of the variable they're interested in. For example, you can't understand the effects of low self-esteem by looking only at people with low self-esteem. If there's a relationship between self-esteem and academic performance, for example, the only way to find that out is to look at people with *different levels* of self-esteem (see Figure 2.1). If there is a relationship, people with low self-esteem should have poor grades and people with higher self-esteem should have better grades.

The last part of that statement is every bit as important as the first part. Knowing that people low in self-esteem have poor grades tells you nothing if people high

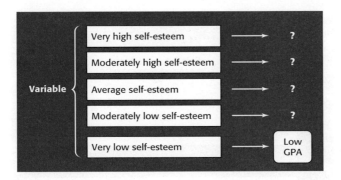

FIGURE 2.1
Whether a relationship exists between variables can be determined only by looking at more than one value on each variable. For instance, knowing that people low in self-esteem have poor academic performances leaves open the question of whether everyone else's performances are just as poor. This question is critically important in establishing a relationship between the two variables.

in self-esteem also have poor grades. It can be hard to keep this in mind. In fact, people often fail to realize how important this issue is. If you don't keep it in mind, though, you can draw seriously wrong conclusions (for illustrations, see Chapman, 1967; Crocker, 1981).

The need to examine people who represent a range of levels of a given variable is a second reason why it's important to go beyond case studies. (The issue of generality was the first one.) The need to examine a range of variability underlies several research methods.

CORRELATION BETWEEN VARIABLES

Two kinds of relationship can be established between variables. The first is called **correlation.** A correlation between two variables means that as you examine the variables across many people or instances, the values on the two tend to go together in a systematic way. There are two aspects of this relationship, which are separate from each other. They are the *direction* of the correlation and the *strength* of the correlation. To clarify what these terms mean, let's return to the example of self-esteem and academic performance.

A correlation between two variables means they covary in some systematic way. Here, there is a correlation between height and place in line.

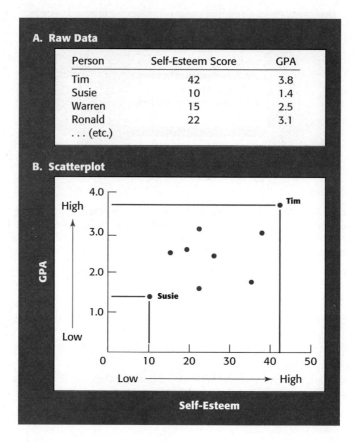

FIGURE 2.2
Thinking about the meaning of correlation (with hypothetical data): (A) For each person (subject), there are two pieces of information: a self-esteem score and a grade-point average (GPA). (B) The data can be arranged to form a scatterplot by plotting each person's self-esteem score along the horizontal dimension and his or her GPA along the vertical dimension, thereby locating the combination in a two-dimensional space.

Suppose you've decided to study whether these two variables go together. You've gone out and found 40 students. They've completed a measure of self-esteem and given you their current grade point average (GPA). You now have two pieces of information for each person (see Figure 2.2, A). One way to organize this information is called a *scatterplot* (see Figure 2.2, B). In a scatterplot, the variables are represented by lines at right angles (the axes of the graph). The point where the lines meet is zero for both variables. Being farther away from zero on each line means having a larger value on that variable. Because the lines are at right angles, the combination of any score on one variable and any score on the other variable can be portrayed as a point in two-dimensional space. For example, in Figure 2.2, Tim has a self-esteem score of 42 (and is toward the right side on the horizontal line) and a GPA of 3.8 (and is toward the top on the vertical line). The scatterplot for your study would be the points that represent the combinations of self-esteem scores and GPAs for all the people in the study.

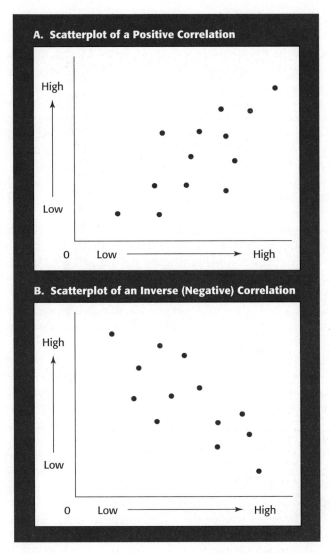

FIGURE 2.3
(A) If high numbers on one dimension tend to go with high numbers on the other dimension (and low with low), there is a positive correlation. (B) If high numbers on one dimension tend to go with low numbers on the other dimension, there is an inverse, or negative, correlation.

To ask whether the two variables are correlated means (essentially) asking the following question about the scatterplot: When you look at points that represent low versus high values on the *horizontal* dimension, do they differ in how they line up regarding the *vertical* dimension? If low values tend to go with low values and high values tend to go with high values (as in Figure 2.3, A), the variables are said to be *positively* correlated. If people low in self-esteem tend to have low GPAs and people high in self-esteem tend to have high GPAs, you would say that self-esteem correlates positively with GPA.

Sometimes, however, a different kind of pattern occurs. Sometimes, high values on one dimension tend to go with low values on the other dimension (and vice versa). When this happens (see Figure 2.3, B), the correlation is termed *inverse* or *negative*. This kind of correlation might emerge if you studied the relationship between GPA and the frequency of going to parties. That is, you might find that students who party the most tend to have lower GPAs, whereas those who party the least tend to have higher GPAs.

The *direction* of the association between variables (positive versus negative) is one aspect of correlation. The second aspect—entirely separate from the first—is the *strength* of the correlation. Think of strength as the "sloppiness" of the association between the variables. More formally, it refers to the degree of accuracy with which you can predict values on one dimension from values on the other one. For example, assume a positive correlation between self-esteem and GPA. Suppose that you know that Victoria has the second-highest score on self-esteem in your study. How accurate a guess could you make about her GPA?

The answer to this question is dictated by how strong the correlation is. Because the correlation is positive, knowing that Victoria is on the high end of the self-esteem dimension would lead you to predict that she has a high GPA. If the correlation is also *strong,* you're very likely to be right. If the correlation is weaker, you're less likely to be right. A perfect positive correlation—the strongest possible—means that the person who has the very highest value on one variable also has the very highest value on the other, the person next highest on one is also next highest on the other, and on so throughout the list (see Figure 2.4, A).

The strength of a correlation is expressed by a number called a **correlation coefficient** (often labeled with a lowercase r). An absolutely perfect positive correlation (as in Figure 2.4, A) is expressed by the number 1.0. This is the largest numerical value a correlation can take. It indicates a totally accurate prediction from one dimension to the other. If you know where the person is on one variable, you can tell with complete confidence where he or she is on the other.

The scatterplot of a somewhat weaker correlation is shown in Figure 2.4, B. As you can see, there's more "scatter" among the points than in the first case. There's still a noticeable tendency for higher values on one dimension to match up with higher ones on the other and for lows to match up with lows, but the tendency is less exact. As the correlation becomes weaker, the number expressing it becomes smaller (thus, virtually all correlations are decimal values). Correlations of 0.6 to 0.8 are strong. Correlations of 0.3 to 0.5 are moderately strong. Below 0.3 or 0.2, the prediction from one variable to the other is getting poorer. As you can see in Figure 2.4, C, weak correlations have even more scatter. The tendency toward a positive relation is there, but it definitely isn't strong. A correlation of 0.0 means the two variables aren't related at all. The scatterplot of a zero correlation is random dots.

As we said before, a correlation's strength is entirely separate from its direction. *Strength* refers only to degree of accuracy in prediction. Thus, it is eminently sensible to talk about a perfect negative correlation as well as a perfect positive correlation. A perfect negative correlation (see Figure 2.4, D) means that the person who had the highest value on one variable also had the very lowest value on the other variable, the person with the next-highest value on one had the next-to-lowest value on the other, and so on.

Negative correlations are expressed in numbers, just like positive correlations. But to show that the relationship is an inverse one, a minus sign is placed in front. Thus, an r value of -0.75 is precisely as strong as an r value of 0.75. The first expresses an inverse correlation, though, whereas the second expresses a positive correlation.

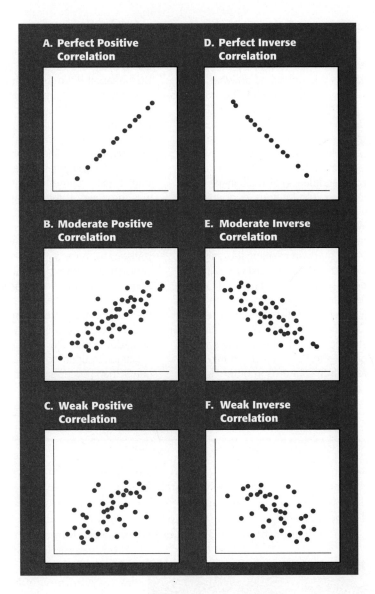

Figure 2.4
Six correlations: (A) Perfect positive correlation, (B) Moderate positive correlation, (C) Weak positive correlation, (D) Perfect inverse correlation, (E) Moderate inverse correlation, and (F) Weak inverse correlation. The weaker the correlation, the more "scatter" in the scatterplot.

TWO KINDS OF SIGNIFICANCE

We've been describing the strength of correlations in terms of the size of the numbers that represent them. Although the size of the number gives information about its strength, the size of the number by itself doesn't tell you whether the correlation is believable or real. Maybe it's a fluke. This is a problem for all kinds of statistics. You can't tell just by looking at the number or looking at a graph whether the result is real. You need to know whether the result is **statistically significant**.

Box 2.1 STATISTICS AND STATISTICS

Description versus Inference

When people think of *statistics,* they often think of the statistics that portray a set of events—for example, "The average American earns $37,000 a year" or "She averaged 21.6 points per game." These are called **descriptive statistics,** because their purpose is to give a description.

Psychologists also use different kinds of statistics, called **inferential statistics,** because they let the researcher make inferences. The information they provide guides the scientist in deciding whether to believe something is true. Interestingly enough, it isn't possible to *prove* something is true. What statistics do is show how likely the finding was, if there was no true relation. If it can be shown that the effect was very *unlikely* to have occurred, the researcher can infer that it's real.

An example of the ability of inferential statistics to reveal patterns, as well as the limitations on what they can say, took place after the 2000 U.S. presidential election. Voters in Palm Beach County, Florida, had encountered an unfamiliar and confusing ballot format on election day. Many later reported accidentally voting for one candidate (Pat Buchanan) while trying to vote for another one (Al Gore). The election, won by George W. Bush, was extremely close. Its outcome might have turned on the errors made in marking the ballot. Were these people just complaining because their candidate lost? Or was there really a problem with the ballot?

Social scientists Greg Adams and Chris Fastnow (2000) used inferential statistics to test whether the pattern of votes in Palm Beach County differed from patterns in other Florida counties. In every county but Palm

Beach, the more votes cast for Bush, the more votes also cast for Buchanan. If Palm Beach had been like every other county in Florida, Buchanan would have gotten around 600 votes instead of 3,407. The inference was clear: It was extremely unlikely that this difference in pattern would have occurred if there were no true relation. Something apparently was throwing off the voting pattern in Palm Beach.

We say "apparently" to emphasize that whenever you use inferential statistics to make a judgment, the conclusion is always probabilistic. The odds that the inference was wrong in this case are *extremely* small. But the possibility does exist. Inferential statistics are thus best viewed as procedures that allow us to attach "confidence units" to our judgments, rather than procedures that lead infallibly to correct choices.

Significant in this context has a very specific meaning: It means that the correlation would have been that large or larger only rarely if no true relationship exists. When the probability is small enough (just under 5%), the correlation (or whatever statistic it is) is said to be *statistically significant* (see also Box 2.1). At that point, the researcher concludes that the relationship is a real one, rather than a random occurrence.

Random assignment is an important hallmark of the experimental method. The experimenter randomly assigns participants to a condition, much as a roulette wheel randomly catches the ball in a black or red slot.

A second use of the word *significant* is also common in psychology, which more closely resembles the use of the word in day-to-day language. An association is said to be **clinically significant** or **practically significant** if the effect is both statistically significant (so it's believable) and large enough to have some practical importance. How large is large enough to be practically important varies from case to case. It's possible, though, for an association to be statistically significant but to account for only a tiny fraction of the behavior. The practical significance of such an association usually isn't very great.

CAUSALITY AND A LIMITATION ON INFERENCE

Correlations tell us whether two variables go together (and in what direction and how strongly). But they don't tell us *why* the variables go together. The *why* question takes us beyond the realm of correlation to a second kind of relationship. This one is called **causality**—the relationship between a cause and an effect. Correlational research isn't able to provide evidence on this second kind of relationship. A correlational study often gives people strong *intuitions* about causality, but no more.

Why? The answer is shown in Figure 2.5. Each arrow there represents a possible path of causality. What this figure shows is that there are always three ways to account for the results of a correlation. Consider the correlation between self-esteem and academic performance. What causes it? Your intuition may say the best explanation is that bad academic outcomes cause people to develop lower self-esteem, whereas having good outcomes causes people to feel good about themselves (arrow 1 in Figure 2.5). Or maybe you think the best explanation is that having low self-esteem causes people not to try as hard, resulting in poorer performance (arrow 2). Both of these explanations are plausible, though they go in the opposite directions.

It could also be, however, that a third variable—not measured, perhaps not even thought of—actually has a causal influence over both variables that were measured (the pair of arrows labeled 3). Perhaps having a high level of intelligence

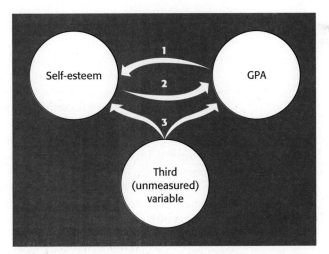

FIGURE 2.5
Correlation does not imply cause and effect, because there are always three possibilities: (1) variations in one variable (academic performance) may be causing variations in the second (self-esteem); (2) variations in the second may be causing variations in the first; or (3) a third variable may actually be causing both observed effects. Knowing only the single correlation between self-esteem and GPA doesn't allow you to distinguish among these possibilities.

causes a positive sense of self-esteem and also causes better academic perform-ance. In this scenario, both self-esteem and academic performance are effects, and something else is the cause.

The possible involvement of another variable in a correlation is sometimes called the **third-variable problem.** It's a problem that can't be handled by correlational research. That method cannot tell which of the three possibilities in Figure 2.5 is actually correct.

SEARCH FOR CAUSALITY: EXPERIMENTAL RESEARCH

There *is* a method that demonstrates cause and effect, however. It's called the **experimental method.** Think of it as having two defining characteristics. First, in an experiment, the researcher manipulates one variable—creates the existence of at least two levels of it. The one the researcher is manipulating is called the **independent variable.** It's the one the researcher is testing as the possible *cause* in a cause–effect relationship. When we say the researcher is "creating" two (or more) levels of this variable, we mean exactly that. There's some kind of event that *actively creates* a difference between the experience of some people and the experience of other people.

Sometimes researchers do experiments in order to better understand what they've seen in correlational studies. Let's illustrate the experimental method by doing just that. Let's pursue further the example we just discussed. Suppose you have a hunch that variations in academic performance have a causal effect on self-esteem. To study this possibility, you conduct an experiment, in which you hypothesize (predict) that academic outcomes cause effects on self-esteem.

You're not going to be able to manipulate GPA in this experiment, but it's fairly easy to manipulate other things with overtones of academic performance. For instance, you could arrange to have some people experience a success and others a failure on a cognitive task (using one rigged to be easy or impossible). By arranging this, you would *create* the difference between success and failure. You'd manipulate it—not measure it. You're sure that a difference now exists between the two sets of people in your experiment, because you *made* it exist.

As in all research, you'd do your best to treat every participant in your experi-ment exactly the same in all ways other than that one. Treating everyone the same—making everything exactly the same except for what you manipulate—is called **experimental control.** Exerting a high degree of control is important to the logic of the experimental method, as you'll see momentarily.

Control is important, but you can't control everything. It's rarely possible to have every person do the experiment at the same time of day or the same day of the week. More obviously, perhaps, it's impossible to be sure the people in the experiment are exactly alike. One of the main themes of this book, after all, is that people differ. Some people in the experiment are just naturally going to have higher self-esteem than others when they walk in the door. How can these differ-ences be handled?

This question brings us to the second defining characteristic of the experimental method: Any variable that can't be controlled—such as an individual difference—is treated by **random assignment.** In your experiment, you would randomly assign each participant to either the success experience or the failure experience. Random assignment is often done by such means as tossing a coin or using a list of random numbers.

The use of random assignment rests on a specific assumption: that if you study enough people in the experiment, any important differences between people (and from other sources as well) will balance out between the groups. Each group is likely to have as many tall people, fat people, depressed people, and confident people as the other group—*if* you have a fairly large number of participants and use random assignment. Anything that matters should balance out.

So, you've brought people to your research laboratory one at a time, randomly assigned them to the two conditions, manipulated the independent variable, and exerted experimental control over everything else. At some point, you would then measure the variable you think is the effect in the cause-and-effect relationship. This one is termed the **dependent variable.**

In this experiment, your hypothesis was that differences in success and failure on academic tasks cause people to differ in self-esteem. Thus, the dependent measure would be a measure of self-esteem (for example, self-report items asking people how they feel about themselves). After getting this measure for each person in the experiment, you would compare the groups to each other (by statistical procedures that need not concern us here). If the difference between groups was statistically significant, you could conclude that the experience of success versus failure *causes* people to differ in self-esteem.

What would make you so confident in that cause-and-effect conclusion? The answer, despite all the detail, is really quite simple. The logic is displayed graphically in Figure 2.6 on page 26. At the start of the experiment, you separated people into two groups. (By the way, the reasoning applies even if the independent variable has more than two levels or groups.) If the assumption about the effect of random assignment is correct, then the two groups don't differ from each other at this point. Because you exercise experimental control, the groups still don't differ as the experiment unfolds.

At one point, however, a difference between groups is introduced—when you manipulate the independent variable. As we said before, you know there's a difference now, and you know *what* the difference is, because you created it yourself. For this reason, if you find the groups differ from each other on the dependent measure at the end, you know there's only one thing that could have caused the difference (see Figure 2.6). It *had* to come from the manipulation of the independent variable. That was the only place where a difference was introduced. It was the only thing that could have been responsible for causing the effect.

This reasoning is straightforward. We should note, however, that this method isn't entirely perfect. Its problem is this: When you do an experiment, you show that the *manipulation* causes the difference on the dependent measure—but you can't always be completely sure *what it was* about the manipulation that did the causing. Maybe it was the aspect of the manipulation that you were focused on, but maybe it was something else.

For example, in the experiment we've been considering, low self-esteem may have been caused by the failure and the self-doubt to which it led. But it *might* have been caused by other things about the manipulation. Maybe the people who failed were worried that they had spoiled your experiment by not solving the problems.

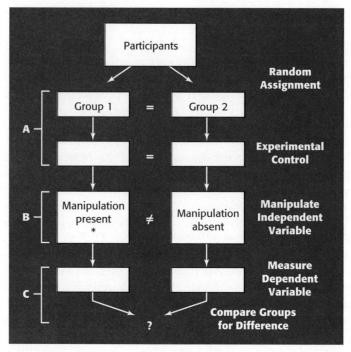

FIGURE 2.6
The logic of the experimental method: (A) Because of random assignment and experimental control, there is no systematic difference between groups at first; (B) The experimental manipulation creates—for the first time—a specific difference, (C) If the groups then are found to differ in another fashion, the manipulation must have caused this difference.

They didn't feel a sense of *failure* but were angry with themselves for creating a problem for you. This interpretation of the result wouldn't mean quite the same thing as your first interpretation of it. This issue requires us always to be a bit cautious in how we view results, even from experiments.

RECOGNIZING TYPES OF STUDY

When you read about correlational studies and experiments in this book, how easy is it going to be to tell them apart? At first glance, it seems simple. An *experiment* makes a comparison between groups, and a *correlational study* gives you a correlation, right? Well, no. Results of correlational studies aren't always reported as correlations. Sometimes the study compares two (or more) groups with each other on a dependent measure, and the word *correlation* is never even mentioned.

Suppose you studied some people who were 40% overweight and some who were 40% underweight. You interviewed them individually and judged how sociable they were, and you found that heavy people were more sociable than thin people. Would this be an experiment or a correlational study? Recall the two defining characteristics of the experiment: manipulation of the independent variable and random assignment of people to groups. You didn't randomly assign people to be heavy or thin (and you didn't *create* these differences). Therefore, this is a correlational study. The limitation on correlational research (the inability to conclude cause and effect) applies to it.

A good rule of thumb is that any time groupings reflect *naturally occurring differences* or are formed on the basis of some *characteristic that you measure*, the study is correlational. This means that all studies of personality differences are, by definition, correlational.

Why do personality researchers make their correlational studies look like experiments? Sometimes it's because they study people from categories, such as cultural groups or genders. It has the side effect, however, of making it hard to express the finding as a correlation. The result is correlational studies that look at first glance like experiments.

What Kind of Research Is Best?

Which kind of research is better: experiments or correlational studies? Both have advantages, and the advantage of one is the disadvantage of the other. The advantage of the experimental method, of course, is its ability to show cause and effect, which the correlational method cannot do.

But experiments also have drawbacks. One drawback (as noted) is that there's sometimes uncertainty about which aspect of the manipulation was important. Another drawback is that experiments on people usually involve events of relatively short duration, in carefully controlled conditions. The correlational method, in contrast, lets you examine events that take place over long periods (even decades) and events that are much more elaborate. Correlational studies also let you get information about events in which experimental manipulation would be unethical—for example, how being raised by divorced parents affects people's personality.

Personality psychologists sometimes also criticize experiments on the grounds that the kinds of relationships they obtain often have little to do with the central issues of personality. Even experiments that seem to bear on important issues in personality may tell less than they seem to. Consider the hypothetical experiment described earlier, in which you manipulated academic success and failure and measured self-esteem. Assume for the moment that those given a failure had lower self-esteem afterward than those given a success. You might be tempted to conclude from this that having poor academic outcomes over the course of one's life causes people to develop low self-esteem.

This conclusion, however, may not be justified. The experiment dealt with a brief task outcome, manipulated in a particular way. The broader conclusion you're tempted to reach deals with a basic, ingrained quality of personality. This latter quality may differ in many ways from the momentary state you manipulated. The "reasoning by analogy" that you're tempted to engage in can be misleading.

To many personality psychologists, the only way to really understand personality is to look at naturally occurring differences between people (Underwood, 1975). These researchers are willing to accept the limitation on causal inference that's inherent in correlations; they regard it as an acceptable price to pay. On the other hand, many of these psychologists are comfortable *combining* the correlational strategy with experimental techniques, as described next.

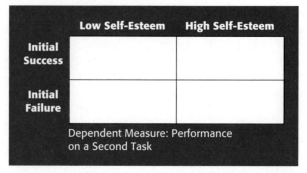

FIGURE 2.7
Diagram of a hypothetical two-factor study. Each square represents the combination of the value listed above it and the value listed to the left. In multifactor studies, all combinations of values of the predictor variables are created in this fashion.

MULTIFACTOR STUDIES

We've been describing studies as though they always involve predicting a dependent variable from a single predictor variable (an experimental manipulation or an individual difference). In reality, however, studies often look at several predictors at once by using multifactor designs. In a **multifactor study,** two (or more) variables are varied *separately*, which means creating all combinations of the various levels of the predictor variables. The study shown in Figure 2.7 has two factors, but more than two can be used. The more factors in a study, of course, the larger the resulting array of combinations, and the trickier it is to keep track of things.

Sometimes, the factors are all experimental manipulations. Sometimes, they're all personality variables. Often, though, experimental manipulations are crossed by individual-difference variables. The example shown in Figure 2.7 is such a design. The self-esteem factor is the level of self-esteem the people had when they came to the study. This is a personality dimension (thus correlational). The success–failure factor is an experimental manipulation, which takes place during the session. In this particular experiment, the dependent measure is performance on a second task, which the participants attempt after the success–failure manipulation.

These designs allow researchers to examine how different types of people respond to variations in situations. They thus offer a glimpse into the underlying dynamics of the individual-difference variable. Because this type of study combines experimental procedures and individual differences, it's often referred to as **experimental personality research.**

READING FIGURES FROM MULTIFACTOR RESEARCH

Because multifactor designs are more complex than single-factor studies, what they can tell you is also potentially more complex. Indeed, people who do experimental personality research use these designs precisely for this reason.

You don't *always* get a complex result from a multifactor study. Sometimes you find only the same outcomes you would have found if you had studied each predictor separately. When you find that a predictor variable is linked to the outcome in a systematic way, completely separate from the other predictor, the finding is called a **main effect.** For example, the study outlined in Figure 2.7 might find simply that people of both initial self–esteem levels perform worse after a failure than after a success.

The complexity occurs when a study finds what's termed an **interaction.** Figure 2.8 portrays two interactions, each a possible outcome of the hypothetical study of Figure 2.7. In each case, the vertical dimension portrays the dependent

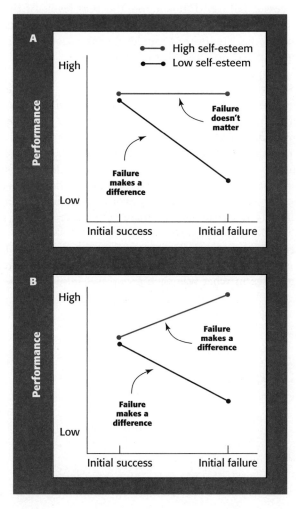

FIGURE 2.8
Two hypothetical outcomes of a two-factor study looking at self-esteem and an initial success-versus-failure experience as predictors of performance on a second task. (A) This graph indicates that experiencing a failure causes people low in self-esteem to perform worse later on than if they had experienced a success, but that experiencing a failure does not have any effect at all on people high in self-esteem. (B) This graph indicates that experiencing a failure causes people low in self-esteem to perform worse later on, but that experiencing a failure causes people high in self-esteem to perform better later on. Thus, the failure influences both kinds of people but does so in opposite ways.

measure: performance on the second task. The two marks on the horizontal line represent the two values of the manipulated variable: initial success versus failure. The color of the line depicts the other predictor variable: the color line represents people high in self-esteem, and the black line represents those low in self-esteem.

We emphasize that these graphs show *hypothetical* outcomes. They are intended only to give you a clearer understanding of what interactions mean. Figure 2.8, A, portrays a finding that people who are low in self-esteem perform worse after an initial failure than after a success. Among people high in self-esteem, however, this doesn't occur. Failure apparently has no effect on them. Thus, the effect of one variable (success versus failure) differs across the two levels of the other variable (degree of self-esteem). That is the meaning of the term *interaction*. In the case in Figure 2.8, A, a failure has an effect at one level of the second variable (in the low self-esteem group) but has no effect at the other level of the second variable (the high self-esteem group).

Two more points about interactions: First, to find an interaction, it's *absolutely necessary* to study more than one factor at a time. It's impossible to find an interaction unless both variables involved in it are studied at once. This is one reason researchers often use multifactor designs: They allow the possibility for interactions to emerge.

The second point is revealed by comparing Figure 2.8, A, with 2.8, B. This point is that interactions can take many forms. In contrast to the interaction just described, the graph in panel B says that failure has effects on both kinds of people—but opposite effects. People low in self-esteem perform worse after failure (as in the first graph), but people high in self-esteem actually perform better after a failure, perhaps because the failure motivates them to try harder.

These two graphs aren't the only forms interactions can take. Exactly what an interaction means always depends on its form. Thus, exploring interactions always requires checking to see in what way each group was influenced by the other variable under study.

· SUMMARY ·

Research in personality relies on observations of both the self and others. The desire to understand a person as an integrated whole led to *case studies*: in-depth examinations of specific persons. The desire for *generalizability*—conclusions that would apply to many rather than to a few people—led to studies involving systematic examination of many people.

Gathering information is only the first step toward examining relationships between and among variables. Relationships among variables are examined in two ways, corresponding to two kinds of relationships. *Correlational research* determines the degree to which two variables tend to go together in a predictable way when measured at different levels along the dimensions. This technique determines two aspects of the relationship: its direction and its strength. The special relationship of cause and effect cannot be determined by this kind of study, however.

A second technique, called the *experimental method,* allows testing for cause and effect. In an experiment, an independent variable is manipulated, other variables are controlled (made constant), and anything that cannot be controlled is treated by random assignment. An effect caused by the manipulation is measured in the dependent variable. Experimental and correlational techniques are often combined in multifactor studies. When the study contains a personality variable and an experimental manipulation, it's termed *experimental personality research*. Multifactor studies permit the emergence of interactions.

· GLOSSARY ·

Case study   An in-depth study of one individual.

Causality (causal relationship)   A relationship such that variation in one dimension produces variation in another.

Clinically significant   An association large enough to have some practical importance.

Correlation   A relationship in which two variables or dimensions covary when measured repeatedly.

Correlation coefficient   A numeric index of the degree of correlation between two variables.

Dependent variable   The variable measured as the outcome of an experiment; the effect in a cause–effect relationship.

Descriptive statistics   Statistics used to describe or characterize some group.

Experience sampling   A method in which people report repeatedly on their current experiences.

Experimental control   The holding constant of variables that are not being manipulated.

Experimental method   The method in which one variable is manipulated to test for causal influence on another variable.

Experimental personality research   A study involving a personality factor and an experimental factor.

Generality (generalizability) The degree to which a conclusion applies to many people.

Idiographic   Relating to an approach that focuses on a particular person across situations.

Independent variable   The variable manipulated in an experiment and tested as the cause in a cause–effect relationship.

Inferential statistics   Statistics used to judge whether a relationship exists between variables.

Interaction   A finding in which the effect of one predictor variable differs depending on the level of another predictor variable.

Main effect   A finding in which the effect of one predictor variable is independent of other variables.

Multifactor study   A study with two (or more) predictor variables.

Personology   The study of the whole person, as opposed to the study of only one aspect of the person.

Practical significance   An association large enough to have practical importance.

Random assignment   The process of putting people randomly into groups of an experiment so their characteristics balance out across groups.

Statistical significance   The likelihood of an obtained effect occurring when there is no true effect.

Third-variable problem   The possibility that an unmeasured variable caused variations in both of two correlated variables.

Variable   A dimension along which two or more variations exist.

Issues in Personality Assessment

THE MEASURING OF PERSONALITY is called **assessment.** It's something we all do informally all the time. We want to know what the people we interact with are like, so we know what to expect of them. For this reason, we develop various ways of gauging people, judging what they're like. You probably don't think of this as "assessment," but what you're doing informally is much the same—in principle—as what psychologists do more formally.

Forming impressions of what other people are like can be hard. It's easy to get misleading impressions. Personality assessment is also hard for psychologists. All the problems you have, they have. But personality psychologists work hard to deal with those problems.

Sources of Information

Informal assessment draws information from many sources, and so does formal assessment.

OBSERVER RATINGS

As suggested in Chapter 2, many measures of personality come from someone other than the person being assessed (Funder, 1991; Paunonen, 1989). The name for this approach is **observer ratings.**

There are many kinds of observer ratings. Some of them involve interviews. People being assessed talk about themselves, and the interviewer draws conclusions from what's said and how it's said. Sometimes people being interviewed talk about something *other than* themselves. In doing so, they reveal something indirectly to the interviewer about what they're like.

Other kinds of observer ratings don't require that kind of complexity. Observers may make judgments about a person based on watching his or her actions. Or observers may be people who already know the person being assessed well enough to say what he or she is like, and their ratings are simply those summary judgments. Observers can even observe a person's belongings and draw conclusions about what the person is like (see Box 3.1).

There are many different types of observer ratings. Here, an observer is directly rating a research participant's overt behavior.

Box 3.1   What Does Your Stuff Say about You?

Many people assume that the vast reach of the web and popular media has completely homogenized American culture. Everyone buys more or less the same stuff, and everyone's personal space therefore looks more or less the same. Not so. Not even close.

Sam Gosling and his colleagues have found that people "portray and betray" their personalities by the objects and mementos they surround themselves with (Gosling, 2008). Practicing a research technique they refer to as "snoopology" (the science of snooping), these researchers have extensively studied people's offices, bedrooms, and other personal domains. They've found evidence of three broad mechanisms that connect people to their spaces. They refer to these as identity claims, feeling regulators, and behavioral residue.

Identity claims are symbolic statements about who we are. Photos, awards, bumper stickers, and other objects that symbolize a past, current, or hoped-for identity (e.g., cheerleader pompoms) are identity claims. They are indicators of how we want to be regarded. They can be directed to other people who enter our space, or they can be directed to ourselves, reminders to ourselves of who we are (or want to be). Photos can be particularly revealing. They say, "Here I am being me" (Gosling, 2008, p. 16).

Feeling regulators aren't intended to send messages about our identities but to help us manage our emotions. Being in a particular desired emotional state can be important for a variety of life's activities, and emotions can be regulated in a wide variety of ways. You can improve your mood by looking at a picture that reminds you of a time when you were very happy. You can soothe yourself with pictures of tranquil nature

scenes and with readily available music playing through a high-quality sound system. A bathtub surrounded by candles and scented oils can be eminently relaxing. And if you're the sort of person who thrives on excitement, there are plenty of things that can be included in your surroundings to stimulate those feelings, as well.

Behavioral residues are in some ways less interesting than either of these. Behavioral residues are physical traces left in our surroundings by everyday actions (trash is a special case of residue that is discarded repeatedly). What can these residues tell about you? A simple thing is how much residue you've accumulated. The more the residue, the less organized you probably are. A separate issue is what *kinds* of residue show up. As noted in Chapter 1, personality is displayed in consistencies. Similarly, behavioral residue tends to give an indication of what sorts of things take place repeatedly in your life space.

SELF-REPORTS

Another category of assessment technique is **self-report.** In self-reports, people themselves indicate what they think they're like or how they feel or act. Self-reports thus resemble the process of introspection described in Chapter 2. Although self-reporting can be done in an unstructured descriptive way, it's usually not. Most self-reports ask people to respond to a specific set of items.

Self-report scales can be created in many formats. An example is the true–false format, where you read statements and decide whether each one is true or false for you. Another common one is a multipoint rating scale. Here, a wider range of response options is available—for example, along a 5-point response scale ranging from "strongly agree" to "strongly disagree."

Some self-reports focus on a single quality of personality. Often, though, people who develop assessment devices want to assess *several* aspects of personality in the same test (as separate scales). A measure that assesses several dimensions of personality is called an **inventory.** The process of developing an inventory is pretty much the same as that for developing a single scale. The difference is that for an inventory, you go through each step of development for *each scale of the inventory,* rather than just one.

IMPLICIT ASSESSMENT

Also of increasing interest over the past decade (though they've been around for a long time) are techniques called **implicit assessment.** These techniques attempt to find out what a person is like from the person (like self-reports) but not by asking him or her directly. Rather, the person is given a task of some sort that involves making judgments about stimuli. The pattern of responses (e.g., reaction times) can inform the assessor about what the person is like.

An example of such a procedure is called the Implicit Association Test (IAT; for review, see Greenwald, McGhee, & Schwartz, 2008). It measures links among semantic properties in memory that are believed to be hard to detect by introspection (and thus are "implicit"). The IAT can be applied to virtually any kind of association. As applied to properties of personality, it would go like this. Your job is to categorize a long series of stimuli as quickly as you can. Each can be categorized according to either of two dichotomies: "me" versus "not me" or (for example) "plant" versus "mineral." You don't know which dichotomy makes sense until the item appears. Some items pertain to qualities of personality. If one of those items is strongly associated in your memory with you, your "me" response will be faster than if it isn't strongly associated with you. Thus, reaction times across a large number of stimuli can provide information about your implicit sense of self.

Implicit assessment techniques have been particularly important in the motive approach to personality. Accordingly, we will spend more time on that technique in Chapter 5.

As indicated by the preceding sections, the arsenal of assessment techniques is large. All require two things, though. First, in each case, the person being assessed produces a sample of "behavior." This may be an action, which someone observes; it may be internal behavior, such as a change in heart rate; it may be the behavior of answering questions; or it may be the accumulation of possessions over an extended period. Second, someone then uses the behavior sample as a guide to some aspect of the person's personality.

SUBJECTIVE VERSUS OBJECTIVE MEASURES

One more distinction among measures is important. Some measures are termed **subjective**, and others are termed **objective.** In subjective measures, an interpretation is part of the measure. An example is an observer's judgment that the person he or she is watching looks nervous. The judgment makes the measure subjective, because it's an *interpretation* of the behavior. If the measure is of a concrete physical reality that requires no interpretation, then it's objective. For example, you could count the number of times a person stammers while talking. This would involve no interpretation. Although this count might then be used to infer nervousness, the measure itself is objective.

To some extent, this issue cuts across the distinction between observer ratings and self-reports. An observer can make objective counts of acts, or can develop a subjective impression of the person. Similarly, a person making a self-report can report objective events as they occur (as in experience sampling) or can report a subjective overall impression of what he or she is like. It should be apparent, though, that self-reports are particularly vulnerable to incorporating subjectivity. Even reports of specific events permit unintentional interpretations to creep in.

Reliability of Measurement

All techniques of assessment confront several kinds of problems or issues. One issue is termed **reliability** of measurement. The nature of this issue can be conveyed by putting it as a question: Once you've made an observation about someone, how confident can you be that if you looked again a second or third time you'd see about the same thing?

When an observation is reliable, it has a high degree of *consistency* or *repeatability*. Low reliability means that what's measured is less consistent. The measure isn't just reflecting the person being measured. It's also including a lot of randomness, termed **error.**

All measurement procedures have sources of error (error can be reduced, but not eliminated). When you use a telescope to look at the moon, a little dust on the lens, minor imperfections in the glass, flickering lights nearby, and swirling air currents all contribute error to what you see. When you use a rating scale to measure how self-reliant people think they are, the way you phrase the item can be a source of error, because it can lead to varying interpretations. When you have an observer watch a child's behavior, the observer is a source of error because of variations in how closely he or she is paying attention, thinking about what he or she is seeing, or being influenced by a thousand other things.

How do you deal with the issue of reliability in measurement? The general answer is to repeat the measurement—make the observation more than once. Usually, this means measuring the same quality from a slightly different angle or using a slightly different "measuring device." This lets the diverse sources of error in the different devices cancel each other out.

Reliability actually is a family of problems, not just a single problem, because it crops up in several different contexts. Each version of the problem has a separate name, and the tactic used to treat each version differs slightly from the tactics used for the others.

INTERNAL CONSISTENCY

The simplest act of assessment is the single observation or measurement. How can you be sure it doesn't include too much error? Let's take an illustration from ability assessment. Think about what you'd do if you wanted to know how good someone was at a particular type of problem—math problems or word puzzles. You wouldn't give just a *single* problem to solve, because whether the person solved it easily or not might depend too much on some quirk of that particular problem. If you wanted to know (reliably) how well the person solves that kind of problem, you'd give *several* problems.

The same strategy applies to personality assessment. If you were using a self-report to ask people how self-reliant they think they are, you wouldn't ask just once. You'd ask several times, using different items that all reflect self-reliance, but in different words. In this example, *each item* is a "measuring device." When you go to a new item, you're shifting to a different measuring device, trying to measure the same quality. In effect,

Human judges are not infallible. They sometimes perceive things inaccurately.

BOX 3.2   NEW APPROACHES TO ASSESSMENT: ITEM RESPONSE THEORY AND COMPUTER ADAPTIVE TESTING

The idea that having lots of items increases a scale's internal consistency comes from classical test theory, which guided scale construction for years. More recently, a different approach has emerged called *item response theory (IRT)*. IRT is an attempt to increase the efficiency of assessment (Reeve, Hays, Change, & Perfetto, 2007), while reducing the number of items

IRT focuses on determining the most useful items, and the most useful response choices, for the concept being measured. Determining which responses choices are most useful starts with creation of response curves. These show how frequently each response is used, and whether each choice is measuring something different from other choices (Streiner, 2010). For example, consider a scale where the response choices indicate

the frequency of something: "always," "often," "sometimes," and "never." Analysis might find that "often" and "sometimes" are actually treated the same. If so, there's no point in offering these responses as separate alternatives.

IRT also determines the "difficulty" of an item (Streiner, 2010). For instance, on a scale assessing anxiety, the item "I worry" would be easier to endorse than the item "I get panicky." Why? Because the second item requires more anxiety. A more difficult item concerning anxiety will better distinguish people who have anxiety from those who do not.

One widely used application of IRT is *computerized adaptive testing (CAT;* Bjorner, Chang, Thissen, & Reeve, 2007; Cook, O'Malley, & Roddey, 2005). As a person completes a measure on a computer, the CAT program selects the best items for that person from a bank of questions.

The items selected are based on the person's responses to prior items. For example, if someone endorses "I am always hopeful," it would not be useful to ask questions of less "difficulty," such as, "I am sometimes hopeful." CAT ensures that less difficult items are not given after an item of medium difficulty has been endorsed.

IRT and CAT have been applied to a diverse range of assessments including those for personality (e.g., Samuel, Simms, Clark, Lively, & Widiger, 2010; Walton, Roberts, Krueger, Blonigen, & Hicks, 2008) and psychological disorders (e.g., Gelhorn et al., 2009; Purpura, Wilson, & Lonigon, 2010; Uebelacker, Strong, Weinstock, & Miller, 2009). One interesting finding from these analyses is that there is more overlap between measures of normal versus abnormal personality patterns than expected (Samuel et al., 2010; Walton et al., 2008).

you're putting down one telescope and picking up another. The reliability question is whether you see about the same thing through each of the different telescopes.

This kind of reliability is termed **internal reliability** or **internal consistency.** This is reliability within a set of observations of a single aspect of personality. Because different items have different sources of error, using many items should tend to balance out the error. The more observations, the more likely the random error will cancel out. Because people using self-report scales want good reliability, most scales contain many items (but see Box 3.2). If the items are reliable enough, they're then used together as a single index of the personality quality.

How do you find out whether the items you're using have good internal reliability? Just having a lot of items doesn't guarantee it. Reliability is a question about the correlations among people's responses to the items. Saying that the items are highly reliable means that people's responses to the items are highly correlated.

As a practical matter, there are several ways to investigate internal consistency. All of them examine correlations among people's responses across items. Perhaps the best way (although it's cumbersome) is to look at the average correlation between each pair of items taken separately. A simpler way is to separate the items into two subsets (often odd– versus even–numbered items), add up people's scores for each subset, and correlate the two subtotals with each other. This index is called **split–half reliability.** If the two halves of the item set measure the same quality, people who score high on one half should also score high on the other half, and people who score low on one half should also score low on the other half. Thus, a strong positive correlation between halves is evidence of internal consistency.

INTER-RATER RELIABILITY

As noted, personality isn't always measured by self-reports. Some observations are *literally* observations, made by one person watching and assessing someone else. Use of observer ratings creates a slightly different reliability problem. In observer ratings, the *person making the rating* is a "measuring device." There are sources of error in this device, just as in other devices. How can you judge reliability in this case?

Conceptually, the answer is the same as it was in the other case. You need to put down one telescope and pick up another. In the case of observer ratings, you need to check this observer against another observer. To the extent that both see about the same thing when they look at the same event, reliability is high. This dual observation is logically the same as using two items on a questionnaire. Raters whose judgments correlate highly with each other across many ratings are said to have high **inter-rater reliability.**

In many cases, having high inter-rater reliability requires the judges to be thoroughly trained in how to observe what they're observing. Judges of Olympic diving, for example, have seen many thousands of dives and know precisely what to look for. As a result, their inter-rater reliability is high. Similarly, when observers assess personality, they often receive much instruction and practice before turning to the "real thing," so their reliability will be high.

STABILITY ACROSS TIME

There's one more kind of reliability that's important in the measurement of personality. This type of reliability concerns repeatability across time. That is, assessment at one time should agree fairly well with assessment done at a different time.

Why is this important? Remember, personality is supposed to be stable. That's one reason people use the word—to convey a sense of stability. If personality is really *stable*—doesn't fluctuate from minute to minute or from day to day—then *measures* of personality should be reliable across time. People's scores should stay roughly the same when measured a week later, a month later, or four years later.

If all judges are seeing the same thing when they rate an event, then inter-rater reliability will be high.

Table 3.1 Three Kinds of Reliability. Each assesses the consistency or repeatability of an observation by looking a second time, either with the same measuring device or with a slightly different one.

Type of Reliability	Measuring Device	Type of Consistency
Internal reliability	Test item	Consistency within the test
Inter-rater reliability	Rater	Agreement between raters
Test–retest reliability	Entire test	Consistency across time

This kind of reliability is termed **test–retest reliability.** It's determined by giving the test to the same people at two different times. A scale with high test–retest reliability will yield scores the second time (the retest) that are fairly similar to those from the first time. People with high scores the first time will have high scores the second time, and people with lower scores at first will have lower scores later on. (For a summary of these three types of reliability, see Table 3.1.)

Validity of Measurement

Reliability is a starting point in measurement, but it's not the only issue that matters. It's possible for measures to be highly reliable but completely meaningless. Thus, another important issue is what's called **validity.** This issue concerns whether what you're measuring is what you *think* you're measuring (or what you're *trying* to measure). Earlier, we portrayed reliability in terms of random influences on the image in a telescope as you look through it at the moon. To extend the same analogy, the validity issue is whether what you're seeing is really the moon or just a streetlight (see also Figure 3.1).

How do you decide whether you're measuring what you want to measure? There are two ways to answer this question. One is an "in principle" answer, and the other is a set of tactics. The "in principle" answer is that people decide by comparing two kinds of "definitions" with each other. When you see the word *definition,* what probably comes to mind is a conceptual definition, which spells out the word's meaning in terms of conceptual qualities or attributes (as in a dictionary). It tells us what information a word conveys, by consensus among users of the language. Psychologists also talk about another kind of definition, however, called an **operational definition.** This is a description of a physical event.

The difference between the two kinds of definition is easy to illustrate. Consider the concept *love.* Its conceptual definition might be something like "a strong affection for another person." There are many ways, however, to define *love* operationally. For example, you might ask the person you're assessing to indicate on a rating scale how much she loves someone. You might measure how often she looks into that person's eyes when interacting with him. You might measure how willing she is to give up events she enjoys in order to be with him. These three measures differ considerably from one another. Yet each might be taken as an operational definition (or operationalization) of love.

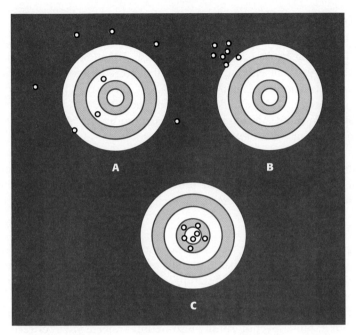

FIGURE 3.1
A simple way to think about the difference between reliability and validity, using the metaphor of target shooting. (A) Sometimes when people shoot at a target their shots go all over. This result corresponds to measurement that's neither reliable nor valid. (B) Reliability is higher as the shots are closer together. Shots that miss the mark, however, are not valid. (C) Good measurement means that the shots are close together (reliable) *and* near the bull's-eye (valid).

The essence of the validity issue in measurement can be summarized in this question: How well does the *operational* definition (the event) match the *conceptual* definition (the abstract quality you have in mind to measure)? If the two are close, the measure has high validity. If they aren't close, validity is low.

How do you decide whether the two are close? Usually, psychologists poke at the conceptual definition until they're sure what the critical elements are and then look to see whether the same elements are in the operationalization. If they aren't (at least by strong implication), the validity of the operationalization is questionable.

The validity issue is critically important. It's also extremely tricky. It's the subject of continual debate in psychology, as researchers try to think of better and better ways to look at human behavior (Borsboom, Mellenbergh, & van Heerden, 2004). The reason the issue is important is that researchers and assessors form conclusions about personality in terms of what *think* they're measuring. If what they're measuring isn't what they think they're measuring, they will draw wrong conclusions. Likewise, a clinician may draw the wrong conclusion about a person if the measure doesn't measure what the clinician thinks it measures.

Validity is important whenever anything is being observed. In personality assessment, the validity question has been examined closely for a long time. In trying to be sure that personality tests are valid, theorists have come to distinguish several aspects of validity from one another. These distinctions have also influenced the practical process of establishing validity.

CONSTRUCT VALIDITY

The idea of validity you have in mind at this point is technically called **construct validity** (Campbell, 1960; Cronbach & Meehl, 1955; Strauss & Smith, 2009). Construct validity is an all-encompassing validity, and is therefore the most important kind (Hogan & Nicholson, 1988; Landy, 1986). Construct validity means that the measure (the assessment device) reflects the construct (the conceptual quality) that the psychologist has in mind. Although the word *construct* sounds abstract, it just means a concept. Any trait quality, for example, is a construct.

Establishing construct validity for a measure is a complex process. It uses several kinds of information, each treated as a separate aspect of the validation process. For this reason, the various qualities that provide support for construct validity have separate names of their own. Several are described in the following paragraphs.

CRITERION VALIDITY

An important part of showing that an assessment device has construct validity is showing that it relates to other manifestations of the quality it's supposed to measure (Campbell, 1960). The "other manifestation" usually means a behavioral index, or the judgment of a trained observer, as an external *criterion* (a standard of comparison). The researcher collects this information and sees how well the assessment device correlates with it. This aspect of validity is sometimes referred to as **criterion validity** (because it uses an external criterion) or **predictive validity** (because it tests how well the measure predicts something else it's supposed to predict).

As an example, suppose you were interested in criterion validity for a measure of dominance you were developing. One way to approach this problem would be to select people who score high and low on your measure and bring them to a laboratory one at a time to work on a task with two other people. You could tape each group's discussion and score the tape for the number of times each person made suggestions, gave instructions, took charge of the situation, and so on. These would be viewed as behavioral criteria of dominance. If people who scored high on your measure did these things more than people who scored low, it would indicate a kind of criterion validity.

Another way to approach the problem would be to have a trained interviewer spend 20 minutes with each person who completed your scale and rate each person's dominance after the interview. The interviewer's ratings would be a different kind of criterion for dominance. If the ratings related to scores on your measure, it would indicate a different kind of criterion validity for the measure.

Criterion validity is regarded as the most important way to support construct validity. A controversy has arisen over the process of establishing it, however. Howard (1990; Howard, Maxwell, Weiner, Boynton, & Rooney, 1980) pointed out that people often assume the criterion that's used is a perfect reflection of the construct. In reality, though, this is almost never true. In fact, far too often, researchers choose criterion measures that are *poor* reflections of the construct.

We raise this point to emphasize how important it is to be careful in deciding what criterion to use. Unless the criterion is a good one, associations with it are meaningless. Despite this issue, criterion validity remains the keystone of construct validation.

CONVERGENT VALIDITY

Another kind of support for a measure's construct validity involves showing that the measure relates to characteristics that are similar to, but not the same as, what it's supposed to measure. How is this different from criterion validity? It's just a very small step away from it. In this case, though, you know the second measure aims to assess something a little different from what your measure assesses. Because this kind of information gathering often proceeds from several angles, it's termed **convergent validation** (Campbell & Fiske, 1959). That is, the evidence "converges" on the construct you're interested in, even though any single finding by itself won't clearly reflect the construct.

For example, a scale intended to measure dominance should relate at least a little to measures of qualities such as leadership (positively) or shyness (inversely). The correlations shouldn't be perfect because those aren't quite the same constructs, but they shouldn't be zero either. If you developed a measure to assess dominance and it didn't correlate at all with measures of leadership and shyness, you'd have to start wondering whether your measure really assesses dominance.

Discriminant Validity

It's important to show that an assessment device measures what it's intended to measure. But it's also important to show that it does *not* measure qualities it's *not* intended to measure—especially qualities that don't fit your conceptual definition of the construct (Campbell, 1960). This aspect of the construct validation process is termed **discriminant validation** (Campbell & Fiske, 1959).

The importance of discriminant validity can be easy to overlook. However, discriminant validation is a major line of defense against the third-variable problem in correlational research, discussed in Chapter 2. That is, you can't be sure why two correlated variables correlate. It may be that one influences the other. But it may be that a third variable, correlated with the two you've studied, is really responsible for their correlation. In principle, it's always possible to attribute the effect of a personality dimension on behavior to some other personality dimension. In practice, however, this can be made much harder by evidence of discriminant validity. That is, if research shows that the dimension you're interested in is unrelated to another variable, then that variable can't be invoked as an alternative explanation for any effect of the first.

To illustrate this, let's return to an example used in discussing the third-variable problem in Chapter 2: a correlation between self-esteem and academic performance. This association *might* reflect the effect of an unmeasured variable—for instance, IQ. Suppose, though, that we know this measure of self-esteem is unrelated to IQ, because someone checked that possibility during the process of its validation. This would make it hard to claim that IQ underlies the correlation between self-esteem and academic performance.

The process of discriminant validation is never ending, because new possibilities for third variables always suggest themselves. Ruling out alternative explanations is thus a challenging task, but it's also a necessary one. Earlier in the chapter (in Box 3.2), we discussed implications of item response theory for internal consistency. Item response theory also provides safeguards that help ensure that items measure only what they are intended to measure. This new method therefore offers a valuable tool to enhance discriminant validity and help reduce the third-variable problem.

Face Validity

One more kind of validity should be mentioned. It's much simpler and a little more intuitive, and most people think it's less important. It's called **face validity**. Face validity means that the assessment device appears, on its "face," to be measuring the construct it was intended to measure. It *looks* right. A test of sociability made up of items such as "I prefer to spend time with friends rather than alone" and "I would rather socialize than read books" would have high face validity. A test of sociability made up of items such as "Green is my favorite color" and "I prefer imported cars" would have low face validity.

Many researchers regard face validity as a convenience, for two reasons. First, some believe that face-valid measures are easier to respond to than measures with less face validity. Second, researchers sometimes focus on distinctions between qualities of personality that differ in subtle ways. It often seems impossible to separate these qualities from each other except by using measures that are high in face validity.

On the other hand, face validity can occasionally be a detriment. This is true when the assessment device is intended to measure something that the person being assessed would find threatening or embarrassing to admit. In such cases, the test developer usually tries to obscure the purpose of the test by reducing its face validity.

Whether face validity is good, bad, or neither, it should be clear that it does not substitute for other aspects of validity. If an assessment device is to be useful in the long run, it must undergo the laborious process of construct validation. The "bottom line" is always construct validity.

CULTURE AND VALIDITY

Another important issue in assessment concerns cultural differences. In a sense, this is a validity issue; in a sense, it's an issue of generalizability. Let's frame the issue as a question: Do the scores on a personality test have the same meaning for a person from an Asian culture, a Latino culture, or an African American culture as they do for a person from a middle-class European-American culture?

There are at least two aspects to this question. The first is whether the psychological construct *itself* has the same meaning from one culture to another. This is a fundamental question about the nature of personality. Are the elements of personality the same from one human group to another? Many people assume the basic elements of personality are universal. That may, in fact, be a dangerous assumption.

The second aspect of the question concerns how people from different cultures *interpret* the items of the measure. If an item has one meaning for middle-class Americans, but a different meaning in some other culture, responses to the item will also have different meanings in the two cultures. A similar issue arises when a measure is translated into a different language. This usually involves translating the measure into the new language and then translating it back into the original language by someone who's never seen the original items. This process sometimes reveals that items contain idiomatic or metaphorical meanings that are hard to translate. Adapting a measure from one culture for use in another culture is a complex process with many difficulties (Butcher, 1996). It must be done very carefully, if the measure is to be valid in the new culture.

RESPONSE SETS AND LOSS OF VALIDITY

Any discussion of validity must also note that there are problems in self-reports that can interfere with the validity of the information collected. We've already mentioned that biases in recall can distort the picture and render the information invalid. In the same way, people's motivational tendencies can also get in the way of accurate reporting.

The tendency to provide socially desirable responses can sometimes mask a person's true characteristics or feelings.

There are at least two biases in people's responses in assessment. These biases are called **response sets.** A response set is a psychological orientation, a readiness to answer in a particular way (Jackson & Messick, 1967). Response sets create distortions in what's assessed. Personality psychologists want their assessments to provide information that's free from contamination. Thus, response sets are problems.

Two response sets are particularly important in personality assessment. One of them emerges most clearly when the assessment device is a self-report instrument that, in one fashion or another, asks the person questions that require a "yes" or "no" response (or a response on a rating scale with "agree" and "disagree" as the opposite ends of the scale). This response set, called **acquiescence,** is the tendency to say "yes" (Couch & Keniston, 1960).

Everyone presumably has a bit of this tendency, but people vary greatly on it. That's the problem. If the set isn't counteracted somehow, the scores of people who are highly acquiescent become inflated. Their high scores reflect the response set, instead of their personalities. People who have extreme personalities but not much acquiescence will also have high scores. But you won't know whose high scores are from personality and whose are from acquiescence.

Many view acquiescence as an easy problem to combat. The way it's handled for self-reports is this: Write half the items so that "yes" means being at one end of the personality dimension. Write the other half of the items so that "no" means being at that end of the personality dimension. In the process of scoring the test, then, any bias that comes from the simple tendency to say "yes" is canceled out.

This procedure takes care of the problem of overagreement, but not everyone is convinced it's a good idea. Negatively worded items often are harder to understand or more complicated to answer than positively worded items. The result can be responses that are less accurate (Converse & Presser, 1986; Schriesheim & Hill, 1981). For this reason, some people feel it's better to live with the acquiescence problem than to introduce a different kind of error through complex wording.

A second response set is perhaps more important than acquiescence and also more troublesome. It's called **social desirability.** It reflects the fact that people tend to portray themselves in a good light (in socially desirable ways) whenever possible. Once again, this tendency is stronger among some people than others (Crowne & Marlowe, 1964; Edwards, 1957). As with acquiescence, if it isn't counteracted, people with strong concerns about social desirability will produce scores that reflect the response set, rather than their personalities.

For some personality dimensions, this isn't much of a problem. The reason is that there's really no social approval or disapproval at either end of the dimension. In other cases, though, there's a consensus that it's better to be one way (for example, honest or likable) than the other (dishonest or unlikable). In these cases, assessment becomes tricky.

In general, psychologists deal with this problem by trying to phrase items so that the issue of social desirability isn't salient. As much as anything else, this is a process of trying to avoid even bringing up the idea that one kind of person is approved of more than the other. Sometimes this means phrasing undesirable responses in ways that makes them more acceptable. Sometimes it means looking for ways to let people admit the undesirable quality indirectly. A different way to deal with the problem is to include items that assess the person's degree of concern about social desirability and use this information as a correction factor in evaluating the person's responses to other items. In any event, this is a problem that personality psychologists must constantly be aware of and constantly guarding against in trying to measure what people are like.

Two Rationales behind the Development of Assessment Devices

Thus far, this chapter has considered issues that arise when measuring any quality of personality. But how do people decide what qualities to measure in the first place? This question won't be answered fully here, because the answer depends partly on the theoretical perspective underlying the assessment. We will, however, address one general issue. In particular, development of personality measures usually follows one of two approaches or strategies, each of which has its own kind of logic.

RATIONAL OR THEORETICAL APPROACH

One strategy is termed a **rational** or **theoretical approach** to assessment. This strategy is based on theoretical considerations from the very start. The psychologist first develops a theoretical basis for believing that a particular aspect of personality is important. The next task is to create a test in which this dimension is reflected validly and reliably in people's answers. This approach to test development often leads to assessment devices that have a high degree of face validity.

It's important to realize that the work doesn't stop once a set of items has been developed. Instruments developed from this starting point must be shown to be reliable, to predict behavioral criteria, and to have good construct validity. Until these steps have been taken, the scale isn't considered a useful measure of anything.

It's probably safe to say that the majority of personality measurement devices that exist today were developed using this path. Some of these measures focus on a single construct, others are inventories with scales focusing on multiple constructs. Most of the measures discussed in later chapters were created by first deciding *what* to measure and then figuring out *how* to measure it.

EMPIRICAL APPROACHES

A second strategy is usually characterized as an **empirical**, or data-based, approach. Its basic characteristic is that it relies on data, rather than on theory, to decide what items go into the assessment device.

There are two important variations on this theme. In one of them, the person developing the measure uses the data to decide what qualities of personality even *exist* (e.g., Cattell, 1979). Because that line of thought is an important contributor to trait psychology, we're going to wait to discuss it until Chapter 4. We'll focus here on another empirical approach—one that reflects a very pragmatic orientation to the process of assessment. It's guided less by a desire to understand personality than by a practical aim: to sort people into categories. If a quick or inexpensive technique can be found to do this, the technique is useful.

Instead of developing the test first and then validating it against a criterion, this approach works in the opposite direction. The criterion is the groups into which people are to be sorted. To develop the test, you start with a huge number of possible items and find out which ones are answered differently by one criterion group than by other people. This is called the **criterion keying** approach. This label reflects the fact that the items retained are those that distinguish between the criterion group and other people. If an item set can be found for each group, then the test (all item sets together) can be used to tell who belongs to which group. In this view, it doesn't matter at all what the items look like. Items are chosen solely because members of a specific group (defined on some other basis) tend to answer them differently than other people.

This method underlies the Minnesota Multiphasic Personality Inventory, or MMPI (Hathaway & McKinley, 1943), revised in 1989 as the MMPI-2 (Butcher, Dahlstrom, Graham, Tellegen, & Kaemmer, 1989). This is a very long true–false inventory that was developed to assess abnormality. A large number of self-descriptive statements were given to a group of normal persons and to groups of psychiatric patients—people already judged by clinicians to have specific disorders. Thus, the criterion already existed. If people with one diagnosis either agreed or disagreed with an item more often than normal people and people with different diagnoses, that item was included in the scale for that diagnosis.

The MMPI-2 has become controversial in recent years, for several reasons. Most important for our purposes in this book, it is increasingly recognized that different diagnostic categories are not as distinct as they were formerly thought to be. As a result, scores on the MMPI tend to be elevated (if at all) on several scales, rather than just one. Once consequence of the recognition of this pattern is a broad (and intense) reconsideration of the nature of psychiatric diagnosis.

Better Assessment: A Never-Ending Search

No test is perfect, and no test is ever considered finished, just because it's widely used. Most personality scales in wide use today have been revised and restandardized periodically. The process of establishing construct validity requires not just a single study but many. It thus takes time. The process of establishing discriminant validity is virtually never ending. Tremendous effort is invested in creating and improving tests of personality. This investment of effort is necessary if people are to feel confident of knowing what the tests measure. Having that confidence is an important part of the assessment of personality.

The characteristics of personality tests discussed in this chapter distinguish these tests from those you see in newspapers and magazines, on TV, online, and so forth. Sometimes, the items in a magazine article were written specifically for that article. It's unlikely, though, that anyone checked on their reliability. It's even less likely that anyone checked on their validity. Unless the right steps have been taken to create an instrument, you should be careful about putting your faith in the results that come from it.

· SUMMARY ·

Assessment (measurement of personality) is something that people constantly do informally. Psychologists formalize this process into several distinct techniques. Observer ratings are made by someone other than the person being rated—an interviewer, someone who watches, or someone who knows the people well enough to make ratings of what they are like. Observer ratings often are somewhat subjective, involving interpretations of the person's behavior. Self-reports are reports about themselves made by the people being assessed. Self-reports can be single scale or multiscale inventories. Implicit assessment is measuring patterns of associations within the self that are not open to introspection. Assessment devices can be subjective or objective. Objective techniques require no interpretation as the assessment is made. Subjective techniques involve some sort of interpretation as an intrinsic part of the measure.

One issue for all assessment is reliability (the reproducibility of the measurement). Reliability is determined by checking one measurement against another (or several others). Self-report scales usually have many items (each a measurement device), leading to indices of internal reliability or internal consistency. Observer judgments are checked by inter-rater reliability. Test–retest reliability assesses the reproducibility of the measure over time. In all cases, high correlation among measures means good reliability.

Another important issue is validity (whether what you're measuring is what you want to measure). The attempt to determine whether the operational definition (the assessment device) matches the concept you set out to measure is called *construct validation*. Contributors to construct validity are evidence of criterion, convergent, and discriminant validity. Face validity isn't usually taken as an important element of construct validity. Validity is threatened by the fact that people have response sets (acquiescence and social desirability) that bias their responses.

Development of assessment devices follows one of two strategies or approaches. The rational strategy uses a theory to decide what should be measured and then figures out the best way to measure it. Most assessment devices developed this way. The empirical strategy involves using data to determine what items should be in a scale. The MMPI was developed this way, using a technique called *criterion keying,* in which the test developers let people's responses tell them which items to use. Test items that members of a diagnostic category answered differently from other people were retained.

· GLOSSARY ·

Acquiesence   The response set of tending to say "yes" ("agree") in response to any question.

Assessment   The measuring of personality.

Construct validity   The accuracy with which a measure reflects the underlying concept.

Convergent validity   The degree to which a measure relates to other characteristics that are conceptually similar to what it's supposed to assess.

Criterion keying   The developing of a test by seeing which items distinguish between groups.

Criterion validity   The degree to which the measure correlates with a separate criterion reflecting the same concept.

Discriminant validity   The degree to which a scale does *not* measure unintended qualities.

Empirical approach (to scale development)   The use of data instead of theory to decide what should go into the measure.

Error   Random influences that are incorporated in measurements.

Face validity   The scale "looks" as if it measures what it's supposed to measure.

Implicit assessment   Measuring associations between the sense of self and aspects of personality that are implicit (hard to introspect about).

Internal reliability (internal consistency)   Agreement among responses made to the items of a measure.

Inter-rater reliability   The degree of agreement between observers of the same events.

Inventory   A personality test measuring several aspects of personality on distinct subscales.

Objective measure   A measure that incorporates no interpretation.

Observer ratings   An assessment in which someone else produces information about the person being assessed.

Operational definition   The defining of a concept by the concrete events through which it's measured (or manipulated).

Predictive validity   The degree to which the measure predicts other variables it should predict.

Rational approach (to scale development)   The use of a theory to decide what you want to measure and then deciding how to measure it.

Reliability   Consistency across repeated measurements.

Response set   A biased orientation to answering.

Self-report   An assessment in which people make ratings pertaining to themselves.

Social desirability   The response set of tending to portray oneself favorably.

Split-half reliability   Assessing internal consistency among responses to items of a measure by splitting the items into halves and then correlating them.

Subjective measure   A measure incorporating personal interpretation.

Test-retest reliability   The stability of measurements across time.

Theoretical approach   *See* **Rational approach.**

Validity   The degree to which a measure actually measures what it's intended to measure.

The Trait Perspective

"I want you to meet a friend of mine from high school. He's really outgoing. He's friendly, but he doesn't go along with the crowd all the time. You might say he's sociable, but he's also independent."

"My psychology professor is smart, but he's totally hopeless. He must spend all his time in his office. I can't imagine him doing anything interesting or fun. He can't help it, I guess. It's just who he is."

THE TRAIT APPROACH TO personality exemplifies two points made in Chapter 1 about the concept of personality. One is the view that people are consistent in their actions, thoughts, and feelings over time and situations. Indeed, the concept of trait provides a way of saying that people remain the same people, even as time passes and they move from one situation to another. Traits are qualities that people carry around with them, that belong to them, that are part of them.

A second point is that people differ from each other in many ways. The field of personality psychology is guided, in part, by an emphasis on such differences among people. This emphasis is particularly central to the trait perspective. From this view, a personality consists, in part, of a pattern of trait qualities. The composition of the pattern differs from one person to another. The intersection among these traits in any given person defines his or her personality.

Types and Traits

The idea that people differ in fundamental ways goes back at least to Hippocrates (about 400 BC), whose ideas were later embellished by Galen (about AD 150). Back then, the idea was more specifically that people can be divided into different types, or categories. People were put in four groups: *choleric* (irritable), *melancholic* (depressed), *sanguine* (optimistic), and *phlegmatic* (calm). Each type was thought to reflect an excess of one of four basic bodily fluids.

More recently, Jung (1933) argued that people are either introverts or extraverts. An **introvert** tends to prefer solitary activities. When facing stress, introverts tend to withdraw into themselves. An **extravert** prefers to spend time with others. When facing stress, extraverts tend to seek out other people.

In a true typology, the **types** are seen as distinct and discontinuous categories (Figure 4.1, A). Type theories have faded over the years (although there remain some supporters of the idea: for discussions, see Gangestad & Snyder, 1985; Meehl, 1992; Robins, John, Caspi, Moffitt, & Stouthamer-Loeber, 1996; Strube, 1989; York & John, 1992).

In contrast to typologies, **trait** theories assume that people occupy different points on continuously varying dimensions (Figure 4.1, B). For that reason, this is sometimes called a *dimensional* approach. In trait theories, differences among people are seen as *quantitative*, rather than qualitative. People are seen as differing in *how much* various characteristics are incorporated in their personalities.

NOMOTHETIC AND IDIOGRAPHIC VIEWS OF TRAITS

Thus far, we've implied that traits pertain to every person and that people just vary in how much of each quality they have. The belief that traits exist in the same way in every person is called a **nomothetic** view (Allport, 1961). The term *nomothetic* derives from the Greek word meaning "law." This view holds that everyone stands somewhere on each trait that exists. This allows comparisons among people.

In contrast is the **idiographic** view (Allport, 1961), which emphasizes each person's uniqueness. In Chapter 2, we used this term to refer to an approach to research that focuses on how one person's experience varies across situations. In this context, the term implies that traits are individualized. A given trait may exist for only one person in the world. Even if the same term applies to two people, its connotations

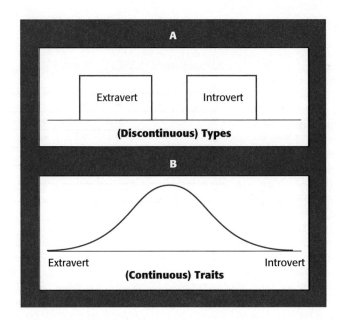

FIGURE 4.1
(A) Early type theories assumed a discontinuity between or among categories of people. (B) Trait theories assume that traits are continuous dimensions of variability on some characteristic and that the degree of presence versus absence of the characteristic is distributed across a population.

differ from one to the other (Dunning & McElwee, 1995). Even if the connotations are the same, the trait may differ in importance, so the people can't be compared meaningfully (Britt & Shepperd, 1999).

Some people like the idiographic view, because they think the nomothetic view provides no place for uniqueness. In reply, those who favor the nomothetic view say that uniqueness arises from unique *combinations* of levels on many trait dimensions, though the dimensions themselves are the same for everyone. As Eysenck put it, "the unique individual is simply the point of intersection of a number of quantitative variables" (1952, p. 18).

Psychologists who emphasize the idiographic view believe that nomothetic views are always oversimplifications (even though they sometimes use them). Allport (1961) believed we should never lose sight of the fact that even traits shared by people always have a special flavor (maybe from differences in how the traits are expressed) that varies from person to person.

What Traits Matter?

Thinking of personality in terms of traits quickly leads to this question: What are the traits that make up personality?

This is a hard question to answer with complete certainty. In fact, there have been serious disagreements about where to *start* in answering it. Before we describe this disagreement, let's back up and consider a problem that all trait theorists share, along with a tool that helps deal with it.

Box 4.1 A Closer Look at Factor Analysis

The process of factor analysis is complex, but its logic is fairly simple. It's an attempt to find patterns of association in a set of variables.

The first step is collecting data. This is more complicated than it might seem. First you have to decide what aspects of behavior you want to measure. Do you want self-reports? Observer ratings? As you can see, the first step—collecting data—entails many decisions.

Let's use an example. Imagine you're interested in how people cope with stress. You've decided to use self-reports: people's ratings of how much they did certain things during their most stressful event of the past year. To collect data, get 300 or so of your friends to recall a stressful event and respond to each of 28 items (listing things people sometimes do under stress). Here are some of the items.

1. Took action quickly, before things could get out of hand
2. Refused to believe that it was real
3. Did something concrete to make the situation better
4. Tried to convince myself that it wasn't happening
5. Went on thinking things were just like they were
6. Changed or grew as a person in a new way
7. Tried to look on the bright side of things

The second step is to compute the correlation of every item with every other item (panel A, top). Each correlation reflects the degree to which the 300 people tended to answer one item the same as the other item. There are strong correla tions between items 1 and 3; between 6 and 7; and between 2 and both 4 and 5 (which also strongly relate to each other). The others are quite weak.

Because you had people rate 28 items (instead of just these 7), your correlation matrix is huge. Interpreting the pattern of correlations would be a real chore. The chore is lessened by the third step, called *factor extraction*. It reduces your matrix to a smaller number of underlying dimensions (for example, the links among items 2, 4, and 5 would contribute to one dimension). These dimensions of underlying commonality are called *factors*. Factors are hazy entities you can imagine but can't see.

The next step is to compute the *factor loadings* of each item on each factor. Loadings tell you the relations between the items and the factors (panel B, right). Each loading indicates how much the item reflects the underlying dimension. A large number (a high loading) means the item is closely linked to that dimension, a small number means it's not. As shown, items 1 and 3 load on factor A, items 6 and 7 load on factor B, and items 2, 4, and 5 load on factor C. Similar loadings emerge for all your 28 items, letting you know which items go together.

Once it's clear which items form factors, you're at the final step: naming the factors. You want to convey the essence of the underlying quality, but your only guide is which items load on it. Often the items are ambiguous, clouding the picture. In our example, a couple of factors are easy. The items on factor A show a tendency to try to solve the problem. This might be called *problem-focused coping*. Given the content of items 2, 4, and 5, factor C might be *denial*. Factor B seems to be *positive reinterpretation* or *posttraumatic growth* or *looking on the bright side,* but it's hard to be sure which is best. It's important to be careful, though, because the name you use will guide your future thinking.

A. Hypothetical Correlation Matrix

Item	1	2	3	4	5	6	7
1	*	0.10	0.75	−0.05	0.03	0.12	0.00
2		*	−0.02	0.52	0.61	−0.007	−0.08
3			*	0.17	0.00	0.09	0.15
4				*	0.71	0.11	0.08
5					*	0.06	−0.04
6						*	0.59
7							*

B. Hypothetical Factor Loadings

Factor	A	B	C
Item 1	0.62	0.15	0.01
Item 2	0.03	−0.08	0.49
Item 3	0.54	0.04	0.20
Item 4	0.10	0.11	0.56
Item 5	0.07	0.08	0.50
Item 6	−0.02	0.72	0.12
Item 7	0.08	0.48	0.08

A KEY TOOL: FACTOR ANALYSIS

Personality is reflected in many ways—for example, in descriptive words. If each word that describes personality meant a different trait, a psychologist would go crazy trying to organize things. That, in a nutshell, is a problem trait psychologists face: bringing order to such diversity. Perhaps, however, the many words reflect a small number of underlying trait dimensions. If so, how do you figure out what the dimensions are?

A tool that's often used for this is a statistical technique called **factor analysis**. The basic idea is simple: If two qualities correlate when assessed across many people, they may reflect a trait that contributes to both of them. *Patterns* of correlation, then, may reveal trait dimensions that lie beneath the measured qualities. Factor analysis is essentially a more complex version of correlation. Instead of looking at one correlation between *two* variables, a factor analysis looks at correlations among *many* variables.

Because the process of factor analysis is very complex, it wasn't widely used until the computer age. The huge rise in computing power over the years has led to far greater sophistication in such procedures (Bentler, 1990; Jöreskog & Sörbom, 1979).

The process starts by collecting measurements on many variables (typically self-reports or observer ratings) from large numbers of people. Once the data have been collected, correlations are computed between every pair of variables (see Box 4.1). The set of correlations is then put through a procedure called *factor extraction*. This distills the correlations to a smaller set of **factors**. Each factor represents shared variations (underlying commonalities) among several of the measures (rather than just two at a time).

Once the factors have been extracted, each can be described by a set of **factor loadings**. Think of these as correlations between the factor and each item (rating) that contributes to its existence. Items that correlate strongly with the factor (usually higher than 0.40 or so) are said to "load on" that factor. Items that don't correlate strongly with the factor are said not to load on it. The items that load on the factor tell you what the factor is "about."

The final step in the analysis is labeling the factors. Remember that a factor is defined by which items load on it. Thus, you choose a label to denote as closely as possible the essence of those items, particularly those with the highest loadings. In personality, the factor is viewed as the statistical reflection of a trait. When you name the factor, you are naming the trait.

Factor naming is very subjective. Several names might seem equally good, but which name is chosen can have important consequences. People often forget that the label is an inference from the correlations, and they rely on the label to tell them what the trait is. If the label you choose is misleading, it can create problems later.

Factor analysis as a tool in trait psychology does three things. First, it reduces the multiple reflections of personality to a smaller set of traits. Second, it provides a basis for arguing that some traits matter more than others. That is, if a factor accounts for a lot of variability in the ratings, it reflects an important trait; if it accounts for less, it's less important. Third, it helps in developing assessment devices. You keep items (or ratings) that load strongly (greatly reflect the trait) and discard items that don't. Through repeated item creation and testing, items that don't do a good job of measuring a particular trait are replaced by better ones.

Factor analysis is a very useful tool. It's only a tool, though. What we've told you has a big hole in it. We haven't said anything about *what measures to collect in the first place*. A factor analysis can tell you only about what you put into it. Thus, the decision about what to measure has a huge impact on what emerges as traits.

Whereas extraverts prefer exciting activities involving other people, introverts prefer solitary activities and being alone.

How do you decide what measures to collect? As noted earlier, different people have started off differently. Let's now return to that question.

LET REALITY REVEAL ITSELF

The answer some give to that question is that researchers should determine *empirically* what traits make up personality. If you start with preconceptions, you'll lead yourself astray. This was the argument of Raymond Cattell, an early contributor to trait psychology and one of the first to use factor analysis (Cattell, 1947, 1965, 1978; Cattell & Kline, 1977).

One empirical approach focused on language as a source of information (see Goldberg, 1982). A language that's evolved over thousands of years has words to describe many human qualities. Presumably, any trait that matters has words that describe it. In fact, the more words for a quality of personality, the more it probably matters. This is called the **lexical criterion** of importance. Following this idea, Cattell (1947, 1965) took a set of trait terms, collected ratings on them, and factor analyzed the ratings. The emerging factors were the traits he believed mattered.

Cattell thought that personality is captured in a set of 16 dimensions. The dimensions reemerged in analyses across various types of data, and he saw them as the primary traits in personality. These 16 primary factors provided a name for his personality inventory: the 16 Personality Factor inventory, or 16PF (Cattell, Eber, & Tatsuoka, 1977).

START FROM A THEORY

Not everyone agreed that an empirical starting point is best. Another major contributor to trait psychology, Hans Eysenck (1967, 1970, 1975, 1986; Eysenck & Eysenck, 1985) argued that we should begin instead with well-developed ideas about what we want to measure. Then we should set about measuring those qualities well. In framing his ideas, Eysenck began with the typology of Hippocrates and Galen and observations made by Jung and Wundt (Eysenck, 1967). He set out to study whether the types identified by Hippocrates and Galen (and re-identified by others) could be created by combining high and low levels of two supertraits.

The two supertraits Eysenck posed as the key dimensions of personality are *extraversion* (vs. introversion) and *neuroticism* (also called *emotional stability*). The extraversion dimension concerns tendencies toward sociability, liveliness, activeness, and dominance (all of which characterize extraverts). The neuroticism dimension concerns the ease and frequency with which the person becomes upset and distressed.

Table 4.1 Traits That Are Common among Four Categories of People Deriving from the Two Major Personality Dimensions Proposed by Eysenck. Each category results from combining moderately extreme levels of introversion or extraversion with either a high or a low level of neuroticism. (The colored labels are the names given to personality types by Galen in the second century AD.) *Source:* Adapted from Eysenck, 1975.

	Low Neuroticism		High Neuroticism	
Introvert	Passive Careful Thoughtful Peaceful Controlled Reliable Even tempered Calm	**Phlegmatic**	Quiet Pessimistic Unsociable Sober Rigid Moody Anxious Reserved	**Melancholic**
Extravert	Sociable Outgoing Talkative Responsive Easygoing Lively Carefree Leaderly	**Sanguine**	Active Optimistic Impulsive Changeable Excitable Aggressive Restless Touchy	**Choleric**

These dimensions can create more diversity than you might guess. Table 4.1 portrays four sets of people with combinations of highs and lows on these dimensions. The ancient type label for each group is printed in color. In looking at these people, keep two things in mind: First, although the form of Table 4.1 suggests discontinuity, both dimensions are continuous. Second, the descriptions are of fairly extreme and clear-cut cases. Most people are closer to the middle on both dimensions and thus have less extreme characteristics.

As Table 4.1 indicates, people who are introverted and also emotionally stable (low in neuroticism) tend to be careful, controlled, calm, and thoughtful in their actions. The combination of introversion and high neuroticism, on the other hand, creates a more pessimistic and anxious quality. Thus, introverts can differ substantially, depending on their levels of neuroticism. So can extraverts. When extraversion combines with low neuroticism, the result is an easygoing, carefree sociability. High neuroticism in an extravert introduces an excitable aggressive quality. Thus, the impact of one dimension differs as a function of the person's location on the other trait dimension. In the terms used in Chapter 2, the traits interact.

Eysenck assessed these dimensions using self-report measures (Eysenck & Eysenck, 1975). He also used factor analysis to help create these measures, but he did so with a different goal in mind than Cattell had. Cattell used factor analysis to find out what dimensions *exist*. Eysenck used factor analysis to refine his scales, by

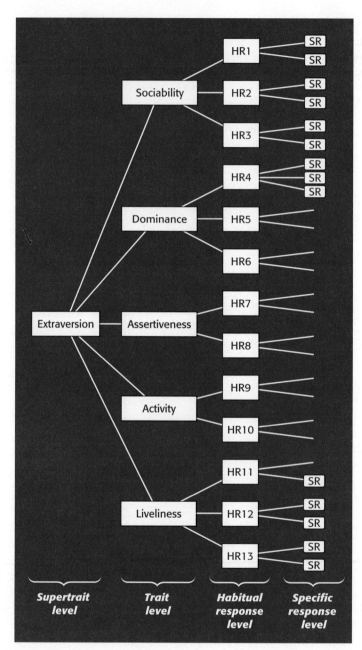

FIGURE 4.2

Eysenck's hierarchical view of personality as applied to extraversion. The top level of the model (supertraits) subsumes the elements represented at the next-lower level (traits). These elements, in turn, are made up of yet lower-order qualities (habits), which are made up of associations between stimulus and response.

Source: Adapted from The Biological Basis of Personality (1967, p. 36), by H. J. Eysenck. Reprinted courtesy of Charles C Thomas, Publisher, Springfield, IL.

selecting items that loaded well, and to confirm that the scales measure two factors, as he intended.

Although Eysenck and Cattell started out very differently, the trait structures they produced have distinct similarities. The two dimensions Eysenck saw as supertraits resemble two of the first three factors of Cattell's 16PF. The similarities are even stronger in **second-order factors** from the 16PF. A second-order analysis tells whether the factors *themselves* form factors (correlate in clusters). One second-order factor from the 16PF is virtually identical to extraversion (Cattell & Kline, 1977); another is similar to neuroticism.

Another reflection of the convergence can be seen in Eysenck's view that extraversion is at the top of an unfolding hierarchy of qualities (see Figure 4.2), as is neuroticism. Each supertrait is made of component traits (which resemble Cattell's primary traits). Component traits, in turn, reflect habits, which derive from specific responses. Eysenck believed all levels are involved in behavior, but he saw supertraits as the most important.

Two more points about Eysenck's view: First, he believed that extraversion and neuroticism link to aspects of nervous system functioning. (This aspect of his theory comes up in Chapter 7.) Second, there's a third dimension in Eysenck's view, called *psychoticism*, which has received less attention than the others (Eysenck & Eysenck, 1976). It involves, in part, a tendency toward psychological detachment from, and lack of concern with, other people. People high in this trait tend to be hostile, manipulative, and impulsive (Eysenck, 1992).

ANOTHER THEORETICAL STARTING POINT: THE INTERPERSONAL CIRCLE

Another theoretical starting point emphasized interpersonal aspects of personality. Jerry Wiggins and his colleagues (Wiggins, 1979; Wiggins, Phillips, & Trapnell, 1989) argued that the core human traits concern interpersonal life. Wiggins proposed a set of eight patterns, which he called the **interpersonal circle**, arrayed around two dimensions underlying human relations (see Figure 4.3). The core dimensions are dominance (or status) and love.

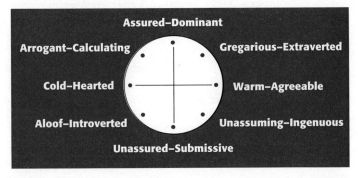

FIGURE 4.3
The *interpersonal circle,* a set of personality patterns portrayed in terms of their relative prevalence of two traits: love (the horizontal dimension) and dominance (the vertical dimension). The midpoint of each trait is the point where the lines cross.
Source: Adapted from Wiggins, Phillips, & Trapnell, 1989.

Wiggins argued (as did Eysenck) that diverse personalities arise from combinations of values on the two core dimensions. A person who's high in dominance and toward the cold-hearted end of love will seem arrogant and calculating. Put the same degree of dominance with warmth on the love dimension, though, and you get a person who's gregarious and extraverted.

Introversion and extraversion appear on this interpersonal circle (in the lower-left and upper-right corners of the figure), but here, they don't represent a fundamental dimension. Instead, they are seen as resulting from the intersection of two other qualities.

The Five-Factor Model: The Basic Dimensions of Personality?

Despite the different starting points taken by various people, a substantial consensus has begun to emerge about what traits are basic. The emerging consensus has overtones of several ideas already presented, but it extends beyond them. The emerging consensus is that the structure of personality may incorporate five superordinate factors. These are often referred to as the *five-factor model* or the *big five* (Goldberg, 1981; McCrae & Costa, 2003; Wiggins, 1996).

Evidence for a five-factor view of personality structure accumulated slowly for a long time (Digman, 1990). In 1949, Fiske couldn't reproduce Cattell's 16 factors but instead found 5. That finding sat in obscurity until the early 1960s, when Norman (1963), Borgatta (1964), and Smith (1967) all addressed the same general issue with different measures. Each reached the same conclusion: Five factors provided the best account of the data.

During the decades of the 1980s and 1990s, there was an explosion of work on this topic. Diverse samples have been studied, including teachers' ratings of children (Digman & Inouye, 1986); peer ratings (McCrae & Costa, 1987); frequencies with which people engage in particular kinds of actions (Botwin & Buss, 1989); and nonverbal assessments (Paunonen, Jackson, Trzebinski, & Forsterling, 1992). The model was also tested against measures developed from entirely different lines of thought (Costa & McCrae, 1988a; McCrae & Costa, 1989). Peabody and Goldberg (1989; Peabody, 1984) used scales that were chosen to be sure there were enough *common* trait words, instead of words that mean more to psychologists than to other people. Haas (2002) even explored the idea that proverbs capture the five factors.

Data have now been collected from many cultures and languages. The findings, as a group, suggest that the five factors may transcend many boundaries of language and culture (e.g., Benet-Martínez & John, 1998; Church, 2001; Katigbak, Church, Guanzon-Lapeña, Carlota, & del Pilar, 2002; McCrae & Costa, 1997; McCrae, Zonderman, Costa, Bond, & Paunonen, 1996; Paunonen et al., 1992; Saucier & Ostendorf, 1999; Somer & Goldberg, 1999; Stumpf, 1993). The cultures examined in this work are as diverse as those of Turkey (Somer & Goldberg, 1999) and the Philippines (Katigbak et al., 2002). One study of observer ratings collected data in 50 cultures (McCrae et al., 2005). It has even been argued (Gosling, 2001) that the factors (or at least some of them) apply to lower animals!

There have been some failures to find the pattern and some imperfections in the findings (e.g., Benet & Waller, 1995; Church & Burke, 1994; Di Blas & Forzi, 1999; Lanning, 1994). And Saucier and Simonds (2006) caution that the pattern is clearest in Western languages and hard to find in some other languages. Yet the

Table 4.2 Labels Used by Various Authors to Refer to the "Big Five" Factors in Personality. Labels in the rows are from (in order) Fiske (1949), Norman (1963), Borgatta (1964), Digman (1990), and Costa and McCrae (1985). The final row provides a characterization by Peabody and Goldberg (1989) of the life domain to which the trait pertains.

1	2	3	4	5
Social adaptability	Emotional control	Conformity	Will to achieve	Inquiring intellect
Surgency	Emotionality	Agreeableness	Conscientious-ness	Culture
Assertiveness	Emotionality	Likeability	Responsibility	Intelligence
Extraversion	Neuroticism	Friendly compliance	Will to achieve	Intellect
Extraversion	Neuroticism	Agreeableness	Conscientious-ness	Openness to experience
Power	Love	Work	Affect	Intellect

body of work, as a whole, is impressive in its fit to the five-factor model (Digman, 1990; John, 1990; McCrae & Costa, 1997, 2003; McCrae & John, 1992; Ozer & Reise, 1994).

What *Are* the Five Factors?

Given what we've said so far, what comes next may surprise you. There's still a certain amount of disagreement as to exactly what the five dimensions *are* (Briggs, 1989; John, 1990; Johnson & Ostendorf, 1993; Pytlik Zillig, Hemenover, & Dienstbier, 2002; Saucier, 1992).

The disagreement has at least two sources. First, recall that naming factors can be hard. You do it by looking at the items that load on the factor and trying to extract the underlying thread that connects them. But most words have several connotations, and trait words often portray blends of factors rather than only one factor per word (Hofstee, de Raad, & Goldberg, 1992). Naturally, then, there are disagreements in interpretation.

Second, exactly what a factor looks like depends on what items are in the study. If a particular quality is left out or is not well represented in the items, its importance to a trait will be missed (Peabody & Goldberg, 1989). Thus, studies with slightly different measures can lead to different conclusions about what defines the factors, even when there's agreement that more or less the same factors have emerged.

Table 4.2 displays the five traits, using a variety of names for each. Peabody and Goldberg (1989) suggested that the five factors are the metaphorical equivalent of a piece of music in which there's a theme and a series of variations on it. That's pretty much what you see in Table 4.2. The labels listed under each factor all share a theme, but there are also variations. Some of the basis for the variation is displayed in Table 4.3, which lists examples of the descriptive terms that loaded on the five factors in one study or another.

The first factor is usually called *extraversion*, but there's a good deal of variation in what it includes. This helps account for the different labels. Sometimes it seems based in assertiveness, sometimes in spontaneity and energy. Sometimes it's based in dominance and confidence, sometimes in a tendency toward happiness. It often conveys a

Table 4.3 Bipolar and Unipolar Adjective Sets Reflecting the Five Major Personality Factors.

Factor		Item
Extraversion	Bold-timid	Gregarious
	Forceful-submissive	Outspoken
	Self-confident-unassured	Energetic
	Talkative-silent	Happy
	Spontaneous-inhibited	Seclusive (inverse)
Neuroticism	Nervous-poised	Concerned
	Anxious-calm	Nervous
	Excitable-composed	Fearful
	Relaxed-high strung	Tense
Agreeableness	Friendly-unfriendly	Jealous (inverse)
	Warm-cold	Considerate
	Kind-unkind	Spiteful (inverse)
	Polite-rude	Touchy (inverse)
	Good natured-irritable	Complaining (inverse)
Conscientiousness	Cautious-rash	Neat
	Serious-frivolous	Persevering
	Responsible-irresponsible	Planful
	Thorough-careless	Careful
	Hardworking-lazy	Eccentric (inverse)
Intellect	Imaginative-simple	Knowledgeable
	Intellectual-unreflective	Perceptive
	Polished-crude	Imaginative
	Uncurious-curious	Verbal
	Uncreative-creative	Original

Source: Based on Digman & Inouye, 1986; McCrae & Costa, 1987; Norman, 1963; Peabody & Goldberg, 1989.

sense of sociability (Watson, Clark, McIntyre, & Hamaker, 1992), but some argue that that's actually a by-product of other features of extraversion (Lucas, Diener, Grob, Suh, & Shao, 2000). Extraverts do, however, interact more with others in day-to-day life (Srivastava, Angelo, & Vallereaux, 2008).

There's a great deal of agreement (though still not unanimity) about the meaning of the second factor. *Neuroticism*, or *emotional stability*, is regarded by most people as being what Eysenck referred to with those labels. Though there are other overtones, what's at the heart of this factor is the subjective experience of anxiety and general distress.

The third factor in Table 4.3 is most commonly called *agreeableness*. This trait is often characterized as reflecting a concern with maintaining relationships. It can also imply nurturance and emotional supportiveness, which requires inhibition of negative affect (Graziano & Eisenberg, 1999). Indeed, such inhibition seems to occur automatically among persons high in agreeableness (Haas, Omura, Constable, & Canli,

2007). The opposite pole of this dimension has an oppositional or antagonistic quality verging toward hostility (Digman, 1990). Fitting this, people low in agreeableness choose displays of power as a way of resolving social conflict more than people higher in agreeableness (Graziano, Jensen-Campbell, & Hair, 1996). There's also evidence that they actually *experience* more conflicts (Asendorpf & Wilpers, 1998).

The essence of the fourth factor is also a little hard to capture. The most commonly used label is *conscientiousness*. However, this label doesn't fully reflect the qualities of planning, persistence, and purposeful striving toward goals (Digman & Inouye, 1986). Indeed, because the word *conscientious* itself has two shades of meaning, that word loads both on this factor and on agreeableness. That hints that conscientiousness may not be a perfect name for this factor. Digman (1990) suggested that it be thought of as the *will to achieve* or simply *will*. Other suggested names include *constraint* and *responsibility*. Roberts, Walton, and Bogg (2005) recently examined the qualities that various theorists consider part of conscientiousness and concluded that no single measure of the trait includes all of them.

The largest disagreement may concern the last factor. The disagreement stems at least partly from differences in measures. Early on, Cattell measured aspects of intelligence. Then he stopped doing so and started using the term *culture* to refer to the qualities that remained. The label stuck. Peabody and Goldberg (1989) pointed out, though, that when intelligence-related measures are reintroduced, they join with culture. These researchers suggest the factor should more properly be labeled *intellect*. Costa and McCrae (1985) favored yet another label: *openness* to experience.

Peabody and Goldberg (1989) argued that Costa and McCrae's measure of this factor taps one aspect of intellect (the imaginative side) but misses the other side (the logical side). They said that when both sides are measured, they merge (implying that this factor is really intellect). On the other hand, there's evidence that qualities of intellect and openness rely on different aspects of the brain (DeYoung, Shamosh, Green, Braver, & Gray, 2009).

Reflections of the Five Factors in Behavior

For some time, most work on the five-factor model was aimed at the factors themselves: showing that they exist in diverse cultures and emerge from many ways of assessment. More recently, however, researchers have turned more to looking at how these five traits are reflected, or expressed, on the broader canvas of people's lives.

SOCIAL TRAITS: EXTRAVERSION AND AGREEABLENESS

Let's start with the traits that are most social in nature: extraversion and agreeableness. Several projects have suggested that extraversion and agreeableness are both tied to social situations, but in different ways. Extraversion seems to relate to *having social impact*; agreeableness seems to relate to *maintaining positive relations with others* (Jensen-Campbell & Graziano, 2001). Fitting this, extraversion predicts being prominent in fraternities and sororities (Anderson, John, Keltner, & Kring, 2001), but agreeableness does not. In a study of adolescents (Jensen-Campbell et al., 2002), extraversion and agreeableness both related to peer acceptance, but agreeableness also protected against being victimized by peers. Adults high in agreeableness also report greater social support from family members (Branje, van Lieshout, & van Aken, 2004). All of this makes sense, if agreeableness is largely about maintaining good relations.

People high in agreeableness care about maintaining positive relations with others.

A variety of other findings fit this idea, as well. Agreeableness predicts endorsement of conflict resolution tactics among children (Jensen-Campbell, Gleason, Adams, & Malcolm, 2003). Agreeable adults get less angry over bad outcomes caused by other people than do less agreeable adults (Meier & Robinson, 2004). Thus, agreeableness short-circuits aggressive responses (Meier, Robinson, & Wilkowski, 2006). Agreeableness has been related to greater responsiveness in parenting (Clark, Kochanska, & Ready, 2000), less negativity in marital interactions (Donnellan, Conger, & Bryant, 2004), and less seeking of revenge after being harmed (McCullough & Hoyt, 2002). Agreeableness also predicts less poaching of romantic partners, less responsiveness to poaching attempts by others (Schmitt & Buss, 2001), and greater cooperation in resolving social dilemmas over resources (Koole, Jager, van den Berg, Vlek, & Hofstee, 2001). Agreeableness has also been linked to less substance abuse (Chassin, Flora, & King, 2004; Lynam, Leukefeld, & Clayton, 2003; Walton & Roberts, 2004) and less antisocial behavior (Miller, Lynam, & Leukefeld, 2003).

Extraversion can also be helpful socially, in ways that differ from effects of agreeableness. Extraverted men interact better with women they don't know than introverts do (Berry & Miller, 2001), and extraverts have the firm handshake that conveys confidence (Chaplin, Phillips, Brown, Clanton, & Stein, 2000). When extraverts and introverts tell catch-up stories to their friends, extraverts construct the stories along with their friends, whereas introverts construct the plots solo (Thorne, Korobov, & Morgan, 2007). On the other hand, extraverts are less cooperative than introverts when facing social resource dilemmas (Koole et al., 2001).

Studies have also found that these two trait dimensions relate in consistent ways to personal values and life goals. Extraversion relates to valuing achievement and stimulation; agreeableness relates to valuing benevolence and tradition (Roccas, Sagiv, Schwartz, & Knafo, 2002). Extraversion relates to desires for a high-status career, political influence, an exciting lifestyle, and children; agreeableness relates to desires for group welfare and harmonious family relations and actually relates inversely to desires for wealth, political influence, and an exciting lifestyle (Roberts & Robins, 2000).

CONSCIENTIOUSNESS, OPENNESS, AND NEUROTICISM

Conscientiousness has also received a good deal of attention in recent years. Greater conscientiousness predicts less unsafe sex (Trobst, Herbst, Masters, & Costa, 2002) and other risky behaviors (Markey, Markey, & Tinsley, 2003). Conscientious people are less likely to try to steal someone else's romantic partner and are less responsive to being lured away (Schmitt & Buss, 2001). Conscientiousness has been linked to more responsive parenting of young children (Clark et al., 2000) and to use of negotiation as a conflict-resolution strategy (Jensen-Campbell & Graziano, 2001). Conscientiousness has also been shown to be important in the development of relationships in adolescence (Jensen-Campbell & Malcolm, 2007).

Conscientiousness has been related to the desire for a career but not necessarily a high standard of living (Roberts & Robins, 2000). Conscientiousness in adolescence predicts higher academic achievement (Chamorro-Premuzic & Furnham, 2003; Noftle & Robins, 2007; Poropat, 2009; Wagerman & Funder, 2007) and relates to higher religiousness in adulthood (McCullough, Tsang, & Brion, 2003). Conscientiousness also predicts peer ratings of social influence in organizational settings (Harms, Roberts, & Wood, 2007).

Conscientiousness also seems to have health implications. In a study of cancer risk factors, conscientiousness led to more restrictive household bans on smoking (Hampson, Andrews, Barckley, Lichtenstein, & Lee, 2000). People who are high in conscientiousness live longer (Kern & Friedman, 2008; Martin, Friedman, & Schwartz, 2007), presumably because they take better care of themselves (Christensen et al., 2002). Consistent with this, conscientiousness relates to various kinds of health-linked behaviors (Bogg & Roberts, 2004; Roberts et al., 2005). In fact, conscientiousness in childhood has been related to health behaviors 40 years later (Hampson, Goldberg, Vogt, & Dubanoski, 2006). Conscientiousness has also been related to less substance abuse (Chassin et al., 2004; Lynam et al., 2003; Roberts & Bogg, 2004; Walton & Roberts, 2004) and to less antisocial behavior more generally (Miller, Pedersen, Earleywine, & Pollock, 2003).

Openness to experience has been linked to a range of social experience (McCrae, 1996). Openness to experience has been found to predict greater engagement with the existential challenges of life (Keyes, Shmotkin, & Ryff, 2002). Openness relates to more favorable inter-racial attitudes (Flynn, 2005) and less likelihood of stigmatizing others (McCrae et al., 2007). Openness relates to greater sexual satisfaction in marriage (Donnellan et al., 2004). People high in openness say they desire artistic expression and devalue the possibility of an easy, lazy life (Roberts & Robins, 2000). They also react less intensely to stress (Williams, Rau, Cribbet, & Gunn, 2009). On the other hand, openness has also been found to predict more prior arrests among prisoners (Clower & Bothwell, 2001).

Neuroticism has been studied for decades. A high level of neuroticism relates to distress in a wide variety of difficult circumstances. For instance, it relates to more difficult interactions among married partners (Donnellan et al., 2004) and less satisfaction in the relationship. People who are highly neurotic are also more likely to distance themselves from their partners after a negative event (Bolger & Zuckerman, 1995). Neuroticism impairs academic performance (Chamorro-Premuzic & Furnham, 2003), and it even predicts a negative emotional tone when writing stories about oneself (McAdams et al., 2004). Neuroticism also predicts earlier death (Hampson & Friedman, 2008), partly (but not exclusively) because people higher in neuroticism smoke more (Mroczek, Spiro, & Turiano, 2009). Death comes even sooner if one develops an even higher level of neuroticism over time (Mroczek & Spiro, 2007).

Relations to Earlier Trait Models

Today, when people think of trait psychology, they generally think first of the five-factor model. However, recall from earlier in the chapter that some other trait models preceded this one. Let's consider how the five-factor model relates to them.

The easiest comparison is to Eysenck's theory. It's obvious from Table 4.2 that two of the "big five" are virtually the same as Eysenck's supertraits: extraversion and emotional stability. It's been suggested that Eysenck's third dimension, psychoticism, is a blend of agreeableness and conscientiousness (Goldberg, 1993b; Zuckerman, Kuhlman, Joireman, Teta, & Kraft, 1993).

A second similarity to Eysenck is that the five factors are superordinate traits, incorporating narrower traits. For example, Paul Costa and Robert McCrae (1985, 1992) developed a measure called the NEO Personality Inventory (NEO-PI-R; NEO stands for neuroticism, extraversion, and openness; agreeableness and *conscientiousness* were added after the name was coined; the R stands for *revised*.) The NEO-PI-R includes measures of six narrow traits for each domain of the five-factor model. The six narrow traits combine into a score for that supertrait. Thus, many people who use the five-factor model share with Eysenck the idea that the core traits are supertraits, which are, in turn, composed of more specific facet traits.

Another useful comparison is with the interpersonal circle of Wiggins and his colleagues. The basic dimensions of the circle are dominance and love. Love may be equivalent to agreeableness. If dominance were seen as roughly equivalent to extraversion, the interpersonal circle would comprise two factors of the five-factor model (McCrae & Costa, 1989; Peabody & Goldberg, 1989). Trapnell and Wiggins (1990) expanded a measure of the interpersonal circle to have additional scales and an even better fit to the five-factor model (see also Saucier, 1992).

This comparison with the interpersonal circle also raises an issue, however. As noted earlier (see Figure 4.3), Wiggins saw extraversion as a combination of two qualities in the circle, not as a basic dimension. Doesn't this conflict with the five-factor model? It depends on how you define *extraversion*. Remember, there are diverse opinions on how to view that factor. If it's really about dominance and assertiveness, it would fit with the interpersonal circle.

To summarize some of the points made thus far, the five-factor model of personality structure has emerged as a candidate for integrating a variety of earlier models. The data make this set of broad traits look very much as though they represent universal aspects of personality (McCrae & Costa, 1997). Remember, though, that what comes out of a factor analysis depends on what goes into it. It can be dangerous to draw conclusions too fast. Nonetheless, at present the five-factor model seems to offer the best promise of a consensus about the dimensions of personality that trait psychology has ever seen.

Other Variations

Consensus is not unanimity, however. People have disagreed with this view for a variety of reasons (e.g., Block, 1995, 2001; Eysenck, 1992, 1993; Zuckerman, 1992). Several other trait models also exist that differ from the five-factor model in various ways.

One is Tellegen's (1985) model. It greatly resembles Eysenck's (1975, 1986) in having three supertraits, though with somewhat different origins and overtones. Tellegen (1985) recast neuroticism slightly as a tendency to experience negative emotions, and he recast extraversion as a tendency to experience positive emotions. Positive emotionality (like extraversion) has been tied to social success, and negative emotionality (like neuroticism) has been tied to indices of poor adjustment (Shiner, Masten, & Tellegen, 2002). Tellegen's third factor, constraint, resembles psychoticism in Eysenck's model but viewed from the opposite direction. It also predicts similar outcomes: Low constraint has been linked to criminal and antisocial behavior (Krueger, 2002; Shiner et al., 2002) and (in interaction with high negative affectivity) to drug use (Shoal & Giancola, 2003).

The idea of five factors was adopted but carried in another direction by Zuckerman and his colleagues (1993), who proposed an "alternative 5." Once again, remember that what comes out of a factor analysis depends partly on what goes into it. These theorists put slightly different things in. The sociability factor in this model resembles extraversion (if you view extraversion as mostly social). Neuroticism–anxiety is most of neuroticism but without the hostility that others include there. Hostility is in aggression–hostility, which otherwise looks like agreeableness (reversed). Impulsive sensation seeking looks like conscientiousness (reversed). The last factor in this model is Activity. What may be the most important difference between this and the other five-factor model is that Zuckerman et al. located hostility outside neuroticism. There are several reasons why that may actually be a better location for it (Carver, 2004; Jang, Livesley, Angleitner, Riemann, & Vernon, 2002; Peabody & DeRaad, 2002; Saucier & Goldberg, 2001).

EXPANDING AND CONDENSING THE FIVE-FACTOR MODEL

The idea that what comes out depends on what goes in is also reflected in a viewpoint that builds on the five-factor model by adding another factor. Ashton and his colleagues believe that the five-factor model is incomplete. In tests involving seven languages, they found a sixth supertrait that they call *honesty–humility* (Ashton, Lee, Perugini, et al., 2004). Subsequent work established that this factor can also be found in analyses of English words (Ashton, Lee, & Goldberg, 2004). Ashton and his colleagues suggest that this trait tends to be absorbed by agreeableness in some measures but is a distinct quality that stands out on its own, if it's allowed to do so. They developed a measure (and model) that they call the HEXACO framework (Ashton & Lee, 2007), and they have shown that this additional factor adds predictive validity above and beyond the five-factor framework (Ashton & Lee, 2008).

Some have made an opposite argument: that the five-factor model can be condensed into two dimensions. That is, putting the five traits into a higher-order analysis yields two factors. The first is defined by (low) neuroticism, agreeableness, and conscientiousness. Digman (1997) called it *socialization*, because these qualities all influence whether people get along in social units. The second is defined by extraversion and openness. Digman characterized it as reflecting *personal growth*, because these qualities influence whether people expose themselves to new things, thereby fostering growth. DeYoung (2006) found the same two higher-order factors and called them *stability* and *plasticity*. He argued that they reflect, respectively, an organismic need to maintain a stable organization of psychological functioning and a need to explore and grow.

ARE SUPERORDINATE TRAITS THE BEST LEVEL TO USE?

There remains at least one more question to raise, even for people who accept the five-factor model. As we said, this is a model of supertraits. Supertraits have facets. As noted earlier, Costa and McCrae's NEO-PI-R measures six facets of each factor. Those who use the five-factor model sometimes point to the utility of examining patterns of traits within each factor (Costa & McCrae, 1995; Goldberg, 1993a).

Is anything lost when lower-level traits are combined to form the supertraits? This is essentially what Cattell and Eysenck argued about when they disagreed about the meaning of second-order factors (see also Briggs, 1989; H. E. P. Cattell, 1993;

Funder, 1991; John, 1990). The evidence suggests that something is indeed lost when facet traits are merged.

Paunonen and Ashton (2001a) compared the "big five" factors to specific facet scales as predictors of 40 behaviors, which were measured by self-reports and peer ratings. The behaviors were chosen because they had some social importance (altruistic behavior, smoking, alcohol consumption, religiosity, and so on). For a substantial number of these behaviors, facet scales added significantly to prediction after the five factors had been entered as predictors. Thus, something is lost if only the "big five" are used. Conceptually similar findings have come from a number of other studies (Mershon & Gorsuch, 1988; Paunonen, 1998; Paunonen & Ashton, 2001b; Schimmack, Oishi, Furr, & Funder, 2004; Wolfe & Kasmer, 1988).

Better prediction from specific, narrow traits comes at a cost, though. The cost is that to understand the findings, you have to hold a larger number of traits in mind at once. In general terms, that's the trade-off: Using supertraits creates a picture that's more intuitive and easier to hold in mind, whereas using narrower traits may often give greater accuracy.

An in-between position has also been suggested (DeYoung, Quilty, & Peterson, 2007). This position derives from evidence that a broad set of facets within a given supertrait can be reduced to two aspects per trait. DeYoung et al. suggest that this intermediate position provides many of the benefits of the facet approach but keeps the number of variables manageable.

Traits, Situations, and Interactionism

We turn now to a very different issue pertaining to the trait perspective on personality. Trait psychology experienced an important controversy over a period from about 1970 to about 1990. How researchers reacted to this controversy had a big impact on today's views of traits, although this impact is distinct from anything we've discussed so far.

IS BEHAVIOR ACTUALLY TRAITLIKE?

The question that shook the foundations of trait psychology in the early 1970s is whether behavior actually shows traitlike consistency. As we said at the start of this chapter, traits are assumed to be *stable* aspects of personality that influence behavior in a *wide range of settings*. The reason for assuming traits in the first place was to account for consistency in thoughts and actions across time and circumstances (see also Box 4.2). Differences on a trait should predict differences in trait-related behaviors.

It was somewhat surprising, then, that trait measures and behavior often didn't correlate well (Mischel, 1968; Vernon, 1964). Mischel (1968) pointed out that correlations between trait self-reports and actual behavior typically were modest—around 0.30. This means that the trait accounts for about 9% of the variation in the behavior, with the remaining 91% unaccounted for. Later estimates ranged a little higher, but even so, the proportion of variance accounted for didn't seem high.

What, then, were we to think about traits? If traits don't predict people's actions, then why should the trait concept be considered useful?

SITUATIONISM

Indeed, some people went so far as to ask why the concept of personality should be considered useful. The extreme form of this view was called **situationism**: the idea that

Box 4.2 How Stable Is Personality over Long Periods?

Discussions of consistency and stability in personality often focus on fairly short time periods. However, the trait concept implies stability over much longer periods. Do people's personalities stay the same, even years later?

Although research on this question is hard (it requires following people for years), several projects have contributed information on it (for reviews, see Caspi, Roberts, & Shiner, 2005; Roberts, Walton, & Viechtbauer, 2006). As a whole, the evidence is impressive in showing both continuity and change. This may sound contradictory, but it isn't.

When investigators look at a given trait across a large number of people across a period of time, they usually find a high degree of stability in people's rankings on the trait dimensions (thus, a strong positive correlation over time). Indeed, a review of 152 longitudinal studies found that correlations of traits grow increasingly stronger from college, through middle adulthood, to later adulthood (Roberts & Del Vecchio, 2000; see also Costa & McCrae, 1988b, 1989; McCrae, 1993). Thus, if Rachel is more agreeable than most other people in the sample when she's a senior in high school, she's very likely to be more agreeable than most of the same people when they're all 4 years out of college and when they're all 50.

It's also possible to ask a second question concerning stability, however: Is there an absolute change in a person's standing on a trait dimension over time? That is, if Rachel is a 6 on a scale of 10 on agreeableness at age 18, will she still be about a 6 when she's 28? The answer to this question is that there tend to be systematic overall (mean level) changes over time. These changes occur both in adolescence and throughout adulthood. Interestingly, although we tend to think of adolescence as a time of great change, Roberts et al. (2006) reported that the largest changes in traits occur in young adulthood (from 20 to 40 years old).

As a group, adolescents tend to become higher on agreeableness and lower in neuroticism from about age 12 to about age 17 (Klimstra, Hale, Raaijmakers, Branje, & Meeus, 2009). These changes are consistent with development of greater maturity during this period. Across adulthood, people tend to become even higher in agreeableness up to about age 60 and even lower in neuroticism up to about age 40—the ages when the curves flatten out (Roberts et al., 2006). People also become more conscientious as they age, even up to age 70. Openness to experience tends to be stable across adulthood until about age 50, then drifts downward.

Extraversion is perhaps the most puzzling case. Results from several studies appear conflicting. Roberts et al. (2006) may have solved the puzzle by splitting extraversion into subcomponents of *social vitality* (sociability and positive emotion) and *social dominance* (assurance and agency). Social dominance goes up in adolescence and early adulthood, then stabilizes. Social vitality goes up in adolescence, falls until about age 25, and then falls again starting at about age 55 (Roberts et al., 2006). Thus, even as rank orders stay very stable, overall levels show considerable change.

---

situational forces determine behavior, not personality. This view was promoted by some social psychologists, who traditionally emphasize the role of the environment, rather than personality, as causing people's actions. This view argued that correlations between traits and behavior were low because situational variables overwhelm the effect of personality.

This turned out to be quite wrong. Funder and Ozer (1983) pointed out that effects of situations and traits usually are reported with different statistics, making them hard to compare. These researchers returned to several famous studies of the impact of situations on behavior and converted the original statistics to correlations. To the astonishment of many, these correlations were *about the same size* as the personality coefficients that had been criticized so sharply.

INTERACTIONISM

Another approach to understanding weak links between traits and actions is **interactionism** (e.g., Ekehammer, 1974; Endler & Magnusson, 1976; Magnusson & Endler, 1977; Ozer, 1986; Pervin, 1985). Interactionism is the idea that traits and situations interact to influence behavior. Neither the setting alone nor the person alone provides a complete account.

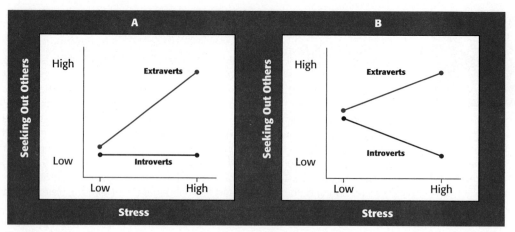

FIGURE 4.4

Interactionism. (A) Sometimes there's an interaction between a situation and a trait variable, such that variations in the situation affect some people but not others. (B) Sometimes the interaction is even more interesting, with some people being affected one way and other people being affected the opposite way.

The term *interactionism* is tied in part to an analysis-of-variance understanding of how two variables (or in this case, two classes of variables) influence an outcome. Recall from Chapter 2 how experimental personality research often combines two variables as factors in a single study. We now restate that point in terms of persons and situations. When a situation and a trait are examined in the same study, there are three sources of influence on behavior. Sometimes, variations in the *situation* have an effect on all persons; for example, stressful situations may cause everyone to seek out other people for social support. Sometimes, variations on a *trait* have an effect in all situations; for example, extraverts may always spend more time with other people than introverts.

It's also possible, however, for the situation and trait to *interact* (see Figure 4.4). An interaction here means that variations in the situation affect some people in one way and others in a different way. For example, stress may cause extraverts to seek out others more, but not affect introverts. This interaction might occur *in addition to* one or both of the overall effects, or it may occur *instead of* them. In the latter case, it would create a picture of weak effects for both the trait and the situation.

Some situations act to constrain behavior and hide individual differences. Other situations allow the free expression of personality.

People exercise choice over the settings they enter, which influences the behaviors they engage in. Some people choose to go to football games; other people do not.

In this view, situations and dispositions can interact in several ways to determine behavior. Perhaps most obvious (the case in Figure 4.4, A) is that a situation may influence one kind of person but not other kinds. Sometimes a situational change causes one kind of behavior change in one person and a *different* behavior change in another person. For example, a stressful situation may cause extraverts to seek out others and introverts to withdraw from others (Figure 4.4, B).

Here's another way to describe such interactions: Some situations permit easy expression of personality. Other situations force behavior into channels, thus preventing expression of personality (Monson, Hesley, & Chernick, 1982; Schutte, Kenrick, & Sadalla, 1985). The first set are called *weak* situations, the second set are called *strong* situations (Mischel, 1977). As an example, the lawn of a college campus on a Sunday afternoon is a weak situation. Individual differences can be expressed easily; in fact, the situation seems to invite it. An army boot camp is a strong situation. It dampens any expression of individual differences.

OTHER ASPECTS OF INTERACTIONISM

The analysis-of-variance model derives from lab research, a context in which researchers put people into identical situations. It tends to assume that people outside the lab also enter identical situations. This, of course, is wrong—a point made by a number of authors (e.g., D. M. Buss, 1984; Emmons & Diener, 1986; Emmons, Diener, & Larsen, 1986; Magnus, Diener, Fujita, & Pavot, 1993; Scarr & McCartney, 1983). In life outside the lab (and rarely, but occasionally, even in the lab), people exercise considerable choice over which environments they enter.

Some people choose to go to church, others choose not to. Some people choose to go to basketball games, some to rock concerts, some to country meadows. By exercising choice over the settings they enter, people thereby influence the behaviors they engage in. Indeed, there's evidence that people choose their marriage partners partly by whether the partner lets them be who they are (Caspi & Herbener, 1990). The choices that people make about what situations to enter depend partly on their personalities (Brandstätter, 1983; Emmons & Diener, 1986; Emmons et al., 1986).

Another way persons and situations interact is that people differ in the kinds of responses they elicit from others (Scarr & McCartney, 1983). Some people naturally bring a smile to your face, others can make you frown just by entering the room. Introverts tend to steer conversations in one direction, extraverts in another (Thorne, 1987). Indeed, people actively manipulate each other, using such tactics as charm, coercion, and silence (Buss, Gomes, Higgins, & Lauterbach, 1987). All these effects change the situation, so *the situation is actually different for one person than it is for another.* This reciprocal influence is another way persons and situations interact.

WAS THE PROBLEM EVER REALLY AS BAD AS IT SEEMED?

Trying to understand why there were weak links from trait to behavior led to uncovering a great deal of information about how they relate. In the process, however, doubt arose about whether the problem ever was actually as bad as it seemed to be.

After Mischel (1968) wrote that personality correlated with behavior around 0.30, others pointed out that the studies leading to that conclusion weren't the best of studies (Block, 1977; Hogan, DeSoto, & Solano, 1977). More recent studies, which were more carefully designed (e.g., Conley, 1985; Deluty, 1985; Funder & Block, 1989; Funder & Colvin, 1991; Moskowitz, 1994), have found much stronger relationships than that.

There also turn out to be statistical reasons why a correlation of 0.30 isn't so bad! Many actions are influenced by more than one trait. For example, when you get to a party where you don't know anyone, what you do will depend not only on how extraverted you are but also on how anxiety prone you are. As it happens, whenever a behavior is influenced by several traits at once, the *mere fact of multiple influence* puts limits on how strong a correlation can be for any single trait (Ahadi & Diener, 1989). This limit looks, in fact, very nearly the same as the much-maligned 0.30 correlation coefficient.

Maybe the core problem really wasn't ever as bad as it seemed in 1968. But the work addressing the problem has told us a lot about how behavior emerges. Indeed, this work has led many people to hold a more elaborate view of traits than they might otherwise have developed. We consider this view next.

Interactionism Becomes a New Trait View: Context-Dependent Expression of Personality

Psychologists put a lot of effort into developing the ideas known collectively as *interactionism.* Nonpsychologists, however, seem to naturally approach traits with an interactionist mentality. That is, people seem to know intuitively that whether a trait influences behavior varies from setting to setting. In reality, you shouldn't expect a given trait to operate all the time—only in situations to which it's relevant.

This is reflected in the fact that people often use verbal hedges in discussing personality (Wright & Mischel, 1988). A *hedge* (in this context) means a word or phrase that limits a trait's applicability. As examples, you might describe someone as "shy *with strangers*" or "aggressive *when teased.*" The ultimate hedge is *sometimes.* Using a hedge implies that you think the trait-based behavior occurs only in some kinds of situations (see also Shoda, Mischel, & Wright, 1989).

Such evidence, along with the insights of interactionism more generally, led Mischel and Shoda (1995) to a deeper analysis of how traits affect behavior (see also Cervone, 1997, 2004; Mischel, Shoda, & Mendoza-Denton, 2002). In this view, traits are not freestanding tendencies to act, but patterns of linkages between situation and action. Given situation x, action y is likely. A key point is that a given action shouldn't be expected to occur all the time, because the situation that elicits it isn't always present. Thus, a behavior may appear inconsistent across situations—especially situations that differ a lot. But in situations that seem similar to the person, the behavior *is* consistent (Furr & Funder, 2004). Thus, there's a lot of consistency, despite the variability.

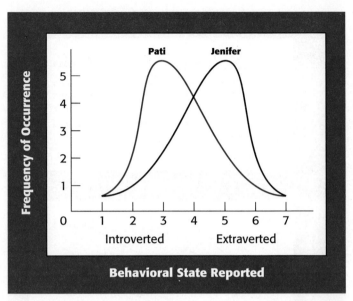

FIGURE 4.5
Traits as situation-linked frequency distributions of states. People occasionally act extraverted, even if they are essentially introverts (such as Pati); people occasionally act introverted, even if they are essentially extraverts (such as Jenifer). The person's generalized trait is reflected in the fact that particular sorts of behavioral states are most frequent. *Source:* Based on Fleeson, 2001.

Another key point in this theory is that the pattern of linkage between situation and behavior differs from one person to another. This is a source of individuality, uniqueness: the pattern of situation–behavior links the person has established over time and experience. This pattern is referred to as the person's **behavioral signature**. Even if two people tend toward the same kind of behavior, the situations that elicit that behavior may differ from one person to the other. If so, these two people will act differently in many situations, despite having the same trait. This, in fact, may be a way for idiographic traits to exist. Each person's unique pattern of links from situation to action creates a trait that's just a little different from that of any other person.

The idea that traits represent patterns of situation–action links opens other possibilities, as well. For example, imagine a person who's mostly an introvert but occasionally acts like an extravert—for example, by becoming talkative. From the perspective of the linkage model, this would mean that there are classes of situations (perhaps infrequent) that link to those actions for this person. From this way of thinking, there would be no contradiction in the idea that a person can display qualities from one end of a trait dimension in one situation and qualities from the opposite end of the dimension in another.

Fleeson (2001) has reported considerable support for this argument. For example, he found that most people do things that reflect the entire range of a trait dimension. It's just that the things they do most often reflect a narrower portion of that dimension (see Figure 4.5). In the same way, other research (Fleeson, Malanos, & Achille, 2002) has shown that the positive emotions tied to extraversion vary from hour to hour, right along with the degree of extraverted behavior the person is engaging in.

The linkage viewpoint seems to deal well with some problems people have had in thinking about traits. It doesn't distort the trait concept, but it clearly adds some-

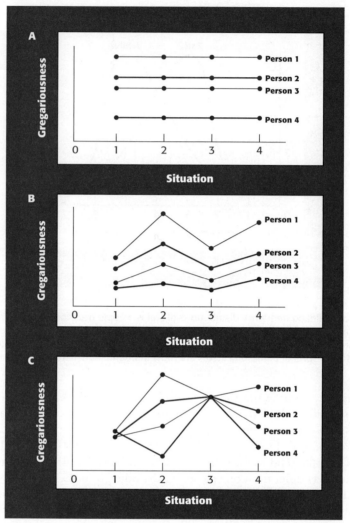

FIGURE 4.6
Three views of the effects of traits on behavior (portrayed for the trait of gregariousness). (A) A naive model, in which people are assumed to display their traits at a relatively constant level, no matter what situation they're in (what Magnusson & Endler, 1977, called *absolute consistency*). (B) A model in which situations influence the overall levels at which the trait is displayed, but people retain the same ordering (*relative consistency*). (C) An *interactionist model*, in which some situations (2 and 4) permit or even elicit individual differences, whereas others (1 and 3) don't do so.

thing to the concept that was discussed in the first part of this chapter. This theory has other elements that are considered in Chapter 12. For now, the point is that the impact of traits seems context dependent (see also Fleeson & Leicht, 2006). This conclusion is quite consistent with the interactionist view.

FITTING THE PIECES TOGETHER: VIEWS OF TRAITS AND BEHAVIOR

Let's put these ideas together with what we discussed earlier. If you had read only the first half of this chapter, you might have been tempted to assume that most trait theorists hold the view portrayed in Figure 4.6, A or B, in which traits have a *constant* influence on behavior. People who discuss the five-factor model tend not to talk much about how traits and situations interact. It can be easy to infer from their statements that panel A or B is what they assume.

But traits don't work that way. The research just described makes that clear. Traits sometimes influence behavior a lot, and sometimes not at all. Whether the trait matters depends on the situation (Figure 4.6, C). This dynamic approach to the role of traits in the constantly varying social environment recognizes complexities in the creation of behavior.

This picture is certainly more compelling than the simple ones. Interestingly enough, though, the core idea isn't all that new. Some trait theorists of earlier eras said much the same thing, but not in as much detail as is used today. As early as 1937, Gordon Allport wrote that "traits are often aroused in one situation and not in another" (p. 331). His conception of a trait explicitly included the assumption that the trait doesn't influence all behaviors and that it may not influence a given category of behavior at all times (Zuroff, 1986). Rather, the effect of the trait depends on whether it's evoked in that situation. Allport even believed that people have *contradictory* traits. The fact that the contradictory traits are aroused by different situations keeps this from being a problem (Fleeson, 2001, 2004).

Allport also anticipated another contemporary theme when he noted that people choose the situations they enter and actively change the situations they're in (Zuroff, 1986). Thus, the ideas that would become known as *interactionism* go back a long way.

Assessment

The trait approach focuses on assessment more than do most other viewpoints on personality. Indeed, the first part of this chapter discussed how various theorists developed measures. In this section, we consider briefly how the measures are used.

COMPARING INDIVIDUALS: PERSONALITY PROFILES

The trait approach makes extensive use of self-report inventories, which ask people to describe their views of themselves by making ratings of some kind. The most common ratings involve indicating whether an adjective applies to you or not, or where on a dimension or continuum (anchored by opposing adjectives) you'd fall, or whether you agree or disagree with a statement. The ratings may be made as "yes–no" or "agree–disagree" decisions, or they may be made using multipoint scales.

Recall that traits are seen as fundamental qualities of personality, reflected in diverse behaviors. For this reason, self-reports usually include ratings for several reflections of each trait being measured. A scale using adjectives would have several adjectives for each trait; a scale made up of statements would include statements implying diverse ways the trait might be expressed.

Regardless of the exact form of the inventory, nomothetic trait psychology assumes that everyone can be placed somewhere along each trait dimension. Inventories measuring these traits are used to create *profiles*. A personality profile describes a person's place on each dimension the inventory measures (see Figure 4.7). Knowing the dimensions and the person's place on each can create a sense of what he or she is like and how he or she will act.

The profile in Figure 4.7 illustrates the kind of information provided by a personality inventory. At first glance, a profile can seem like nothing more than a string of beads

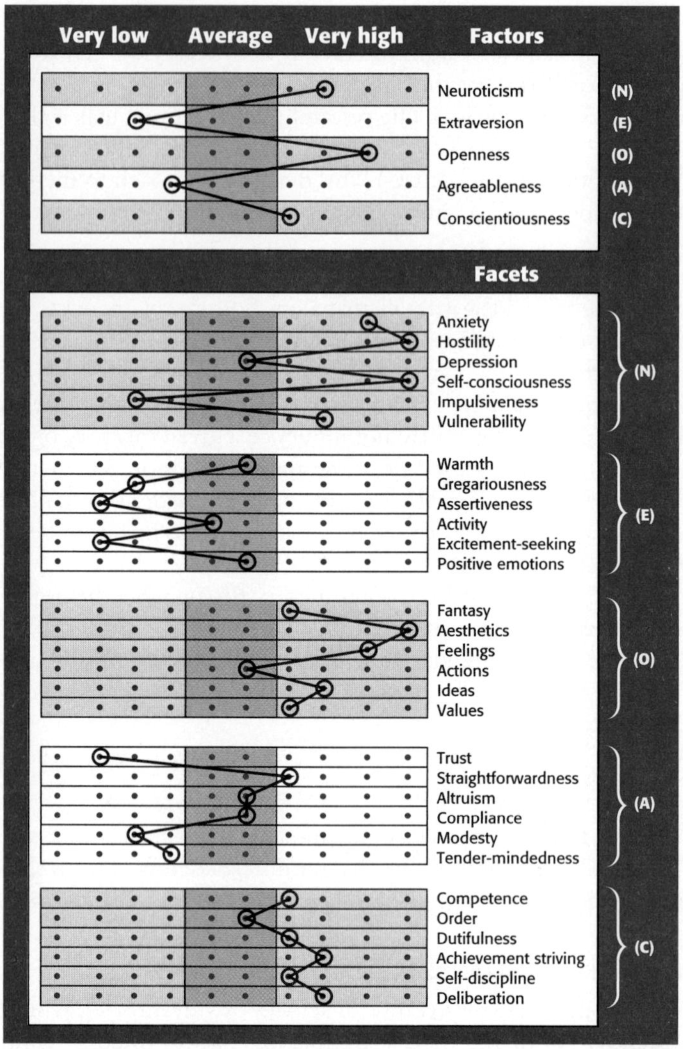

	Very low	Average	Very high	Factors
				Neuroticism	(N)
				Extraversion	(E)
				Openness	(O)
				Agreeableness	(A)
				Conscientiousness	(C)

Facets

(N) Anxiety, Hostility, Depression, Self-consciousness, Impulsiveness, Vulnerability

(E) Warmth, Gregariousness, Assertiveness, Activity, Excitement-seeking, Positive emotions

(O) Fantasy, Aesthetics, Feelings, Actions, Ideas, Values

(A) Trust, Straightforwardness, Altruism, Compliance, Modesty, Tender-mindedness

(C) Competence, Order, Dutifulness, Achievement striving, Self-discipline, Deliberation

FIGURE 4.7

An illustration of a personality profile, adapted from the NEO-PI-R. The NEO-PI-R provides both an overall profile of the five major factors (top portion) and a profile of the facets within each of the "big five" (lower portion). The top profile provides a quick and simple summary for the person's personality; the other provides a more detailed picture.

Source: Reproduced by special permission of the Publisher, Psychological Assessment Resources Inc, 16204 North Florida Avenue, Lutz, Florida 33549, from the NEO Personality Inventory Revised by P. T. Costa, Jr., and R. R. McCrae, PhD, copyright 1978, 1985, 1989, 1992 by Psychological Assessment Resources, Inc. (PAR). Further reproduction is prohibited without permission of PAR.

(indeed, Allport [1961] said that's exactly what they are). Perhaps a better metaphor is a bar code. Nomothetic theorists believe that the profile is where uniqueness lies. You can see from Figure 4.7 that a shift on a single trait changes the balance of a person's qualities. It can thereby change how the person will act in various settings and how the person will seem to someone else. Since every person has a unique combination of trait levels, everyone is different from everyone else.

Further, trait theorists believe traits can *interact* with one another. To put it differently, how a given level of one trait influences behavior may differ from person to person, as a function of where each person is on other traits. For example, two adventuresome people may display their boldness differently as a function of how sociable they are. The highly sociable one may engage in risky interpersonal exchanges, the less sociable one may climb mountains. Thus, a given trait can be reflected in unique ways for each person because of the modifying effect of differences on *other* traits. (Recall the earlier discussion of extraversion and neuroticism and Table 4.2.) This is true even though any particular trait dimension is the same from one person to another.

Problems in Behavior, and Behavior Change

The trait approach was the starting point for some of the earliest efforts to assess disorder. Those efforts were based on the idea that problems directly reflect people's traits. Differences among categories of problems occur because each trait (or group of traits) relates to a different kind of problem.

The attempt to understand psychopathology from this trait-based viewpoint was largely an attempt to categorize it. Categorizing was a matter of determining the trait indicators in people's behavior that relate to a given class of problem. This led to a taxonomy for identifying and labeling problems (Wiggins, 1973), which has been revised several times.

Some traits relate to problems because the traits themselves are problematic. As noted earlier, Eysenck's model has a dimension termed *psychoticism. Psychoticism* is a tendency toward certain kinds of problem behaviors, such as antisocial actions and alcohol and drug abuse (Sher, Bartholow, & Wood, 2000). Because people vary in psychoticism, they vary in the degree to which they will likely display those problems. *Neuroticism* is a tendency toward emotional distress. Many disorders are characterized by a high level of distress. Thus, people who are high in neuroticism are more likely to display those problems than people lower in neuroticism.

THE FIVE-FACTOR MODEL AND PERSONALITY DISORDERS

The emerging influence of the five-factor model of personality has led to renewed interest in the traits related to disorders, especially personality disorders (see Clark, 2007; Costa & Widiger, 2002; Widiger & Mullins-Sweatt, 2009; Widiger & Trull, 2007). Personality disorders are stable, enduring patterns of behavior that deviate from normal cultural expectations and interfere with the person's life or the lives of others. Many theorists suspect that personality disorders are essentially extreme manifestations of several of the "big five" traits (Larstone, Jang, Livesley, Vernon, & Wolf, 2002; Markon, Krueger, & Watson, 2005; Widiger, Trull, Clarkin, Sanderson, & Costa, 2002).

Recent research indicates this might be the case. For example, O'Connor and Dyce (2001) found that all personality disorders are represented within the five-factor model. Reynolds and Clark (2001) also found that the "big five" did a good job of representing personality disorder, and that the facet scales (the narrow scales within the five domains) did an even better job. An edited volume containing diverse reviews of relevant evidence and theoretical statements on the relation between the "big five" and the personality disorders is now in its second edition (Costa & Widiger, 2002). One recent study even found that clinicians find the "big five" more useful clinically than the categories of the diagnostic system (Samuel & Widiger, 2006).

Even a person prone to being afraid will not experience fear unless he or she encounters a fear-producing situation.

This exploration of the five factors and disorders is not limited to personality disorders. The question is being raised more generally about abnormalities of all types (Krueger, Watson, & Barlow, 2005; Nigg et al., 2002; O'Connor, 2002). Might they turn out to reflect extremes of specific traits? This area of work will likely continue to be an important focus for more exploration in future years.

INTERACTIONISM IN BEHAVIOR PROBLEMS

As described earlier in the chapter, evidence suggesting a poor relationship between traits and actions led to development of *interactionism*. The logic of interactionism is useful not just for understanding normal behavior but also for understanding problems.

One tenet of interactionism is that individual differences matter in some situations but not others. As applied to problems, this idea takes on a slightly different connotation. Think of a trait as a *vulnerability* or *susceptibility* to a problem. Saying a person is susceptible to a problem doesn't mean that he or she *has* the problem. Rather, it means the problem will emerge more easily for this person than for someone else. To put it in terms of interactionism, the susceptibility matters in some situations but not in others (recall Figure 4.4).

The susceptibility usually matters in situations involving a lot of stress. Therefore, this approach to problems is called a **diathesis-stress model**. (*Diathesis* means "susceptibility.") In this model, an interaction is required between the diathesis and a stress for the problem to develop (Meehl, 1962). Diathesis-stress models have been quite common in thinking about psychological problems.

Behavior Change

What about the process of therapeutic behavior change? The trait approach is inherently a little pessimistic about change. If traits define a person's personality, how can problems be resolved without changing the person's personality? Traits are stable. Any change that therapy produces will likely be in how the traits are displayed, not in the traits themselves.

On the other hand, the interactionist approach also has an implication here. If problems arise through an interaction between susceptibilities and difficult situations, it should be helpful for the susceptible person to avoid entering situations in which the relevant stresses are likely to occur. Avoiding such situations should help prevent the problems from arising.

This, of course, is something that people often do on their own. As we said earlier in the chapter, people exercise some control over what situations they choose to enter. Just as some people choose to go to church and some do not, some people choose to avoid situations in which their vulnerabilities place them at risk. Shy people may avoid singles bars, for example. People with short tempers may try to avoid arguments. People who routinely overspend their credit cards may cancel the cards and switch to using only cash. Avoidance isn't always possible. Yet if people learn which stressors they can and cannot handle, this knowledge should make them more effective in managing their lives.

Trait Psychology: Problems and Prospects

The trait view is, in many respects, the most basic of all the approaches to personality. The very concepts of type and trait arose literally thousands of years ago to account for consistency in behavior across time and circumstances. The concepts have been elaborated and embellished over the years, but in some ways their core remains the same.

On the other hand, some people find this view unsatisfying. It's been criticized on several grounds (Block, 1995; for more opinions on both sides, see Block [2010] and the commentaries that follow it). One problem is that in their early years, trait theories had little to say about how personality works or how the person gets from trait to action. To put it differently, the trait approach had little to say about intrapersonal functioning. This resulted in a picture of personality that seems static and empty. McAdams (1992) called trait psychology the "psychology of the stranger," because it provides information that would be important if you knew nothing about a person but doesn't portray the dynamic aspects of personality. Labeling a person as *friendly, sociable,* or *dominant* gives a name to what you see. But it doesn't tell you much about how or why the person acts that way. This has been a major criticism of the trait concept.

Several responses have been offered to this criticism. One response is that trait psychology doesn't claim to present a complete picture of the person but rather one angle of view (McAdams & Walden, 2010; McCrae, 2010). Another response is that recent years have seen far more serious attempts to develop an understanding of how traits operate on behavior. One example described earlier is the work of Mischel and Shoda (1995), their colleagues, and others pursuing their ideas. This work doesn't much resemble the trait approach of years past, but it may be the trait approach of the future. Another response is that the trait perspective is developing links to other perspectives that are providing more of a sense of mechanism behind the influence of traits (see Chapter 7).

The idea that the trait viewpoint has had little to say about the process side of personality is often made jointly with a second criticism: that trait theories sometimes resort to circular explanations. As an example, imagine a woman who acts in a dominant manner—not just occasionally but often, and not just in one situation or with one set of people but in many situations, with whoever else is around. You may feel justified in concluding from this that she has a high level of the trait of dominance.

But ask yourself two questions and think about your natural responses. Question 1: Why does she behave that way? (Answer: Because she's dominant.) Question 2: How do you know she's dominant? (Answer: Because she behaves that way.) The problem here is that the information about the behavior is being used to infer the existence of a trait, which is being used, in turn, to explain the behavior. This is called *circular reasoning,* because it can go around and around in an endless circle. The circularity can be broken if the trait is used to predict something new, and sometimes, trait theorists do that. However, this view on personality is more vulnerable than most to the criticism of circularity.

A final point, which favors the future of the trait approach, is this: No matter how hard various people have tried to dispense with the use of traits as explanatory mechanisms, the trait concept has retained an active place in the working vocabulary of the personality psychologist. The long history of these concepts attests to their hardiness. Somehow, it seems as though the personality psychologist needs them. The fact that they've endured the test of time seems to imply a fundamental correctness that's hard to deny.

• SUMMARY •

The trait approach begins with the assumption that personality consists of stable inner qualities, which are reflected in behavior. Types are discontinuous categories of personalities, with each person falling into one category or another. This concept is no longer prominent in personality psychology, however. Traits are continuous dimensions of variability, along which any person can be placed. Most trait approaches are nomothetic, emphasizing how people differ but assuming that the trait dimensions are the same for everyone. An idiographic approach emphasizes uniqueness and treats some dimensions as unique to specific persons.

Factor analysis is a tool used by many trait psychologists. It tells what items (or ratings, etc.) go together. Further, the more variability in ratings that a factor accounts for, the more important the factor. Factor analysis also reveals which observations do and don't reflect a factor well, thus helping refine scales.

An important question in trait psychology is what traits are basic and important. Some researchers believe we must let reality tell us the structure of personality. Others believe we must start with a theory. Several theoretical views have been developed, including one that emphasizes traits that have a long history in ideas about personality (extraversion and neuroticism) and one that emphasizes traits that are relevant to social interaction (the interpersonal circle).

Many now favor the idea that there are five major factors in personality. Evidence for this view is strong, and the five factors have a reasonable fit to aspects of preexisting models of personality structure. There is disagreement about the precise nature of the five factors, but commonly used labels for them are *extraversion, agreeableness, conscientiousness, emotionality,* and *openness.* Recent research has examined how these traits relate to behaviors and experiences in people's lives.

The usefulness of the trait concept was questioned by the finding that people's behavior often wasn't well predicted from self-reports of traits. This led some to doubt whether traits actually influence behavior. Situationism—the idea that behavior is controlled primarily by situational influences—proved wrong. Interactionism holds that personality and situations interact in several ways to determine behavior. For example, some situations permit or even elicit individual differences, whereas other situations don't. People also choose which situations to enter, and then they influence the nature of the situations by their own actions. Indeed, people also vary in how consistent they are, and they often know whether they're consistent or not.

The idea that the influence of traits on behavior is dependent on situations has expanded into a broader view of personality structure, in which traits are individualized linkages between situations and actions. This view accounts for stability over time within the person, as well as for variability across situations. This view of the nature of traits provides a sense of process for trait models.

Personality assessment from the viewpoint of trait psychology is a matter of developing a personality profile of the person being assessed—a description of where the person falls on all the dimensions being measured by the inventory. To these psychologists, the profile holds the key to understanding the person's uniqueness.

Regarding problems in behavior, trait theorists say that some problems result from having a trait that's intrinsically problematic, such as psychoticism or neuroticism. Other kinds of problems stem from having an extreme position on some trait dimension. Interest in the relationship between personality disorder and the five-factor model is growing. The interactionist position suggests the following possibility (termed a *diathesis-stress model*): Certain dispositions may create a susceptibility to some kind of problem, but the problem occurs only under certain conditions, usually involving stress. Therapeutic behavior change, from the trait perspective, may mean changing how a trait is reflected in behavior, because a person's traits aren't easily altered. Alternatively, it may mean avoiding situations in which the problem behavior arises.

• GLOSSARY •

Behavioral signature The pattern of situation–behavior links the person has established over experiences in some specific domain.

Diathesis–stress model A theory holding that a vulnerability plus stress creates problems in behavior.

Extravert A person who's outgoing and prefers social and exciting activities.

Factor A dimension that underlies a set of interrelated measures, such as items on a self-report inventory.

Factor analysis A statistical procedure used to find basic dimensions underlying a set of measures.

Factor loading A correlation between a single measure and the factor to which it's being related.

Idiographic Pertaining to an approach that focuses on an individual person's uniqueness.

Interactionism The idea that situations and personality interact to determine behavior.

Interpersonal circle Personality patterns deriving from varying levels of dominance and love.

Introvert A person who prefers solitary activities.

Lexical criterion An index of the importance of a trait based on the number of words that refer to it.

Nomothetic Pertaining to an approach that focuses on norms and on variations among persons.

Second-order factor A factor that emerges from a factor analysis performed on a set of previously found factors.

Situationism The idea that situations are the primary determinants of behavior.

Traits Continuous dimensions of personality on which people vary.

Types Distinct and discontinuous categories of persons.

The Motive Perspective

"I'm in the pre-med program, and I really want to get into a good medical school. The courses aren't that easy for me, so I have to study more than some people. I can't even take time off on weekends, because I'm taking an extra-heavy load. I don't mind, though, because when I do well, I feel really satisfied."

MOST COLLEGE STUDENTS spend at least part of their time planning what they will do after college. Some have ambitions they're already pursuing full speed (like the pre-med student, above). Most college students also devoted part of their energies to close relationships. Some are already thinking about being married in the years to come and building a life together with someone.

These two concerns are probably familiar to you. Work and love are issues in everyone's life. But people vary quite a lot in how central each of these issues is. And not even these issues are everything, of course. Some people have a deep desire to influence others—maybe in politics, or in show business, or by running a successful company. Some people want to find order and meaning in life. Some seek truth, some seek beauty.

There's a lot of diversity in the concerns people focus their lives around. Yet despite the diversity, all have something in common: They imply the existence of needs and motives behind people's thoughts and actions. How do people describe their preoccupations? "I *need* to find a soul mate. I *need* to accomplish things in my life. I *want* to do well in school. I *need* to feel in control." There are also individual differences here. For any aspect of life you might imagine, some people feel a deep need within it; others don't.

If needs and motives influence people's thoughts and actions this way, they're important. It can even be argued that a person's needs define who the person is. This idea forms the basis for the viewpoint on personality that's examined in this chapter.

Basic Theoretical Elements

NEEDS

The fundamental principle of this approach is that behavior is best understood as a reflection of the strength of the person's needs. A **need** is an internal state that's less than satisfactory, a lack of something necessary for well-being. Henry Murray (1938), who began this approach to personality, defined a *need* as an internal directional force that determines how people seek out or respond to objects or situations in the environment.

Some needs are biological (needs for food, water, air, sex, and pain avoidance). Others—such as the needs for power, achievement, and intimacy—either derive from biological needs or are inherent in our *psychological* makeup. It's easiest to start with biological needs, because biology is a good model for how needs work. Biological needs must be satisfied repeatedly over time. As time passes, the needs gradually become more intense, and the person acts to cause the needs to be satisfied. For example, over time, your body starts to need food. When the need gets strong enough, you'll do something to get some food. That reduces the need.

The strength of a need influences the intensity of the related behavior. The stronger the need, the more intense the action. Intensity can be reflected in several ways, such as vigor, enthusiasm, and thoroughness. But intensity can also be expressed in less obvious ways. For example, need strength can help set priorities—which action you do first versus put off until later. The stronger the need, the sooner it's reflected in action. Figure 5.1 shows how this prioritizing can create a continually changing stream of actions, as need strengths build and subside. The need that's greatest at any given point is the one that shows up in behavior.

Every need has associated with it some category of *goal objects.* When you're thirsty, you need water, not food.

Needs are directive: They help determine which of many possible actions occurs at a given time. They are directive in two senses. First, when you have a need, it concerns something in particular. When you need water, you don't just *need*; you need *water.* Needs thus pertain to classes of goal objects or events. Needs are also directive in that they create movement either *toward* the object or *away* from it. A need aims to get something or to avoid something. Thirst reflects a water-related need, but it's more than just water *related.* Fear of going swimming also reflects a water-related need. Thirst reflects a need to *get* water. Moving toward versus moving away is part of the directionality of all needs.

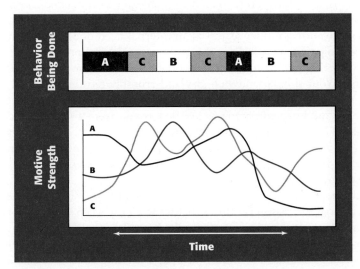

FIGURE 5.1
A graphic display of how changes in behavior over time can be explained by variations in the relative strengths of several motives over the same time. The letters at the top of the diagram indicate which of three activities the person is engaged in at any given time (shifting from one to the other). The three lines indicate the levels of the three motives related to these three activities. As one motive rises above the other two, the behavior changes.

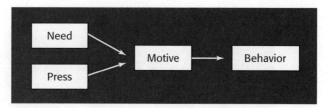

FIGURE 5.2
Internal need states and external press can both influence motives to engage in particular kinds of action, which in turn become realized in overt behavior.

MOTIVES

Needs work through **motives**. Motives are a step closer to behavior. David McClelland (1984), an important contributor to this view of personality, said motives are clusters of *cognitions with affective overtones, organized around preferred experiences and goals*. Motives appear in your thoughts and preoccupations. The thoughts pertain to goals that are either desired or undesired. Thus, they are emotionally toned. Motives eventually produce actions.

To illustrate the relationship between need and motive, the need for food occurs in the tissues of the body. But the need results in a motive state called *hunger*. Unlike the need for food, hunger is experienced directly. It creates mental preoccupation and leads to behavior that will reduce the hunger (and the need for food). Thus, we distinguish needs from motives partly by the existence of a subjective experience. A need is a physical condition you don't sense directly. It creates a motivational state that you *do* experience.

PRESS

Motives are influenced by needs, but they're also influenced by external events. Murray (1938) used the term **press** to refer to such external influences. A press (plural is also *press*) is an external condition that creates a desire to get (or avoid) something. It thus has a motivational influence, just as an internal need does (see Figure 5.2).

It may be easiest to get a feel for the effects of need and press by considering a biological motive. Imagine your need for food creates a hunger motive. You respond by eating lunch. Your simple sandwich, dry and crumbly, satisfies the need for food. But just as you finish, someone walks in with an extra-large pizza (or whatever you find irresistible). Suddenly you aren't as satisfied as you were a moment before. The motive to eat has been rekindled—not by a need but by a press. The idea also applies to purely psychological motives. Seeing someone else receive an honor can increase your motive for recognition. Being around someone who's engaged may increase your motive to be in a close relationship.

Although needs and motives clearly *can* be distinguished from each other, people don't always do so. One reason for this is that it's harder to keep the concepts distinct for psychological needs than biological needs. A need for achievement involves no deficit in the body. It's hard to say how the need to achieve differs from the motive to achieve. For this reason, it's common for people writing about needs and motives in personality to use the two terms interchangeably.

Needs, Motives, and Personality

When motives are strong, they influence behavior. Motives vary across time and situations. But people also vary in *dispositional* motives. That is, some people naturally

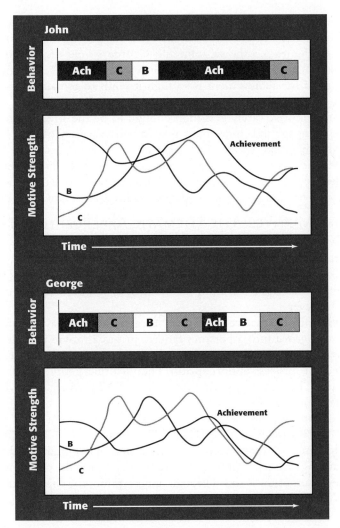

FIGURE 5.3
John has a high dispositional need for achievement; George's is lower. Assume this need fluctuates for both of them in the same pattern across time. John's and George's levels of two other needs are identical (and also fluctuate). The difference in the dispositional need for achievement creates a great difference in the overt actions John and George display (the bars above the lines).

have more of a given motive much of the time than other people do. Such **motive dispositions** begin to form a picture of the person's personality.

MOTIVE STATES AND MOTIVE DISPOSITIONS

We've already shown how to think about temporary fluctuations (see Figure 5.1, earlier). People shift from doing one thing to doing something else, as one need is satisfied and others build up. Ongoing behavior reflects whichever need is now greatest. That model provides a sense of how people shift from one action to another over time.

Now let's add the idea that people vary in their dispositional levels of needs. This can be portrayed as differences in the overall heights of the lines. Such differences can have large effects on moment-to-moment behavior. For example, John has a high dispositional need for achievement, whereas George's dispositional need for achievement is lower. Assume that this motive goes up and down in the same pattern for both across time. Assume also that they have identical patterns in all their other needs. As Figure 5.3 shows, John and George would display quite different patterns of behavior over time. Why? Because even when John's other needs are also elevated, his need for achievement is so high it tends to remain above the others. As a result, he tends to do achievement-related things a lot of the time. For George, the achievement motive rarely gets high enough to be the strongest motive. Thus, George doesn't engage in achievement-related behavior very often.

Henry Murray (1938) was the first to develop a view of personality organized in terms of needs and motives. He and his colleagues generated a list of needs that they believed underlie personality. Murray believed that all people have the same basic needs, but that everyone has a dispositional tendency toward *some particular level* of each need.

MEASURING MOTIVES: THE THEMATIC APPERCEPTION TEST OR PICTURE STORY EXERCISE

To develop the motive approach to personality, researchers had to measure motives. For several reasons, they began not by asking people about their motives but by using another strategy. This was a fortuitous decision. *Why* it was fortuitous gets us ahead of our story, however.

What was this alternative strategy? Morgan and Murray (1935) suggested that needs are *projected* into a person's fantasy, just as a movie is projected onto a screen. (This idea derives from psychoanalytic theory, the subject of Chapter 8.) Murray called this process **apperception**. The idea that people do this easily and often led to the **Thematic Apperception Test (TAT)** (Morgan & Murray, 1935; Murray, 1938; Smith, 1992).

When your motives are being assessed by TAT, you view a set of pictures and are asked to create a story about each one. The pictures are ambiguous. Your story is supposed to describe what's happening, the characters' thoughts and feelings, the relationship among characters (if there's more than one), and the outcome of the situation. The key assumption is this: Through apperception, the themes in your stories will reflect your implicit motives.

Do fantasy stories really reflect people's needs? Early studies tested the procedure by creating situational needs. One such study looked at the need for food. People were deprived of food for varying lengths of time, so they would have different needs for food. They subsequently differed in their food-related TAT imagery (Atkinson & McClelland, 1948).

Another early study manipulated the achievement motive, by giving some people a success and others a failure. A failure should temporarily increase the achievement need by creating an achievement deficit. As expected, the failure caused greater achievement imagery than occurred in a group that had not experienced the failure (McClelland, Atkinson, Clark, & Lowell, 1953). Unexpectedly, though, achievement imagery was also elevated in a group that had experienced a success. This finding led McClelland to conclude that deprivation isn't necessary to arouse a motive (Winter, 1998). The motive can be aroused by any circumstances that point to the motive's relevance.

Studies of Specific Dispositional Motives

Once tested in studies of situational motives, the apperception procedure was used to measure motive *dispositions*. The TAT pictures were used in some of this work, but variations on the TAT with other pictures were also developed. The procedure in its various forms is now often referred to as the **picture story exercise (PSE)**. Researchers have used this procedure to study several motive dispositions in detail, as outlined in the next sections.

Persons high in achievement motivation have a strong need to succeed.

NEED FOR ACHIEVEMENT

Of the various needs identified by Murray, the first to receive research attention was the **need for achievement**. This motive was studied for decades by David McClelland, John Atkinson, and many others (e.g., Atkinson & Birch, 1970; Atkinson & Raynor, 1974; Heckhausen, 1967; Heckhausen, Schmalt, & Schneider, 1985; McClelland et al., 1953).

Achievement motivation is *the desire to do things well, to feel pleasure in overcoming obstacles*. Need for achievement is reflected in PSE responses that mention performing well at something, reaching goals or overcoming obstacles to goal attainment, having positive feelings about success, or negative feelings about failure.

People who differ in achievement motivation differ in several ways in achievement-related situations. Consider the very act of choosing a task. Tasks (or problems within a task) can be easy, hard, or somewhere in between. Given a choice, which would you prefer? (When you plan your course schedule for next semester, do you choose easy courses and professors, hard ones, or ones in between?)

People low in need for achievement prefer tasks that are either very easy or very hard (Atkinson, 1957). It's easy to understand the easy ones. There isn't much achievement pressure in an easy task, and it's nice to get something right, even if everyone else gets it right too. Why, though, would people with a low achievement need choose a hard task? Clearly, it's not for the challenge. It seems to be more that doing poorly on a hard problem doesn't reflect badly on them. And there's always the possibility (however remote) that they will get lucky and succeed. In contrast, people high in need for achievement tend to prefer tasks of moderate difficulty. They also work harder on moderately difficult tasks than on very hard or very easy ones (Clark & McClelland, 1956; French, 1955).

Why do people high in achievement motivation prefer tasks of middle difficulty? Maybe it's because these tasks give the most information about ability (Trope, 1975, 1979). If you do well at an easy task, you don't learn much about your ability, because everyone does well. If you *fail* at a *hard* task, you don't learn much about your ability, because almost *no one* does well. In the middle, though, you can find out a lot. Perhaps people high in achievement motivation want to find out about their abilities. Trope (1975, 1980) tested this by having people choose test items. He figured out a way to manipulate (separately) the items' difficulty and their **diagnosticity** (how much they tell about ability). People with a high achievement need had a strong preference for

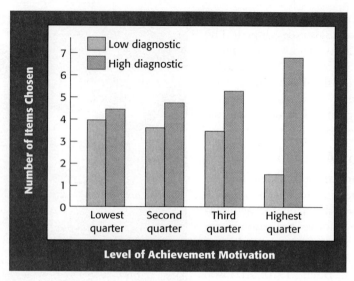

FIGURE 5.4
Participants in this study chose items to work on that they expected to be either highly diagnostic of their abilities or not diagnostic. This figure divides participants into four levels of achievement motive, ranging from very low to very high. There is an increasingly strong preference for highly diagnostic items among those with higher levels of achievement motivation.   *Source:* Based on Trope, 1975.

diagnostic items (see Figure 5.4), whereas difficulty in itself turned out not to be important.

Effects of achievement motivation have been studied in lots of domains over the years. The need for achievement relates to greater persistence in the face of failure (e.g., Feather, 1961), better task performances (e.g., Lowell, 1952), higher grades (Schultz & Pomerantz, 1976), and greater educational achievement among 20,000 students in Holland (Hustinx, Kuyper, van der Werf, & Dijkstra, 2009). Indeed, it's even been suggested that the need for achievement plays a role in the economic rise and decline of entire cultures.

This idea led to studies of literature from several civilizations, at several distinct points in their history. The literature is interpreted for its themes, in much the same way as PSE responses are interpreted. The economic growth and decline of that civilization are then plotted over the same period. One impressive study of this sort (Bradburn & Berlew, 1961) examined the history of England from 1500 to just after 1800. The researchers divided this period into 50-year segments and coded achievement imagery and economic development in each. Achievement imagery was stable for 100 years, fell off, and then rose sharply. The index of economic development followed a nearly identical pattern of falling then rising—but 50 years later. This suggests that shifts in achievement motives had economic consequences.

Another even more complex study of this sort was done by McClelland (1961). This study focused on a much narrower period—1925 to 1950—but looked at 23 cultures across the world. McClelland coded achievement imagery from children's schoolbooks at both points in history. He developed two measures of economic growth over the intervening period and compared the achievement imagery to economic growth. A moderately strong association emerged between achievement imagery in 1925 and economic growth from 1925 to 1950. As in the earlier study, there was virtually no relation between economic growth and later achievement imagery. This pattern suggests that motivation (reflected in the imagery) produced the economic achievement, instead of vice versa.

Achievement motivation predicted economic success in these studies, but in some situations a need for achievement is less helpful. For example, people in high-level politics have the task of mobilizing others (which draws on a different need), and they often have little personal control over outcomes (Winter, 2010). As a result, the need for achievement is frustrated, rather than producing good outcomes. Indeed, the achievement motive has been linked to lower effectiveness among U.S. presidents (Spangler & House, 1991). Winter (2010) has also found that need for achievement is valuable in the business world only when control is relatively high.

An interesting aspect of the literature on the achievement motive is that, at first, far more was known about its effects among men than among women, because most early studies looked only at men. Moreover, even when studies did address achievement motivation across gender, they typically focused on stereotypically masculine pursuits (e.g., work income), rather than look at a variety of areas for achievement (e.g., family roles; Duncan & Peterson, 2010). Eventually, however, researchers looked at achievement needs among women. Some of this work suggests that achievement needs are expressed in varying ways among women, depending on the direction they take in their lives.

Elder and MacInnis (1983) recruited two sets of 17- to 18-year-old girls. One group was family oriented, the other group had a mix of family and career interests. Achievement motives, assessed at the same time, predicted different outcomes in the two groups as they moved into adulthood. Among family-oriented women, those with a high achievement need invested energy in activities leading to marriage and family. In effect, they expressed achievement by creating and sustaining a family. Among career-minded women, having a high achievement need led to putting off marriage and families. Presumably, this was because they were focusing on their careers. Thus, what women value as a goal determines what behaviors follow from their achievement needs.

Another way of putting this is to say that women with achievement needs pursue achievement in ways that fit their views of themselves and the world they live in. It seems reasonable that this principle should also influence what careers women consider. Jenkins (1987) looked at career choices made by women who were college seniors in 1967. Those high in the need for achievement were likely to become teachers but not to go into business. Why? Teaching gave them an outlet for their achievement needs but didn't conflict with traditional women's roles. Business careers didn't fit those roles as well. Thus, the achievement needs of these women were channeled by other aspects of their social environments.

NEED FOR POWER

Another motive that's been studied extensively by David Winter (1973) and others is the **need for power**. Need for power is *the motive to have impact on others, to have prestige, to feel strong* compared to others. PSE responses that reflect the need for power have images of forceful, vigorous action—especially action that evokes strong emotional responses in others. Responses showing concern about status or position also reflect the need for power.

What kinds of behavior reflect the power motive? Not surprisingly, people high in need for power seek out positions of authority and influence and surround themselves with symbols of power (Winter, 1972, 1973). For example, students high in the power motive are likely to be office holders in student organizations (Greene & Winter, 1971). The power motive also predicts the likelihood of holding execu-

The need for power is often expressed in the tendency to acquire high-status positions and to surround oneself with symbols of power.

tive positions in organizations (Harms, Roberts, & Wood, 2007). People high in the need for power are concerned about controlling the images they present to others (McAdams, 1984). They want to enhance their reputations. They want others to view them as authoritative and influential. Not surprisingly, they tend to be somewhat narcissistic, absorbed in their importance (Carroll, 1987). They also are more sexually active than persons lower in this motive (Schultheiss, Dargel, & Rohde, 2003).

The power motive can be helpful in many contexts. People high in the power motive are less likely to make concessions in diplomatic negotiations than those lower in this motive (Langner & Winter, 2001); this can yield better outcomes in the negotiations. When power-motivated people win, they learn implicitly (outside their awareness) to continue what they had been doing. When they lose, they learn implicitly not to continue what they had been doing (Schultheiss, Wirth, Torges, Pang, Villacorta, & Welsh, 2005).

There's evidence that the power motive also enhances effectiveness in managing others. For example, U.S. presidents high in the power motive were more effective than those who were lower (Spangler & House, 1991). Winter (2010) has argued that what makes the power motive effective in politics (where the achievement motive is ineffective) is that people high in the power motive aren't bothered by the lack of control in political situations. They just keep adjusting their behavior in a continuing effort to have influence.

In their personal lives, men with high power needs are inclined to say that the ideal wife is a woman who's dependent (Winter, 1973). An independent woman is a potential threat. A dependent woman allows the man to feel superior. A later study found that the wives of men high in the need for power were indeed less likely to have a career outside the home (Winter, Stewart, & McClelland, 1977).

This isn't to say that the need for power is something that matters only among men. Women vary in this need, as well, and studies have proven that it predicts important outcomes among women. One study (Jenkins, 1994) found that women high in the need for power have more power-related job satisfactions than women lower in this need but also more *dis*satisfactions. These women also made greater strides in career development over a 14-year period—but only if they were in power-relevant jobs.

The level of a person's need for power can also influence the manner in which he or she relates to others. The need for power relates to taking an active, assertive, controlling orientation in peer interactions (McAdams, Healy, & Krause, 1984). People

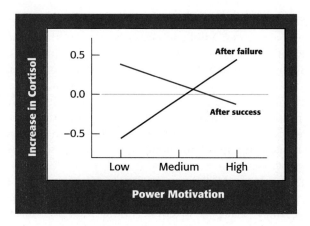

FIGURE 5.5
Increase in the stress hormone cortisol after a failure was greater among persons higher in the need for power; increase in cortisol after a success was greater among persons lower in the need for power. *Source:* Based on Wirth et al., 2006.

high in the need for power are rewarded by low-dominance expressions from others (indeed, are especially attentive to them; Schultheiss & Hale, 2007), and they're disrupted by high-dominance expressions from others (Schultheiss, Pang, Torges, Wirth, & Treynor, 2005). These people are also more angered when others don't respond well to their efforts to exert influence (Fodor & Wick, 2009). The dominating style of interacting that characterizes the need for power can also have more ominous overtones: Men high in power needs are more likely than men with lower power needs to physically abuse their female partners during arguments (Mason & Blankenship, 1987).

The desire for dominance often leads to success, but sometimes it's frustrated by failure. People with a high need for power have an increase in the stress hormone cortisol after a failure (Wirth, Welsh, & Schultheiss, 2006). Interestingly, people with a low need for power have an increase in cortisol after a success! Apparently, what constitutes a stressor differs between these two sorts of people (see Figure 5.5). Both success and failure can be stressful but they're stressful for different people. Stress seems to follow when the outcome *isn't* the one you are motivated for or accustomed to.

Oliver Schultheiss and his colleagues have found that the need for power also relates to the sex hormone testosterone (we say more about this hormone's influence on personality in Chapter 7). There's a slight link between power needs and baseline testosterone (Schultheiss et al., 2005). More interesting, however, is what happens to testosterone after success and failure. Among men, a high need for power relates to both a larger increase in testosterone after a success and a greater reduction in testosterone after failure. Among women, however, the associations were much more complex.

On the other hand, there's also evidence that the sex hormone estradiol (which is closely related to testosterone chemically) plays a role in women similar to that played by testosterone in men (Stanton & Schultheiss, 2007). First, high power motivation was related to a higher level of estradiol at baseline. More striking, after a competition, the changes in estradiol were very similar to those shown in testosterone by the men in the earlier study. Among winners, estradiol increased most among those who were highly power motivated. Among losers, estradiol decreased most among those who were highly power motivated. A similar pattern emerged in a later study by Stanton and Edelstein (2009), showing that women not taking oral contraceptives had an even higher correlation between estradiol and power motivation than other women.

Is the power motive a good thing or a bad thing? Winter has suggested that the power motive is manifested in two paths, depending on whether or not the person acquires a sense of responsibility during socialization (Winter, 1988; Winter & Barenbaum, 1985). For those high in the sense of responsibility, the motive yields a conscientious pursuit of prestige, in which power is expressed in socially accepted ways. For those without this sense of responsibility, though, the motive leads to problematic ways of influencing others, including aggressiveness, sexual exploitation, and alcohol and drug use.

Winter and Barenbaum (1985) reported considerable support for this reasoning. In one sample, among men low in responsibility, the need for power related to drinking, fighting, and sexual possessiveness. Among men high in responsibility, the need for power related inversely to all these tendencies. Similarly, Magee and Langner (2008) found that the two forms of the power motive resulted in antisocial and prosocial decisions, respectively. Men with a high need for power without the sense of responsibility also displayed a notable rise in testosterone when imagining and experiencing a power-related success (Schultheiss, Campbell, & McClelland, 1999; Schultheiss & Rohde, 2002).

All of this suggests that the power motive can be "tamed" by proper socialization. There's an important qualifier to this conclusion, however: Prosocial decisions promote the good of one's group. But sometimes, larger issues intrude. Winter (2007) analyzed communications of various sorts that occurred during a set of crises that developed into wars and a matched set that were peacefully resolved. Results showed that the war crises involved higher displays of the power motive but also—paradoxically— higher levels of responsibility. Winter noted that in many circumstances, going to war seems to be the responsible thing to do. Thus, the carefully socialized sense of responsibility may tame the power motive, but only up to a point.

NEED FOR AFFILIATION

Another motive that received a good deal of attention early in the development of the motive perspective is the motive to affiliate. The **need for affiliation** is *the motive to spend time with others and form friendly social ties.* This isn't a need to dominate others but to be in social relationships, to interact with others (for a review, see Sokolowski, 2008). In this need, social interactions aren't a means to an end; they're a goal in their own right. In PSE responses, the need for affiliation is reflected in concern over acceptance by others and by active attempts to establish or maintain positive relations with others.

Studies have uncovered several manifestations of this motive. For example, people who want to affiliate want to be seen as agreeable. If a group exerts pressure on them, they're more likely to go along than people with lower affiliation needs (Hardy, 1957). These people get nervous if they think others are judging their interpersonal skills (Byrne, McDonald, & Mikawa, 1963). They prefer interaction partners who are warm, compared to those who are reserved (Hill, 1991). They're more likely to make concessions in negotiations (Langner & Winter, 2001), and they're more likely to initiate contacts and try to establish friendships (Crouse & Mehrabian, 1977). They're especially sensitive to angry expressions from others (Schultheiss et al., 2005).

The active initiation of social contact suggests that affiliative needs go beyond worrying about acceptance from others. These needs can also lead to active participation in social events. For example, Sorrentino and Field (1986) studied the emergence of leadership in discussion groups that met in five weekly sessions. At the end, group members were asked to indicate whom they viewed as group leaders. People high in the need for affiliation were nominated more often than people lower in the need for affiliation.

As suggested by Sorrentino and Field's research, people with a strong affiliation motive spend more time engaged in social activities than people lower in this motive. These people make more phone calls (Lansing & Heyns, 1959), and when they're paged they're more likely to be engaged in some social activity—conversing or letter writing, for example (Constantian, 1981; McAdams & Constantian, 1983). When they're alone, they're more likely to express the wish to be interacting with others (McAdams & Constantian, 1983; Wong & Csikszentmihalyi, 1991).

Need for intimacy is the desire to experience warm, close, and meaningful relationships with others.

Links between the affiliation motive and relationship satisfaction are complex (Meyer & Pepper, 1977). Happiness depends partly on the balance of affiliation needs between partners. That is, well-adjusted husbands and wives have affiliation needs that *correlate* with each other. To put it concretely, if you have a low affiliation need, you're best off with someone who has a similarly low affiliation need. If your affiliation need is high, you're best off with someone whose affiliation need is also high.

NEED FOR INTIMACY

Another motive that has emerged as a research focus is the **need for intimacy**. It's been studied intensively by Dan McAdams (1982, 1985, 1989) and his collaborators. Intimacy motivation is *the desire to experience warm, close, and communicative exchanges with another person, to feel close to another person.* Intimacy motivation shares with affiliation motivation a wish to be with others as an end, rather than a means. It goes beyond the need for affiliation, though, in its emphasis on closeness and open sharing with another person.

McAdams proposed this need partly because he felt the need for affiliation didn't focus enough on the positive, affirmative aspects of relationships. Additionally, the need for affiliation is an active, striving, "doing" orientation, whereas the need for intimacy, as McAdams views it, is more of a "being" orientation (McAdams & Powers, 1981). The two aren't fully distinct, of course. McAdams and Constantian (1983) reported a correlation of 0.58 between them.

What kinds of behaviors reflect the intimacy motive? In one study, people higher in the need for intimacy reported having more one-to-one exchanges with other people, though not more large-group interactions (McAdams et al., 1984). The interactions reported by intimacy-motivated people involved more self-disclosure, as well.

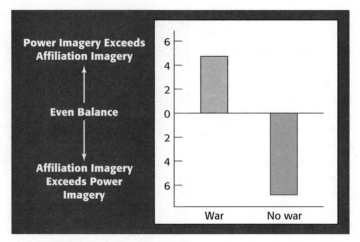

FIGURE 5.6
Balance of power motive imagery versus affiliation motive imagery in sovereign's speeches during the year before Great Britain entered a war (18 cases) compared to the year before Britain did *not* enter a war (36 cases). *Source:* Based on Winter, 1993, Table 3.

To put it differently, people with a high intimacy need are more likely to share with friends their hopes, fears, and fantasies. The sharing goes both ways: People with a high intimacy need report doing more *listening* than people with a low intimacy need, perhaps because they are more concerned about their friends' well-being. Indeed, intimacy seems to entail both self-disclosure and partner disclosure (Laurenceau, Barrett, & Pietromonaco, 1998).

Because having close interactions is important to people with high intimacy needs, it should be no surprise that these people define their lives partly in terms of such interactions. McAdams (1982) collected autobiographical recollections among students high and low in intimacy needs. They were asked to report a particularly joyful or transcendent experience from their past and then an important learning experience. Content was coded several ways. For instance, some events involved considerable psychological or physical intimacy with another person; others did not. Analysis revealed that intimacy motivation was strongly correlated with memory content that also implied intimacy.

How do people high in the intimacy motive act when they're with others? They laugh, smile, and make more eye contact when conversing than do people with lower intimacy needs (McAdams, Jackson, & Kirshnit, 1984). They don't try to dominate the social scene (which is what people with the need for power do). Instead, they seem to view group activities as chances for group members to be involved in a communal way (McAdams & Powers, 1981).

The desire for intimacy is good for people, based on evidence from a study in which men wrote narrative fantasies at age 30 and were assessed 17 years later (McAdams & Vaillant, 1982). Men with higher intimacy motives at 30 had higher marital and job satisfaction at 47 than did those with lower intimacy motives. Another study found that women high in the intimacy motive reported more happiness and gratification in their lives than those low in the intimacy motive—unless they were living alone (McAdams & Bryant, 1987).

Interestingly, intimacy needs (needing to be close) don't seem to coexist well with power needs (needing to influence or dominate others). Persons who are high in both needs are often poorly adjusted (Zeldow, Daugherty, & McAdams, 1988).

Patterned Needs: Inhibited Power Motive

Thus far, we've discussed needs individually. Indeed, for many years, that's how they were examined—one at a time. However, some studies have examined patterns involving several needs at once—sometimes, in combination with other characteristics. One well-known pattern combines a low need for affiliation with a high need for power, in conjunction with the tendency to inhibit the expression of the latter. This pattern is called **inhibited power motivation** (McClelland, 1979). The reason for interest in this pattern depends on the context in which it's examined.

One context is leadership. The line of reasoning goes as follows: A person high in need for power wants to influence people. Being low in need for affiliation lets the person make tough decisions without worrying about being disliked. Being high in self-control (inhibiting the use of power) means the person will want to follow orderly procedures and stay within the framework of the organization. Such a person should do very well in the structure of a business.

This pattern does, in fact, relate to managerial success. In one study that spanned a 16-year period, people with the inhibited power pattern moved to higher levels of management than others, but only those who were nontechnical managers (McClelland & Boyatzis, 1982). Among managers whose jobs rested on engineering skills, personality didn't matter. This is understandable, because the managerial value of these people depends heavily on their particular skills.

There's also evidence that people with this pattern are especially effective at persuasion (Schultheiss & Brunstein, 2002). Their persuasiveness stems both from greater verbal fluency and from an effective use of nonverbal cues, such as gesturing. Presumably, being more persuasive helps these people be effective in mobilizing others.

The pattern of high power motivation and low affiliation motivation may be good for getting others mobilized, but even this may be a mixed blessing. Winter (1993) argued that this pattern is conducive to starting wars. Historical data show that high levels of power imagery and low levels of affiliation imagery in the statements of politicians predicted going to war. For example, speeches by the rulers of Great Britain contained more power imagery than affiliation imagery in the year before the country entered a war, whereas the reverse was true during years before a no-war year (see Figure 5.6). In another case involving U.S. leaders—the Cuban missile crisis of 1962—greater affiliation than power imagery occurred before the successful avoidance of a war.

Implicit and Self-Attributed Motives

As noted earlier in the chapter, the motivational view is that personality is a system of multiple motives. Each motive exists in every person. Behavior, at any given time, depends partly on how intense the various motives are, which is determined partly by personality and partly by context.

Incentive Value

This analysis sounds reasonable, but it's missing something. It predicts that if your need for affiliation is more intense than your other needs, you'll engage in an affiliative act. But *what* act? Additional concepts are needed to address this question (McClelland, 1985).

One such concept is **incentive**: the degree to which a given action can satisfy a need for you. It's sort of a personalized weighting of how relevant an act is to the need. Incentive values determine how a motive is expressed behaviorally. For example, a person with a high need for affiliation who loves music will go to clubs and concerts with friends. A person with a high need for affiliation who loves sports will go to football and basketball games with friends. But people don't engage in all conceivable need-related behaviors. They choose ways to satisfy their needs, based on the incentive values that various activities have for them.

We didn't introduce the concept of incentives earlier in the chapter along with the concept of need. Clearly, though, something like it is needed to account for the diversity of behavior. People differ in the activities they engage in, even when satisfying the same need. As noted earlier, some women satisfy the need for achievement through careers, others by achieving strong family lives. These activities differ greatly, yet both can satisfy the need to achieve.

This principle relates to a point made in Chapter 4 regarding interactionism: We said there that people choose for themselves which situations to enter and which to avoid, thus creating an interaction between person and situation. We didn't say *why* different people choose different situations. One answer is that various situations have different *incentive* values to different people, even if the situations fulfill the same need.

Needs and incentives both influence behavior, but in different ways. McClelland (1985) said that need strength relates to long-term *frequencies of need-relevant actions of any type*. Incentive values, on the other hand, should relate to *choices within a domain of action*. In McClelland's view, needs influence behavior primarily at a nonconscious level, whereas values influence the more conscious process of choice.

IMPLICIT MOTIVES ARE DIFFERENT FROM SELF-ATTRIBUTED MOTIVES

The last paragraph was deceptively simple, but it has a great many implications. Earlier in the chapter, we described development of the TAT or PSE to assess motives. We said there that the decision to use that strategy, instead of asking people about their motives, was fortuitous. Why? Because it allowed the discovery of something that today seems very important indeed.

The PSE procedure was used in the vast majority of the work described thus far. And from the wide range of findings, we feel relatively confident that it does assess people's motives. Given the large effort required to score the PSE, however, other researchers created self-report scales to assess motives, which were far simpler. They intended those self-reports to measure the same motives as the PSE. But the self-reports turned out to correlate poorly with PSE assessment (McClelland, Koestner, & Weinberger, 1989; Pang & Schultheiss, 2005; Schultheiss & Brunstein, 2001). Why? What's going on?

McClelland and his colleagues argued that the two kinds of assessments are, in fact, measuring different things (McClelland et al., 1989). They used the term **implicit motive** to refer to what the PSE measures (Schultheiss & Brunstein, 2010). They called the motives *implicit* because the person may or may not be aware of them. They used the term **self-attributed motive** to refer to what's measured by self-reports (also now termed *explicit motive*). An increasing body of evidence indicates that implicit motives and self-attributed motives are different. *Implicit motives* are what we have been calling *motives*. *Self-attributed motives* are closer to what was described in the preceding section as *incentives*.

McClelland et al. (1989) held that implicit motives are more basic. They are the recurrent preferences for classes of affective experiences that McClelland believed lie at the heart of motives (the feeling of "doing better" for the achievement motive, the feeling of "being strong" for the power motive, the feeling of "being close" for the intimacy motive). Implicit motives are seen as primitive and automatic (Schultheiss, 2002; Schultheiss & Brunstein, 2010). Because they are basic, they are good predictors of broad behavioral tendencies over time. In contrast, self-attributed motives relate to specific action goals. They tell how a person will act in a particular situation. For this reason, they're better at predicting responses in structured settings.

This distinction has been pursued further in several projects. Brunstein and Maier (2005) expanded on the idea that both implicit and self-attributed achievement motives play important but distinct roles in achievement behavior. They found evidence that the implicit achievement motive acts primarily as an energizer, boosting effort when the person falls behind. The self-attributed achievement motive, in contrast, acts primarily as an influence on decision making, influencing how people seek information about their skills compared to other people (for example, by choosing to continue a task or not).

Evidence that these qualities are distinct also comes from research in which people completed PSE and self-report measures and then kept records of memorable experiences over 60 days (Woike, 1995). The records were coded for motive relevance and for feelings. Strength of implicit motives (PSE) related to the frequency of reporting feelings that relate to that motive. Strength of self-attributed motives did not. Self-attributed motives related instead to the frequency of reporting motive-related events with no feelings (but PSE scores did not).

It seems, then, that the two aspects of motivation link to different aspects of memory. Further evidence that they link to different aspects of memory comes from studies showing that self-attributed motives predict recall of general memories related to the self-concept, whereas implicit motives predict recall of specific events (Woike, Mcleod, & Goggin, 2003).

Another example of the value of distinguishing between implicit and self-attributed motives comes from a set of studies by Baumann, Kaschel, and Kuhl (2005). They argued that people sometimes have motive-related intentions (explicit) that fit poorly with their implicit motive dispositions. When this happens, the person is stressed, which has adverse effects on his or her well-being. They argued further that this tendency is particularly pronounced among persons who are also poor at regulating negative emotions. Evidence from three studies fits that picture.

The idea that incongruence between one's implicit and explicit motives can be problematic has been studied in several other contexts. As in Baumann et al.'s (2005) work, the idea is that the motive discrepancies create stress by having conflicting influences on behavior. There's evidence, for example, that motive discrepancy of this sort can lead to unhealthy eating (Job, Oertig, Brandstätter, & Allemand, 2010). More generally, it's been proposed that optimal well-being follows from having explicit motives that are congruent with one's implicit motives and acting in way that satisfies both motives (Schüler, Job, Fröhlich, & Brandstätter, 2008).

McClelland believed that both the implicit motive and the self-attributed motive are important, but that they should be viewed separately. The evidence appears to support that belief. Sometimes it makes sense to expect an implicit motive to predict an outcome but not a self-attributed motive. Sometimes the opposite is true. For this reason, it's important to be sure which one you want to measure and to measure it

Table 5.1 Sample Hypothesis about the Interaction between the Affiliation–Intimacy Motive and the Trait of Introversion–Extraversion.

	Affiliation–Intimacy Motive	
	Low	High
Extravert	Intimate relationship not salient as a desire	Desire for intimate relationship leads to single stable relationship
Introvert	Intimate relationship not salient as a desire	Desire for intimate relationships but difficulty maintaining them, because having a high focus on one's inner world is disruptive of a connection to the other person

Source: Based on Winter et al., 1998.

correctly (McClelland, 1989). The distinction between implicit and self-attributed motives is one aspect of the motive view on personality that is receiving increasingly close attention.

Approach and Avoidance Motives

Another distinction that's also increasingly important is the distinction between approach and avoidance. As noted early in the chapter, a motive is either a readiness to approach something or a readiness to avoid something. Thus far, we've written only about approach. For example, people motivated to achieve try to approach success. But any achievement task also holds a possibility of failure. It seems likely that the desire to avoid failure also plays a role here. Just as Atkinson (1957) tied the need for achievement to the capacity to feel pride in success, the need to avoid failure relates to a tendency to feel shame after failure (McGregor & Elliot, 2005).

A simple way to avoid failure is to avoid achievement situations altogether. *Never trying* keeps you from failing. Another way to avoid failing is *the very act of succeeding*. It may be that some people who struggle to achieve don't care so much about gaining success as they care about the fact that gaining success lets them avoid failure.

Much of the early research on achievement actually measured both of these motives. A lot of it derived from Atkinson's (1957) theory of achievement behavior. That theory makes its clearest predictions for people whose only motivation is to approach success and people whose only motivation is to avoid failure. Predictions are less clear for people high in both motives and people low in both motives. For that reason, studies often included only the two groups who were high in one motive and low in the other.

That strategy was guided by theory, but it has a bad side effect: It completely confounds the two motives. This causes ambiguity in interpretation (Chapter 2). If the groups act differently, is it because of the difference in the motive to approach success or because of the difference in the motive to avoid failure? There's no way to know, although interpretations tend to focus on the motive to approach success.

In recent years, the distinction between approach and avoidance motivation has re-emerged as a focus for research on achievement, much of it by Andrew Elliot and his colleagues (e.g., Elliot, 2005; Elliot & Harackiewicz, 1996; Elliot & McGregor, 2001). Part of their theory is that achievement can reflect either of these motives. Which motive is central, however, will influence many aspects of the person's experience.

Elliot and McGregor (2001) found that the motive to succeed in mastering course material (approach) related to study strategies that involve thoughtfully elaborating on the material. The avoidance motive related to memorization. Avoidance motivation also related to having trouble organizing study time effectively. Elliot and Sheldon (1997) found that the motive tendencies also have different effects on subjective experiences. People who focus their effort on trying to avoid failure report less emotional well-being and less satisfaction with their performance than people who are trying to approach success.

Though it might generally be better to approach than to avoid, there's also evidence that people do better when they're doing what's familiar to them. Specifically, people with a high fear of failure are made uneasy and upset by imagining success (Langens & Schmalt, 2002). As suggested in the context of the power motive, it may be that what's stressful to you is what you're unfamiliar with.

APPROACH AND AVOIDANCE IN OTHER MOTIVES

Once you grasp the idea of separate approach and avoidance motives, you realize that the idea has implications for every motive you can think of (see also Carver, Lawrence, & Scheier, 1999; Higgins, 1997; Ogilvie, 1987). Try it out. Pick a motive. Identify a behavior that reflects that motive. Then see if you can spot the opposing motive that might create the same behavior. For example, acts of affiliation can come from the desire to be with others (need for affiliation) but they can also come from the desire to avoid being alone (Boyatzis, 1973; Pollak & Gilligan, 1982). These aren't the same. One is a motive to approach; the other is a motive to avoid. The same issue can be raised for any motive you can think of.

Box 5.1 THE PROCESS UNDERLYING THE TAT OR THE PSE

Take a good look at the picture on the right. Something's happening, but what? Decide for yourself. Make up a story that fits the picture. Include the following information (and whatever else you want to include):

- What's just happened to these people?

- What's the relationship between them?

- What are their present thoughts and feelings?

- What will be the outcome of the situation?

Take your time, and make your story as long and detailed as you wish.

What you've just done is similar to what people do when completing the Thematic Apperception Test (TAT; Morgan & Murray, 1935) or picture story exercise (PSE; McClelland et al., 1989). The idea is that people's motives show up in what comes from their minds when they try to make sense of an ambiguous picture. The ambiguity makes it less likely that press will dictate your story's content and more likely that your motives will influence what you write.

When people complete a PSE, they write stories for several pictures. Different pictures tend to elicit stories with different themes. Some pictures naturally elicit achievement-related stories; others are more amenable to stories with affiliation themes. Over the course of several pictures, however,

dispositional tendencies emerge in people's narratives. Presumably, these storytelling tendencies reflect the motives that underlie the person's personality.

If you're interested in the motives that dominate your own personality, look at the story you wrote to see if there's evidence of any of the motives discussed in this chapter.

Illustration by Stephen P. Scheier. Reproduced by permission.

Just as with achievement behavior, evidence is beginning to accumulate that approach and avoidance motives have different consequences in other domains. A powerful example is a study of commitment between romantic partners (Frank & Brandstätter, 2002). This study found that commitment based in approach predicted more relationship satisfaction 6 and 13 months later. However, commitment based in avoidance (i.e., avoiding the process of breaking up) predicted lower relationship satisfaction at the follow-ups.

The idea that a given behavior can be based on either an approach motive or an avoidance motive (or some combination of the two) raises very broad questions about why people do the things they do. Are people generally moving toward goals, or are they trying to avoid or escape from things? Do actions differ depending on which motive is more prominent? Do the feelings that go with the actions differ?

The general idea that any approach motive has a corresponding avoidance motive has very broad implications. It complicates the picture of human behavior enormously. We will put this idea aside for the rest of this chapter, but you should keep in mind that it's always in the background.

Motives and the Five-Factor Trait Model

When thinking about motive dispositions as the core of personality, a question that naturally arises concerns the relation between the motive view and the trait view described in Chapter 4. Does the five-factor model absorb the qualities that motive theorists see as important?

One way this question can be approached is to analyze measures of self-attributed motives. Stumpf (1993) used one such measure, the Personality Research Form (PRF; Jackson, 1984), and concluded that it captured all of the "big five" except neuroticism. Costa and McCrae (1988a) also found that many PRF scales reflect underlying qualities of the five-factor model. On the other hand, several PRF scales loaded on two or more of the five factors rather than one, suggesting that those motives relate to several traits. This general pattern was also found by Paunonen et al. (1992). In contrast, somewhat better support for a fit to the five-factor model has been found in a different measure of needs (Piedmont, McCrae, & Costa, 1992).

TRAITS AND MOTIVES AS DISTINCT AND COMPLEMENTARY

The attempt to fit motives to the five-factor model can be seen as an effort to integrate across theoretical boundaries. However, many believe that the effort is misguided and that traits and motives are fundamentally different (Winter, John, Stewart, Klohnen, & Duncan, 1998). Note that the evidence reviewed just above involved self-attributed motives, not implicit motives. The fact that self-attributed and implicit motives are not strongly related is reason enough to be wary about concluding that traits and motives are the same. There's also separate evidence that implicit motives relate poorly to the five-factor model (Schultheiss & Brunstein, 2001).

Winter et al. (1998) proposed an integration but of a different sort: They proposed that motives are fundamental desires and that traits channel how those desires are expressed. Thus, they argued, motives and traits interact to produce behavior. In some respects, this resembles the argument described earlier in the chapter about implicit motives and incentive values. In the view taken by Winter et al., traits may represent patterns of incentive preferences.

In support of their argument, Winter et al. presented two studies of extraversion and (PSE-derived) motives. The studies examined women's lives across many decades. Winter et al. argued that intimacy needs would have different effects among introverts and extraverts (see Table 5.1). For women with low intimacy needs, it shouldn't matter much whether they are introverts or extraverts. Intimacy isn't a big need for them. The complicated situation occurs among those with high intimacy needs. An extravert with high intimacy needs should do fine in relationships, because extraverts are comfortable with, and good at, various kinds of social interaction. In contrast, introverts with high intimacy needs should have problems. Their highly inner-directed orientation should interfere with relationships. Their partners may see them as remote or withholding. The result should be a greater likelihood of marital problems. That's exactly what was found.

The bottom line here appears to be that implicit motives exist at a different level of abstraction than traits. Exactly how these constructs relate to each other doubtlessly will be a subject for continued research.

Personology and the Study of Narratives

Research on the effects of motive dispositions tends to take one of two approaches. Some studies examine how people respond to particular events, in the laboratory or in the field. Other studies collect evidence of a dispositional motive (or set of motives) at one time and relate the motive to some outcome that occurs considerably later.

Both of these approaches differ greatly from the one favored by Murray, the father of this viewpoint. Murray believed that the way to understand personality is to study the *whole person* and to do so over an extended period. The work on which he based his theory was an intensive study of 51 college men (Murray, 1938). Each was tested in many ways and interviewed by a staff of professionals, who came to know each man's personality quite thoroughly.

This approach was idiographic. It focused on the pattern of qualities that made each person unique. Murray disliked nomothetic methods. He thought their focus on comparison keeps them from probing deeply into a person's life. To Murray, the nomothetic approach yields only a superficial understanding. Murray's concerns led him to coin the term **personology** to refer to the approach he preferred. He defined *personology* as the study of individual lives and the factors that influence their course. He believed that personology was more meaningful than other approaches because of its emphasis on the person's life history. According to Murray (1938), "the history of a personality *is* the personality" (p. 604).

Recent years have seen a resurgence of interest in this way of thinking about personality. For example, Dan McAdams, whose work on intimacy motivation was described earlier, has written extensively on the idea that identity takes the form of an extended narrative—a life story that each of us writes and lives out over time (McAdams, 1985; McAdams & Pals, 2006). This narrative has chapters, heroes, and thematic threads that recur and permeate the story line (see also Rabin, Zucker, Emmons, & Frank, 1990).

Here's an example of how narratives can differ from person to person. Some themes emphasize growth ("I found out how to make our relationship better"), others emphasize safety ("I hope that never happens again") (Bauer, McAdams, &

Sakaeda, 2005). As another example of a narrative focus, McAdams (2006) identified a constellation of themes focused on personal redemption—a transition from a state of suffering to a better psychological state—which characterizes the lives of some middle-aged Americans.

From this point of view, the person's identity lies in keeping a coherent narrative going across time (McAdams & Pals, 2006; Singer, 2004). This way of thinking speaks directly to the uniqueness of each person, because every life story is unique (Singer, 2005). Whether this approach will become more prominent in personality psychology in the future remains to be seen, but it's surely a development that Murray would have applauded.

Assessment

Assessment of personality from the motive viewpoint is a matter of determining the levels of a person's motive dispositions. The assessment technique most associated with assessment of these dispositions is the PSE (Smith, 1992; Winter, 1996).

Earlier in the chapter, we described the essence of the procedure by which the PSE is administered (see also Box 5.1). People who are completing it view a set of ambiguous pictures, in which it isn't clear what's happening. They're asked to create a story about each picture. The story should describe what's happening, the characters' thoughts and feelings, their relationship to each other (if there's more than one character), and the outcome of the situation. Through apperception, the themes that are manifested in the stories reflect implicit motives.

Scoring people's responses can be complex (Winter, 1994), but here's a simplified version. Look to see what kinds of events take place in the story and what themes and images are in it. Events that involve overcoming obstacles, attaining goals, and having positive feelings about those activities reflect the achievement motive. Events in which people choose to be with other people and stories that emphasize relationships among people reflect the affiliation motive. Stories with images of one person controlling another reflect the power motive. More than one theme can occur in a given story. These can be scored separately, so the stories can be used to assess several different motives at the same time.

The use of stories written about ambiguous pictures is the core method for assessing motives in research deriving from this theoretical viewpoint. It's not just stories that can be scored for motive imagery, of course. Anything that's written—speeches, diaries, letters—can be scored in the same way (Winter, 1994). However, variations on the PSE remain the most popular method of assessing implicit motives.

The PSE is widely used to measure motives, but it has had its share of criticism. Questions have been raised about its relatively low internal consistency and test–retest reliability (Entwisle, 1972; Lilienfeld, Wood, & Garb, 2000). Defenders of the technique reply that there are good reasons for both of these to be low. The pictures in any PSE vary considerably in content, so it's not surprising that they bring out different kinds of stories. That reduces internal consistency. It also may be that being told to tell several stories in the same session creates implicit pressure to avoid repetition. This can reduce both internal consistency and test–retest reliability (Atkinson & Raynor, 1974). There's evidence, though, that the reliability of the PSE need not be as low as was once believed (Lundy, 1985; Schultheiss, Liening, & Shad, 2008; Schultheiss & Pang, 2007).

Another criticism of the PSE is far more pragmatic: It takes a lot of time and effort to give and score it. This is a key reason why people wanted to develop self-report measures of motives. As noted earlier in the chapter, however, there's now substantial evidence that self-attributed motives (assessed by self-report scales) and implicit motives (assessed by story imagery) are not the same. Each captures something about human motivational experience, but what is being captured differs from one to the other.

OTHER IMPLICIT ASSESSMENTS

People working within the motive tradition in personality have relied heavily on the PSE as the primary tool of implicit assessment. In recent years, however, other ways of assessing implicit constructs have been developed (which were discussed in Chapter 3). The reasoning behind them doesn't rely on the concept of projection, but rather on the idea that a good deal of people's knowledge is associative in nature (largely due to processes of conditioning, discussed in Chapter 10). If you ask people to introspect about that knowledge, they won't be able to give you accurate answers, because the knowledge isn't explicit (able to be verbalized). Instead, it's in the pattern of associations. It may well represent different sources of information than create explicit knowledge (Rudman, Phelan, & Heppen, 2007).

An example of a procedure derived from this reasoning is the implicit association test (IAT; Greenwald, McGhee, & Schwartz, 2008). It measures links among semantic properties in memory that are believed to be hard to detect by introspection. As noted in Chapter 3, the IAT can be applied to virtually any kind of association. When it's applied to properties of personality, reaction times for various associations can be informative about the implicit sense of self. Just as explicit and implicit motives predict different aspects of behavior, explicit and implicit (IAT) measures of self-concept contribute separately to predicting behavior (Back, Schmukle, & Egloff, 2009).

Some research has compared the TAT and IAT (Sheldon, King, Houser-Marko, Osbaldiston, & Gunz, 2007). The two measures were correlated and had similar patterns of correlations with other scales. This suggests that they may be measuring similar things.

Problems in Behavior, and Behavior Change

People working within the motive approach to personality have been interested in specific domains of human activity (e.g., achievement, affiliation, power, intimacy) and in the more general idea of motivation as a concept. They haven't spent nearly as much effort analyzing problems in behavior. Nevertheless, the literature has at least tentative links to some problems.

THE NEED FOR POWER AND ALCOHOL ABUSE

It's been suggested that the need for power can play a role in developing a drinking problem (McClelland, Davis, Kalin, & Wanner, 1972). This idea stems partly from the finding that drinking alcohol leads to feelings of power. Thus, a person with a need for power can satisfy that need, at least somewhat, by drinking. This doesn't satisfy the need for long, of course, because the feeling of power is illusory. It goes away when the person sobers up.

The idea that alcohol abuse may reflect a need for power leads to some recommendations for treatment. In particular, it suggests that people who are using alcohol this way aren't aware of doing so. They would probably benefit from realizing what

Motivation seminars are often used to enhance achievement motivation among people in business.

they're doing. By encouraging other ways to satisfy the power motive, therapists can treat the issue productively, rather than simply treating a symptom. One study (Cutter, Boyatzis, & Clancy, 1977) found that this approach can be more effective than traditional therapies, yielding nearly twice the rate of rehabilitation at one-year follow-up.

FOCUSING ON AND CHANGING MOTIVATION

Psychologists contributing to the motive approach to personality have also had relatively little to say about therapeutic behavior change. Murray, the father of this approach, was a therapist, but he didn't develop new techniques. In general, he applied the currently existing psychodynamic techniques to people's problems.

It would seem, however, that the study just discussed makes some suggestions about behavior change. As noted, some people appear to use alcohol as a way of temporarily satisfying a desire for power. A treatment program developed for these people focused on two things: It made them more aware that this motive was behind their drinking, and it helped them find other ways to satisfy the need for power, thus making drinking unnecessary.

A broader implication of this discussion is that people may *often* be unaware of the motives behind their problem behaviors. Many problem behaviors may reflect needs that are being poorly channeled or reactions to conflicts between implicit motives and self-attributed motives. If so, taking a close look at the person's motive tendencies might reveal something about the source of the problem. Knowing the source may make it easier to make changes.

Another program of study, conducted by McClelland and his colleagues (McClelland, 1965; McClelland & Winter, 1969), has also had indirect implications for therapy. It was a training program developed to raise achievement motivation among businesspeople (see also Lemann, 1994). The program was rooted in the idea that thinking a lot about achievement-related ideas increases your motive to achieve.

The program began by describing the nature of the achievement motive and instructing people on how to score TAT protocols for achievement imagery. People were then taught to use achievement imagery in their thoughts as much as possible. By teaching themselves to think in terms of achievement, they increased the likelihood of using an achieving orientation in whatever activity they undertook.

Achievement-related thinking is important, but it isn't enough by itself. A second goal of the training was to link these thoughts to specific, concrete patterns of action. It was also important to be sure the patterns worked outside the training program. The people were encouraged to think in achievement terms everywhere—not just in the training sessions—and to put the action patterns into motion. People in the course wrote down their plans for the next two years. They were taught to plan realistically and to set goals that were challenging but not out of reach. This planning provided a way of turning the achievement orientation they learned into a self-prescription for a course of activity. This prescription then could be used in guiding actual achievement later on.

Was the course effective? The answer seems to be yes. In a two-year follow-up, participants had higher business achievements, were more likely to have started new business ventures, and were more likely to be employing more people than before, compared to control participants (McClelland & Winter, 1969).

This program showed that it's possible to change people's achievement-related behavior, but a question remains about whether it changes their underlying needs. It also remains uncertain how much these effects can be generalized to the domain of therapy. Nonetheless, the studies do seem to provide intriguing suggestions about behavior change.

Motive Theories: Problems and Prospects

The theorists represented in this chapter look to motivational processes and the pressures they place on people as a way to specify how dispositions influence actions. By providing a way to think about how dispositions create behavior—by specifying a type of intrapersonal functioning—this approach to dispositions evades one of the criticisms of trait theories.

A criticism that's harder to evade is that decisions about what qualities to study have been arbitrary. Murray developed his list of needs from his own intuition (and other people's lists). Others working in this tradition have tended to go along uncritically. Yet McAdams noted one omission from that list—the need for intimacy—that's strikingly obvious as a human motive. This suggests that Murray's intuitive list was incomplete. A response to this criticism is that the motives that have been examined most closely are those that fit with ideas appearing elsewhere in psychology, as well. This convergence suggests that the needs really are fundamental.

Another criticism bears less on the theory than on its implementation. Murray was explicit in saying that the dynamics of personality can be understood only by considering multiple needs at once. However, research from the motive approach to personality has rarely done that. More often, people study one motive at a time to examine its dynamics. Occasionally, researchers have stretched to the point of looking at particular clusters of two or three needs, but even that has been rare.

Despite these limitations, work on personality from the viewpoint of motive dispositions has continued into the present. Indeed, this area of work has enjoyed a resurgence in the past decade or so. The idea that people vary in what motivates them has a good deal of intuitive appeal. Further appeal derives from the idea that motive states wax and wane across time and circumstances. These ideas provide a way to incorporate both situational influences and dispositional influences in an integrated way. Given these "pluses" and a growing interest in understanding how implicit motives and self-attributed motives work together, the future of this approach seems strong.

• SUMMARY •

The motive approach to personality assumes that behavior reflects a set of underlying needs. As a need becomes more intense, it's more likely to influence behavior. Behavior is also affected by press: external stimuli that elicit motivational tendencies. Needs (and press) vary in strength from moment to moment, but people also differ in patterns of chronic need strength. According to this viewpoint, this difference is the source of individual differences in personality.

Murray catalogued human motives, several of which later received systematic study by others. One (studied by McClelland, Atkinson, and others) was the need for achievement: the motive to overcome obstacles and to attain goals. People with high levels of the achievement motive behave differently from those with lower levels in several ways: the kinds of tasks they prefer, the level of task difficulty they prefer, their persistence, and their performance levels. Early research on achievement tended to disregard how approach and avoidance motives might separately influence behavior. More recent work has begun to examine those distinct influences.

The need for power—the motive to be strong, compared to other people—has also been studied extensively. People who score high in this need tend to seek out positions of influence, to surround themselves with the trappings of power, and to become energized when the groups they're guiding have difficulties. People with high levels of the power motive tend to choose as friends people who aren't influential or popular, thereby protecting themselves from undesired competition. The power motive can lead to unpleasant forms of social influence, unless it's tempered by a sense of responsibility.

The need for affiliation is the desire to spend time with other people—to develop and maintain relationships. People who score high in this need are responsive to social influence, spend a large proportion of their time communicating with other people, and when alone, often think about being with others. A related motive that isn't represented in Murray's list but has received attention in recent years is the need for intimacy. People high in this need want warm, close, and communicative relationships with others. People with strong intimacy needs tend to spend more time in one-to-one interaction and less time in groups. They tend to engage in interactions that involve a lot of self-disclosure and are concerned about their friends' well-being.

Research has also investigated patterns of motives, such as inhibited power motive. This pattern is defined by having more of a need for power than a need for affiliation and by restraining the power need. People with this pattern do well in managerial careers, but the pattern has also been linked to political stances that preceded wars.

Theorists of this view use other concepts besides motives in talking about behavior. Incentive value—the extent to which a given action will satisfy a given need for a person—helps to explain why people with the same motive express it in different ways. Indeed, the concept of incentive provides an opening into a broader issue. Specifically, assessment of motives by the picture story exercise (PSE) technique does not relate well to assessment by self-report. What's assessed by the PSE has come to be called implicit motives, and what's assessed by self-report has come to be called self-attributed or explicit motives. Implicit motives are thought to function mostly unconsciously, and self-attributed motives are thought to function mostly consciously. One active area of interest is how these two aspects of motives function and relate to one another.

Murray emphasized the study of individual lives in depth over extended periods of time. He coined the term *personology* to refer to the study of the whole person, and personology was his goal. This emphasis has not been strong in the work of most others, but it has re-emerged more recently in the work of McAdams and his colleagues.

The contribution to assessment that's most identified with the motive approach is the PSE. It's based on the idea that people's motives are reflected in the imagery they "apperceive"—that is, read into ambiguous stimuli, such as a set of pictures depicting people in ambiguous situations. There are also self-report measures of motives, but they appear to measure something different from what the PSE measures.

The motivational approach to personality has largely ignored the issue of analyzing problems in behavior, although at least some evidence links the need for power to the misuse of alcohol. It's possible to infer from this evidence, however, that many problems in behavior stem from inappropriate channeling of motives. It's also reasonable that people can be helped by increasing their awareness of the motive that underlies the problem and then channeling the motive in alternative ways. Research on increasing the need for achievement suggests that it may be possible to alter people's dispositional levels of the motives that make up personality.

• GLOSSARY •

Apperception   The projecting of a motive onto an ambiguous external stimulus via imagery.

Diagnosticity   The extent to which a task provides information about something.

Implicit motive   A motive assessed indirectly because it's relatively inaccessible to consciousness.

Incentive   The degree to which an action can satisfy a particular need for a person.

Inhibited power motivation   The condition of having more need for power than for affiliation but restraining its use.

Motive   Cognitive–affective clusters organized around readiness for a particular kind of experience.

Motive disposition   The dispositional tendency toward a high or low level of some motive.

Need   An unsatisfactory internal condition that motivates behavior.

Need for achievement   The need to overcome obstacles and attain goals.

Need for affiliation   The need to form and maintain relationships and to be with people.

Need for intimacy   The need for close communication and sharing with someone else.

Need for power   The need to have influence over other people.

Personology   Study of the entire person.

Picture story exercise (PSE)   Any one of a family of tests that uses stories written about pictures to assess motive strength through narrative fantasy.

Press   An external stimulus that increases the level of a motive.

Self-attributed motive   A motive that's consciously reported.

Thematic Apperception Test (TAT)   A particular method of assessing the strength of a motive through narrative fantasy.

Genetics, Evolution, and Personality

Two newborn babies are lying in cradles behind the glass window of the hospital nursery. One lies peacefully for hours at a time, rarely crying and moving only a little. The other thrashes his arms and legs, screws up his face, and rends the air with piercing yowls. What could possibly have made them be so thoroughly different from each other so soon in life?

A group of young men, 16 to 18 years old, have been hanging around the pool hall, acting cool, eyeing women who pass by, and trying to outdo one another with inventive insults. Occasionally, tempers flare, the lines of faces harden, and there's some pushing and taunting. This time, though, the one doing the taunting has gone too far. A glint of dark steel, and the air is shattered by gunshots. Later, the dead one's grieving mother cries out, "Why do men do these things?"

P ART OF WHO YOU ARE is the body you walk around in. Some people have big bodies, some have small ones. Some bodies are strong, some are frail. Some bodies are coordinated, some are klutzy. Some bodies turn toward dolls at a certain stage of life, others turn to Legos.

Your body isn't your personality. But does it influence the personality you have? This idea goes back at least to Hippocrates and Galen. As noted in Chapter 4, Hippocrates proposed four personality types. Galen added the idea that each reflects an excess of a bodily fluid. The idea that people's physical makeup determines their personalities has come up repeatedly ever since.

The term *physical makeup* has meant different things at different times, however. In the early and mid-twentieth century, it meant physique or body build (see Box 6.1). Today, physical makeup means genes. Many people now believe that most qualities of personality are partly genetically determined.

CHAPTER 6

Determining Genetic Influence on Personality

How do we decide whether a given personality quality is inherited? Family resemblance is a starting point, but it has a serious problem. Family members could be similar because of inheritance. But they also could be similar because they're around each other a lot and have learned to act like each other (see Chapter 10).

To get a clearer picture requires better methods. Psychologists turned to the discipline of genetics for ideas. The result was a mix of psychology and genetics called **behavioral genetics**. This is the study of genetic influences on behavioral qualities, including personality (Plomin, 1997; Plomin, DeFries, & McClearn, 1990; Plomin & Rende, 1991).

TWIN STUDY METHOD

A method that's been widely used in behavioral genetics is the **twin study**. It takes advantage of two unusual reproductive events, which produce two types of twins. One kind of event occurs shortly after conception. A fertilized egg normally divides into two cells, then four, then eight, and eventually forms a person. Sometimes, though, the first two cells become separated, and each grows *separately* into a person. These persons are identical twins, or **monozygotic (MZ) twins**. Because they came from what was a single cell, they are 100% alike genetically.

Comparisons between identical and fraternal twins can provide information about the heritability of characteristics.

Box 6.1 Early Biological Views: Physique and Personality

The idea that people's bodies relate to their personalities is reflected in popular stereotypes: the jolly fat man; the strong, adventurous hero; the frail intellectual. Is there any truth to it?

The idea has had a long life. Kretschmer (1925) classified people as *thin*, *muscular*, or *obese* and found that each group was prone to a different set of disorders. W. H. Sheldon (1942) expanded the idea from categories to dimensions and looked at normal personality. He believed each quality relates to one of three layers of the embryo. For that reason, he named them after the layers:

Endomorphy is the tendency toward plumpness (reflecting digestion). Endomorphs are soft and round.

Mesomorphy is the tendency toward muscularity (reflecting predominance of bone and muscle). Mesomorphs are rectangular, hard, and strong.

Ectomorphy is the tendency toward thinness (reflecting the skin and nervous system). Ectomorphs are delicate and frail, easily overwhelmed by stimulation.

Most people have a little of each quality.

In parallel with the physical dimensions, Sheldon proposed three aspects of *temperament*. *Viscerotonia* means qualities such as relaxation, tolerance, sociability, love of comfort, and easygoingness. *Somatotonia* means qualities such as boldness, assertiveness, and a desire for adventure and activity. *Cerebrotonia* means avoidance of interaction, restraint, pain sensitivity, and a mental intensity approaching apprehensiveness.

As he had predicted, Sheldon found that temperaments and somatotypes go together. Mesomorphy related to somatotonia, endomorphy to viscerotonia, and ectomorphy to cerebrotonia. Later studies also supported this view.

These studies all said that body types relate to personality. But why?

Does physique cause personality? Is the link more roundabout? The body types reflect well-known stereotypes, which include expectations about how people act. If we have such expectations, we may induce people to act as expected (Gacsaly & Borges, 1979). This can produce an association between physique and behavior. It would stem from social pressure, though, not body type per se.

It's hard to know why associations exist between body type and personality. Partly because of this, many people were skeptical about the associations and interest in them gradually waned. Sheldon's ideas are no longer influential in personality psychology, but he stressed a theme that re-emerged only a couple of decades later. He believed that personality, along with body type, was inherited. He didn't test this belief. Indeed, in his time, it wasn't widely understood *how* to test it. Others found ways to do so, however, leading to the findings presented in the first half of this chapter.

The second kind of event occurs in conception itself. Usually, only one egg is released from the mother's ovary, but occasionally two are. If both happen to be fertilized and develop simultaneously, the result is fraternal twins, or **dizygotic (DZ) twins**. Genetically, DZ twins are like any pair of brothers, pair of sisters, or brother and sister. They just happen to be born at the same time, rather than separately. As with any pair of **siblings** (brothers or sisters), DZ twins are, on average, 50% alike genetically (though specific pairs range from 0% to 100%). Interestingly enough, many twins are wrong about which kind they are, and errors are just as common for MZ as DZ twins. One study found that in about 30% of pairs, one twin was wrong, and in about 12% of pairs, both twins were wrong (Scarr & Carter-Saltzman, 1979).

In a twin study, a correlation is computed between sets of identical twins and their co-twins on some quality (see Figure 6.1). The same is done with pairs of same-sex fraternal twins. The two *correlations* are then compared. If identical twins are more similar to each other than fraternal twins, presumably it's because of the difference in degree of genetic similarity.

The index of genetic influence on a trait is termed a **heritability** estimate. This index represents the amount of variability in the population that's accounted

FIGURE 6.1
A basic twin study method examines pairs of identical and same-sex fraternal twins raised together. Members of each twin pair are assessed on the variable of interest, and a separate correlation is computed for each type of twin. The correlation for fraternal (DZ) twins is subtracted from the correlation for identical (MZ) twins. Multiplying this difference by 2 gives an index of the heritability of the characteristic—an estimate of the proportion of variance in that characteristic that is accounted for by inheritance.

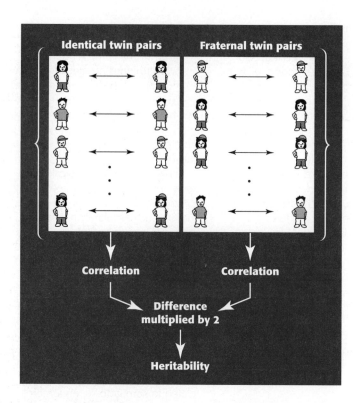

for by inheritance in the trait under consideration. The higher the heritability, the stronger the evidence that genes matter. It's important to be careful here, because people sometimes read too much into this term. It does not represent the *amount* of a behavioral characteristic that's inherited by any one person. Nor does it explain *why* genes matter.

The twin study method is based on the assumption that the degree of similarity of the life experiences of co-twins raised together is just as great for DZ twins as for MZ twins. This is critically important. You couldn't conclude that a difference between correlations comes from heredity if parents treated DZ twins differently from MZ twins. The difference in genetic overlap would be confounded with the difference in treatment.

Are the two kinds of twin pairs treated more or less the same? The answer is a very cautious yes. MZ twins are more likely than DZ twins to be dressed alike, but the differences are slight (Plomin et al., 1990). MZ twins also wouldn't resemble each other in personality more if they were treated alike than if they were not (Loehlin & Nichols, 1976). Even so, one study found that DZ twins who *thought* they were MZ twins were more alike than other DZ twins (Scarr & Carter-Saltzman, 1979). A later study found that MZ pairs recalled somewhat more similar experiences than DZ twin pairs, but these similarities didn't relate to personality similarity (Borkenau, Riemann, Angleitner, & Spinath, 2002).

ADOPTION RESEARCH

Another way to study inheritance is an **adoption study**, which looks at how adopted children resemble the biological parents and the adoptive parents. Resemblance to biological parents is genetically based, whereas resemblance to adoptive parents is environmentally based.

Another method combines features of the twin study with features of the adoption study. It's sometimes possible to study MZ twins who were adopted and raised separately. Because they grew up in different homes, environmental impacts should make them *different*, rather than similar. Similarity between these pairs can be contrasted with MZ twins raised together and DZ twins raised together. If heredity is important, then MZ twins—even if they were raised apart—should be more similar than DZ twins. If heredity is *really* important, then MZ twins raised apart should be nearly as similar as MZ twins raised together.

What Personality Qualities Are Genetically Influenced?

Twin and adoption study methods have been used for more than five decades to study genetic effects on personality (Johnson, Vernon, & Feiler, 2008). Early work focused on **temperaments**.

TEMPERAMENTS: ACTIVITY, SOCIABILITY, AND EMOTIONALITY

Arnold Buss and Robert Plomin (1984) used the term *temperament* to refer to *an inherited personality trait present in early childhood.* They looked for signs of possible temperaments in observations of the behaviors of young children. Further work indicated that three dimensions of individual differences in normal personality deserve to be called temperaments: *activity level, sociability,* and *emotionality*.

Temperaments influence many kinds of behavior; for example, activity level expresses itself through the kinds of leisure activities people choose to engage in.

Activity level is the person's overall output of energy or behavior. It has two highly correlated aspects: *vigor* (the intensity of behavior) and *tempo* (its speed). People high in activity level prefer high-intensity, fast-paced activities. Those who are lower in activity level take a more leisurely approach to things. *Sociability* is the tendency to prefer being with other people, rather than alone. Sociability is a desire for sharing activities, along with the responsiveness and stimulation that are part of interaction. To be sociable is to value intrinsically the process of interacting with others. *Emotionality* is the tendency to become emotionally aroused—easily and intensely—in upsetting situations.

Early evidence that these temperaments are inherited came from twin studies in which parents rated their children (Buss & Plomin, 1975; Plomin, 1974; Plomin & Rowe, 1977). Correlations between parent ratings of activity, emotionality, and sociability were strong for MZ twins; they were next to nonexistent for DZ twins, however. Adoption research also indicated genetic influences (Loehlin, Willerman, & Horn, 1985).

MORE RECENT VIEWS OF TEMPERAMENTS

Developmental researchers have become increasingly interested in temperaments over the past three decades, but they now approach the nature of the temperaments a little differently. Mary Rothbart and her colleagues argue for **approach** and **avoidance temperaments**, which reflect tendencies to approach rewards and avoid threats, respectively (e.g., Derryberry & Rothbart, 1997; Rothbart, Ahadi, & Evans, 2000; Rothbart, Ahadi, Hershey, & Fisher, 2001; Rothbart & Bates, 1998; Rothbart, Ellis, Rueda, & Posner, 2003; Rothbart & Posner, 1985; see also Eisenberg, 2002; Eisenberg et al., 2004; Kochanska & Knaack, 2003; Nigg, 2000). The avoidance temperament, in some ways, resembles Buss and Plomin's (1984) emotionality. There also seems some resemblance between the approach temperament and sociability, though that one is less clear.

The newer theorists also posit a third temperament that's generally termed **effortful control**. This temperament is about being focused and restrained. In part, it reflects attentional management (persistence of attention during long tasks). It also reflects the ability to suppress approach behavior when approach is situationally inappropriate. This temperament seems to imply a kind of planfulness versus impulsiveness. High levels of this temperament early in life relate to fewer problems with antisocial behavior later in life (Kochanska & Knaack, 2003).

INHERITANCE OF TRAITS

Early twin studies were done before trait theorists had begun to converge on the idea that personality has five basic factors (see Chapter 4). With the emergence of the five-factor model, work has increasingly focused on whether those five dimensions are genetically influenced (Bergeman et al., 1993; Heath, Neale, Kessler, Eaves, & Kendler, 1992; Jang, Livesley, & Vernon, 1996; Jang, McCrae, Angleitner, Riemann, & Livesley, 1998; Loehlin, 1992; Tellegen et al., 1988; Viken, Rose, Kaprio, & Koskenvuo, 1994). The answer is clearly yes. The effects are substantial and remarkably consistent across factors (Bouchard, 2004). Indeed, there's evidence of an invariant genetic influence on the five factors across cultures. Yamagata et al. (2006) concluded that the five factors may represent a common genetic heritage of the human species.

Most twin studies of adult personality use self-reports or reports of people close to the twins. This approach has led to criticism of possible bias. To deal with this concern, Borkenau, Riemann, Angleitner, and Spinath (2001) did a twin study in which adult participants were videotaped and then rated by people who didn't know them. That study also found evidence of genetic influences on all five traits of the five-factor model.

TEMPERAMENTS AND THE FIVE-FACTOR MODEL

The supertraits that make up the five-factor model are broad and pervasive in influence. In that respect, they're a lot like temperaments. In fact, the five factors have considerable conceptual similarity to qualities that others call *temperaments* (Caspi, Roberts, & Shiner, 2005; Digman & Shmelyov, 1996; Halverson, Kohnstamm, & Martin, 1994). One obvious similarity is that the temperament Buss and Plomin (1984) called *emotionality* and Rothbart and Posner (1985) called *avoidance* temperament very closely resembles *neuroticism*.

Extraversion, from the "big five," also has overtones of an approach temperament. (Some people think extraversion is about approaching social rewards.) Extraversion suggests a preference for being with others, implying a possible link to sociability (Depue & Morrone-Strupinsky, 2005). Eysenck (1986) included activity in his view of extraversion, suggesting that extraversion may blend sociability with activity.

Another of the five factors—agreeableness—also has overtones of sociability, although again, the two are not identical. Agreeableness suggests liking to be with people. It goes beyond that, however, in having connotations of being easy to get along with. Whether agreeableness derives from a temperament of sociability is an open question.

The trait of conscientiousness is defined partly by the absence of impulsiveness. That is, conscientiousness is a planful, persistent, focused orientation toward life's activities. Given the possibility that impulsivity, or effortful control, is a temperament (Pedersen, Plomin, McClearn, & Friberg, 1988; Rothbart et al., 2003), this would suggest another link between temperaments and the five-factor model.

The last of the "big five" is openness to experience, or intellect. Recall from Chapter 4 that it's been hard to pin this trait down, so there are several labels for it. Some see links from this trait to intelligence. Intelligence is another quality that might be thought of as a temperament (and, interestingly, there are arguments about exactly what intelligence is, too). Intelligence has the characteristics Buss and Plomin used to define temperaments: It's genetically influenced (Bouchard, Lykken, McGue, Segal, & Tellegen, 1990; Plomin, 1989), and its effects on behavior are broad, manifest early in life, and continue throughout the life span. If we thought of intelligence as a temperament, the relationship between it and the fifth trait of the five-factor model would represent yet another link between temperament and trait models.

In sum, although the fit isn't perfect, the set of qualities proposed as biologically based temperaments bears a strong resemblance to the qualities in the five-factor model. The places where the resemblance is less clear raise interesting questions. For example, why should activity and sociability be considered fundamental, rather than extraversion? Is extraversion really one trait, or two? As we said in Chapter 4, there are many ways to divide up the qualities of behavior, and it's sometimes hard to know which is best.

GENETICS OF OTHER QUALITIES: HOW DISTINCT ARE THEY?

The evidence that genes influence behavior extends quite broadly. Many effects have emerged, some of which relate fairly easily back to personality. For example, there's a genetic effect on risk of divorce (McGue & Lykken, 1992), which operates through personality (Jockin, McGue, & Lykken, 1996). There's a genetic effect on having adverse life events, which again appears to operate via personality (Saudino, Pedersen, Lichtenstein, McClearn, & Plomin, 1997). Heredity influences how much social support people have (Kessler, Kendler, Heath, Neale, & Eaves, 1992), which may reflect personality (Brissette, Scheier, & Carver, 2002; Kendler, 1997). People's attitudes on various topics are also genetically influenced (Eaves, Eysenck, & Martin, 1989; Olson, Vernon, Harris, & Jang, 2001; Tesser, 1993), which again may reflect personality.

Findings such as these raise a question: To what extent are the various effects distinct and separate? The temperaments and supertraits discussed earlier are very broad. When evidence is found that some behavior is genetically influenced, one has to wonder whether this is a *separate* effect, or whether the effect is there because the behavior relates to a temperament or supertrait. For example, happiness has high heritability, but its heritability is fully accounted for by the heritability of neuroticism, extraversion, and conscientiousness (Weiss, Bates, & Luciano, 2008).

The question of how many distinct qualities are *separately* influenced by inheritance hasn't been explored much. However, it's an important question in understanding genetic influences on personality. One study has explored it, within the framework of the five-factor model (Jang et al., 1998). This study found that not only were the five supertraits heritable, but so were most of the facet traits. Indeed, the genetic influences on facets were separate from the genetic influences on the overall traits. This suggests that *many* distinct qualities are genetically influenced, not just a few broad ones.

ENVIRONMENTAL INFLUENCES

The studies that establish a powerful role for genetics in personality also show an important role for environmental factors. Surprisingly, however, the environment doesn't generally make twins alike, as you might assume. The environment seems to affect personality mostly by making twins *different* (Plomin & Daniels, 1987). This is called a **nonshared environmental effect**.

What might be the sources of nonshared environmental influence? There isn't a lot of information on this. Several guesses sound reasonable, though (Dunn & Plomin, 1990; Rowe, 1994). For example, siblings often have different sets of friends, sometimes totally different. Peers have a big influence on children. Having different friends may cause twins' personalities to diverge. If that happens, it's an environmental influence, but it's not shared by the twins.

Another point is that siblings in families develop roles that play off each other (e.g., Daniels, 1986; Hoffman, 1991). For example, if one child often helps another child with schoolwork, the two are developing styles of interacting that diverge. As another example, parents sometimes favor one child over another. This can affect the children's relationship, perhaps inducing differences between them. Again, the effects would be environmental, but they would differ from one child to the other.

Questions still remain about environment effects. There are methodological reasons to believe that the importance of nonshared environment has been overstated (Rutter, 2006). In addition, when behavior measures are used instead of rating scales, shared effects are stronger (Turkheimer, 1998). For example, in the study in which videotaped behavior was rated by strangers, Borkenau et al. (2001) found a far larger shared environment effect than is typically found. Thus, variations in research methods may also influence what conclusions emerge.

New Approaches to Genetics and Personality

Many aspects of personality have high heritability. In recent years, however, it's become apparent that this is less informative than it might seem (Johnson, Turkheimer, Gottesman, & Bouchard, 2009). One reason is that the size of genetic and environmental influences depends partly on how much variability there is in each domain. That is, a heritability index pertains to a specific population in a specific environment. If one or the other changes substantially, the heritability index can also change substantially.

This point is illustrated by a study of genetic and environmental effects on a vocabulary IQ test (Rowe, Jacobson, & Van den Oord, 1999). As illustrated on the left side of Figure 6.2, among families in which the parents had little education, the shared environment had a large effect but genetics had no effect at all. On the right side of the figure, where parental education was very high, there was a very large genetic effect and no

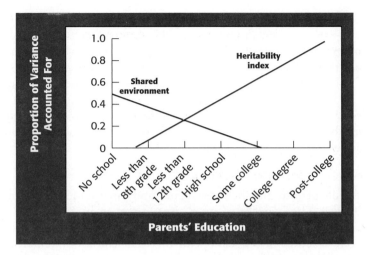

FIGURE 6.2
Variability in vocabulary IQ accounted for by genetic factors and by shared environment factors, when examined as a function of parents' education level. Heritability is very low among children with poorly educated parents, but it is very high among children with highly educated parents
Source: Adapted from Rowe et al., 1999.

environmental effect. This sort of pattern means we have to be cautious about generalizing estimates of heritability from one sample to the universe of people.

CORRELATIONS BETWEEN GENETIC AND ENVIRONMENTAL INFLUENCES

It is also increasingly recognized that two kinds of interplay between genes and environment are important (Rutter, 2006). One of them is a correlation between a genetic influence and an environmental one. It was originally assumed that genetic and environmental influences are distinct and independent. But that turned out to be a naïve assumption.

Dickens and Flynn (2001) illustrated this point using intelligence as an example. People with high intelligence (more than people with less intelligence) gravitate to environments that foster learning. In those environments, they learn more. As a result, their IQs go up. The *environment* had the actual effect on their IQ. But the possibility for it to happen stemmed from their genetic makeup. Thus, the two influences are correlated.

Why does this matter? It makes it very hard to sort out causal responsibility. The size of an environmental effect is judged by how much variability is not explained by the genetic effect. If an environmental effect is mistaken to be a genetic effect (because they're correlated), the genetic effect gets the credit for what the environment is doing. On the other hand, sometimes the environment would not have the chance to exert an effect if not for the genetic influence.

Dickens and Flynn (2001) made this argument in the context of IQ, but it can easily be applied to personality. As we said in Chapter 4, people gravitate to environments that suit their interests—that let them be who they are. Maybe those environments even induce people to develop more of what first led them there. Someone who's slightly introverted who starts reading more may discover the joys of solitary pursuits and become even more introverted. Someone who's slightly extraverted who gets involved in group activities may discover he or she likes being in charge of groups and develop greater extraversion.

This issue arises any time a genetic factor makes it more likely that a person will experience an environment different from the environments other people experience. Sometimes, the impact is from outsiders' genes, as when parents' genetic makeup leads them to create adverse environments for their children. Sometimes, the impact comes when people's own genetic makeup influences what environments they seek out. Sometimes, it comes when people's genetic makeup influences the responses they induce from people around them. (As we said in Chapter 4, some people always bring a smile to your face, while others can make you frown just by entering the room.)

GENE-BY-ENVIRONMENT INTERACTIONS

A different kind of interplay between genes and environment is an interaction between the two. The concept of interaction came up in Chapters 2 and 4. In Chapter 4, we talked about trait-by-situation interactions. We said that situations may cause one reaction in a person with one trait and a different reaction in a person with a different trait. The point here is the same, but substitute *genetic makeup* for *trait*.

Geneticists long believed that gene-by-environment **(GxE)** interactions were rare and unimportant (Rutter, 2006). This also appears to have been a naïve assumption. A number of studies have provided evidence of GxE interactions (see Rutter, 2006; Chapter 9). Most of these studies have looked at how genetic factors interact with situations of life adversity or stress, such as childhood maltreatment. How to test properly for such effects raises several technical issues (see Moffitt, Caspi, & Rutter, 2006), and there's a great deal of debate about the usefulness of research looking for them (Caspi, Hariri, Holmes, Uher, & Moffitt, 2010). However, it now appears that this will be an important part of the field in the future.

ENVIRONMENTAL EFFECTS ON GENE EXPRESSION

The idea of a GxE interaction is that genes render some people more susceptible than others to environmental influences. However, environments also influence how genes act. Environments don't change the strands of DNA that make up the gene, but they do affect their ability to function. **Gene expression** is the term used when the gene engages in the processes that create a protein. Interestingly, gene expression is not the same throughout the body. Gene expression varies by region and type of cell involved (e.g., brain cells, blood cells).

Gene expression is influenced by several factors that affect the gene's accessibility to other chemicals. One influence is **methylation**: the attachment of methyl chemical groups to what's called the gene's *promoter region* (its "on" switch). When there's more methylation, there's less gene expression. This effect doesn't involve a change in the gene itself. For that reason, it's called an **epigenetic** effect (meaning "in addition to genetic"). Methylation can be affected by stress level and even by diet (Champagne & Mashoodh, 2009; Gilbert & Epel, 2009).

There's growing evidence that gene expression can be affected by many variations in the environment (Cole, 2009; Gilbert & Epel, 2009; Rutter, 2006). Most of this evidence comes from research with laboratory animals, but more and more is being done with humans. Much of the human research thus far has involved genes implicated in stress responses. For example, chronic social isolation can greatly alter the expression of genes that are involved in immune responses (Cole, 2009).

An astonishing aspect of research into gene expression is the discovery that epigenetic changes (patterns of methylation) can be passed from one generation to the next, just as genetic influences are passed onward (Gilbert & Epel, 2009). Now, put that together in your mind with the fact that the epigenetic changes reflect experience with the environment. The inescapable conclusion is that changes caused by experience with the environment can be inherited (Champagne & Mashoodh, 2009)—an idea that would have prompted ridicule 40 years ago.

MOLECULAR GENETICS

Another issue has gradually crept into the discussion in the preceding sections. There now are ways to study genetic influences that weren't available even a short time ago. The effort to map the human **genome**—the genetic blueprint of the body—was wildly successful. The "first draft" was completed in 2000, years ahead of schedule. The identification of gene sequences is becoming faster and less expensive all the time. It's increasingly possible to identify specific genes that influence differences among people—from vulnerability to disorders to normal personality qualities. Many researchers believe the ability to identify genes linked to such differences will revolutionize medicine, psychiatry, and psychology (Plomin, 1995; Plomin & Crabbe, 2000; Plomin, DeFries, Craig, & McGuffin, 2003).

A huge proportion of the human genome is identical for everyone. Interest focuses on the parts that vary. When different patterns of DNA (genetic material) can occur at a particular location, they are called **alleles**. The existence of a difference is called a **polymorphism**. A **genotype** difference between persons means they have different alleles at some particular location. Whereas twin research is referred to as **quantitative genetics**, the attempt to relate differences in particular gene locations to other measurable differences among persons is called **molecular genetics** (Carey, 2003) or **genomics**. In the not too distant past, for most practical purposes genes were treated as abstractions, inferred from patterns of inheritance. Now, they are increasingly viewed as what they are: specific DNA sequences in specific locations of chromosomes (Cole, 2009).

The question for personality is whether specific locations influence a given personality quality. The answer to this question isn't likely to be at all simple. It's very likely that many genes relate to any given personality quality (Plomin & Crabbe, 2000). Despite this, the first genomic studies on this topic used what's called a **candidate gene strategy**. This means that particular gene locations were examined selectively, based on evidence linking those genes to particular biological processes, as well as theoretical reasoning linking those biological processes to personality.

Several genes have been identified that have clear relevance to normal personality. One example is a gene called *DRD4*, which relates to receptors for dopamine in the brain. It has several alleles, one longer than the others. Two research teams found almost simultaneously that people with the long allele have high scores on personality scales that relate to novelty seeking (Benjamin et al., 1996; Ebstein et al., 1996). Another candidate gene related to dopamine function, called *DRD2*, has also been linked to a personality measure of fun seeking (Reuter, Schmitz, Corr, & Hennig, 2006). These findings fit with the view that dopamine is involved in reward pursuit (a view that's discussed in Chapter 7).

Another candidate gene relates to the use of serotonin in the brain. It's called the serotonin transporter gene, or *5HTTLPR*. Several groups of researchers have found a link of the short allele of that gene to high scores on neuroticism and low scores on agreeableness (e.g., Greenberg et al., 2000; Lesch et al., 1996; Sen et al., 2004). Others have related it to impulsivity and aggressiveness (for review, see Carver, Johnson, & Joormann, 2008). The associations with neuroticism have been somewhat difficult to replicate. Evidence is beginning to accumulate that the 5HTTLPR polymorphism is more about impulse versus constraint than about neuroticism per se (Carver et al., 2008; Carver et al., 2011).

Single-gene discoveries are very exciting. We repeat, though, that it's very likely that most genetic influences on behavior will involve small contributions from many genes (Plomin & Crabbe, 2000). Indeed, that may be one reason why the single-gene discoveries have been hard to replicate. Even though the media continue to trumpet every new discovery as "the gene for" something or other, that's misleading (Kendler, 2005). Some researchers worry that candidate gene studies, in particular, are vulnerable to false positives.

In part for that reason and in part because of the rapid advance of technology, other molecular geneticists argue that the candidate gene strategy should be abandoned. It's now possible to conduct **genome-wide association studies (GWAS)**, in which the entire genome is examined for any and all differences that relate to an outcome of interest. Done properly, this kind of study involves a huge number of research participants (there are so many genes to test that the large number alone creates the potential for false positives). This kind of study also is very costly. Some believe, however, that this is the path of the future in behavioral genomics.

Whether candidate gene studies continue or GWAS take their place, it's clear that the tools of molecular genomics radically change the nature of genetic research bearing on many topics, including personality. It's of some interest that this newer genetic approach (like the older one) doesn't really specify what aspects of personality matter. Rather, it provides tools for testing genetic contribution to whatever aspect of personality a researcher is interested in.

Evolution and Human Behavior

We now change directions somewhat. Human beings are all members of a species that evolved across millennia. The view that humans are a product of evolution leads to the possibility that ancient evolutionary processes have a major influence on present-day

Evolutionary psychologists believe that even acts of altruism, such as doing disaster relief work for the Red Cross, may have a genetic basis.

Box 6.2 Theoretical Issue: Universal Adaptations and Why There Are Individual Differences

The basic concepts of natural selection and population genetics are simple. If a characteristic differs from person to person, it means that each gene behind that characteristic has several potential forms, or alleles. *Selection* means that one allele is more likely to show up in the next generation because it *helped* with survival or reproduction, or is less likely to show up because it *interfered* with survival or reproduction. This is **directional selection**: a shift toward a higher proportion of the adaptive allele in the population's next generation. If it goes on long enough, directional selection can even eliminate individual differences. Over many generations, those without the adaptive allele fail to reproduce, and a larger proportion of the next generation has the adaptive one. In principle, this is how a characteristic can become universal in the population.

Many characteristics influence survival. For example, in a world where strength matters (which probably was true during human evolution), strength makes you more likely to survive long enough to reproduce. That sends genes for strength into the next generation. As long as these genes are well represented in the population, the population will tend to survive and create yet another generation.

But wait. If some characteristics are more adaptive than others, why are there individual differences at all? Why aren't we all large and strong and smart and stealthy and whatever else is good to be? A tricky thing about selection is that whether a value is adaptive depends on the context. Sometimes, a value that's useful in one environment is not just useless—but fatal—in another. For example, openness to experience is adaptive in a benign environment, but if there are lots of diseases around, it's adaptive not to be so open. Indeed, there's evidence that higher prevalence of disease in particular environments relates to lower level of openness among the population living there (Schaller & Murray, 2008).

In the long run, genetic variability in the population is necessary for the population to survive in a world that changes. Thus, the importance of another kind of selection, termed **stabilizing selection**, which maintains genetic variability (Plomin, 1981). Stabilizing selection occurs when an intermediate value of a characteristic is more adaptive than the value at either extreme. Presumably, intermediate values reflect combinations of alleles, rather than specific alleles, and probably involve multiple genes. Predominance of intermediate values thus implies genetic variability.

How can an intermediate value of a characteristic be more adaptive than an extreme value? Here's an example. It's important for people to have some sociability, because humans are such a social species. Having too little sociability isn't adaptive. But neither is it adaptive to have *too much* sociability. A person with extremely high sociability can hardly bear to be alone, and life sometimes requires people to be alone.

Intermediate values are especially adaptive in many of the domains that are relevant to personality. That's why personality traits vary from person to person: There's genetic diversity on those traits. Otherwise, there would be only a single personality, which everyone would have.

---

human behavior. This line of thought is tied to several labels, including *sociobiology* and *evolutionary psychology* (Barkow, Cosmides, & Tooby, 1992; Bjorklund & Pellegrini, 2002; D. M. Buss, 1991, 1995; Caporael, 2001; Heschl, 2002; Segal, 1993; Tooby & Cosmides, 1989, 1990). Work deriving from this group of ideas has grown rapidly in recent years.

SOCIOBIOLOGY AND EVOLUTIONARY PSYCHOLOGY

Sociobiology was proposed as the study of the biological basis of social behavior (Alexander, 1979; Barash, 1986, 2001; Crawford, 1989; Crawford, Smith, & Krebs, 1987; Dawkins, 1976; Lumsden & Wilson, 1981; Wilson, 1975). The core assumption underlying this field is that many—perhaps all—forms of social interaction are products of evolution. That is, the patterns were retained genetically because at some point in prehistory they conferred an adaptive advantage.

Sociobiologists focused on the question of how behavior patterns might get built in (see also Box 6.2). Their work led in some surprising directions. For example, it led to a way to account for altruism, a tendency that seems very hard to explain in evolutionary terms. *Altruism* is acting for the welfare of others, to the point of sacrificing one's own well-being (potentially one's life) for someone else. Altruism would seem to confer a biological *dis*advantage. That is, being altruistic may help someone, but it also might get you killed. This would prevent your genes from being passed on to the next generation. If the genes aren't passed on, a genetically based tendency toward altruism should disappear very quickly.

Some point out, however, that the process of evolution isn't really entirely a matter of individual survival (Wilson & Wilson, 2008). What ultimately matters is a *gene pool,* over a population. If one *group* in a population survives, prospers, and reproduces at a high rate, its genes move onward into subsequent generations more than other groups' genes.

This means there are ways to get your genes carried forward besides reproducing on your own. Your genes are helped into the next generation by anything that helps *your part of the gene pool* reproduce, an idea called **inclusive fitness** (Hamilton, 1964). If you act altruistically for a relative, it helps the relative survive. If an extremely altruistic act (in which you die) saves a great many of your relatives, it helps aspects of your genetic makeup be passed on because your relatives resemble you genetically. This phenomenon is sometimes called *kin selection.*

Thus, it's argued, the tendency to be altruistic may be genetically based. This argument implies that people will be more altruistic toward those in their kinship group than strangers (especially competitors). This seems to be true (Burnstein, Crandall, & Kitayama, 1994). Also fitting this view, there seems to be a genetic contribution to empathic concern for others, which may underlie altruism (Burnstein et al., 1994; Matthews, Batson, Horn, & Rosenman, 1981; Rushton, Fulker, Neale, Nias, & Eysenck, 1986). Indeed, there's evidence that emotional closeness, which increases with genetic relatedness, underlies the effect of relatedness on altruism (Korchmaros & Kenny, 2001).

The idea that altruistic tendencies are part of human nature has been extended to suggest an evolutionary basis for cooperation even among nonrelatives. The idea is essentially that our remote ancestors survived better by cooperating than by being individualistic. Thus, they acquired a tendency toward being helpful more generally. One person helps the other in the expectation that the help will be returned, an idea termed **reciprocal altruism** (Trivers, 1971).

Can this possibly have happened? Wouldn't people cheat, and take without giving? Sometimes. But those who do get punished (Fehr & Gächter, 2002). From an evolutionary view, the issue is whether cooperation leads to better outcomes for the group. There's evidence that it does, at least in the situations studied by psychologists (Axelrod & Hamilton, 1981). This has led some to conclude that a tendency to cooperate is part of human nature (Guisinger & Blatt, 1994; Kriegman & Knight, 1988; McCullough, 2008). There's also evidence that punishing people who don't cooperate leads to better group outcomes (Fehr & Gächter, 2002). Maybe punishing those who don't go along with the group is also genetically built into human nature.

GENETIC SIMILARITY AND ATTRACTION

The idea that people act altruistically toward relatives has been extended by Rushton and his colleagues (Rushton, 1989a; Rushton, Russell, & Wells, 1984) to **genetic similarity theory**. The idea is what we've said already: A gene "survives" (is represented in the next generation) by any action that brings about reproduction of any organism in which copies of the gene exist. That may mean altruism to your kinship group, but Rushton says it means other things, as well.

Both men and women are in competition for desirable mates.

Rushton and his colleagues (1984) argued that genetic similarity has an influence on who attracts you. Specifically, you're more attracted to strangers who resemble you genetically than those who don't. How does this help the survival of the gene? If you're attracted to someone, you may become sexually involved, which may result in offspring. Offspring have genes from both parents. By making you attracted to someone with genes like yours, your genes increase the odds that genes like themselves will be copied (from one parent or the other or both) into a new person, surviving into the next generation.

Are people attracted to others whose genes resemble their own? Maybe. Rushton (1988) had couples take blood tests that give a rough index of genetic similarity. He found that sexually involved couples had in common 50% of the genetic markers. When he took the data and paired people randomly, the pairs shared only 43% of the markers—significantly less. Rushton went on to compare couples who had had children with those who hadn't. Those with children shared 52% of the genetic markers; those with no children shared only 44%. Thus, among sexually active couples, those who were most similar were also most likely to have reproduced.

This attraction effect isn't limited to the opposite sex. People also tend to form friendships with others who are genetically similar to them. Rushton (1989b) repeated his study with pairs of men who were close friends (all heterosexual). The pairs of friends shared 54% of the genetic markers, and the random pairs shared only 48%. Again, genetic similarity related to attraction.

How would friendships with genetically similar people of the same sex be adaptive? The point is to get the genes into offspring. Having same-sex friends won't do that directly. There are two ways it can help, though. The first is similar to the idea discussed earlier about altruism and kin selection. You're more likely to be altruistic for a close friend than a stranger, making the friend more likely to live to reproduce. The second possibility is that you may meet the same-sex friend's opposite-sex sibling. If the sibling is also genetically similar to you, an attraction may develop that may have the potential for sexual activity, resulting in offspring.

How do people detect genetic similarity in others? It's not clear. One possibility is that we are drawn to others who share our facial and body features. People who look like us seem like family and therefore attract us. Another possibility is that genetic similarity is conveyed by smell. Consistent with this, there's evidence that women prefer the odor of men who are genetically similar to their fathers (Jacob,

McClintock, Zelano, & Ober, 2002). Outside your awareness, you may recognize those who are like you by subtle physical cues.

It's also likely that culture plays a role here. If you are descended from eastern Europeans, you may feel more comfortable around people who share your (eastern European) traditions. It might be the familiar traditions that bring you close, but the result is that you are drawn to people who come from your part of the gene pool.

There's at least one finding that contradicts this principle. Garver-Apgar et al. (2006) looked at genes that help the immune system to distinguish the self from pathogens. It's most adaptive to be able to detect as many pathogens as possible, so your immune system can neutralize them. The researchers reasoned that this is a case in which you should be attracted not to others who resemble you but to others who differ from you. As predicted, they found that women who differed from their partners in these specific genes were more sexually responsive to them and less attracted to other men.

The general idea that people choose mates on the basis of particular character-istics is called **assortative mating** (Thiessen & Gregg, 1980). Mating definitely isn't random. People select their mates on the basis of a variety of characteristics, though there are limitations on how fine grained this selection is (Lykken & Tellegen, 1993). Often, the features that influence mate selection are similarities to the self (Buss, 1985; Rushton & Bons, 2005).

MATE SELECTION AND COMPETITION FOR MATES

We've talked at some length about the importance of getting genes to the next gen-eration. (From this viewpoint, it's sometimes said that a person is just a gene's way of creating another gene [Barash, 2001].) Obviously, then, the evolutionary view on personality focuses closely on mating (Gangestad & Simpson, 2000). Indeed, from this view, mating is what life's all about (although other issues do arise when you think about the complexities of mating). Just as certain qualities confer survival advantage, certain qualities also confer reproductive advantage.

Mating involves competition. Males compete with one another; females compete with one another. But what's being competed for differs between the sexes. Trivers (1972) argued that males and females evolved different strategies, based on their roles in reproduction. Female humans have greater investment in offspring than males: They carry them for nine months, and they're more tied to caring for them after birth. The general rule in biology is that the sex with the greater investment can generate fewer offspring over the life span, because of the commitment of time and energy to each. It thus is choosier about a mate (though not everyone agrees on this; see Small, 1993). The sex with less investment can create more offspring and is less discriminating.

Given the difference in biological investment, the strategy of women is to tend to hold back from mating until they identify the best available male. *Best* here is defined as quality of genetic contribution, parental care, and material support for the mate and offspring. In contrast, the strategy of males is to maximize sexual opportunities, copulating as often as possible. This means seeking partners who are available and fer-tile (Buss, 1994a, 1994b). In this view, men tend to view women as *sex objects*, whereas women tend to view men as *success objects*.

These differences in orientation should produce different strategies for trying to get the opportunity to mate. David Buss and David Schmitt (1993) examined differ-ences in how men and women compete for and choose mates and how the strategies differ from short to long term (see also Buss, 1994a, 1994b; Feingold, 1992; Schmitt &

Buss, 1996). If men are interested in finding fertile partners, women should compete by stressing attributes that relate to fertility—youth and beauty. If women want to find partners that will provide for them and their babies, men should compete by stressing their status, personal dominance and ambition, and wealth or potential for wealth (Sidanius, Pratto, & Bobo, 1994; Sprecher, Sullivan, & Hatfield, 1994).

What do men and women actually *do* to compete for mates? College students report doing pretty much what we just described (Buss, 1988). Women enhance their beauty with makeup, jewelry, clothing, and hairstyles. They also play hard to get, to incite widespread interest among many males. This permits women to be choosy once candidates have been identified (see also Kenrick, Sadalla, Groth, & Trost, 1990). Men, on the other hand, brag about their accomplishments and earning potential, display expensive possessions, and flex their muscles. In fact, just seeing women around makes men display these qualities even more (Roney, 2003). Consistent with this picture, people selectively attend to signs of dominance among males and to signs of physical attractiveness among females (Maner, DeWall, & Gailliot, 2008).

Buss (1989) examined mate preferences in 37 different cultures around the world. Cultural

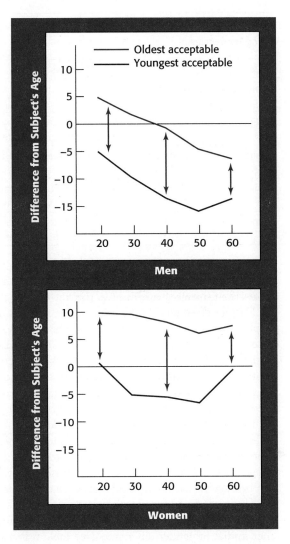

FIGURE 6.3
Singles' ads placed by men and women often specify the age range of persons of the opposite sex whom the placer of the ad would like to meet. In this sample of ads, as men aged, they expressed an increasing preference for younger women. Women tended to prefer men slightly older than they were, and the extent of that preference didn't change over time.
Source: Adapted from Kenrick & Keefe, 1992.

differences were relatively rare. The preferences of U.S. college students didn't differ much from those of people elsewhere. Males (more than females) were drawn to cues of reproductive capacity. Females (more than males) were drawn to cues indicating resources (see also Singh, 1995). The resource issue may not be a case of "more is better." It may just be that men who don't have an acceptable level of resources will be out of the running (Kenrick, Sundie, Nicastle, & Stone, 2001). Females are also drawn to cues of dominance and high status (Cunningham, Barbee, & Pike, 1990; Feingold,

Table 6.1 Summary of Predictions from Evolutionary Psychology for Sex Differences in Mating Tendencies.

Issue	Females	Males
Reproductive constraints	Can produce only a limited number of children over life	Can reproduce without limit through life
Optimal reproductive strategy	Locate and hold onto best-quality mate	Mate as widely and often as possible
Desired quality in potential mate	Resources to protect and support them and offspring	Childbearing capability
Basis for evaluating mate potential	Earning capacity, status, possessions, generosity	Physical attractiveness, health, youth
Prime basis for jealousy	Partner's emotional attachment to another	Partner's sexual infidelity

1992; Kenrick et al., 1990; Sadalla, Kendrick, & Vershure, 1987), especially dominance expressed in socially positive ways (Jensen-Campbell, Graziano, & West, 1995).

Despite these gender differences, the qualities just listed don't always rank high in people's lists of desired characteristics. This leads some to be skeptical of their importance. But rankings can also be deceiving. Other research gave people tight "budgets" for getting what they want in a partner (Li, Bailey, Kenrick, & Linsenmeier, 2002). In this situation, men saw attractiveness as a necessity rather than an option, women saw status and resources as necessities, and both saw kindness and intelligence as necessities. That is, given that they couldn't be choosy about everything, they went for these qualities first.

Researchers have investigated implications of the evolutionary model in several ways. For example, research shows that men prefer younger women—especially as they grow older—consistent with the seeking of reproductive capacity. This comes from a study of the age ranges specified in singles' ads (Kenrick & Keefe, 1992). As illustrated in Figure 6.3, men past age 25 specified an age range that extended increasingly below their own age. Women, in contrast, tended to express a preference for men slightly older than themselves.

Also consistent with predictions from the evolutionary model are results from several other studies of gender differences (see Table 6.1). Compared to women, men are more interested in casual sex (Bailey, Gaulin, Agyei, & Gladue, 1994; Buss & Schmitt, 1993; R. D. Clark & Hatfield, 1989; Oliver & Hyde, 1993), want more sexual variety (Schmitt, 2003), and are less selective in their criteria for one-night stands (Kenrick, Groth, Trost, & Sadalla, 1993). Men also are more easily turned on by visual erotica than women are (Bailey et al., 1994). Men's commitment to their relationship is shaken by exposure to a very attractive woman, whereas women's commitment is shaken by exposure to a very dominant man (Kenrick, Neuberg, Zierk, & Krones, 1994). Men's confidence in their own value as a mate is shaken by exposure to a very dominant man (but not an attractive one), and women's confidence in their value as a mate is shaken by exposure to a very attractive woman (but not a dominant one) (Gutierres, Kenrick, & Partch, 1999). Men overinterpret women's smiles and touches as implying sexual interest, and women are overly conservative in judging men's commitment in relationships that are forming (Buss, 2001).

Both men and women experience jealousy, but it's been suggested that there's a difference in what creates this emotion. In theory, it's evolutionarily important for men to be concerned about paternity. (They want to support their *own* children, not someone else's.) Thus, men should be especially jealous about sexual infidelity. In theory, women are most concerned about whether the man will continue to support her and her children. Thus, women should be jealous about a man's having emotional bonds with another woman, rather than sex per se.

Data from several studies fit this view: Men were more disturbed by thoughts of sexual infidelity, and women were more disturbed by thoughts of emotional infidelity (Buss, Larsen, Westen, & Semmelroth, 1992; see also Bailey et al., 1994). This particular finding has been challenged, however, partly because asking the question differently erases the gender difference (DeSteno, Bartlett, Braverman, & Salovey, 2002; Harris, 2002, 2003) and partly because it's been hard to obtain the effect in nonstudent samples (Sabini & Green, 2004).

Jealousy is partly about what your partner may have done, but it's partly about the presence of rivals. Again, there's evidence of a gender difference in what qualities matter. Men are more jealous when the potential rival is dominant than when he is physically attractive; women are more jealous when the potential rival is physically attractive (Dijkstra & Buunk, 1998).

MATE RETENTION AND OTHER ISSUES

The first challenge in mating is *getting* a mate. The next challenge is *keeping* the mate. Men and women both have the potential to stray, and other people sometimes try to make that happen (Schmitt, 2004; Schmitt & Buss, 2001). People use various tactics to prevent this (Buss & Shackelford, 1997). Some tactics are used by men and women alike, but others differ by gender. For example, men report spending a lot of money and giving in to their mates' wishes. Women try to make themselves look extra attractive and let others know their mate is already taken.

Use of retention tactics also relates predictably to other factors in the relationship but differently for men and women. Men use their tactics more if they think their wife is physically attractive. Men also work harder at keeping a wife who is young—independent of the man's age and the length of the relationship. In contrast, women work harder at keeping a husband with a high income. They also make more efforts if their husband is striving for high status (independent of current income).

Although mating strategies are the starting point for much of this research on gender differences, other researchers have applied the theme more broadly. (As noted earlier, issues involved in mating lead to several other complexities in life.) Several have suggested that evolutionary differences cause men and women to have very different styles—indeed different *needs*—in communication (e.g., J. Gray, 1992; Tannen, 1990). Men are seen as having an individualistic, dominance-oriented, problem-solving approach. Women are seen as having an inclusive, sharing, communal approach. The argument is also made that these differences in goals and patterns of communication lead to a good deal of misunderstanding between men and women.

We should note that our discussion has emphasized gender differences, not similarities. There are, of course, many similarities. Both genders are looking for partners who have a good sense of humor and a pleasing personality (Feingold, 1992), who are agreeable and emotionally stable (Kenrick et al., 1993), intelligent (Li et al., 2002), and kind and loving (Buss, 1994b). Both also seem to prefer partners whose faces are symmetrical (Grammer & Thornhill, 1994). The way men and women look at each other goes far beyond seeing each other as sex objects and success objects (Buss, 1994b). Nevertheless, gender differences also seem important.

AGGRESSION AND THE YOUNG MALE SYNDROME

Competition for mating opportunities leads to a lot of male posturing. It's also been blamed for many problem aspects of young men's behavior, including their risky driving (Nell, 2002). But it can also lead to more. When males face hard competition for scarce resources (females), the result sometime is confrontation and potentially serious violence (Hilton, Harris, & Rice, 2000).

This pattern has been referred to as the *young male syndrome* (Wilson & Daly, 1985). It's viewed as partly an effect of evolutionary pressures from long ago and partly a response to situations that elicit the pattern. That is, although the pattern of behavior may be coded in every man's genes, it's most likely to emerge when current situations predict reproductive failure. The worst case would be a single man who's unemployed and thus a poor candidate as a mate.

In line with this analysis, there's clear evidence that homicide between competitors is primarily a male affair (Daly & Wilson, 1990). Figure 6.4 displays the homicide rates in Chicago during a 16-year period, omitting cases in which the person killed was a relative. Males are far more likely to kill one another than are females. It's also obvious that the prime ages for killing are the prime ages for mating. According to Daly and Wilson, these killings come largely from conflicts over "face" and status (see also Wilson & Daly, 1996). Trivial events escalate into violence, and someone is killed.

Why killing instead of a ritualized display of aggressiveness? No one knows for sure. It's certain that easy access to guns in the United States plays a role. When weapons aren't available, the same pressures are more likely to result in punching and shouting. Deadly violence certainly is possible without weapons, but weapons make it far more likely.

We should point out explicitly that the theory underlying this area of study is very different from the ideas about aggression and human nature of only a few years ago. This view isn't that aggression is part of human nature, expressed indiscriminately. Rather, physical aggression is seen as largely a male phenomenon, which occurs specifically as a result of sexual selection pressures in the competition for mates (Buss, 2005). Recent laboratory results confirm that men become more aggressive when status is an issue, and that mating motives also matter when men are around other men (Griskevicius et al., 2009).

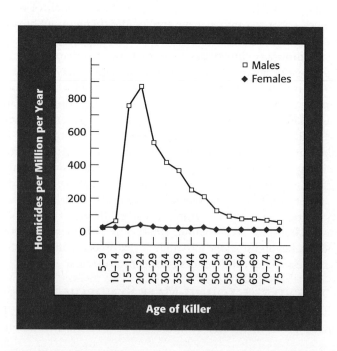

FIGURE 6.4
Homicide rates for males and females killing nonrelatives of the same sex in Chicago during the period 1965–1981. *Source:* Adapted from Daly & Wilson, 1990.

BOX 6.3 LIVING IN A POSTGENOMIC WORLD

The human genome is mapped. Researchers today know more than ever about the makeup of the human body and the functions of some of our genes (Plomin et al., 2003). The technology behind these advances is continuing its rapid development, with no signs of slowing down.

Mapping the human genome will surely yield benefits. Some disorders are caused by single genes. Knowing the map makes it easier to find those genes. This information can be used in genetic counseling. People can be warned if they carry a gene for a disorder they may pass on to a child. Another benefit is genetic therapies, which now exist for some disorders— for example, to correct defects in producing blood cells. Some say having the map of the genome and using it to identify genetic weaknesses will usher in a new era of preventive medicine, dramatically changing the way we deal with disease (Lewin, 1990).

The mapping of the genome excites imaginations, but it also raises concerns (Buchanan, Brock, Daniels, & Wikler, 2000; Fukuyama, 2002; Lynn, 2001; Stock, 2002). Knowing what genes control behavior raises serious ethical issues. For example, a great deal of pressure will doubtlessly arise to modify genes to create specific characteristics in new children, creating so-called designer babies (Plomin & Crabbe, 2000; Stock, 2002). Should this happen? Who is to decide what characteristics should be created? What happens to people whose genetic characteristics are viewed by society as inferior?

Knowledge about disorders also raises ethical issues. Will there be discrimination against people with particular genetic profiles? What happens to the cost of medical insurance when it's possible to know who's susceptible to specific diseases? Will insurance even be *available* to people with susceptibilities? This isn't an idle question. Insurance policies have been cancelled for entire families because of genetic problems in specific family members

(Stolberg, 1994). The issue is serious enough that a federal law was passed in 2009 banning use of genetic tests to set insurance rates or deny coverage.

The same issue arises with respect to psychological disorders. If it's known that your genes predispose you to mania or antisocial behavior, will you be able to get a job? Will you be able to have insurance against the possibility of needing treatment? The other side of this issue, however, is that it's likely that many patterns now seen as disorders are actually extremes of personality (Plomin & Crabbe, 2000). Clarity on this issue would follow from knowing what genes are involved in both the problem patterns and the normal patterns. Such a realization might go a long way toward removing the stigma from disorders.

In short, the project to map the genome holds out much promise, but it also raises very difficult issues that will have to be addressed. You may want to start thinking about them, because they're issues that are in your future—and the future of your children.

Our focus here is on violence by young men toward their genetic competitors. It's worth noting that genetic competition also may play a role in violence within families. In particular, children—especially very young children—are far more likely to be killed by stepparents than by genetic parents (Daly & Wilson, 1988, 1996). The overall frequency of this event is low; most parents don't kill children. Yet if it happens, a stepparent is far more likely to be guilty than a biological parent. As is true of the young male syndrome, this finding may reflect a deep-rooted desire to help one's own genes into the next generation instead of a competitor's genes.

We noted earlier that part of mating is retaining one's mate. People have a variety of tactics for doing this. Most of them are quite benign. Some can even be viewed as efforts at solidifying the relationship to make it resistant to temptation. However, some tactics of mate retention are coercive. Some men are so concerned about losing their mates—or unknowingly supporting a rival's child—that they become quite controlling. Tactics to control the woman sometimes escalate to violence against her (Hilton et al., 2000; Wilson & Daly, 1996). Sometimes that violence is a warning: Don't stray! Sometimes the violence is murder, ending all possibility of straying (Buss, 2005). When killings occur *within* families, most of the victims are wives.

Although male violence against women is cause for great concern, we should also be clear that it isn't just men who do this. Aggression against partners also occurs among women (Hilton et al., 2000).

Assessment

The genetic orientation to personality, discussed in the first part of this chapter, tends to approach assessment of personality in much the same way as the trait view. What it offers, primarily, is some further ideas about what traits to assess. As we said earlier, those who take this view on personality believe that certain temperaments are inherited as biological substrates of personality. These, then, are the qualities to assess.

Given the rise in influence of molecular genetics, some researchers raise the possibility that gene assessment will eventually become a common way of assessing personality. Although it's far too soon to be sure, many people who are prominent in this area see this as unlikely (e.g., Plomin & Crabbe, 2000). They argue that personality traits are influenced by many, many genes, each exerting a small effect. It will be hard enough to identify those genes, never mind use them as convenient personality tests—at least, not any time soon.

Problems in Behavior, and Behavior Change

The genetic approach has made a major contribution to the analysis of problems in behavior. Behavior geneticists have examined the possibility that several kinds of vulnerabilities to problems may be influenced by inheritance (see also Box 6.3). Molecular genetics is also starting to weigh in, but with the same problem it has with respect to normal personality: that many genes are likely to be involved in any given problem, not just one or two.

SCHIZOPHRENIA AND BIPOLAR DISORDER

For many years, research on the behavior genetics of problems focused mainly on schizophrenia and bipolar disorder. Most of the research has been on schizophrenia, which is characterized by disorientation, confusion, cognitive disturbances, and a separation from reality.

A well-known early study of genetic influence on schizophrenia by Gottesman and Shields (1972) began by recruiting twins admitted to a hospital with a diagnosis of schizophrenia. The researchers sought out each one's co-twin and evaluated the

Some people believe that our cultural evolution has out-stripped the ability of our biological evolution to keep up.

co-twin's status. The term **concordance** is used to describe similarity of diagnosis. A pair of twins were concordant if they were both diagnosed as schizophrenic. This study found concordance rates of 50% among identical twins and 9% among fraternal twins. It thus appears that inheritance plays a role in schizophrenia. Indeed, this conclusion follows from over a dozen studies similar to this one.

It should be noted that the twin study data also indicate that life circumstances play a role in determining who shows schizophrenic symptoms openly (Plomin & Rende, 1991). Some people have the genetic susceptibility but don't develop the disorder. This interaction between a susceptibility and a suitable context to touch it off reflects a diathesis-stress view of disorder (a GxE interaction). This is a theme that recurs in studying genetics and disorder.

Molecular genetic studies have also been done to try to isolate gene locations that relate to schizophrenia. Several locations have been suggested (Faraone, Taylor, & Tsuang, 2002; Owen, Williams, & O'Donovan, 2004; Straub et al., 2002). However, as with candidate gene studies of personality traits, findings from these studies are often very difficult to replicate (DeLisi et al., 2002). Thus, there remains great uncertainty about what genes are involved in schizophrenia.

A second disorder that appears to be affected by heredity is bipolar (manic–depressive) disorder. *Mania* is characterized by episodes of frenetic, hyperactive, grandiose, and talkative behavior, accompanied by a rush of ideas. Often the manic pattern is accompanied by positive emotion, but anger is also common. The onset of this disorder is usually sudden. As with schizophrenia, twin studies reveal very strong evidence of genetic contribution (McGuffin et al., 2003).

There has also been molecular genetic research on this problem. One study linked bipolar disorder to a specific dominant gene on chromosome 11 in a group of Amish families (Egeland, Gerhard, Pauls, Sussex, & Kidd, 1987). Two other studies, however, found no link from the disorder to that gene, so it can't be the only one responsible for the disorder (Detera-Wadleigh et al., 1987; Hodgkinson, Sherrington, Gurling, Marchbanks, & Reeders, 1987). Scientists continue to look for genetic markers of bipolar disorder using the techniques of molecular genetics (Badner & Gershon, 2002).

It's clear that biology plays a major role in bipolar disorder. However, it's also clear that events in the environment are important to how the disorder is expressed. In this case, at least a little is known about what environmental influences matter. For example, lack of sleep makes people with the disorder especially vulnerable to manic episodes. So does experiencing success in attaining goals (S. L. Johnson, 2005; S. L. Johnson et al., 2000). Once again, at least in the short term, there is a GxE interaction.

SUBSTANCE USE AND ANTISOCIAL BEHAVIOR

Another focus of research on the genetics of problems is substance abuse. Quite some time ago, Eysenck (1964b) found that MZ twins were more likely to share tendencies toward alcoholism than DZ twins. Similar findings, along with information about the metabolic processes that underlie the difference, were reported by Schuckit and Rayses (1979). A more recent finding has provided an interesting reflection of the interweaving of genetic and environmental influences. In a study by Dick and Rose (2002), genetic contributions increased from about one-third of the variance at age 16 to one-half the variance—in the same sample—at age 18.

Recent research has also implicated a specific gene in the craving for alcohol that some people experience after having a small amount (Hutchison, McGeary, Smolen, Bryan, & Swift, 2002). The gene turns out to be the long allele of the DRD4 gene described earlier in the chapter—the gene that relates to measures of reward seeking.

That allele has also been linked to heroin addiction (Kotler et al., 1997; Li et al., 1997; Shao et al., 2006).

Another fast-growing area of research concerns genetics and antisocial behavior. Long ago, Eysenck (1964a) reported higher concordance rates among MZ than DZ twins on childhood behavior problems and adult crime. Further research on adult criminality tends to fit the picture of a genetic influence (DiLalla & Gottesman, 1991; Wilson & Herrnstein, 1985). Other research suggests that antisocial personality disorder is genetically influenced (Rowe, 1994; Vandenberg, Singer, & Pauls, 1986; Willerman, Loehlin, & Horn, 1992), and most observers now believe there are clear and strong genetic influences on antisocial behavior (Baker, Jacobson, Raine, Lozano, & Bezdjian, 2007; Moffitt, 2005a, 2005b; Rhee & Waldman, 2002).

Once again, however, there appears to be evidence of an interaction between predisposition and environment. Moffitt (2005a, 2005b) reviewed research on antisocial behavior, looking specifically for GxE interactions. One of her conclusions was that we should not frame questions in terms of whether genes influence this disorder but rather who is at greatest risk when placed in circumstances that elicit problem behavior. The search for GxE interactions will likely remain an important focus for studies of problems, including this one (Moffitt, Caspi, & Rutter, 2006).

EVOLUTION AND PROBLEMS IN BEHAVIOR

A somewhat different view of certain behavior problems is suggested by evolutionary psychology. Barash (1986) argued that many difficulties in human life stem from the fact that two kinds of evolution influence people. There is biological evolution, a very slow process that occurs over millennia. There is also cultural evolution, which is much faster. Your experiences of life stem partly from what biological evolution shaped humans to be during prehistory and partly from the cultural circumstances in which you live.

Barash (1986) pointed out that biological evolution prepared us to live in a world very different from the one we live in now. Cultural evolution has raced far ahead, and biological evolution can't keep up. Living in a world in which we don't quite belong, we are conflicted and alienated. Barash's point is a general one—not specific to a particular disorder—but it's an interesting one: That is, problems emerge when behavioral tendencies that have been built in as part of human nature conflict with pressures that are built into contemporary culture.

BEHAVIOR CHANGE: HOW MUCH IS POSSIBLE?

The genetic perspective raises a major question about therapeutic behavior change. Biologically based personality qualities—whether temperaments or not—are, by definition, firmly anchored in the person's constitutional functioning. How easy can it be to alter these aspects of personality in any major way, through *whatever* therapeutic processes are used? Psychotherapy may change the person to some extent. But how far against their biological nature can people be expected to bend?

This is an interesting issue, about which little is known. It's been suggested that even true temperaments can be modified, within limits. But what are the limits? It seems likely that some kinds of change are more difficult to create and sustain for some people than for others. For example, it will be harder for a therapy aimed at reducing emotional reactions to be effective for someone high in emotionality than for someone lower in that temperament. In fact, there may be some people whose temperaments make some kinds of therapy so difficult as to be impractical.

Nonetheless, it should also be recognized that the heritability of personality, though strong, is not complete. There's a good deal of influence from experiences. Thus, the data that establish a genetic influence on personality also show that genetic determination is not total. The extent to which genetic tendencies limit behavior change is an important issue. It's clear, however, that psychological processes matter, even for disorders that are strongly influenced by inheritance, such as bipolar disorder. Although medication is very important in the management of this disorder (see Chapter 7), psychological treatments of various kinds have also proven beneficial (Johnson & Leahy, 2003).

Genetics and Evolution: Problems and Prospects

The genetic perspective on personality has roots that go far back in the history of ideas. Yet in many ways, today's views are quite new. Research on heritability of personality makes a strong case, but complex issues still remain in understanding how genes interact with the environment to influence personality. With advances in molecular genetics, researchers are now trying to link particular genes with qualities of personality—an approach that's newer still. The ideas that form evolutionary personality psychology are also fairly recent.

In considering the usefulness of these ideas in thinking about personality, several issues arise. For example, temperaments are broad tendencies reflected in fundamental aspects of behavior. The fact that temperaments are so basic, however, raises a question about how to view their role. Does it make more sense to think of temperaments as all of personality, as part of personality, or as the bedrock on which personality is constructed? Since many personality traits seem heritable and many of the traits relate conceptually to temperaments, perhaps we should view temperaments as the starting points from which the conceptually related traits emerge (Caspi et al., 2005).

Here's another question: How many traits are genetically influenced, and how many just *look* heritable because they derive from the first group? Recent evidence suggests that facets of the five supertraits are separately heritable. This puts a different twist on the question. Maybe we should be asking whether temperaments are unitary, broad qualities that are just displayed in diverse ways or whether they instead are convenient aggregates of what are really separate traits.

A final question concerns the fact that the genetic approach to personality intrinsically takes no position on how personality should be conceptualized or what aspects of personality matter. Rather, it provides tools for testing genetic contributions to diverse aspects of personality. Ultimately, the theoretical viewpoint being tested by the genetic research must be rooted somewhere else. One such place is trait psychology (see Chapter 4). Another is biological process model (see Chapter 7).

Another aspect of the viewpoint discussed in this chapter is sociobiology and evolutionary psychology. This view on personality has been controversial during its relatively brief existence, and it has been criticized on several grounds (e.g., L. C. Miller, Putcha-Bhagavatula, & Pedersen, 2002). The early arguments were very theoretical and had little supporting evidence. Sociobiology was seen by some as a game of speculation, rather than a serious science. More than a few people scorned the ideas under discussion as unfalsifiable and indeed untestable.

In the past decade and a half, however, this situation changed dramatically. As more precise ideas were developed about the implications of evolutionary theory, this way of thinking led to a surge of studies. Evolutionary psychology is now an area of vigorous research activity. It seems clear that evolutionary ideas provide a wealth of hypotheses for researchers. Moreover, the hypotheses are becoming more and more sophisticated.

Nevertheless, there remains concern about whether the hypotheses being studied by these researchers really *depend on* evolutionary theory, as opposed to merely *being consistent* with it. Indeed, some recent critics argue that support for many key evolutionary hypotheses is highly ambiguous and does not support the conclusions drawn (Buller, 2005a, 2005b; Richardson, 2007). One challenge evolutionary psychology faces today is that of making clear predictions that resist alternative interpretations. This issue, of course, is faced by all views on personality. The issue, however, seems likely to remain an especially important one for this approach for some time.

Evolutionary psychology has also been criticized because its statements sometimes have disturbing political and social overtones. Some regard arguments about how human nature evolved as thinly veiled justifications for unfair social conditions in today's world (see Kitcher, 1987, and the succeeding commentaries; Lewontin, Rose, & Kamin, 1984). That is, the ideas explain why men are bullies, why there's a double standard of sexual behavior for men and women, and why race and class differences exist. These explanations provide a basis for considering such conditions as natural, which is only a small step away from saying they should continue to exist (Pratto & Hegarty, 2000). Some people view these overtones of evolutionary thinking as racist and sexist, and some have shown considerable hostility toward the theories themselves.

One response to this sort of criticism is to point out that evolution is a natural force that works dispassionately, based on the principles of reproduction and survival. In the arena of evolution, issues of equal rights and equal opportunities have no meaning. It may well be that in today's world, some of the results of evolution work against some people, because evolution prepared us to fit not this world but the world of prehistory. If people are disadvantaged by the consequences of evolution, it's something that must be dealt with by the cultures that people have built. The fact that the theory explains why inequity exists can't be used as an argument that the theory is wrong. As you might expect, though, this response isn't entirely satisfying to critics.

Despite controversies such as these, there remains a huge interest in evolutionary ideas in today's personality psychology. These ideas will not go away any time soon.

• SUMMARY •

The approach to personality rooted in inheritance and evolution has two facets. One emphasizes that your personality is tied to the biological body you inherit. This idea goes far back in history, but today's version of the idea is quite different, emphasizing the role of genes.

Behavior genetics provides ways to find out whether personality differences are inherited. In twin studies, correlations among identical twins are compared with correlations among fraternal twins; in adoption studies, children are compared with their biological and adoptive families. Studies of identical twins raised apart provide yet a different look at the effects of inheritance and environment.

Twin research has been used to look at genetic contributions to a variety of dispositions, starting with temperaments: broad, inherited traits that appear early in life. Early evidence supported genetic influences on activity level, emotionality, and sociability. Other views of temperaments have also bee n suggested, including temperaments for approach, avoidance, and effortful control. There's also evidence of genetic influence in the "big five" supertraits and other variables. It's unclear whether the "big five" derive from (or duplicate) the temperaments studied under other names. It's also unclear whether hereditary influences on other variables depend on associations between the other variable and a temperament. Recent developments in molecular genetics provide a new tool in the search for genetic influences on personality. Now, there's evidence of specific genes playing roles in traits, including novelty seeking, neuroticism, and perhaps effortful control or impulsivity.

The idea that dispositions are genetically influenced can be extended to suggest that many aspects of human social behavior are products of evolution. This idea is behind an area of work termed *sociobiology* or *evolutionary psychology*. Sociobiologists propose ways to account for various aspects of human behavior—even behavior that, on the face of it, seems not to provide an evolutionary advantage. Altruism, for example, is understood as people acting for the benefit of their family groups, so that the family's genes are more likely to be continued (kin selection). This idea has been extended to the notion that people are attracted to other people who share their genetic makeup.

The evolutionary view also has implications concerning mate selection, including the idea that males and females use different strategies. The male strategy is to mate whenever possible, and males are drawn to signs of reproductive capability. The female strategy is to seek the best male available, and females are drawn to signs of resources. People use the relevant strategies and act in ways that make them seem better candidates as mates. Mating pressures also may lead to aggression among young men. Theory suggests that violence is most likely among men of reproductive age who are in poor reproductive circumstances. Evidence seems to bear this out, along with the idea that much violence concerns conflicts over status.

The genetic approach to personality says little about assessment except to suggest what dispositions are particularly important to assess—those that have biological links. Assessment directly from genes will not likely occur soon, due to the probable involvement of many genes in any given trait. With regard to problems in behavior, there is substantial evidence that schizophrenia and manic–depressive disorder are affected by heredity, as are tendencies toward substance abuse and antisocial behavior. Like other topics, the study of disorder is beginning to use the tools of molecular biology to search for genetic influences.

With regard to therapeutic behavior change, this approach raises a question on the basis of studies of temperament: How much can people be expected to change, even with therapy, in directions that deviate from their biological makeup?

• GLOSSARY •

Adoption study   A study of resemblances between children and their adoptive and biological parents.

Allele   Some version of a particular gene.

Approach temperament   The temperamental tendency to approach rewards.

Assortative mating   Mating based on the choice of specific characteristics, rather than at random.

Avoidance temperament   The temperamental tendency to avoid threats.

Behavioral genetics   The study of the inheritance of behavioral qualities.

Candidate gene strategy   Testing specific genes because evidence links them to particular biological processes and theory links those processes to personality.

Concordance   Agreement on some characteristic between a twin and a co-twin.

Directional selection   Evolution in which one extreme of a dimension is more adaptive than the other.

Dizygotic (DZ) twins   Fraternal twins (overlapping genetically 50%, on average).

Ectomorphy   A tendency toward frail thinness.

Effortful control   A tendency to be focused, restrained, and planful.

Endomorphy   A tendency toward obesity.

Epigenetic   An effect that isn't on DNA but affects DNA functioning and can be inherited.

Gene expression   Activity in which the gene engages in the processes that create a protein.

Genetic similarity theory   The idea that people work toward reproducing genes similar to their own.

Genome   The sequence of the genes contained in the full complement of chromosomes.

Genome-wide association study (GWAS)   Study in which all genes are tested at once.

Genomics   *See* Molecular genetics.

Genotype   The particular version of a gene that a given person or group has.

GxE   Gene-by-environment interaction, in which the environment produces different outcomes depending on genetic composition.

Heritability   An estimate of how much variance of some characteristic is accounted for by inheritance.

Inclusive fitness   The passing on of genes through the survival of relatives.

Mesomorphy   A tendency toward muscularity.

Methylation   The attachment of methyl chemical groups to a gene or surrounding material.

Molecular genetics   The study of how alleles of specific genes relate to other observed differences.

Monozygotic (MZ) twins   Identical twins (overlapping genetically 100%).

Nonshared environment effect   An effect of the environment that makes twins differ.

Quantitative genetics   The study of how much variance in a characteristic is attributable to genetics versus environment.

Polymorphism   The characteristic of having more than one allele for a given gene.

Reciprocal altruism   Helping others with the expectation the help will be returned.

Siblings   Brothers and sisters.

Sociobiology   The study of the evolutionary basis for social behavior.

Stabilizing selection   Evolution in which intermediate values of a dimension are most adaptive.

Temperaments   Inherited traits that appear early in life.

Twin study   A study comparing the similarity between MZ twins against the similarity between DZ twins.

Biological Processes and Personality

Gina craves adventure. She always seems to be widening her circle of friends and activities. It's as though she needs the stimulation to keep her alive and happy. Her boyfriend shies away from it. All the noise and action are too much for him. He's more comfortable when things are less intense and he can plan his activities. Oddly enough, both feel their bodies are telling them what's best for them, even though "what's best" is quite different for one versus the other.

Laboratory studies suggest that introverts may do better than extraverts at tasks that require the monitoring of slowly changing visual displays, as is required in the work of air traffic controllers.

HUMANS ARE CARD-CARRYING members of the animal kingdom. We have all the characteristics implied by membership in that kingdom. We eat, drink, breathe, void wastes, and engage in the sexual activities that ensure the continuation of our species.

How deeply rooted are these animal pressures? How pervasive is their influence? The biological process approach to personality assumes that human behavior reflects the operation of a complex biological system. The processes that make up this system reflect the way we're organized as living creatures. In this view, biological processes have systematic influences on behavior and experience. To understand these influences, theorists first examine biological systems, to see what they're about and how they work. Then they consider how the workings of these systems might influence the kinds of phenomena identified with personality.

This chapter takes the same starting point as did Chapter 6: the idea that personality is embedded in our bodies. Now, though, the focus is on the idea that personality is influenced by the *workings* of the body. Here, we consider some ideas about what the body is organized to do and think about how personality reflects these processes of the body.

As in Chapter 6, there's room for both similarities and differences among people. The similarities reflect the fact that everyone has a nervous system and an endocrine system. The systems have the same basic structure and functions from one person to another. The differences reflect the fact that parts of the nervous system and endocrine system are more active or more responsive in some people than in others.

Early Ideas: Eysenck's Views on Brain Functions

One of the first modern attempts to link personality to biological functions was made by Hans Eysenck. Recall from Chapter 4 that Eysenck saw personality as composed largely of two supertraits: neuroticism and extraversion. He saw both of these as rooted in the body.

Introverts are quiet and retiring; extraverts are outgoing, uninhibited, and immersed in social activity. Eysenck (1967, 1981) argued that this difference derives from differences in activation of the cerebral cortex. When the cortext is activated, the person is alert. When it's not, the person is drowsy. Eysenck proposed that introverts normally have higher cortical arousal than extraverts. Thus, they avoid social interaction because it gets them overstimulated. Extraverts, with lower baseline levels, seek stimulation to bring their arousal up.

Some evidence fits the idea that introverts and extraverts differ in alertness. Consider vigilance tasks. They require you to be alert for specific stimuli. For example, you might have to listen to a long series of numbers and press a button whenever you hear three odd ones in a row. If your mind wanders, you'll miss some of what you're listening for. Introverts miss less than extraverts (Claridge, 1967). Another source of evidence is drug effects. If introverts are already alert, they shouldn't need as much of a stimulant to reach a given level of arousal. On the other hand, introverts should need *more* of a depressant drug to reach a given level of unalertness. Both of these observations seem true (Claridge, 1967; Eysenck, 1983).

Eysenck also proposed a neural basis for neuroticism. He said that people who are high on this trait are easily aroused in the brain's emotion centers. He thought this emotional arousal intensifies the manifestations of both extraversion and introversion—that is, it causes both to emerge more fully in behavior. This arousal causes both extraverts and introverts to become "more of what they are."

Eysenck's effort to link personality to brain function was a path-breaking one. However, at the time in which he wrote, brain functioning wasn't understood remotely as well as it is now. Changes in knowledge have elaborated people's views of how brain functions and personality are related.

Incentive Approach System

Within the past 25 years or so, a number of theorists have proposed ideas about how the nervous system relates to personality. The ideas vary in focus. Some concern what parts of the brain are involved in certain kinds of actions. Some concern what brain chemicals are involved in certain kinds of actions. All take what might be called a *functional approach*. That is, they ask, What *functions* do particular kinds of behavior serve? The various types of behavior are then linked to ideas about brain processes, and both are also linked to personality.

Many people are working hard on this topic, and the literature is growing explosively. There are broad areas of agreement, but there are also disagreements. There's a lot of consensus about major themes, but there are also lots of ways to slice the pie.

BEHAVIORAL APPROACH

Most theorists of this group believe there's a set of brain structures that cause animals to approach **incentives**: things they desire. Several theorists have made assertions about parts of the brain involved in this system, but they're not in full agreement (Cloninger, 1988; Davidson, 1992, 1995; Davidson, Jackson, & Kalin, 2000; Depue & Collins, 1999; Depue & Iacono, 1989; J. A. Gray, 1982, 1991). Although there's a great deal of ongoing effort to figure out what parts of the brain are involved, we will say only a little about that. We will focus instead on functional properties of the brain systems—how they're reflected in behavior and experience.

The structures involved in approach behavior have been given several names: *activation system* (Cloninger, 1987; Fowles, 1980), *behavioral engagement system* (Depue, Krauss, & Spoont, 1987), *behavioral facilitation system* (Depue & Iacono, 1989), and **behavioral approach system (BAS)** (J. A. Gray, 1987, 1990, 1994a, 1994b). You might think of this system as regulating the psychic gas pedal, moving you toward what you want. It's a "go" system—a reward-seeking system (Fowles, 1980).

This set of brain structures is presumed to be involved whenever a person is pursuing an incentive. It's likely that certain parts of the brain are involved in the pursuit of food, others in the pursuit of sex, and others in the pursuit of shade on a hot summer day. But it is thought that the separate parts also link up to an overall BAS. Thus, the BAS is seen as a general mechanism to go after things you want. The BAS doesn't rev you up "in neutral," though, with no incentive in mind (Depue & Collins, 1999). It's engaged only in the active pursuit of incentives.

The BAS is also held to be responsible for many kinds of positive emotions (e.g., hope, eagerness, and excitement), which can be seen as reflecting the anticipation of getting a reward. Evidence comes from studies of brain activity. Richard Davidson and his colleagues (and others) have studied brain activity by recording electrical activity on the scalp (Davidson, 1988, 1992, 1995; Davidson & Sutton, 1995) and by using imaging techniques that capture activity in other ways. While this is happening, the people are exposed to stimuli such as video clips or still images that were chosen to create specific kinds of emotional reactions. The question is which parts of the brain become more active in various situations.

A variety of evidence indicates that incentives (and, presumably, positive feelings) activate the left prefrontal cortex. More left-prefrontal activity has been found in adults presented with incentives (Sobotka, Davidson, & Senulis, 1992), or positive emotional adjectives (Cacioppo & Petty, 1980), and in 10-month-olds viewing their mothers approaching (Fox & Davidson, 1988). Higher *resting* levels in this area predict positive responses to happy films (Wheeler, Davidson, & Tomarken, 1993). Self-reported BAS sensitivity also relates to higher resting levels in this area (Harmon-Jones & Allen, 1997; Sutton & Davidson, 1997). Such findings led Davidson and his colleagues to two conclusions: First, the tendency to experience many positive emotions relates to an approach system. Second, that system is based partly in the left prefrontal cortex.

MORE ISSUES IN APPROACH

Recent evidence suggests that what underlies left-prefrontal activation is not positive feelings per se but something else about the approach process (Carver & Harmon-Jones, 2009; Harmon-Jones, Lueck, Fearn, & Harmon-Jones, 2006). Sometimes, a desire to approach is thwarted. In this case, the approach system is engaged, but the emotions—frustration and anger—have a negative valence, rather than a positive one. Several studies have linked such experiences to left-prefrontal activation and BAS sensitivity (for review, see Carver & Harmon-Jones, 2009).

Another project has linked BAS sensitivity to learning. Because the BAS responds selectively to incentives, BAS sensitivity should relate to learning involving *positive* outcomes but not to learning involving *negative* outcomes. In a study supporting this idea, a self-report measure of BAS sensitivity predicted speed at learning cues of reward in a conditioning task (Zinbarg & Mohlman, 1998). This scale did not relate to speed at learning cues of punishment.

As noted earlier, there may also be specialized subsystems here. Some neurobiological evidence suggests that there may be social incentive and social threat systems, which overlap partially but not entirely with the more general approach and avoidance systems (Depue & Morrone-Strupinksy, 2005; Panksepp, 1998). Thus, there may be specialized sensitivities to incentives and threats *within relationships*. This idea has been supported in research on couples (Laurenceau, Kleinman, Kaczynski, & Carver, 2010).

To sum up, people with reactive approach systems are highly sensitive to incentives, or to cues of good things about to happen. Those whose approach systems are less reactive don't respond as much (either behaviorally or emotionally) to such cues. For example, suppose two people have tickets to an upcoming concert by a band they like. Melanie gets excited just thinking about the concert (although it isn't until next week). Every time she does, she's ready to jump in the car. Melanie is very high in incentive reactivity, BAS sensitivity. Barbara, on the other hand, is more calm. She knows she'll enjoy the concert, but she's not so responsive to thoughts of potential reward. Barbara has less incentive reactivity.

Neurotransmitters and the Approach System

Besides brain regions, operation of the approach system has been tentatively linked to a specific **neurotransmitter** in the brain. A *neurotransmitter* is a chemical involved in sending messages along nerve pathways. There are many neurotransmitters, and they seem to have somewhat different roles. Several theorists have argued that a neurotransmitter called **dopamine** is involved in the approach system (Cloninger, 1988; Depue & Collins, 1999; Zuckerman, 1994).

There are several methods to study dopamine function. One is to assess individual differences in dopamine reactivity using biomedical indicators of response to drug challenges. Another is to look at genes relating to dopamine function (see Chapter 6). In several studies, higher dopamine reactivity has been related to higher positive emotionality (Depue, 1995; Depue, Luciana, Arbisi, Collins, & Leon, 1994). Others have related dopamine to novelty seeking (Hansenne et al., 2002). Depue and Collins (1999) linked dopamine to several aspects of extraversion, including social dominance, enthusiasm, energy, and assertiveness. Research on monkeys also linked dopamine function to greater social dominance (Kaplan, Manuck, Fontenot, & Mann, 2002).

It's also been suggested that high dopamine levels produce a flexible shifting among goals (Dreisbach & Goschke, 2004). Of course, what seems like flexible shifting of goals can also be seen as distractibility. Consistent with this, evidence links high levels of dopamine explicitly to distractibility (Frank & O'Reilly, 2006).

It's long been believed that dopamine is involved in reward-based learning (Frank & Claus, 2006; Holroyd & Coles, 2002). This idea has evolved over the years, however. One current view is that bursts of dopamine in response to reward increase the learning (and the execution) of approach responses, and that dips in dopamine after nonreward increase the learning (and the execution) of avoidance responses (Frank, Seeberger, & O'Reilly, 2004).

It may be, however, that the effect of dopamine is more on the performance than on actual learning. Studies of mice seem to show that they don't need dopamine to learn from reward. However, dopamine is necessary for the mice to *want* the reward and *seek* it in goal-directed action (Berridge, 2007; Robinson, Sandstrom, Denenberg, & Palmiter, 2005; Wise, 2004). Some researchers have concluded that dopamine is mainly about motivation, rather than learning—more specifically, that dopamine is involved in approach-related effort (Farrar et al., 2007; Salamone, Correa, Farrar, & Mingote, 2007).

Others have looked at these effects from a different angle. Dopaminergic neurons respond intensely to unexpected rewards but less so to rewards that are expected. When a reward is expected but fails to occur, these neurons decrease responding (Schultz, 2000, 2006). This pattern has been seen as indicating that dopamine neurons are involved in detecting unexpected events of two kinds: better and worse than expected. That is, there's an increase in activity when an event is better than expected, no change when an event occurs as expected, and a decrease in activity when an event is worse than expected (Schultz, 2006).

Behavioral Avoidance, or Withdrawal, System

The previous section described an approach system. Many theorists also assume a somewhat distinct system in the brain that reacts to punishments and threats, rather than incentives. Gray (1987, 1990, 1994a, 1994b) called it the *behavioral inhibition system*. Others have labeled a threat-responsive system as an **avoidance** or **withdrawal system**

(Cloninger, 1987; Davidson, 1988, 1992, 1995). Activity in this system may cause people to *inhibit* movement (especially if they're currently approaching an incentive) or to pull back from what they just encountered. You might think of this system as a psychic brake pedal—a "stop" system. You might think of it instead as a "throw-it-into-reverse" system. Again, there are candidates for brain systems that manage anxiety and avoidance; there also are disputes, though, and we leave that issue aside.

The avoidance system is responsive to cues of punishment and danger. When this system is engaged, the person may stop and scan for further cues about the threat, or the person may pull back. Since this is the system that responds to threats, dangers, and other to-be-avoided stimuli, it's also thought to be responsible for feelings such as anxiety, fear, guilt, and revulsion.

Once again, research on cortical activity is consistent with this general view. We said earlier that left-prefrontal areas are more active when people are happy. Right-prefrontal areas are more active when people are feeling anxiety or aversion—for example, when viewing film clips that induce fear and disgust (Davidson, Ekman, Saron, Senulis, & Friesen, 1990). Higher resting levels in that area predict more negative feelings when seeing such films, and they also relate to self-reports of threat sensitivity (Harmon-Jones & Allen, 1997; Sutton & Davidson, 1997). Findings such as these led Davidson and his colleagues to argue that anxiety relates to a behavioral withdrawal system, which involves the right prefrontal cortex.

Research on learning has also examined the sensitivity of this system. This one is theorized to be reactive to punishments, not incentives. Thus, its sensitivity should relate to learning for *negative* outcomes, not positive ones. This prediction was confirmed by Zinbarg and Mohlman (1998), who found that a self-report measure of threat sensitivity predicted speed at learning cues of punishment (but not cues of reward). Similar results were reported by Corr, Pickering, and Gray (1997).

To sum up this section, people with reactive avoidance systems are sensitive to threat. This dimension reflects a trait of anxiety proneness. As an example of how it influences experiences, think of two people who just took a psychology test and suspect they did badly. Anxiety-prone Randy is almost in a panic about it, but Jessica, who is less anxiety prone, is bothered hardly at all. One of them is reacting emotionally to the sense of threat; the other isn't.

Threat sensitivity and incentive sensitivity are thought to be relatively separate. People presumably differ from each other on both. As a result, all combinations of high and low approach and avoidance sensitivity probably exist. As an example, some might think of sociability as being the opposite of shyness, but that's too simple (Schmidt, 1999). It's possible to be both very sociable (drawn to social incentives) and very shy (fearful of social interaction and avoiding it).

NEUROTRANSMITTERS AND THE AVOIDANCE SYSTEM

As with reward sensitivity, people have tried to link threat sensitivity to a neurotransmitter. Here, there's less consensus. **Serotonin** has long been believed by some to be involved in anxiety or threat sensitivity (Cloninger, 1987; Handley, 1995; Lesch & Mössner, 1998). However, this view has been strongly challenged (Depue, 1995; Depue & Spoont, 1986; Panksepp & Cox, 1986; Soubrié, 1986; Zuckerman, 2005). The dispute isn't over, and the evidence is complex. Our own interpretation of it, however, suggests that serotonin's main influence lies elsewhere (Carver & Miller, 2006; Carver, Johnson, & Joormann, 2008). We return to this issue later on.

Another candidate for involvement in anxiety is *gamma-aminobutyric acid*, more commonly known as **GABA** (Roy-Byrne, 2005). There's some research linking sensitivity of GABA receptors to neuroticism (Glue, Wilson, Coupland, Ball, & Nutt, 1995). However, most of what is known about GABA and anxiety comes from studies of anxiety disorders. In fact, most of the studies focus specifically on panic disorder (Zwanzger & Rupprecht, 2005). People with panic disorder have relatively low levels of GABA (Goddard et al., 2001). Treatments that increase GABA reduce anxiety in panic patients (Zwanzger & Rupprecht, 2005).

Yet another likely contributor to the biology of threat is **norepinephrine**. Norepinephrine is produced in response to stress (Morilak et al., 2005), and evidence links it to panic reactions (Bailey, Argyropoulis, Lightman, & Nutt, 2003). Research has also shown that problems in regulating norepinephrine relate selectively to anxiety disorders (Cameron, Abelson, & Young, 2004). This finding seems to link this chemical specifically to threat sensitivity.

Relating Approach and Avoidance Systems to Traits or Temperaments

Let's stop and look at what we've said thus far in the chapter. Many theorists converge on the idea that one brain system manages approach of incentives and another manages withdrawal from threats. The one that manages approach also creates excitement and enthusiasm. The one that manages withdrawal creates anxiety. How do these ideas fit with ideas from previous chapters? Quite well, in fact.

The avoidance system links easily to the trait of neuroticism. As noted earlier, anxiety is at its core. Thus, Larsen and Ketelaar (1991) found that neuroticism predicts susceptibility to a manipulation of anxiety; Carver and White (1994) found the same effect for a measure of threat sensitivity. In sum, neuroticism and anxiety proneness have a great deal in common (see also Elliot & Thrash, 2002). In fact, there's little doubt that the brain system we've been describing regarding avoidance is critical to neuroticism. As noted in Chapter 6, developmental theorists have also posited an avoidance temperament (e.g., Derryberry & Rothbart, 1997; Eisenberg, 2002; Eisenberg et al., 2004; Kochanska & Knaack, 2003; Rothbart, Ahadi, & Evans, 2000; Rothbart, Ahadi, Hershey, & Fisher, 2001; Rothbart & Bates, 1998; Rothbart & Posner, 1985). Again, there is a good fit.

With respect to approach, there appears to be a link between the approach system and extraversion. Fitting these two together is a bit trickier than matching neuroticism to avoidance, partly because theorists differ about what defines extraversion. Definitions usually include a sense of activity and agency (Morrone, Depue, Scherer, & White, 2000). Extraversion also suggests a preference for being with others, or sociability (Depue & Morrone-Strupinsky, 2005). Sometimes, there's a quality of social dominance or potency (Depue & Collins, 1999). All definitions seem to include a tendency to experience positive emotions.

These various extraversion packages resemble BAS function fairly well. As noted in Chapter 6, contemporary developmental theorists also assume an approach temperament. Measures of extraversion correlate with measures of approach sensitivity (Carver & White, 1994). Zelenski and Larsen (1999) found that measures of extraversion and several BAS constructs were all interrelated, and as a set, they predicted positive feelings. Extraverts are responsive to positive mood manipulations (Larsen & Ketelaar, 1991); those high in BAS sensitivity also have positive feelings to impending reward (Carver & White, 1994). Thus, there's a good deal of consistency.

THE ROLE OF SOCIABILITY

Still, when fitting extraversion to approach sensitivity, there are a couple of areas of uncertainty. Table 7.1 lists several theorists who have written about extraversion and similar traits. The table also lists some qualities the theorists see as belonging to these traits. As you can see, there are two qualities for which differences of opinion arises.

One issue concerns the social quality that's usually considered part of extraversion. That quality is missing from Gray's view of the BAS. In fact, Gray ignored sociability altogether. One way to resolve things would be to view BAS sensitivity as sensitivity to *social* incentives. Given that humans are a very social species, it might make sense to think of human approach primarily in terms of approaching social interaction. As noted earlier in the chapter, however, some postulate a separate approach subsystem that's specialized to regulate social approach. Perhaps extraversion actually is a blend of overall BAS sensitivity and social-specific BAS sensitivity.

On the other hand, several projects seem to suggest that sociality per se is not the core of extraversion. One of these projects, mentioned in Chapter 4, was by Lucas, Diener, Grob, Suh, and Shao (2000). Their studies led them to conclude that the core of extraversion is *reward sensitivity* and the tendency to experience *positive affect*. They inferred that extraverts' social tendencies stem from the fact that social interaction is one source of positive experiences. Indeed, Lucas and Diener (2001) found extraverts were drawn to situations that offered opportunities for pleasant experiences, whether social or nonsocial.

THE ROLE OF IMPULSIVITY

The second issue on which conceptualizations of extraversion have differed in the past concerns impulsivity. In this case, however, the argument is dying down. Gray used the word *impulsivity* for approach sensitivity, but it was an unfortunate choice, as he didn't seem to have issues of impulse control in mind. Eysenck included impulsiveness in extraversion for years, but he moved it, because it consistently related better to psychoticism. Depue and Collins (1999) said that impulsivity with positive affect (the key to extraversion) belongs in extraversion but that impulsivity without it does not.

Table 7.1 Several Theorists and Qualities They Believe Belong to Extraversion (and alternative traits closely related to extraversion). All incorporate pursuit of incentives and a tendency to experience positive emotions. Many, though not all, include a quality of sociability. A couple have also included impulsiveness.

Theorist	Preferred Term	Term Incorporates:			
		Pursuit of Incentives	Sociability	Impulsivity	Positive Emotions
Eysenck	Extraversion	×	×		×
Costa & McCrae	Extraversion	×	×		×
Depue	Extraversion	×	×	×	×
Zuckerman	Sociability	×	×		×
Tellegen	Positive emotionality	×	×		×
Gray	BAS–Impulsivity	×		×	×

Relevant to this issue is the study by Zelenski and Larsen (1999) mentioned earlier. They factor analyzed several personality measures, including measures of impulsivity and threat and incentive sensitivity. They found that measures of impulsivity loaded on a different factor than did extraversion (which loaded on the BAS factor). Also relevant to this issue is evidence from research with monkeys. One study (Fairbanks, 2001) found that social dominance, which many see as part of extraversion, relates to moderate impulsivity—not high or low. On the whole, evidence suggests that impulsivity does not belong in extraversion. Where, then, does it belong?

A Third Dimension: Sensation Seeking, Constraint, and Effortful Control

Many people believe that there's at least one more biologically based dimension of personality. It has had several labels, but in each case, the construct has incorporated a quality of planfulness versus impulsivity. One label for this dimension is **sensation seeking**. Marvin Zuckerman (e.g., 1985, 1991, 1992, 1993, 1994, 2005) and his colleagues have studied this quality extensively.

SENSATION SEEKING

People high in sensation seeking want new, varied, and exciting experiences. Compared to people lower on this trait, they are faster drivers (Zuckerman & Neeb, 1980). They are also more likely to use drugs (Zuckerman, 1979), to increase alcohol use over time (Newcomb & McGee, 1991), to do high-risk sports such as skydiving (Hymbaugh & Garrett, 1974), and to engage in risky antisocial behaviors (Horvath & Zuckerman, 1993). They are more sexually experienced and sexually responsive (Fisher, 1973), and when in relationships, they are more dissatisfied (Thronquist, Zuckerman, & Exline, 1991). When serving in the army, they are more likely to volunteer for a combat unit (Hobfoll, Rom, & Segal, 1989).

We said earlier that theorists of this group tend to use a functional approach—that is, they look for the purpose a given system might serve. What might be the function of sensation seeking? An early view was that this dimension regulates exposure to stimulus intensity (Zuckerman, 1979, 1991, 1994). High sensation seekers open themselves to stimulation; low sensation seekers protect themselves from it. Both have advantages and disadvantages. People high in sensation seeking should function

Sensation seekers like to pursue new, varied, and exciting experiences.

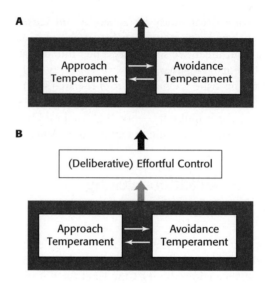

FIGURE 7.1
Two sources of action and restraint. (A) Approach and avoidance temperaments compete for influence over behavior; impulsive approach occurs if the approach process outweighs the avoidance process. (B) Effortful control can countermand whichever of those temperaments is dominating and change the direction of behavior.

well in overstimulating conditions, such as combat, but they may display antisocial qualities in situations that are less demanding. People lower in sensation seeking are better adapted to most circumstances of life, but they may "shut down" psychologically when things get too intense.

A broader view of this trait's function relates it to the demands of social living. Zuckerman (1991, 1993) thinks that what he calls **impulsive unsocialized sensation seeking (IUSS)** concerns the capacity to inhibit behavior in service of social adaptation. People high on IUSS don't do this very well. IUSS relates inversely to sociability and positively to aggressiveness (Zuckerman, 1996; Zuckerman, Kuhlman, Joireman, Tetar, & Kraft, 1993). It's been implicated in antisocial personality disorder (Krueger et al., 1994; Rowe, 2001; Zuckerman, 1994). There's also evidence that it involves a focus on the immediate consequences of behavior, rather than longer-term consequences (Joireman, Anderson, & Strathman, 2003). All of these qualities seem to reflect, in part, qualities of impulse versus restraint.

RELATING SENSATION SEEKING TO TRAITS AND TEMPERAMENTS

How do these ideas fit with ideas from previous chapters? There are strong links to several trait models, discussed in Chapter 4 (see Carver, 2005). IUSS relates inversely to both agreeableness and conscientiousness of the five-factor model (Zuckerman, 1996) and to constraint from Tellegen's (1985) model (constraint being virtually the opposite of IUSS). Recall that low levels of these traits relate to problems in getting along in life. IUSS also relates to psychoticism in Eysenck's model, which concerns disregard of social restraint in pursuit of intense sensations.

In Chapter 6, we noted that properties pertaining to impulsivity have also been discussed as a temperament by Rothbart and her colleagues (e.g., Rothbart et al., 2000; Rothbart et al., 2001; Rothbart, Ellis, Rueda, & Posner, 2003; see also Eisenberg, 2002; Eisenberg et al., 2004; Kochanska & Knaack, 2003). The temperament called *effortful control* bears a good deal of resemblance to IUSS. It's about being focused and

Box 7.1 Research Question: How Do You Assess Neurotransmitter Function?

Researchers are now examining the role of neurotransmitters in a wide range of behavior. Many of the techniques for studying this require a way to assess neurotransmitter functions in research participants. How is this done? It's more complicated than assessing how much of that particular neurotransmitter is lying around in the person's brain. What's actually at issue is how the neurotransmitter is being *used*.

Consider serotonin as an example. Serotonin receptors can vary in sensitivity (as can all receptors for neurotransmitters). If someone has a chronically low serotonin level (call him Eddie), the receptors will adjust to become more sensitive. If someone has a chronically high serotonin level (call him Phil), the receptors will adjust to become less sensitive. Because Eddie's receptors have become very sensitive, they can do their work with relatively little serotonin. Because Phil's receptors have become relatively insensitive, they will respond less to the same amount of serotonin. Phil needs more serotonin to have the same processing effect. Eddie has very responsive serotonin functioning, whereas Phil's functioning is less responsive.

The responsiveness of a neurotransmitter system in humans is often assessed by challenging the system's ability to regulate itself. This is done by administering an agent that perturbs or disrupts its stable state. The drug that's administered stimulates the system to see how big a response occurs.

For example, a drug called *fenfluramine* causes the release of serotonin from presynaptic storage areas and also inhibits its reuptake. Thus, it causes an increase (lasting several hours) in the level of serotonin available for use. Receptors in the hypothalamus sense this increase in serotonin and cause the pituitary gland to release prolactin into circulation. This eventually helps bring the serotonin level back down, but it takes a while. Prolactin concentrations are easy to assess. Researchers track the prolactin level and determine its peak increase over a period of three to five hours after the fenfluramine is taken. That peak prolactin response (the increase over baseline) is an index of how responsive the serotonin system is (Manuck, Flory, Ferrell, Mann, & Muldoon, 2000). A large rise in prolactin means a sensitive or responsive serotonin system.

restrained, and it implies a planfulness and awareness of others' needs. High levels of this temperament early in life predict fewer problems with antisocial behavior later on (Kochanska & Knaack, 2003). This temperament is slower to emerge than the approach and avoidance temperaments and may not be fully operative until adulthood (Casey, Giedd, & Thomas, 2000). It's believed to relate to the part of the brain that manages executive functions: the prefrontal cortex.

In making comparisons to these trait and temperament models, one more thing is worth noting. In each case, the trait under discussion is distinct and separate from the traits relating to extraversion and neuroticism (or approach and avoidance sensitivities). Depue and Collins (1999) reviewed 11 studies in which two or more personality inventories were jointly factor analyzed. All identified a distinct higher-order trait reflecting impulse versus constraint.

Two Sources of Impulse and Restraint

The emergence of the third dimension provides a second way for impulses to be restrained. With only an approach and an avoidance system, there's only one force to restrain impulses (Figure 7.1, A). A person with strong appetites and little anxiety will approach impulsively (Arnett, Smith, & Newman, 1997; Avila, 2001); a person with weak appetites and strong anxiety won't behave impulsively.

The addition of a third system for effortful control (Figure 7.1, B) allows the decision between action and restraint to have a different source. Now, people can restrain themselves to get along better with others or to get better outcomes over the long term (Carver, 2005). They can also make themselves do things they don't want to do, such as look happy when they get a gift they don't really like (Kieras, Tobin, Graziano, & Rothbart, 2005). These influences on behavior need not involve anxiety at all. Interestingly, a study of brain responses among persons high and low in sensation seeking found support for the view that highs have both especially strong approach reactions and relatively weak self-control over such responses (Joseph, Liu, Jiang, Lynam, & Kelly, 2009).

NEUROTRANSMITTERS AND IMPULSE VERSUS CONSTRAINT

Is a particular brain chemical tied to impulse versus constraint? Zuckerman (1994, 1995) suggested a role for **monoamine oxidase (MAO)**, which helps regulate several neurotransmitters. MAO levels relate to personality traits such as sensation seeking and novelty seeking (Ruchkin, Koposov, af Klinteberg, Oreland, & Grigorenko, 2005; Zuckerman, 1994). MAO also relates to dominance, aggression (Rowe, 2001; Zuckerman, 1995), and drunk driving (Paaver, Eensoo, Pulver, & Harro, 2006). Genes related to MAO levels have been linked to aggression and impulsivity (Manuck, Flory, Ferrell, Mann, & Muldoon, 2000; Raine, 2008). Maybe MAO is one key to this system.

On the other hand, some researchers consider MAO level to be mostly an indicator of the activity of neurons of the serotonin system (Oreland, 2004). Perhaps the key actually lies in serotonin function. There is, in fact, a good deal of evidence linking low serotonin function to impulsivity (reviewed by Carver et al., 2008; see also Carver et al., 2011). Much of the research assesses serotonin function by responses to drug challenges of various sorts (see Box 7.1). Sometimes, serotonin function is even manipulated.

In one such study, experimentally lowering serotonin led to greater hostility and aggressiveness among persons who were already high in aggressive tendencies, but it didn't do anything among persons lower in aggressiveness (Cleare & Bond, 1995). In a later study, lowering serotonin created higher aggressiveness among highly aggressive men but had the opposite effect among those low in aggressiveness (Bjork, Dougherty, Moeller, & Swann, 2000). These findings suggest that low serotonin function made people act more the way they tend to be anyway. That would fit with the idea that low serotonin means loosening restraint of one's basic tendencies.

Another source of information is cross-sectional studies linking qualities of personality to serotonin function. Many of these studies focus on patient samples, typically comparing patients to controls. A popular group for this kind of study is people who display impulsive aggression. A good number of studies have related lower serotonin function to a history of fighting and assault (Coccaro, Kavoussi, Cooper, & Hauger, 1997), domestic violence (George et al., 2001), and impulsive aggression more generally (Cleare & Bond, 1997). Although there's a lot of evidence linking low serotonin function to aggressiveness, most researchers seem to believe that the link is more directly to impulsiveness or volatility than to hostility per se.

Studies have also examined personality and serotonin function among nonclinical samples. Several early studies (Cleare & Bond, 1997; Depue, 1995; Netter, Hennig, & Rohrmann, 1999) found relations between low serotonin function and elevated aggression—hostility traits, similar to the findings just described. Depue (1995) also found links from low serotonin function to the impulsivity facet of Tellegen's constraint scale, the aggression facet of Tellegen's negative emotionality scale, to two sensation-seeking subscales, and to several indices of impulsiveness. Depue also looked more closely at hostility and found the strongest relations of low serotonin function to subscales reflecting impulsive, action-oriented aggression. A more recent study produced similar results (Hennig Reuter, Netter, Burk, & Landt, 2005).

Other research has had a broader focus. Several studies have been done using personality inventories, sometimes along with other measures. One of them (Manuck et al., 1998) used the NEO-PI-R plus additional measures in a community sample.

All effects that emerged did so only among men. Low serotonin function related to greater life history of aggression and impulsiveness, consistent with previous results. Low serotonin function also related to higher neuroticism (from the NEO-PI-R) and the neuroticism facet angry hostility. High serotonin function related to higher conscientiousness (from the NEO-PI-R).

There's also one more interesting twist to the evidence. Zald and Depue (2001) argued that serotonin should inhibit positive reactions as well as negative. To test this, they had men track their emotions for two weeks. Then they computed averages separately for positive and negative feelings and related them to the men's levels of serotonin function. Higher serotonin function related to less negative affect, consistent with the findings just reviewed. However, higher serotonin function also related to lower levels of *positive* feelings (interested, active, attentive, and enthusiastic). Thus, serotonin may provide a constraining influence over the biological systems that manage affects of both sorts.

The pattern from this research as a whole seems consistent with the view that serotonergic pathways are involved in impulse control (Depue, 1995; Depue & Collins, 1999; Depue & Spoont, 1986; Manuck, Flory, Muldoon, & Ferrell, 2003; Soubrié, 1986; Zuckerman, 2005). Further, it appears to be consistent with a view in which the resulting restraint (when it does occur) is effortful, rather than an involuntary reaction to anxiety.

Hormones and Personality

We turn now to a different part of the biological process view on personality: the relationship between hormones and personality. An important group of hormones is sex hormones. We won't explore all the ways sex hormones influence behavior (e.g., Le Vay, 1993; Tavris & Wade, 1984), but we'll examine a few of them, focusing primarily on **testosterone**.

HORMONES, THE BODY, AND THE BRAIN

From very early in life, sex hormones are important in a variety of ways. Normal males have higher testosterone than normal females from week 8 to week 24 of gestation, from about the first through the fifth month after birth, and again after puberty (Le Vay, 1993). Testosterone differences in gestation are essential to changes in the nervous system that create normal male and female physical development. Many researchers believe the hormones also change the brain in ways that result in behavioral differences (Breedlove, 1994; Le Vay, 1993).

The basic template for a human body is female. Only if hormones cause specific changes to occur does a body emerge that looks male. If a genetic male isn't exposed to androgen ("male-making") hormones at critical points in development, the result will be an exterior that looks female. If a genetic female is exposed to testosterone at the same points, the result will be an exterior that looks male (Breedlove, 1994). During typical fetal development, only males are exposed to enough androgen to be masculinized.

The hormones that guide the body in its sexual development also affect nerve cells (Breedlove, 1992; Le Vay, 1993). They organize the developing brains of males and females differently, in subtle ways (Cohen-Bendahan, van de Beek, & Berenbaum, 2005). Animal research suggests there aren't just two patterns but a broad range of variation, with male and female patterns as the extremes (Panksepp, 1998). The genders tend to differ in linkages among synapses and in the size of some brain structures.

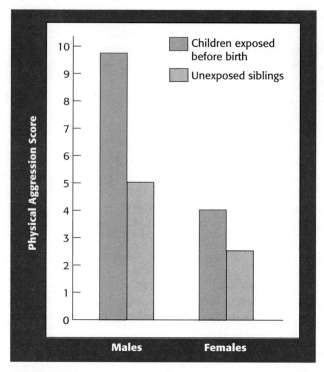

FIGURE 7.2
Average (self-report) physical aggression scores during childhood for boys and girls who had been exposed to synthetic hormones before birth and for their sex-matched siblings who had not been exposed. Exposure to the hormone produced elevated aggression scores for both boys and girls. *Source:* Adapted from Reinisch, 1981.

For example, the two sides of the cortex are more fully interconnected in women than men (Le Vay, 1993). Interestingly, there's evidence that the brains of gay men structurally resemble those of women more than those of heterosexual men (Allen & Gorski, 1992; Le Vay, 1991).

How might these differences in the nervous system relate to personality? We said earlier that exposure to androgens masculinizes the nervous system. Several things may follow from this.

EARLY HORMONAL EXPOSURE AND BEHAVIOR

Early exposure to hormones, even prenatal exposure, can influence later behavior. One study (Reinisch, 1981) looked at children whose mothers had received synthetic hormones that act like testosterone while being treated for complications in their pregnancies. Each child thus was exposed to the hormones prenatally during a critical phase of development. The other group was the children's same-sex siblings (to match as closely as possible on genetic and environmental variables).

An average of 11 years after exposure, each child completed a self-report measure in which six situations were described, each involving interpersonal conflict. The children made decisions about what they would do in each situation. Of interest was the likelihood of responding with physical aggression versus other responses.

The study yielded two separate effects, both bearing on the choice of physical aggression as a response to conflict (see Figure 7.2). The first was a sex difference: Boys chose this response more than girls did. There was also an effect of prenatal

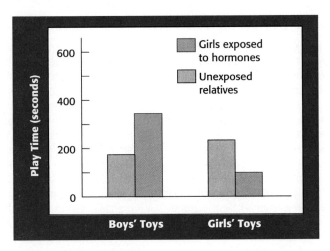

FIGURE 7.3
Amount of time two groups of girls played in a free-play setting with toys generally preferred by boys and toys generally preferred by girls. Some of the girls had been exposed to masculinizing hormones before birth and shortly afterward: the others had not been exposed. *Source:* Adapted from Berenbaum & Hines, 1992.

exposure to the hormone. Children who had been exposed chose physical aggression more than children who hadn't been exposed. This was true both for boys and for girls.

This study is intriguing for a couple of reasons. It's clear that a biological variable—the hormone—influenced the behavior. It's less clear *how* it did so. Animal research indicates that exposure to male hormones during early development increases aggressive displays (Reinisch, 1981). But this study measured no aggressive actions, just self-reports indicating the choice of aggression. Thus, any masculinizing influence on the nervous system had to filter through a lot of cognition to be displayed.

In another project, Berenbaum and Hines (1992) studied children with a genetic disorder that causes high levels of masculinizing hormones prenatally and soon after birth. Years later (ages 3 to 8), these children (and unaffected same-sex relatives) were observed as they played individually. Available to them were toys that had been determined to be generally preferred by boys and by girls. The question was who would play with which toys. The androgen-exposed girls spent more time with the boys' toys and less time with the girls' toys than did unexposed girls (see Figure 7.3). In fact, they displayed a preference pattern like that of boys.

Androgens come from several sources. Exposure through a mother's medical treatment during pregnancy is one. Another is the adrenal glands, which secrete androgen normally. High levels of natural androgen in girls has been related to greater involvement in sports that involve rough body contact (Kimura, 1999), activities that are more typical of boys. Another study found that higher levels of naturally occurring fetal testosterone predicted lower levels of empathy at age 4 (Knickmeyer, Baron-Cohen, Raggatt, Taylor, & Hackett, 2006).

The findings are somewhat mixed, but they appear generally consistent with the idea that early exposure to masculinizing hormones can influence behavior. It can increase the potential for aggression, lead to preference for masculine toys, and enhance boldness.

Box 7.2 Steroids: An Unintended Path to Aggression

Discussing the effects of testosterone on behavior brings up a related topic: bodybuilding and its excesses. The appeal of bodybuilding comes partly from its result: a body that looks chiseled from rock. Cultural expectations of men's bodies (as reflected in *Playgirl* photos) have shifted over the decades, becoming increasingly dense and muscular (Leit, Pope, & Gray, 2001). These expectations create pressure on men to look that way.

The desire for a well-formed body has led many people to use **anabolic steroids**. The word *anabolic* means "building up." Anabolic steroids are chemicals that mimic the body's tendency to rebuild muscle tissue that has been stressed or exercised. Your body gives you small doses of such chemicals, producing growth in muscle size. Using steroids gives you a much bigger dose. Steroids thus let you speed up and exaggerate the building of muscles in ways that exercise alone cannot do. That's why people use steroids. In a survey of male gym users, 18% said they used adrenal hormones, 25% used ephedrine, and 5% used anabolic steroids (Kanayama, Gruber, Pope, Borowiecki, & Hudson, 2001). Indeed, some people are using steroids and steroidlike substances without fully realizing it. So-called dietary supplements, which many people use, often are potent drugs.

Many users don't realize that steroids are synthetic hormones. Steroids are related to testosterone (that's why men's muscles tend to be larger than women's). Testosterone is involved in many things, not just building muscle tissue. Consequently, people who use steroids to produce larger muscles are in for a surprise: There can be unintended and unpleasant side effects.

Some of these effects are physical. If you're a man, part of your body sees the steroids as testosterone. It reacts to what looks like too much testosterone by shutting down the production of more. The results are a lowered sperm count and a decreased sex drive. (The steroids don't act like testosterone in these respects.) If you're a woman, taking steroids causes masculinizing effects: shrinking breasts, a deepening voice, and an increase in facial and body hair (Gruber & Pope, 2000).

Steroids also have behavioral effects, which are of particular interest here. As you've read in the main text, studies have linked testosterone to dominance and aggressiveness. Steroids do much the same (even among hamsters; Grimes, Ricci, & Melloni, 2006). Because the doses tend to be large, so are the effects. Heavy steroid use can yield irrational bursts of anger, popularly referred to as "roid rages." Adverse behavioral and psychological responses aren't limited to men, either. Among women users, 56% reported manic symptoms during steroid use, and 40% reported depressive symptoms during steroid withdrawal (Gruber & Pope, 2000). Evidence from animal research suggests that steroid use during adolescence can create aggressive tendencies that remain after the steroid has been withdrawn (Harrison, Connor, Nowak, Nash, & Melloni, 2000).

These effects are bad enough in the average person. But bodybuilding and steroid use aren't limited to the average person. Bodybuilding has considerable appeal for people who already have a strong streak of dominance and aggressiveness. Add steroids to an already aggressive personality, and the result is a potential for serious violence.

Testosterone and Adult Personality

A good deal of research on sex hormones and personality examines how current levels of testosterone relate to behavior. That research is several steps away from examining the idea that testosterone masculinizes the nervous system. Yet it shares with it the theme that testosterone is involved in regulating important qualities of behavior. Much of the pioneering research in this area was conducted by James Dabbs and his colleagues (see Dabbs & Dabbs, 2000).

Testosterone is a sex hormone, but research on its behavioral effects has focused more on dominance and antisocial behavior than sexual behavior. One study of men in prison (Dabbs, Frady, Carr, & Besch, 1987) found that inmates high in testosterone had violated prison rules more often and were more dominant than those lower in testosterone. They were also more likely to have committed violent crimes. Similar results have come from female inmates (Dabbs, Ruback, Frady, Hopper, & Sgoutas, 1988). In a sample of men who had committed murder, those high in testosterone were more likely to have planned the act ahead of time and to have killed people they knew (Dabbs, Riad, & Chance, 2001).

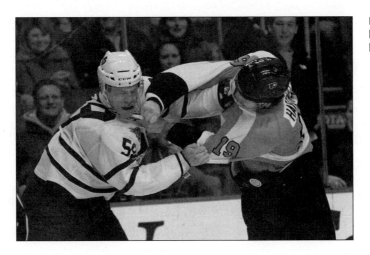

Recent research suggests a link between testosterone level and aggression.

Another study examined testosterone and antisocial behaviors in a noncriminal population: military veterans (Dabbs & Morris, 1990). Men higher in testosterone had larger numbers of sex partners and were more likely to abuse alcohol and other drugs. They were more likely to have gone absent without leave in the military and to have assaulted others. They were also more likely to have had trouble with parents, teachers, and classmates while growing up (see also Box 7.2). These effects were strongest, by far, among men of low socioeconomic status (SES).

Not only can having low SES increase the ill effects of high testosterone, but high testosterone tends to lead men *into* lower-SES occupations (Dabbs, 1992a). This seems to occur because high testosterone promotes antisocial behavior and disruption of education. Both factors then lead people away from white-collar occupations.

Differences in testosterone relate to occupations in other ways, as well, fitting a link between testosterone and social dominance (Mazur & Booth, 1998). For example, trial lawyers (of both genders) are higher in testosterone than nontrial lawyers (Dabbs, Alford, & Fielden, 1998). Actors and professional football players have high levels of testosterone (Dabbs, de La Rue, & Williams, 1990), and ministers have low levels. (College professors, if you must know, are in the middle.)

Why are actors so different from ministers? After all, they're both on stage. Dabbs et al. (1990) suggested that actors must be dominant constantly, because their reputation is only as good as their last show. Ministers are in a framework that tolerates more variability. Further, the actor's role is to seek and hold onto glory, whereas the minister's role is to be self-effacing.

Effects of testosterone occur in many small ways that are related to social potency and dominance. In one study, testosterone related to deeper voices among men (Dabbs & Mallinger, 1999). In studies of brief interactions with strangers, participants higher in testosterone entered more quickly, focused more directly on the other person, and displayed more independence and confidence than those with less testosterone (Dabbs, Bernieri, Strong, Campo, & Milun, 2001). Even young children high in testosterone are more independent on the playground than those with lower testosterone (Strong & Dabbs, 2000).

The role of testosterone in dominance is displayed in other ways, as well. What happens if people low in testosterone are put into positions of high status? What happens if people high in testosterone are put into positions of low status? In both

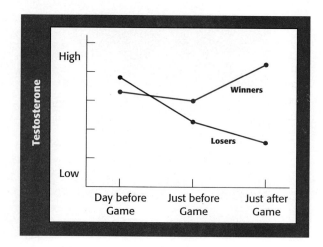

FIGURE 7.4
Testosterone levels among chess players who won or lost close matches in a citywide tournament.
Source: Adapted from Mazur et al., 1992.

cases, the people become upset and perform poorly (Josephs, Sellers, Newman, & Mehta, 2006). When the situations are reversed, however, everyone feels better and performs better.

The dominance that's linked to high testosterone is useful in many contexts, but it can interfere with relationships. Booth and Dabbs (1993) found that men with higher testosterone were less likely to have married. If they did marry, they were more likely to divorce. They were also more likely to have had extramarital sex and to commit domestic abuse. Men high in testosterone have smiles that are less friendly than those of men lower in testosterone, and they express more dominance in their gaze when in conversation (Dabbs, 1992b, 1997). Members of low-testosterone fraternities are friendly and smile a lot, whereas members of high-testosterone fraternities are more wild and unruly (Dabbs, Hargrove, & Heusel, 1996).

Several studies have related testosterone to personality. In two studies, personality data and testosterone data were factor analyzed (Daitzman & Zuckerman, 1980; Udry & Talbert, 1988). In both cases, a factor formed around testosterone, with overtones of impulsiveness, sensation seeking, and dominance. The factor included these self-ratings: *cynical, dominant, sarcastic, spontaneous, persistent,* and *uninhibited.* This pattern of characteristics also appears to relate back to work on brain functions and impulsivity, discussed earlier in the chapter.

CYCLE OF TESTOSTERONE AND ACTION

It may be most obvious to think about testosterone in terms of stable individual differences. However, testosterone is also part of a dynamic system that changes over time and events (Dabbs, 1992b). Levels of testosterone shift in response to social situations of several types. These shifts may, in turn, go on to influence the person's later behavior.

Testosterone rises after positive experiences. As shown in Figure 7.4, it rises after success at a competitive event (Mazur, Booth, & Dabbs, 1992) and falls after a failure or humiliation. It rises when your team wins and falls when your team loses (Bernhardt, Dabbs, Fielden, & Lutter, 1998). It also rises, though, when you are confronted with an insult (Nisbett & Cohen, 1996). It rises (for both men and women) after sexual intercourse (Dabbs & Mohammed, 1992). It goes up among men skateboarding in front of an attractive woman (Ronay & von Hippel, 2010). Even fooling around with a gun for a few minutes can make testosterone increase (Klinesmith, Kasser, & McAndrew, 2006).

Such changes in testosterone also have implications for subsequent behavior. Increases in testosterone make people more sexually active (Dabbs, 1992b). An increase in testosterone can also make a person seek out new competition and chances to be dominant (Mazur, 1985; Mazur et al., 1992). It makes people more responsive to possible rewards and less responsive to possible losses (van Honk, Schutter, Hermans, Putman, Tuiten, & Koppeschaar, 2004). It makes them less empathic (Hermans, Putman, & van Honk, 2006) and less able to detect anger on another person's face (van Honk & Schutter, 2007). A decrease in testosterone after a failure may cause a person to be less assertive and avoid new competition. Thus, in either case (success or failure), there's a tendency toward a spiraling effect: A given outcome tends to promote more of the same outcome.

TESTOSTERONE, DOMINANCE, AND EVOLUTIONARY PSYCHOLOGY

Let's step back from these studies to consider a broader implication. The findings, as a group, seem to fit with one of the themes of evolutionary psychology, discussed in Chapter 6.

Recall that evolutionary thinking includes the idea that selection pressures lead to certain gender differences. These differences stem from the fact that human females have greater investment than males in offspring (through the long period of pregnancy and mothering). Females are believed to be choosy about mates for this reason—trying to find one who will provide resources for her children. A gender difference in dominance and aggression is also believed to follow from the differing selection pressures.

In this view, aggression can increase males' opportunities to mate. Aggressiveness helps males establish dominance and status. One study found that when male monkeys in a troupe were threatened by an outside rival, their testosterone went up, facilitating displays of aggression and dominance (Cristóbal-Azkarate, Chavira, Boeck, Rodríguez-Luna, & Veàl, 2006). An extensive review of literature in humans supports that conclusion and others, as well (Archer, 2006). For example, when men are required to care for offspring, testosterone decreases.

There are also interesting individual differences in testosterone effects. For example, after being insulted, men from the American South have a greater increase in testosterone than men from the North (Cohen, Nisbett, Bowdle, & Schwarz, 1996). This has been interpreted as indicating that there is a stronger culture of honor in the South, which increases the impact of an insult.

Overt aggressiveness in females doesn't confer the same advantage as it does to men and may even be a disadvantage. It can create the potential for damage to an unborn or young child. It also interferes with women's more important activities (bearing and raising children). Nonetheless, testosterone does relate to aggression among women as well as men (Archer, 2006). That this can be a problem for women is suggested by findings that this assertive style interferes with forming alliances in female groups (Archer & Coyne, 2005).

Dabbs (1992b, 1998) noted an interesting irony about testosterone effects. In the evolutionary view, males are high in testosterone and dominance, because physical domination over other males brought access to mates. In recent millenia, however, the rules have changed, at least a little. Success is now defined partly by socioeconomic status, rather than physical dominance. A man who's too preoccupied with displays and posturing may have trouble gaining the skills needed for economic and social power. Thus, a quality that was important in prehistory may actually interfere with success in today's world.

RESPONDING TO STRESS: MEN, WOMEN, AND OXYTOCIN

Another hormonal influence has drawn considerable attention in recent years. It concerns responses to stress, but extends far beyond. A phrase that's well known in psychology, coined long ago by Cannon (1932), is the *fight-or-flight response*. It refers to the fact that when an animal confronts a predator or competitor, it has two adaptive choices: to attack (hoping to overcome the other) or to flee (hoping to escape). Presumably, the flight response connects in some way to the avoidance that was discussed earlier in the chapter. Apparently, there's a link between the fight response and the system of impulsivity, also discussed earlier in the chapter.

It's often been assumed that these are the only important responses to threat. Shelley Taylor (2002, 2006) and her colleagues (Taylor et al., 2000) argue that this assumption is wrong. As they point out, most of the evidence for that view comes from studies of males (and mostly male rats, at that). Females have been studied in a few stressful contexts, but the behavior examined in those studies hasn't been about fight or flight. Rather, the behavior has concerned affiliation—particularly, affiliation with other women.

Taylor et al. (2000) argued that focusing on male behavior caused an important set of responses to be widely ignored. They refer to these responses, which are stronger in females than in males, with the phrase *tend and befriend*. Taylor et al. think the existence of these responses reflects a difference in evolutionary pressures on males and females, due to differing investment in offspring. That is, as just noted, fighting and fleeing may make good sense for males, who aren't carrying offspring (or pregnant), but it makes less sense for females. Females thus may have evolved strategies that benefit both themselves and their offspring.

Tending refers to calming offspring. This protects them from harm. That is, if they don't cry, they (and you) fade into the background, where the threat is less. By extension, you do the same for close adults who are stressed. By soothing them, you put them into a situation of less threat. *Befriending* means affiliating and bonding with others. This reduces certain kinds of risk (because there's greater safety in numbers) and increases the chances of receiving tending from each other when needed (Taylor, 2002).

This pattern of response is believed to derive from the system that produces attachment between infant and caregiver. Attachment is often discussed from the perspective of the infant's bond to a caregiver (see Chapter 9). It's less often discussed the other way around. Yet there's a good deal of research on this topic, and aspects of the biological mechanism that creates it have been identified (Panksepp, 1998).

This system involves a hormone called **oxytocin**. It acts to relax and sedate (e.g., Light et al., 2000), to reduce fear, and to enhance mother–infant bonding (Feldman, Weller, Zagoory-Sharon, & Levine, 2007). Both males and females have this hormone, but females seem to have more of it. Further, androgens inhibit its release under stress, and estrogen increases its effects (see Taylor et al., 2000). Thus, men and women react somewhat differently to stress. Men tend to remove themselves from social interaction; women immerse themselves in nurturing those around them (Repetti, 1989).

The idea that oxytocin is involved in mother–infant bonding is a starting point. But it also seems to be involved in social bonding more generally (Carter, 1998; Panksepp, 1998; Taylor et al., 2000; Turner, Altemus, Enos, Cooper, & McGuinness, 1999). Animal research shows that oxytocin plays a key role in adult pair bonding in some species. It's released during orgasm, childbirth, massage, and breastfeeding (Matthiesen, Ransjö-Arvidson, Nissen, & Uvnäs-Moberg, 2001; Turner et al., 1999).

Greater partner support relates to higher levels of oxytocin (Grewen, Girdler, Amico, & Light, 2005). There's also evidence that receiving a jolt of oxytocin causes people to experience an increase in trust, a willingness to take on risks in the context of a social bond with a stranger (Kosfeld, Heinrichs, Zak, Fischbacher, & Fehr, 2005). It also improves the ability to empathically infer other people's mental states (Domes, Heinrichs, Michel, Berger, & Herpertz, 2007).

And what of personality? One recent study found oxytocin related to lower lifetime aggression (Lee, Ferris, Van de Kar, & Coccaro, 2009). But to date, there's not much evidence linking oxytocin to personality traits. Human research on oxytocin is just gaining momentum, partly because it's harder to study than some other hormones. If oxytocin is important in the formation of social bonds, though, it's a key biological influence on human experience. Undoubtedly, its influence on personality will be the subject of work in the years to come.

Assessment

The biological view on personality discussed in this chapter assumes that personality derives from events in the nervous system and hormonal system. If personality is biological, then why not just assess the biological characteristics?

There are a couple of problems with this. In many cases, no one's quite sure what the biological mechanism is, so it's hard to know what to measure. It's also hard to assess biological functions in a way that doesn't require a sensor in the body or the drawing of blood. Nonetheless, some biological methods of assessment are now in use.

ELECTROENCEPHALOGRAMS

An indirect indication of brain activity can be obtained by recording electrical activity from the scalp. The record is called an **electroencephalogram (EEG)**. The reasoning behind the EEG is that neurons in the brain fire at various intervals, creating fluctuations in voltage. Electrodes on the scalp sense these changes, giving a view of aspects of the activity in the cerebral cortex. Cortical activity is very complex, but it forms patterns that relate to different subjective states.

EEGs have been used for some time as a way of investigating normal personality. In fact, some of the work discussed earlier in the chapter used EEGs. Various regions of the cortex are active to different degrees when people are in different psychological states. Mapping EEG activities in different locations shows what areas of the brain are involved in what kinds of mental activity. For example, it's possible to identify a person who's dominated by incentive motivation or by avoidance motivation by looking at left- versus right-prefrontal activation levels at rest (Harmon-Jones & Allen, 1997; Sutton & Davidson, 1997).

NEUROIMAGING

Mapping of brain activities has also moved inside the brain. One technique, called **positron emission tomography (PET)**, derives a picture of brain functioning from metabolic activity. The person receives a radioactive form of glucose (the brain's energy source). Then later, radioactivity in different brain areas are recorded. Presumably, more active areas use more glucose, resulting in higher radioactivity there. A computer color codes the intensities, producing a brain map in which colors represent levels of brain activity.

An MRI creates an image of the inside of the brain.

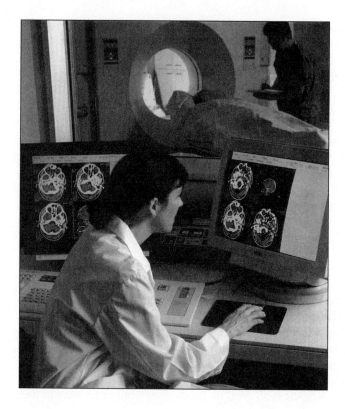

Another technique, called **magnetic resonance imaging (MRI)**, relies on a very subtle property of nerve activity. Functioning nerve cells create magnetic fields. With a good deal of computer assistance, the magnetic resonances of a person's brain can be translated into a visual image. Typically, the image is of slices across the brain, as seen from above. Different slices give different information, because they show different parts of the brain.

At first, MRI images were used primarily to look for structural problems in the brain. For example, if you were having blackouts after an auto accident, you might be asked to undergo an MRI to look for possible damage. MRIs are also now being used in a different way. People are being studied to assess levels of activation in various brain structures, both at rest and in other mental states. The picture from this sort of study, called **functional MRI (fMRI)**, is much more detailed than what comes from EEG recordings. Of particular importance is that it lets the brain be viewed in slices at different levels. The result is a very detailed three-dimensional picture about what brain centers are active during the scan. As with PET scans, the images are usually created in multiple colors, with each color representing a different level of activity.

Use of fMRI has increased at an incredible rate over the past decade and a half. It's very expensive (because it requires a giant, powerful magnet, plus a lot of skilled technical support). But the fact that it can provide a three-dimensional picture means it can show precise locations of increases and decreases in neural activity as a function of what the person is doing. People can be placed in different motivational and emotional states while in the device and can engage in diverse tasks. This lets researchers determine which parts of the brain are involved in those various experiences.

More and more researchers are thinking of possible uses for this tool. This is a research area that unquestionably will continue to grow enormously in the years to come.

Problems in Behavior, and Behavior Change

Let's now turn to problems in behavior. The biological process approach has made large contributions to the understanding of disorders. We focus here on contributions that relate to the ideas discussed earlier in the chapter.

BIOLOGICAL BASES OF ANXIETY AND DEPRESSION

Recall that a basic assumption of these models is that two motivational systems in the brain manage the approach of incentives and avoidance of threats, respectively. People presumably vary in the strength or sensitivity of these systems. Being too extreme on one or the other system may set a person up for problems.

Perhaps the easiest problem to link to this view is anxiety disorders. The avoidance system creates anxiety in the presence of cues of impending punishment. A person with a very sensitive threat system will experience anxiety easily and frequently (Blackford, Avery, Cowan, Shelton, & Zald, 2010; Haas, Omura, Constable, & Canli, 2007). This creates fertile ground for an anxiety disorder to develop. If these people are exposed to frequent punishment during childhood, they learn anxiety responses to many stimuli. The result may be the development of such clinical symptoms as phobias, panic attacks, and obsessive–compulsive disorders.

A related problem is depression. There's less consensus on the biological roots of depression than on those of anxiety (Davidson, Pizzagalli, Nitschke, & Putnam, 2002). Some researchers see depression as a variant of anxiety, reflecting an oversensitive avoidance system. Others tie depression to a weak BAS (e.g., Allen, Iacono, Depue, & Arbisi, 1993; Henriques & Davidson, 1990, 1991). In this view, a person with weak BAS activation has little motivation to approach incentives. The result is the lifeless, weary behavioral qualities that typify depression.

Both problems—anxiety and depression—are likely to be worse if the person also has deficits in the third system: the one that corresponds to constraint or effortful control (Carver et al., 2008). When that system isn't operating effectively, emotions feel more intense and demanding, and it's harder for the person to escape from them (Spoont, 1992). Indeed, the argument is now being made by some that hyper-responsiveness to emotions characterizes a wide variety of disorders (Johnson-Laird, Mancini, & Gangemi, 2006).

BIOLOGICAL BASES OF ANTISOCIAL PERSONALITY

Another problem that's often discussed in terms of biological systems is **antisocial personality**. As noted earlier, this personality involves impulsivity and an inability to restrain antisocial urges. It's often argued that people with this personality have an overactive BAS (Arnett et al., 1997; Joseph et al., 2009). Thus, they pursue whatever incentive comes to mind. It's also sometimes argued that they have deficits in the threat system (Fowles, 1980). Thus, they fail to learn from punishment or aren't motivated to avoid it.

Some think the failure to learn from punishment stems not from a deficient avoidance system but from a failure to stop and think before plowing ahead in pursuit of an incentive (Bernstein, Newman, Wallace, & Luh, 2000; Patterson & Newman, 1993; Schmitt, Brinkley, & Newman, 1999). This would tend to link the antisocial personality to the system that underlies impulsiveness and sensation seeking (Krueger et al., 1994; Rowe, 2001; Zuckerman, 1994). This would represent yet another case in which the problem appears to reflect an over-responsiveness to emotions (Johnson-Laird et al., 2006) but a different set of emotions.

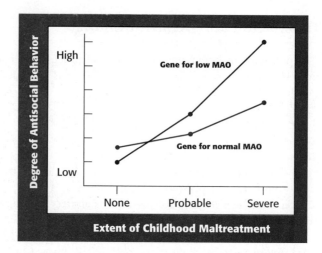

FIGURE 7.5
Scores on an index of antisocial behavior among men with a gene causing low MAO and men with a gene for normal MAO who had experienced either no maltreatment (abuse) during childhood, probably some maltreatment, or severe maltreatment. *Source:* Adapted from Caspi et al., 2002.

Insufficient MAO (associated with this system) may be a vulnerability, interacting with an adverse environment (Raine, 2008). In one study (Caspi et al., 2002), boys with genes causing low MAO engaged in more antisocial behavior—but only if they also were maltreated while growing up (see Figure 7.5). Although men with the combination of low MAO gene and severe maltreatment were only 12% of the male birth cohort, they accounted for 44% of the cohort's violent convictions. Indeed, a full 85% of this group developed some sort of antisocial behavior.

Some discussions of antisocial behavior involve other biological systems, as well. Recall that high levels of testosterone relate to various kinds of violent and antisocial behavior (Dabbs & Dabbs, 2000; Dabbs et al., 2001). There's even evidence that high testosterone relates to disruptive behavior in boys as young as 5 to 11 years of age (Chance, Brown, Dabbs, & Casey, 2000). Thus, this set of problems seems to relate to both hormonal and neural processes.

MEDICATION IN THERAPY

The biological process approach to personality also has relatively straightforward implications for therapy. Many manifestations of problems reflect biological functions. It follows that changing the action of these biological functions should change the manifestation of the disorder. There are several disorders for which this approach seems effective. Because the treatments typically involve administering drugs, they are often called **pharmacotherapy**.

It has long been known that bipolar, or manic–depressive, disorder can be relieved by taking lithium. About 80% of people with bipolar disorder respond to lithium (Depue, 1979). Besides treating existing symptoms, repeated doses can ward off new symptoms. Unfortunately, lithium has serious unpleasant side effects. Nevertheless, its effectiveness supports two ideas: that the disorder is biological and that its treatment should be (at least in part) biologically based.

A similar case can also be made for the treatment of schizophrenia. One long-standing hypothesis is that the symptoms of schizophrenia reflect too much dopamine (Grace, 2010; Walker & Diforio, 1997). With too much dopamine, transmission in certain parts of the nervous system is too easy. When too many messages are being sent, communication is disrupted.

This hypothesis is supported by some studies of biochemical treatments for schizophrenic symptoms. As it turns out, drugs that remove the symptoms of schizophrenia also lower the levels of usable dopamine in the brain. Apparently, the effectiveness of these drugs is related to their ability to block dopamine use. Once again, this finding suggests that the disorder is biological and that the treatment should also be biologically based (at least in part).

Drug treatments are also used for disorders that are far less extreme than the two just discussed. Antianxiety drugs are among the most often prescribed of all medications. Current antidepressants—*selective serotonin reuptake inhibitors (SSRIs)*—are used by many people with moderate to mild depression. Indeed, development of this set of antidepressants has led to a far wider use of mood-altering medication than ever before.

The widespread use of these drugs raises a number of questions and issues (Kramer, 1993). One issue concerns the fact that responses to these medications often are much broader than the mere lifting of a depressed mood. People's personalities undergo changes that are subtle but profound and pervasive. People become more confident, more resilient, more decisive—almost more dominant—than they were before. In a sense, they aren't quite the same people as they were before taking the medication. Their very personalities have changed.

Seeing these changes in personality as a function of a slight alteration in brain chemistry raises questions about where personality resides. Personality may consist of the person's biological functioning and the experiences to which it gives rise. Personality may not be a stable entity that stands apart from the symptoms that bring people for therapy. Personality, in the form of the person's biological systems, may be the *source* of the symptoms.

Researchers have gone on to ask whether SSRIs affect people who don't have a disorder. One study (Knutson et al., 1998) gave people either an SSRI or a placebo for four weeks and assessed them before and afterward. Those who were given the medication later reported less hostility and negativity (but not greater positive feelings). They also displayed more positive social behavior while working on a cooperative task. Another study (Tse & Bond, 2001) found an increase on a measure of self-direction, which assesses such qualities as purposefulness and resourcefulness.

The availability of drugs with these broad effects on personality raises more questions: How widely should they be prescribed? Should people whose problems aren't severe be given medication if it will make their lives more enjoyable? Should all people have the option of changing their personalities by taking pills? Researchers are a long way from answering these questions.

Biological Processes and Personality: Problems and Prospects

This chapter has discussed the idea that patterns of biological processes have important things to tell us about personality. We wouldn't blame you if you came away feeling that the presentation was a little fragmented. In truth, the ideas themselves are somewhat fragmented. The pieces are coming together, but they're not there yet. As a result, this way of thinking about personality has something of a disjointed feel.

One reason for this is that theories about how the nervous system and hormones influence behavior rely, in part, on knowledge from other sciences. Ideas in those sciences are continually evolving, causing changes in the ideas about personality. Further, work on these topics is as new as the methodological advances that permit a closer look at how the biological systems function. These methodological advances continue to march forward (Davidson et al., 2000; Lane & Nadel, 2000; Posner & DiGirolamo, 2000). The result is a kaleidoscope of new looks at biological functioning that sometimes have unexpected implications for personality.

For example, many psychologists now have access to PET scans and fMRIs, which illuminate brain functioning in ways only dreamed of a few years ago. However, the findings generated from these techniques have raised as many new questions as they have answered. Sorting out the picture that such methods reveal will likely be a complex process.

It's clear that there's been progress in these areas of research and thought. To a large extent, theorists agree about what they're trying to account for. There's a general consensus that approach and avoidance (and positive and negative feelings) are important focal points for biological theory building. Almost everyone seems to feel the need to include something more than that, but there's been less of a consensus about what else to include. Partly for this reason, this way of thinking doesn't yet stand as a fully developed personality theory. It's more of a vantage point—a place from which to look at and consider the nature of personality.

Lest you be tempted to conclude from the disagreements that these theorists aren't doing their homework carefully enough, let us point out that it's hard to tell what's going on in the nervous system. To really know what connects to what in the brain means tracing neural pathways, which can't be done in human subjects. When animal research is done, the animals can't report directly on the psychological effects of what the researcher is doing. Thus, information often is indirect, and progress can be slow. The functions of the nervous system are being sorted out by research of several types, but there's a long way to go. Until the nature of the organization of the nervous system becomes clearer, personality psychologists of this orientation are unlikely to have definitive models.

Although criticisms can be made of various aspects of this way of thinking about personality, this line of work is one of the most active areas of personality psychology today. Many people believe that the mysteries of the mind will be revealed by a better understanding of the brain. They are committed to unraveling those mysteries and their implications for personality. The prospects of this viewpoint seem quite bright indeed.

• SUMMARY •

The idea that personality is tied to the biological functions of the body leads to a variety of possibilities involving the nervous system and the hormone system. An initial approach of this sort was Eysenck's theory that brain processes underlie extraversion and neuroticism. He argued that introverts are more cortically aroused than extraverts and that people high in neuroticism are emotionally aroused.

Others have taken a different path, relying on newer knowledge. It's now often argued that personality rests on an approach system (BAS) that responds to incentives and an avoidance system that responds to threats. Work on emotions suggests that the approach system involves (in part) the left prefrontal cortex and that the withdrawal system involves (in part) the right prefrontal cortex. The threat system seems to represent the biological basis for the trait of neuroticism. Some researchers suggest that the BAS represents the biological basis for extraversion.

Many people now believe it's useful to assume that another biological system is responsible for variations in impulsiveness and sensation seeking (the tendency to seek out novel, complex, and exciting stimuli). Sensation seeking relates to Eysenck's psychoticism dimension and Tellegen's constraint dimension, and both relate to the temperament of effortful control. Variation in these qualities may be grounded in differences in the functions that cause people to take into account other people and long-term goals.

Another aspect of the biological view on personality focuses on the influences of hormones on behavior. Exposure to male hormones before birth can cause people years later to choose more aggressive responses to conflict and can increase girls' preference for boys' toys. Testosterone in adults relates to dominance behavior, sometimes expressed in antisocial ways. Testosterone also fluctuates with the context, increasing with challenges and victories and decreasing with failures.

An emerging area of work examines the possibility that another hormone, called *oxytocin*, is important in human social behavior. Oxytocin appears to relate to female responses to stress, termed a *tend-and-befriend response*. The roots of this response may be in the attachment system, and it may relate to social bonding more generally.

The biological process approach to personality suggests it may be possible to assess personality through biological functions. Although the attempt to do this is in its infancy, some researchers believe recordings of brain activity—particularly fMRIs—hold great promise for the future.

With regard to problems in behavior, high levels of threat sensitivity activity promote disorders involving anxiety. Either a high threat response or a low approach response may contribute to depression. High approach–low avoidance can yield symptoms of antisocial personality, which also relates to impulsive sensation seeking and testosterone. This orientation to personality suggests that therapy based, in part, on medication is a means to bring about behavioral change. The idea is that medication can influence the underlying biological system, thereby altering the person's behavior and subjective experience.

• GLOSSARY •

Anabolic steroids Chemicals that mimic the body's tendency to rebuild muscle tissues.

Antisocial personality A person who displays impulsive action with little thought to consequences.

Avoidance or **withdrawal system** The part of the brain that regulates responses to punishment.

Behavioral approach system (BAS) The part of the brain that regulates pursuit of incentives.

Dopamine A neurotransmitter believed to be especially important to approach regulation.

Electroencephalogram (EEG) A record of overall electrical activity in higher regions of the brain.

Functional MRI (fMRI) Use of magnetic resonance imaging (MRI) to create a picture of activity inside the brain in different mental states.

GABA A substance, low levels of which appear to be linked to anxiety disorders.

Impulsive unsocialized sensation seeking (IUSS) A trait involving the capacity to inhibit behavior in the service of social adaptation.

Incentives Things that people desire.

Magnetic resonance imaging (MRI) A picture of activity inside the brain based on the brain's electro-magnetic energy.

Monamine oxidase (MAO)   A substance that helps regulate several neurotransmitters and seems to be involved in constraint over impulses.

Neurotransmitter   A chemical involved in sending messages along nerve pathways.

Norepinephrine   A neurotransmitter that some researchers believe is important in anxiety responses.

Oxytocin   A hormone that appears to be important in social bonding.

Pharmacotherapy   A therapy based on use of medication.

Positron emission tomography (PET)   A picture of activity in the brain based on the brain's metabolism.

Sensation seeking   The tendency to seek out varied, unusual, and exciting stimuli.

Serotonin   A neurotransmitter that some researchers believe is involved in anxiety and others believe is involved in constraint over impulses.

Testosterone   A male sex hormone that influences a wide range of behaviors.

The Psychoanalytic Perspective

Dan and Jamie are talking about a club they'd been to last night, where one of their friends had gotten totally drunk—something she's done weekly for the past year. At that moment, Robin rounds the corner, practically running into them.

"Hey Robin, you recovered from last night?" Jamie asks.

"What are you talking about?" replies Robin.

"Come on, Robin." Dan throws in. "Aren't you concerned about how much you've been drinking?"

Robin looks offended. "Look, guys, I don't have a clue what you're talking about."

WHEN YOU look at your actions, do you see them for what they really are? Or have you distorted them to yourself for some reason? Most of us probably think we're aware of what we do and why. Accidents may happen, but accidents are random.

There's a perspective on personality, though, that sharply challenges this view. It sees behavior as determined partly by inner forces that are outside your awareness and control. Accidents? Not likely. What seems an accident, you've usually done on purpose—you just aren't *aware* of the purpose.

This approach to personality is called *psychoanalysis*. Psychoanalysis originated in the writings of an Austrian physician named Sigmund Freud. His impact on personality psychology was huge. His view emerged just as behavioral science was getting its start (his theory evolved from 1885 to 1940). Because it came to prominence before other views of personality had been widely circulated, many people think of Freud as the father of personality psychology.

Basic Themes

One theme underlying Freud's view, which gives rise to the term *psychodynamic*, is the idea that personality is a set of processes that are always in motion. Personality is a dynamo—or a bubbling spring. Forces emerge that can be channeled, modified, or transformed. Personality is not one process but several, which sometimes work against each other—competing or wrestling for control over the person's behavior. The idea that pressures within the personality can *conflict* with each other is another theme that's prominent in the psychoanalytic view.

The idea that personality is filled with conflict brings up another theme: defense as a key aspect of human functioning. The psychoanalytic view assumes that everyone experiences threats about aspects of himself or herself. Maybe you have desires you think are shameful; maybe you've done things you regret; maybe you feel unworthy as a human being. Whatever most threatens you, your defensive processes keep it from overpowering you. This idea of continual defense is an important aspect of psychoanalytic thought.

Yet another theme in psychoanalytic theory is that human experience is suffused with qualities of lust and aggression, sexuality and death. These ideas link Freud to evolutionary theory (Ritvo, 1990) and serve as a reminder that humans are—first of all—animals whose purpose in life is reproduction. The extent to which Freud emphasized the role of sexuality was very unusual at the time, however, and many found it shocking.

The psychoanalytic perspective on personality is extremely metaphorical. It does not rely on a single metaphor but multiple metaphors. Freud was a physician, and the idea of biological processes underlying mental processes often appeared in his writing. His concepts of life and death instincts resemble the dual processes of metabolic functioning—continually tearing down and building up. Freud also used many other metaphors. Sometimes he compared the mind to a sociopolitical system, making reference to censors, economics, compromises, and repression. Sometimes he turned to physics, treating personality as an energy system or the competition among forces as hydraulic systems. His fascination with metaphor was consistent with his view of personality. Freud's fascination with symbol and metaphor is also seen in the theory's content. He came to believe that human behavior itself is highly symbolic. People's acts are rarely quite what they seem to be. Instead, they symbolize other more hidden qualities.

Psychoanalytic theory is very complex. Underlying the complexity, however, is a fairly small number of principles (Kahn, 2002). The theory can be confusing because its concepts are deeply interwoven. Thus, it's hard to talk about any aspect of the theory separate from other aspects. Perhaps the best place to start, though, is Freud's view of how the mind is organized, a view that is often termed his **topographical model** of mind.

The Topographical Model of Mind

Many people assume the mind has two regions. One holds conscious experience: the thoughts, feelings, and behaviors you're aware of right now. The other contains memories, now outside awareness but able to come to awareness easily. Drawing on ideas of other theorists of his time, Freud added a third region. Taken together, the three form what Freud viewed as the mind's topography—its surface configuration.

Freud used the term **conscious** much as we do today: to refer to the part of the mind that holds what you're now aware of. The part of the mind representing ordinary memory he called **preconscious**. Things in the preconscious can be brought to awareness easily. For example, when you think of your phone number or the last movie you saw, you're bringing that information from the preconscious to conscious.

Freud used the term **unconscious** in a way different from its everyday use. He used it to mean a part of the mind that's not directly accessible to awareness. Freud saw the unconscious as the source of desires and as a repository for urges, feelings, and ideas that are tied to anxiety, conflict, or pain (Rhawn, 1980). Yet despite being stored away in the unconscious, these things aren't gone. They exert a continuing influence on later actions and conscious experience.

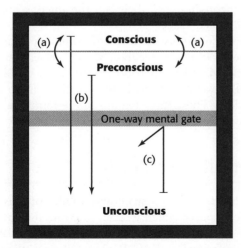

FIGURE 8.1
Graphic representation of Freud's topographical model of the mind. (A) Material can pass easily back and forth between the conscious and preconscious portions of the mind. (B) Material can also move from the conscious and preconscious into the unconscious. But once material is in the unconscious, the person is prevented from having conscious access to it because (C) a mental gate prevents retrieval.

BOX 8.1 EGO PROCESSES AND DELAY OF GRATIFICATION

A key function of the ego is to delay gratification of impulses and urges until a later time. Delay of gratification is a mark of a mature personality. It's also a major goal of socialization. To become full and productive members of society, children must learn to wait for rewards (work now but be paid later). Inability to delay gratification predicts use of cigarettes, alcohol, and marijuana among high school students (Wulfert, Block, Santa Ana, Rodriguez, & Colsman, 2002) and may play a role in development of criminal behavior.

Delay of gratification has been studied from a variety of angles (in fact, it comes up several more times in this book). Most of the research was prompted by ideas other than psycho-

analytic theory, but the findings are relevant to psychodynamic processes. In most studies of this phenomenon, children are given the following choice: They can have a smaller, less desired reward now, or they can wait for a while and then get a larger, more desired reward. A focus of this research is on determinants of delay (for reviews, see Mischel, 1966, 1974). It's harder for children to delay when the desired object is right in front of them (Mischel & Ebbesen, 1970). Delay is easier if the children can mentally transform the situation to make it seem as though the object isn't really there—for example, to imagine it is only "a color picture in their head" (Mischel & Baker, 1975; Moore, Mischel, & Zeiss, 1976). More generally, delay is easiest when children distract themselves, shifting attention away from the desired reward (Mischel, Ebbesen, & Zeiss, 1973). In effect, the

ego tricks the id by getting it involved in something else.

A second line of research on delay of gratification concerns personality correlates of the ability to delay. Children who are better able to delay are more concerned with achievement and social responsibility (Mischel, 1961), fitting the idea that they have a well-defined ego. The basis for delay also differs slightly from boys to girls (Funder, Block, & Block, 1983). Among boys, it's closely related to the ability to control emotional impulses, to concentrate, and to be deliberate in action. This fits the idea that delay of gratification is an ego function, aimed at control over id impulse expression. Delay among girls, in contrast, is more related to intelligence, resourcefulness, and competence, suggesting that they recognize delay as being the situationally appropriate response.

In this view, the mind is like an iceberg. The tip of the iceberg is the conscious part of the mind. The much larger part—the part below the water line—is outside awareness. Some of it (the part you can see through the water) is the preconscious. The vast majority of it, however (the part you can't see), is the unconscious. Although the conscious and preconscious both influence behavior, Freud saw them as less important than the unconscious, He believed the unconscious is where the core operations of personality take place.

The three levels of consciousness form the topographical model of the mind (see Figure 8.1). Material (thought, feelings, desires) passes easily from conscious to preconscious and back. Material from both of these can slip into the unconscious. Unconscious material, however, can't be brought voluntarily to awareness because of forces that keep it hidden. These three regions of the mind are the theater in which the dynamics of personality are played out.

Aspects of Personality: The Structural Model

Freud (1962/1923) also developed a **structural model** of personality. He saw personality as having three aspects, which interact to create the complexity of behavior. They aren't physical entities but are perhaps best thought of as labels for three aspects of functioning (Grigsby & Stevens, 2000). We know them as the id, ego, and superego.

Id

The **id** is the original component of personality, present at birth. The *id* (the Latin word meaning "it") is all the inherited, instinctive, primitive aspects of personality. The id functions entirely in the unconscious. It's closely tied to basic biological processes, which underlie life. Freud believed that all psychic energy comes through it. Thus the id is the "engine" of personality.

The id follows what's called the **pleasure principle**: that all needs should be satisfied immediately (Freud, 1949/1940). Unsatisfied needs create aversive tension states. To prevent that tension, the person seeks to reduce needs as soon as they begin to arise. According to the pleasure principle, any increase in hunger should cause an attempt to eat. Any twinge of sexual desire should cause an effort to get sexual gratification.

The id satisfies needs via the **primary process**: forming an unconscious mental image of an object or event that would satisfy the need. In the case of a hungry infant, the primary process might produce an image of mother's breast or a bottle. In the case of being separated from someone you love, the primary process produces images of that person. The experience of having such an image is called **wish fulfillment**.

Ego

Tension reduction by primary process has a drawback, however. It doesn't connect well with reality. As a result, a second set of functions develops, termed the **ego** (the Latin word for *I*). The ego evolves from the id and harnesses part of the id's energy for its own use. The ego tries to make sure the id's impulses are expressed *effectively*, by taking into account the external world. Because of this concern with the outside world, most ego functioning is in the conscious and preconscious. Given the ego's ties to the id, however, it also functions in the unconscious.

The ego follows the **reality principle**. This means taking into account external reality along with internal needs and urges. Because the ego orients you toward the world, it leads you to weigh the risks of an action before acting. If the risks seem too high, you'll think of another way to meet the need. If there's no safe way to do so immediately, you'll delay it to a later, safer, or more sensible time.

Thus, a goal of the ego is to *delay the discharge* of the id's tension until an appropriate object or context is found (see Box 8.1). The ego uses the **secondary process**: matching the unconscious image of a tension-reducing object to a real object. Until such an object can be found, the ego keeps the tension in check. The ego's goal is *not* to block the id's desires permanently. The ego wants the id's urges to be satisfied. But it wants them satisfied at a time and in a way that's safe—that won't cause trouble because of some danger in the world (Bergmann, 1980).

The ego—using the reality principle and secondary process thought—is the source of intellectual processes and problem solving. The capacity for realistic thought allows the ego to form plans of action to satisfy needs and test the plans mentally to see whether they will work. This is called **reality testing**. The ego is often described as having an "executive" role in personality, as it mediates between the desires of the id and the constraints of the external world.

The ego can seem to be a positive force, because it exercises restraint over the id. That can be misleading, though. The ego has no moral sense. It's entirely pragmatic, focused on getting by. The ego wouldn't be bothered by cheating or stealing or setting loose the pleasure principle, as long as no danger is involved. The moral sense resides in the third part of personality.

Superego

The final aspect of personality—the last to develop—is the **superego** (a joining of two Latin words meaning "over I"). Freud held that the superego develops while the person resolves a particular conflict during development (discussed later in the chapter).

The superego has two parts. The conscience holds an image of undesirable behavior, and the ego-ideal holds an image of desirable behavior. DENNIS THE MENACE® used by permission of Hank Ketcham and © by North America Syndicate.

DENNIS THE MENACE

"MOM TELLS ME THE STUFF I SHOULDN'T DO AND MY DAD TELLS ME THE STUFF I *SHOULD* DO!"

The superego is the embodiment of parental and societal values. The values in your superego stem mostly from the values of your parents. To obtain the parents' love, the child comes to do what its parents think is right. To avoid pain, punishment, and rejection, the child avoids what its parents think is wrong. The process of "taking in," or incorporating, the values of the parents (and wider society) is called **introjection**.

The superego is further divided into two subsystems. The **ego ideal** comprises rules for good behavior or standards of excellence. The **conscience** comprises rules about what behaviors the parents disapprove of and punish (Janoff-Bulman, Sheikh, & Hepp, 2009; Sederer & Seidenberg, 1976). Doing these things causes the conscience to punish you with feelings of guilt. Thus, the ego ideal reflects things you strive for, and the conscience reflects things to avoid. (This distinction also arose in the context of approach and avoidance motivation in Chapters 5 and 7.)

The superego also operates at all three levels of consciousness. It has three interrelated goals. First, it tries to prevent (not just postpone) any id impulse that would be frowned on by one's parents. Second, it tries to force the ego to act morally, rather than rationally. Third, it tries to guide the person toward perfection in thought, word, and deed. The superego exerts a "civilizing" influence on the person, but its perfectionism is quite removed from reality.

BALANCING THE FORCES

Once the superego has developed, the ego has a hard road. It must deal simultaneously with the desires of the id, the moral dictates of the superego, and the constraints of

Ego strength refers to a person's ability to deal effectively with competing demands and taxing situations.

Box 8.2 Freud's Ideas Have Likely Been Distorted by Translation and Cultural Distance

Sigmund Freud was Austrian and lived in a time and culture that were very different from ours. He wrote entirely in German, and his ideas were later translated into English. Translation of any complex or subtle idea is hard, and there is great potential for error. Less than perfect word choices can greatly distort meaning. It's hard for any translator to know precisely what the original writer intended to convey, and it's likely that no translation is entirely faithful to the original.

How faithful are the translations of Freud's writings? Not very, according to Bruno Bettelheim (1982), an important analyst in his own right. Bettelheim had the background to judge. He came from Vienna, spoke German from childhood, and lived in the same cultural context as Freud. He was distressed by many aspects of the English translations of Freud. Here are some, as illustrated by the following examples.

Whenever possible, Freud tried to communicate his ideas in words that his readers had used since childhood, adding new insights to those common words. Two names he chose for aspects of personality are among the first words learned by every German-speaking child. In German, the words are personal pronouns. In the pronoun I (Ich), Freud chose a word that virtually forces you to think of yourself, adding the emotional qualities related to your assertive affirmation of your own existence. The translated word ego, in contrast, is lifeless and sterile.

In the pronoun it (Es), Freud made an allusion that's completely lost to people who speak only English. In German, the word that means "child" is neuter. Thus, in early childhood, each German or Austrian child is referred to as an it. This word, as applied to yourself, has clear emotional overtones: It's what you were called when you were so young that you hadn't learned to stifle your impulses or feel guilty about them. A sense of personalized infancy is conveyed in the original, whereas the translated id has no intrinsic associations at all.

Another common word used by Freud was Trieb, which is commonly translated as instinct. Bettelheim says drive is better, because Freud used a different word when he wanted to refer to the instincts of animals. By Trieb, he meant to convey an inner propulsion, a basic urge, an impulse, but—not the sense that the drive was an animal instinct, inborn and unalterable.

Among the few non-German terms Freud used are Eros and Psyche. These are the names of characters in a Greek myth. They were characters Freud knew intimately, as did most people to whom he was writing. (At the time, educated people read classic works of literature.) When Freud wrote of "erotic" qualities, he referred to these characters and their qualities: Eros's charm and cunning and the deep love he had for Psyche. Psyche had at first been tricked into believing that Eros was disgusting, and the message of the myth is that this was an error. For sexual love to be true erotic pleasure, it must be filled with beauty (symbolized by Eros himself) and express the longings of the soul (symbolized by Psyche). These are connotations Freud wanted to convey with the word erotic. When they are stripped away (because readers don't know the myth), the word not only loses its true meaning, but even takes on connotations opposite to Freud's intention.

Indeed, Bettelheim argued that the word psyche itself has also been misrepresented. We are used to thinking of the psyche as the mind, because that's how the word has been translated. The German word for psyche, however, is Seele, which means "soul." Thus, said Bettelheim, Freud's focus was on the metaphysical, but this has been misread as a focus on the mental.

In sum, Bettelheim argued that much of the sense of Freud's ideas has been missed. Freud chose his language to evoke responses not just at an intellectual level but at an emotional level, as well. This has been lost. Because we don't live in the cultural context in which Freud wrote, we also miss many of his nods to ideas that were common at the time. Bettelheim also argued that Freud was aware of the distortions and chose not to correct them. Why? Apparently, Freud was annoyed at the U.S. medical establishment, which seemed intent on making psychoanalysis part of medicine, which he opposed.

reality. To satisfy all these demands, the ego would have to release tension immediately in a way that's both socially acceptable and realistic. This, of course, is highly unlikely, because these forces often conflict. In the psychoanalytic view, such conflicts are part of life. The term **ego strength** refers to the ego's ability to be effective despite them (Barron, 1953). With little ego strength, the person is torn among competing pressures. With more ego strength, the person can manage the pressures.

It's important to realize that no aspect of personality is "better" than the others. Rather, there should be a balance among them. A person whose superego is too strong may feel guilty all the time or act in an insufferably "saintly" way. A person whose id is too strong may be obsessed with self-gratification and completely uninterested in other people. The healthiest personality is one in which the influences of all three aspects are integrated and balanced.

Motivation: The Drives of Personality

At several points, we've talked in general terms about energy, impulses, tension states, drives, and urges. Let's now consider these forces more explicitly.

In thinking about motivation, Freud borrowed heavily from prevailing views in the biological and physical sciences. He saw people as complex energy systems, in which the energy used in psychological work (thinking, perceiving, remembering, planning, dreaming) is generated and released through biological processes. These biological processes, operating via the id, have been called *instinct* and *drive*. These two terms differ from each other in other contexts (see Box 8.2), but they're used interchangeably here.

A drive has two related elements: a biological need and its psychological representation. For example, a lack of sufficient water in the body's cells is a need that creates a psychological state of thirst, a desire for water. These elements combine to form a drive to drink water. (This portrayal isn't much different from the view of motives in Chapter 5.)

These processes are continuous. Drive states build until an action causes their tension to be released. If a drive isn't expressed, its pressure continues to build. This view of motives is called a *"hydraulic"* model. In this view, trying to prevent a drive from being expressed only creates more pressure toward its expression.

TWO CLASSES OF DRIVES: LIFE AND DEATH INSTINCTS

As with many aspects of Freud's work, his ideas about drives evolved over time. Ultimately, he contended that all drives form two classes (Freud, 1933). The first is termed **life or sexual instincts** (collectively called **Eros**). Eros is a set of drives that deal with survival, reproduction, and pleasure. Not all life instincts deal with erotic urges per se. Hunger and pain avoidance, as well as sex, are life instincts. Collectively, the energy of the life instincts is known as **libido**.

A second set of drives is **death instincts** (also termed **Thanatos**). Freud's view of these instincts is reflected in his statement that "the goal of all life is death" (Freud, 1955/1920). He believed that life leads naturally to death and that people desire (unconsciously) to return to nothingness. The expression of death instincts is usually held back by the life instincts, however. Thus, the effects of the death instincts aren't always visible.

Freud never coined a term for the energy of death instincts, and the death drive has received less attention than Eros. Interestingly, however, today's biology assumes a death instinct in human physiology. That is, there is an active gene-directed suicide process, termed **apoptosis**, which occurs in human cells in certain circumstances. It's critical in development (W. R. Clark, 1996), and it seems to be involved in the body's defense against cancer (Tyner et al., 2002). The cell-death function is coded in your cells (Hopkin, 1995). This fact suggests that death is an ultimate goal for parts of the body. Perhaps the principle extends more broadly into personality, as well.

An aspect of the death instinct that *has* received attention from psychologists concerns aggression. In Freud's view, aggression isn't a basic drive but stems from the thwarting of the death drive. That is, if Eros blocks expression of the death drive, tension remains. Energy is unspent. It can be used in aggressive or destructive actions against others. In this view, acts of aggression express *self*-destructive urges but turned outward onto others.

CATHARSIS

We said earlier that if the tension of a drive isn't released, the pressure remains and even grows. At some point, the buildup of energy may be so great that it can't be restrained any longer. At this point, the impulse is unleashed. The term **catharsis** is used to refer to the release of emotional tension in such an experience. (This term also has a slightly different use, discussed later on.)

The idea of catharsis has been studied mostly with respect to aggression. The principle leads to two predictions there. First, engaging in aggression should reduce tension, because the aggressive urge is no longer being bottled up. Second, because this act dissipates the urge's energy, the person should be less likely to be aggressive again in the near future.

This view of aggressive energy and its release is echoed in the ideas of other theorists. Megargee (1966, 1971; Megargee, Cook, & Mendelsohn, 1967) argued that people with strong inhibitions against aggressing rarely blow off steam, even when provoked. Over time, though, their feelings build until their restraints can no longer hold. Because so much energy has built up, the aggression that's released may be quite brutal. Ironically, the final provocation is often trivial (see also Miller, Pederson, Earleywine, & Pollock, 2003). Once the episode is over, these people (whom Megargee terms *overcontrolled aggressors*) revert to their overcontrolled, passive ways.

What evidence supports the catharsis hypothesis for aggression in *most* people? People seem to *think* aggression will make them feel better (Bushman, Baumeister, & Phillips, 2001), but the evidence is mixed (Baron & Richardson, 1994). Aggression can help dissipate arousal (Geen, Stonner, & Shope, 1975; Hokanson & Burgess, 1962a, 1962b; Hokanson, Burgess, & Cohen, 1963), but it's less clear why. Some of the evidence suggests that actual retaliation produces this effect, but not symbolic or fantasy retaliation.

In sum, although some evidence suggests catharsis effects, the effects occur only under very specific circumstances. Moreover, other evidence seems to contradict catharsis. As a whole, the evidence doesn't support this aspect of psychoanalytic theory very well.

Anxiety and Mechanisms of Defense

Much of the activity of personality—in people who are perfectly normal, as well as people with problems—concerns **anxiety**. Freud (1936/1926) didn't view anxiety as a drive per se but as a warning signal to the ego that something bad is about to happen. Nonetheless, people seek to avoid or escape anxiety.

Freud (1959/1926) distinguished three types of anxiety, reflecting three kinds of bad things. The simplest is **reality anxiety**, which arises from a danger in the world. You experience it when you realize you're about to be bitten by a dog, crash your car, be yelled at for a mistake at work, or fail an exam. As its name implies, reality anxiety is rooted in reality. We deal with it by fixing, avoiding, or escaping from the situation that creates the feeling.

The second type, **neurotic anxiety**, is an unconscious fear that your id impulses will get out of control and make you do something that will get you punished. This isn't a fear of expressing the id impulses but a fear of the punishment that will result from expressing them. Because punishment often follows impulsive actions

Box 8.3 Unintended Effects of Thought Suppression

People sometimes consciously try to keep particular thoughts out of their minds. If you want to quit smoking, you'll try to avoid thinking about cigarettes. If you want to lose weight, you'll try not to think of food. If you've just broken up with someone, you'll try to avoid thinking about the things you did together. These all involve efforts to keep ideas out of your consciousness.

Sometimes thought suppression works. But trying *not* to think of something can have unintended side effects. Dan Wegner and his colleagues have conducted a program of studies on thought suppression (Wegner, 1989, 1994; Wenzlaff & Wegner, 2000), and their conclusions may surprise you. Trying not to think about something can actually make that thought become *more* likely later on, especially if the thought is an emotionally arousing one (Wegner, Shortt, Blake, & Page, 1990).

The idea of conscious thought suppression contains a paradox. Thought suppression requires two steps: deciding to suppress the thought and then getting rid of all evidence of the thought—including the plan to suppress it. This seems to require that

you be conscious of your intent and not conscious of it, at once. (If repression occurs unconsciously, of course, this problem is avoided, because the plan to get rid of the thought is unconscious.)

So what happens when people try to suppress a thought? Initial research taught people a think-aloud technique, in which they reported all thoughts that came to mind. Then they used this technique for periods of 5 minutes under two different conditions. In one condition, they tried *not* to think of a white bear, and every time a white bear came to mind, they rang a bell in front of them. In the other condition, they were to *think* of a white bear and to ring the bell whenever they did. For some people, the suppression came first, then the thinking. For others, the order was reversed.

Two findings emerged. First, it was hard for people to avoid thinking of a white bear. (The most effective strategy is focusing on something else.) Interestingly, most intrusions of the unwanted thought occurred when the person had just finished another thought and was silent. It was as though the suppressed thought could be kept out as long as the mental machinery was fully occupied, but when an opening came up the

thought leaped in. Suppression is hard unless you have a distractor to think of instead (recall discussion in Box 8.1 on how distraction helps in delay of gratification).

The second finding was that people who suppressed showed a rebound effect. That is, when they were later asked to think of the bear, they did so more frequently and consistently than did the other people. Their reports of the white bear were stable over the 5-minute period. In contrast, those who had started by thinking of the bear wore out fairly quickly, and their reports fell off over the 5-minute period. Rebound effects have been found repeatedly, even in dreams (Wegner, Wenzlaff, & Kozak, 2004)!

In practical terms, what are the implications of findings such as these? What should you do if you want *not* to think about something? Wegner (1989) argues that, as odd as it may sound, the best medicine is to let the thoughts in. Experience the feelings associated with the intrusion, and let the experience run its course. Only by relaxing mental control, he says, can we regain it. By lowering your defenses, you eventually reduce the pressure of the unwanted thought, and it will go away on its own (perhaps through the mechanisms of the unconscious).

---

that society disapproves of, neurotic anxiety has a kind of basis in reality. However, the danger ultimately is rooted inside, in the urges of the id. For this reason, neurotic anxiety is harder to deal with than reality anxiety. You can avoid dangerous dogs, drive carefully, do your best at work, and prepare for exams, but you can't escape from your id. It always has the potential to get out of control.

The third type of anxiety is **moral anxiety**. This is the fear people have when they have violated (or are about to violate) their moral code. If your moral sense forbids cheating and you're tempted to cheat, you feel moral anxiety. If your moral sense forbids having sex before marriage and you're just about to have sex, you experience moral anxiety. Moral anxiety is felt as guilt or shame. Again, it's important to be clear about the difference between this type of anxiety and reality anxiety. The threat of punishment from society isn't the source of moral anxiety. Its source is internal, in your conscience. As with neurotic anxiety, it's hard to deal with. Just as you can't escape your id, you can't run away from your conscience.

If your ego did its job perfectly, you would never feel anxiety. External dangers would be avoided or dealt with, preventing reality anxiety. Id impulses would be released at appropriate times and places, preventing neurotic anxiety. You would never let yourself do anything (or even *want* to do anything) that your superego prohibited, preventing moral anxiety. No one's ego works this well, though. As a result, most people experience some anxiety, and many people experience a lot. This is part of normal life.

When anxiety arises, the ego responds in two ways. First, it increases problem-oriented coping efforts. It tries to deal (consciously) with the source of the threat. This works pretty well for reality anxiety. Second, the ego engages **defense mechanisms**: tactics it develops to help avoid the other kinds of anxiety. When defenses work well, they keep anxiety away. Defense mechanisms share two characteristics: First, they all can operate unconsciously. Second, they all distort or transform reality in one way or another.

Varying defenses have been proposed. The most comprehensive discussion of these mechanisms came from Freud's daughter Anna (A. Freud, 1966). The next sections outline some of the defense mechanisms identified by Anna Freud and others.

REPRESSION

The central mechanism of defense is **repression**. Indeed, Sigmund Freud often used the terms *defense* and *repression* interchangeably. In repression, a certain amount of energy available to the ego is used to keep unacceptable impulses out of consciousness. Repression can be done consciously (which Anna Freud called *suppression*), as the person tries to force something out of awareness (see also Box 8.3). Most discussions of repression, however, focus on it as an unconscious process.

Repression can be used to block from awareness not only id impulses but also information that's painful or upsetting. Sometimes this is the memory of impulses you already expressed. If you did something you're ashamed of, the memory might be pushed into the unconscious. Eventually you may be unable to recall doing it (as in the example opening the chapter). Threat can come from things about yourself that you see as failings—for example, the fact that you're unpopular or the fact that you can't dance. It can come from being part of a group that others put down (Steele, 1997) or from the realization you will eventually die (Pyszczynski, Greenberg, & Solomon, 2000). Threat can come from conflicts with your superego's standards—for example, the fact that you're not doing anything to help the people in the world who are starving.

Repression need not be total. It's easiest to talk about defenses in all-or-nothing terms, but that can be misleading. You can partly hide a moderately distressing memory, so you don't think about it often. In essence, you simply avoid retrieving it (Shane & Peterson, 2004). You haven't forgotten it, however. If reminded of it, you're still aware it's there. But you'd just as soon not be reminded of it. This would be a partial repression.

DENIAL

Another simple defense occurs when people are overwhelmed by a threatening reality. This defense is **denial**: refusal to believe an event took place or a condition exists. An example is the mother who refuses to believe that her son has been killed in combat. Another is a child abused by a parent who goes on as if nothing were wrong (Freyd, 1996). A less extreme case is a student who receives a failing grade and

Denial prevents us from becoming aware of unpleasant things in our lives.

assumes there's been some sort of mistake or the idea that your parents have an active sex life with certain preferred positions for intercourse.

Denial resembles repression in many ways. Both keep from awareness what the person feels unable to cope with. They differ in the source of the threat. Repression deals with threats that originate within the dynamics of the mind. Denial deals with threats with other sources.

It is said that people use repression and denial because they work (Erdelyi, 2006). They save you from pain or anxiety. They create problems in the long run, though, because they take up energy that could be used in other ways. You have only so much energy to go around at any given time (Baumeister, 2002; Muraven & Baumeister, 2000). If too much of it is tied up in these defenses, your ego has little left for anything else. When resources are lacking, behavior becomes less flexible and accommodating (Finkel & Campbell, 2001). If an act of repression continues for a long time, the energy is more or less permanently tied up. Thus, despite the fact that repression and denial are sometimes needed, they can eventually work against you.

Perhaps for that reason, other defenses develop. They operate in combination with repression (and with one another). They free up some of the energy, while keeping unacceptable impulses, thoughts, or feelings from registering in your consciousness.

PROJECTION

In **projection**, your reduce anxiety by ascribing your own unacceptable qualities to someone else. You project traits, impulses, desires, or even goals onto another person (Kawada, Oettingen, Gollwitzer, & Bargh, 2004). Projection provides a way to hide your knowledge of a disliked aspect of yourself while still expressing that quality, though in a highly distorted form (Mikulincer & Horesh, 1999). For example, if you feel hostile toward others, you repress the feeling. The feeling is still there, however. In projection, you develop a perception that others hate you or are out to get you. In this way, your hostile impulse is expressed but in a way that's not threatening to you (Schimel, Greenberg, & Martens, 2003).

Thus, projection serves two purposes. It helps to get true desires into the open in one form or another, releasing some of the energy required to repress them (Schimel et al., 2003). Just as importantly, though, the desire emerges in such a way that the ego and superego don't recognize it as belonging to you. Thus, the threat is sidestepped (see Figure 8.2).

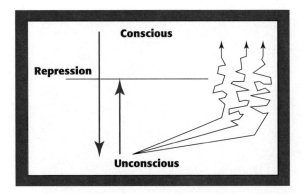

Figure 8.2
Defenses begin with repression, removing threatening material from the conscious region of the mind to the unconscious. What has been repressed cannot be brought out directly because it's too anxiety provoking. Repressed material can sneak around the barrier, however, by being transformed so as to make it less recognizable. Though these distortions permit the repressed urges to gain expression, the expression is weaker and less effective than the initial urge. Thus, pressure to express the urge remains.

RATIONALIZATION AND INTELLECTUALIZATION

Another important defense is **rationalization**. In rationalization, you reduce anxiety by finding a rational explanation (or excuse) for a behavior that you really did for unacceptable reasons. For example, the man who cheats on his income tax may rationalize his behavior as reducing the amount of money spent on weapons in the world.

Rationalization also protects against other kinds of threats. For example, after a failure, rationalization maintains self-esteem. If you don't get into medical school, you may convince yourself that you really didn't want to be a doctor anyway. A man who's turned down for a date may convince himself that the woman really wasn't so great after all. Rationalization is very common in responses to success and failure. It's been shown repeatedly that people tend to take credit for good performances and blame bad performances on forces outside their control (e.g., Krusemark, Campbell, & Clementz, 2008; Ross & Fletcher, 1985; Wilson, Smith, Ross, & Ross, 2004).

Another defense is **intellectualization**: the tendency to think about threats in cold, analytical, and emotionally detached terms. Thinking about events in this way allows people to dissociate their thoughts from their feelings. It separates and isolates the threatening event from the feeling that normally would accompany it (Barrett, Williams, & Fong, 2002). For example, a woman who finds out her husband is dying of cancer may learn as much about cancer and its treatment as she can. By focusing on the disease intellectually and compartmentalizing that information, she shields herself from distress.

DISPLACEMENT AND SUBLIMATION

Two more defense mechanisms are generally considered less neurotic and more adaptive than the others. **Displacement** is shifting an impulse from one target to another. This often happens when the intended target is threatening. Displacement is a defense in such cases because substituting a less threatening target for the original one reduces anxiety. For example, the student who's angry with her professor and takes it out on her very

One view of surgery is that it allows unacceptable aggressive energy to be sublimated and released through a more socially acceptable form of activity.

understanding boyfriend avoids the anxiety that would arise from attacking her professor. The person with an inappropriate lust who displaces that urge onto a permissible target avoids the anxiety that would arise from expressing the desires toward the true target.

Sublimation also lets impulses be expressed, by transforming them to an acceptable form. In this case, it's not something about the target that creates the threat but something about the impulse. Anxiety goes down when a transformed impulse is expressed, instead of the initial one. Freud felt that sublimation, more than any other mechanism, reflects maturity. Sublimation is a process that keeps problems from occurring, rather than functioning after anxiety is aroused.

RESEARCH ON DEFENSES

Although much of psychoanalytic theory has been untested, a fair amount of research has been done on defenses, and interest in this topic is growing again (Cramer, 2000). Consider one study of projection (Halpern, 1977). People who did or did not seem sexually defensive (by a self-report scale) either were or were not exposed to erotic photos; then they made ratings of someone else. Sexually defensive people rated the other person as more "lustful" if they'd seen erotic photos than if they hadn't. Those who weren't defensive about sexual issues didn't do this. This pattern makes sense from a psychoanalytic view. You project only about things that threaten you.

People often express impulses in symbolic form. Sometimes, people live out their impulses through their children or even their pets!

Research has also tested the idea that projection occurs when people actively try to suppress thoughts about something they don't like about themselves (Newman, Duff, & Baumeister, 1997). The active effort to suppress causes thoughts about the unwanted trait to push back and become more accessible (recall Box 8.3). This, in turn, makes the thoughts ready to use when someone else's behavior even remotely fits the trait. There's also evidence that when a stereotype involving that trait applies to someone else, projection is more likely (Govorun, Fuegen, & Payne, 2006).

These studies seem supportive of the idea of defense. But the literature as a whole is ambiguous, and it's often easy to find alternative interpretations. As a result, different readers have drawn different conclusions. Sherwood (1981) found substantial evidence of projection, whereas Holmes (1981) did not. Many are convinced that repression occurs in the short term (e.g., Erdelyi, 1985, 2006; Paulhus & Suedfeld, 1988), others are convinced it does not (Hayne, Garry, & Loftus, 2006).

Psychosexual Development

Freud derived his ideas primarily from a few case histories of adults in therapy. Despite this, he wrote a lot about how personality develops during childhood. He believed that early experiences are critical in determining adult personality.

Freud viewed personality development as movement through a series of stages. Each is associated with an **erogenous zone**: an area of the body that's the focus of sexual energy in that period. For this reason, the stages are called *psychosexual stages*. In Freud's view, the child has conflicts at three stages. If the conflict isn't well resolved, too much energy gets permanently invested in that stage, a process called **fixation**. Because the energy for personality functioning is limited, this means less energy is available to handle conflicts in later stages. As a result, it's harder to resolve later conflicts. In this sense, each stage builds on previous stages.

Fixation can occur for two reasons. A person who's overindulged in a stage may be reluctant to leave it and move on, and a person whose needs are deeply frustrated in a stage *can't* move on until the needs are met. In either case, personality is partly stuck at this stage, as the libido remains partly invested in the concern of that stage. The stronger the fixation, the more libido is invested in it. In a very strong fixation, the person is so preoccupied—albeit unconsciously—that little energy is left for anything else.

THE ORAL STAGE

The **oral stage** is from birth to roughly 18 months. During this time, much of the infant's interaction with the world occurs through the mouth and lips, and gratification focuses

Although oral gratification may be most important during infancy, the pleasure it provides continues throughout life.

in that area. The mouth is the source of tension reduction (eating) and pleasurable sensations (tasting, licking, and sucking). Further, infants are completely dependent on others for their survival. The conflict here concerns the ending of this arrangement: the process of weaning, literal and figurative. That is, toward the end of this stage, children are under increasing pressure to let go of their mother and become less reliant on her.

There are two oral substages. During the first (lasting roughly 6 months), the infant is helpless and dependent. Because he or she is more or less limited to taking things in (food and other experiences), this part is called the *oral incorporative phase*. Freud thought that several traits develop here, depending on what the infant was exposed to. If the infant experienced a benign world, traits such as optimism and trust emerged. If the infant experienced a world that was less supportive, pessimism and mistrust evolved. If the world was too helpful, the infant might develop a strong dependency on others.

The second part of the oral stage starts with teething. It's called the *oral sadistic phase*. Sexual pleasure now comes from biting and chewing (and even inflicting pain—thus sadistic). During this time, the infant is weaned from the bottle or breast and begins to bite and chew food. Traits arising during this phase trace to this newly acquired ability. This phase is thought to determine who will be verbally aggressive later on and who will use "biting" sarcasm.

In general terms, oral individuals should relate to the world orally. They should be more preoccupied than others with food and drink. When stressed, they should be more likely than others to smoke, drink, or bite their nails. When angry, they should be verbally aggressive. Oral characters should be concerned with getting support from others, and they should do things to ease interactions with people.

Is this depiction accurate? Joseph Masling and his colleagues found that tests of oral imagery relate to both obesity (Masling, Rabie, & Blondheim, 1967; Weiss & Masling, 1970) and alcoholism (Bertrand & Masling, 1969). Orality has also been related to measures of interpersonal interest and social skills. For example, oral imagery has been related to the need to nurture others (Holt, 1966) and to interpersonal effectiveness (Masling, Johnson, & Saturansky, 1974). Persons high in oral imagery also volunteer readily for interpersonal tasks (Bornstein & Masling, 1985; Masling, O'Neill, & Jayne, 1981) and rely on other people's judgments during ambiguous tasks (Masling, Weiss, & Rothschild, 1968).

More generally, people who display oral imagery seem highly motivated to gain closeness and support from others and are sensitive to others' reactions. They react physiologically to social isolation (Masling, Price, Goldband, & Katkin, 1981) and to cues of rejection (Masling, O'Neill, & Katkin, 1982)—more than people who display less oral imagery. They also use more physical contact during social interaction (Juni, Masling, & Brannon, 1979) and are more self-disclosing (Juni, 1981) than less oral people.

THE ANAL STAGE

The **anal stage** of development begins at about 18 months and continues into the third year. During this period, the anus is the key erogenous zone, and pleasure comes from defecation. The big event of this period is toilet training. For many children, toilet training is the first time that external constraints are systematically imposed on their satisfaction of internal urges. When toilet training starts, children can no longer relieve themselves whenever and wherever they want. They must learn that there's an appropriate time and place for everything.

The personality characteristics said to arise from fixations during this period depend on how toilet training is approached by parents. Two orientations are typical. One involves urging the child to eliminate at a desired time and place and praising the child for suc-

An anal retentive personality might be displayed in an excessively neat and tidy workplace.

cess. This places a lot of attention on the elimination process and the reward for it. This convinces the child of the value of producing *things* (in this case, urine and feces) at the *right* time and place. To Freud, this provides a basis for adult productivity and creativity.

The second approach to toilet training is more harsh. Rather than praise for a job well done, the emphasis is on punishment, ridicule, and shame for failure. This practice yields two patterns, depending on how the child reacts. If the child adopts an active pattern of rebellion, eliminating forcefully when the parents least want it, a set of *anal expulsive traits* develop. These are tendencies to be messy, cruel, destructive, and overtly hostile.

If the child tries to get even by withholding feces and urine, a set of *anal retentive* traits develops. Anal retentive personality is a rigid, obsessive style. The characteristics that form this pattern are sometimes called the *anal triad*: stinginess, obstinacy, and orderliness. Stinginess reflects the desire to retain feces. Obstinacy reflects the struggle of wills over toilet training. Orderliness is a reaction against the messiness of defecating. This pattern does seem to exist. In one study (Rosenwald, 1972), male students assessed as having the most anal anxiety were also the most compulsively neat (see also Juni & Fischer, 1985; Juni & Lo Cascio, 1985).

THE PHALLIC STAGE

The **phallic stage** begins during the third year and continues through the fifth year. During this period, the focus shifts to the genital organs. This is also the period when most children begin to masturbate, as they become aware of the pleasure that results.

At first, the awakening sexual desires are completely *autoerotic*; that is, sexual pleasure comes totally from self-stimulation. Gradually, however, the libido shifts toward the opposite-sex parent, as boys develop an interest in their mothers and girls develop an interest in their fathers.

Boys' desire to possess their mothers and replace their fathers is termed the **Oedipus complex** (after the character in the ancient Greek play *Oedipus Rex*, who unwittingly marries his mother after killing his father). Comparable feelings in girls are sometimes called an Oedipus complex and sometimes an *Electra* complex (after the Greek character Electra, who persuades her brother to kill both their mother and their mother's lover in revenge for the death of their father). These patterns reflect forces that are similar in many ways, but the forces are displayed differently for boys and girls.

Consider first what happens to boys. Two changes take place: His love for his mother transforms into sexual desire, and his feelings for his father shift toward hostility and hatred, because his father is a rival for his mother's affection. Over time, the boy's jealousy and competitiveness toward his father may become extreme. Such thoughts may induce feelings of guilt. The boy also fears that his father will retaliate against him. In traditional psychoanalytic theory, the boy's fear is quite specific: He

Box 8.4 THE THEORIST AND THE THEORY: FREUD'S OWN OEDIPAL CRISIS

The idea that theorists' personal experiences influenced the very forms taken by their theories is vividly illustrated by the life of Sigmund Freud. In fact, it's widely believed that several aspects of Freud's life had a direct impact on his theories.

Freud's father Jakob, a merchant, was 40 years old at the time of Sigmund's birth (1856). By all accounts, he was a strict and authoritarian father. Given this, it would be no surprise that Freud's feelings about him were ambivalent. In fact, Freud's memories were of hating his father as well as loving him. A hint of scandal concerning Sigmund's birth may also have strained their relationship. Two different dates are indicated in various places as his birth date. Was this a clerical error? Maybe. But some believe that the later date was an effort to disguise the fact that Freud's mother was

pregnant when she and Jakob married (Balmary, 1979).

Jakob Freud had had two sons in a prior marriage and was a grandfather by the time Sigmund was born. His wife Amalie, on the other hand, was only 20. Sigmund was her first child and her special favorite. Sigmund responded by developing a highly idealized image of his mother and a strong affection for her. They had a very close relationship.

In short, the relationships of Freud's childhood had all the elements of what he would later call the *Oedipal conflict*. There was a deep attachment to his mother, which some have said had sexual overtones. He also had a strong ambivalence toward his father. (Freud was even late for his father's funeral, an act he later saw as having been unconsciously motivated.) It seems hard to ignore the possibility that Freud used his own experiences as a model for what he

came to argue were universal aspects of development.

The Oedipal crisis wasn't the only aspect of Freud's thinking to be influenced by events in his own life. World War I, in which 10 million people died, deeply disillusioned him, along with many other Europeans. Newspapers were filled with accounts of the slaughter, which seemed truly purposeless. Two of Freud's sons fought in the war, and his fears for their safety must have placed a great strain on him. Shortly after the end of the war Freud wrote his view of the death instinct: that people have an unconscious wish to die, which they turn outward toward others in murderous actions such as war. It seems likely that this view was partly Freud's attempt to understand how the atrocities of that war could have come to happen. Again, the elements of the theory seem formed by the experiences of the theorist.

---

fears that his father will castrate him to eliminate the source of his lust. Freud termed this **castration anxiety**.

Ultimately, castration anxiety causes the boy to repress his desire for his mother. Castration anxiety also causes the boy to identify with his father. In this context, **identification** refers to the tendency to develop feelings of similarity to and connectedness with someone else. This does several things. First, it gives the boy a kind of "protective coloration." Being like his father makes it seem less likely that his father will harm him. Second, by identifying with the father, the boy reduces his ambivalence toward him. Identification thus paves the way for development of the superego, as the boy introjects his father's values. Finally, by identifying with the father, the boy gains vicarious expression of his sexual urges toward his mother. That is, he gains symbolic access to his mother *through* his father. The more the boy resembles the father, the more easily he can fantasize himself in his father's place.

For girls, the conflict here is more complicated. As we said earlier, girls abandon their love relationship with their mother for a new one with their father. This shift occurs when the girl realizes she has no penis. She withdraws affection from her mother and blames her for her castrated condition (because her mother has no penis either). At the same time, the girl's affection is drawn to her father, who does have a penis. Ultimately, the girl comes to wish that her father would share his penis with her through sex or that he would provide her with the symbolic equivalent of a penis—a baby.

Freud referred to these feelings as **penis envy**. Penis envy is the female counterpart of castration anxiety in boys. As do boys, girls resolve the conflict through identification. By becoming more like her mother, the girl gains vicarious access to her father. She also increases the chances that she will marry someone just like him.

Fixations during the phallic stage result in personalities that reflect the Oedipal conflicts. For example, men may go to great lengths to demonstrate that they haven't been castrated. The way to do that is to seduce as many women as they can or to father many children. Men's attempt to assert their masculinity may also be expressed symbolically by attaining great career success. Alternatively, they may fail sexually and professionally (purposely but unconsciously) because of the guilt they feel over competing with their father for their mother's love.

Among women, the continued Oedipal conflict is displayed by relating to men in a way that's seductive and flirtatious but with a denial of the sexuality. This style of relating first develops toward her father. She was attracted to him first but by now has repressed the sexual desire that first drew her. The pattern then applies to later interactions. This is a woman who excites men with her seductive behavior and is then surprised when they want sex with her.

Freud felt that identifying the Oedipus complex was one of his key contributions (but see Box 8.4). This brief span holds great turmoil: love, hate, guilt, jealousy, and fear. Freud believed that how children negotiate the conflicts and difficulties of the phallic stage determines their attitudes toward sexuality, interpersonal competitiveness, and personal adequacy.

THE LATENCY PERIOD

Fixations that develop during the first three stages presumably form much of the basis of adult personality. At the close of the phallic stage, the child enters a period of relative calm, termed the **latency period**. This period, from about age 6 to the early teens, is a time when sexual and aggressive drives are less active. The lessening of these urges results partly from the emergence of ego and superego. During this period, children turn their attention to other pursuits, often intellectual or social in nature.

With the onset of puberty (toward the end of the latency period), sexual and aggressive urges again intensify. Adolescents have adult sexual desires, but sexual intercourse isn't socially sanctioned for them. This is a time, then, when the ego's coping skills are severely tested.

THE GENITAL STAGE

In later adolescence and adulthood, the person moves into the **genital stage**. If earlier stages have been negotiated well, the person enters this stage with libido still organized around the genitals, and it remains focused there throughout life. Sexual gratification during this stage differs, however, from that of earlier stages. Earlier sex was narcissistic. The child cared only about his or her own sexual pleasure. In the genital stage, a desire develops to share mutual sexual gratification with someone. Thus, the person becomes capable of loving others not just for selfish reasons. This ability to share with others in a warm, caring way and to be concerned with their welfare is the hallmark of the genital stage.

Freud believed that people don't enter the genital stage automatically and that this transition is rarely achieved in its entirety. Most people have less control over their impulses than they should, and most have difficulty in gratifying sexual desires in a completely satisfying and acceptable way. In this sense, the genital personality is an ideal to strive for, rather than an end point to be taken for granted. It is the perfect culmination of psychosexual development, from the analytic point of view.

Exposing the Unconscious

Given the importance of unconscious processes in psychoanalytic theory, it becomes critical to be able to access the urges, impulses, and feelings that are contained there. This might seem a difficult task, considering that what you are trying to access is actively being kept from awareness. Freud believed, though, that it's not as hard as it seems. He thought that unconscious impulses are revealed constantly in everyday events. You just have to look for them.

THE PSYCHOPATHOLOGY OF EVERYDAY LIFE

One way such motives are revealed is in people's mistakes. We all make mistakes. We forget things, get our words jumbled, and have accidents. Freud (1960/1901) referred to such events as the *psychopathology of everyday life* (a phrase that also conveys his belief that all normal life contains a little of the abnormal). He believed such events, far from being random, stem from urges in the unconscious. The urges emerge in a distorted form as mistakes. Thus, memory lapses, slips of speech, and accidents, collectively termed **parapraxes**, provide insights into a person's true desires (for a contrasting opinion, however, see Reason & Mycielska, 1982). Indeed, this idea has been so identified with psychoanalysis that people use the term *Freudian slip* to refer to an error in speech that seems to suggest an unconscious feeling or desire.

As another example, consider forgetting. In the psychoanalytic view, forgetting is an attempt to keep something from consciousness. Sometimes it's easy to see why (e.g., the student who forgets to return an important book to someone she doesn't like, thereby preventing herself from becoming aware of her hostility). At other times, it's harder to see the motive. Yet a motive can often be found, if enough is known about the situation.

If forgetting is a successful attempt to keep thoughts from awareness, slips of the tongue are *un*successful attempts to do the same thing. That is, the person expresses all or part of the unconscious thought or wish, despite the effort to keep it hidden. As with forgetting, the hidden meaning may be obvious to observers. Consider the

Freud believed that accidents often result from an unconscious desire to cause harm.

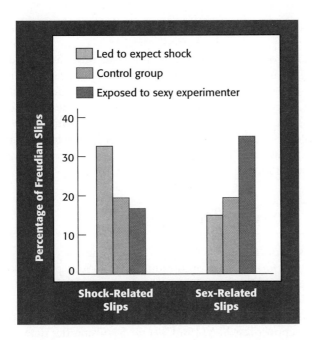

FIGURE 8.3
Freudian slips induced in the laboratory. When participants expected to receive electric shocks, they made more shock-related slips (left side). When participants had been exposed to a provocatively dressed experimenter, they made more sex-related slips (right side).   *Source:* Based on Motley, 1985.

woman who reveals her ambivalent feelings toward her lover by telling him he's exactly the kind of person she'd like to "bury" (instead of "marry"). At other times, the meaning of the slip is less clear.

There's evidence that verbal slips are related to anxiety, although the evidence falls short of indicating that the anxiety is unconscious. Motley (1985) and his colleagues induced people to make a certain kind of slip, in which a pair of words was read as a different word pair (for example, saying "flute fry" instead of "fruit fly"). The research required creating specific pairs that are easy to misread, producing slips with particular overtones. The research involved creating specific anxieties and seeing whether those anxieties increase relevant slips.

For example, in one case men were made to feel anxious about receiving electric shocks. In another, the session was run by a provocatively dressed woman to arouse anxiety over sexual issues. Both conditions included word pairs that could be misread as shock related (e.g., "damn shock" instead of "sham dock") and pairs that could be misread as sex related (e.g., "happy sex" instead of "sappy hex"). As illustrated in Figure 8.3, men led to be nervous about shocks made more shock-related slips than anyone else, and men led to think about sex made more slips with sexual connotations than anyone else. Sexual slips were also more frequent among men high on a measure of sex guilt (Motley, 1985).

DREAMS

Freud (1953/1900) believed the unconscious also reveals itself through dreams, which he called "the royal road to the unconscious." Dreams have two kinds of content. **Manifest content** is the sensory images—what most of us think of as the dream. More interesting to Freud, though, was the **latent content**—the unconscious thoughts, feelings, and wishes behind the manifest content. Latent content tells why a dream takes the form it does.

Latent content has three sources. The first is the *sensory stimulation* that bombards us as we sleep: a thunderstorm, a passing siren, or the barking of a dog. Such sounds can prompt dreams and be absorbed into them. The second source is the thoughts, ideas, and feelings connected to waking life—**current concerns**. For example, you may have been thinking about an upcoming exam, an interesting person you just met, or a financial problem you have. The third source is unconscious impulses, which are blocked from expression while you're awake and are often related to core conflicts. For this reason, the impulse is often infantile in form and primitive in content. Freud believed this aspect of latent content reveals the most about a person's personality.

Assessment: Projective Techniques

The preceding section focused on ways in which the unconscious reveals itself in everyday life. More formal ways of assessing unconscious processes have also been developed. Collectively, they are called **projective techniques**. They confront people with ambiguous stimuli. Because there is no obvious response, responses are believed to reflect unconscious feelings, attitudes, desires, and needs. (Recall discussion of the Thematic Apperception Test [TAT] in Chapter 5.) Using the defense mechanism of projection, people perceive aspects of themselves in the stimulus. What's projected presumably reflects the unconscious.

FIGURE 8.4
Example of inkblot similar to those used in the Rorschach test. *Source:* Courtesy of Jeremy Matthews Scheier and Meredith Matthews Scheier

The best-known projective technique, developed by Hermann Rorschach (1942), is the **Rorschach inkblot test**. Rorschach used the criterion keying approach to test development (described in Chapter 3) to select a set of ten inkblots. Each inkblot is bilaterally symmetrical (approximately the same on both sides of an imaginary center line; see Figure 8.4). The ink on five of them is all black, but the intensity is uneven, ranging from solid black to light gray. Two have both black and red ink. Three have pastel colors, including blue, green, yellow, pink, and orange.

The Rorschach usually is administered to one person at a time in a two-stage procedure. First, the person views the inkblots in a predetermined order and indicates what he or she sees in them—or what the inkblot resembles or suggests—while the examiner records what's being said. Then the person views all ten cards again. The examiner reminds the person what he or she said earlier and asks what it was about the card that made the person say that.

Several systems have been devised for scoring the Rorschach test, the most popular being that of John Exner (1974, 1993). In Exner's system, the responses are first compared against those of people with known personalities. Then, the responses are examined as a progression from one card to the next. Finally, responses are analyzed in terms of location (where the response focuses), determinants (form, color, shading, or perceived movement), and content (the response's subject). Analyses of these features is thought to reveal information about the person's unconscious motivations and feelings.

Although the Rorschach generates interesting information, it has serious psychometric problems (Lilienfeld, Wood, & Garb, 2000). Exner and his collaborators have tried to improve the scoring, but their efforts have not been entirely well received (Lilienfeld et al., 2000; Wood, Nezworski, & Stejskal, 1996a, 1996b). On the other side, data have suggested that the Rorschach is better at identifying depressed and psychotic persons than the MMPI-2, a widely used tool of psychological assessment (Ganellen, 1996).

Many psychologists who favor projective tests respond to criticisms by saying that psychometric criteria are irrelevant to the Rorschach's usefulness. In their view, its value is in the insights it gives the examiner. Perhaps psychologists should stop treating the Rorschach as a test and think of it as a tool. From that angle, it's an interview aid in the hands of a trained clinician, suggesting hypotheses worth further investigation. Even if the Rorschach is seen only as a clinical aid, though, it won't likely be discarded soon as part of the psychoanalytic assessment battery.

Problems in Behavior, and Behavior Change

Our discussion of problems and how they can be dealt with emphasizes the themes stressed throughout the chapter. Freud believed the unconscious holds the secrets of people's difficulties in life. Only by delving into the unconscious can those difficulties be identified and resolved. This section begins by considering the psychoanalytic perspective on ways in which problems arise.

ORIGINS OF PROBLEMS

Problems have several possible origins. One origin is childhood experiences. As described earlier, Freud believed adult personality is determined by early psychosexual development. He considered it rare for a person to enter the later stages of development unmarked. Most people are partly fixated at earlier stages. If those fixations are strong, a lot of energy is invested in them. In a very strong fixation, the preoccupation (albeit unconscious) leaves the person with little energy for anything else. This is one source of problems: overinvestment of energy in a fixation. This prevents flexible adult functioning by depleting energy the ego needs (Baumeister, 2002).

Another source of problems is broad repression of basic drives and urges. If an overly punitive superego or a harsh environment causes too many urges to be buried, the person's basic nature will be distorted and denied. The repressed needs will be able to squeeze their way past the repression only in twisted forms. This isn't really effective in terms of meeting the needs. And again, the repression required to keep the needs hidden is a constant drain on energy available to the ego.

A third source of problems is buried trauma. Although traumatic incidents can occur at any point in life, most discussion of trauma focuses on early childhood. Indeed, at one point early in the evolution of his thinking, Freud believed most of his patients had suffered childhood sexual abuse. The "seduction theory," as it came to be known, was later abandoned when Freud decided the seductions hadn't actually taken place.

It was this change in thinking that led to Freud's theory of the Oedipal conflict, in which children deal with a sexual attraction to their opposite-sex parent. The Oedipal theory accounted for sexual imagery among patients, and it did so in a way that didn't require Freud to believe that large numbers of parents had seduced their children. Despite this change, Freud's theory clearly holds a place for traumas such as sexual and physical abuse. His altered view simply reflects his conclusion that abuse isn't common. Still, a child who experiences physical abuse, especially repeated abuse, has a deeply unpleasant part of reality to deal with. The same is true of a child who is sexually abused.

These three points of origin for problems differ, and the problems that result can also differ. All three paths, however, share one mechanism: In each case, the original fixation, urge, or trauma is repressed. This repression may protect the person, but it does so at a cost.

BEHAVIOR CHANGE

What can be done about this situation? The therapeutic methods of psychoanalysis developed by trial and error in Freud's practice. After initially trying hypnosis, Freud stumbled on a procedure in which the person was simply to say aloud whatever came to mind—a procedure called **free association**. He discovered that this procedure enabled material hidden in the unconscious to gradually emerge. This procedure also helped convince Freud that what emerged often wasn't literally true, and it led him to rethink how he viewed the content of free association. Free association was producing something important, but it wasn't quite what it had seemed to be.

In Freud's newer view, unconscious material emerges through free association in *symbolic* form. The symbolism makes it less threatening, thus letting it emerge. However, free association often creates a jumble of symbols that makes no sense on the surface. Yet, as in a crossword puzzle, they provide a partial context from which missing elements can be inferred.

As noted earlier, many problems serious enough to be manifested in behavior are thought to stem from repressed conflicts and urges and from suppressed libidinal energy. The goal of therapy is to uncover the conflicts and loose the restrained energy (see also Box 8.5). Free association is a first step, because it allows symbolic access to the problem. It rarely gets to the heart of the problem, though, because of the threat in the repressed material.

BOX 8.5 REPRESSION, DISCLOSURE, AND PHYSICAL HEALTH

Our main discussion focuses on the idea that repression has a psychological cost. Evidence is accumulating, however, that holding back thoughts and feelings can also have a *physical* cost.

An early study of women undergoing breast biopsies (Greer & Morris, 1975) found that those who reported suppressing their emotions (most notably, anger) were more likely to have cancer than those who didn't (see also Jensen, 1987). Another study found that women who said they suppressed their anger had more atherosclerosis over a 10-year period (Matthews, Owens, Kuller, Sutton-Tyrrell, & Jansen-McWilliams, 1998). Not all evidence supports the view that suppression relates to disease (O'Donnell, Fisher, Rickard, & McConaghy, 2000; Price et al., 2001). But enough support exists to make the idea worth further study.

The flip side of this idea is that releasing distressing thoughts and feelings can have physical benefits. James Pennebaker and his colleagues have been at the forefront of research on disclosure of suppressed thoughts and feelings (Pennebaker, 1989;

Pennebaker & Chung, 2007; Sexton & Pennebaker, 2009; see also Smyth, 1998). In these studies, participants described (anonymously, in most studies) their deepest thoughts and feelings about a specific nontraumatic event or about "the most upsetting or traumatic experience of your entire life." Ideally, the event the participant talked about (or wrote about) was one that he or she had not talked about much with others. Thus, it was more likely to be something the participant had repressed, at least partially. The disclosure of thoughts and feelings typically took place for about 20 minutes at a time across 4 successive days.

The short-term effect of disclosing trauma is that people feel more distress. In the longer term, however, self-disclosure seems to have health benefits. In an early study, students who disclosed about traumatic events were less likely to visit the health center in the next 6 months than those not asked to disclose (Pennebaker & Beall, 1986). The results of other work suggest that disclosure influences the functioning of the immune system (Pennebaker, Kiecolt-Glaser, & Glaser, 1988). In a study of Holocaust survivors, those who seemed to "let

go" the most during disclosure were least likely to visit their physicians later (Pennebaker, 1989).

Why might disclosure of painful memories have health benefits? Pennebaker has pursued the idea that the mechanism lies in the cognitive changes that occur during and after the disclosures. He has found that people who come to organize their experiences into causal narratives benefit more than people who do not (Pennebaker & Graybeal, 2001). It apparently isn't *having* a coherent story that helps, but rather the process of *creating* the story.

Pennebaker (1993) argued that the body expresses itself linguistically and biologically at the same time. As we struggle to create meaning from trauma, we create beneficial changes in biological functions, as well. The result is better physical functioning and better health. This view of the effects of emotional expression surely will continue evoke controversy and interest. It's a viewpoint with many important implications. If it continues to be supported by research evidence, it will change the way many people think about therapy and even about such activities as keeping a journal.

Indeed, people in therapy sometimes actively fight against becoming aware of repressed conflicts and impulses. This struggle is called **resistance**. Resistance can be conscious or unconscious. In either case, it's usually a sign that something important is nearby, that the person is close to revealing something sensitive. Resistance provides an illustration of how emotionally wrenching psychoanalytic therapy can be. The person in therapy is trying to uncover distressing truths—truths that have been buried in the unconscious precisely *because* they're too painful to admit. It's no wonder that the process of uncovering them is hard.

An important element in psychoanalytic therapy is **transference**. Transference is a set of *displacements*. Specifically, feelings toward other people in the patient's life are displaced (transferred) onto the therapist. The feelings can be love or hatred. Transference serves as another defense, in that the therapist provokes less anxiety than do the original objects of the feelings. Transference can help point out the significance of the feelings that are being displaced. When transference occurs, then, its interpretation is an important part of the therapy process.

Table 8.1 Three Origins of Problems in Personality and the Goal of Psychoanalysis in Treating Each.

Origin	Goal
Fixation	Relive prior conflict to work through
Repressed trauma	Relive experience for catharsis of feelings
Repressed basic needs	Gain emotional insight into the needs and their acceptability

The goal of psychoanalytic psychology is **insight**. This term doesn't mean an intellectual understanding. Rather, it implies the re-experiencing of the emotional reality of repressed conflicts, memories, or urges, previously unconscious parts of one's personality (see Table 8.1). Intellectual understanding has no power to change the person. For a cognitive reorganization to be useful, it must come in the context of an emotional catharsis, a freeing of pent-up energy. On the other hand, emotional release doesn't help unless there is also reorganization (Kelly, Klusas, von Weiss, & Kenny, 2001).

DOES PSYCHOANALYTIC THERAPY WORK?

Psychoanalytic therapy is long (literally years), expensive, and usually painful. Given these costs, how effective is it? Early reviews concluded that therapy in general, including psychoanalysis, isn't very helpful (Eysenck, 1961; Feldman, 1968; Wolpe, 1981). Other reviews, however, found that therapy works and that analytic therapy works about as well as other techniques (Smith & Glass, 1977; Smith, Glass, & Miller, 1980). Very recent evidence indicates that long-term psychoanalysis may reduce the use of medical care (Berghout, Zevalkink, & Hakkaart-Van Roijen, 2010; de Maat, Philipszoon, Schoevers, Dekker, & De Jonghe, 2007).

Part of the difficulty in interpreting studies is that success can be defined in several ways, and what definition is used can affect the conclusions drawn. Psychoanalysts tend to define success by how much insight patients gain into their conflicts and dynamics. This insight may or may not yield less distress. Given that many psychoanalysts believe the goal is to produce insight (and not necessarily reduce stress), it's hard to be sure what negative findings say about the success of psychoanalytic therapy (for details, see Fisher & Greenberg, 1977).

The Psychoanalytic Perspective: Problems and Prospects

The psychoanalytic view on personality has been both influential and controversial. From the start, people were reluctant to accept certain aspects of it. Many were incensed by the prominence of sexual themes, being shocked that anyone would suggest that the behavior of young children is sexually motivated.

The scientific community has faulted psychoanalysis on other grounds. The problem here is that the theory is very hard to test, partly because many of its concepts are defined ambiguously. An example is *libido*. Freud used this term to refer to sexual energy, a psychological quality arising from physiological processes. We know little else about it. Where does it come from? What makes it sexual? How do you measure it? Without a way to measure it, you can't study it.

Much of the ambiguity of psychoanalytic concepts comes from the fact that Freud thought about personality in such a metaphorical way. This metaphorical approach is deeply embedded in descriptions of the theory. It's very difficult to know when to read Freud literally and when to read him metaphorically. Consider, for example, the Oedipal complex. Should we believe Freud meant literally that every boy comes to desire his mother sexually at around age 4? Or should we assume he was using the Oedipal theme as a metaphor for the conflict between young children and their parents? Freud wrote at one point that many of the specific explanatory devices he used could be replaced or discarded without damaging the theory (Silverman, 1976). Clearly, then, parts of what he wrote shouldn't be taken literally. Unfortunately, we don't know which parts.

A related problem arises for mechanisms of defense. Here, the problem is that defenses provide limitless flexibility. Defenses can be invoked to explain virtually anything that might occur. If a defense is working poorly and threatening material is coming too close to awareness, a different defense emerges, potentially creating even the opposite effect. Flexibility is good, because it lets a theory account for a lot, but it also makes prediction hard. If a theory is too flexible, *any* finding can be reconciled with it. If it can explain any outcome, its predictions can never be disconfirmed. Unfortunately, if a theory can never be disconfirmed, it can never really be confirmed, either. Interestingly, despite these criticisms, the idea that humans have defenses has been absorbed deeply into the fabric of today's understanding of personality. This idea has been widely accepted, even by people who accept nothing else about the psychoanalytic viewpoint.

Another criticism that scientific psychologists make against psychoanalytic theory concerns the kind of evidence on which it rests. Critics disparage Freud's heavy reliance on case studies in developing his ideas, particularly those involving infantile sexuality. It's hard to be sure whether different observers would draw the same conclusions, even when looking at the same case. The problem of reliability is even further compounded by the fact that Freud acted both as theorist–researcher and as therapist. Freud's actions as a participant observer may have biased the kinds of things his patients said even more than usual (Powell & Boer, 1994). Indeed, there's even evidence that Freud was sometimes highly directive with patients (Esterson, 1998).

Freud's reliance on patients allowed bias in another way, as well. The number of cases Freud relied on for a database was distressingly small. In all his writings, Freud described the case histories of only a dozen or so people. He carefully screened potential patients and allowed into therapy only those he thought were good candidates. Thus, he developed his ideas from observing a very small set of cases that were selected in a biased way. We can't be sure how much or in what ways these people differed from the overall population, but they certainly weren't chosen randomly.

Another criticism of psychoanalytic ideas is the tendency of its proponents to mix facts with inferences. For example, observations led Freud to infer the existence (and universality) of an Oedipal complex. He then went on to discuss the Oedipal complex as though its existence were a fact. This tendency to mix fact with inference has contributed to an intellectual climate in psychoanalytic circles in which basic concepts have gone untested—because it was thought they didn't *need* to be tested (Crews, 1996; Esterson, 1993).

Despite these problems, there's been a resurgence of interest in the ideas that make up both the topographic model and the structural model (Bargh, 1997). With respect to the topography of the mind, many who start from different perspectives now argue that important aspects of memory cannot be brought to consciousness voluntarily. In some cases, this is because the thing we're looking for (by its very nature) can be used but not viewed. In other cases, it's because the thing we might be looking for has become so automatic that it's fallen out of our mental "address book." Although these aren't quite the same as the unconscious phenomena Freud emphasized, they represent new interest in the idea that the mind has more than two regions.

With respect to the structural model, it is being re-emphasized that we shouldn't get too distracted by the idea that the mind has three components. Rather, it has three modes of functioning (Grigsby & Stevens, 2000). Moreover, we should take the descriptions of the modes less literally. The id is simply the psychological nature of the infant. Infantile qualities are overlaid in all of us by effects of socialization, but those infantile qualities remain, in some sense, the basic structure from which we grew. The id is the part that *wants*—wants as the 1-year-old wants, without regard to dangers or disapprovals. We all still have that part, and it still makes its presence known. The ego is the set of restraints we learn, restraints that diminish the pain we experience from grabbing too fast for what we want without looking for danger. The superego is the abstract rules we learn, to become part of a society in which we can't always have our way, even if we wait patiently.

The idea that humans begin life grabbing for what they want when they first want it, and only gradually learn to restrain themselves, makes a lot of sense. The idea that people later learn abstractions concerning morality also makes sense. So does the idea that the moral abstractions can conflict with the wants. In sum, the structural model expresses a fair amount of truth about the human experience. Indeed, you will encounter similar ideas in other perspectives.

Given the problems just outlined, why has psychoanalysis been so popular? Indeed, there's been a resurgence of interest in it in recent years (e.g., Bargh, 1997; Grigsby & Stevens, 2000). There seem to be at least three reasons for its enduring popularity. One is that it was the first major theory of personality. Whenever something comes first, its influence persists for a long time. Second, Freud spoke to questions that lie at the heart of personality: How does childhood influence later life? What is mental health? To what extent are people's motives accessible to them? The questions he posed began to stake out the territory of what would become personality psychology.

A final reason concerns the intuitive appeal of the major themes of psychoanalysis. Apart from their scientific status, notions such as unconscious motivation, psychosexual development, and the intrapsychic tug-of-war of conflicting pressures from the id, ego, and superego have an emotional appeal. These ideas are novel, exciting, and interesting. In a word, they are *seductive*. Psychoanalytic theory undoubtedly took root partly because it portrayed personality in a way that people found—and continue to find—interesting.

• SUMMARY •

Freud's topographical model assumes three regions of mind: the conscious, the preconscious (ordinary memory), and the unconscious (a part of mind that isn't accessible to consciousness). The unconscious holds threatening or unacceptable ideas and urges.

Freud's structural model assumes three facets of personality. The id (the original part) is the source of all energy. It follows the pleasure principle (that all needs should be immediately gratified), exists only in the unconscious, and uses primary process thinking (primitive and separate from reality). The ego eventually develops because the id ignores the demands of the external world, and those demands cannot adaptively be ignored. The ego follows the reality principle (that behavior must take into account external reality), operates in all three regions of the mind, and tries to see that the id's impulses are gratified in a realistic way. The ego uses secondary process (reality-based) thought. The third facet, the superego, is a representation of the rules by which parents reward and punish the child. It has two parts: Ego ideal is standards of moral perfection, and conscience is a representation of the behaviors that are considered bad. Both function in all three regions of the mind. Once the superego develops, the ego must mediate among the id, superego, and reality.

Id impulses form two categories: Life instincts aim for self-preservation and sexual pleasure. Death instincts are self-destructive and may turn outward as aggression. Evidence of a death instinct may exist in cell biology, in the form of apoptosis. Catharsis is the emotional release resulting from the release of an impulse.

Anxiety is a warning signal to the ego. Reality anxiety is fear of a threat in the world. Neurotic anxiety is fear that id impulses will get out of control and get you in trouble. Moral anxiety is fear of violating the superego's moral code. The ego deals with anxiety (and sometimes prevents it from arising) by employing defense mechanisms.

The basic defense is repression: forcing id impulses and other threatening material out of consciousness. Denial is a refusal to acknowledge the reality of something that lies outside the mind. Other defenses, which typically act along with repression, are projection (attributing an unacceptable impulse to someone else), rationalization (developing an acceptable but incorrect explanation for your action), intellectualization (separating your thoughts from your feelings and allowing the thoughts but not the feelings to be in awareness), displacement (shifting an impulse from one target to another, usually a safer one), and sublimation (transforming an unacceptable impulse to an acceptable one).

Freud argued that child development proceeds through psychosexual stages and that adult personality is influenced by how crises are resolved at each stage. In the oral stage, sexuality centers on the mouth, and the crisis involves being weaned. In the anal stage, sexuality centers on the anus, and the crisis involves toilet training. In the phallic stage, sexuality centers on the genitals, and the crisis experienced there (which results in Oedipal and Electra complexes) involves lust for the opposite-sex parent and fear of and rivalry with the same-sex parent. The latency period is a calm interval with no serious conflict. The genital period is maturity, in which genital sexuality shifts from selfish narcissism to mutual sharing.

The psychoanalytic orientation holds that the unconscious is the key to personality. Freud believed that the unconscious reveals itself in many ways in day-to-day life. *Parapraxes* are acts of forgetting and slips of the tongue and pen that occur when unconscious desires cause you to act in a way other than as you consciously intend. The unconscious is also revealed in dreams, which have manifest content (what's in the dream) and latent content (the determinants of the dream, many of which are unconscious).

The unconscious can also be revealed more formally, through projective assessment techniques, such as the Rorschach inkblot test. Projective techniques allow the person's unconscious to release symbolic versions of threatening material while describing ambiguous stimuli. The Rorschach is controversial, in that its reliability and validity have not been well supported by research evidence.

In the psychoanalytic view, behavioral problems may derive from fixations (unresolved conflicts during psychosexual development), from a general repression of libido, or from repressed traumas. An important aspect of psychoanalytic therapy is free association: saying whatever comes to mind without censoring it in any way. This approach typically produces an incomplete matrix of symbolic meanings, from which other elements can be inferred.

People in therapy often display resistance, which implies that the ego is trying to defend itself against something the therapy is starting to touch on. Often, the person in therapy displays transference, displacing onto the therapist unacceptable feelings that actually pertain to someone else. The goal of the therapy is insight, an emotional experiencing of previously unconscious parts of personality.

Research on the effectiveness of psychoanalytic therapy has produced mixed results. Yet even in the absence of strong support for the usefulness of psychoanalytic therapy, many people continue to undertake it because they believe it provides benefits that are not adequately assessed by the measures used in outcome research.

• GLOSSARY •

Anal stage   The second stage of development, centered around issues in toilet training.

Anxiety   A feeling warning the ego that something bad is about to happen.

Apoptosis   Biologically programmed cell death.

Castration anxiety   A boy's fear (during the phallic stage) that his father will perceive him as a rival and castrate him.

Catharsis   The release of emotional tension.

Conscience   The part of the superego that punishes violations of moral standards.

Conscious   The part of the mind that holds what you are currently aware of.

Current concerns   Preoccupations in your current waking life.

Death instincts (Thanatos)   Self-destructive instincts, often turned outward as aggression.

Defense mechanism   An ego-protective strategy to hide threats from yourself and thereby reduce anxiety.

Denial   A refusal to believe that some real condition exists.

Displacement   The shifting of an impulse from its original target to a different one.

Ego   The rational part of the personality that deals pragmatically with reality.

Ego ideal   The part of the superego that represents perfection and rewards for good behavior.

Ego strength   The ability of the ego to function despite competing demands of the id, superego, and reality.

Erogenous zone   A sexually responsive area of the body.

Eros   *See* Life instincts or sexual instincts (Eros).

Fixation   The condition of being partly stuck in a stage of psychosexual development.

Free association   A therapy procedure of saying without hesitation whatever comes to mind.

Genital stage   The final stage of development, characterized by mature and mutual sexual involvement with another.

Id   The original, primitive component of personality; the source of all energy.

Identification   Developing feelings of similarity to and connectedness with another person.

Insight   An emotional re-experiencing of earlier conflicts in your life that occurs during therapy.

Intellectualization   The process of thinking about something clinically and without emotion.

Introjection   Absorbing the values of your parents into your superego.

Latency period   The period in which the crises of the phallic stage give way to a temporary calm.

Latent content   The underlying sources of symbolic dream images.

Libido   The collective energy of the life instincts.

Life instincts or sexual instincts (Eros)   Survival and sexual instincts.

Manifest content   The images that make up the dream experience as it's recalled.

Moral anxiety   The fear of behaving in conflict with the superego's moral code.

Neurotic anxiety   The fear that your id impulses will get out of control and get you into trouble.

Oedipus complex   The mix of desire for the opposite-sex parent and fear of or hatred for the other parent.

Oral stage   The first stage of psychosexual development, in which oral needs create a crisis over weaning.

Parapraxis   A slip of the tongue, behavior, or memory.

Penis envy   A girl's envy of males resulting from feelings of having been castrated.

Phallic stage   The third stage of development, in which a crisis occurs over sexual desire for the opposite-sex parent.

Pleasure principle   The idea that impulses should be gratified immediately.

Preconscious   The region of the mind that corresponds to ordinary memory.

Primary process   The id process that creates an unconscious image of a desired object.

Projection   Ascribing a threatening urge or quality in yourself to someone else.

Projective techniques   An assessment in which you project from the unconscious onto ambiguous stimuli.

Rationalization   Finding a plausible but incorrect explanation for an unacceptable action or event.

Reality anxiety   The fear caused by real danger in the world.

Reality principle   The idea that actions must take into account the constraints of external reality.

Reality testing   The ego's checking to see whether plans will work before they are put into action.

Repression   The process of preventing an idea or impulse from becoming conscious.

Resistance   An attempt to avoid becoming conscious of threatening material in therapy.

Rorschach inkblot test   A projective test that uses inkblots as ambiguous stimuli.

Secondary process   The ego process of rationally seeking an object to satisfy a desire.

Structural model   Freud's model of three components of personality.

Sublimation   Alteration of an id impulse into a socially acceptable act.

Superego   The component of personality that seeks moral perfection.

Thanatos   *See* Death instincts (Thanatos).

Topographical model   Freud's model of three regions, or areas, of the mind.

Transference   The displacement onto your therapist of feelings that are tied to an object of conflict.

Unconscious   The region of the mind that's not accessible to consciousness.

Wish fulfillment   The creation of an unconscious image of a desired object.

Psychosocial Theories

Ever since high school, Christina has had a particular pattern in her love relationships with men. She is close and clingy as the relationship is first being established. Later on, an ambivalent quality emerges. She wants closeness, but at the same time, she does things that drive her lover away: She gets upset with him, gets into arguments over nothing, and isn't satisfied by anything he does to calm her. As he gets more and more irritated by this and their relationship becomes more and more strained, Christina makes her final move: She breaks up. "Why can't I ever find the right kind of man?" she wonders.

THE PSYCHOSOCIAL perspective on personality has its roots partly in the psycho-analytic perspective. Freud attracted many followers, all of whom differed from him in important ways. The group that made the most impact—and evolved into an active part of today's personality psychology—focused on the idea that people's primary tasks in life concern relationships.

This perspective started by examining how infants interact with and are affected by other people. Eventually, it grew to carry that theme onward to the rest of life, viewing adult personality as a reflection of the same forces that are critical in infancy. This chapter describes these ideas.

Object Relations Theories

We begin with a group of theories that have diverse origins and terminologies yet are strikingly similar. They are referred to with the phrase **object relations** (for overviews, see Klein, 1987; Masling & Bornstein, 1994; St. Clair, 1986). In the phrase *object relations*, the "object" is a *person*. Thus, these theories focus on one person's relations to others.

The core theme derives from Freud's idea (Eagle, 1984) that the ego develops bonds to external objects to release id energies effectively. Object relations theories focus on these bonds but only for people as objects. In these theories, the point isn't to satisfy the id. Instead, the bond is a basic *ego function*. It is personality's main focus (Fairbairn, 1954). As in many other neoanalytic theories, the emphasis is on the ego, rather than the id (see Box 9.1).

Object relations theories were developed by several people. They share two broad themes (Klein, 1987; St. Clair, 1986). First, they all emphasize that a person's pattern of relating to others is laid down in early childhood. Second, they all assume that the patterns tend to recur over and over throughout life.

One influential object relations theorist was Margaret Mahler (1968; Mahler, Pine, & Bergman, 1975; see also Blanck & Blanck, 1986). She believed that newborns begin life in a state of psychological fusion with others. In her view, personality development is a process of breaking down this fusion, of becoming an individual who's separate and distinct. The period when the infant is fused with its mother is called **symbiosis**. Boundaries between mother and self haven't arisen yet (e.g., the infant doesn't distinguish its mother's nipple from its own thumb). At around 6 months of age, the child starts to become aware of its separate existence. Mahler called this process **separation–individuation**. It involves gradual exploration away from mother.

The child experiences a built-in conflict between two pressures during this time. The first is a wish to be taken care of by mother and united with her. The second is a fear of being overwhelmed in a merger with her and a desire to establish one's own selfhood. Thus, the child strives for individuation and separation but also wants the earlier sense of union. This conflict is important in adult behavior, as well.

The mother's behavior during this period is important to the child's later adjustment. She should combine emotional availability with a gentle nudge toward independence. If the mother is too present in the child's experience, the child won't be able to establish a separate existence. If the mother pushes too much toward individuation, the child will experience a sense of rejection and loss called *separation anxiety*.

Eventually (at about age 3), the child develops a stable mental representation of its mother. Now, mother will be with the child all the time symbolically. The *object*

Box 9.1 Ego Psychology

Many people who followed Freud came to believe that he didn't give enough attention or credit to the ego. As a result, many neoanalytic theories were proposed that focused on the ego and its functions. Although the theories are diverse, they all emphasize development of the ego for its own sake.

Robert White (1959, 1963) introduced two motivational concepts to discuss the ego. **Effectance motivation** is the motive to have an effect or an impact on your surroundings. White believed effectance is a basic motive. During early childhood, it's the major outlet for the ego's energies. This motive evolves into **competence motivation**, the motive to be effective in dealing with the environment. This motive underlies adaptive ego functioning. Competence motivation can be exercised endlessly, as there are always new competencies to attain. The competence motive thus moves the person toward ever-new challenges and masteries.

Alfred Adler (1927, 1929, 1931), another ego psychologist, also argued that people strive for greater competence, but for different reasons. Adler proposed that whenever a person has **feelings of inferiority** (any sense of inadequacy), a compensatory process is activated and the person strives for superiority. Adler believed that inferiority feelings and superiority strivings continue to cycle with each other constantly. The result is that people keep working to get better, more proficient at what they do. Adler viewed the struggle for increased competence to be an important part of healthy ego functioning, calling it the "great upward drive." He believed that healthy people continue to function this way throughout life.

In both of these views, the primary goal of the ego is to better adapt to the world. Adaptation has two aspects. The first is learning to restrain impulses. Doing so lets you gain better command of your transactions with the world and avoid trouble from acting impulsively. Part of adaptation, though, is being flexible in dealing with the world. Thus, the

second aspect of adaptation is knowing when to restrain yourself and when to behave more freely.

These issues lie at the heart of the work of ego psychologists Jeanne H. Block and Jack Block (1980; J. Block, 2002; J. Block & Block, 2006). They called the first aspect of adaptation **ego control**. This is the extent to which the person inhibits impulses. At one extreme are people who undercontrol—who can't delay gratification, who express their feelings and desires immediately. At the other end are people who overcontrol—who delay gratification endlessly, inhibit their actions and feelings, and insulate themselves from outside distractions. The other aspect of ego functioning is **ego resiliency**. This is flexibility. It's the capacity to modify your usual level of ego control—in either direction—to adapt to a given situation. People low in ego resilience can't break out of their usual way of relating to the world, even when it's temporarily good to do so. People who are ego resilient are resourceful and adapt well to changing circumstances.

---

relation is internalized. In the future, the child will view its mother through this image and will generalize it to other people. In many ways, the child will act toward others as though they were its mother (and father).

Often, the early years include some stresses—a sense of rejection from a parent or too much smothering fusion. If so, the stresses are carried by the child's internal object representations into later life. Because the internalization derives from infant experiences, there can be a lot of distortion. What matters, though, isn't what *happens* in childhood but what the child *experiences* as happening.

You may not be very persuaded by the idea that you relate to others as though they were your mother and father. You may think you treat everyone uniquely. An object relations theorist would reply that you think this because you're looking at yourself from *inside* your patterns (Andersen & Chen, 2002). Being inside them, you don't notice them. You notice only variations *within* the patterns. You think the variations are big, but in many ways, they're really quite minor.

In this view, the pattern of relating to others that you develop in early childhood forms the core of your way of relating to others for the rest of your life. Indeed, this pattern forms the very core of your personality. You take it for granted, as much as any other aspect of your personality. It's the lens through which you view not just your parents but the entire world.

SELF PSYCHOLOGY

Another important neoanalyst was Heinz Kohut. Because Kohut felt that relationships form the structure of the self, his theory is called **self psychology** (A. Goldberg, 1985). Despite this label, his theory focuses on experiences that others termed *object relations*.

Kohut began with the idea that people have an essential **narcissism**: a pattern of self-centered needs that must be satisfied through others. He coined the term **selfobject** to refer to someone who helps satisfy your needs. In early childhood, selfobjects (parents) are experienced as extensions of the self. Later, *selfobject* means any person *as he or she is experienced within the structure of the self*. Even then, a selfobject exists from the self's point of view and to serve the self's needs.

Kohut thought the child acquires a self through interaction with parents. Parents engage in **mirroring**: giving support to the child and responding in an empathic, accepting way. Mirroring gratifies the child's narcissistic needs, because it makes the child temporarily the center of the universe. The child's sense of self is grandiose at first. The illusion of all importance must be sustained to some degree throughout development, to create a sense of self-importance to be carried into adulthood. It also must be tempered, though, so the child can deal with difficulties and frustrations later in life.

In a healthy personality, the grandiosity is modified and channeled into realistic activities. It turns into ambition and self-esteem. If there are severe failures of mirroring, though, the child never develops an adequate sense of self. Later in life, this child will have deeper narcissistic needs than other people, because his or her needs have gone unmet. As a result, the child will continue relating to other people immaturely. A delicate balance is required here: The parents must give the child enough mirroring to nurture development but not too much. This is similar, in some ways, to the balance in Mahler's theory regarding separation–individuation and fusion with the other.

Mirroring continues to be important in relationships throughout life (Tesser, 1991). Later mirroring involves **transference** from parents to other selfobjects. This use of the term means that you *transfer* the orientation you've developed to your

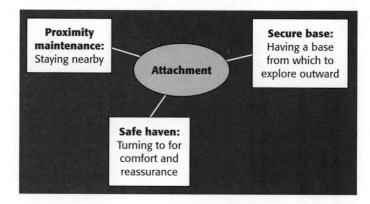

FIGURE 9.1
Three defining features of attachment and three functions of attachment. Attachment provides a secure base for exploration, keeps the infant nearby and safe, and provides a source of comfort.
Source: Based on Hazan & Shaver, 1994.

Early attachment patterns can influence the quality of later social relationships.

parents to other people, using it as a frame of reference for them (Andersen & Chen, 2002). In effect, other people become parent substitutes, and you expect them to mirror you as your parents did. This is like Mahler's idea that the internal object relation corresponding to a parent is used in forming later relationships.

Attachment Theory and Personality

The ideas discussed thus far fit, in many ways, with the ideas proposed by theorists interested in the infant's **attachment** to its mother (e.g., Ainsworth, Blehar, Waters, & Wall, 1978; Bowlby, 1969, 1988; Sroufe & Fleeson, 1986). Attachment is an emotional connection. The need for such a connection is a basic part of the human experience (Baumeister & Leary, 1995).

The first attachment theorist was John Bowlby. He pointed out that the clinging and following of the infant serve an important biological purpose: They keep the infant close to the mother. That, in turn, increases the infant's chances of survival.

A basic theme in attachment theory is that mothers (and others) who are responsive to the infant create a secure base for the child. The infant needs to know that the major person in his or her life is *dependable*—is there when needed. This sense of security provides a place of comfort (a safe haven) when the child is threatened (see Figure 9.1). It also gives the child a base from which to explore the world. Thus, temporary dependence on the caregiver fuels future exploration.

Attachment theory also holds that the child builds implicit mental "working models" of the self, others, and the nature of relationships. These working models are later used to relate to the world (Bowlby, 1969). This idea resembles Mahler's beliefs about object representations and Kohut's beliefs about selfobjects.

To assess infant attachment, Mary Ainsworth and her colleagues devised a procedure called the **strange situation** (Ainsworth et al., 1978). It comprises a series of events involving the infant's mother and a stranger. Of special relevance are two times when the infant is left alone with the stranger and then the mother returns. Assessors observe the infant throughout, paying special attention to its responses to the mother's return.

The strange situation procedure identified several patterns of infant behavior. *Secure attachment* was shown by normal distress when the mother left and happy enthusiasm when she returned. Two main types of *insecure attachment* were revealed, as well. An *ambivalent* (or *resistant*) infant was clingy and became very upset when the mother left. The response to the mother's return mixed approach with rejection and anger. The infant sought contact with the mother but then angrily resisted all efforts to be soothed. In the *avoidant* pattern, the infant stayed calm when the mother left and responded to her return by ignoring her. It was as though this infant expected to be abandoned and was retaliating in kind.

Observations made in the home also suggested a basis for variations in attachment (Ainsworth, 1983; Ainsworth et al., 1978). Mothers of securely attached infants responded quickly to their infants' crying and returned their smiles. They showed *synchronous* behavior—making replies to a variety of infant actions (Isabella, Belsky, & von Eye, 1989). Mothers of ambivalent babies were inconsistent: sometimes responsive and sometimes not. Mothers of avoidant babies were distant, radiating a kind of emotional unavailability and sometimes being outright rejecting or neglectful. In other research, women with secure infants spoke to their children using richer language than they used when speaking with a stranger (Ritter, Bucci, Beebe, Jaffe, & Maskit, 2007). Not surprisingly, the personality of the mother predicts how she interacts with the infant (Kochanska, Friesenborg, Lange, & Martel, 2004).

Interestingly enough, it's not always the actions themselves that differ between groups but rather the timing. For example, mothers of secure and avoidant infants don't differ in how much total time they spend holding their babies. Mothers of avoidant babies, however, are less likely to hold their babies *when the babies signal they want to be held*. Timing can be very important.

On the basis of findings such as these, Hazan and Shaver (1994) characterized the secure, ambivalent, and avoidant attachment patterns as reflecting three possible answers to the question, Can I count on my attachment figure to be available and responsive when needed? The possible answers—"yes," "no," and "maybe"—correspond to the secure, avoidant, and ambivalent patterns.

In theory, it's possible to get past an insecure attachment by forming a better one with someone later on. This is hard, however, because insecure attachment leads to actions that alienate others. This interferes with creating a new attachment. The clinginess mixed with rejection in the ambivalent pattern can be hard to deal with. (Recall the chapter opening, which describes an adult version of this.) So can the aloofness and distance of the avoidant pattern. Both patterns cause others to react negatively. That, in turn, reconfirms the perceptions that led to the patterns in the first place. Indeed, people with an insecure attachment pattern appear to distort their memory of interactions over time to make them more consistent with their working models (Feeney & Cassidy, 2003). An insecure pattern thus has a self-perpetuating quality.

The patterns seem fairly stable early in life, though they take slightly different forms (see Table 9.1). In one study, infant attachment coded at age 1 could be identified by responses to parents at age 6 for 84% of the children (Main & Cassidy, 1988, Study 1). Secure children were still acting secure, avoidant ones were still withdrawn, and ambivalent ones were still being both dependent and sullen. A more recent project (Simpson, Collins, Tran, & Haydon, 2007) reported on children from early childhood to their early 20s. Securely attached infants were more socially competent in elementary school (by teacher ratings). That, in turn, predicted secure relations with close friends at age 16, which predicted more positive emotional experiences in adult romantic relationships.

ATTACHMENT PATTERNS IN ADULTS

Attachment behavior in childhood is interesting, but more relevant at present is how these ideas relate to adult personality. Research on this question began with the

Table 9.1 Three Forms of Attachment-Related Behavior, Viewed at 1 Year and 6 Years of Age.

Name of Pattern at 1 Year	Behavior at 1 Year	Behavior at 6 Years
Secure	Seeks interaction, closeness, contact with returning parent. Readily soothed by parent and returns to play.	Initiates conversation with returning parent or responds to parent's overture. Remains calm throughout.
Avoidant	Actively avoids and ignores returning parent; looks away; remains occupied with toys.	Minimizes opportunity for interaction with returning parent, looking and speaking only briefly; returns to toys.
Ambivalent	Distress over separation isn't soothed by parent. Wants contact but shows subtle to overt signs of anger.	Posture and voice exaggerate sense of intimacy and dependency. Shows some resistance, subtle signs of hostility.

Source: Based on Main & Cassidy, 1988.

idea that the working models of relationships formed in childhood are carried into adulthood (with adjustments along the way). These working models influence the adult's social relationships. In that way, they represent the core of personality.

During the past two decades, research on adult attachment patterns has exploded (see Cassidy & Shaver, 1999; Feeney, 2006; Mikulincer & Goodman, 2006; Mikulincer & Shaver, 2007; Rholes & Simpson, 2004). The first study was done by Cindy Hazan and Phillip Shaver (1987). Participants classified themselves (from descriptions) as being secure, ambivalent, or avoidant. Then they described the most important romance of their life (past or current) on several scales (see Figure 9.2).

Secure adults described their most important love relationship as more happy, friendly, and trusting, compared with adults in the other two groups. Their relationships also had lasted longer. Avoidant adults were less likely than the others to report accepting their lovers' imperfections. Ambivalents experienced love as an obsessive preoccupation, with a desire for reciprocation and union, extreme emotional highs and lows, and extremes of both attraction and jealousy. These people were also more likely than others to report that a relationship had been "love at first sight."

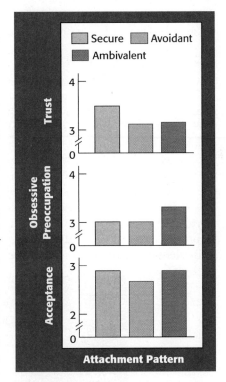

FIGURE 9.2
Adults with a secure attachment pattern report higher levels of trust in their romantic partner than do adults, those with an ambivalent pattern report greater obsessive preoccupation, and those with an avoidant pattern report lower levels of acceptance of their partners' imperfections. *Source:* Based on Hazan & Shaver, 1987.

Hazan and Shaver (1987) also investigated the mental models these people held on the nature of relationships. Secure adults said, in effect, that love is real and when it comes, it stays. Avoidants were more cynical, saying love doesn't last. Ambivalents showed their ambivalence: They said falling in love is easy and happens often, but they also agreed that love doesn't last.

Other research confirms that ambivalent college students are most likely to have obsessive and dependent love relationships (Collins & Read, 1990). Their obsessive reassurance seeking leads to greater conflict and stress in their relationships (Eberhart & Hamman, 2009). They are also the most obsessive about lost loves (Davis, Shaver, & Vernon, 2003).

Avoidants are the least likely to report being in love in the present or in the past (Feeney & Noller, 1990), the least interested in knowing their partners' intimate thoughts and feelings (Rholes, Simpson, Tran, Martin, & Friedman, 2007), the least comfortable with sex (Birnbaum, Reis, Mikulincer, Gillath, & Orpaz, 2006), and the most likely to cope in self-reliant ways after a breakup (Davis et al., 2003).

Secures show the most interdependence, commitment, and trust (Mikulincer, 1998; Simpson, 1990). If they experience a breakup, they turn to family and friends as safe havens (Davis et al., 2003). The many ways in which adult attachment affects the course of romantic relationships has become the focus of a great deal of additional research in the past few years (Mikulincer & Goodman, 2006).

HOW MANY PATTERNS?

The proliferation of work on adult attachment has raised many issues, complicating the picture (see also Box 9.2). Early studies used the three main categories from infancy work, but another approach also emerged. Bartholomew and Horowitz (1991) started with Bowlby's notion of working models, and focused on models of self and other. They argued for two dimensions: a positive-versus-negative model of the self (the self is lovable or not) and a positive-versus-negative model of others (others are trustworthy or not). The dimensions that result are termed *anxiety* and *avoidance*, respectively (Brennan, Clark, & Shaver, 1998).

With this approach, hypotheses typically are tested using the two dimensions. Less often, groups are formed by combining extremes on models of self and others (see Figure 9.3). Two of the groups that result from this are equivalent to the secures and ambivalents from the three-group approach. However, avoidants from that approach

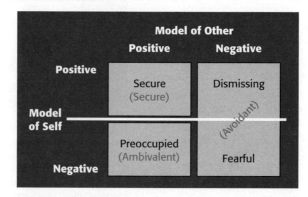

FIGURE 9.3

Combinations of positive and negative views of self and other, yielding four types of attachment patterns. In color are shown the names of the comparable patterns from the three-category model. *Source:* Based on Bartholomew & Horowitz, 1991.

Box 9.2 How Do You Measure Adult Attachment?

People who study attachment patterns in adults measure attachment in two quite different ways. One procedure is to ask people to respond to a series of statements expressing various opinions about their current close relationships. Such self-report scales include items that reflect greater versus lesser attachment ambivalence and items that reflect greater versus lesser attachment avoidance. Most of the research on attachment described in this chapter used some measure of this general sort.

A very different way to measure adult attachment is called the Adult Attachment Interview (AAI; Main, Kaplan, & Cassidy, 1985). This interview asks people to talk about their early experiences with caregivers.

When the information that's gathered is coded, however, it's not so much what people recall that's coded but whether the person has arrived at a coherent narrative regarding the childhood experiences. Key issues are whether people either lack childhood memories or idealize their caregivers (both of which are taken as signs of avoidance) and whether people seem preoccupied by unresolved loss or abuse (taken as a sign of anxious attachment).

Although there are conceptual parallels between these measurement procedures, there is very little empirical overlap (Roisman, 2009; Roisman et al., 2007). Put differently, people who score as secure on a self-report are only barely more likely to score as secure on the AAI than other people. Yet despite this almost complete lack of convergence, both measures predict outcomes that are relevant to the theory.

How can this be? Roisman et al. (2007) concluded that self-reports were most reliably associated with the quality of adult relationships under conditions of high interpersonal stress; in contrast, the AAI was linked to relationship quality whether stress was high or low.

It's tempting to speculate that these measures differ in the same way that implicit versus self-ascribed measures of motives differ (see Chapter 5). However, there is at least some evidence that self-reports of attachment relate to implicit attachment related attitudes (Shaver & Mikulincer, 2002), which would tend to contradict that view. Nonetheless, it remains an intriguing possibility that how adults perceive their current relationships and how they talk about their early lives derive from different sets of experience and are represented differently in the mind.

---

split into two separate groups in this approach, which are called *dismissive* and *fearful*, depending on whether attachment anxiety is also involved.

Each approach has a conceptual strength. The three-category approach nicely conveys the sense that a significant other can be available, unpredictable, or unavailable. The two-dimensional approach nicely conveys the sense that two separate issues are involved in the attachment response. However, the literature appears to have moved largely to the two-dimensional approach.

STABILITY AND SPECIFICITY

Two more questions about this view of personality concern its stability and its generality. If the attachment pattern is part of personality, it should remain fairly stable. Does it? If attachment concerns key figures in one's life, are the same patterns used in casual interactions or groups?

First, let's consider stability. Although the findings are mixed, attachment seems moderately stable over fairly long periods. Fraley (2002) concluded from a review of studies that a prototype for close relations arises in infancy and doesn't go away, despite new experiences. On the other hand, *moderate* stability is not *total* stability. Some people change more than others. People who vary in self-portrayal over time seem to be insecure at the core but periodically feel more secure (Davila, Burge, & Hammen, 1997). Research on longer-term stability is ongoing (Grossmann, Grossmann, & Waters, 2005; Mikulincer & Shaver, 2007).

What about specificity? Does each person have one pattern of relating to others, or do people have many patterns for different relationships? The answer seems to be that people have many patterns. Even infants may display one pattern to one parent and a different pattern to the other parent. This diversity in relational behavior also appears in adults (Baldwin, Keelan, Fehr, Enns, & Koh-Rangarajoo, 1996; Bartholomew & Horowitz, 1991; Cook, 2000; La Guardia, Ryan, Couchman, & Deci, 2000; Overall, Fletcher, & Friesen, 2003; Pierce & Lydon, 2001).

For example, one study had participants define each of their 10 closest relationships in terms of the three categories. Across the 10 descriptions, almost everyone used at least two patterns and nearly half used all three (Baldwin et al., 1996). There's also evidence that people have patterns of attachment to groups that are distinct from their patterns for close relationships (Smith, Murphy, & Coats, 1999). There's even evidence that religious beliefs involve yet another pattern of attachment (Kirkpatrick, 1998).

Thus, the ways people relate to others in their lives—even significant others—does seem to have variability. There is likely a general orientation for approaching new relationships (Feeney, Cassidy, & Ramos-Marcuse, 2008) or a central tendency among the various orientations that a person takes (Crittenden, 1990; Pierce & Lydon, 2001), and it may well derive from early childhood experiences. But adult behavior definitely is more complex than would be the case if each person had only a single way of relating to others.

Other Reflections of Adult Attachment

A surprising range of behaviors has been tied to people's attachment patterns. Hazan and Shaver (1990) studied links to people's orientations to work. Recall that ambivalence involves a sense of insecurity. Consistent with this, ambivalents reported unhappiness with the recognition they got at work and their degree of job security. They were also most likely to say their work was motivated by a desire for others' approval. Avoidants reported a desire to keep busy with work, and they socialized less during leisure time. Hazan and Shaver suggested that avoidants use work as a way to escape from their lack of relationships.

A good deal of research has looked at how attachment patterns relate to both comfort seeking and caregiving in stressful situations (Collins, Ford, Guichard, & Feeney, 2006). In one study (Simpson, Rholes, & Nelligan, 1992), women were told they were going to do a task that creates anxiety. They then waited for 5 minutes with their boyfriends, who were to do a different task. As anxiety increased, secure women sought support from their partners, talked about being nervous, and so on. Avoidant women did the opposite: The more anxious they got, the *less* they sought support. The men also varied. Among secure men, the more anxiety their partners showed, the more reassuring they were. Among avoidant men, the more anxiety their partners showed, the *less* reassuring they were (see also Kobak & Hazan, 1991). Other researchers have found that avoidant men even get angry if their partners show signs of distress (Rholes, Simpson, & Oriña, 1999). Interestingly, avoidance also predicts greater stress reactivity during discussion of a relationship conflict (Powers, Pietromonaco, Gunlicks, & Sayer, 2006).

This pattern of results has been confirmed and extended in several ways. The tendency to give less support to stressed partners has been shown among avoidant women as well as men (Simpson, Rholes, Oriña, & Grich, 2002). These patterns have also been confirmed by Feeney and Collins (2001) using different methods. They found that avoidance related inversely to a measure of responsive caregiving; avoidance also related inversely to reports of a prosocial orientation, trust, and interdependence. Anxiety related to compulsive caregiving and also to higher levels of egoistic motivation and lower levels of trust. Higher anxiety and avoidance have also been linked to lower sexual and marital satisfaction among married persons (Butzer & Campbell, 2008).

Seeking and supplying support have been looked at in many situations. Fraley and Shaver (1998) observed couples at an airport, where one person was leaving on a flight. They found that avoidant women sought contact less, did less caregiving, and displayed more behavioral avoidance than secure women. Westmaas and Silver (2001) looked at how students reacted to a stranger they thought was being treated for cancer. Avoidants were less supportive in interacting with her than were others. Another study looked at the experience of becoming a new parent (Rholes, Simpson, & Friedman, 2006). Avoidants experienced more stress and found parenting less satisfying compared to people with other attachment patterns. Yet another study looked at parental adjustment after the loss of a child (Wijngaards-de Meij et al., 2007). Both types of attachment insecurity were associated with elevated levels of grief.

Additional research suggests that the sense of attachment security makes people more compassionate and responsive to the needs of others in general (Mikulincer & Shaver, 2005). This is true even if the sense of security is increased experimentally, rather than varying naturally (Mikulincer, Shaver, Gillath, & Nitzberg, 2005). Thus, the sense of attachment security promotes altruism for others in need.

Not surprisingly, people's motivation for helping others depends on their attachment style. Avoidants are more likely to report helping because they want something in return or they feel obligated and want to avoid the negative consequences of not helping. They're less likely to report helping because they enjoy it or have a genuine concern over their partner's well-being (Feeney & Collins, 2003). Secure attachment is related to having autonomous motives for engaging in family caregiving and also to finding benefits in caregiving (Kim, Carver, Deci, & Kasser, 2008). On the receiving side, secures explain away a partner's unsupportive behavior, while insecures exaggerate the negative implications of a partner's failure to offer help.

Other research has looked at how people cope with stress. In a study of war veterans and their wives, anxious attachment was linked to severity of posttraumatic stress disorder symptoms in veterans and secondary traumatic stress in their wives (Ein-Dor, Doron, Solomon, Mikulincer, & Shaver, 2010). Another study concerned threats of missile attacks in Israel (Mikulincer, Florian, & Weller, 1993). Avoidants used more distancing-type coping (trying not to think about the situation) than did other people. Ambivalents had higher levels of ineffective emotion-focused reactions (e.g., self-criticism, wishing they could change how they felt). Secure people used their social support resources more than did the other groups.

Recall that one aspect of secure infant attachment is the sense of having a secure base. This has also been studied among adults. Security relates to an exploratory orientation (Feeney, 2004; Feeney & Thrush, 2010; Green & Campbell, 2000), perhaps because security causes people to react more positively to stimuli (Mikulincer, Hirschberger, Nachmias, & Gillath, 2001). When secure people must temporarily be dependent, they use the reassurance to help move to greater self-sufficiency afterward (Feeney, 2007). Having a partner who acts as a secure base helps people perform better on exploratory tasks and increases their self-esteem afterward (Feeney & Thrush, 2010). Security also reduces the typical negative reaction to outgroups (Mikulincer & Shaver, 2001), suggesting willingness to explore. In contrast, the avoidant pattern leads people to perceive hostile intent behind others' behavior (Mikulincer, 1998).

Also of interest is how people with various attachment patterns relate to one another. Not unsurprisingly, secures are most desired as partners, and they tend to wind up with each other (Collins & Read, 1990). Relationships in which the man is avoidant and relationships in which the woman is ambivalent are unsatisfying to both partners. On the other hand, there's evidence that avoidant men with ambivalent women tend to be stable pairings (Kirkpatrick & Davis, 1994), despite the dissatisfactions. Why? Avoidant men avoid conflict, which may help the relationship run smoothly; ambivalent women may work harder at holding things together.

Pairings of avoidants with avoidants and of ambivalents with ambivalents are rare (Kirkpatrick & Davis, 1994). This fits with the idea that people with insecure attachment patterns steer away from partners who would treat them as they were treated in infancy. Avoidants avoid partners who will be emotionally inaccessible, and ambivalents avoid partners who will be inconsistent (Collins & Read, 1990; Kirkpatrick & Davis, 1994; Pietromonaco & Carnelley, 1994; Simpson, 1990).

ATTACHMENT PATTERNS AND THE FIVE-FACTOR MODEL

Recall that many people are interested in how various views of personality relate to the five-factor model of traits. This has also been examined with adult attachment patterns. Several studies using the three-category view of attachment found strong links between measures of adult attachment and two traits from the five-factor model (Carver, 1997; Shaver & Brennan, 1992). Avoidants are introverted, secures are extraverted, and ambivalents are high in neuroticism.

An even stronger correspondence seems implied by the alternate approach to attachment. As noted earlier, it rests on two dimensions, which are sometimes termed *attachment avoidance* and *attachment anxiety*. Although the focus in each case is on relationships, the dimensions strongly resemble introversion–extraversion and neuroticism. Maybe avoidants aren't that interested in social connections because they're introverts. This would be consistent with the finding that avoidants encode less than do secures when listening to a tape about relationships (Fraley, Garner, & Shaver, 2000). If we add the twist of viewing extraversion as a desire for social incentives (from Chapter 7) and the idea that neuroticism is essentially anxiety proneness, the fit is even closer. It might even be argued that the attachment patterns represent relationship-focused versions of extraversion and neuroticism.

This reasoning has been supported with regard to attachment anxiety and neuroticism, but the situation is a little more complex with regard to avoidance. Avoidance, measured by the scale that pits avoidance against security, has associations with both extraversion and agreeableness (Noftle & Shaver, 2006).

Another question that might be raised is whether the correlated measures (attachment and "big five" scales) overlap in predicting outcomes or contribute separately. The answer appears to be that they make partially separate contributions to such experiences as relationship quality (Noftle & Shaver, 2006) and distress during bereavement (Wijngaards-de Meij et al., 2007). Simpson et al. (2002) also reported that measures of extraversion and neuroticism did not duplicate the effects of attachment patterns. So even though there is overlap, the attachment dimensions don't seem identical with the "big five" traits.

Do these patterns in personality arise from patterns of parenting (as held by psychosocial theorists)? Or are they manifestations of genetically determined traits—manifestations that simply happen to be social? One study of a large national adult sample found that reports of interpersonal trauma (e.g., abuse, threat with a weapon, parental violence) related to insecure adult attachment (Mickelson, Kessler, & Shaver, 1997). So did a history of parental depression and anxiety. These findings suggest a social origin to the patterns. However, another study found that overlap of adult attachment with "big five" traits rested on shared genetic influences (Donnellan, Burt, Levendosky, & Klump, 2008). So the jury apparently is still out.

Erikson's Theory of Psychosocial Development

We turn now to what is probably the most elaborate of psychosocial theories: that of Erik Erikson (1950, 1963, 1968). Erikson adopted Freud's view that personality develops in a series of stages. However, whereas Freud's is a theory of psycho*sexual* development, Erikson's is a theory of psycho*social* development. It describes the impact of social phenomena across life.

Another difference pertains to the age span involved. The stages that Freud described unfold in the first few years of life. In contrast, Erikson believed that personality evolves throughout life, from birth through maturity to death. He also believed no part of life is more important than any other. Erikson was thus one of the first to propose the idea of **life–span development**.

EGO IDENTITY, COMPETENCE, AND THE EXPERIENCE OF CRISIS

The central theme of Erikson's theory is **ego identity** and its development (Erikson, 1968, 1974). *Ego identity* is the consciously experienced sense of self. It derives from transactions with social reality. A person's ego identity changes constantly in response to events in the social world. To Erikson, forming and maintaining a strong sense of ego identity is critical.

A second major theme in Erikson's theory concerns competence and personal adequacy. His stages focus on aspects of mastery. If a stage is managed well, the person emerges with a sense of competence. If not, the person has feelings of inadequacy. This theme in Erikson's theory—that a desire for competence is a motivating force behind people's actions—is similar in many ways to White's ideas about competence, discussed in Box 9.1. One difference is that Erikson focused more specifically on competence in the social environment.

Erikson viewed development as a series of periods in which some issue is prominent. In his view, people experience a **psychosocial crisis,** or **conflict**, during each stage. The terms *crisis* and *conflict* are interchangeable here. They have a special meaning, though, that differs from the use of either word in everyday speech. Here, a crisis is a *turning point*: a period when the potential for growth is high but the person is also quite vulnerable. Each crisis is fairly long (none is shorter than about a year), and some are quite long (perhaps 30 years). Thus, Erikson's use of the word conveys the sense of crucial importance more than the sense of time pressure.

According to the principle of life-span development, all periods of a person's life are important, infancy through adulthood—even old age.

The conflict in each crisis isn't a confrontation between persons, nor is it a conflict within personality. Rather, it's a struggle between attaining some psychological quality versus failing to attain it. To Erikson, the conflict never ends. Even handling it in the period when it's most intense doesn't mean having mastered it, once and for all. The conflict is always there to some degree, and you confront it repeatedly in different forms throughout life.

Erikson identified eight stages. Each focuses on some aspect of transactions with social reality. Each has a conflict, or crisis. Each conflict pits two possibilities against each other, as a pair of opposed psychological qualities. One of the pair is obviously adaptive; the other appears less so. The labels that Erikson gave to the two qualities indicate the nature of the crisis.

People negotiate each stage by developing a balance between the qualities for which the stage is named. The point isn't just to acquire the good quality. In fact, it's important that the ego incorporate *both* sides of the conflict, at least a little. Having only the quality that seems good creates problems. For example, if you had only *basic trust* and absolutely no sense of *basic mistrust*, you'd be unable to deal effectively with a world that's sometimes *not* trustworthy.

Nonetheless, successful negotiation of a stage does imply that the balance is weighted more toward the positive value than the negative one. If this occurs, the person emerges from the crisis with a positive orientation toward future events concerning that conflict. Erikson used several terms to refer to this positive orientation: **ego quality, ego strength,** and **virtue** (Erikson, 1964; Stevens, 1983). Once established, these qualities remain part of your personality.

Erikson was very reluctant to specify age norms for stages. He believed that each person has a unique timetable. Thus, it's hard to say when each stage will begin and end for a person. The ages given in the following sections are only rough approximations.

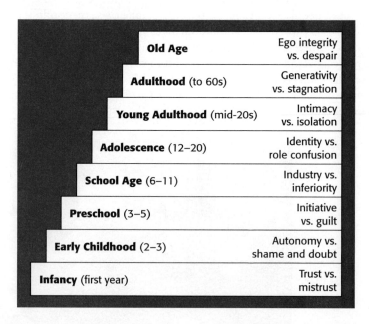

FIGURE 9.4
Erikson's eight psychosocial stages, the approximate age range in which each occurs, and the crisis that dominates each stage.

INFANCY

The first four stages parallel stages of psychosexual development outlined by Freud. The first is infancy, roughly the first year (see Figure 9.4). The conflict at this stage—the most fundamental crisis of life—is between a sense of *basic trust versus basic mistrust*. In this stage, the infant is totally dependent on others to meet its most basic needs. If the needs are met, the infant develops a sense of security and trust. This is reflected by the infant's feeding easily, sleeping well, and eliminating regularly. Caretakers can leave the infant alone for short periods without causing too much distress, because the infant has learned to trust that they'll return. Mistrust is reflected by fitful sleep, fussiness in feeding, constipation, and greater distress when the infant is left alone.

Children often seem driven to figure things out on their own. Successful mastery of the environment is important in developing feelings of competence.

The sense of trust is extremely important. It provides a basis for believing that the world is predictable—especially relationships. Trust is enhanced by interactions in which caregivers are attentive, affectionate, and responsive. A sense of mistrust is created by inconsistent treatment, emotional unavailability, or rejection. This portrayal closely resembles ideas concerning object relations and attachment patterns. A predominance of trust over mistrust gives rise to the ego strength of *hope*. Hope is an enduring belief that wishes are attainable. It's optimism about life.

EARLY CHILDHOOD

The second stage is early childhood (the second and third years of life), as children focus on gaining control over their actions. The crisis of this stage concerns these efforts. It's about creating a sense of *autonomy in actions versus shame and doubt* about being able to act independently.

Erikson agreed with Freud that toilet training is an important event, but for different reasons. To Erikson, acquiring control over bladder and bowels helps create feelings of autonomy (self-direction). Achieving control over these functions means you're not at the mercy of your body's impulses. But that's just one way to gain these feelings. Feelings of autonomy and competence emerge when children interact effectively with others. If the efforts lead to failure, ridicule, or criticism—or if parents don't let children act on their own—the result is shame and self-doubt. Managing this conflict leads to the ego quality of *will*: a determination to exercise free choice.

Much of the research on Erikson's theory focuses on the idea that successful management of one crisis prepares you to deal with the next one. Consider how this idea applies to the first two stages. The sense of basic trust is reflected in secure attachment. In one study (Hazen & Durrett, 1982), attachment was assessed at 1 year; then at 2½ years the children and their mothers came to a laboratory. While

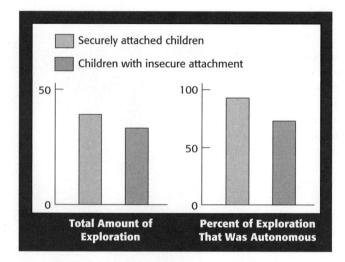

FIGURE 9.5
Children with a greater sense of basic trust and security at 1 year explore more at 2½ years of age than do less securely attached children, and a higher proportion of their exploration is self-initiated, or autonomous. This finding suggests that successful management of the first crisis of Erikson's theory prepares the child to do better with the second crisis. *Source:* Based on Hazen & Durrett, 1982.

they explored a play area there, observers coded how many times the child went alone (or led the mother) to a new part of the area—action that reflects autonomy and self-initiation of behavior. They also coded how often the child *was led by* the mother into new parts of the area—action that's *not* autonomous.

As shown in Figure 9.5, children who had been securely attached a year and a half earlier explored more than those who had been less securely attached. Further, more of the exploration was self-initiated (autonomous) among the securely attached. Similar results have been reported by others (e.g., Matas, Arend, & Sroufe, 1978). Thus, a sense of basic trust seems to promote more autonomy later on.

PRESCHOOL

The next period is preschool (from about 3 to 5). Being autonomous and capable of controlling your actions is an important start, but it's only a start. An ability to manipulate objects in the world leads to an increasing desire to exert influence, to make things happen—in short, a desire for *power* (McAdams, 1985). This period is the time when Freud saw Oedipal conflicts emerging. As we said earlier, people who are skeptical about the Oedipal conflict tend to view Freud's depiction as a metaphor for a more extensive power struggle between parents and child, who by now has become willful. Erikson focused on this power struggle.

The conflict at this stage concerns *initiative versus guilt*. Children who take the initiative are seeking to impose their newly developed sense of will on their surroundings. They express and act on their curiosity as they explore and manipulate their world and ask about things going on around them. Acts and words can also be perilous, however. Action that's too powerful can cause others pain (e.g., grabbing a toy you want can distress another child). Asking too many questions can become tiresome to adults. If taking the initiative leads to disapproval, feelings of guilt will result. Because constantly exerting power does tend to produce some disapproval, initiative eventually must be tempered by restraint. If this crisis is managed well, the child emerges with the ego quality of *purpose*: the courage to pursue valued goals without fear of punishment.

Does attaining a sense of basic trust during the first year foster later initiative? In one study (Lütkenhaus, Grossmann, & Grossmann, 1985), attachment was assessed at age 1 and the children were studied again (at home) at age 3. Those securely attached at age 1 were quicker to show initiative in interacting with a stranger than those who had been insecurely attached. During a game involving a failure, securely attached children responded by increasing their efforts, but the other children decreased their efforts. Thus, the sense of basic trust seems to provide groundwork for the sense of initiative and purpose.

SCHOOL AGE

The next stage corresponds to Freud's latency period (from about 5 to 11). Erikson held that this period also has a conflict, which he called *industry versus inferiority*. The term *industry* reflects the fact that the child's life remains focused on doing things that have an impact. But now the nature of those efforts acquires a different shade of meaning. It's no longer enough to take the initiative and assert power. Now there's pressure to do things that others judge to be *good*, in two senses. Industriousness isn't just *doing* things; it's doing things that others *value*. It's also doing things in ways that others regard as appropriate and commendable.

The crisis over this sense of industry begins about when the child enters elementary school. School is aimed at teaching children to become productive and responsible members of society. The school years are also the period when intellectual skills are first tested. Children are urged to do well in school, and the adequacy of their performance is explicitly evaluated.

The school experience also involves learning social roles. Children are beginning to learn about the nature of adult work. They're also being exposed to some of the tools of adult work. In former times, these were tools of farming, carpentry, and homemaking; today, it's more likely to be computers and other technology. Another role children are acquiring is that of citizenship. Thus, the child's sense of industry is being judged partly by the acceptability of his or her behavior to the social group.

Children with a strong sense of industry differ in several ways from children with less industry (Kowaz & Marcia, 1991). They tend to prefer reality-based activities over fantasy, and they are more able to distinguish the role of effort from that of ability in producing outcomes. These children get better grades, and they tend to agree more with statements that are socially desirable.

To emerge from this stage successfully, children must feel they are mastering their tasks in a fashion that's acceptable to those around them. The danger at this stage is developing feelings of inferiority. Such feelings can arise when children are led by others to view their performance as inadequate or morally wrong. Managing the conflict between industry and inferiority results in the ego quality termed *competence*: the sense that one can do things that are valued by others.

ADOLESCENCE

Next comes adolescence, a period that begins with the physical changes of puberty and lasts until roughly age 20. This stage is a larger break with the past than any stage up to this point. Part of the sense of separation comes from the physical changes of puberty. Your body doesn't just get larger during this period but also changes in other ways. You also have desires you never had before. You're not quite the same person you used to be. But who *are* you?

Box 9.3 The Theorist and the Theory: Erikson's Lifelong Search for Identity

Erik Erikson's life had a distinct impact on the form his theory took, particularly his emphasis on the importance of attaining a sense of identity (see Friedman, 1999). Erikson was born in Germany in 1902 to Danish parents. His father abandoned his mother before he was born, and three years later she married Theodor Homburger, a Jewish physician. Erik wasn't told for years that Homburger wasn't his real father. He later referred to that as an act of "loving deceit."

He grew up as Erik Homburger, a Jew with the appearance of a Scandinavian. Jews saw him as a gentile; gentiles saw him as a Jew. For this reason, he wasn't accepted by either group and began to form an image of himself as an outsider. By adolescence, he had been told of his adoption, and his identity confusion was further complicated by the realization that his ancestry was Danish, rather than German.

As Erik wandered Europe during his early twenties, his feelings of a lack of identity deepened. He worked as a portrait painter but never developed a clear sense of identity as an artist. Eventually, he took a teaching job in Vienna at a school created for children of Freud's patients and friends. There, he became familiar with a number of psychoanalysts, including Anna Freud, with whom he went on to train as an analyst. In 1933, he moved to the United States, where he established a practice as a child analyst. As Erik Homburger, he was also in the research team that Henry Murray brought together, which led to development of the motive approach to personality described in Chapter 5.

In 1939, Homburger became a U.S. citizen. At that time, he took the name *Erikson*. This was an event—and a choice of name—that unquestionably had much personal meaning, symbolizing his full attainment of the sense of identity.

In later years, Erikson spent time studying methods of childrearing and

other aspects of cultural life among the Sioux of South Dakota and the Yurok of northern California. These studies were important for two reasons. First, they led to themes that would permeate Erikson's thinking concerning the importance of culture and society in identity. Second, they revealed to him symptoms of dislocation, feelings of having been uprooted and separated from cultural traditions. The members of these tribes appeared to have lost their sense of identity, much as Erikson had done earlier in his life. Erikson also saw similar qualities in the lives of veterans of World War II who returned with emotional difficulties.

From all these experiences, Erikson came to believe that the attainment and preservation of a sense of identity—not wholly separate from but rather embedded in one's own society—was the critical task of growing up. This idea would emerge as one of the major themes of his viewpoint on personality.

Part of the break with the past reflects the fact that you're now beginning to think explicitly about yourself and your life in relation to the adult world. You'll have to find your place in that world. Doing so requires you to decide what roles fit your identity. This, in turn, means knowing who you are.

The crisis of this stage is *identity versus role confusion*. *Identity* reflects an integrated sense of self. It's the answer to the question *Who am I?* The phrase *role confusion* reflects the fact that every self has many facets that sometimes seem incompatible. The greater the incompatibility, the harder it is to pull the facets together, and the more confused you are. Worse yet, you can even be in a position where *no* role seems to fit your identity.

To emerge from adolescence with a strong sense of identity requires the person to evolve in two ways. First, you must consolidate the self-views from the previous stages, merging them in a way that's sensible. Second, this integrated self-view must be integrated with the view of you that others hold. This reflects the fact that identity is something you develop in a consensus with the people you relate to. Only by considering both views does a full sense of identity emerge.

Thus, from Erikson's perspective, identity derives from a blending of private and social self-conceptions. The result is a sense of personal continuity or inner congruence. Erikson placed great emphasis on the importance of developing a sense of identity. In many ways, he saw this as each person's major life task (see also Box 9.3).

If the person fails to form a consolidated identity, the result is *role confusion*: an absence of direction in the sense of self. Role confusion is reflected in an inability to select a career (or a college major that will take you toward a career). Role confusion can also lead people to identify with popular heroes or groups (or even antiheroes) to try to fill the void. The virtue associated with successful identity formation is *fidelity*. Fidelity means truthfulness. It's the ability to live up to who you are, despite the contradictions that inevitably occur among the values you hold.

YOUNG ADULTHOOD

The next stage in Erikson's theory is young adulthood (through the mid-20s). The conflict here concerns the desire for *intimacy versus isolation*. *Intimacy* is a close, warm relationship with someone, with a sense of commitment to that person. Erikson saw intimacy as an issue in relationships of all kinds, nonsexual as well as sexual.

True intimacy requires you to approach relationships in a caring and open way and to be willing to share the most personal aspects of yourself with others. You also must be open and receptive to others' disclosures. Intimacy requires the moral strength to live up to a commitment even when it requires sacrifice. Erikson believed people are capable of intimacy only if they have a strong sense of identity.

The opposite pole is *isolation*: feeling apart from others and unable to make commitments to them. A person can drift into isolation if conditions aren't right for intimacy—if no one's there who fills his or her needs. Sometimes, though, people withdraw into isolation on their own—for instance, if they feel a relationship threatens their sense of separate identity. Withdrawing can have other results, however. People can become self-absorbed to the point that they aren't able to establish intimate relationships in the future (Erikson, 1982). The ego quality associated with the ability to be intimate is *love*. This is a mutuality that subdues the conflicts of separate identities.

The theme that handling one crisis prepares you for the next one continues here. Erikson said people need a strong sense of identity to be able to attain intimacy. This idea was supported in a study that followed adolescents to early adulthood (Beyers & Seiffge-Krenke, 2010). It found that identity development at age 15 predicted intimacy at age 25. Another study looked at identity in college and intimacy in middle age (Kahn, Zimmerman, Csikszentmihalyi, & Getzels, 1985). Intimacy was assessed as whether subjects had married and, if so, whether the marriage had been disrupted by divorce. There was a clear link between a strong identity and a later capacity for intimacy. The effect differed slightly, however, between men and women (see Figure 9.6). Men with stronger identities were more likely to have married. Identity didn't predict whether the women married, but among those who *had* married, those with a strong identity were less likely to divorce. Conceptually similar findings have been reported by others (e.g., Orlofsky, Marcia, & Lesser, 1973; Schiedel & Marcia, 1985; Tesch & Whitbourne, 1982).

The other pole of the conflict of this stage—isolation—has drawn interest in its own right (e.g., Peplau & Perlman, 1982; Shaver & Rubenstein, 1980; Weiss, 1973). Two aspects of it are distinguishable from each other. *Social isolation* is a failure to be integrated into a society. People who stand apart from social groups fail to develop

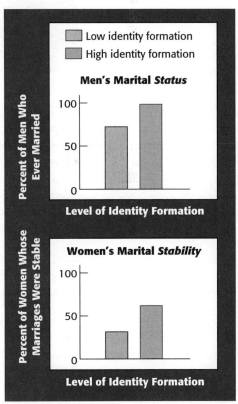

FIGURE 9.6
Percentage of men who had ever been married during the 18-year period after art school and percentage of women who had married and whose marriages remained intact during the same period, as a function of previously assessed identity formation. *Source:* Based on Kahn et al., 1985.

One way in which feelings of generativity are displayed is by helping the next generation learn about life.

a sense of belonging. In contrast, the failure to have intimacy in your life is termed *emotional isolation*—more simply, loneliness.

Emotional isolation feeds on itself. Recall that experiencing intimacy requires self-disclosure, opening oneself to others. Lonely people don't do this (W. H. Jones, Hobbes, & Hockenberg, 1982; Mikulincer & Nachshon, 1991). They're also less responsive, ask fewer questions, and seem less interested in what the other person is saying. As a result, they are hard to get to know and are likely to remain lonely.

ADULTHOOD

Young adulthood is followed by adulthood, the longest of the psychosocial stages, which typically lasts into the mid-60s. The crisis of adulthood centers around being able to generate or nurture. For this reason, the central conflict in this stage is termed *generativity versus stagnation*.

The desire for generativity is the desire to create things in the world that will outlive you (Kotre, 1984)—children, for example. By creating a new life tied to yours, you symbolically ensure your continuation into the future. Consistent with this idea, McAdams and de St. Aubin (1992) found that men who'd had children scored higher on a self-report measure of generativity than did childless men. Generativity also relates to having a view of the self as a role model and source of wisdom for one's children (Hart, McAdams, Hirsch, & Bauer, 2001) and to a parenting style that fosters autonomy (Pratt, Danso, Arnold, Norris, & Filyer, 2001).

Although generativity is partly a matter of creating and guiding the growth of the next generation, the concept is broader than that. It includes creating ideas or objects, teaching young people who aren't your own children, and anything that influences the future in a positive way (see Table 9.2). Erikson believed that the desire for generativity reflects a shift in focus from a close relationship with one other person (intimacy) to a broader concern with society as a whole.

Table 9.2 Aspects of Generativity.

Aspect	Description
Biological	Creating, bearing, and nursing an infant
Parental	Raising, nurturing, shaping, and socializing children; providing them with family traditions
Technical	Teaching the skills that make up the body of a culture; training a new generation in techniques for doing things
Cultural	Creating, changing, and maintaining a symbol system that represents the mind of a culture; passing it on to the next generation

Source: Based on Kotre, 1984, p. 12.

Consistent with this idea, highly generative persons express commitment to assisting the next generation; they also show an integration between that commitment and a sense of agency (Mansfield & McAdams, 1996; see also de St. Aubin, McAdams, & Kim, 2004; McAdams, Diamond, de St. Aubin, & Mansfield, 1997). Once the quality of generativity emerges, it may continue through the rest of one's life (Zucker, Ostrove, & Stewart, 2002).

Adults who fail to develop this sense of generativity drift into *stagnation*. Stagnation is an inability or unwillingness to give of oneself to the future. These people are preoccupied with their own concerns. They have a self-centered or self-indulgent quality that keeps them from deeper involvement in the world around them. Such an absence of generativity is related to poorer psychological well-being (Vandewater, Ostrove, & Stewart, 1997).

If there's a positive balance of generativity, the ego quality that emerges is *care*. Care is a widening concern for whatever you've generated in your life, be it children, something in your work, or something that has emerged from your involvement with other people.

OLD AGE

The final stage is maturity, or old age. This is the closing chapter of people's lives. It's a time when people look back and review the choices they made and reflect on their accomplishments (and failures) and on the turns their lives have taken. The crisis here is termed *ego integrity versus despair*. If you emerge from this review feeling that your life has had order and meaning, accepting the choices you made and the things you did, a sense of ego integrity emerges. This is a sense of satisfaction—a feeling that you wouldn't change much about your life.

The opposite pole is despair—the feeling that your life was wasted. It's a sense of wishing you had done things differently but knowing it's too late. Instead of accepting your life's story as a valuable gift, there's bitterness that things turned out as they did. As Erikson predicted, there's evidence that people who have greater generativity at age 53 have greater ego integrity at age 62 (Torges, Stewart, & Duncan, 2008).

Emerging from this life review with a sense of integrity creates the ego quality of *wisdom*. Wisdom involves meaning making and benevolence (Helson & Srivastava, 2002). It's an active concern with life and continued personal growth, even as one confronts the impending reality of death (see also Baltes & Staudinger, 1993; Kunzmann & Baltes, 2003).

THE EPIGENETIC PRINCIPLE

One more issue to address about Erikson's theory is that a given conflict is presumed to exist outside the stage in which it's focal. In embryology, **epigenesis** is the process by which a single cell turns into a complex organism. For this process to occur requires a "blueprint" at the start, with instructions for all the changes and their sequencing. Erikson applied this idea to his theory, saying that there's a readiness for each crisis at birth. The core issue of each crisis is especially focal during a particular stage, but all of the issues are always there.

This principle has several implications. For one, as we already said, it means that your orientation to a particular crisis is influenced by the outcomes of earlier ones. It also means that in resolving the core crisis of any stage, you're preparing solutions (in simple form) for the ones to come. As you deal in adolescence with the conflict between identity and role confusion, you're also moving toward handling the crisis of intimacy versus isolation. Finally, this principle means that crises aren't resolved once and for all. Your resolutions of previous conflicts are revisited and reshaped at each new stage of life (Sneed, Whitbourne, & Culang, 2006; Whitbourne, Sneed, & Sayer, 2009).

IDENTITY AS LIFE STORY

The sense of the epigenetic principle is well conveyed in some of the work of Dan McAdams. His work focuses partly on motivations that underlie personality (discussed in Chapter 5) and partly on the idea that people construct their identities as **narratives**, or life stories (McAdams, 1985, 1993, 2001). In his view, your story is not completed until the end of your life. It's constantly being written. Indeed, it's constantly under revision, just as your identity is constantly evolving.

As in any good book, the opening chapters of your narrative set the stage for things that happen much later. Sometimes, future events are foreshadowed; sometimes, things that happen in early chapters create conditions that have to be reacted to later on. As the chapters unfold, characters reinterpret events they experienced earlier or understand them in different ways. All the pieces eventually come together into a full and integrated whole, and the narrative that results has qualities from everything that's happened throughout the story. McAdams thus sees the broad crisis of identity as one that continues to occupy each person throughout life (McAdams, 2001).

Of interest is how categories of narrative themes show up in many people's lives. McAdams and his colleagues have found that highly generative midlife adults often report life stories in which they had early advantages, became aware of the suffering of others, established a personal belief system that involved prosocial values, and committed themselves to benefiting society. McAdams calls these *commitment stories*. Often, these commitment stories also contain *redemption themes*, in which a bad situation somehow is transformed into something good (McAdams, 2006; McAdams, Reynolds, Lewis, Patten, & Bowman, 2001). Indeed, the link from the sense of redemption to the quality of generativity appears quite strong (McAdams, 2006). Adults who are low in generativity sometimes have stories involving *contamination themes*, in which a good situation somehow turns bad.

LINKING ERIKSON'S THEORY TO OTHER PSYCHOSOCIAL THEORIES

Let's look back to the theories discussed earlier in this chapter to make a final point. Those theories represent contributions of their own. Yet in a sense, the fundamental theme of each is the one reflected in the first crisis in Erikson's theory: basic trust versus basic mistrust. That's a big part of security in attachment. It seems implicit in object relations theories. This issue is also the core of Erikson's own theory, providing the foundation on which the rest of personality is built.

Humans seem to need to be able to trust in the relationships that sustain their lives. In the minds of many theorists, that trust is necessary for adequate functioning. People who are deeply mistrustful of relationships or are constantly frightened about possibly losing relationships have lives that are damaged and distorted. The damage may be slight, or it may be major. Avoiding such mistrust and doubt (or recognizing and overcoming it, if it's already there) seems a central task in human existence.

Assessment

Let's turn now to assessment from the psychosocial viewpoint. Two aspects of assessment are specific to this view.

OBJECT RELATIONS, ATTACHMENT, AND THE FOCUS OF ASSESSMENT

One difference concerns what's being assessed. The psychosocial approach places a greater emphasis than other approaches on assessing the person's orientation to relationships.

There are several ways in which a person's mental model of relationships might be assessed. Measures range from some that are open ended in nature (e.g., Blatt, Wein, Chevron, & Quinlan, 1979) to structured self-reports (e.g., Bell, Billington, & Becker, 1986). Some measures assess a range of issues pertaining to relationships (Bell et al., 1986). Others focus specifically on the attachments you have to other people in close relationships (e.g., Bartholomew & Horowitz, 1991; Carver, 1997; Collins & Read, 1990; Griffin & Bartholomew, 1994; Simpson, 1990).

The object relations measure of Bell et al. (1986) is a good illustration of content assessed from this viewpoint. It has four scales. The *alienation* scale measures a lack of basic trust and an inability to be close. People high on this scale are suspicious, guarded, and isolated, convinced that others will fail them. This resembles avoidant attachment. Another scale measures *insecure attachment*, which resembles the ambivalent pattern—a sensitivity to rejection and concern about being liked and accepted. The third scale, *egocentricity*, assesses narcissism, a self-protective and exploitive attitude toward relationships and a tendency to view others only in relation to one's own needs and aims. The final scale measures *social incompetence*, or shyness and uncertainty about how to engage in even simple social interactions.

A different approach to assessment is the open-ended measure of Blatt et al. (1979), which uses a coding system to assess the maturity of people's perceptions of social relations. This measure asks you to describe your mother and father. If you're at a low level of maturity, you tend to focus on how your parents acted to satisfy your needs. If you're at a higher level, your descriptions focus more on your parents' values, thoughts, and feelings apart from your needs. At a very high level, the description takes into account internal contradictions in the parents and changes over time. This measure reflects a person's level of separation and individuation from the parents.

Children often reveal their feelings through play.

PLAY IN ASSESSMENT

Another facet of the psychosocial view on assessment reflects its emphasis on child-hood experiences as determinants of personality. Because of that, this view deals with child assessment more than others. Assessment of children tends to use play as a tool. It's often said that children's play reveals their preoccupations (e.g., Axline, 1947, 1964; Erikson, 1963; Klein, 1935, 1955a, 1955b). Play lets them express their concerns in ways they can't do in words.

Erikson (1963) devised a play situation using a specific set of toys on a table. The child was to imagine that the table was a movie studio and the toys were actors and sets. The child then created a scene and described what was happening. Other techniques have used less structured settings, but the elements almost always include a variety of dolls (e.g., mother, father, older person, children, baby). This permits children to choose characters that relate to their own concerns or preoccupations.

The play situation is projective, because the child imposes a story on ambiguous stimuli. It often has two objective characteristics, however. First is a *behavioral record*, which includes what the child says about the scene and a description of the scene and the steps taken to create it. Second, the face value of the child's behavior receives more attention than is usual in projective tests. It isn't automatically assumed that the child's behavior has deeply hidden meanings.

Problems in Behavior, and Behavior Change

Given that psychosocial theorists focus on the nature of people's relationships, it's natural that they see problems as reflecting relationship difficulties. Here are two examples.

NARCISSISM AS A DISORDER OF PERSONALITY

One psychosocial view focuses specifically on narcissism as a disorder. Indeed, this disorder was the starting point for Kohut's work on the self. Pathological narcissism is a sense that everyone and everything is an extension of the self or exists to serve the self. It entails a grandiose sense of self-importance and need for constant attention. Narcissists show a sense of *entitlement*, of deserving others' adulation. As a result, they often exploit others.

Recall that Kohut said everyone begins life with a grandiose narcissism, which is tempered during development. Some people never escape it, however. Kohut (1977) said that inadequate mirroring by parents frustrates the narcissistic needs and prevents formation of an adequate self structure. Similarly, Kernberg (1976, 1980) said that narcissism arises from parental rejection. The child comes to believe that the only person who can be trusted (and therefore loved) is himself or herself. Fitting this picture, narcissists prefer romantic partners who are admiring over those who offer intimacy (Campbell, 1999). They're also less committed in their relationships—always on the lookout for someone better (Campbell & Foster, 2002).

Unmet narcissistic needs can cause a person to distort reality in several ways in an effort to satisfy those unmet needs. For example, narcissistic people are more likely to inflate their judgments of their performances in various arenas of life than are less narcissistic people (John & Robins, 1994). If threatened by being told that someone else has outperformed them, they're more likely to criticize or ridicule that other person (Morf & Rhodewalt, 1993).

Narcissists may seem quite agreeable at first, but they wear on other people after a while (Paulhus, 1998). They are quite responsive to opportunities for self-enhancement (Wallace & Baumeister, 2002). In addition, they love to take credit for successes but respond to failure or criticism with anger (Rhodewalt & Morf, 1998). Indeed, narcissists may erupt in extreme rage if their desires are thwarted (Bushman & Baumeister, 1998; Stucke & Sporer, 2002) or they experience social rejection (Twenge & Campbell, 2003). This can be a real problem, because they are especially likely to view themselves as victims (McCullough, Emmons, Kilpatrick, & Mooney, 2003).

ATTACHMENT AND DEPRESSION

Another window on the nature of problems comes from the idea that interpersonal rejection is an important cause of depression. This idea has a good deal of support (Blatt & Zuroff, 1992). Recall that the avoidant attachment pattern is also believed to be produced by neglectful or rejecting parenting, resulting in sadness, despair, and eventual emotional detachment (Carnelley, Pietromonaco, & Jaffe, 1994; Hazan & Shaver, 1994).

The avoidant attachment pattern has also been linked to development of emotional distress when under stress (Berant, Mikulincer, & Florian, 2001). Participants in this study were women who had found out two weeks earlier that their newborns had congenital heart disease. Those with avoidant (and those with anxious) attachment patterns were most distressed. Having an avoidant pattern also predicted further deterioration in well-being a year later. Other research also supports the idea that avoidant attachment is a risk factor for depression (Hankin, Kassel, & Abela, 2005; Lee & Hankin, 2009).

It's been suggested that both the avoidant attachment pattern and the depression to which it relates can be passed from one generation to another. This argument is based on behavior, however, not genetics. The pattern you acquire as a child is the working model you bring to bear when you have children of your own. If you're an avoidant adult (due to parental rejection) and especially if you're a *depressed* avoidant adult, what kind of parent will you be? An emotionally distant one. You are likely to be experienced as a rejecting parent—not because you dislike your child but because you're so distant. Being emotionally unavailable, you may then create an avoidant child—someone just like you.

Thus, parents may transfer to the next generation precisely the attachment qualities that made them unhappy themselves. There's support for this line of reasoning regarding rejection and depression (Besser & Priel, 2005; Whitbeck et al., 1992). There's also support regarding an erratic pattern of adult behavior that may be tied to the ambivalent attachment pattern (Elder, Caspi, & Downey, 1986).

BEHAVIOR CHANGE

People in the psychosocial tradition have also added a few techniques to the arsenal of therapy. We noted earlier that interest in development led to the use of play in assessment. In the same way, psychologists such as Erik Erikson (1963), Virginia Axline (1947), and Melanie Klein (1955a, 1955b) developed **play therapy** techniques for use with children. These techniques give the child the opportunity to do as he or she wishes, without pressuring, intruding, prodding, or nagging. Under these conditions, children can have distance from others (if they're worried about being smothered by a too ever-present parent), or they can play out anger or the wish for closeness (if they're feeling rejected or unwanted). The playroom is the child's world. In it, the child has the chance to bring feelings to the surface, deal with them, and potentially change working models of relationships and the self in positive ways (Landreth, 1991).

Because object relations and self theories emphasize the role of relationships in problems, they also emphasize relationships as part of the therapeutic process. Therapists try to provide the kind of relationship the patient needs so he or she can reintegrate problematic parts of the self. Healing is brought about by providing a successful experience of narcissism or attachment (almost a kind of re-parenting), replacing the earlier emotional failure.

These therapy techniques can be seen as representing a way of restoring to the person's life a sense of connectedness to others. By modifying the representations of relationships that were built in the past, they permit the development of more satisfying relationships in the future. The optimism that this approach holds about being able to undo problematic experiences from the past is reflected in the saying "It's never too late to have a happy childhood."

Psychosocial Theories: Problems and Prospects

The psychosocial approach to personality is home to many theorists. Although they had different starting points, there's a remarkable consistency in the themes behind their work. Each assumes that human relationships are the most important part of human life and that how relationships are managed is a core issue in personality. Each tends to assume that people develop working models of relationships in early experience, which then are used to frame new ones. Also implied is the idea that health requires a balance between being separate and being closely connected to someone (see also Helgeson, 1994, 2003, in press; Helgeson & Fritz, 1998).

A strength of psychosocial theories is that they point us in directions that other theories don't. Thinking about personality in terms of attachment patterns, for example, suggests hypotheses that aren't readily derived from other viewpoints. Work based in attachment theory is leading to a better understanding of how personality plays out in social relations. The picture of this aspect of personality would very likely not have emerged without having the attachment model as a starting point. Furthermore, linking the themes of attachment to models of greater complexity, such as Erikson's, creates a picture of change and evolution across the life span that would be nearly impossible to derive from other viewpoints. The psychosocial viewpoint clearly adds something of great importance to our understanding of personality.

This isn't to say that the psychosocial approach has no unresolved issues. One important issue concerns a clash between this view and the views of of trait psychologists and behavior geneticists. Adult attachment patterns correspond well to genetically influenced traits. Avoidants are like introverts, secures like extraverts, and anxious–ambivalents like people high in neuroticism. Do these patterns result from parenting, or are they genetically determined? There are strong opinions on both sides of this question. It's a question that will surely continue to be examined closely.

In considering the prospects of this viewpoint for the future, we should note explicitly that research on psychosocial approaches is continuing at full speed. Indeed, adult attachment and related ideas represent one of the most active areas of research in personality psychology today, and the recent flood of research on this topic shows no sign of abating (Mikulincer & Shaver, 2007; Rholes & Simpson, 2004). Research on the implications of attachment patterns for the life of the child—and the adult— promises to yield interesting new insights into the human experience. The prospects of this area of work seem very bright, as do the prospects for the approach more generally.

• SUMMARY •

Psychosocial theories emphasize the idea that personality is intrinsically social and that the important issues of personality concern how people relate to others. Several psychosocial theories focus on early life. Mahler's object relations theory proposes that infants are psychologically merged with their mothers and that they separate and individuate during the first 3 years of life. How this takes place influences later adjustment.

Kohut's self psychology resembles object relations theory. He said humans have narcissistic needs that are satisfied by other people, represented as *selfobjects*. If the child receives enough mirroring (positive attention) from selfobjects (chiefly, the mother), his or her sense of self develops appropriately. If there's too much mirroring, the child won't be able to deal with frustrations. If there's too little, the development of the self will be stunted.

Some of these ideas are echoed in the work of attachment theorists such as Bowlby and Ainsworth. Secure attachment provides a solid base for exploration. There are also patterns of insecure attachment (ambivalent and avoidant), which stem from inconsistent treatment, neglect, or rejection. There's increasing interest in the idea that infant attachment patterns persist and influence adult personality. A great deal of work is currently being done on this topic, assessing adult attachment in several ways. Although people do display diverse ways of relating across their social connections, a core tendency seems to exist. Adult attachment patterns influence many aspects of behavior, including how people relate to work activities, how they seek and give emotional support, and how they relate to romantic partners.

Another important theory of the psychosocial group is Erikson's theory of psychosocial development. Erikson postulated a series of crises from infancy to late adulthood, giving rise to ego strengths that influence one's ego identity: the consciously experienced sense of self. Erikson assumed that each crisis becomes focal at one stage but that each is present in a less obvious form throughout life.

The first crisis concerns the development of a sense of *basic trust*. The child then becomes concerned with control over its body and the sense of *autonomy* that comes with that. The next issue is *initiative*, as the child seeks to exercise its power. As the child enters the school years, he or she begins to realize that the social environment demands being *industrious*. With adolescence, the child enters a new stage of life and has a crisis over *identity*. In young adulthood, identity issues give way to concern over *intimacy*. In adulthood, the person's concern is over *generativity*. Finally, in the last stage of life, the individual confronts the *integrity* of life as a whole.

Assessment techniques from the psychosocial view are similar to those of ego psychology but focus more on relationships. This approach also leads to use of play for assessment with children. The psychosocial view of problems focuses on the idea that problems are rooted in relationship issues. Kohut suggested that pathological narcissism stems from inadequate childhood mirroring. Insecure attachment seems to create a risk for depression.

These theories approach therapy in ways similar to those of ego psychology, but there are additional variations. One of them is play therapy for children. Object relations and attachment theories also suggest that a relationship with a therapist is critical in permitting reintegration of the sense of self or establishing a sense of secure attachment.

• GLOSSARY •

Attachment   An emotional connection to someone else.

Competence motivation   The need to be effective or successful in dealing with the environment.

Effectance motivation   The need to have an impact on the environment.

Ego control   The extent to which a person controls or inhibits impulses.

Ego identity   The overall sense of self that emerges from your transactions with social reality.

Ego quality (ego strength or virtue)   The quality that becomes part of your personality through successful management of a crisis.

Ego resiliency   The ability to flexibly modify your typical level of ego control to adapt to new contexts.

Epigenesis   The idea (adopted from embryology) that an internal plan for future development is present at the beginning of life.

Feelings of inferiority   The feeling that you are deficient in some way.

Life-span development   The idea that developmental processes continue throughout life.

Mirroring   The giving of positive attention and supportiveness to someone.

Narcissism   A sense of grandiose self-importance and entitlement.

Narrative   A story you compose for yourself about about life to create a coherent sense of identity.

Object relations   An individual's symbolized relations to other persons (such as parents).

Play therapy   The use of play as a procedure for conducting therapy with children.

Psychosocial crisis (or conflict)   A turning point in a developmental period when some interpersonal issue is being dealt with and growth potential and vulnerability are both high.

Self psychology   Kohut's theory that relationships create the structure of the self.

Selfobject   The mental representation of another person who functions to satisfy your needs.

Separation–individuation   The process of acquiring a distinct identity; separating from fusion with the mother.

Strange situation   A procedure used to assess the attachment pattern of the infant to the mother.

Symbiosis   A period in which an infant experiences fusion with the mother.

Transference   The viewing of other people through selfobject representations originally developed for parents.

The Learning Perspective

Lisa has a fondness for pastels. When asked why, she looks sort of blank and says she doesn't know, except she's felt that way at least since her eighth birthday, when she had the most wonderful surprise party, decorated all in pale pink, green, and violet.

I was watching my 2-year-old the other day in the kitchen, when he popped open the childproof latch on one of the cabinet doors, just like that, and reached in for a pan. I never taught him how to do that. I wonder how he figured it out. Maybe he was watching me.

WHY DO people have the preferences they have? How do people acquire new ways to act in the world? A common answer is that these aspects of behavior arise through learning. From this perspective, personality consists of all the tendencies you've learned over all the experiences of your life.

If personality is the residue of learning, it's important to know how learning works. Disagreement remains about whether learning is one process that has several manifestations or whether several distinct processes are involved (e.g., Locurto, Terrace, & Gibbon, 1980; Rescorla, 1987; Staats, 1996). For ease in presentation, we'll adopt the view that there are distinct types of learning that have their own rules.

The first part of this chapter focuses on basic forms of learning called *conditioning*. Much of the work on these processes uses animals other than humans. Nonetheless, many people think these processes underlie the qualities we know as personality. As the study of learning progressed, learning began to appear more complex than it seemed at first. The result was a need for more elaborate theories, reflecting the fact that human knowledge can accumulate in great leaps, rather than just small increments. The elaborated theories also proposed a larger role for cognition in learning. The later part of this chapter discusses these types of learning that are more specific to humans.

Classical Conditioning

An early discovery about learning was that reactions could be acquired by associating one stimulus with another. This type of learning is called **classical conditioning**. It's sometimes also called *Pavlovian conditioning*, after the Russian scientist Ivan Pavlov, whose work opened the door to understanding it (e.g., Pavlov, 1927, 1955).

BASIC ELEMENTS

Classical conditioning seems to require two things. First, the organism must already respond to some class of stimuli reflexively. That is, the response must occur reliably and automatically whenever the stimulus occurs. A **reflex** is an existing connection between a stimulus and a response, such that the first causes the second. For example, when you put something sour in your mouth (perhaps a tart candy), you start to salivate. When you touch a hot oven, you pull your hand away. These reactions happen reflexively for most people. Some reactions are innate; others were learned in the past. But in each case, a stimulus leads reliably to a particular response.

The second condition for classical conditioning is that the stimulus in the reflex must become associated in time and place with another stimulus. The second stimulus is usually (though not always) neutral at first. That is, by itself it causes no particular response beyond being noticed. In principle, there are no special requirements for this stimulus. It can be pretty much anything—a color, a sound, an object, a person.

People often describe classical conditioning in stages (see Figure 10.1). The first stage is the situation *before* conditioning. At this point, only the reflex exists—a stimulus causing a response. The stimulus is termed the **unconditioned** or **unconditional stimulus (US),** and the response it creates is called the **unconditioned** or **unconditional response (UR).** The word *unconditional* here means no special condition is required for the response to occur. It's automatic when the stimulus occurs (see Figure 10.1, A).

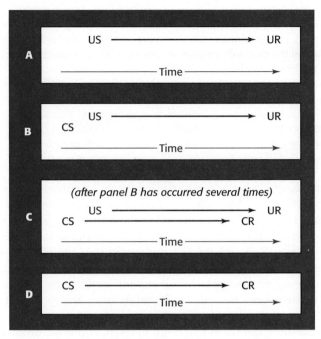

FIGURE 10.1

The various stages of a typical classical conditioning procedure (time runs left to right in each panel): (A) There is a pre-existing reflexive connection between a stimulus (US) and a response (UR). (B) A neutral stimulus (CS) is then paired repeatedly in time and space with the US. (C) The result is the development of a new response, termed a *conditioned response* (CR). (D) Once conditioning has occurred, presenting the CS by itself will now lead to the CR.

The second stage is conditioning. In this stage, the neutral stimulus occurs along with, or slightly before, the US (see Figure 10.1, B). The neutral stimulus is now termed a **conditioned** or **conditional stimulus (CS)**. Here are two ways to keep track of what that means. First, this is the stimulus that's becoming *conditioned*. Second, a response occurs in its presence only under a specific condition: that the US is there, as well. When the US comes, the UR follows automatically, reflexively (and remember that it does so *whenever* the US is presented, whether something else is there or not).

When the US and the CS are paired frequently, something gradually starts to change (see Figure 10.1, C). The CS starts to acquire the ability to produce a response *of its own*. This response is termed the **conditioned response (CR)**. The CR is often very similar to the UR. Indeed, in some cases, they look identical (see Table 10.1, row A), except that the CR is less intense. In other cases, the two can be distinguished. Even so, there is a key similarity: If the UR has an unpleasant quality, so will the CR (see Table 10.1, row B). If the UR has a pleasant quality, so will the CR (see Table 10.1, rows C and D).

How does any of this apply to you? Suppose you've started squandering your evenings at a restaurant that specializes in Italian food and Sicilian folk music. One night while you're there, you meet a person (US) who induces in you an astonishingly high degree of sexual arousal (UR). As you bask in candlelight, surrounded by crimson wallpaper and the soft strains of a Sicilian love song (CSs), you may be acquiring a conditioned sexual response (CR) to these previously neutral features of the setting. Candlelight may never be the same for you again, and the song you're hearing may gain a special place in your heart.

Table 10.1 Illustrations of the Elements of Classical Conditioning in Two Common Research Procedures (A and B), in One Common Childhood Experience (C), and in One Common Adult Experience. (Note that the elements are arranged here in terms of stimulus and the associated response, not in time sequence.)

	US	UR	CS	CR
A.	Lemon juice in mouth	Salivation	Tone	Salivation
B.	Shock to foot	Pain	Light	Fear
C.	Ice cream in mouth	Pleasant taste	Sight of ice cream	Happiness
D.	Romantically enticing partner	Sexual arousal	Mood music	Sexual arousal

If you know that a US has occurred repeatedly along with a neutral stimulus, how do you know whether conditioning has taken place? To find out, present the CS by itself—without the US (see Figure 10.1, D). If the CS (alone) gets a reaction, conditioning has occurred. If there's no reaction, there's been no conditioning. The more frequently the CS is paired with the US, the more likely conditioning will occur. If a US is very strong, however—causing a very intense UR—conditioning may occur with only one pairing. For example, cancer patients undergoing chemotherapy often experience extreme nausea from the medication and develop very strong CRs to surrounding stimuli after only one exposure.

Once conditioning has taken place, the CS–CR combination acts just like any other reflex. That is, once it's there, this combination can act as reflex for another instance of conditioning. Returning to our example, once Sicilian music has been conditioned to induce sexual arousal, Sicilian music can be used to condition that arousal to other things, such as a particular photograph in the place where you listen to Sicilian songs. This process is termed **higher-order conditioning**.

DISCRIMINATION, GENERALIZATION, AND EXTINCTION IN CLASSICAL CONDITIONING

Classical conditioning provides a way for new responses to become attached to CSs (though see Box 10.1 for questions about this). Yet the CS almost never occurs later in precisely the same form as during conditioning. You will, however, run across many stimuli later that are somewhat similar to the CS. What happens then?

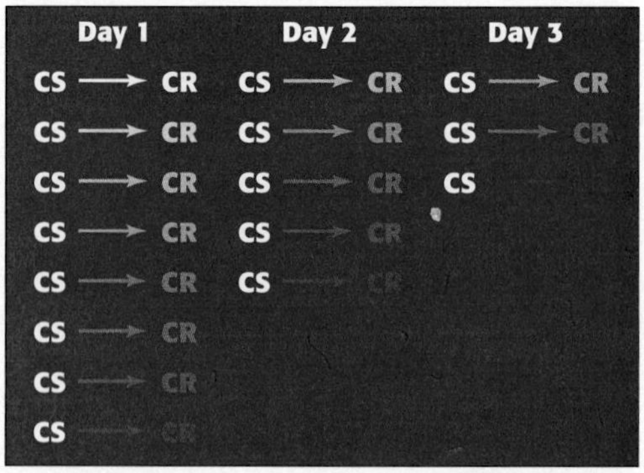

FIGURE 10.2
Extinction and spontaneous recovery in classical conditioning. When a CS appears over and over without the US, the CR becomes progressively weaker and eventually disappears (or nearly does). If the CS is repeated again after the passage of time, the CR returns at a lower level than it was initially but at a higher level than it was when the CS was last presented. Over repeated occasions, the spontaneous recovery also diminishes.

Box 10.1 What's Going On in Classical Conditioning?

Classical conditioning has been part of psychology courses for decades. In most accounts, it's presented as a process that was well mapped out early in the development of learning theory and to which little new has been added since then. Not everyone agrees with this, however (Mineka & Zinbarg, 2006).

Classical conditioning is usually portrayed as a low-level process in which a response gets spread from one stimulus to another because they occur close in time. But Robert Rescorla (1988) has argued that's not the way it is. He says that organisms use their experiences of relations between parts of the world to represent reality (see also Mowrer & Klein, 2001). Association in time and place isn't what makes conditioning occur, in his view. Rather, it's the information one stimulus gives about the other. To Rescorla, learning is a process by which the organism's representation of the world is brought into line with the actual state of the world. Organisms learn only when they're "surprised" by something that happens to them.

As a result, two stimuli experienced together sometimes don't become associated. Consider two animals. One has had a series of trials in which a light (as a CS) was paired with a shock (as a US). The other hasn't had this experience. Both animals then get a series of trials in which both the light and a tone (as *two* CSs) are paired with the shock. The second animal acquires a CR to the tone, but the first one doesn't. Apparently, the first animal's earlier experience with the light has made the tone redundant. Because the light already signals that the US is coming, there's no need to condition to the tone, and it doesn't happen.

In the same way, cancer patients undergoing chemotherapy can be induced to form conditioned aversions to specific unusual foods by giving those foods before chemotherapy (Bernstein, 1985). Doing this can make that specific food a "scapegoat," and prevent conditioning of aversions to other foods, which otherwise is very common.

Rescorla (1988) has also challenged other aspects of the traditional view. He argues against the idea that classical conditioning is a slow process requiring many pairings. He says learning commonly occurs in five to six trials. He says that classical conditioning "is not a stupid process by which the organism willy-nilly forms associations between any two stimuli that happen to co-occur. Rather, the organism is better seen as an information seeker using logical and perceptual relations among events, along with its own preconceptions, to form a sophisticated representation of the world" (p. 154).

The position taken by Rescorla (and others) is clearly different from that expressed in the body of this chapter: that classical conditioning reflects learning of an association between stimuli. The views these researchers have expressed also heralds a broad issue that's prominent in a later part of this chapter: the role of cognition in learning.

Suppose your experiences in the Sicilian restaurant have led you to associate candlelight, crimson wallpaper, and Italian food (as CSs) with sexual arousal (as CR). What would happen if you walked into a room with muted lamplight, burgundy-painted walls, and Spanish food? These aren't quite the stimuli that got linked to sexual arousal, but they're similar. Here a process called **generalization** occurs. Generalization is responding in a similar way to similar-but-not-identical stimuli. In this setting, you'd probably start to feel the glow of arousal, although probably not as much as in the first room. Your reaction would fall off even more if the new room differed even more from the first room.

Why would it fall off more? The answer lies in a concept called **discrimination**. Discrimination means responding differently to different stimuli. If you walked into a room with fluorescent lights and blue walls, the mellow glow associated with the Sicilian restaurant would surely not emerge. You would *discriminate* between the two sets of stimuli. Discrimination and generalization are complementary. Generalization gives way to discrimination, as the stimuli become more different from the initial CS.

Do conditioned responses go away? Discussions of conditioning don't use words such as *forgetting*. CRs do weaken, however, by a process called **extinction**. This occurs when a CS appears repeatedly without the US (Pavlov, 1927). At first, the CS leads reliably to the CR (see Figure 10.2). But gradually, over repeated presentations, the CR grows weaker. The CR doesn't actually disappear, however. Even when a response stops in a session, there's a "spontaneous recovery" the next day (Wagner, Siegel,

BOX 10.2 CLASSICAL CONDITIONING AND ATTITUDES

Where do attitudes come from? The answer provided in this chapter is that you develop attitudes through classical conditioning. A neutral stimulus (CS) begins to produce an emotional reaction (CR) after it's paired with a stimulus (US) that already creates an emotional reaction (UR). This approach says that people acquire emotional responses to attitude objects (classes of things, people, ideas, or events) exactly that way. If the attitude object is paired with an emotion-arousing stimulus, it comes to evoke the emotion itself. This response, then, is the basis for an attitude.

A good deal of evidence fits this depiction. More than 65 years ago, Razran (1940) presented political slogans to people and had them rate how much they approved of each. Later, he presented the slogans again under one of three conditions: while

the people were eating a free lunch, while they were inhaling noxious odors, or while they were sitting in a neutral setting. Then the people rated their approval of the slogans a second time. Slogans paired with a free lunch were now rated more positively than before. Slogans paired with unpleasant odors were now rated more negatively than before. Many other studies have found similar results (De Houwer et al., 2001). Attitudes toward people can form the same way. Walther (2002) found that pairing photos of neutral persons with liked or disliked persons led to positive and negative attitudes, respectively, toward the neutral persons.

There's also the potential for higher-order conditioning here. Negative attitudes formed by associating a neutral person with a disliked person can produce further conditioning from that person to another neutral person (Walther, 2002). And think about the fact that words such as *good* and *bad* are tied in most people's experiences

with positive and negative events (Staats & Staats, 1957, 1958) and thus probably cause emotional responses themselves. People use such words all the time around others, creating many opportunities for higher-order conditioning.

A large number of studies have shown that classical conditioning *can* be involved in the development of attitudes. However, they have not shown whether attitudes *are* usually acquired this way. But events that arouse emotions are common in day-to-day life, which provides opportunities for conditioning. For example, the "business lunch" is remarkably similar to Razran's experimental manipulation. It therefore seems reasonable that classical conditioning may underlie many of people's preferences for persons, events, things, places, and ideas. Given that preferences are important aspects of personality, conditioning seems an important contributor to personality.

Thomas, & Ellison, 1964). In fact, it is now now believed that classical conditioning leaves a permanent record in the nervous system, and that its effects can be muted but not erased (Bouton, 1994, 2000).

EMOTIONAL CONDITIONING

As you may have realized already, a lot of the classical conditioning in humans involves responses with emotional qualities. That is, many of the stimuli that most clearly cause reflexive reactions are those that elicit positive feelings (hope, delight, excitement) or bad feelings (fear, anger, pain). The term **emotional conditioning** is sometimes used to refer to classical conditioning in which the CRs are emotional reactions.

An interesting aspect of emotional conditioning is emotional reactions to properties such as colors. Andrew Elliot and his colleagues (e.g., Elliot & Maier, 2007) argued that the color red evokes negative emotions in academic contexts, because it's been associated with poor grades. (Teachers tend to use red ink to mark errors in students' work.) Their studies found that exposing test takers to red (compared to other colors) caused performance to drop (Elliot, Maier, Moller, Friedman, & Meinhardt, 2007; Lichtenfeld, Maier, Elliot, & Pekrun, 2009). Elliot suggested that this occurred because the color red induced avoidance motivation (Elliot, Maier, Binser, Friedman, & Pekrun, 2009), but emotional conditioning was also involved (Moller, Elliot, & Maier, 2009).

Conditioning of emotional responses is important to the learning view on personality. It's argued that people's likes and dislikes—all the preferences that help define

One purpose of a business lunch is to associate your company and its products (as CSs) with positive feelings produced by a good meal in a nice restaurant.

personality—develop through this process (De Houwer, Thomas, & Baeyens, 2001). Linking a neutral stimulus to a pleasant event creates a "like." Linking a stimulus to an upsetting event creates a "dislike." In fact, just hearing someone describe a good or bad trait in someone else can link that trait in your mind to the person who's doing the describing (Skowronski, Carlston, Mae, & Crawford, 1998).

Different people experience different bits of the world and thus have different patterns of emotional arousal. Different people also experience the same event from the perspective of their unique "histories." As noted in Chapter 6, children from the same family experience the family differently (Daniels & Plomin, 1985). As a result, people can wind up with remarkably different patterns of likes and dislikes (see Box 10.2). Thus, emotional conditioning can play a major role in creating the uniqueness of personality (Staats & Burns, 1982).

Instrumental Conditioning

A second form of learning is called **instrumental conditioning**. (This term is often used interchangeably with **operant conditioning**, despite slight differences in meaning.) Instrumental conditioning differs in several ways from classical conditioning. For one, classical conditioning is passive. When a reflex occurs, conditioning doesn't require you to *do* anything—just to be there and be aware of other stimuli. In contrast, instrumental conditioning is active (Skinner, 1938). The events that define it begin with a behavior (even if the behavior is the act of remaining still).

THE LAW OF EFFECT

Instrumental conditioning is a simple process, although its ramifications are widespread. It goes like this: If a behavior is followed by a better (more satisfying) state of affairs, the behavior is more likely to be done again later in a similar situation (see Figure 10.3, A). If a behavior is followed by a worse (less satisfying) state of affairs, the behavior is less likely to be done again later (see Figure 10.3, B).

This simple description—linking an action, an outcome, and a change in the likelihood of future action—is the *law of effect* deduced by E. L. Thorndike more than a century ago (Thorndike, 1898, 1905). It is simple but profound. It accounts for regularities in behavior. Any situation allows many potential acts (see Figure 10.3, C). Some acts come to occur with great regularity; others happen once and disappear,

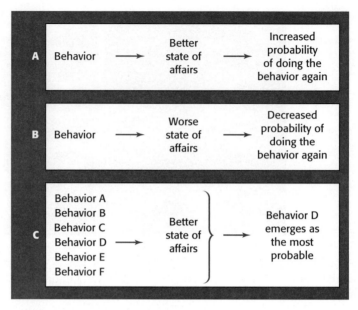

FIGURE 10.3
Instrumental conditioning: (A) Behavior that is followed by a more satisfying state of affairs is more likely to be done again. (B) Behavior that is followed by a less satisfying state of affairs is less likely to be done again. (C) This principle accounts for the fact that (over time and experiences) some behaviors emerge from the many possible behaviors as habitual responses that occur in specific situations.

never to return; still others turn up occasionally—but only occasionally. Why? Because some have been followed by satisfying outcomes whereas others haven't.

As outcomes are experienced after various behaviors, a **habit hierarchy** evolves (Miller & Dollard, 1941). The order of responses in the hierarchy derives from prior conditioning. Some responses are very likely (high on the hierarchy), because they've often been followed by more satisfying states of affairs. Others are less likely (lower on the hierarchy). The form of the hierarchy shifts over time, as outcome patterns shift.

REINFORCEMENT AND PUNISHMENT

Today, the term **reinforcer** replaces the phrase *satisfying state of affairs*. This term conveys that it strengthens the tendency to do the act that preceded it. Reinforcers can reduce biological needs (food or water) or satisfy social desires (smiles and acceptance). Some get their reinforcing quality indirectly (money).

Different kinds of reinforcers have different names. A *primary reinforcer* diminishes a biological need. A *secondary reinforcer* has acquired reinforcing properties by association with a primary reinforcer (through classical conditioning) or by virtue of the fact that it can be used to *get* primary reinforcers (Wolfe, 1936; Zimmerman, 1957).

The term **punisher** refers to unpleasant outcomes. Punishers reduce the tendency to do the behavior that came before them, although there's been controversy about how effective they are (Rachman & Teasdale, 1969; Solomon, 1964; Thorndike, 1933). Punishment can also be primary or secondary. That is, some events are intrinsically aversive (e.g., pain). Others are aversive because of their associations with primary punishers.

Another distinction is also important but a little tricky. Reinforcement always implies moving the state of affairs in a positive direction. But this can happen in two ways. The more obvious way is by receiving something good (food, gifts, money). Getting these things is termed **positive reinforcement**. "Positive" implies *adding* something good. When positive reinforcement occurs, the behavior that preceded it becomes more likely.

There's also a second kind of reinforcement, called **negative reinforcement**. Negative reinforcement occurs when something *unpleasant* is *removed*. For instance, when your roommate stops playing his annoying CD of "Polka Favorites" over and over, that might be a negative reinforcer for you. Removing something unpleasant moves the state of affairs in a positive direction—from unpleasant to neutral. It thus is reinforcing and will cause the behavior that preceded it to become more likely to occur.

Time out is an effective way of discouraging unwanted behavior in children.

Punishment also comes in two forms. Most people think of punishment as adding pain, moving the state of affairs from neutral to negative. But sometimes punishment involves removing something good, changing from a positive to a neutral state of affairs (thus less satisfying). This principle—punishing by withdrawing something good—underlies a tactic that's widely used to discourage unwanted behavior in children. It's called a **time out**, short for "time out from positive reinforcement" (Drabman & Spitalnik, 1973; Risley, 1968).

A time out takes the child from whatever activity is going on to a place where there's nothing fun to do. Many find this practice appealing, because it seems more humane than punishments such as spanking. In principle, however, a time out creates a "less satisfying state of affairs" for the child and thus should have the same effect on behavior as any other punishment.

DISCRIMINATION, GENERALIZATION, AND EXTINCTION IN INSTRUMENTAL CONDITIONING

Several ideas introduced in the discussion of classical conditioning also apply to instrumental conditioning, with slight differences in connotation. For example, discrimination still means responding differently in the presence of different stimuli. In this case, however, the difference in response results from variations in prior reinforcement.

Imagine that when a stimulus is present, a particular action is always followed by a reinforcer. When the stimulus is absent, the same action is *never* followed by a reinforcer. Gradually, the presence or absence of the stimulus gains an influence over whether the behavior takes place. It becomes a **discriminative stimulus**: a stimulus that turns the behavior on and off. You use the stimulus to discriminate among situations and thus among responses. Behavior that's cued by discriminative stimuli is said to be "under stimulus control."

Earlier we said that a habit hierarchy (an ordering of the likelihood of doing various behaviors) can shift because of the ongoing flow of reinforcing (and non-reinforcing) events. It shifts constantly for another reason, as well: Every change in situation means a change in cues (discriminative stimuli). The cues suggest what behaviors are reinforced in that situation. Thus, a change in cues rearranges the list of behavior probabilities. Changing contextual cues can disrupt even very strong habits (Wood, Tam, & Witt, 2005).

The principle of generalization is also important here. As you enter new settings and see objects and people you've never seen before, you respond easily and automatically, because there are similarities between the new settings and previous discriminative stimuli. You generalize behaviors from the one to the other, and your actions flow smoothly forward. For example, you may never have seen a particular style of spoon before, but you won't hesitate to use it to eat the soup. You may never have driven a particular make of car before, but if that's what the rental agency gives you, you'll probably be able to handle it.

The principle of generalization gives conditioning theorists a way to talk about trait-like qualities. A person will behave consistently across time and circumstances if discriminative stimuli stay fairly similar across the times and circumstances. Because key stimulus qualities often *do* stay the same across settings (even if other qualities differ greatly), the person's action tendency also stays the same across the settings. The result is that, to an outside observer, the person appears to have a set of traits. In this view, however, behavioral consistency depends on similarities of environments (an idea that's not too different from the discussion of consistency late in Chapter 4).

Extinction in instrumental conditioning occurs when a behavior that once led to a reinforcer no longer does so. As the behavior is done over and over—with no reinforcer—its probability falls. Eventually it's barely there at all (though just as in classical conditioning there's a tendency for spontaneous recovery, causing some to believe that it hasn't gone away; Bouton, 1994; Lansdale & Baguley, 2008; Rescorla, 1997, 1998). Thus, extinction is a way in which behavioral tendencies fade.

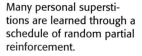

Many personal superstitions are learned through a schedule of random partial reinforcement.

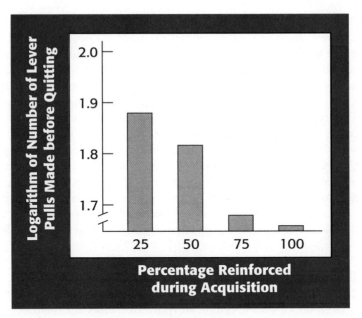

FIGURE 10.4
Effect of partial reinforcement and continuous reinforcement on persistence. People first played on a slot machine that paid off 25%, 50%, 75%, or 100% of the time. Then they were allowed to continue playing for as long as they liked, but they never again won. As can be seen, partial reinforcement leads to greater resistance to extinction. Those initially rewarded less than 100% of the time persist longer when all reward is removed. The lower the percentage of partial reinforcement, the greater the persistence. *Source:* Based on Lewis & Duncan, 1956.

SCHEDULES OF REINFORCEMENT

In reading about instrumental conditioning, people often assume that reinforcement occurs every time the behavior occurs. But common sense and your own experience should tell you life's not like that. Sometimes reinforcements are frequent, but sometimes not. Variations in frequency and pattern are called *schedules of reinforcement*. One simple variation is between continuous and partial (or intermittent) reinforcement. In **continuous reinforcement**, the behavior is followed by a reinforcer every single time. In **partial reinforcement**, the behavior is followed by a reinforcer only some of the time.

Continuous and partial reinforcement differ in two ways in their effects on behavior. The first is that new behaviors are acquired faster when reinforcement is continuous than when it's not. Eventually, even infrequent reinforcement results in high rates of the behavior, but it may take a while. The other effect is less intuitive, but more important. It's often called the **partial reinforcement effect**. It shows up when reinforcement stops (see Figure 10.4). Take away the reinforcer, and a behavior acquired by continuous reinforcement will go away quickly. A behavior built in by partial (less frequent) reinforcement remains longer—it's more *resistant* to extinction (Amsel, 1967; Humphreys, 1939).

REINFORCEMENT OF QUALITIES OF BEHAVIOR

One final point about learning through instrumental conditioning: It's most intuitive to think that the reinforcer makes a particular *act* more likely in the future. However, there's evidence that what becomes more likely isn't always an act but rather some *quality* of action (Eisenberger & Selbst, 1994). For example, reinforcing *effort* in one setting can increase *effortfulness* in other settings (Mueller & Dweck, 1998). Reinforcing accuracy on one task increases accuracy on other tasks. Reinforcing speed on one task increases speed elsewhere. Reinforcing creativity yields more creativity (Eisenberger & Rhoades, 2001). Reinforcing focused thought produces more focused thinking elsewhere (Eisenberger, Armeli, & Pretz, 1998). Reinforcing variability produces greater variability in behavior (Neuringer, 2004). Indeed, reinforcement can influence the process of selective attention (Libera & Chelazzi, 2006, 2009).

Thus, reinforcement can change not just particular behaviors but whole dimensions of behavior. This idea broadens considerably the ways in which reinforcement principles may act on human beings. It suggests that reinforcers act at many levels of abstraction. In fact, many aspects of behavior at many different levels may be reinforced *simultaneously* when a person experiences a more satisfying state of affairs. This possibility creates a far more complex picture of change through conditioning than one might initially imagine.

Social and Cognitive Variations

The basic principles of conditioning are powerful tools for analyzing behavior. They account for large parts of human experience. They explain how attitudes and preferences seem to derive from emotional reactions, and they explain how behavior tendencies strengthen and fade as a result of good and bad outcomes.

Powerful as these ideas are, however, many came to believe that they were insufficient to account for the learning exhibited by humans. Some became disenchanted with conditioning theories because they ignored aspects of behavior that seem obvious outside the lab. For example, people often learn by watching others. Moreover, people often decide whether to do something by thinking about what would happen if they did it. Existing theories didn't seem wrong, exactly, but they seemed incomplete.

From these dissatisfactions (and the work they prompted) came what might be seen as another generation of learning theories. They emphasize mental events more than the earlier ones do. For this reason, they're often called *cognitive* learning theories. They also emphasize social aspects of learning. Thus, they're often called *social* learning theories. One aspect of this second generation of theories was some elaborations on conditioning principles.

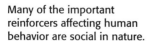

Many of the important reinforcers affecting human behavior are social in nature.

Empathy causes us to experience other's emotions. For example, others' grief elicits sadness from us, and their happiness elicits our joy. As you look at this picture, you are probably beginning to feel the same emotions that the people in the picture are experiencing.

SOCIAL REINFORCEMENT

As learning theory evolved, some researchers began to think more carefully about *human* learning. This led, in part, to a different view of reinforcement. Many came to believe that reinforcement in human experience (beyond infancy, at least) has little or nothing to do with reduction of physical needs. Rather, people are most affected by **social reinforcers**: acceptance, smiles, hugs, praise, approval, interest, and attention from others (Bandura, 1978; Kanfer & Marston, 1963; Krach, Paulus, Bodden, & Kircher, 2010; Rotter, 1954, 1982). The idea that the important reinforcers for people are social is one of several senses in which these learning theories are social (Brokaw & McLemore, 1983; A. H. Buss, 1983; Turner, Foa, & Foa, 1971).

A description of social reinforcement should also mention **self-reinforcement**. This term has two meanings. The first is the idea that people may give themselves reinforcers after doing something they've set out to do (Bandura, 1976; Goldiamond, 1976; Heiby, 1982). For example, you might reward yourself with a pizza for studying 6 straight hours, or you may get yourself a new piece of stereo equipment after a semester of good grades.

The second meaning derives from the concept of social reinforcement. It's the idea that you react to your own behavior with approval or disapproval, much as someone else reacts to your behavior. In responding to your actions with approval, you reinforce yourself. In responding with disapproval, you punish yourself. This sort of internal self-reinforcement and self-punishment plays a role in social–cognitive learning theories of behavior and behavior change (Bandura 1977a, 1986; Kanfer, 1977; Kanfer & Hagerman, 1981; Mischel, 1973, 1979).

VICARIOUS EMOTIONAL AROUSAL

Another elaboration on conditioning comes from the fact that people can experience events vicariously—through someone else. Vicarious processes represent a second sense in which human learning is social. That is, vicarious processes involve two people: one to experience something directly, another to experience it indirectly.

One type of vicarious experience is **vicarious emotional arousal**, or empathy. This occurs when you observe someone feeling an intense emotion and experience the same feeling yourself (usually less intensely). Empathy isn't the same as sympathy, which is a feeling of concern for someone else who's suffering (Gruen & Mendelsohn, 1986;

Box 10.3 Modeling and Delay of Gratification

Social–cognitive learning theories emphasize that people's acts are determined by cognitions about potential outcomes of their behavior (Kirsch, 1985). This emphasis returns us to the concept of **self-control**, the idea that people sometimes restrain their own actions.

As noted in earlier chapters, people often face the choice of getting a desired outcome immediately or getting a better outcome later on. The latter choice—delay of gratification—isn't all that easy to make. Imagine that after saving for four months, you have enough money to go to an oceanside resort for two weeks. You know that if you saved for another ten months, you could take the trip to Europe you've always wanted. One event is closer in time. The other is better, but getting it

requires more self-control. Ten more months with no vacation is a long time.

Also as noted earlier, many variables influence people's ability to delay. Especially relevant to this chapter is the role played by modeling (Mischel, 1974). Consider a study by Bandura and Mischel (1965) of fourth- and fifth-graders who (according to a pretest) preferred either immediate or delayed reward. Children of each preference were put into one of three conditions. In one, the child saw an adult model make a series of choices between desirable items that had to be delayed and less desirable items that could be had immediately. The model consistently chose the opposite of the child's preference. Children in the second condition read about the model's choices. In the third condition (a control group), there was no modeling.

All the children had a series of delay-of-gratification choices just

afterward and again a month later. Seeing a model choose an immediate reward made delay-preferring children more likely to choose an immediate reward. Seeing a model choose a delayed reward made immediate-preferring children more likely to delay. These effects were still observed a month later.

How do models exert this influence on self-control? One possibility is through vicarious reinforcement. In the Bandura and Mischel (1965) study, for example, the model vocalized reasons for preferring one choice over the other. The model's statements implied that he felt reinforced by his choices (see also Bandura, Grusec, & Menlove, 1967; Mischel & Liebert, 1966; Parke, 1969). Thus, people obtain information from seeing how others react to experiences and use that information to guide their own actions.

Wispé, 1986). When you empathize, you feel the same feeling, good or bad, as the other person. Everyone has this experience, but people differ in how intensely they empathize (Eisenberg et al., 1994; Levenson & Ruef, 1992; Marangoni, Garcia, Ickes, & Teng, 1995).

Examples of empathy are easy to point out. When something wonderful happens to a friend, putting her in ecstasy, you feel happy, as well. Being around someone who's frightened makes most people feel jumpy. Laughter is often contagious, even when you don't know what the other person is laughing at. There's even evidence that being around someone who's embarrassed can make you feel embarrassed too (Miller, 1987).

Experiencing vicarious emotional arousal doesn't constitute learning, but it creates an opportunity for learning. Recall emotional conditioning, from earlier in the chapter. Feeling an emotion in the presence of a neutral stimulus can cause that stimulus to become capable of evoking a similar emotion (Olsson, Nearing, & Phelps, 2007). The emotion can be caused by something you experience directly, but it can also arise vicariously. Thus, vicarious emotional arousal creates a possibility for classical conditioning. Such an event is called **vicarious classical conditioning**.

Vicarious Reinforcement

Another vicarious process may be even more important. This one, called **vicarious reinforcement**, is very simple: If you observe someone do something that's followed by reinforcement, you become more likely to do the same thing yourself (Kanfer & Marston, 1963; Liebert & Fernandez, 1970). If you see a person punished after doing something, you're less likely to do it. The reinforcer or punishment went to the other person, not to you. But your own behavior will be affected as though you'd received it yourself (see also Box 10.3).

How do vicarious reinforcement and punishment influence people? Presumably, seeing someone reinforced after a behavior leads you to infer that you'd get the same reinforcer if you acted the same way (Bandura, 1971). If someone else is punished, you conclude the same thing would happen to you if you acted that way (Bandura, 1973; Walters & Parke, 1964).

What Is Reinforcement?

Note that the effect of vicarious reinforcement just described appears to involve developing an expectancy—a mental model of links between actions and reinforcers. Such a mental model of a link from action to expected outcome is called an **outcome expectancy** (Bandura, 1977a). The idea that people hold expectancies and that expectancies influence action wasn't new when it was absorbed into social learning theory (e.g., Brunswik, 1951; Lewin, 1951b; Postman, 1951; Tolman, 1932). But an emphasis on expectancies became a cornerstone of this view of personality (Rotter, 1954; see also Bandura, 1977a, 1986; Kanfer, 1977; Mischel, 1973).

In fact, this concept became important enough to raise questions about what direct reinforcement does. We said earlier in the chapter that reinforcers strengthen the tendencies to do the behaviors that preceded them. Yet Albert Bandura (1976, 1977a), a prominent social learning theorist, explicitly rejected this sense of the reinforcement concept, while continuing to use the term (see also Bolles, 1972; Brewer, 1974; Rotter, 1954).

If reinforcers don't strengthen action tendencies, then what do they do? Bandura said they do two things: First, by providing information about outcomes, reinforcers lead to expectancies about what actions are effective in what settings. In addition, reinforcers provide the potential for future motivational states through anticipation of their recurrence in the future. Many people would agree that these functions are important. But they clearly represent a very different view of what reinforcement is about, compared to the view discussed earlier in the chapter.

Efficacy Expectancies

Another variation on the theme of expectancies derives partly from clinical experience. Bandura (1977b) argued that people with problems generally know exactly what actions are needed to reach the outcomes they want. Just knowing what to do, however, isn't enough. You also have to be confident of being able to *do* the behavior. This confidence in having the ability to carry out a desired action is what Bandura termed **efficacy expectancy**, or **self-efficacy**. To Bandura, when therapy works, it's because the therapy restores the person's sense of efficacy about being able to carry out actions that were troublesome before.

Research on efficacy expectancies began by focusing on changes associated with therapy, but the work quickly expanded to examine a wide range of other topics (Bandura, 1986, 1997, 2006). Here are some examples: Wood and Bandura (1989) found that self-efficacy influenced how well business students performed in a management task. Bauer and Bonanno (2001) found that efficacy perceptions predicted less grief over time among persons adapting to bereavement. Efficacy expectancies predict whether drug users stay clean during the year after treatment (Ilgen, McKellar, & Tiet, 2005). There's even evidence that acquiring a sense of efficacy can have a positive influence on immune function (Wiedenfeld et al., 1990).

Beyond these direct associations, perceptions of efficacy may underlie the positive effects found for other variables. For example, efficacy perceptions may be a pathway by which social support gives people a sense of well-being (Major et al., 1990). There's also evidence that self-esteem and optimism operate through perceptions of efficacy (Major, Richards, Cooper, Cozzarelli, & Zubek, 1998).

ROLE OF AWARENESS

A final elaboration on conditioning principles comes from considering the role of awareness in conditioning. It's long been assumed that conditioning happens whether you're paying attention or not. There's reason to believe, though, that this assumption is wrong. Several old studies found that people show little or no classical conditioning from repeated pairings of stimuli unless they realize the stimuli are *correlated* (Chatterjee & Eriksen, 1962; Dawson & Furedy, 1976; Grings, 1973). Newer studies have found that people are conditioned only if they are aware of the US (Dawson, Rissling, Schell, & Wilcox, 2007) or at least its valence (Stahl, Unkelbach, & Corneile, 2009). There's also evidence that people change their behavior after reinforcers only when they're aware of what's being reinforced (Dulany, 1968; Spielberger & DeNike, 1966).

On the other hand, sometimes just expecting an aversive event (as a US) can produce what look like conditioned responses to other stimuli (Bridger & Mandel, 1964; Spacapan & Cohen, 1983). After classical conditioning of a fear response, a statement that the painful US will no longer occur sometimes eliminates fear of the CS (Bandura, 1969; Grings, 1973). All of these findings suggest that conditioning is about noting rule-based regularities (recall Box 10.1).

There is also a viewpoint that takes something of a middle ground on this issue. In this view, experiences are processed in two different ways in different areas of the nervous system. The result is learning that creates records of two different forms (Daw, Niv, & Dayan, 2005). One mode acquires what might be thought of as an "actuarial" record of experiences, a totaling of all the associations across all instances of experience. The other mode, in contrast, tries to develop a predictive model. Instead of just piling things up, it tries to generate expectancies. Presumably, the second mode is more advanced than the first one. Consistent with that, toddlers operate according to the first mode of learning (Thomason-Schill, Ramscar, & Chrysikou, 2009). Perhaps awareness matters in the second but not the first way of learning.

Observational Learning

Although many aspects of the social–cognitive learning approach can be viewed as elaborations on classical and instrumental conditioning, there is one part of this approach that leaves those concepts behind. This part is called **observational learning**. Two people are involved in this process, providing yet another basis for the term *social learning theory*.

Observational learning takes place when one person performs an action, and another person observes it and thereby acquires the ability to repeat it (Bandura, 1986; Flanders, 1968). For such an event to represent observational learning unambiguously, the behavior should be one the observer doesn't already know. At a minimum, the behavior should be one the observer had not previously associated with the context in which it's now occurring.

Observational learning allows people to pack huge amounts of information into their minds quickly. This makes it very important. Observational learning occurs as early as the first year of life (Jones, 2007; Meltzoff, 1985). What's most remarkable about it is how simple it is. It seems to require little more than the observer's noticing and understanding what's going on.

Table 10.2 Four Categories of Variables (and specific examples of each) That Influence Observational Learning and Performance.

Attention for Encoding
- *Characteristics of the model:* Is the model attractive or powerful or an expert?
- *Characteristics of the behavior:* Is the behavior distinctive, clear, and simple?
- *Characteristics of the observer:* Is the observer motivated to attend and capable of attending?

Retention
- Use of imagery as an encoding strategy
- Use of language as an encoding strategy
- Use of mental rehearsal to keep in memory

Production
- Observer's capacity to produce necessary responses
- Observer's prior experience with overall behavior
- Observer's prior experience with components of behavior

Performance
- *Consequences to the model:* Is the model rewarded or punished, or are there no consequences?
- *Consequences to the observer:* Is the observer rewarded or punished, or are there no consequences?

Source: Based on Bandura, 1977a, 1986.

ATTENTION AND RETENTION

This last statement requires several qualifications, which will help to give a better sense of what observational learning is (see Table 10.2). Observational learning requires the observer to pay attention to the model (the person being observed). If the person doesn't pay attention to the right aspect of the model's behavior, the behavior won't be encoded well enough to be remembered.

This principle has several implications. For one, it means that observational learning will work better with some models than others. Models that draw attention for some reason—for example, from their power or attractiveness—are most likely to be effective. The role of attention also means that some *acts* will more likely be encoded than others. Acts that are especially salient will have more impact than acts that aren't (cf. McArthur, 1981; Taylor & Fiske, 1978). Other variables that matter here are the observer's capabilities and concentration. For instance, an observer who's distracted by music while viewing a model may miss entirely what he or she is doing.

A second important set of processes in observational learning concern *retention* of what's observed. In some way or other, what's been observed has to be represented in memory (which makes this a cognitive as well as a social sort of learning). Two strategies of coding predominate. One is *imaginal coding*, creating images or mental pictures of what you're observing. The other is *verbal coding*, creating a description to yourself of what you're observing. Either can produce a memory that can later be used to repeat the behavior (Bandura & Jeffery, 1973; Bandura, Jeffery, & Bachicha, 1974; Gerst, 1971).

PRODUCTION

Once an action is in memory, one more thing is needed for it to occur. Specifically, you have to translate what you observed into a form you can *produce* in your own actions. How well you can do this depends partly on whether you already know some of the components of the act. It's easier to reproduce a behavior if you have skills

Having readily available summary labels for action sequences greatly simplifies the task of storing things in memory.
Reprinted by permission: Tribune Media Services.

that underlie it or know bits of action involved in it. That's why it's often so easy for experienced athletes to pick up a new sport. They often already know movements similar to those used in the new sport.

The importance of having components available also applies to the encoding process (see Johnson & Kieras, 1983). For example, if you already know names (or have good images) for components of the modeled activity, you'll have less to put into memory. If you have to remember every little thing, it will be harder to keep things straight. Think of the difference in complexity between the label "Sauté one onion" (or "Remove the brake pad assembly") and the set of physical acts the label refers to. Now think about how much easier it is to remember the label than the sequence of acts. Using the label as mental shorthand simplifies the task for memory. But you can do this only if you know what the label refers to (see the cartoon).

ACQUISITION VERSUS PERFORMANCE

Observational learning permits fast learning of complicated behaviors. Given what we've just discussed, it also seems to be a case of "the more you already know, the easier it is to learn." There's an important distinction to be made, however, between *acquisition* of a behavioral potential and *performance* of the behavior. People don't always repeat the actions they see. People learn a great many things that they never do.

To know whether observational learning will result in behavior, we need to know something else. We need to know what outcome the person expects the behavior to lead to (Bandura, 1977a, 1986). An illustration of this comes from an early study by Bandura (1965). Children saw a 5-minute film in which an adult model performed a series of distinctive aggressive acts toward an inflated doll. The model accompanied each act with a verbalization. For example, while pounding the doll on the head with a mallet, the model said, "Sockeroo—stay down."

Many complex behaviors are acquired by children through observational learning.

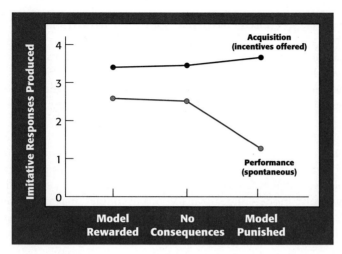

FIGURE 10.5

Acquisition and Performance. Participants observed a model display a series of aggressive acts that led to reward, no consequences, or punishment. Participants then had an opportunity to imitate the model spontaneously (performance). Finally, they were asked to demonstrate what they could remember of the model's behavior (acquisition). The study showed that reinforcement of the model played no role in acquisition but did influence spontaneous performance. Source: *Based on Bandura & Walters, 1963.*

At this point, three experimental conditions were created, using three versions of the film. In one condition, another adult entered the picture, praised the model, and gave the model a candy treat. In a second condition (the no-consequence control group), this final scene was omitted. In a third condition, this scene was replaced by one in which the second adult came in and punished the model verbally and with a spanking.

After seeing one of these three films, the child in the study was taken to an observation room that contained a wide range of toys. Among the toys was an inflated doll identical to the one in the film. The child was left alone for 10 minutes. Hidden assistants noted whether the child performed any of the previously modeled aggressive acts. The number of acts the child did was the measure of spontaneous *performance.*

Ten minutes later, the experimenter returned. At this point, the child was offered an incentive (juice and stickers) to show the experimenter as many of the previously viewed acts as he or she could remember. The number of behaviors shown was the measure of *acquisition.*

The results of this study are very instructive. The top line in Figure 10.5 shows how many acts children reproduced correctly in the three experimental conditions, when given an incentive to do so (the measure of acquisition). It's obvious that there isn't a trace of difference in acquisition. Reinforcement or punishment for the model had no impact here. Spontaneous performance, though, shows a different picture. The outcome for the model influenced what the observers did spontaneously. As in many studies (Thelen & Rennie, 1972), the effect of punishment was greater than the effect of reward, although other evidence shows that both can be effective in this sort of situation (e.g., Kanfer & Marston, 1963; Liebert & Fernandez, 1970; Rosekrans, 1967).

In conclusion, vicarious reinforcement influences whether people spontaneously do behaviors they've acquired by observation. This effect is the same as any instance of vicarious reinforcement. It thus reflects vicarious instrumental learning. In contrast, reinforcement to the model has no influence on acquisition of the behavioral potential. Thus, observational learning and vicarious instrumental learning are distinct processes.

Modeling of Aggression and the Issue of Media Violence

The processes described in this chapter provide a set of tools for analyzing behavior. To indicate how broadly they can be used, this section describes one area in which the processes play a key role. The processes tend to get tangled up with one another. Nevertheless, they can be distinguished conceptually, and we'll do so as we go along.

There's a great deal of concern in the United States about the impact of media violence on real-life aggression. Social–cognitive learning theories have been applied to this issue for some time. Observational learning occurs with **symbolic models** as well as live models. Indeed, the influence of symbolic models is pervasive. Symbolic models appear on TV and in movies, magazines, books, video games, and so on. The actions they portray—and the patterns of reinforcement around the actions—can have a big impact on both acquisition and performance of observers.

All the ways models influence observers are implicated here, to one degree or another (Anderson et al., 2003). At least three processes occur. First, people who observe innovative aggressive techniques acquire the techniques as behavior potentials by observational learning. Wherever observational learning *can* occur, it *does* occur (Geen, 1998; Heller & Polsky, 1975; recall Figure 10.5). This principle looms large, as producers strive to make movies new and different every year. A common source of novelty is new methods for inflicting pain.

A second process is that observing violence that's condoned or even rewarded helps promote the sense that aggression is an appropriate way to deal with disagreements. Vicarious reinforcement thus increases the likelihood that viewers will use such tactics themselves. (By implication, this is also why some worry about sex on TV and in movies.)

When the suggestion is made that violence is reinforced in the media, a common reply is that the "bad guys" in TV and movie stories get punished. Two things must be noted, however. First, the punishment usually comes late in the story, after a lot of short-term reinforcement. As a result, aggression is linked more closely to reinforcement than to punishment. Second, the actions of the heroes usually are also aggressive, and these actions are highly reinforced. From that, there's a clear message that being aggressive is a good way to deal with problems. Does viewing so-called acceptable aggression make people more likely to use aggression in their own lives when they're annoyed? Yes. Whether the model is live (e.g., Baron & Kempner, 1970) or symbolic (e.g., Bandura, 1965; Liebert & Baron, 1972), exposure to aggressive models increases the aggression of observers.

The final point here is more diffuse: Repeated exposure to violence *desensitizes* observers to human suffering. The shock and upset that most people would associate with acts of extreme violence are extinguished by repeated exposure to violence. In 1991, the police chief of Washington, DC, said, "When I talk to young people involved with violence, there's no remorse, . . . no sense that this is morally wrong." Exposure to violence in video games creates a similar desensitizing effect (Bartholow, Bushman, & Sestir, 2006; Bartholow, Sestir, & Davis, 2005; Carnagey, Anderson, & Bushman, 2006).

The long-term consequences of this desensitizing process are profoundly worrisome. As people's emotional reactions to violence diminish, being victimized (and victimizing others) is coming to be seen as an ordinary part of life. It's hard to study the impact of this process in its full scope, but the effects are pervasive enough that they represent a real threat to society. Indeed, there is a growing awareness across the nation that bullying in schools is on the rise.

Does this mean that all video games are bad? No. In fact, prosocial video games seem to increase prosocial behavior (Gentile et al., 2009). What matters is entirely the content that people are exposed to during the game.

Assessment

As described throughout the chapter, conditioning theories and social–cognitive theories tend to focus on different aspects of the learning process. It should not come as a surprise, then, to learn that their approaches to assessment are also slightly different.

CONDITIONING-BASED APPROACHES

From the view of conditioning theories, personality is largely the accumulation of a person's conditioned tendencies (Ciminero, Calhoun, & Adams, 1977; Hersen & Bellack, 1976; Staats, 1996). By adulthood, you have acquired a wide range of emotional responses to various stimuli, which you experience as attitudes and preferences. Many assessment techniques from the conditioning approach measure the affective quality of people's experience.

Two techniques have evolved. One focuses on assessment of emotional responses through **physiological assessment**. Physiological assessment (which also relates to biological process views of personality, Chapter 7) follows from the fact that emotional responses are partly physiological. When you experience an emotion (especially if it's intense), changes take place in your body: changes in muscle tension, heart rate, blood pressure, brain waves, sweat gland activity, and more. Some think the measurement of such responses is useful in assessing problems such as posttraumatic stress disorder (Keane et al., 1998; Orr et al., 1998).

A second technique that can be used to assess emotional responses is called **behavioral assessment** (Barlow, 1981; Haynes & O'Brien, 2000; Staats, 1996). It entails observing overt behavior in specific situations. Emotions such as fear can be assessed by behavioral indicators—trembling, paleness, avoidance, and so on. This technique can also be applied more broadly to assess what kinds of activities people undertake, for how long, and in what patterns.

Behavioral assessment varies widely in how it's actually done. Sometimes, the observer simply counts acts of specific types, checks possibilities from a prearranged list, or watches how far into a sequence of action a person goes before stopping (Lang & Lazovik, 1963; O'Leary & Becker, 1967; Paul, 1966). In other cases, the procedure is more elaborate—for instance, using automated devices to record how long a person engages in various behaviors.

SOCIAL–COGNITIVE APPROACHES

In considering the social–cognitive approach to assessment, two characteristics stand out. First, the social–cognitive approach tends to use self-report devices, rather than behavioral observation. Given that the cognitive learning view emphasizes the role of thoughts, it's only natural to take people's reports of their tendencies to act in various ways and to have various kinds of thoughts and feelings as useful sources of information.

The second issue concerns what variables are measured. Assessment from this view tends to focus on *experiential* variables. Instead of charting actions, assessments frequently ask people how they feel or what kinds of thoughts go through their minds, in certain situations. Particularly important are expectancies: expectancies of coping and expectancies of personal efficacy. This should be no surprise, because expectations are regarded as so important in this view of behavior.

Assessment in the social–cognitive learning view tends to emphasize responses to *specific* categories of situations, as does the rest of the learning perspective. This reflects the fact that behavior varies greatly from one situation to another. The social–cognitive learning view differs from the conditioning view, however, in its emphasis on personal views of situations, rather than objective definitions of situations. According to this approach, people's representations determine how they act. This must be taken into account in assessment.

Problems in Behavior, and Behavior Change

If personality can derive from learning, so can problems. People sometimes learn things that interfere with their lives, and they sometimes fail to learn things that would make their lives easier. These phenomena suggest a basis for several kinds of problems, along with ways of treating them. As a group, the techniques are termed **behavior modification** or **behavior therapy** (Craighead, Kazdin, & Mahoney, 1981). These terms reflect the fact that the emphasis is on changing the person's actual *behavior*.

CLASSICAL CONDITIONING OF EMOTIONAL RESPONSES

One class of problems is emotional reactions that interfere with effective functioning. People sometimes have intense anxiety when exposed to specific stimuli, called **phobias**. Although a phobic reaction can become tied to virtually any stimulus, some are more common than others. Common focal points for phobias are animals such as dogs, snakes, and spiders; closed-in spaces such as elevators; open or exposed spaces such as railings on high balconies; and germs and the possibility of infection.

The conditioning view is that phobic reactions are classically conditioned. This view also leads to ideas about how to treat phobias. One technique is **systematic desensitization**. People are first taught to relax thoroughly. That relaxation response is then used to counteract or replace fear in the presence of the phobic stimulus, a process termed **counterconditioning**. Once the person has learned to relax, he or she can work with a therapist to create an anxiety hierarchy—a list of situations involving the feared stimulus, ranked by how much anxiety each creates (see Table 10.3).

In the desensitization process, you relax fully. Then you visualize a scene from the least-threatening end of the hierarchy. The anxiety aroused by this image is allowed to dissipate. Then, while you continue to relax, you imagine the scene again. You do this repeatedly, until the scene provokes no anxiety at all (i.e., until your fearful reaction to the stimulus has been extinguished). Then you move to the next level on the anxiety hierarchy. Gradually, you're able to imagine increasingly threatening scenes without anxiety. Eventually, the imagined scenes are replaced by the actual feared stimulus. As the anxiety is countered by relaxation, you're able to interact more and more effectively with the stimulus that previously produced intense fear. Systematic desensitization has proven very effective in reducing fear reactions, particularly for fears that focus on a specific stimulus (e.g., Brady, 1972; Davison & Wilson, 1973).

Table 10.3 An Anxiety Hierarchy Such as Might be Used in Systematic Desensitization for One Type of Acrophobia (fear of heights). Each scene is carefully visualized while the person relaxes completely, working from the least threatening scene (at the bottom) to those that produce greater anxiety (toward the top).

Looking down from the top of the Empire State Building
Walking around the top floor of the Empire State Building
Looking out the window of a 12-story building
Looking over the balcony rail of a 4-story building
Looking out the window of a 4-story building
Looking up at a 30-story building from across a small park
Reading a story about the construction of a skyscraper
Reading a story that mentions being on top of the Statue of Liberty
Hearing a news story that menions the tall buildings of a city
Seeing a TV news story in which tall buildings appear in the background

More recently, desensitization has been taken in a different direction. Many therapists now use treatments in which the person is exposed to a more intense dose of the feared stimulus and endures it—while anxiety rises then gradually falls. Exposure to the feared stimulus is maintained well after the physical aspects of the anxiety have subsided. It seems that extinction occurs more quickly when a state of rest occurs after the anxiety has fallen off. Such **exposure treatments** for phobias can sometimes be done in as little as one session (Öst, Ferebee, & Furmark, 1997). This sort of treatment has also proven to be superior for severe posttraumatic disorders (Foa & Meadows, 1997; Powers, Halpern, Ferenschak, Gillihan, & Foa, 2010).

CONDITIONING AND CONTEXT

The purpose of procedures based on extinction and counterconditioning is to replace an undesired response with a neutral one or with a response opposite the original one. Often, however, the response will disappear in the treatment setting but return when the person is in his or her everyday environment. How can that be made less likely?

Context plays an important role is this effect. That is, the context of the original conditioning often differs from the context of the therapy. In effect, each context is a set of discriminative stimuli. People acquire a neutral response (via extinction) to the target stimulus in the therapy room. But when they return to the setting where the response was learned, the old response may reappear (Bouton, 1994, 2000). Why? Because the stimuli in the original setting *weren't there during the extinction*. As a result, they still serve as cues for behavior.

For the new response to carry over to the person's life outside the therapy room, one of two things must happen. First, the person can acquire the new response in a setting that resembles the setting where the old response was acquired. This will cause the new response to generalize to the original setting. Alternatively, the person can avoid the original setting. That's why many approaches to avoiding relapse emphasize staying away from settings that resemble those where the original response was acquired and maintained.

As a concrete example, consider work on smoking relapse. Withdrawal from nicotine isn't the sole problem in quitting (Perkins, 1999). Relapse rates are as high as 60% even if smokers get nicotine other ways (Kenford, Fiore, Jorenby, & Smith, 1994). Many who quit smoking return to it well after the end of nicotine withdrawal (Brandon, Tiffany, Obremski, & Baker, 1990). Why? The smoking is linked by conditioning to particular contexts (after meals, after sex, being at a bar, and so on). The context itself is a discriminative stimulus for smoking long after the craving for nicotine is gone (Carter & Tiffany, 1999; Conklin, 2006). Contexts can create cravings even when no specific smoking cues are present, such as cigarettes or a lighter (Conklin, Robin, Perkins, Salkeld, & McClernon, 2008).

Programs to quit smoking now emphasize efforts to extinguish responses to the cues linked to smoking. The contextual cues are presented alone, with no smoking. The hope is that the nonsmoking response will condition to those cues, and the person will thereby become resistant to relapse. Such programs have had only limited success (Conklin & Tiffany, 2002), perhaps because they've used "normative" smoking cues, rather than personalized ones. Because everyone has a unique smoking history, individualizing the cues may promote better success (Conklin, Perkins, Robin, McClernon, & Salkeld, in press; Conklin & Tiffany, 2001).

INSTRUMENTAL CONDITIONING AND MALADAPTIVE BEHAVIORS

Another set of problems in behavior relates to the principles of instrumental conditioning. The reasoning here is that undesirable behavioral tendencies are built in by reinforcement. Indeed, they can be acquired in ways that make them resistant to extinction.

Imagine that a certain class of behavior—for instance, throwing tantrums when you don't get your way—was reinforced at one period of your life, because your parents gave in to them. The reinforcement strengthened the tendency to repeat the tantrum. If reinforced often enough and with the right pattern of partial reinforcement, the behavior becomes frequent and persistent.

Later on (when you are older), the behavior is less appropriate. It isn't reinforced as often now, although people do give in to it occasionally. (It's surprising how often people reinforce the exact behaviors they wish would go away.) Although the reinforcement is rare, the behavior continues (thanks to the partial reinforcement effect). The behavior seems irrational to observers, but from the conditioning view, it's just showing resistance to extinction.

The principles of instrumental conditioning suggest that the way to change such undesired behavior is to change the patterns of reinforcement. One good approach is to reinforce desired alternative actions and simultaneously reduce even further (if possible) any reinforcement of the undesired action. This should shape the behavior toward greater adaptiveness or suitability. This approach is sometimes called **contingency management**.

An example comes from the literature of health psychology. Childhood obesity is a risk factor for several serious health problems later on. It stems partly from habits such as watching TV instead of being active and partly from having a poor diet. Research has shown that reinforcing less sedentary activities causes both an increase in those activities and a decrease in sedentary activities (Epstein, Saelens, Myers, & Vito, 1997). Similarly, reinforcing the choice of fruits and vegetables over snack foods causes an increase in the tendency to choose healthy foods (Goldfield & Epstein, 2002).

Contingency management has also been used in efforts to keep people from abusing drugs and alcohol. It can be used to shape undesired behavior in the direction of abstinence over time before quitting (Preston, Umbricht, Wong, & Epstein, 2001; Reback et al., 2010). It also can be useful in treating alcohol dependence (Petry, Martin, Cooney, & Kranzler, 2000) and in supporting abstinence from cocaine use (Higgins, Wong, Badger, Ogden, & Dantona, 2000; Rash, Alessi, & Petry, 2008).

SOCIAL–COGNITIVE APPROACHES

Social–cognitive approaches suggest further influences on problems and their treatment, using the three key principles of vicarious conditioning, expectancies, and observational learning.

Vicarious processes suggest two changes to the analyses described thus far. First, you don't have to have direct experience with a stimulus to develop an emotional response toward it (such as fear). You can acquire emotional responses vicariously. Second, your patterns of action can be influenced by watching outcomes that other people experience. Vicarious reinforcement can build in behavior, even if the behavior isn't desirable. Vicarious punishment can reduce your tendency to do a behavior, even if it's a behavior that's actually adaptive.

All these effects can be seen as mediated, in part, by expectancies (see Bandura, 1986). If you expect to experience strong fear in high places, you'll avoid high places. If you expect to get social approval for bullying someone else, you may do it. If you expect to be rejected, to do badly on an exam, or even to do badly at "life," you may not even try (Carver, Scheier, & Segerstrom, 2010; Scheier & Carver, 1992). Expectancies can develop from direct experience, from vicarious experience, from things that other people tell you, or from putting two and two together in your own head.

Another source of behavior problems, in the social learning view, is more specific. Problems sometimes reflect **skill deficits**. A person with a skill deficit is literally unable to do something that's necessary or desirable. Some skill deficits reflect deficits in observational learning. That is, in some cases, people never had good models to learn from. Without being able to learn how to do important things (such as cooking, taking notes in class, dancing, and many others), people can have gaps in the ability to function.

Note that having a skill deficit can influence the development of expectations. People who know they lack particular skills anticipate bad outcomes in situations in

Seeing someone else cope successfully with something that you fear can help you develop the ability to cope successfully yourself.

which the skills are relevant. For example, people who see themselves as lacking social skills come to expect the worst in social situations.

MODELING-BASED THERAPY FOR SKILL DEFICITS

Not surprisingly, modeling plays an important role in the therapy techniques identified with the social–cognitive viewpoint. Techniques involving modeling have been used in two areas: skill deficits and emotion-based problems.

When people lack specific types of adaptive behavior, they can often develop the needed skills by watching a good model. The model is put in the situation for which the skill is lacking and makes an action appropriate to the situation. The observer (the person in therapy) is then encouraged to repeat the action. This repetition can be overt (action), or it can be covert (mentally practicing the action). Indeed, the modeling can also be covert, with the subject told to imagine someone else doing a particular behavior within a particular scenario (Kazdin, 1975).

In principle, modeling can be used to supply missing skills any place there are deficits. Research on this subject, however, commonly focuses on such areas as basic social skills (e.g., La Greca & Santogrossi, 1980; La Greca, Stone, & Bell, 1983; Reichow & Volkmar, 2010; Ross, Ross, & Evans, 1971) and assertiveness (Goldfried & Davison, 1976; Kazdin, 1974, 1975; McFall & Twentyman, 1973; Rosenthal & Reese, 1976). Assertiveness is acting to make sure your rights aren't violated while at the same time not violating someone else's rights. It can be hard to know just how to respond to problem situations in a manner that's properly assertive. But having models who illustrate responses (combined with practice, to make sure you can do the same thing) can make a big difference.

In therapies for skill deficits, observational learning is often blended with vicarious reinforcement. In certain cases, though, one or the other seems most relevant. In some cases, people literally don't know what to do in a given situation. Observational learning is most relevant here, because it provides new responses. In other cases, it's not so much that people don't know what to do but that they have doubts about whether doing it will work. In these cases, vicarious reinforcement seems to play a larger role.

MODELING AND RESPONSES TO FEAR

In discussing modeling and fear-related behavior problems, a distinction is made between two kinds of models: those who exhibit mastery and those who exhibit coping (e.g., Meichenbaum, 1971). A **mastery model** seems to be completely without fear regarding what the person in therapy is afraid of. This model presumably creates vicarious extinction of the conditioned fear, as the observer sees that the model experiences no distress. In contrast, a **coping model** is one who initially displays fear but overcomes it and eventually handles the situation. The effect of this model presumably depends on the fact that the model is in the *same situation* as the observer but is noticeably able to overcome the fear through active effort.

The effect of a coping model seems more cognitive than that of the mastery model. And although the evidence isn't entirely consistent, coping models seem more effective than mastery models in therapy for fears (Kornhaber & Schroeder, 1975; Meichenbaum, 1971). This effectiveness attests to the powerful role that cognitive processes can play in coping with fear.

Another distinction to be made here is between modeling in which the observer just observes and **participant modeling**, in which the model (often, the therapist) performs the behavior in front of the other person, who then repeats it. Participant modeling usually involves a lot of verbalization, instruction, and personalized assurance from the model. It takes more of the therapist's time, but it's more powerful as a behavior change technique (e.g., Bandura, 1982; Bandura, Adams, & Beyer, 1977; Davis, Ollendick, & Öst, 2009).

In a typical modeling therapy for a specific fear, a model approaches, engages, and deals with the feared stimulus. While doing so, the model describes the feelings that develop and the mental strategies that are being used to cope. Then the observer tries to do the same thing—first with the therapist's help, then alone. This procedure is effective at reducing fear and increasing coping in a variety of domains, including fears aroused by animals such as dogs and snakes (Bandura et al., 1977; Bandura, Grusec, & Menlove, 1967; Bandura & Menlove, 1968), by surgery, injections, and dental work (Melamed & Siegel, 1975; Melamed, Weinstein, Hawes, & Katin-Borland, 1975; Vernon, 1974); and by test taking (Cooley & Spiegler, 1980; Malec, Park, & Watkins, 1976; Sarason, 1975).

THERAPEUTIC CHANGES IN EFFICACY EXPECTANCY

The research just outlined indicates that models who display an ability to cope with difficulties can help people to overcome their own fears. But how does it happen? Bandura (1977b) suggested these effects illustrate a broader principle behind behavior change. In his view, when therapy is effective (through whatever technique), it works by increasing the person's sense of efficacy for a given class of situations. When a model shows an ability to overcome fear, it helps give observers the sense that they can also overcome their fear. This enhanced perception of personal efficacy results in greater effort and persistence.

These ideas, introduced earlier in the chapter, have been tested in many studies of the therapy process (e.g., Avia & Kanfer, 1980; Bandura et al., 1977; Bandura, Adams, Hardy, & Howells, 1980; Bandura & Schunk, 1981; DiClemente, 1981; Gauthier & Ladouceur, 1981). Across many such tests, participant modeling has been effective in changing people's efficacy expectancies and changing their behavior. Such outcomes also generalize to new situations.

In Bandura's (1986, 1997) view, such results make several points. The broadest is that change in efficacy expectancy mediates behavior change. That is, the behavior changes *because* of a change in expectancy. Two other points concern factors that determine efficacy perceptions. Expectancy ratings typically change most among people who have an opportunity to show themselves that they can cope (by participant modeling). This fits with Bandura's belief that performance accomplishments are the strongest influence on efficacy perceptions.

Research also demonstrates a second influence on efficacy perceptions, however: vicarious experiences. That is, modeling-only groups typically report greater efficacy and outperform control groups. Vicarious consequences don't have as strong an impact as personal outcomes, but they definitely play a role. Bandura (1977b) also suggested that verbal persuasion and emotional arousal can influence efficacy perceptions.

The Learning Perspective: Problems and Prospects

The learning perspective on personality has been particularly influential among two groups: researchers involved in the experimental analysis of behavior in the laboratory and clinicians trained when behavior therapies were at their height of popularity. The learning view is attractive to these groups for two different reasons, which in turn represent two strengths of this view.

First, the learning viewpoint emerged—as had no other perspective before it—from the crucible of research. The ideas that form this approach to behavior were intended to be given close scrutiny, to be either upheld or disconfirmed through investigation. Many of the ideas have been tested thoroughly, and the evidence that supports them is substantial. Having a viewpoint on the nature of personality that can be verified by careful observation is very satisfying to researchers.

A second reason for the impact of learning ideas is the effectiveness of behavioral and cognitive–behavioral therapy techniques. Research has shown that several kinds of problems can be treated with fairly simple procedures. With this realization, clinicians began to look closely at the principles behind the procedures. The learning perspective has an aura of credibility among some psychologists because of its good fit with these effective techniques of behavior change.

Although many find this viewpoint congenial, it also has its critics. One criticism concerns researchers' tendency to simplify the situations they study. Simplification ensures experimental control, and having control helps clarify cause and effect. Yet sometimes, the simplification results in situations that offer very few options for behavior. There can be a nagging suspicion that the behavior occurred because there were so many pressures in its direction and so little chance to do anything else. But what happens to behavior when the person leaves the laboratory? This concern is far less applicable to the social–cognitive learning approach. People working from it have examined behavior in very diverse settings and contexts.

Another problem with the learning view is that it isn't really so much a theory of personality as a view of the determinants of behavior. Some people think this view is too simplistic to provide a meaningful view of personality. The processes of learning presumably operate continuously in a piecemeal and haphazard fashion. The human experience, on the other hand, seems highly complex and orderly. How do the haphazard learning processes yield such an orderly product?

To put it another way, conditioning theories tell us a lot about how a specific behavior becomes more or less probable, but they don't tell us so much about the person who is doing the behavior. The processes are very mechanistic. There seems little place for the subjective sense of personhood, little focus on the continuity and coherence that characterize the sense of self. In sum, to many, this analysis of personality doesn't convey the subjective experience of what it means to *have* a personality. Again, this criticism is less applicable to the social–cognitive learning theories. Concepts such as the sense of personal efficacy have a great deal to do with the sense of personhood, even if the focus is on only a limited part of the person at any given time.

Another problem for the learning perspective concerns the relationship between conditioning ideas and social–cognitive ideas about learning. The two approaches to learning are split by a core disagreement. We minimized this issue while presenting the theoretical principles, but it deserves mention. The issue is this: Conditioning theories tend to focus on observable events. Behavioral tendencies are explained from patterns of prior experiences and present cues. Nothing else is needed. Cognitions are irrelevant. The social–cognitive learning approach is quite different. Expectations cause behavior. Actions follow from thinking.

Treating cognitions as causes of behavior may mean rejecting fundamental tenets of the conditioning approach. In the more cognitive view, classical and instrumental conditioning aren't necessarily incremental processes occurring outside awareness; they depend on expectancies and mental models. Reinforcement is seen as providing information about future incentives, instead of acting directly to strengthen behavioral tendencies.

How are we to think about this situation? Are the newer theories extrapolations from the previous theories, or are they quite different? Can they be merged, or are they competitors for the same theoretical niche? Some people would say the newer version of the learning perspective should *replace* the conditioning version—that the conditioning view was wrong, that human learning simply doesn't occur that way.

Some people have abandoned any effort at integration and simply stepped away from the issue altogether. For example, years ago, Bandura dropped the word *learning* from the phrase he used to characterize his theory. He now calls it *social–cognitive theory* (Bandura, 1986). This raises the question of whether his ideas about efficacy expectancies should be seen as belonging to the learning perspective at all.

Bandura's change of label reflects a more general trend among people who started out within the social learning framework. Over the past 35 years, many of these people have been influenced by the ideas of cognitive psychology. Many people who used to call their orientation to personality a *social learning view* would hedge in using that term today. Some would now give their orientation a different label. There has been a gradual fraying of the edge of the social learning approach, such that it has tended to combine with the cognitive and self-regulation theories, discussed in later chapters. This blurring and blending between bodies of thought raises a final question for the learning approach: Will this approach retain its identity as an active area of work in the years to come, or will it disperse and have its themes absorbed by other viewpoints?

• SUMMARY •

Conditioning approaches emphasizes two types of learning. In classical conditioning, a neutral stimulus (CS) is presented along with another stimulus (US) that already elicits a reflexive response (UR). After repeated pairings, the CS itself comes to elicit a response (CR) that's similar to the UR. The CR appears to be an anticipatory response that prepares for the US.

This basic phenomenon is modified by discrimination (different stimuli leading to different responses) and extended by generalization (different stimuli leading to similar responses). CRs fade if the CS is presented repeatedly without the US, a process termed *extinction*. Classical conditioning is important to personality primarily when the responses being conditioned are emotional reactions (emotional conditioning). Classical conditioning thus provides a basis for understanding people's unique preferences and aversions, and it provides a way of analyzing certain psychological problems, such as phobias.

In instrumental conditioning, a behavior is followed by an outcome that's either positively valued or aversive. If the outcome is positively valued, the tendency to perform the behavior is strengthened. Thus, the outcome is called a *reinforcer*. If the outcome is aversive (a *punisher*), the tendency to perform the behavior is reduced. *Discrimination* in instrumental conditioning means responding in different ways to different situational cues; *generalization* is responding in a similar way to different cues;

extinction is the reduction of a behavioral tendency through nonreinforcement of the behavior. Reinforcers can occur in many patterns, termed *schedules*. An important effect of variations in reinforcement schedules is that behavior learned by intermittent (partial) reinforcement is more persistent (under later conditions of nonreinforcement) than is a behavior learned by continuous reinforcement.

Another generation of learning theories has evolved. They are called *cognitive* because they emphasize the role of thought processes in behavior and *social* because they emphasize the idea that people often learn from one another. Several aspects of these theories represent elaborations on conditioning principles, including an emphasis on social reinforcement (rather than other sorts of reinforcement) in shaping behavior. Because humans have the capability for empathy (vicariously aroused emotions), we can experience classical conditioning vicariously. We can also experience reinforcement and punishment vicariously, causing shifts in action tendencies on the basis of someone else's outcomes. This view also holds that humans often learn expectancies and then apply them to new situations.

The idea that expectancies about outcomes play an important part in determining behavior is a central part of social–cognitive learning models. Another important idea is that perceptions of personal efficacy determine whether a person will persist when in stressful circumstances.

One part of this approach to personality stands as distinct from conditioning principles: the process of acquiring behavior potentials through observational learning. This process requires that an observer attend to a model (who is displaying a behavior), retain some memory of what was done (usually a visual or verbal memory), and have component skills to be able to reproduce what was modeled. This process of acquisition isn't directly influenced by reinforcement contingencies. On the other hand, spontaneous performance of the acquired behavior is very much influenced by perceptions of reinforcement contingencies.

Assessment, from a conditioning point of view, emphasizes observation of various aspects of behavior as they occur in specific situations. Assessment can focus on people's physiological responses, their overt behaviors, or their reports of emotional reactions in response to different kinds of stimuli. Assessment from a social–cognitive learning point of view is more reliant on self-reports.

The conditioning approach assumes that problems in behavior are the result of the same kinds of processes as result in normal behavior. Classical conditioning can produce intense and irrational fears, called *phobias*; instrumental conditioning can produce behavior tendencies that persist even when they are no longer adaptive. These various problems can be treated by means of conditioning procedures, collectively termed *behavior therapy* or *behavior modification*. Systematic desensitization counterconditions fear reactions with relaxation. Exposure treatments keep people focused on distressing situations until long after the burst of anxiety calms down.

Problems in behavior can also develop through vicarious learning, or when people haven't had the opportunity to learn needed behaviors from models. Therapy based on the social–cognitive learning approach often involve modeling, whether as an attempt to remedy skill deficits through observational learning or as an attempt to show the utility of coping skills through vicarious reinforcement.

• GLOSSARY •

Behavior modification or behavior therapy   A therapeutic approach in which conditioning processes are used to change behavior.

Behavioral assessment   An assessment made by observing a person's overt behavior.

Classical conditioning   The pairing of a neutral stimulus with an unconditioned stimulus.

Conditioned or conditional stimulus (CS)   A neutral stimulus that's paired with a US to become conditioned.

Conditioned or conditional response (CR)   A response to the CS that's acquired by classical conditioning.

Contingency management   Programs in which reinforcement is increased for desired behaviors and withheld after undesired behaviors.

Continuous reinforcement   A schedule in which reinforcement follows each instance of the behavior.

Coping model   A model that displays fear but ultimately handles it.

Counterconditioning   The linking of an emotion to a stimulus that differs from the emotion the stimulus now causes.

Discrimination   Responding in a different manner to different stimuli.

Discriminative stimulus   A cue that controls the occurrence of behavior.

Efficacy expectancy   Confidence of being able to do something successfully.

Emotional conditioning   Classical conditioning in which the CR is an emotional reaction.

Exposure treatments   Treatments in which people stay focused on the distressing topic until well after their anxiety reaction dissipates

Extinction   In classical conditioning, the reduction of a CR by repeating the CS without the US; in instrumental conditioning, the reduction of a behavioral tendency by removing reinforcement.

Generalization   Responding in a similar manner to somewhat different stimuli.

Habit hierarchy   The ordering of a person's potential responses by their likelihood.

Higher-order conditioning   An event in which a former CS now acts as a US in a new instance of conditioning.

Instrumental or **operant conditioning**   Conditioning in which a behavior becomes more likely because it's followed by a desirable event or less likely because it's followed by an undesirable event.

Mastery model   A model that displays no fear.

Negative reinforcement   The removal of an aversive stimulus.

Observational learning   Acquiring the ability to do a new behavior by watching someone else do it.

Operant conditioning *See* Instrumental conditioning.

Outcome expectancy   A judgment about how likely a specific behavior is to attain a specific goal.

Partial reinforcement   A schedule in which the behavior is reinforced less often than every time it occurs.

Partial reinforcement effect   The fact that a behavior acquired through partial reinforcement is resistant to extinction.

Participant modeling   The act of practicing a behavior that's hard for you while using the therapist as a model.

Phobia   An inappropriately intense fear of some specific class of stimuli.

Physiological assessment   The measuring of physiological aspects of emotional reactions.

Positive reinforcement   A reinforcement involving the addition of a desired stimulus.

Punisher   An undesired event that makes the behavior that came before it less likely to occur again.

Reflex   An event in which a stimulus produces an automatic response.

Reinforcer   An event that makes the behavior that came before it more likely to occur again.

Self-control   The regulation and sometimes restraint of one's own activities.

Self-efficacy *See* Efficacy expectancy.

Self-reinforcement   The approval you give yourself for your own behavior.

Skill deficit   The absence or insufficiency of a needed behavior or skill.

Social reinforcer   Praise, liking, acceptance, or approval received from someone else.

Symbolic models   Models in print, movies, TV, and so on.

Systematic desensitization   A therapeutic procedure intended to extinguish fear.

Time out   A punishment in which a child is temporarily removed from an enjoyable activity.

Unconditioned or unconditional response (UR)   A reflexive response to an unconditioned stimulus.

Unconditioned or unconditional stimulus (US)   A stimulus that causes a reflexive (unconditioned) response.

Vicarious classical conditioning   Conditioning in which the unconditioned response occurs via empathy.

Vicarious emotional arousal   The tendency to feel someone else's feelings along with him or her; also called *empathy*.

Vicarious reinforcement An event in which a reinforcement experienced by someone else has a reinforcing effect on your own behavior.

Self-Actualization and Self-Determination

Julia spends most of her waking hours doing things for others. She talks often with her mother, who always wants more than Julia can give. She sometimes feels as though she's being drawn into quicksand, but she never complains. Then there's Eric, a guy she used to date. Eric's life is a mess, and he often calls her late at night for advice. Although she needs her sleep, she never refuses him a sympathetic ear. Julia always seems to be setting her own life aside for the benefit of others, as though she thinks she's unworthy unless she does so. Deep inside, a small voice says she's wrong about that (but she's usually too busy to hear). And sometimes, just sometimes, she has the feeling that a different destiny awaits her, if she could only free herself to find it.

THE EXPERIENCE of being human is mysterious and challenging. You experience events, feelings, thoughts, and choices that are different from those of any other person who ever has lived or ever will live. You are continuously "becoming," evolving from a simpler version of yourself into a more complex version. It's sometimes mystifying, because you don't always understand why you feel what you're feeling. But the fact that the life you're living is your own—a set of sensations that belongs to you and nobody else—makes the experience also vivid and compelling.

How does your self know *how* to "become"? As you change, how do you still remain yourself? Why do you sometimes feel as though part of you wants to grow in one direction and another part wants to grow in another direction? What makes this experience of being human so special? What are our responsibilities to ourselves? These are among the questions raised by the theorists whose ideas about self-actualization and self-determination are taken up in this chapter.

Some of the theories discussed in this chapter are referred to using the term **humanistic psychology** (Schneider, Bugental, & Pierson, 2001). This term reflects the idea that everyone has the potential for growth and development. No one—*no one*—is inherently bad or unworthy. A basic goal of humanistic psychology is to help people realize this about themselves, so they'll have the chance to grow. Some of the ideas in this chapter are also referred to with the term **phenomenological**. This term reflects an emphasis on the importance of one's own personal experiences.

Self-Actualization

An important figure in humanistic psychology was Carl Rogers. His ideas provide a way to talk about how potential is realized and also how that can fail to happen. In his view, the potential for positive, healthy growth expresses itself in everyone if there are no strong opposing influences. This growth is termed **actualization**. Actualization is the tendency to develop capabilities in ways that maintain or enhance the organism (Rogers, 1959).

In part, the actualizing tendency is reflected physically. For example, your body actualizes when your immune system kills disease cells. Your body actualizes when it grows bigger and stronger. The actualizing principle also applies to personality. Maintenance or enhancement of the self is called **self-actualization**. Self-actualization enriches your life experiences and enhances creativity. It promotes **congruence**, wholeness or integration within the person, and it minimizes disorganization or incongruence.

Rogers believed that the actualizing tendency is part of human nature. This belief is also reflected in another term he used: the **organismic valuing process**. This term refers to the idea that the organism automatically evaluates its experiences to tell whether they are enhancing actualization. If they aren't, the organismic valuing process creates a nagging sense that something isn't right.

Rogers used the phrase **fully functioning person** to describe someone who is self-actualizing. Such people are open to experiencing their feelings and not threatened by them, no matter what the feelings are. Fully functioning people trust their feelings. They are also open to experiencing the world. Rather than hide from it, they immerse themselves in it. The result is that they live lives filled with meaning, challenge, and excitement but also a willingness to risk pain. A fully functioning person isn't a particular *kind of person*. It's a way of *functioning* that can be adopted by anyone who chooses to live that way.

The Need for Positive Regard

Self-actualization isn't the only big influence on human behavior, however. People also need to have the acceptance, love, friendship, and the affection of others—particularly, others who matter to them (*significant others*). Rogers referred to this acceptance using the term **positive regard**.

Positive regard can come in two ways. Affection given without special conditions—with "no strings attached"—is called **unconditional positive regard**. Sometimes, though, affection is given only if certain conditions are satisfied. The conditions vary from case to case, but the idea is the same: I'll like you and accept you, but only if you act in a particular way. This is **conditional positive regard**. Much of the affection people get in their day-to-day lives is conditional.

We all have a strong need to experience positive regard from others—to feel wanted, appreciated, and respected.

Another term used here is **conditions of worth**. These are the conditions under which people are judged worthy of positive regard. When people act to conform to a condition of worth, they're doing so not because the act is intrinsically desirable, but to get positive regard from other people (see the cartoon).

Rogers argued that having conditions of worth applied to us by people around us causes us to start applying the conditions to *ourselves* (Sheldon & Elliot, 1998). We give ourselves affection and acceptance only when we satisfy those conditions. This pattern is called **conditional self-regard**. Conditional self-regard makes you behave so as to fit the conditions of worth you're applying to yourself (Crocker & Wolfe, 2001).

Conditions of worth and conditional regard have an important effect: Choosing your behavior, values, or goals to get acceptance can interfere with self-actualization. Because self-actualizing is more important than fulfilling conditions of worth, it should get first priority. But the need for positive regard is so salient that its influence is often felt more keenly.

Consider a couple of examples. Joel has decided to give up a possible career in music because his father needs help in the family business. In doing this, Joel is reacting to conditions of worth imposed by his family. Bowing to these conditions of worth, however, may mean denying something that's important inside him, something that's truly a part of who he is.

The same kind of conflict is being experienced by Julia, the woman in the chapter opening. Recall that Julia spends much of her time and energy giving to others. Her actions, however, seem driven by a need to prove she's worthy as a human being. She seems to be applying conditions of worth to herself. By trying to live up to them, Julia prevents herself from hearing the voice of self-actualization and from growing in her own way.

People sometimes attempt to impose conditions of worth on other people.
Reprinted by permission: Tribune Media Services.

SHOE by Jeff MacNelly

Mary feels a strong desire for a career, but her parents want her to marry and raise a family. If her parents won't fully accept her unless she bends to their wishes, they're creating a condition of worth for her. Accepting this condition may interfere with Mary's self-actualization. Remember, though, that conditions of worth aren't always imposed from outside. It's possible that Mary's desire for a career may be a condition of worth—a self-imposed condition (just like Julia's need to prove her worthiness by giving to others). Mary may have decided she won't accept herself as a complete person unless she has a career.

It can be very hard to distinguish a true desire from a condition of worth (Janoff-Bulman & Leggatt, 2002). What defines a condition of worth is that it's a *precondition for acceptance,* either by others or by oneself. A condition of worth is always coercive: It pushes you into doing things. Such conditions can prevent self-actualization. When parents place such conditions on their children, the result is resentment and less well-being (Assor, Roth, & Deci, 2004).

CONTINGENT SELF-WORTH

Jennifer Crocker and her colleagues have conducted a good deal of research on the idea that people place such conditions of worth on themselves (Crocker & Knight, 2005; Crocker & Park, 2004; Crocker & Wolfe, 2001). People who use their performance in some area of life as a condition for self-acceptance are said to have **contingent self-worth** (which means essentially the same thing as *conditional self-regard*). Conditions of worth come in many forms. Some people are demanding about their academic performance and others about their appearance.

Contingencies can be motivating. People who impose an academic condition of worth do study more than other people; people who have an appearance-based condition of worth exercise more and shop for clothes more often than others (Crocker, Luhtanen, Cooper, & Bouvrette, 2003). When a failure happens, though, it's more upsetting if you have a contingency in that domain. The failure can then result in loss of motivation.

Consistent with the view expressed by Rogers, holding oneself to these conditions has costs. It is stressful and disrupts relationships (Crocker & Knight, 2005). It causes people to be more upset by negative interpersonal feedback (Cambron & Acitelli, 2010; Cambron, Acitelli, & Steinburg, 2010; Park & Crocker, 2008). It can also make people more likely to become victims of relationship violence (Goldstein, Chesir-Teran, & McFaul, 2008). Perhaps most important, it keeps people focused on a particular condition of worth, rather than letting them grow freely.

Self-Determination

Rogers's ideas are echoed in a more recent theory of **self-determination** proposed by Ed Deci and Richard Ryan (1980, 1985, 1991, 2000; Ryan, 1993; Ryan & Deci,

2001; see also Vallerand, 1997). Deci and Ryan believe that having a life of growth, integrity, and well-being means satisfying three needs. The needs are for autonomy (self-determination), competence, and relatedness. People in general also see these needs as being most important to them (Sheldon, Elliot, Kim, & Kasser, 2001).

The theory begins with the idea that behavior can reflect several underlying dynamics. Some actions are *self-determined:* done either because they have intrinsic interest or are of value to you. Other actions are *controlled:* done to gain payment or to satisfy some pressure. A behavior can be controlled even if the control occurs entirely inside your own mind. If you do something because you know you'd feel guilty if you didn't do it, you're engaging in controlled behavior.

Whether behavior is controlled or self-determined can have several consequences. One of them concerns how long you'll stay interested in the behavior. People stay interested longer when they see their actions as self-determined. In fact, people lose interest in activities when promised some reward for working on them (Deci, Koestner, & Ryan, 1999). This effect has been found in children as well as adults. In children, it's been called "turning play into work" (Lepper & Greene, 1975, 1978).

It's not the reward itself that does this. Rather, it's whether people see their actions as self-determined. Telling people they're going to be paid for something often seems to make them infer that their behavior isn't self-determined. As a result, they lose interest. In some circumstances, however, expecting reward increases motivation instead of undermining it (Elliot & Harackiewicz, 1994; Harackiewicz, 1979; Henderlong & Lepper, 2002). Why? Because reward has two aspects (Deci, 1975). It has a *controlling* aspect, telling you that your actions are not autonomous. It can also have an *informational* aspect, informing you about yourself. If a reward tells you that you're competent, it increases your motivation (Eisenberger & Rhoades, 2001; Koestner, Zuckerman, & Koestner, 1987). It's even possible for a reward to promote a sense of self-determination, under the right conditions (Henderlong & Lepper, 2002). If the reward implies a condition of worth, however, or if it implies that you're acting just for the reward, then the controlling aspect will stand out and your motivation will fall off.

Deci and Ryan believe that people want to feel a sense of self-determination in everything they do. In this view, accomplishments such as doing well in your courses are satisfying only if you feel self-determination in them. If you feel forced or pressured to do these things, then you'll be less satisfied (Flink, Boggiano, & Barrett, 1990; Grolnick & Ryan, 1989). Indeed, pressuring *yourself* to do well can also reduce motivation (Ryan, 1982). This fits the idea that people can impose conditions of worth on themselves.

INTROJECTION AND IDENTIFICATION

Deci and Ryan and their colleagues have used several more terms to describe degrees of control and self-determination (see Figure 11.1). Especially important are *introjected* and *identified* regulation.

Introjected regulation occurs when a person treats a behavior as a "should" or an "ought"—when the person does it to avoid guilt or gain self-approval. If you try to do well in a class so you won't feel guilty about wasting your parents' tuition money, that's introjected behavior. Introjected behavior is controlled, but the control is exerted from inside. If you try to do well so your parents won't look down on you, that's also controlled, but it's externally regulated rather than introjected, because the control is outside you (see Figure 11.1).

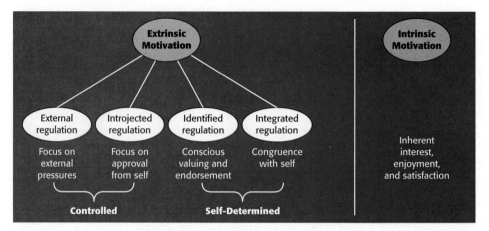

FIGURE 11.1

Degrees of control versus self-determination. In Deci and Ryan's view, regulation of behavior can range from extremely controlled (left side) to extremely self-determined (right side). The ideal is intrinsic motivation, but extrinsically motivated actions can also be self-determined if the person consciously values them or has integrated them in the self-structure. Other types of extrinsic motivation (external and introjected regulation) are controlled behavior. *Source:* Based on Ryan & Deci (2000).

In *identified regulation*, in contrast, the person has come to hold the behavior as personally meaningful and valuable. If you try to do well in a class because you believe learning is important to your growth, that's identified regulation. Identified regulation is self-determined. It's not quite as self-determined as integrated regulation (in which the goal is integrated within the self) or intrinsically motivated behavior (for which the interest is naturally there), but it's pretty close (see Figure 11.1). In general, as people mature, they regulate less by introjected values and more by identified and integrated (autonomous) values (Sheldon, 2005).

These ideas have many applications. For example, think about what you want out of life. There's evidence that wanting financial success (which generally reflects controlled behavior) relates to poorer mental health, whereas wanting community involvement relates to better mental health (Kasser, 2002; Kasser & Ryan, 1993). Of course, *why* the person has the aspiration is also important (Carver & Baird, 1998). Wanting community involvement for controlling reasons (e.g., because it will make people like you) is bad. Wanting financial success for truly self-determined reasons (because the process itself is intrinsically enjoyable) can be good.

The pressures that lead to introjected behavior stem from the desire to be accepted by others or to avoid a sense of guilt over doing things you think others won't like. This fits with Rogers's belief that the desire for positive regard can disrupt self-actualization. A lot depends on whether others place conditions of worth on you. Restrictive parenting produces adults who value conformity instead of self-direction (Kasser, Koestner, & Lekes, 2002).

Having a sense of autonomy also seems to foster further autonomy. In one project, medical students who thought their professors were supportive of their own autonomy became even more autonomous in their learning over time (Williams & Deci, 1996). They also felt more competent, and they acted toward others in ways that supported the others' autonomy.

NEED FOR RELATEDNESS

Deci and Ryan also believe that people have an intrinsic need for relatedness (see also Baumeister & Leary, 1995). At first glance, it might seem that a need for relatedness should conflict with the need for autonomy. However, it's important to realize that Deci and Ryan's definition of *autonomy* doesn't mean being separate from or independent of others. Rather, it means having the sense of free self-determination (Deci & Ryan, 1991, 2000). True relatedness doesn't conflict with this.

Several studies have confirmed that autonomy and relatedness can exist side by side. One project, involving several studies, found that autonomy and relatedness were complementary: Each related independently to well-being (Bettencourt & Sheldon, 2001; see also Beiswenger & Grolnick, 2010). Another study found that a measure of behaving autonomously was tied to *more* relatedness, in the form of having open and positive communication with significant others. People who regulated their lives in a controlled way were the ones who interacted defensively with others (Hodgins, Koestner, & Duncan, 1996). Other research has found that being autonomous promotes the use of relationship-maintaining coping strategies and positive responses in discussing relationships (Knee, Patrick, Vietor, Nanayakkara, & Neighbors, 2002). The result was less defensiveness and more understanding responses when conflict did occur (Knee, Lonsbary, Canevello, & Patrick, 2005).

Support for autonomy is a powerful force (see Sheldon & Gunz, 2009). When relationship partners are supportive of autonomy, the relationship is experienced as being better and richer (Deci, La Guardia, Moller, Scheiner, & Ryan, 2006). The relationship also feels better to *you* when you support your partner's autonomy (Deci et al., 2006).

Still, the need for relatedness has some resemblance to the need for positive regard. Why, then, doesn't it interfere with self-actualization? The answer seems to be that Deci and Ryan's conception of relatedness implies a genuine connection to others, an unconditional acceptance, rather than a connection based on pressure and demand. It might be more accurate to equate this need to a need for *unconditional* regard.

SELF-CONCORDANCE

Self-determination theory has important implications for thinking about the goals people pursue in their lives. Elsewhere in this book, you'll read about personality being expressed in the goals people take up (see Chapters 5 and 13). But goals are not equal in their contributions to well-being. The key is that it's good to pursue goals that are **self-concordant**, or consistent with your core values (Sheldon & Elliot,

When we are prevented from doing something that we want to do, our desire to do it increases even more.

1999). You care more about such goals, and you benefit more from attaining them than from attaining goals that don't connect to your core values. Support for this reasoning comes from several sources (Brunstein, Schultheiss, & Grässmann, 1998; Greguras & Diefendorff, 2010; Sheldon & Elliot, 1999; Sheldon & Kasser, 1998).

There's even evidence that pursuit of self-concordant goals can create a longer-term spiral of benefit (Sheldon & Houser-Marko, 2001). When you try to reach self-concordant goals, you try harder, you have more satisfying experiences, and you attain better well-being. This experience promotes greater motivation for the next self-concordant goal, and the cycle continues.

FREE WILL

Humanistic psychologists emphasize the idea that people have freedom to decide for themselves how to act and what to become. In Rogers's view, people are free to choose whether to act in self-actualizing ways or to accept conditions of worth. In Deci and Ryan's view, people exert their will when they act in self-determination.

The concept of *free will* is interesting and controversial. It's nearly impossible to know for sure whether people have free will, but they certainly seem to *think* they do. Consider **reactance** (Brehm, 1966; Brehm & Brehm, 1981). Reactance happens when you expect to have a particular freedom and you see it as being threatened. The result is an attempt to regain or reassert it. Thus, young children who've been told they can't do something want to do it all the more. In a romantic relationship, "playing hard to get" can increase another person's attraction to you. Certainly, people often resist being told what to do. Much evidence supports the idea that reactance leads to reassertion of freedom (Brehm & Brehm, 1981).

Although people think they have free will, some question whether they actually do. In a complicated study, Wegner and Wheatley (1999) showed that people could be led to believe they had intentionally caused something to happen that someone else had actually caused. Put differently, they claimed to have exerted their will in a situation in which they had not. This and other evidence led Wegner (2002) to argue that free will is an illusion. This issue, of course, will continue to be debated.

The Self and Processes of Defense

We now turn to the concept of *self*. Rogers is sometimes called a *self theorist*, because he stressed the importance of the self. As the person grows, the self becomes more elaborate and complex. It never reaches an end state but continues to evolve.

Rogers used the term self in several ways. Sometimes, he used it to refer to the subjective awareness of being (Rogers, 1965). At other times, he used it interchangeably with *self-concept*. The self-concept is the set of qualities a person views as being part of himself or herself (much like *ego identity*; see Chapter 9). Many distinctions can be made among the elements of the self-concept. One of them is between the actual (or real) self and the ideal self. The **ideal self** is the image of the kind of person you want to be. The **actual self** is what you think you're really like.

Recall that self-actualizing is supposed to promote congruence. *Congruence* means "fitting together." One kind of congruence is between actual and ideal selves. Thus, as self-actualization occurs, it creates a closer fit between the actual and the ideal. It leads you to become more like the self you want to be.

A second kind of congruence that's important is between the actual self and experience. That is, the experiences you have in life should fit with the kind of person

Box 11.1 How Can You Manage Two Kinds of Congruence Simultaneously?

This section of the chapter emphasizes the importance of two kinds of congruence: between the actual self and the ideal self and between the self-concept and one's experience. Often, these two kinds of congruence can be managed at the same time. In some circumstances, though, the desire to avoid one kind of incongruence can plunge you right into the other.

What circumstance would do that? An example is suggested by the work of William Swann and his colleagues on what they call *self-verification* (e.g., Swann, 1987, 1990). The idea is that once people have a picture of what they're like, they want to have that self-concept confirmed by other people's reactions to them. That is, people want their experience to be congruent with their self-concept. For example, if you think you're a good athlete, you want others to think so, too. If you think you're shy, you want others to realize it. It may seem odd, but the desire to verify beliefs about yourself applies even to beliefs that are unflattering

(Swann, Wenzlaff, & Tafarodi, 1992). If you think you're homely, you'd rather have someone else agree than say the opposite.

Here's the problem: For the person with a negative self-view, there's a built-in conflict between self-verification and self-protection. *Self-verification* is trying not to have incongruity between self and experience. *Self-protection* is trying not to be aware of incongruity between one's desired self and actual self. Attempts to diminish these two incongruities can pull a person in opposite directions.

Swann and his colleagues have argued that both of these forces operate in everyone. Which force dominates at a given moment depends on your options. Keep in mind that most people's self-concept has both positive and negative qualities (Swann, Pelham, & Krull, 1989). Suppose, then, you had the chance to obtain information about yourself (say, from another person or from a personality test). Would you prefer to get information about what you view as your best quality or about what you view as your worst? Given

this option, most people would prefer to learn about something they view as desirable. This fits the self-protection tendency. But suppose you know that the information you're going to get is about a quality you perceive as bad. Would you rather get information that says you're bad in that quality or that says you're good? The answer obtained by Swann et al. (1989) was that people tend to seek unfavorable information.

In sum, the self-protection and self-enhancement tendencies seem to influence where you look (and where you don't look) when you consider the relationship between your actual and desired selves. People prefer to look at their favorable self-aspects. Even so, when they look at some self-aspect in particular, the self-verification tendency influences the kind of information they focus on. They want information that confirms their view of who they are—that fits the experienced self to the actual self. In each case, the effect is to enhance perceptions of congruence, consistent with the ideas proposed by Rogers.

you think you are. For example, if you think you're a kind person and you find yourself doing something insensitive and unkind, there's an incongruity between self and experience. If you think you're a smart person but find yourself doing poorly in a course, there's an incongruity between self and experience. Self-actualization should tend to promote a closer congruence here, as well (see also Box 11.1).

INCONGRUITY, DISORGANIZATION, AND DEFENSE

Incongruence is disorganization, a fraying of the unitary sense of self. You don't always know it consciously, but your organismic valuing process senses it. Rogers said that incongruence—either perceiving a gap between real and ideal or experiencing something that doesn't fit your self-image—leads to anxiety.

The experience of incongruence can also make people vulnerable to yet further problems. Incongruity between the actual and ideal selves leads people to underestimate how much their significant others care for them (Murray, Holmes, & Griffin, 2000; Murray, Holmes, Griffin, Bellavia, & Rose, 2001). This misperception can make them react poorly to their partners. They feel pessimistic about the relationship and may act in ways that aren't genuine. Ultimately, the relationship is less likely to flourish.

It isn't always possible to have complete congruence. Rogers assumed that people defend themselves against even the *perception* of incongruence, to avoid the anxiety it creates. Defenses against perceptions of incongruity form two categories, which aren't so different from some of the defenses addressed by psychoanalytic theory (see Chapter 8).

One kind of defense involves *distortion of experience*. Rationalization is one such distortion: creating a plausible but untrue explanation for why something is the way it is. Another distortion is seeing an event as being different from how it really is. For instance, if you say something that makes someone else feel bad, you may protect yourself by believing the other person wasn't really upset.

The second kind of defense involves *preventing threatening experiences from reaching awareness*. Denial—refusing to admit to yourself that a situation exists or an experience took place—serves this function. A woman who ignores overwhelming evidence that her boyfriend is unfaithful to her is doing this.

You can also prevent an experience from reaching awareness indirectly by not letting yourself be in a situation in which the experience would be *possible*. By taking steps to prevent it from occurring, you prevent its access to consciousness. This is a subtle defense. For example, a person whose self-image is threatened by having sexual feelings toward attractive strangers may avoid going to the beach or nightclubs, thereby preventing the feelings from arising.

SELF-ESTEEM MAINTENANCE AND ENHANCEMENT

Defenses act to maintain and enhance the congruity or integrity of the self. Another way to put it is that defenses protect and enhance self-esteem. The idea that people go out of their way to protect self-esteem has been around for a long time. It's been an active area of study under several labels (for review, see Alicke & Sedikides, 2010).

It's often said that two conditions are required for someone to become concerned about maintaining or enhancing self-esteem (Snyder, Stephan, & Rosenfield, 1978). First, an event must be attributable to the person. An event that's outside your control is not relevant to you. Second, the event must be good or bad, thereby having a potential connotation for the person's self-esteem.

What happens when there's a threat to self-esteem? Just as Rogers argued, people either distort their perceptions or distance themselves from the threat. They minimize the negativity of the event. They also try to prevent the event from being attributed to permanent qualities of the self, thereby denying its relevance.

Consider failure. Failure (academic, social, or otherwise) can make most of us feel inadequate. What do people do when they fail? They make excuses (Snyder & Higgins, 1988). They blame it on things beyond their control. They attribute it to task difficulty, to chance, to other people, or (in a bind) to a lack of effort (e.g., Bradley, 1978; Snyder et al., 1976, 1978). People respond in these ways whether the event is as trivial as failure on a laboratory task or as profound as the experience of divorce (Gray & Silver, 1990). Blaming something or someone else creates distance between the failure and you. Given enough distance, the failure doesn't threaten your self-esteem.

People can also protect their self-esteem after failure by distorting perceptions in another way. An event is relevant to self-esteem only if its impact is either good or bad. You can protect your self-esteem, then, by discounting the impact. Making a bad impression on someone isn't a problem if that person isn't worth bothering with. Doing poorly on a test doesn't matter if the test isn't important or valid. People who are told they did poorly on a test say exactly that: It's not so important and not so valid (Greenberg, Pyszczynski, & Solomon, 1982).

When you experience success, on the other hand, you have the chance to enhance your self-esteem. You can do this by ascribing the success to your abilities (Agostinelli, Sherman, Presson, & Chassin, 1992; Snyder et al., 1976, 1978; Taylor & Brown, 1988). Indeed, there's even evidence that people think that any positive personal qualities they have are under their own control, allowing them to claim credit for being the way they are (Alicke, 1985).

Self-Handicapping

People protect their self-esteem in some very strange ways. One of them is called **self-handicapping** (e.g., Arkin & Baumgardner, 1985; Higgins, Snyder, & Berglas, 1990; Jones & Berglas, 1978; Jones & Pittman, 1982). Self-handicapping is acting to create the very conditions that tend to produce a failure. If you have a test tomorrow, it's self-handicapping to party all night instead of studying. If you want to make a good impression on someone, it's self-handicapping to show up drunk or drenched in sweat from playing basketball.

Why would you do such a thing? If you want to reach a goal, why create conditions that make it harder? The theory is that failing to attain a goal threatens self-esteem. You can't really fail, though, if success is prevented by circumstances beyond your control. Given such conditions, the stigma of failing goes away. If you fail the test or make a poor impression—well, *no one* could do well in those conditions. So it wasn't really a failure. Consistent with this reasoning, people self-handicap more when they expect bad outcomes (Lovejoy & Durik, 2010).

Thus, self-handicapping prevents awareness of failing. Note that for this strategy to be successful, you need to be *unaware that you're using it*. If you realize you're setting up barriers for yourself, they won't have the same meaning.

Self-handicapping may be common, but it's not a good strategy. People who tend to self-handicap cope poorly with stress (Zuckerman, Kieffer, & Knee, 1998). Indeed, self-handicapping and maladjustment reinforce each other (Zuckerman & Tsai, 2005). Further, if people think you're self-handicapping, they react negatively to you (Hirt, McCrea, & Boris, 2003). Finally, don't forget that self-handicapping helps create the very failure it was intended to protect against.

Stereotype Threat

Another concept that connects to the ideas we've been discussing is called **stereotype threat**. It was first proposed and studied by Claude Steele and his colleagues (Pronin, Steele, & Ross, 2004; Steele, 1997; Steele & Aronson, 1995). It begins with the fact that some groups are stereotyped in ways that lead to expectations of poor performance of some sort. For example, the negative stereotype of African Americans includes an expectation that they will perform poorly on intellectual tasks. The negative stereotype of women includes an expectation that they will perform poorly in math. The negative stereotype of elderly people includes an expectation that they will perform poorly on memory tasks. Members of these groups can be threatened by being viewed through the stereotype, rather than as individuals. The sense of being prejudged occupies the person's mind and promotes negative thinking (Cadinu, Maass, Rosabianca, & Kiesner, 2005). All of this can interfere with performance (e.g., Cheung & Hardin, 2010; Chung, Ehrhart, Ehrhart, Hattrup, & Solamon, 2010; Fischer, 2010; Rydell, Shiffrin, Boucher, Van Loo, & Rydell, 2010). When performance is poor, the stereotype is confirmed.

If this happens frequently, even worse things can follow. Steele (1997) argued that the person begins to *disidentify* with the domain in which the threat is occurring—to stop caring about it. This protects self-esteem by denying that the experience is relevant to the self. Failure doesn't matter if the test isn't important. But disidentifying also has negative results. As does self-handicapping, disidentifying makes poor performance more likely (due to lower effort). Further, it ultimately causes people to stop caring about important areas of endeavor in which they may actually have considerable skill (Bergeron, Block, & Echtenkamp, 2006).

Self-Actualization and Maslow's Hierarchy of Motives

Another theorist who emphasized the importance of self-actualization was Abraham Maslow (1962, 1970). He was interested in the qualities of people who seem to get the most out of life—the most fully functioning of persons, the healthiest and best adjusted. Maslow spent most of his career trying to understand how these people were able to be so complete and so well adapted (see Box 11.2).

As part of this effort, Maslow eventually came to examine how diverse motives are organized. His view of motivation was very different from the view discussed in Chapter 5. Maslow came to view human needs as forming a hierarchy (Maslow, 1970), which is often portrayed as a pyramid (see Figure 11.2). He pointed out that needs vary in their immediacy and power. Some are extremely primitive, basic, and demanding. Because they're so fundamental, they form the base of the pyramid. These needs are *physiological*—pertaining to air, water, food, and so on—things obviously necessary for survival.

The needs at the next higher level are also necessary for survival but less demanding. These are *safety and* (physical) *security* needs—shelter from the weather, protection against predators, and so on. Maslow considered this second class of needs less basic than the first class, because they require satisfaction less frequently. You need to get oxygen every few seconds, water every few hours, and food once or twice a day. But once you've found an apartment, you have physical shelter for quite a while (as long as you pay the rent). If

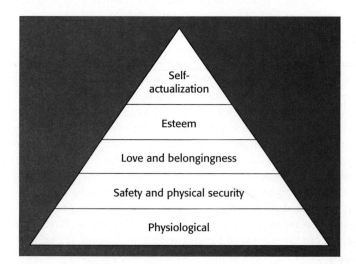

FIGURE 11.2
Maslow's theoretical hierarchy of needs. Needs lower on the hierarchy are more demanding and animalistic. Needs higher on the hierarchy are more subtle but more distinctly human. *Source:* Based on Maslow, 1970.

Box 11.2 The Theorist and the Theory: Abraham Maslow's Focus on the Positive

Abraham Maslow focused his work almost exclusively on the positive side of human experience. He was interested in what causes some people to succeed and even achieve greatness in their lives while others fail. He cared about issues of personal growth and the realization of human potential. It's clear that these interests were influenced by events in his own life.

Maslow was born in 1908 in Brooklyn, New York, the oldest of seven children of Russian Jewish immigrants. His home life definitely did not foster personal growth. His father thought little of him and publicly ridiculed his appearance. This led young Maslow to seek out empty cars whenever he rode the subway, to spare others the sight of him.

If Maslow's father treated him badly, his mother was worse. The family was poor, and she kept a lock on the refrigerator to keep the children

out, feeding them only when she saw fit. Maslow once characterized her as a "cruel, ignorant, and hostile figure, one so unloving as to nearly induce madness in her children" (Hoffman, 1988, p. 7). He later said that his focus on the positive side of personality was a direct consequence of his mother's treatment of him. It was a reaction against the things she did and the qualities she represented (Maslow, 1979, p. 958). Thus, from a life begun in hardship came a determination to understand the best in human experience.

Maslow entered college intending a career in law, but he quickly became disenchanted, because law focuses so much on evil and so little on good. He turned to psychology. According to Maslow, that was when his life really started. His doctoral work, done under the direction of well-known primate researcher Harry Harlow, focused on how dominance is established among monkeys. Thus, even while conducting

animal research, Maslow was interested in what sets exceptional individuals off from others who are less special.

Maslow shifted this research interest to humans during the period surrounding World War II. New York in the 1930s and 1940s was a gathering place for some of the greatest intellectuals of Europe—many of whom were escaping Nazi Germany. Maslow was impressed by several of these individuals and tried to find out everything he could about them. In his search to understand how these people came to be exceptional, Maslow was sowing the seeds of more formal work he would conduct later.

Maslow was deeply moved by the suffering and anguish caused by World War II. He vowed to devote his life to proving that humans were capable of something better than war, prejudice, and hatred. By studying the process of self-actualization, he proceeded to do just that.

---

both your apartment and your air supply became inaccessible, you'd surely try to regain the air first and worry about the apartment later.

At the next level of the hierarchy, the needs start to have more social qualities. The level immediately above safety needs is the category of *love and belongingness*. Here, the needs are for companionship, affection, and acceptance from others (much like the need for positive regard). Needs of this type are satisfied through interaction with other people.

Higher yet on the pyramid are *esteem* needs: needs bearing on evaluation (and self-evaluation). Esteem needs include the need for a sense of mastery and power and a sense of appreciation from others (Leary & Baumeister, 2000). Notice that this differs from acceptance and affection. *Acceptance* may not be evaluative. *Appreciation* is. You're appreciated and esteemed for some quality or qualities that you possess. The need for appreciation is thus more elaborate than the need for acceptance.

At the top of the hierarchy stands *self-actualization*. Maslow used this term much as Rogers did, to mean the tendency to become whatever you're capable of becoming, to extend yourself to the limits of your capacities. This, to Maslow, is the highest of human motives.

The pyramid is a visual analogue for Maslow's core assumptions. He assumed that low-level needs are more primitive and more demanding than needs higher on the hierarchy. The need for air is more demanding than the need for shelter. Maslow's assumption was broader than that, however. He also assumed that the need for physical shelter is more demanding than the need to have a sense of being accepted, and that the need for a sense of belonging is more demanding than the need to be appreciated or powerful. Maslow thus held that the power of the motive force weakens as you move up the pyramid. On the other hand, as you move up, the needs are also more distinctly human and less animalistic.

Thus, Maslow saw a trade-off between the constraints of biology and the uniqueness of being human. We have needs that make us different from other creatures. Self-actualization is the highest and most important. But we can't escape the needs we share with other creatures. Those needs are more powerful when they're unsatisfied than the needs that make us special.

In general, people must deal with the needs they have at lower levels of the pyramid before they can attend to higher needs. Two implications follow. First, if a need begins to develop at a lower level while you're trying to satisfy a higher, *the lower-level need can cause you to be pulled away from the higher-level one*. Your attention, in effect, is pulled downward, and you're forced to do something about the lower need (Wicker, Brown, Wiehe, Hagen, & Reed, 1993).

The second implication concerns how people move up through this of needs. It may be precisely the freeing of your mind from the demands of low-level needs that lets you be attuned to the very quiet voice of self-actualization. Remember, the further up the pyramid you go, the more subtle and less survival-related the motive. Self-actualization—the highest motive—is the last to be taken into account. Only when the other needs have been quieted can this one be attended to.

The levels of the hierarchy also differ in one more sense. Maslow (1955) said that the motives low on the pyramid are **deficiency-based motives**, whereas those high on the pyramid (particularly, self-actualization) are **growth-based motives**. That is, lower needs arise from deprivation. Satisfying them means escaping unpleasant conditions. Self-actualization is more like the distant call of your unrealized potential as a person. Satisfying this isn't a matter of avoiding an unpleasant state. Rather, it's the seeking of growth (see also Sheldon et al., 2001).

Finally, compare Maslow's ideas to those of Rogers. Recall that Rogers emphasized two motives: the self-actualizing tendency and the need for positive regard (affection and acceptance). It's possible to see a similarity between those ideas and Maslow's more elaborate structure (see Figure 11.2). The bottom two levels of Maslow's pyramid refer to needs that Rogers ignored. Rogers focused on social needs, which for Maslow begin at the third level. Maslow believed, as did Rogers, that the need for acceptance could be more demanding than the need for self-actualization. The structure of the pyramid clearly implies that people can be distracted from self-actualization by the need for positive regard.

The intermediate level of Maslow's pyramid—esteem needs—can be viewed as an elaboration on the need for positive regard. Esteem needs seem similar, in many ways, to Rogers's conditions of worth. The two theorists differed in how they saw this motive. To Rogers, bowing to conditions of worth is bad. To Maslow, esteem needs are part of being human, although less important than the need for self-actualization. The two theorists agreed, however, that esteem needs can get in the way of self-actualization. In sum, despite the fact that Rogers and Maslow had unique ideas about personality, their theoretical views also have much in common.

CHARACTERISTICS OF FREQUENT SELF-ACTUALIZERS

The concept of self-actualization is, in many ways, the most engaging and intriguing of these theorists' ideas. Although Maslow painted a broad picture of human motives,

Table 11.1 Characteristics of Frequent Self-Actualizers.

Self-actualizing people…

- are *efficient* and accurate in *perceiving* reality
- are *accepting* of themselves, of other people, and of nature
- are *spontaneous* in thought and emotion, natural rather than artificial
- are *problem centered*, or concerned with eternal philosophical questions
- are *independent* and *autonomous* when it comes to satisfactions
- have a continued *freshness of appreciation* of ordinary events
- often experience so-called *oceanic feelings,* a sense of oneness with nature that transcends time and space
- *identify* with all of *humanity* and are democratic and respectful of others
- form *deep ties* but *with only a few persons*
- *appreciate,* for its own sake, the *process* of doing things
- have a *philosophical,* thoughtful, nonhostile *sense of humor*
- have a childlike and fresh *creativity* and *inventiveness*
- maintain an inner *detachment from* the *culture* in which they live
- are sufficiently *strong,* independent, and guided by their own inner visions that they sometimes appear *temperamental* and even *ruthless*

Source: Based on Maslow, 1968.

self-actualization most fully occupied his interest and imagination. He devoted much of his career to studying it.

According to Maslow, everyone has the potential to self-actualize, and everyone has an intrinsic desire to become more and more the person he or she is capable of being. Because self-actualization is so diffuse a quality, it can appear in virtually any kind of behavior. It isn't just the painter, musician, writer, or actor who can be self-actualizing. It's any person who's in the process of becoming more congruent, more integrated, more complete as a person.

Despite believing that every person has this potential, Maslow also recognized that some people self-actualize more than others. To better understand the process, he sought out those who displayed self-actualizing properties often. He worked hard to describe them—in part, because self-actualization is such a hard concept to grasp. By describing them, he hoped to help others recognize self-actualizing experiences in their own lives.

Maslow came to believe that frequent self-actualizers share several characteristics (Maslow, 1962, 1968). Here are a few of them (for a more complete list, see Table 11.1.) For instance, self-actualizers are *efficient* in their perception of reality; that is, their experience is in extra-sharp focus. Self-actualizers can spot the confused perceptions of others and cut through the tangles. People who frequently engage in self-actualization are also *accepting.* They accept both themselves and others. Their self-acceptance isn't smug self-promotion. They realize they're not perfect. They accept themselves as they are—imperfections and all. They also accept the frailties of the people around them as a part of who those people are.

Another characteristic of self-actualizers is a mental *spontaneity.* This is reflected in a creativity without artificiality. This quality is often linked to having a *fresh appreciation* of life, an excitement in the process of living. The idea that creativity relates to self-actualization has received support. In one study (Amabile, 1985), writers were led to think about the act of creation either from the view of extrinsic incentives (thus, lower on Maslow's hierarchy) or from qualities intrinsic to the act itself (by implication, self-actualization). They then wrote poems. Judges later rated the creativity. The poems written after thinking about external incentives were rated lower in creativity than those written from the self-actualizing orientation.

The self-actualizing person is often said to be *problem centered*, but this phrase is a little misleading. Here, the word *problem* refers to enduring questions of philosophy or ethics. Self-actualizers take a wide view, consider universal issues. Along with this quality is an independence from their culture and immediate environment. Self-actualizers live in the universe, and only secondarily in this apartment, city, or country. In addition, self-actualizers know relationships require effort. They have deep ties because relationships matter to them, but the ties are often limited to a very few others.

Toward the end of his life, Maslow (1971) distinguished between this group of people and another group he called **transcendent self-actualizers**. The people in this second group are so invested in self-actualization that it becomes the most precious aspect of their lives. They are more consciously motivated by universal values or goals outside themselves (such as beauty, truth, and unity). They're more holistic about the world, seeing the integration of all its elements. Self-actualization almost becomes "universe-actualization." All of experience seems sacred to these people. They see themselves as the tools by which capabilities are expressed, rather than as the owners of the capabilities. From this view comes the term *transpersonal* ("beyond the person"), which is sometimes used to refer to this way of viewing human potential.

PEAK EXPERIENCES

In trying to describe the process of self-actualization, Maslow also focused on moments in which self-actualization was clearly occurring. Remember, not every act is self-actualizing, even for a person who self-actualizes a great deal. Maslow used the term **peak experience** to refer to a moment of intense self-actualization.

In a peak experience, the person has a sense of being connected with the elements of his or her surroundings. Colors and sounds seem crisper. Perceptions take on

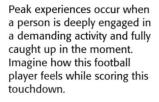

Peak experiences occur when a person is deeply engaged in a demanding activity and fully caught up in the moment. Imagine how this football player feels while scoring this touchdown.

a sharper clarity (Privette & Landsman, 1983). There's also a loss of the sense of time as the experience flows by (Keller & Bless, 2008). The feelings associated with a peak experience often include awe, wonder, and even ecstasy. Having a peak experience tends to take you outside yourself. You aren't thinking about yourself but rather are experiencing whatever you're experiencing as fully as possible.

Peak experiences *can* occur in a passive way—for instance, in examining a great work of art. Usually, though, they occur when people are acting (Csikszentmihalyi, 1975; Privette & Landsman, 1983). Indeed, there's evidence that peak experiences happen more during work than during leisure (Csikszentmihalyi & LeFevre, 1989). The person having a peak experience is so immersed in an activity that it seems to "become" him or her. The term **flow** is also used for such an experience (Csikszentmihalyi, 1990; Csikszentmihalyi & Csikszentmihalyi, 1988).

We should re-emphasize that the activity doesn't have to involve artistic creation or any such thing. What's important isn't *what* is being done but rather *how* it's taking place. If you're completely immersed in it and it's stretching you as a human being, it can be a peak experience.

Existential Psychology: Being and Death

So far, we've focused on the ideas that people have a natural tendency toward growth, that they can exert free will to adjust the course of their lives, that they defend against perceptions of incongruence, and that the motive to grow is at the peak of a hierarchy of motives. However, there's another side to growth and human potential. The possibilities of self-actualization have a cost. They bring responsibilities.

This is a key principle of **existential psychology** (Koole, Greenberg, & Pyszczynski, 2006). The term *existential* is related to the word *existence*. It pertains to a philosophical view which holds that existence is all anyone has. Each person is alone in an unfathomable universe. This view stresses that each person must take responsibility for his or her choices. It fits the phenomenological orientation in emphasizing the importance of the individual's unique experience of reality.

THE EXISTENTIAL DILEMMA

A concept that's central to the existentialist view is *dasein*, a German word that's often translated as meaning "being-in-the-world." The term *dasein* is used to imply the totality of a person's experience of the self as an autonomous, separate, and evolving entity (Binswanger, 1963; Boss, 1963; May, 1958). It also emphasizes that people have no existence apart from the world and that the world has no meaning apart from the people in it.

To existentialists, the basic issue is that life inevitably ends in death, which can come at any time (Becker, 1973). Death is the event no one escapes, no matter how self-actualizing his or her experiences are. Awareness of the inevitability of death provokes *angst*—dread, anguish far deeper than anxiety over incongruity. There exist only being and not-being, and we constantly face the polarity between them.

How should you respond to this realization? To existentialists, this is the key question in life. The choice is between retreating into nothingness or having the courage to *be*. At its extreme, the choice is whether or not to commit suicide, thus avoiding the absurdity of a life that will end in death anyway. To kill oneself is to choose nothingness. But nothingness can also be chosen in less extreme ways. People can choose not to act authentically, not to commit themselves to the goals and responsibilities that are part of who they are. They can drift or go along with some crowd. When people fail to take responsibility for their lives, they're choosing nothingness.

What's involved in the choice to be? To the existentialists, life has no meaning unless you create it. Each person with the courage to do so must assign meaning to his or her existence. You assign meaning to your life by acting authentically, by being who you are. The very recognition of the existential dilemma is an important step to doing this. As May (1958, p. 47) put it, "To grasp what it means to exist, one needs to grasp the fact that he might not exist."

Exercising this freedom isn't easy. It can be hard to know who you are, and it can be hard to stare death in the face. It's often easier to let other people decide what's right and just go along. Existential psychologists believe, though, that we are all responsible for making the most of every moment of our existence and fulfilling that existence to the best of our ability (Boss, 1963; Frankl, 1969; May, 1969). This responsibility is inescapable.

Although people are responsible for their choices, even honest choices aren't always good ones. You won't always deal perfectly with the people you care about. You'll sometimes lose track of your connection to nature. Even if your choices are wise, you'll still have **existential guilt** over failing to fulfill your possibilities. This guilt is strongest when a person who's free to choose fails to do so. But people who are aware are never completely free of existential guilt, because it's impossible to fulfill every possibility. In realizing some capabilities, you prevent others from being expressed. Thus, existential guilt is inescapable. It's part of the cost of being.

EMPTINESS

Existentialists also focus on the problem of life's emptiness. They are concerned that people have lost faith in values (May, 1953). For instance, many people no longer have a sense of worth and dignity, partly because they have found themselves powerless to influence forces such as government and big business. The planet warms, and we do nothing to stop it. Businesses need multibillion-dollar bailouts, and we're stuck with the bill. The leaders of our country commit us to wars without justifying them, or even declaring them as wars, and we bear the consequences.

When people lose their commitment to a set of values, they experience a sense of emptiness and meaninglessness. When people feel this way, they turn to others for answers. The answers aren't there, however, because the problem is really within the person. This illustrates, once again, the existentialist theme that you must be responsible for your own actions and that truth can come only from within and from your actions.

TERROR MANAGEMENT

Some of the ideas of existential psychology are reflected in *terror management* theory (Greenberg, Pyszczynski, & Solomon, 1986). This theory begins with the idea that an awareness of one's eventual death creates existential angst, or terror (Becker, 1973). People respond to the terror by trying to live lives of meaning and value. This much matches what we said about existential psychology.

Terror management theory goes on to suggest, however, that people often don't define the meaning of life on their own. Rather, they use a process of social and cultural consensus. This means that group identity plays an important role in how people affirm the value of their lives. Reminders of mortality lead people to be more protective of their own cultural values (Greenberg, Solomon, & Pyszczynski, 1997). By weaving themselves into a meaningful cultural fabric—a fabric that will last long after they're gone—they affirm their own value as human beings.

People respond to reminders of mortality by holding on more strongly to their social fabric.

This theory has led to a great deal of research over the past two decades (Greenberg et al., 1997). Some of this research has shown that making people aware of their mortality causes them to become more favorable toward those who uphold their worldview and more negative toward those who don't. Mortality salience also makes people adhere more to cultural norms themselves. Americans become more patriotic; jihadists become more devoted to their cause (Pyszczynski, Solomon, & Greenberg, 2002). Mortality salience can make people act more altruistically—for instance, by supporting charities (Jonas, Schimel, Greenberg, & Pyszczynski, 2002)—but only if the charities connect to their own culture. The relationship can also go the other way: Threats to your worldview induce thoughts about death (Schimel, Hayes, Williams, & Jahrig, 2007).

Much of the research on this topic examines how people affirm their cultural worldview after being reminded of their mortality. However, at least one study has looked at how people affirm values of the self (McGregor, Zanna, Holmes, & Spencer, 2001, Study 4). After a manipulation of mortality salience, participants completed a measure of identity seeking and an assessment of their goals for the immediate future. Those whose mortality had been brought to mind were higher on the measure of identity seeking than others. They also reported intending to work at projects that were more self-consistent than the projects reported by others.

Terror management theory leads to a number of other interesting ideas. One is that terror management is the reason people view themselves as separate from other animals. To think of yourself as an animal is to be reminded of your death, because all animals die. Fitting this idea, mortality salience causes people to favor more strongly the idea that humans are distinct from other animals (Goldenberg et al., 2001).

This view also has implications for sexuality (Goldenberg, Pyszczynski, Greenberg, & Solomon, 2000). Sex is one more reminder of your animal nature. This may be one reason many people are nervous about sex: It reminds them of their mortality. People sidestep this reminder in many ways. They ascribe aesthetic value to the sex act. They create romance around it, to distract themselves from its animal qualities (Florian, Mikulincer, & Hirschberger, 2002). They create cultural standards of beauty that are idealized and symbolic. In doing so, the *animal* is transformed to the *spiritual*.

People struggle against existential terror in many ways. According to terror management theory, propping up self-esteem can establish a sense of one's value and stave off existential angst (Pyszczynski, Greenberg, Solomon, Arndt, & Schimel, 2004). Recent research has added the idea that confronting mortality motivates people to

BOX 11.3 SELF-ACTUALIZATION AND *YOUR* LIFE

By now, you've read a lot about the concept of self-actualization, and it may all sound pretty abstract. To get a more concrete feel for the idea, try spending a few minutes interviewing yourself. Think about how issues surrounding self-actualization apply to your own life.

For example, think about how Maslow's hierarchy of needs pertains to your current existence. Which level of the hierarchy dominates your day-to-day experiences? Are you mostly concerned with having a sense of belonging to a social group (or perhaps a sense of acceptance and closeness with a particular person)? Is the need to feel valued and respected what you're currently focused on? Or are you actively trying to grow as close as possible to the blueprint hidden inside you that holds the secret of your possibilities?

Now think back to your junior year of high school and what your life was like then. What were your needs and concerns during that period? Since then, has your focus moved upward on the hierarchy or downward? Or are you focused at about the same level?

Here's another issue: Think about your current mission in life, the goal that gives your life focus and provides it with meaning. Where did it come from? Was it passed down to you by your parents (or someone else)? Or does it come from deep inside you? How *sure* are you that your goal is your own and not someone else's assignment for you, a condition of worth? How sure are you that it isn't an assignment you've given *yourself*? What would it feel like to spend the rest of your life doing "assignments"?

Another question: You can't always do what you want. Everyone knows that. Sometimes, you *have* to do things. But how much of the time? How much of your time—how much of your *self*—should be used up doing your duty—being obedient to conditions of worth—before you turn to your other needs? How dangerous is it to say to yourself that you'll do these assignments—these duties—for a while, just for a little while, and that after a few weeks or months or years, you'll turn to the things you really want? How sure are you that you won't get in a rut and come to see the assignments as the only reality in life? How sure are you that you'll be able to make the decision to turn to your own self-actualization, years down the road, when it's become such a habit to focus on fulfilling conditions of worth?

Not every experience in life is self-actualizing. Even people who self-actualize extensively get stalled sometimes and have trouble with it. When *you* find yourself unable to self-actualize, what's preventing it? What barriers to growth do you confront from time to time? Are they the demands of other needs? Do they stem from your relationships with your parents and family? With your friends? Or are they barriers you place in front of yourself?

Obviously, these questions aren't easy to answer. You can't expect to answer them in just a few minutes. People spend a lifetime trying to answer them. But these questions are important, and thinking about them for a little while should give you a more vivid sense of the issues raised by the self-actualization approach.

---

form close relationships (Mikulincer, Florian, & Hirschberger, 2003). In fact, the push toward affiliation may be even more important than the affirmation of cultural values (Wisman & Koole, 2003).

This theory has prompted a great deal of research, extending in many directions. For our present purpose, however, let's link the theory back to existentialism. The research makes it clear that reminding people of their eventual death makes them try to affirm the value of their lives. People do this mostly (though not entirely) by embracing the values of the culture in which they live. Only a little evidence indicates that people try to create their own personal meanings.

Does this mean that for most people, the response to existential angst is to let others decide what's right and just go along? Surely, this would dismay the existential psychologists. It may simply mean, though, that values are naturally defined more by groups than the existentialists realized.

Assessment

A basic issue in personality assessment is how to go about it. Various perspectives suggest different approaches to assessment. The humanistic perspective suggests yet another one.

INTERVIEWS IN ASSESSMENT

To a self theorist such as Rogers, assessment is a process of finding out *what the person is like*. This orientation is quite compatible with interviewing as an assessment technique. The interview offers maximum flexibility. It lets the person being assessed say whatever comes up. It lets the interviewer follow stray thoughts and ask questions that might not otherwise occur. It lets the interviewer get a subjective sense of what that person is like from *interacting* with him or her (see also Box 11.3).

Finding out what a person is like in this way requires empathy. After all, the interviewer is trying to enter the other person's private world. Empathy isn't automatic. It requires sensitivity to small changes. As an interviewer, you must repeatedly check the accuracy of your sensing to be sure you haven't taken a wrong turn. (Empathy isn't important just for interviewing, by the way. Rogers saw it as important to doing therapy and to being a fully functioning person.)

An extensive interview produces a lot of information. One way to evaluate the information is through **content analysis**. This involves grouping the person's statements in some way and seeing how many statements fall into each group. For example, in an interview, Susan said two things about herself expressing self-approval, eighteen expressing self-disapproval, and fifteen that were ambivalent. One might infer from this that Susan isn't very satisfied with herself.

The flexibility that makes interviews useful also creates problems. Unless an interview is highly structured, it's hard to compare one with another. If Jane expresses more self-disapproval than Sally, is it because Jane dislikes herself more than Sally? Or did the interviewer just happen to follow up a particularly bothersome aspect of Jane's self-image? If Susan expresses less self-disapproval after therapy than before, is it because she's become more satisfied with herself or because the interviewer failed to get into self-critical areas in the second interview?

MEASURING THE SELF-CONCEPT BY Q-SORT

The other core issue in assessment is what qualities to assess. Theorists discussed in this chapter suggest several answers. One answer is to assess the self-concept.

A technique Rogers preferred for assessing self-concept is called the **Q-sort** (e.g., Block, 1961; Rogers & Dymond, 1954). There are many variations on this procedure, but the basic process is the same. It always involves giving the person a large set of items printed on cards. The items often are self-evaluative statements (as shown in Table 11.2), but they can be phrases, words, or other things. The person doing the Q-sort is asked to sort the cards into piles (see Figure 11.3). At one end are just a few cards with statements that are *most like you*, and at the other end are just a few cards with statements that are *least like you*. The piles between the two extremes represent gradations and thus contain more cards.

Table 11.2 Statements Commonly Used in Q-Sort Procedures.

I am intelligent.	I am ambitious.
I often feel guilty.	I am an impulsive person.
I am optimistic.	I get anxious easily.
I express my emotions freely.	I make strong demands on myself.
I understand myself.	I get along easily with others.
I am lazy.	I often feel driven.
I am generally happy.	I am self-reliant.
I am moody.	I am responsible for my troubles.

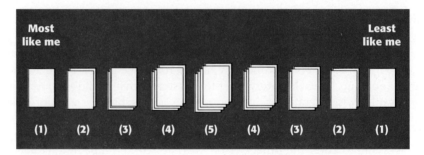

FIGURE 11.3

In the Q-sort procedure, you sort a set of cards containing descriptive statements into a row of piles. At one end of the row might be the card containing the single statement that's most like you; at the other end the card containing the single statement that's least like you. The other piles of cards represent gradations between these two points. As you can see from the numbers in parentheses in this example, the piles toward the middle are permitted to have more cards in them than the piles closer to the end points. Thus, you're forced to decide which items really are very much like and unlike yourself.

There are rules about how many cards can go in a given pile (see Figure 11.3). Usually, people start by sorting very generally (me, not me, neither) and then sorting further. By the time you're done, you've had to look hard at the statements and decide which one or two are most and least descriptive. By comparing qualities, the person is forced into self-evaluation. The Q-sort differs, in this respect, from rating scales in which each response is separate. Rating scales let the person say that all the descriptors apply equally well. This can't possibly happen in a Q-sort.

MEASURING SELF-ACTUALIZATION

A second type of content for assessment is suggested by the emphasis on self-actualization. Given this emphasis, it would seem desirable to measure the degree to which people have characteristics of frequent self-actualization.

The Personal Orientation Inventory (POI) was developed for this purpose (Shostrom, 1964, 1974; see also Knapp, 1976). The POI consists of paired statements. People choose the one from each pair that they agree with more. The POI has two scales. One, called *time competence,* reflects in part the degree to which the person lives in the present, as opposed to being distracted by the past and future. As the word *competence* hints, though, this scale also has other overtones. Time-competent people are able to effectively link the past and future with the present. They sense continuity among these three aspects of time. The second scale assesses the tendency to be *inner directed* in the search for values and meaning. Self-actualizers are believed to have a stronger tendency toward inner direction in determining their values than people who are less self-actualizing.

MEASURING SELF-DETERMINATION AND CONTROL

Yet another quality that's important to the viewpoints presented in this chapter is the extent to which a person's actions tend to be self-determined versus controlled. A number of self-reports assess this difference among people, with varying degrees of breadth.

One of them assesses the extent to which people generally function in a self-determined way in their lives (Sheldon, Ryan, & Reis, 1996). This measure of general self-determination gives a broad sense of a person's behavior across multiple domains. It's been used to show that people high in general self-determination have harmony between their needs and goals (e.g., Thrash & Elliot, 2002).

Several other measures focus on how people behave in some specific domain of life. For example, Ryan and Connell (1989) developed a measure of children's academic behavior and prosocial behavior. The items ask children why they do various things and provide potential reasons that had been chosen to reflect controlled or autonomous motivation. In another project, Black and Deci (2000) developed a measure to ask college students their reasons for learning things in their courses. Again, options are provided for reasons that are controlled and reasons that are self-determined. Another such measure was devised to assess the motives underlying religious behavior (Ryan, Rigby, & King, 1993).

Problems in Behavior, and Behavior Change

How are problems in living conceptualized in this view? Recall that fully functioning people are attuned to the self-actualizing tendency and experience a sense of coherence and consistency. They're not trying to live up to conditions of worth; rather, they're being who they are. To Rogers (and others), lack of congruity within the self creates psychological problems. (For evidence of various kinds, see Deci and Ryan, 1991; Higgins, 1990; and Ryan, Sheldon, Kasser, and Deci, 1996.)

To Rogers, incongruity between experience and self-concept or within the self-concept yields anxiety. Anxiety is a signal of disorganization from the organismic valuing process. Anxiety is especially likely to arise if the person focuses too much on conditions of worth and acts in ways that interfere with self-actualization.

When the holistic self is threatened by uncertainty, the person becomes not only more distressed but also more rigid (McGregor et al., 2001). This response seems to be an effort to hold onto the self that existed before. People faced with incongruity in one aspect of self stress their certainty about other things, apparently trying to compensate for what's been threatened. They become more zealous or extreme in their beliefs and personal values. In fact, McGregor et al. (2001) suggested that this is what happens in the terror management effects discussed earlier in the chapter.

To Rogers, the process of therapy is essentially one of reintegrating a partially disorganized self. It involves reversing the processes of defense to confront the discrepancies between the elements of the person's experience. Doing so isn't easy, however.

Rogers believed that an important condition must be met before such changes can occur. Specifically, the conditions of worth that distorted the person's behavior in the past must be lifted. The person still needs positive regard, but it must be *unconditional*. Only then will the person feel able to confront the discrepancies. Removing the conditions of worth will allow the person to focus more fully on the organismic valuing process, the inner voice that knows what's good and bad for you. This, in turn, allows a reintegration of the self. Consistent with this, people are less defensive when they're accepted for who they are than when they're accepted in an evaluative, conditional way (Arndt, Schimel, Greenberg, & Pyszczynski, 2002; Schimel, Arndt, Pyszczynski, & Greenberg, 2001).

Unconditional positive regard, then, is a key to therapy. But it's a complex key. For it to be effective, it must be given *from the person's own frame of reference*. That is, it means acceptance for who *you* think you are. Someone who knows nothing about you or your feelings can't provide meaningful acceptance. This is a second reason it's important for a therapist to be empathic. The first was that empathy is necessary to get an adequate sense of what the client is like. The second is that it's necessary if the therapist is to show unconditional positive regard for the client in a way that will facilitate reintegration of his or her personality.

There's one more potential problem here. Sometimes, people undertake therapy to *satisfy* a condition of worth. It stands to reason that people who are trying to change for self-determined reasons will do better than people who are trying to make similar changes to satisfy conditions of worth. In at least one domain of change—weight loss—there's evidence that this is true. In one study, people who lost weight for autonomous reasons lost more and kept it off longer than those who had less autonomous reasons (Williams, Grow, Freedman, Ryan, & Deci, 1996).

CLIENT-CENTERED THERAPY

Several approaches to therapy have been derived from the humanistic group of theories (Cain & Seeman, 2002). The one that's best known, developed by Rogers (1951, 1961; Rogers & Stevens, 1967), is called **client-centered therapy** or **person-centered therapy**. As the term implies, the client takes responsibility for his or her own improvement. Recall Rogers's belief that the tendency toward actualizing is intrinsic. If people with problems can be put in a situation in which conditions of worth are removed, they should naturally reintegrate themselves. This is a bit like the rationale for putting a bandage on a wound. The bandage doesn't heal the wound, but by maintaining a sterile environment, it helps the natural healing process take place.

In person-centered therapy, the therapist displays empathy and unconditional positive regard. This lets the client escape temporarily from conditions of worth and begin exploring aspects of experience that are incongruent with the self. Throughout, the therapist remains nondirective and nonevaluative, showing no emotion and giving no advice. The therapist's role is to *remove* the pressure of conditions of worth. By avoiding evaluative comments (e.g., saying that something is good or bad), the effective therapist avoids imposing additional conditions of worth. Rather than be evaluative, the therapist tries to help clients gain clear perspective on their own feelings and experiences. In general, this means reflecting back to the client, in slightly different ways, things the client is saying, so the client can re-examine them from a different angle. There are two variations on this reflection procedure. The first is called **clarification of feelings**. Part of what the client does in the therapy session is to express feelings about things, either directly in words or indirectly in other ways. As the feelings are expressed, the therapist repeats the expressions in different words. The purpose here is to make the client more aware of what his or her true feelings are. Simply being reminded of the feelings can help this to happen.

A moment's reflection should confirm the usefulness of this technique. Feelings are often fleeting. When people express feelings in their words or actions, they often fail to notice them. Moments later, they may be unaware of having had them. If the feelings are threatening, people actively defend against recognizing them. The process of reflecting feelings back to the client allows the nature and the intensity of the feelings to become more obvious to the client. This puts the client into closer touch with the experience.

The second kind of reflection in person-centered therapy is more intellectual and less emotional. It's called **restatement of content**. This is equivalent to what was just described but in terms of the *ideas* in the client's statements—the cognitive content of what he or she says.

BEYOND THERAPY TO PERSONAL GROWTH

To humanistic psychologists, therapy isn't a special process of fixing something that's wrong and then forgetting about it. Rather, it's on a continuum with other life experiences. In this view, a person who's living life to the fullest should always engage in more or less the same processes as occur in therapy. These processes provide a way for people who have average lives—or even very good lives—to further enrich their experiences and to self-actualize even more completely.

Rogers's view of the ideal way of life is captured in the term *fully functioning person*. He believed that personal growth throughout life should be a goal for everyone. Growth requires the same conditions as those needed for effective therapy. It requires that the people with whom you interact be genuine and open, with no holding back and no putting up false fronts. It also requires empathic understanding together with unconditional positive regard.

This view on growth is similar to Maslow's view on self-actualization: Growth isn't a goal that's reached once and then cast aside. It's a way of living to be pursued throughout your lifetime.

Self-Actualization and Self-Determination: Problems and Prospects

Many people see the views described in this chapter as forming an intuitively accessible approach to personality. The appeal of this approach derives partly from its emphasis on the uniqueness and validity of each person's experience. Indeed, this approach treats each person's subjective experience as being of great importance. This emphasis on personal experience fits with what many people bring to mind when they think of the word *personality,* especially when they think of their *own* personality. For this reason, this viewpoint feels comfortable and commonsensical to many.

The humanistic viewpoint also has at least two other virtues. First, it represents an optimistic and positive view of human nature. Psychologists such as Rogers, Maslow, Deci, and Ryan have argued strenuously that people are intrinsically good—naturally motivated to be the best they can be. According to this view, that motive will be expressed in everyone, as long as other circumstances don't interfere too much.

This optimistic outlook on humanity is also reflected in a practical virtue of the humanistic view. This view emphasizes the importance of fully appreciating your own life and maintaining close contact with your own feelings. This emphasis provides a strategy for living that many people have used to enrich their lives. The benefits sometimes come through formal therapy. But remember that many theorists assume there's no real distinction between therapy and the more ordinary "course corrections" that are part of normal living. Thus, the move toward personal enrichment has come for many people in informal ways. It's been sort of a self-guided exploration of how to make one's life better.

Although humanistic psychology certainly has virtues, it has had problems, as well. In the past, one problem was a lack of precision. It was hard to generate research from the theories. For example, to study self-actualization, you need to know the areas of life to which the actualizing tendency is most relevant for each person you're studying. But actualization occurs in different ways within different people. In theory, it might be necessary to study as many types of behavior as there are people being studied.

More recent psychologists of this general orientation have taken many steps to overcome such problems. Deci and Ryan and their co-workers, who share many orienting assumptions with earlier self-actualization theorists, have devised hypotheses that can be tested readily and in a straightforward manner. Findings from research on topics such as self-determination have provided powerful support for many assumptions of the humanistic viewpoint.

A second set of criticisms of humanistic psychology aims at a quality that was just described as a virtue: its optimistic, positive view of human nature. Some critics characterize this view as arbitrary, naïve, sentimental, and romantic. Some say it has no basis other than the theorists' belief that people are inherently good. And not everyone believes that all people are inherently good (Baumeister & Campbell, 1999).

The idea that everyone's self-actualization should be encouraged has also been criticized. Some argue that if this principle were carried to its extreme, it would require that everyone live life to the fullest, regardless of the consequences for anyone else. The result of such unrestrained self-expression would be chaos. Such an approach to life would create serious conflict whenever one person's self-actualization interfered with someone else's self-actualization, which certainly would happen.

It's also worth noting that the optimistic overtones that permeate so much of humanistic psychology are largely missing from the writings of the existentialists. Whereas humanists such as Rogers and Maslow emphasized the fulfilling quality that can come from making your own way in the world, the existentialists emphasize that doing this is hard and can be painful. Living honestly means confronting harsh realities and absurdities and rising above them. This picture is very different from the one painted by Rogers and Maslow. It can be difficult to reconcile the warm, glowing optimism of the one view with the darkness and angst of the other.

Another point of contention about the humanistic view on personality concerns the concept of free will. Theorists who emphasize self-actualization and self-determination tend to assume that people can decide for themselves what to do at any point in their lives. Others regard this conception of free will as a convenient fiction, an illusion that is misleading at best.

What, then, are the prospects for this approach to personality? Although many questions remain to be answered, the future of this way of thinking seems a great deal brighter than it did two decades ago. Several areas of vigorous and enthusiastic research activity have opened up seams of knowledge bearing on assumptions made years earlier by the pioneers of humanism. Topics such as self-determination, stereotype threat, terror management, and self-discrepancies are all being actively explored. The development and exploration of these sorts of ideas is a source of considerable encouragement for the future prospects of this approach.

• SUMMARY •

The theorists discussed in this chapter emphasize that people have an intrinsic tendency toward self-actualization: the tendency to develop your capabilities in ways that maintain or enhance the self. This tendency promotes a sense of congruence, or integration, within the person. Its effectiveness is monitored by the organismic valuing process.

People also have a need for positive regard, acceptance and affection from others. Positive regard may be unconditional, or it may be conditional on your acting in certain ways. These conditions of worth mean that the person is held worthy only if he or she is acting in a desired manner. Conditions of worth, which can be self-imposed as well as imposed by others, can cause you to act in ways that oppose self-actualization.

Self-determination theory focuses on the difference between behavior that's self-determined and behavior that's controlled in some fashion. People enjoy activities more if they feel they're doing them from intrinsic interest, instead of extrinsic reward. People whose lives are dominated by activities that are controlled are less healthy than people whose lives are self-determined.

Many theorists of this group assume that people have free will. This is a very hard idea to test, but people do seem to think they have free will. Studies of reactance have shown that people resist threats to freedoms they expect to have. Other research has questioned whether free will is illusory, though.

Behavior that opposes the actualizing tendency creates *disorganization* in the sense of self. Disorganization can be reduced by two kinds of defenses. You can distort perceptions of reality to reduce the threat, or you can act in ways that prevent threatening experiences from reaching your awareness (for example, by ignoring them). Use of these defenses is seen in the fact that people blame failures on factors outside themselves but take credit for successes. People also engage in self-handicapping strategies, creating esteem-protective explanations for the possibility of failure before it even happens. The use of self-handicapping is paradoxical, because it increases the likelihood of failure.

Maslow elaborated on the idea of self-actualization by proposing a hierarchy of motives, ranging from basic physical needs (at the bottom) to self-actualization (at the top). Basic needs are more demanding than higher needs, which (being more subtle) can affect you only when the lower needs are relatively satisfied. Maslow's intermediate levels appear to relate to the need for positive regard, suggesting why it can be hard to ignore the desire for acceptance from others.

Existential psychologists point out that with freedom comes the responsibility to choose for yourself what meaning your life has. The basic choice is to invest your life with meaning or to retreat into nothingness. When people are reminded of their own mortality, they try harder to connect to cultural values. Even if people try to find meaning, they can't escape existential guilt. No life can reflect all the possibilities it holds, because each choice rules out other possibilities.

The humanistic view on personality uses many assessment techniques, including both interviews and self-reports. Regarding content, it emphasizes the self-concept, self-actualization, and self-determination. One way to assess self-concept is the Q-sort, in which a set of items is sorted into piles according to how much they apply to oneself. Different "sorts" can be compared to obtain additional information.

From the humanistic perspective, problems derive from incongruity, and therapy is a process of reintegrating a partly disorganized self. For reintegration to occur, the client must feel a sense of unconditional positive regard. In client-centered therapy, people are led to refocus on their feelings about their problems. The therapist is nonevaluative and simply helps clients to clarify their feelings. In this viewpoint, the processes of therapy blend into those of ordinary living, with the goal of experiencing continued personal growth.

• GLOSSARY •

Actual self   Your self as you presently view it.

Actualization   The tendency to grow in ways that maintain or enhance the organism.

Clarification of feelings   The procedure in which a therapist restates a client's expressed feelings.

Client-centered or **person-centered therapy**   A type of therapy that removes conditions of worth and has clients examine their feelings and take personal responsibility for their improvement.

Conditional positive regard   Affection that's given only under certain conditions.

Conditional self-regard   Self-acceptance that's given only under certain conditions.

Conditions of worth   Contingencies placed on positive regard.

Congruence   An integration within the self and a coherence between your self and your experiences.

Content analysis   The grouping and counting of various categories of statements in an interview.

Contingent self-worth   Self-acceptance that's based on performance in some domain of life.

Dasein   "Being-in-the-world" the totality of your autonomous personal existence.

Deficiency-based motives   Motives reflecting a lack within the person that needs to be filled.

Existential guilt   A sense of guilt over failing to fulfill all of your possibilities.

Existential psychology   The view that people are responsible for investing their lives with meaning.

Flow   The experience of being immersed completely in an activity.

Fully functioning person   A person who's open to life's experiences and who is self-actualizing.

Growth-based motives   Motives reflecting the desire to extend and elaborate yourself.

Humanistic psychology   A branch of psychology emphasizing the universal capacity for personal growth.

Ideal self   Your perception of how you'd like to be.

Organismic valuing process   The internal signal that indicates whether self-actualization is occurring.

Peak experience   A subjective experience of intense self-actualization.

Person-centered therapy   *See* Client-centered therapy.

Phenomenological   A view that emphasizes the importance of your own personal experiences.

Positive regard   Acceptance and affection.

Q-sort   An assessment technique in which you sort descriptors according to how much they apply to you.

Reactance   A motive to regain or reassert a freedom that's been threatened.

Restatement of content   A procedure in which a therapist rephrases the ideas expressed by a client.

Self-actualization   A process of growing in ways that maintain or enhance the self.

Self-concordance   Pursuing goals that are consistent with your core values.

Self-determination   Deciding for yourself what to do.

Self-handicapping   Creating situations that make it hard to succeed, thus enabling avoidance of self-blame for failure.

Stereotype threat   Having a negative perception of the self because of feeling prejudged.

Transcendent self-actualizers   People whose actualization goes beyond the self to become more universal.

Unconditional positive regard   Acceptance and affection with "no strings attached."

The Cognitive Perspective

Don and Sandy have been shopping for a house. Some houses were easy to turn down: one was way too much money, one was right next to a gas station, and one was ugly. Others were harder. Over time, Don and Sandy became good at noticing things they cared about. They made a list of the pros and cons of each house, sure that by doing that, they would make a rational choice. Last month, though, they went to a house on Forest Hills Drive. It was smaller than they wanted, needed more work than they wanted, and didn't have the pool they wanted. But something about it seemed exactly right. Almost at once, they decided to buy it, and now it's their home.

COGNITIVE PSYCHOLOGY emerged as a major part of the field in the 1970s and 1980s. One topic in cognitive psychology is how people represent experiences mentally. Another is how people make decisions. Hundreds of studies have examined these processes, and many theories have been proposed to account for them. Examination of these processes has also influenced how theorists think about personality.

The cognitive perspective on personality rests implicitly on two assumptions. The first is that it's critical to understand how people deal with the information that surrounds them. Look around the room. You're surrounded by sights and sounds and maybe by other people doing things. Each of these is a source of information. The information comes to you in tiny bits, but you don't experience it that way. You see *walls*, not just patches of color. You hear a *song*, not unconnected bits of sound. You have an *impression* of your roommate, not just a collection of facts. To have these broader experiences, you integrate and organize the bits of information the world provides you.

A second assumption is that the flow of life consists of an elaborate web of decisions. Some of them are conscious, but far more of them occur outside awareness. Your personality is reflected in the decision making that goes on in your mind. It's reflected in the biases that follow from your mental organization and how you use it. The flow of implicit decisions is less predictable than theorists used to think, which has led to some reworking of theories about cognitive processes. This, in turn, has also had implications for thinking about personality.

These two assumptions underlie some of the ideas presented in this chapter. Here, we describe theories about how the mind is organized and how personality thus is structured. The ideas focus on how events are represented in memory and how memories guide your experience of the world. How all this complexity is organized and used is an important issue from the cognitive vantage point.

Although the cognitive perspective emerged as a major force in the 1970s, many of its themes were foreshadowed years earlier by George Kelly (see Box 12.1). For example, as did Kelly, cognitive theorists view people as implicit scientists. You are surrounded by more information than you can use. You can't check every bit of it, so you don't try (Gigerenzer & Goldstein, 1996). Instead, you impose order. You use partial information to make inferences about the rest (J. R. Anderson, 1991; Nisbett & Ross, 1980). This conserves mental resources (Macrae, Milne, & Bodenhausen, 1994). That's important, because you usually have several things on your mind at once and you *need* those resources.

Representing Your Experience of the World

Cognitive theorists are interested in how people organize, store, and retrieve memories of their experiences. How do we do these things?

SCHEMAS AND THEIR DEVELOPMENT

People impose order from recurrences of similar qualities across repeated events. They form **schemas**: mental organizations of information (knowledge structures). Schemas are (roughly) categories. Sometimes, the sense of category is explicit, but sometimes it's only implicit. Schemas can include many kinds of elements, including perceptual images, abstract knowledge, emotion qualities, and information about time sequence (Schwarz, 1990).

Box 12.1 Personal Construct Theory: Foreshadowing the Cognitive Perspective

The same physical world exists for everyone. But people's experience of the world isn't based entirely on physical reality. Three people can see the same movie but have experiences that aren't remotely the same. That's potentially true of all experiences. Physical reality is just the raw material for human experience. No one can examine all the raw material—no one has the time or mental resources. No one can deal with *just* raw material, either. You have to impose organization on it, create order from the chaos. So each person samples the raw material and constructs a personal vision of how reality is organized. You might even say that personality consists of the organization of mental structures through which the person views reality.

That's essentially the position taken by George Kelly (1955). He empha-sized the uniqueness of each person's subjective worldview. In many ways, his ideas also foreshadowed a cognitive view that began to form nearly two decades later. Kelly said the best way to understand personality is to think of people as scientists. Just as scientists, we all need to predict events and understand things that happen around us. You make a prediction about the nature of reality every time you turn on a faucet and expect water to come out. You make a prediction whenever you turn a doorknob (expecting the door to open) or eat (expecting not to get sick).

Just as scientists, all of us develop theories of reality. In Kelly's terms, people generate a set of **personal constructs** and impose them on reality. In his view, people don't experience the world directly but know it through the lens of their constructs. Kelly saw constructs as important, because he believed all events in life are open to multiple interpretations. It's easy to be misled by the fact that people usually can find words for their constructs and that different people use the same words. However, words don't always have precisely the same meanings from one person as to another. Even when two people think they agree about the meaning of a word, it's impossible to be sure they do.

Aspects of Kelly's view are star-tlingly similar to those used later by cognitive psychologists. Oddly, Kelly never saw himself as a cognitive theorist. In fact, he actively distanced himself from the idea (Neimeyer & Neimeyer, 1981). The study of cognitive processes in personality stemmed mostly from other lines of thought (Bruner, 1957; Heider, 1958; Koffka, 1935; Köhler, 1947; Lewin, 1951a). In fact, in what came to be called the "cognitive revolution" in psychology, Kelly was pretty thoroughly ignored. Yet aspects of today's cognitive view of personality greatly resemble his ideas.

Most views assume that schemas include information about specific cases, called **exemplars**, and also information about the more general sense of what the category is. Thus, for any given category (e.g., football players), you can bring to mind specific examples. You can also bring to mind a sense of the category as a whole (a typical football player). This sense of the category as a whole is captured in an idealized best member of the category, often called its **prototype**. In some theories, this is the best *actual* member you've experienced so far. In other theories, it's an *idealized* member— an average of those you've experienced so far.

The word *category* tends to imply that there's a definition for what's in it and what's not, but that's not always so. Features of the category all contribute to its nature, but often they aren't necessary. For example, your *bird* schema probably includes the idea that birds fly. But some birds don't fly (e.g., chickens and penguins). This means flying can't be a defining feature of birds, although flying does make an animal more likely to be a bird. The term **fuzzy set** has been used to convey the sense that a schema is defined in a vague way by a set of criteria that are relevant but not neces-sary (Lakoff, 1987; Medin, 1989). The more criteria that are met by an exemplar, the more likely it will be seen as a category member. But if there's no *required* criterion, members can vary a lot in what attributes they do and don't have.

Theories about schemas differ, but all of them treat schemas as having an organiz-ing quality. Schemas integrate meaning. An *event* is a collection of people, movements, objects in use, and so on. But unless there's a sense of what the event is *about*, the bits might just as well be random. In the same way, the attributes of an *object* are just a collection of bits unless there's an overriding sense of what the object *is*. The schema, in effect, is the glue that holds the bits of information together.

Once schemas have been developed, they're used to recognize new experiences. You identify new events by quickly (and mostly unconsciously) comparing them to the schemas (J. R. Anderson, 1976, 1985; Medin, 1989; Rosch & Mervis, 1975; E. E. Smith, Shoben, & Rips, 1974). If the features of the new event resemble an existing schema, the new stimulus is recognized as "one of those." This is how we recognize objects and events. Each new perception is based partly on incoming information and partly on what you've got as schemas (Jussim, 1991).

EFFECTS OF SCHEMAS

Schemas have several effects. First, they make it easy to put new information into memory. It's as though the schema were Velcro. Once a schema has been evoked, new information sticks to it easily. But what information sticks depends on what schema you use.

The schema tells where in the ongoing experience to look for information. Specifically, you look for information related to the schema. Changing schemas changes what you look for. As a result, you notice different things. For example, Don and Sandy, in the chapter opening, looked at houses as potential buyers. They noticed things about appliances and room layouts. If they had looked as potential burglars, they would have noticed such things as jewelry, TVs, and computers (R. C. Anderson & Pichert, 1978).

These schema-based biases can be self-perpetuating. That is, schemas tell you more than just where to look. They also suggest what you're going to find. You're more likely to remember what *confirms* your expectation than what doesn't. This can make the schema more solid in the future and thus more resistant to change (Hill, Lewicki, Czyzewska, & Boss, 1989).

Another effect of schemas follows from the fact that information is often missing from events. If a schema is evoked, it gives you additional information from *memory*. You assume that what's in the schema is true of the new (schema-related) event, because it's been true before. For example, if you hear about Joe doing laundry, you're likely to assume he put soap in the washer, even if that's not mentioned. In fact, you may even believe later that you had been told so when you hadn't (Cantor & Mischel, 1977). Something you assume is true unless you're told otherwise is called a **default**. A second effect of schemas, then, is to bring default information from memory to fill gaps.

SEMANTIC MEMORY, EPISODIC MEMORY, SCRIPTS, AND PROCEDURAL KNOWLEDGE

Schemas are organizations among memories, but memories are organized in several ways (Tulving, 1972). **Semantic memory** is organized by meaning. It's categories of objects and concepts. For example, most people have a schema for boats, with images of what boats look like and words that describe their nature and function. This schema often incorporates feeling qualities as well—for example, if the person thinks of boats as a source of either fun or danger.

A second type of organization, **episodic memory**, is memory for events or episodes. It's memory for experiences in space and time (Tulving, 1993). In episodic memory, elements of an event are strung together as they happened (Freyd, 1987). Some are long and elaborate—for example, going to high school. Others are brief—for example, hearing the screech of tires on pavement, followed by crashing metal and tinkling glass. A brief event can be stored both by itself and as part of a longer event (e.g., a car crash may have been a vivid episode in your experience of high school).

Scripts refer to well-defined sequences of behavior that tell us what to expect and what to do in certain situations, such as going to a wedding.

If you experience enough episodes of a given type, a schema for that *class* of episodes starts to form. This kind of schema is called a **script** (Schank & Abelson, 1977). A script is a prototype of an event category. It's used partly to perceive and interpret a common event, such as going to the hardware store or mowing the lawn. A script provides a perception with a sense of duration and a sense of flow and change throughout the event.

As with all schemas, scripts have defaults—things you assume to be true. For example, read this: "John went to a Thai restaurant last night. He had chicken curry. After paying his bill, he went home." You understood this description by using your script for dining out. Your defaults added a lot of details. You probably assumed John drove to the restaurant (although you might have assumed he walked). You probably assumed he ordered the chicken before he ate it, rather than snatching it off someone else's table. And you probably assumed that the bill he paid was for his dinner, not for broken dishes. In all these cases, you supplied information to fill gaps in the story. Scripts allow a lot of diversity, but each has a basic structure. Thus, when you encounter a new variation on it, you easily understand what's going on.

It's easy to distinguish between semantic and episodic memory, but most experiences are coded both ways at once. For example, conceptual categories (semantic) develop through repeated exposure to regularities in experiences (episodic). If a young child tries to play with several animals and has varying degrees of success, it may help lead the child to discover that dogs and cats are two different categories of animals.

In recent years, theorists have become more aware of the important role that feelings play in schemas. The involvement of feelings has many implications. For example, having a feeling can evoke particular schemas (Niedenthal, Halberstadt, & Innes-Ker, 1999). Feeling qualities seem especially likely to be part of a schema when the feeling is one of threat (Crawford & Cacioppo, 2002). Presumably, this is because sensing threat is so important for survival that we preferentially code information about it.

In addition to schemas pertaining to semantic categories and episodes of experience, people also have knowledge structures that pertain to actions. These are structures about the process of doing, rather than the more passive process of perceiving and understanding. Knowledge about doing is called **procedural knowledge**. *Doing* sometimes means engaging in specific overt behaviors, but it sometimes means engaging in mental manipulations. For example, dividing one number by another, turning a statement into a question, and making a decision between two alternatives all require use of procedural knowledge. It's harder to gain conscious access to much of this knowledge base, but presumably, it forms schematic structures that are used in different contexts.

SOCIALLY RELEVANT SCHEMAS

Soon after cognitive psychologists began to study categories, personality and social psychologists began to study how the processes involved in forming categories apply to socially meaningful stimuli. The focus of this work came to be called **social cognition** (Fiske & Taylor, 1984; Higgins & Bargh, 1987; Kunda, 1999; Macrae & Bodenhausen, 2000; Schneider, 1991; Wyer & Srull, 1986). People form categories of all sorts of things—for example, people, gender roles, environments, social situations, types of social relations, emotions, and the structure of music.

People differ in how readily they develop schemas (Moskowitz, 1993; Neuberg & Newsom, 1993). People also differ in the content and complexity of their schemas. This comes partly from the fact that people have different amounts of experience in a given domain. For example, some people have elaborate mental representations of the diversity among wines; others know only that some wine is red and some is white.

SELF-SCHEMAS

A particularly important schema is the one you form about yourself (Greenwald & Pratkanis, 1984; Markus, 1977; Markus & Wurf, 1987; T. B. Rogers, 1981), called the **self-schema**. This term is a little like *self-concept*, but it's also a little different. The self-schema, like any schema, makes it easier to remember things that fit it. It provides you with a lot of default information, and it tells you where to look for new information. Your self-schema can even bias your recall, twisting your recollections so they fit better with how you see yourself now (Ross, 1989).

Does the self-schema differ from other schemas? Well, it seems to be larger and more complex (T. B. Rogers, Kuiper, & Kirker, 1977). This makes sense, because you've probably spent more time noticing things about yourself than anything else in the world. The self-schema incorporates both trait labels and information about concrete behaviors (Fekken & Holden, 1992; Schell, Klein, & Babey, 1996), and it has more emotional elements than other schemas (Markus & Sentis, 1982). There are questions, though, about whether the self-schema is truly special. Features that seem special in it are also present in other well-developed schemas (Greenwald & Banaji, 1989; Karylowski, 1990). Perhaps the self-schema seems special only because it's so well developed.

Different people's self-schemas also differ in complexity (Linville, 1987). Some people keep different self-aspects distinct from each other. Each role these people play, each goal they have, each activity they do has its own place in their self-image. These people are high in **self-complexity**. Other people's self-aspects are less distinct, such that everything blends together. These people are lower in self-complexity.

This difference among people has interesting implications. For people low in self-complexity, feelings relating to a bad event in one aspect of life tend to spill over into other aspects of the self (Linville, 1987). Having trouble in a course may make you also feel bad about your social life. This doesn't happen as much for people higher in self-complexity, apparently because the separations and boundaries between their self-aspects prevents it (see also Niedenthal, Setterlund, & Wherry, 1992; Showers & Ryff, 1996).

In the same way, thinking of oneself in a contextualized way—even temporarily—can dampen the emotional reaction to a specific failure. In one study (Mendoza-Denton, Ayduk, Mischel, Shoda, & Testa, 2001), people who had been led to think of themselves in terms of particular classes of situations ("I am _____ when _____") were less affected emotionally by bad outcomes than those who were led to think of themselves in broader terms ("I am _____").

How do people acquire (or fail to acquire) complexity in their self-schemas? It may be partly a matter of how much you think about yourself. Nasby (1985) found that people who say they think about themselves a lot have self-schemas with more complexity and detail than people who say they think about themselves less. Presumably, the very process of thinking about yourself causes more growth and articulation of your self-schema.

Another way of viewing self-complexity is to think of the self as a "family" of self-schemas, rather than one (e.g., Markus & Nurius, 1986). In a sense, you're a different person when you're in different contexts (S. M. Andersen & Chen, 2002; Swann, Bosson, & Pelham, 2002). You make different assumptions about yourself. You attend to different aspects of what's going on. For instance, when you go from being with your friends at college to being with your parents at home, it's as though you're putting aside one schema about yourself and take up another one.

Markus and her colleagues (e.g., Markus & Nurius, 1986) suggested that people have images of themselves that diverge in a different way. People have selves they expect to become, selves they'd like to become (Hewitt & Genest, 1990), and selves they're afraid of becoming (Carver, Lawrence, & Scheier, 1999). People also have disliked selves (Ogilvie, 1987) and selves they think they ought to be (Higgins, 1987, 1990). These various **possible selves** can be brought to bear as motivators, because they provide goals to approach or to avoid.

ENTITY VERSUS INCREMENTAL SCHEMAS

Another variation in self-schemas is in how much stability people assume. An easy example of this is how people think of their abilities (Dweck & Leggett, 1988). To some people, an ability is an *entity*—something they have more of or less of but that doesn't change. To other people, ability is something you can *increment*, increase through experience. Once you establish one or the other of these views, you tend to maintain it as part of your personality (Robins & Pals, 2002).

People who hold an incremental view of ability treat setback as challenges for future improvements.

Both views reflect coherent schemas about ability, but they lead to different experiences. When people have an entity view, performing a task is about *proving* their ability. If they do poorly, they become distressed and want to quit. When people have an incremental view, performing a task is about *extending* their ability. If they do poorly, they see it as a chance to increase the ability.

These views seem to act in ways other schemas do. For example, they guide people's search for new information (Plaks, Stroessner, Dweck, & Sherman, 2001). When people hold an entity view, they attend to (and remember) cues of consistency. When people hold an incremental view, they attend to (and remember) cues of change.

ATTRIBUTION

An important aspect of experiencing events is judging their causes. Inferring a cause tells you whether the event was intentional or accidental. It also tells you something about how likely the event is to occur again. Inferring the cause of an event is called **attribution** (Heider, 1944, 1958). People do this spontaneously, without even knowing they're doing it (Hassin, Bargh, & Uleman, 2002).

The process of making attributions relies partly on schemas about the nature of social situations (Read, 1987). Default values from those schemas help you make inferences beyond the information that's present (Carlston & Skowronski, 1994). And as in other contexts, using different schemas causes people to make different inferences about the causes of events.

An important aspect of attribution is the interpretations people make for good and bad outcomes—successes and failures. Successes and failures can have many causes, but research has focused on four of them: ability, effort, task difficulty, and luck or chance factors. The best-known analysis of this kind of attribution is that of Bernie Weiner (1979, 1986, 1990).

Weiner points out that these four causes can be placed on a dimension of *locus of causality*: Either the cause is *internal*, part of you (ability, effort), or it's *external*, outside you (chance factors, task difficulty, powerful others). Separately from that, causes also vary in *stability*. Some seem fairly stable (ability), whereas others vary from one time to another (effort). In general, people tend to interpret their successes as having internal stable causes—their ability. (Note that this enhances self-esteem, as suggested in Chapter 11.) People generally tend to see their failures as caused by relatively unstable influences, such as bad luck or too little effort.

There are also individual differences in attributional tendencies, which can have big effects. If you see failure as caused by unstable factors, there's no need to worry about the future. That is, since the cause is unstable, the situation probably won't be the same next time. If the cause is stable, though, the picture is quite different. If you failed because you don't have ability or because the world is permanently against you, you're going to face that same situation next time and every time. Your future will hold only more failure.

Your behavior, thoughts, and feelings can be deeply affected by this mindset. Seeing stable and permanent reasons for bad life outcomes is related to depression (e.g., Abramson, Alloy, & Metalsky, 1995; Abramson, Metalsky, & Alloy, 1989; Abramson, Seligman, & Teasdale, 1978; Weiner & Litman-Adizes, 1980) and even sickness and death (e.g., Buchanan, 1995; Peterson, 1995).

Activation of Memories

We've talked about schemas from several angles. Next, let's consider how they are organized and activated.

Do schemas just pile up on top of each other in memory? No. One view is that memories form a vast network (see Figure 12.1). **Nodes,** or areas of storage, are linked if they have a logical connection. Some connections are semantic, linking attributes that contribute to a category (see Figure 12.1, A). Others are episodic, linking attributes that form an event (see Figure 12.1, B). Bits of information that have a lot to do with each other are strongly linked, whereas bits of information that don't have much to do with each other are not strongly linked. From this view, all knowledge is an elaborate web of associations of different strengths among a huge number of nodes of information. (Don't think about distance between nodes, by the way, only strength of association; distance isn't part of this picture.)

When a memory node is activated, the information it contains is in consciousness. A node can be activated by an intentional search (e.g., think of your phone number) or in other ways. As one node becomes active, *partial* activation spreads to other nodes related to it. The stronger the relation, the greater the degree of spreading. Partial activation makes it easier for the related area to come all the way to consciousness. That is, because it's already partly activated, it takes less of a boost to make it fully active.

To use the examples in Figure 12.1, A, thinking of an orange partially activates related semantic nodes. Thinking of an orange tends to remind you of navel oranges, the color and flavor of oranges, orange groves, and maybe orange juice. Since orange groves and orange juice both relate to Florida, you may be slightly reminded of Florida, as well. In the same way, thinking about a bit of an episode partially activates related nodes. Thinking about being in the parking lot tends to remind you vaguely of the person you saw there, which may remind you of the fact that you almost lost control of your driving and ran up over the curb.

These examples involve *partial* activation. The memory may not make it all the way to consciousness without another boost from somewhere. But it's more likely to get there than it was before. An extra boost sometimes comes from another source (e.g., seeing someone who looks a little like the person in the parking lot or hearing the song that was on the radio

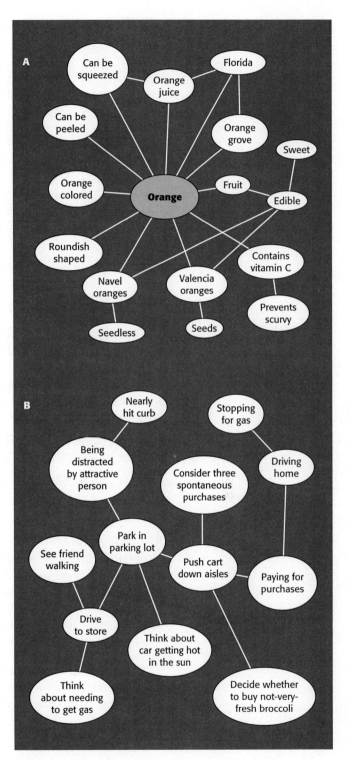

FIGURE 12.1
(A) Part of the network of semantic associations surrounding the concept *orange*. (B) Part of the network of episodic memories surrounding the event *going to the grocery store for broccoli, strawberries, and beer.*

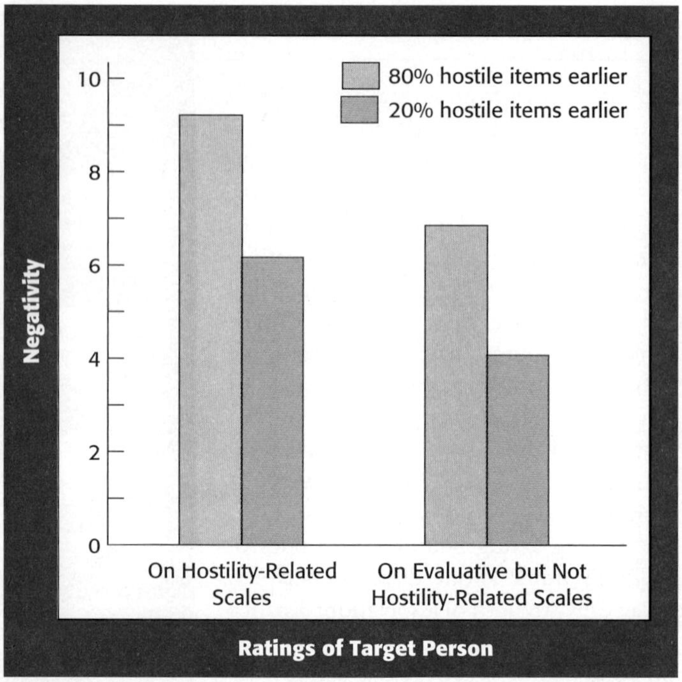

FIGURE 12.2
Effects of priming. Participants read a set of items, 80% of which (or 20% of which) contained words related to *hostility*. Later, in what they thought was a different experiment, they read an ambiguous portrayal of a target person and rated him on two sets of scales: some pertaining to hostility and others evaluative but not directly related to hostility. Reading a larger number of hostile words caused the target person to be seen as more hostile avnd as less pleasant.
Source: Based on Srull & Wyer, 1979, Experiment 1, immediate condition.

while you were parking). Given that extra boost, the node becomes active enough for its content (the image of the person) to pop into awareness. If the node hadn't already been partially active, the boost wouldn't have been enough.

PRIMING AND THE USE OF INFORMATION

The idea that partial activation causes easier access to memories has led to a technique called **priming**. Priming is activating a node by a task that precedes the task of inter-est. This technique was first used to study two questions. One is whether the same information is more accessible later on. That is, it takes a while for the activation to fade. This partial activation would leave the node more accessible than before, until the activation is gone. The other question is whether *related* information becomes more accessible after the priming.

The answer in both cases is yes. For example, Srull and Wyer (1979) had people do a task in which they read words related to hostility. Later, in what was presented as a different study, the people were more likely to see an ambiguously portrayed person as hostile (see Figure 12.2). They rated the person more negatively on other evaluative terms, as well, suggesting a spread of activation to related areas of memory.

These effects occur only if the primed information can plausibly be applied to the later event (Higgins & Brendl, 1995). If you prime *dishonest*, for instance, it won't influence your judgments of *athletic* ability. On the other hand, priming seems to activate the full dimen-sion, not just the end that's primed (Park, Yoon, Kim, & Wyer, 2001). If you prime *honest* and then present a target that might be *dishonest*, people are more likely to see dishonesty.

The technique of priming makes use of the fact that events can make information more accessible. But people also differ in what categories are readily accessible for them (Bargh, Lombardi, & Higgins, 1988; Higgins, King, & Mavin, 1982; Lau, 1989). The most accessible categories are the ones the people use the most. Thus, chronic accessibility reflects people's readiness to use particular schemas in seeing the world (Bargh & Pratto, 1986). Finding out about what schemas are chronically accessible in a particular person, then, can provide information about how that person sees the world (and thus about his or her personality).

As an example, children who grow up in poor neighborhoods are more likely than other children to be exposed to violence. This exposure may lead them to develop social schemas with violent themes. These schemas should be very accessible for children from such neighborhoods and thus likely to be used. Consistent with this, children from low-income neighborhoods see more hostile intent in ambiguous actions than do other children (Brady & Matthews, 2006; Chen & Matthews, 2001; Matthews & Gallo, 2011).

Primes also influence people's actions. A great deal of research shows that activating information that relates to behavior can influence actual behavior. Goals activated by primes range from self-verification goals (Kraus & Chen, 2009) to the eating of snacks (Harris, Bargh, & Brownell, 2009). Priming a particular relationship activates goals that are associated with that person (Morrison, Wheeler, & Smeesters, 2007). Simply mentioning a situation that conflicts with a chronic goal activates behavior relevant to that goal (Custers & Aarts, 2007). Priming a goal makes attitudes more positive toward stimuli that could facilitate achieving the goal (Ferguson, 2008). Priming one behavior also increases tendencies toward different but related behaviors (Maio, Pakizeh, Cheung, & Rees, 2009). Priming of behavior has even been shown in children as young as 18 months (Over & Carpenter, 2009).

It's not just perceptual categories and actions that can be primed. There's also evidence that use of a particular type of procedural knowledge, such as making a comparative decision, primes the use of that same knowledge in the future (Xu & Wyer, 2008). In that research, people were led to make one or another kind of comparative judgment and choice (or not). Afterward, they made a purchase decision (to buy one of two items or to buy neither). The result of making the prior choice was a greater tendency to buy one item or the other, rather than buy neither.

NONCONSCIOUS INFLUENCES ON BEHAVIOR

We've been talking about how information moves from memory to consciousness and is then used in various ways. However, a line of research by John Bargh and his colleagues (e.g., Chartrand & Bargh, 1996; Fitzsimons & Bargh, 2004) makes it very clear that information does not have to reach consciousness to influence what happens next.

In this work, research participants received **subliminal** primes—that is, primes outside their awareness. These subliminal primes often have the same effects as overt primes. For example, people who have the goal of forming an impression pay attention to different things than people who have the goal of memorizing. Activating these purposes subliminally has the same effect as activating them overtly (Chartrand & Bargh, 1996). As another example, recall that goals are often linked to particular relationships (e.g., your father may be linked in your mind with doing well on your exams). Priming the relationship even outside awareness activates the related goal, which you then set about pursuing unconsciously (Fitzsimons & Bargh, 2003). There's also evidence that subliminally priming an emotion causes judgments of subsequent stimuli to take on that emotional quality (Ferguson, Bargh, & Nayak, 2005).

BOX 12.2 WHAT'S IN A NAME?

Priming is a funny process. It happens all the time, though people don't realize it. And it can have some very unexpected effects on people's behavior. For example, consider your name. Your name is part of your self-schema. For most of us, our name indicates our family ties. But does your name have a broader impact on your life? Beyond the fact that some people are teased for having unusual names, most people would probably say no.

Studies have shown, however, that people's names may be involved with important life decisions. Pelham, Mirenberg, and Jones (2002) reported 10 studies of people's names and how they related to where the people lived and what their businesses were. Five studies found that people were more likely than would happen by chance to live in places whose names resembled

their own. For example, men named *Jack* lived in *Jacksonville* in a greater proportion than in, say, Philadelphia. There are more than *twice* as many men named *Louis* in Louisiana than would be expected by chance. Women named *Virginia* were extra likely to move to *Virginia* but not to *Georgia*, whereas the reverse was true of women named *Georgia*.

It's not just where people live. It's also what they do. Pelham et al. (2002) found that people tend to have jobs that have the same first initials as their own names. *Sheri's* odds of owning a *salon* are greater than chance but not *Carol's*. *Carol* is more likely to own a *candle* shop. People named *Thompson* have a greater-than-chance involvement in the *travel* business.

Pelham and his colleagues have also examined these effects in other areas of life (see Pelham et al., 2002). In the 2000 presidential campaign, people whose last names start with

B were more likely to give to the *Bush* campaign, and those whose last names start with *G* were more likely to give to *Gore*. People are also more likely to marry other people whose names resemble their own (J. T. Jones, Pelham, Carvallo, & Mirenberg, 2004).

Why do these things happen? The explanation is that most people have positive feelings about themselves as part of the self-schema. The positive feelings are evoked by anything that reminds them of themselves. This happens even if the reminding is very slight and even if it's unconscious. In effect, if you're named *Ken* and you live in *Kentucky*, you're surrounded by primes to your self-schema. People may gravitate slightly to anything that evokes that warm sense of self. We don't know if there's a *Ken* in *Kentucky* who drives a *Kia*, owns a *kennel*, and is married to a woman named *Karen*. But if there is, we'd bet he's a very contented man.

The findings of this body of work are fascinating. They represent an important reason for a renewed interest in the unconscious (Hassin, Uleman, & Bargh, 2005). This view of the unconscious is very different from that of Freud (described in Chapter 8). Today's theorists talk of the *cognitive* unconscious, as opposed to the *psychodynamic* unconscious (Hassin et al., 2005). Yet they believe (as did Freud) that the impact of forces outside awareness can be quite pronounced. They still view the unconscious as part of the mind to which we don't have ready access, but they posit different reasons.

From today's point of view, consciousness is a workspace, in which you consider information and make judgments, come to decisions, and form intentions. If these processes are routine, they can occur automatically, outside awareness. What makes things routine? Some processes are innately routine. You don't have to think about making your heart beat, for example, and you'd have trouble bringing into awareness the processes by which that happens. Other processes become routine from practice. As you practice anything (a tennis stroke, typing), the first few times you devote lots of attention to it. As you do it over and over, it feels more fluid and smooth. The more you practice, the less attention it needs. When you've done it enough, you disregard it almost totally. It no longer even needs consciousness to start it off. It can be triggered by an unconscious prime.

When you think carefully about what priming is (whether conscious or not), you realize that it happens constantly in life (Carver & Scheier, 2002). Whenever you hear something, read something, think something, or watch something, it makes the corresponding parts of your memories active. This, in turn, causes partial activation in related areas and will leave residual activation in the areas that are now active. That can have a wide range of subtle effects on behavior (see also Box 12.2).

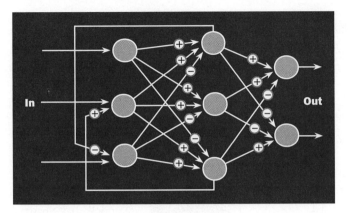

FIGURE 12.3
Example of a connectionist network. The network consists of units that receive and send activation, with two connections (printed in color) that feed activation back to "earlier" units. A given activation can be either excitatory (+) or inhibitory (−). Each unit receives activation from all the units that project to it and sends activation to all the units that it projects to. *Source:* Based on Carver & Scheier, 1998.

Connectionist Views of Mental Organization

For the most part, the way we've been discussing cognition thus far reflects a view in which cognition concerns symbol processing. That view dominated cognitive psychology for many years. In the mid-1980s, however, another view emerged, which now influences how we think about personality. That other view has several labels: *parallel distributed processing* (McClelland, Rumelhart, & PDP Research Group, 1986), *neural networks* (J. A. Anderson, 1995; Levine & Leven, 1992), and (perhaps most common) **connectionism** (J. L. McClelland, 1999).

The connectionist view uses neuronal processes as a metaphor for cognitive processes. Because the nervous system processes information simultaneously along many pathways, parallel processing is one of its key features. This view also holds that representations aren't centralized in specific nodes. Rather, a representation exists in a pattern of activation of an entire network of neurons.

Connectionists describe cognition in terms of networks of simple neuron-like units, in which *processing* means passing activations from one unit to another (see Figure 12.3). Each activation can be either excitatory or inhibitory. Thus, it either adds to or subtracts from the total activity of the unit for which it serves as input. Each unit sums its inputs (pluses and minuses) and passes the total onward. Energy passes in only one direction for each connection, as in neurons. But links are often assumed in which activation goes from a "later" unit back to an "earlier" one, which is also true of neurons. The network reacts to an input with a pattern of activity. This activity goes through the network's layers starting on the input side, through whatever connections exist, to the output side. The pattern that emerges on the output side is the response to the input.

The pattern of activations in the network is updated repeatedly—potentially, quite often. Gradually, the system "settles" into a configuration, and further updates yield no more change. A common way to view this is that the system *simultaneously satisfies multiple constraints* that the units place on each other (Thagard, 1989). For example, if two units inhibit each other, they can't both be highly active at the same time. Each constrains the other's activity. One of them eventually inhibits the other enough to keep it from being active. Diverse constraints settle out during the repeated updating

FIGURE 12.4
An example of an ambiguous figure. This image can be seen either as a young woman turning aside or as an old woman with a protruding nose and chin. Although your perception can easily shift from one to the other, you don't see a blend of images.

of activations. The process is complicated, but here's the bottom line: The parallel constraint satisfaction process creates the greatest organization and coherence it can across the network, given the constraints.

The literature of connectionism in cognitive psychology is large and growing (e.g., J. A. Anderson, 1995; Dawson, 2005; Elman, 2005; Seidenberg, 2005; Smolensky, Mozer, & Rumelhart, 1996; Wendelken & Shastri, 2005). Several authors have also tried to indicate why these ideas are useful for other areas of psychology, including personality (Caspar, Rothenfluh, & Segal, 1992; Kunda & Thagard, 1996; Overwalle & Siebler, 2005; Read & Miller, 1998, 2002; Read, Vanman, & Miller, 1997; Schultz & Lepper, 1996; Smith, 1996).

One interesting application is to social perception and decision making (Read et al., 1997; Thagard & Millgram, 1995). Such phenomena involve selecting one possibility from among two or more. When you view an ambiguous figure (see Figure 12.4), you perceive one or the other possibility, not a blend of the two. The perception of one or the other pops into your mind. In the same way, when you make a decision, you pick one option. You usually don't get to blend options. Again, even if you're trying to be rational, it's often the case that an answer seems to pop into your mind. Think back to Don and Sandy in the chapter opening, who were trying to find a house they liked. They were being rational and orderly, but then a decision just suddenly appeared.

How would connectionists analyze such an experience? They would say the experience is being constructed from bits of input. The bits activate units in the network, and the units place constraints on each other. Activations get transferred from unit to unit, around and around. As the activation pattern is updated over and over, some constraints get stronger and some get weaker. The network, as a whole, settles into a pattern. The pattern is the perception or the decision. Although there may be many cycles, the time involved can be very short. Subjectively, the pattern (perception or decision) emerges as a final product, sometimes abruptly.

These processes can create influences in multiple directions. That is, decisions are made from fitting bits of evidence together despite their constraints on one another. Once a decision has been reached, however, there's also an influence back on your evaluation of the evidence, making it more coherent with the decision (Simon, Snow, & Read, 2004).

Something that's interesting about these networks is that it can be very hard to tell ahead of time how they will settle out. The pattern of constraints can be intricate, and constraints may relate to each other in ways that aren't obvious. The network doesn't care about the "big picture." That's not how it works. Each unit just keeps sending out activations, as a function of how active *it* is. In the pushing and pulling, perceptions and decisions can emerge that seem irrational—and they *are* irrational, in a sense. The decision about buying a house isn't the algebraic sum of the ratings of the good and bad points of each house. It's more interwoven. This aspect of the connectionist approach in particular makes it feel very different from the symbolic approach.

Another thing that's interesting is that although these networks can be very stable, they sometimes reorganize abruptly (Read & Miller, 2002). In many cases, if you change one part of the input, nothing much changes. Reverberations from the change are dampened. Sometimes, though, a change in one part of the input is critical. If the effects of that small change are amplified instead of dampened, there can be profound reverberations over cycles, resulting in a drastic reorganization. Thus, if you're looking at a figure such as the one in Figure 12.4, it can suddenly reorganize and become the alternate image. These ideas have been used to discuss how the self-concept is sometimes resistant to and sometimes responsive to information from outside (Nowak, Vallacher, Tesser, & Borkowski, 2000).

DUAL-PROCESS MODELS

Cognitive psychologists wrestled for some time with differences between the symbol-processing approach and the connectionist approach. Several turned to the idea that cognition involves two kinds of thought, rather than one. Smolensky (1988) argued that a *conscious processor* is used for effortful reasoning and following of programs of instructions and that an *intuitive processor* manages intuitive problem solving, heuristic strategies, and skilled or automatic activities using connectionist processes. This view has also been expressed in several other **dual-process models** in cognitive psychology (De Neys, 2006; Holyoak & Spellman, 1993; Sloman, 1996).

When doing controlled processing, the mind in effect says, "Find a rule, apply it to the situation, carry out its logical steps of inference and action, and make decisions as needed. If no rule is available, use whatever's closest." When the mind is in connectionist mode, the settling process goes on until the elements shake out and a pattern emerges. The activity of this mode fits the experience of insight: A pattern appears suddenly where none existed before.

The idea that people experience the world through two different modes of processing also appears in the literature of personality. Depictions of two modes of processing are very similar to an argument made some time ago by Seymour Epstein (1985, 1990, 1994). Epstein's *cognitive–experiential self-theory* assumes that we experience reality through two systems. The *rational system* operates mostly consciously, uses logical rules, and is fairly slow. This is the symbolic processor that we think of as our rational mind. The *experiential system* is intuitive. It's a "quick and dirty" way of assessing and responding to reality. It relies on shortcuts and readily available information. It functions automatically and largely outside consciousness.

Epstein argued that both systems are always at work and that they jointly determine behavior. Each can also be engaged to a greater degree by circumstances. For example, asking people to give strictly logical responses to hypothetical events tends to place them in the rational mode. Asking them how they would respond if the events happened to them tends to place them in the experiential mode (Epstein, Lipson, Holstein, & Huh, 1992). The more emotionally charged a situation is, the more thinking is dominated by the experiential system.

In Epstein's view, the experiential system resulted from eons of evolution. It dominates when speed is needed (as when the situation is emotionally charged). You can't be thorough when you need to act fast (for example, to avoid danger). Maybe you can't even wait to form an intention. The rational system is more recent in origin. It provides a more cautious, analytic, planful way of proceeding. This approach also

Box 12.3 Delay of Gratification: The Role of Cognitive Strategies

Several previous chapters have discussed the ability to delay gratification—to wait a while for something you want. From a psychoanalytic view (see Chapter 8), this is a matter of the ego holding the id in check until the time is right to fulfill its desires. From the learning perspective (see Chapter 10), whether a person delays or not depends on the reward structure of the situation and the behavior of salient models.

The cognitive point of view provides yet another perspective on the process of delaying gratification. Specifically, an important influence on delay of gratification is the mental strategies people use (Kanfer, Karoly, & Newman, 1975; Mischel, 1974,

1979). *What* people think about—and *how* they think about it—can make delays easier or harder.

Early work showed that preschoolers would wait 10 times longer for a desired food if it wasn't visible than if it was (Mischel & Ebbesen, 1970). Later research showed these effects could be affected by varying how children *thought* about the desired object. Thinking about aspects of a food, such as its taste, made it nearly impossible for children to delay (Mischel & Baker, 1975). In contrast, attending to qualities of the food that weren't related to eating made it possible for children to tolerate delay quite easily (see also Kanfer et al., 1975; Moore, Mischel, & Zeiss, 1976; Toner & Smith, 1977).

Research on how these self-control strategies evolve showed a natural progression over time (Mischel, 1979). At first, children attended to aspects of the reward that were most appealing, such as taste (Yates & Mischel, 1979). Eventually, they generated cognitive strategies to keep these thoughts from their awareness. The result was increased self-restraint. As Mischel (1990) pointed out, it's not what's in front of the children that matters but what's going on in their heads. The same is true for adults (Trope & Fishbach, 2000, 2005). This research thus reinforces one of Mischel's major points: the role of people's mental strategies in determining their behavior.

---

has advantages, of course, when you have enough time and freedom from pressure to think things through.

The dual-process idea has emerged several more times in forms that are very similar to this (for reviews see Carver, 2005; Carver, Johnson, & Joormann, 2008). Metcalfe and Mischel (1999) proposed that there's a "hot" system that's emotional, impulsive, and reflexive and operates in a connectionist manner. There's also a "cool" system that is strategic, flexible, slower, and unemotional. This line of thought derives, in part, from a long line of research on delay of gratification (see Box 12.3). But it obviously applies more broadly.

The dual-process idea has also emerged in a number of other places. For example, Lieberman, Gaunt, Gilbert, and Trope (2002) looked at attributions that are relatively effortful versus those that are automatic (because they'd been made over and over). As did Epstein, these researchers assumed that the reflexive system is attuned to pressured and emotional demands of the world and that it acts very quickly. The other system uses symbolic logic and is slower. After reviewing findings from several sources, Lieberman et al. (2002) concluded that the consciously controlled and automatic versions of attribution are managed by different parts of the brain.

Strack and Deutsch (2004) also proposed a dual-process model of overt social behavior. It is far-reaching model, in which (as in Epstein's theory) action is seen as a joint output of two modes of functioning: reflective and impulsive. These modes of functioning occur simultaneously and may be either mutually supportive or in conflict with each other.

These dual-process models also resemble some ideas that came up in other chapters. We said in Chapter 6 that behavior sometimes reflects automatic impulses and sometimes the oversight of a temperament of constraint or effortful control. Controlled behavior is restrained and socialized. Behavior dominated by automatic processing can be impulsive and may seem unsocialized. In Chapter 7, we described some ideas about biological processes that involved greater control (constraint) versus impulsiveness (sensation seeking). In both cases, those ideas resemble the dual-process models described here. One mode of functioning is clearly recognizable as *thinking*. The other is more like intuitive *reacting* (see also Kuhl, 2000).

Many people have believed thinking is more important and more a part of personality. But intuitive reacting may be a far more potent influence on behavior than most people realize (see also Toates, 2006). The dual-process theories outlined here all assume that it's harder for the effortful process to dominate over the automatic process when the person's mind is relatively full (e.g., when you're trying to do two things at once). Similarly, the automatic process tends to take over when the situation is emotional or pressured. Being cognitively busy and being pressured or emotionally aroused applies to a good proportion of most people's lives.

Explicit and Implicit Knowledge

Another body of research on mental representations also seems to fit a dual-process view of cognition. This research examines the idea that people have both explicit knowledge (which is accessible on demand) and **implicit knowledge** (which isn't). To put it differently, implicit knowledge is the existence of automatic mental associations we aren't really aware of (an idea that came up earlier in Chapter 3 and in Chapter 5).

A topic that helped lead to the emergence of this line of thought concerns prejudices and how they're mentally represented. Many people believe they aren't prejudiced against minorities—that they treat all people equally well. It turns out, though, that many of these same people have stronger mental links from minorities to the semantic quality "bad" than from the minorities to "good" (Greenwald, McGhee, & Schwartz, 1998). These links are called *implicit associations*, because they are measured indirectly (usually through a set of reaction-time trials) and because people are unaware of the links.

The discovery of implicit attitudes has led to a much larger exploration of implicit knowledge of various kinds, including implicit theories of the self (Beer, 2002) and implicit self-esteem (DeHart, Pelham, & Tennen, 2006; Greenwald et al., 2002). Implicit self-esteem has been found to relate to negative feeling states in day-to-day life, independent of any role of explicit self-esteem (Conner & Barrett, 2005). Of particular interest is the fact that *implicit* self-esteem isn't very highly correlated with *explicit* self-esteem (the self-esteem that's reported on self-report scales). The same is often true of attitudes. There's evidence that both implicit and explicit attitudes of various types relate to behaviors, but often to different aspects of behavior (Asendorpf, Banse, & Mücke, 2002).

Why aren't these two aspects of knowledge closely related? One possibility follows from the view that much of implicit knowledge comes from simple association learning—classical and instrumental conditioning—whereas explicit knowledge comes from verbal, conceptual learning. Perhaps the experiences that provide associative versus verbal knowledge are more separate than has often been assumed. For example, parents might treat a child harshly while telling him verbally that he's a wonderful boy. These two sources of experience don't agree well with each other. Over time, this will lead to the boy's having different knowledge at the implicit (associative) and explicit (verbal) levels.

From this, it might follow that implicit knowledge starts forming earlier in life than explicit knowledge. That is, conditioning begins very early, whereas conceptual and verbal learning develop somewhat later. Consistent with this line of thought, negative implicit attitudes toward minorities are displayed as early as age 6. Egalitarian explicit attitudes emerge at about age 10, but the implicit attitudes remain as they were (Baron & Banaji, 2006).

Box 12.4 THE THEORIST AND THE THEORY: MISCHEL AND HIS MENTORS

Professional mentors influence their students in many ways. Most obviously, they impart a set of skills and a way of looking at the world, which the students then apply to topics of their own choosing. Sometimes, however, there's more to it than that. Sometimes an imprint on the mind of a student reverberates for a long time in the student's work. The student absorbs the essence of the mentor's view and recasts it. This seems to characterize the career of Walter Mischel.

Mischel was born in Vienna in 1930 and lived within walking distance of Sigmund Freud's house. When Mischel was 9, his family fled to New York to escape Nazism. He grew up in New York and became a social worker, working with Freud's personality theory. His enthusiasm for psychoanalysis waned, however, when he tried to apply it to juvenile offenders in New York's Lower East Side. After a time, he set off to continue his studies at Ohio State University.

There, he came under the influence of two people who were already making a mark on personality psychology: George Kelly and Julian Rotter. Kelly emphasized personal views of reality, and Rotter emphasized the importance of people's expectations in determining their behavior. Both were also skeptical about a purely dispositional approach to personality.

Mischel's work has displayed all three of these themes, although he took each one in his own direction. For example, as discussed in Chapter 4, Mischel (1968) sparked a controversy in personality psychology over the question of whether behavior has enough cross-situational consistency to justify believing in dispositions. He spent much of his career focusing on issues in the cognitive–social learning perspective, including the role played by expectancies. In the past three decades, his views have evolved to what some see as a resolution of the controversy he sparked in 1968. As we noted earlier in this chapter, today's cognitive view on personality has roots in several places other than Kelly's ideas. Surely, however, one reason for the emergence of this cognitive view is the impact that George Kelly the mentor had on the young Walter Mischel.

In introducing this topic, we said that implicit and explicit attitudes may relate to dual-process models of cognition. It seems possible that what we are referring to here as *implicit knowledge* is the same sort of associative system that others have termed an *experiential* or *reflexive* or *intuitive system*. The *explicit knowledge* seems more related to *a rational, deliberative system*. Fitting that picture, there's evidence that controlled processes are what help people override automatic tendencies to stereotype others (Payne, 2005) and react to cues of stigma (Pryor, Reeder, Yeadon, & Hesson-McInnis, 2004).

Broader Views on Cognition and Personality

Much of the cognitive view of personality concerns specific mental processes that underlie personality. This work tends to be tightly focused on particular issues. As a result, the cognitive approach is fragmented (Funder, 2001). Attempts have been made, however, to create more integrative statements about cognition and personality. Two of the most influential statements were made by Walter Mischel, a theorist with a huge influence on today's cognitive view (see also Box 12.4). Interestingly, these statements were made nearly a quarter century apart.

COGNITIVE PERSON VARIABLES

As is true of many who now hold a cognitive view on personality, Mischel earlier was identified with the *cognitive–social learning* view. The theoretical statement he made in 1973 represents a transition between Mischel the learning theorist and Mischel the cognitive theorist. In it, he proposed that an adequate theory of personality must take into account five classes of cognitive variables in the person, all of which are influenced by learning. Given these criteria, Mischel gave them the long name of *cognitive–social learning person variables*. He intended them to take the place of traits (Mischel, 1990).

One class of variables is the person's *competencies*: the skills that one develops over life. Just as people develop skills for manipulating the physical world, they develop social skills and problem-solving strategies, tools for analyzing the social world. Different people have different patterns of competencies, of course. Some people have the ability to empathize with others, some have the ability to fix brakes, some have the ability to make people laugh, and some have the ability to make people follow them into danger. Situations also vary in what competencies they call for (Shoda, Mischel, & Wright, 1993). Thus, different situations provide opportunities for different persons to take advantage of.

The second class of variables is *encoding strategies and personal constructs*. This covers schemas, as well as what Kelly (1955) said about the unique worldview each person develops. People construe events and people differently, depending on the schema they're using. (As noted earlier, a potential buyer looks at a house one way and a potential burglar, another way.) It's not the objective situation that determines how people react but how they construe it. Two people react to the same situation differently because they literally experience it differently.

Encoding strategies are ways of seeing the world. But to know what people will *do* in that world, you also need to know their *expectancies*. One expectancy is an anticipation that one kind of event typically leads to another event. For example, hearing a siren is often followed by seeing an emergency vehicle. Seeing dark clouds and hearing thunder are often followed by rain. Expectancies about what's connected to what provide continuity in experience.

A second type of expectancy is *behavior-outcome expectancy*: the belief that particular acts typically lead to particular outcomes. These are essentially the same as the outcome expectancies in Bandura's social cognitive learning theory (discussed in Chapter 10). Entering a restaurant (behavior) usually is followed by being greeted by a host or waiter (outcome). Being friendly to others (behavior) is usually followed by friendly responses (outcome). Typing the right code into an ATM (behavior) usually leads to receiving money (outcome). If the expectancies you have match reality, your actions will be effective. But if you've learned a set of behavior-outcome expectancies that don't fit the real world, you'll be less effective.

Expectancies begin to specify what people do: People do what they think will produce outcomes. The fourth part of the puzzle is knowing what outcomes the person wants to produce: the person's *subjective values*. These values are what cause people to use their expectancies in action. If the available outcome isn't one the person cares about, the expectancies won't matter.

The fifth set of variables Mischel (1973) discussed is what he called *self-regulatory systems and plans*. People set goals, make plans, and do the various things that need to be done to see that the plans are realized in action. This covers a lot of ground. Since Mischel proposed his five categories, this category has taken on something of a life of its own. In part for this reason, we'll talk about it separately, in Chapter 13.

PERSONALITY AS A COGNITIVE–AFFECTIVE PROCESSING SYSTEM

Mischel and Shoda (1995) later proposed a model that extends and elaborates Mischel's earlier statement (we discussed this model briefly in Chapter 4.) They proposed what they called a *cognitive–affective processing system*. The linking of *cognitive* to *affective* in this term reflects the recognition that emotion plays a key role in much of cognitive experience.

Mischel and Shoda (1995) said that people develop organizations of information about the nature of situations, other people, and the self. These schemas are more complex, in one sense, than what we've described thus far. Specifically, Mischel and Shoda said that these schemas have a kind of *if ... then* property—a conditional quality. Saying that someone is aggressive doesn't mean you think he or she is aggressive all the time. It means you think the person is more likely than most people to be aggressive in a certain class of situations.

Evidence from several sources supports this view. For example, in describing others, we often use *hedges*: conditions under which we think others act a particular way (Wright & Mischel, 1988). This suggests that people normally think in conditional terms about each other. In fact, the better you know someone, the more likely you are to think about him or her in conditional terms (Chen, 2003).

Mischel and Shoda (1995) said that people also think conditionally about themselves. That is, each person's behavior also follows an *if ... then* principle. Schemas to construe situations include information about appropriate actions in those situations. Norms are mentally represented as links between settings and the behaviors that relate to those settings (Aarts & Dijksterhuis, 2003). If a situation is identified that's linked to a particular behavior, then that behavior will tend to occur (*if ... then*).

In this view, individuality arises from two sources. First, people differ in the accessibility of their various schemas and the cues that evoke the schemas. Thus, different schemas are likely to pop up for different people in a given setting. People literally perceive different things in the same situation. Second, people differ in their *if ... then* profiles. When a schema is active, the person will act in ways that fit it. But that may mean different actions for different people.

For example, some people will view an ambiguous remark made by another person as a rejection, some as a provocation, some as an indication that a "power play" is underway, and some as an indication that the other person was out too late last night and is hung over. If Marty sees a power play—even if no one else in the room does—he erupts in bluster and bravado. If he doesn't see it that way, he doesn't do that. Ed is also sensitive to power plays, but he has a different *if ... then* link. If Ed sees a power play, he gets very quiet and starts looking for cues about who's likely to win. Thus, even if Ed and Marty identify the same situation—a power play—they will act quite differently from each other.

To predict consistency of action, then, you need to know two things. First, you need to know how the person construes the situation (which depends on the person's schemas and their accessibility). Second, you need to know the person's *if ... then* profile. In this view, the unique profile of *if ... then* relations is seen as a **behavioral signature** for a person's personality (Shoda, Mischel, & Wright, 1994). Indeed, these profiles of *if ... then* relations may, in some sense, *define* personality (Mischel, Shoda, & Mendoza-Denton, 2002). These profiles are relatively stable over time (Shoda et al., 1994) and thus account for temporal consistency in behavior. Consistency over time, of course, is a key element in conceptions of personality.

Andersen and Chen (2002) applied this line of thought to the core social relationships in a person's life. They argued that we develop schematic knowledge of people who are significant to us early in life. When we encounter new people who resemble one of those significant people enough to activate that schema, it evokes the *if … then* profile associated with that significant person. You act more like the version of yourself that you displayed to that significant other.

This general viewpoint on behavior suggests that schemas are deeply interconnected to one another. Schemas about what people are like relate to schemas about the nature of situations. Both of these are tied to schemas for acting. Although you may focus on one schema at a time, the use of one implicitly involves the use of the others as well (Shoda et al., 1989).

Consistent with this line of thought, there's evidence that some brain structures are involved in both perception–cognition and related actions. For instance, certain neurons that are active when a monkey *does* an action are also active when the monkey *sees* the same action (Gallese, 2001; Rizzolatti, Fogassi, & Gallese, 2002). They are called **mirror neurons**. Similar evidence has also been found in humans (Buccino et al., 2001). Later work extended the finding to sound. Neurons that are active when the monkey does or sees the action are also active when the monkey *hears* sounds associated with that action (Kohler et al., 2002). Related findings indicate that just reading a story activates areas of the brain that are associated with both watching and doing the actions in the story (Speer, Reynolds, Swallow, & Zacks, 2009). Such findings have led to the idea that perceptual memories may actually be organized in terms of potentials for action (Fadiga, Fogassi, Gallese, & Rizzolatti, 2000).

Assessment

From the cognitive viewpoint, personality assessment emphasizes assessing people's mental structures. There are many ways to assess mental structures (e.g., Merluzzi, Glass, & Genest, 1981), called **cognitive assessment** techniques. These techniques range from interviews and self-reports to *think-aloud protocols*, in which a person says what comes to mind while doing an activity. A variation on this is *experience sampling*, which is more intermittent.

THINK-ALOUD, EXPERIENCE SAMPLING, AND SELF-MONITORING

The technique used is often determined by the nature of the event of interest. For example, think-aloud approaches are used to assess cognition during problem solving (Ericsson & Simon, 1993). They're aimed at finding out what thoughts occur at various stages of problem solving. The idea is to consider such questions as which strategies are effective and which are not and how the strategies of experts and novices differ (Simon & Simon, 1978).

Experience sampling typically has somewhat different purposes. In this technique, people report at certain times what they've been thinking and doing. Sometimes, the reports are made at scheduled times, and sometimes, people are randomly paged and asked to report (e.g., Gable, Reis, & Elliot, 2000; Hormuth, 1990; Laurenceau, Barrett, & Pietromonaco, 1998; Pietromonaco & Barrett, 1997). This procedure allows researchers to sample across a wide range of events in a person's day. That way, they can find out what cognitions and emotions go along with which kinds of events. The result is a picture of what various events feel like to the person who is taking part in them.

For example, Csikszentmihalyi and Csikszentmihalyi (1988) paged people at irregular intervals and had them record their activities, thoughts, and feelings. As noted in Chapter 11, a focus of that work was on optimal experience. There were several interesting findings: Positive feelings related mostly to *voluntary* actions, not things people *had* to do. Satisfaction, freedom, alertness, and creativity related to events in which people's attention was tightly focused on what they were doing (Csikszentmihalyi, 1978). Interestingly, positive feelings of immersion were very likely during work.

More recent research has extended experience sampling methodology into many new domains. Further, it's now common to collect people's reports of their thoughts and feelings on hand-held computers (Gable et al., 2000; Laurenceau et al., 1998; Pietromonaco & Barrett, 1997). This makes collecting these sorts of cognitive assessments extremely easy. This technique is now being used to study ideas from a wide variety of theoretical perspectives.

Another technique, termed *event recording* or *self-monitoring*, focuses not on particular moments of the day but on particular classes of events. In this technique, the person records instances of specific event types (Ewart, 1978; Mahoney, 1977; Nelson, 1977), noting the behavior, emotion, or thought pattern and documenting information about what was going on at that moment (e.g., the time of day, whether the person was with others or alone, what the situation was). Doing this lets the person see regularities in the contexts that surround particular thoughts and emotions. This provides a better understanding of what schemas he or she is automatically using.

CONTEXTUALIZED ASSESSMENT

Another aspect of the cognitive view on assessment is the idea that personality should be assessed for specific classes of contexts. This element is shared with the cognitive–social learning view. Several studies indicate that doing this adds important information.

Research on this issue by Wright and his colleagues focused on assessment of children with problems. In one study (Wright, Lindgren, & Zakriski, 2001), teachers rated boys on two measures. One was a commonly used measure of problem behaviors (aggression and social withdrawal) that didn't identify the context in which they happen. The other measure assessed how often the behaviors occur in response *to specific situations*. The broad measure was able to distinguish aggressive children from others but didn't distinguish between two groups of boys whose aggression occurred in very different contexts. Thus, the contextualized measure provided fine-grained information that the other did not.

In another study (Wright, Zakriski, & Drinkwater, 1999), children were observed in a residential setting over a 6-week period. Elaborate recordings were made of their behaviors and the contexts in which they occurred. Each child was also rated on the measure of problem behaviors that ignores context. Each child was classified by the latter measure as being an *externalizer* (displaying behaviors such as aggression), an *internalizer* (displaying behaviors such as social withdrawal), a *mixed case* (displaying both types of behaviors), or *not a clinical case* (not fitting a diagnosis).

The behavioral signatures of these groups differed in ways that couldn't have been predicted by the global ratings. When teased or threatened by a peer, externalizers tended to hit and boss, whereas internalizers whined and withdrew. Outside these specific situations, these groups of children didn't differ from nondiagnosed children. The mixed cases didn't do any of these things in response to teasing, but they did tend to both hit and withdraw socially when a peer simply talked to them. Again, contextualized assessment gave much more information about those being assessed (see also Wright & Zakriski, 2003).

Problems in Behavior, and Behavior Change

The focus on cognitive structure that's been so apparent throughout this chapter is also involved in how this view conceptualizes psychological problems and therapeutic behavioral change.

INFORMATION-PROCESSING DEFICITS

One implication of the cognitive view is that some problems reflect deficits in basic cognitive or memory functions: attending, extracting and organizing information, and so on. For example, people with schizophrenia need more time than others to recognize stimuli such as letters (Miller, Saccuzzo, & Braff, 1979; Steronko & Woods, 1978). It isn't clear whether this implies a deeper problem or whether it bears only on perceiving. Just by itself, however, this problem would account for some of the difficulty schizophrenic people have in life.

Another simple idea is that there's a limit on attentional capacity. If you pay too much attention to things other than what you're trying to do, you become less efficient at what you're trying to do. Attending too broadly can also make it hard to learn. For example, anxiety takes up attention. For that reason alone, being anxious can make it harder to process other things (Newman et al., 1993; Sorg & Whitney, 1992). People with test anxiety or social anxiety thus become less efficient when their anxiety is aroused. A related argument has been used to explore deficits related to depression (Conway & Giannopoulos, 1993; Kuhl & Helle, 1986).

Some styles of *deploying* attention may also create problems (Crick & Dodge, 1994). For example, children who are overly aggressive don't attend to cues of other children's intentions (Dodge, 1986; Dodge & Crick, 1990). As a result, they often misjudge others' intentions and act aggressively. Indeed, they often strike out preemptively (Hubbard, Dodge, Cillessen, Coie, & Schwartz, 2001). This may also be true of violent adults (Holtzworth-Munroe, 1992). More generally, social exclusion seems to bias people to perceive neutral information as hostile, leading to greater aggression (DeWall, Twenge, Gitter, & Baumeister, 2009).

Why do people deploy their attention in ineffective ways? Their schemas lead them to do so. Recall that one effect of schemas is to tell you where to look for information in a new event: You look for information that fits the schema. Thus, a biased schema can bias the search for cues, which can lead to incorrect inferences and inappropriate actions.

DEPRESSIVE SELF-SCHEMAS

A broad implication of the cognitive view is that many problems stem from schemas that interfere with effective functioning in more complex ways. This reasoning has been applied to several problems—most notably, depression. Theorists hold that people sometimes develop ideas about the world that are inaccurate or distorted, which lead to adverse effects (e.g., Beck, 1976; Ellis, 1987; Meichenbaum, 1977; Young & Klosko, 1993). Aaron Beck (1972, 1976; Beck, Rush, Shaw, & Emery, 1979) is one theorist who thinks that depression and other problems follow from such distortions. In effect, people with these problems use faulty schemas to interpret events. They rely on negative preconceptions (their schemas) and ignore information that's available in the environment.

In Beck's view, the inaccurate schemas are used quickly and spontaneously, producing a stream of **automatic thoughts**. These automatic thoughts (e.g., "I can't do this," "What's the point of trying?" "Everything's going to turn out wrong") influence feelings and behaviors. The pattern has a run-on quality, because the negative feelings lead to more use of negative schemas, which in turn leads to more negative affect, and so on (cf. Nolen-Hoeksema, Morrow, & Frederickson, 1993; Wenzlaff, Wegner, & Roper, 1988). Indeed, just expecting emotional distress makes distress more likely (Kirsch, 1990; Kirsch, Mearns, & Catanzaro, 1990).

People who are prone to depression or anxiety seem to over-rely on information in memory and under-rely on the reality of the situation. This creates problems because the self-schemas of these people are negative (Kuiper & Derry, 1981; Segal, 1988). When people use these negative schemas, they naturally expect bad outcomes. They don't look at the situation with an open mind but attend to and encode the worst side of what's happening (Gotlib, 1983).

Beck uses the term **cognitive triad** to refer to negative thinking about the self, the world, and the future. Depressed people also use other distortions. They overgeneralize in a negative way from a single bad outcome to their overall sense of self-worth (Carver, 1998; Carver, La Voie, Kuhl, & Ganellen 1988; Hayes, Harris, & Carver, 2004). They make *arbitrary inferences*, jumping to negative conclusions when there isn't evidence for them (Cook & Peterson, 1986). They *catastrophize*, anticipating that every problem will have a terrible outcome and interpreting bad outcomes as permanent (Abramson et al., 1978; Abramson et al., 1989). The result of all this is a sense of low self-worth and hopelessness for the future (Haaga, Dyck, & Ernst, 1991; J. E. Roberts, Gotlib, & Kassel, 1996; J. E. Roberts & Monroe, 1994).

A few paragraphs back, we said that Beck views the use of negative mental structures as automatic. This argument has taken on new overtones in recent years in light of the emerging idea that implicit and explicit aspects of the self compete for influence on behavior (described earlier in the chapter). This emerging idea suggests that the negative mental structures are in a part of the brain that's different from the part guiding conscious, effortful action. The negative patterns may have come from conditioning or just become automatic over the years. Regardless, in the dual-process view, they influence behavior unless overridden by a more effortful process (Carver, Johnson, & Joormann, 2008).

This is essentially the argument that Beevers (2005) made about vulnerability to depression. Specifically, a person with negative associations in the implicit self is likely to often be subject to negative feelings. This person needs to make an effortful corrective process to counter those negative associations in the implicit self. If that effortful process doesn't occur, the implicit self maintains control over the person's experiences and depression is more likely.

COGNITIVE THERAPY

In Beck's view, therapy should help people to put faulty schemas aside and build new ones. People must learn to recognize automatic self-defeating thoughts and substitute other self-talk . This is termed **cognitive restructuring** or **reframing**. People must also learn to focus on the information in the situation and rely less on their preconceptions. To put it differently, these people should become more *controlled* in processing what's going on and less *automatic* (cf. Barber & DeRubeis, 1989; Kanfer & Busemeyer, 1982).

The procedures used for changing faulty schemas and their consequences are known broadly as **cognitive therapies** (Beck, 1976, 1991; Beck et al., 1979; DeRubeis, Tang, & Beck, 2001). There are several different techniques. A surprising one is getting people to go ahead and do things they expect (unrealistically) to have bad consequences. If the bad outcome doesn't happen, the people are thereby led to re-examine—and perhaps change—their expectations.

More generally, people are encouraged to view their thought patterns as hypotheses to be tested, instead of as certainties. They're also encouraged to go ahead and test the hypotheses. For example, if you're a person who thinks having a single failure means you can't do anything right, you might be told to examine your skills in other domains immediately after a failure. If you're a person who thinks everyone will despise you if you do anything wrong, you might be told to test this assumption by being with friends the next time you do something wrong.

Even a small amount of this sort of testing of reality can have a large impact on how people view themselves. In one study (Haemmerlie & Montgomery, 1984), students with strong social anxiety were given a simple treatment. The treatment was having a conversation with a member of the opposite sex who'd been told to initiate conversation topics, use the pronoun *you* fairly often, and avoid being negative. These *biased interactions* were held twice, a week apart, for about an hour each time. The result was a large reduction in signs of anxiety.

The Cognitive Perspective: Problems and Prospects

Some psychologists find the cognitive view on personality exciting. Others find it less so, however, believing that it's disorganized and not yet mature (Funder, 2001). Even those who find the cognitive view interesting acknowledge that it has many loose ends. Some critics of this view, on the other hand, think it's a passing fad, a misguided effort to graft a very different part of psychology someplace it just doesn't belong.

More specifically, one criticism of the cognitive view is that it's nothing more than a transplantation of cognitive psychology into the subject matter of personality. What's gained by knowing that a person's knowledge is schematically organized? What does it tell us about personality to know that these knowledge structures can be brought into use by priming them?

One answer is that these aspects of the mind's functioning do seem to have important implications for the kinds of day-to-day behaviors we usually think of in terms of personality. People absorb new experiences in terms of their current understanding of the world. Thus, it's useful to know what biases are created by their current understanding (i.e., schemas). How people interpret their experiences is also influenced by the goals they have in mind. Because different people have different goals, they experience events in very different ways.

The fact that people's interpretations can be influenced by priming is of special interest, partly because it relates to an idea of Freud's but with a very different spin. The idea is that people do things for reasons they're unaware of. Priming studies show that this definitely happens, but the reason for it need not reside in the psychoanalytic unconscious. The process may be far more superficial (and for that reason, less ominous). But because it's superficial, it may also be far more common than previously realized (Bargh & Chartrand, 1999; Carver & Scheier, 2002; Hassin et al., 2005).

The broadest answer to criticisms of the cognitive view, however, may be this: The cognitive viewpoint on personality is part of a broad attempt to understand the operating characteristics of the mind. A better understanding of those characteristics can't help but illuminate important aspects of personality. From this view, the intrapersonal functioning of personality is a reflection of the complexities of the mind and its workings. It's not possible to fully understand the former without understanding the latter.

• SUMMARY •

The cognitive orientation to personality considers how people attend to, process, organize, encode, store, and retrieve information. Schemas are mental organizations of information that develop over experience and are used to identify new events. Some theorists think schemas organize around prototypes (best members), and others believe that schemas have fuzzy, or inexact, definitions. Schemas make new events easy to remember. They also provide default information to fill in the gaps of events. Schemas can represent concepts (in semantic memory) and events (in episodic memory). Each aspect of memory holds exemplars and generalities. Stereotypic event categories are called *scripts*.

The term *social cognition* refers to cognitive processes bearing on stimuli relevant to social behavior. People develop schematic representations of many kinds of socially relevant categories. People also develop self-schemas, representations of themselves. The self-schema is more elaborate than other schemas, but it seems to follow the same principles. The self-schema may have several facets (e.g., possible selves). Some social schemas imply permanence (entity); some imply potential for change (incremental).

Many psychologists view memory as a vast set of content nodes, linked to each other by various associations. Activating one node in memory causes partial activation of related nodes (priming), causing that information to become more accessible. Priming can even happen outside awareness. Connectionist models view memory in terms of patterns in overall networks. A given pattern reflects the satisfaction of many constraints simultaneously. This view applies nicely to social perception and decision making. Some theorists believe there are two distinct kinds of thought processes: one quick, intuitive, and connectionist, the other slower, rational, and linear. Research on implicit attitudes suggests that people have knowledge at two levels, which may correspond to the two modes of thought processes.

Broad statements on cognitive views of personality emphasize the importance of people's schemas, encoding strategies, personal competencies, expectancies about how things are related in the world, values or incentives, and self-regulatory systems. People's behavior is seen as following *if … then* contingencies, in which the *if* describes a situation and the *then* describes a behavioral response. In this view, personality is a profile of these contingencies, forming a unique "behavioral signature" for each person.

Assessment, from this viewpoint, is the process of determining the person's cognitive tendencies and contents of consciousness. Cognitive assessment techniques include think-aloud procedures, thought sampling, and monitoring of the occurrence of particular categories of events. These procedures give a clearer idea of what sorts of thoughts are coming to mind in various kinds of situations—typically, situations that are problematic. Also important is the idea that assessment be contextualized to capture the person's *if … then* contingencies.

Problems in behavior can come from information-processing deficits (e.g., difficulty encoding, ineffective allocation of attention). Problems can also arise from development of negative self-schemas. In this view, depression results from various kinds of cognitive distortions, all of which cause events to seem more unpleasant or have more negative implications than is actually true. Cognitive therapy involves, in part, attempting to get people to stop engaging in these cognitive distortions and to develop more adaptive views of the events they experience. This may entail correcting automatic, intuitive processes through oversight from consciousness, effortful processes.

• GLOSSARY •

Attribution   The process of making a judgment about the cause or causes of an event.

Automatic thoughts   Self-related internal dialogue that often interferes with behavior.

Behavioral signature   The pattern of situation–behavior links the person has established over time and experiences in some specific domain.

Cognitive assessment   Procedures used to assess cognitive processes, mental structures, and contents of consciousness.

Cognitive restructuring or reframing   The process of taking a different and more positive view of your experience.

Cognitive therapies   Procedures aimed at reducing cognitive distortions and the distress that results from them.

Cognitive triad   Negative patterns of thinking about the self, the world, and the future.

Connectionism   An approach to understanding cognition based on the metaphor of interconnected neurons.

Default   Something assumed to be true until you learn otherwise.

Dual-process models   Models assuming two different modes of cognition—one effortful, one automatic.

Episodic memory   Memory organized according to sequences of events.

Exemplar   A specific example of a category member.

Fuzzy set   A category defined by a set of attributes that aren't absolutely necessary for membership.

Implicit knowledge   Associations between things in memory that aren't directly accessible.

Mirror neurons   Neurons that are active both when perceiving an action and when doing the action.

Node   An area of memory that stores some element of information.

Personal construct   A personal mental representation used to interpret events.

Possible self   An image of yourself in the future (expected, desired, feared, etc.).

Priming   Activating an element in memory by using the information contained in it, leaving it partly activated.

Procedural knowledge   Knowledge about doing, about engaging in specific behaviors and mental manipulations.

Prototype   The representation of a category in terms of the best member of the category.

Schema   An organization of knowledge in memory.

Script   A memory structure used to represent a highly stereotyped category of events.

Self-complexity   The degree to which your self-schema is differentiated and compartmentalized.

Self-schema   The schematic representation of the self.

Semantic memory   Memory organized according to meaning.

Social cognition   Cognitive processes that focus on socially meaningful stimuli.

Subliminal   Occurring too fast to be consciously recognized.

The Self-Regulation Perspective

As Susan awakes, thoughts come to mind about the presentation she's to give this morning. While dressing, she rehearses the points she intends to make. She catches herself skipping too quickly from one point to another and makes a mental note that if she speeds up in that section she should take a deep breath and concentrate. She has planned what to wear to make the impression she wants to make, and just before leaving, she checks her appearance in the hall mirror. As she opens the door, she runs through a mental checklist of what she needs to have with her: notes for her presentation, money, purse, keys. Check to see that the door's locked. Check to be sure there's enough gas in the car. Check to see if there's time to take the scenic route to campus. And she's off. "Good" Susan thinks. "Things are going just the way I want them to. Everything's right on track."

PEOPLE SHIFT from one task to another as the day proceeds, yet there's usually coherence and continuity as well. Your days are usually planful (despite disruptions and impulsive side trips) and include many activities. How do you move so easily from one thing to another, keep it all organized, and make it all happen? These are some of the questions behind this chapter.

The approach to personality discussed here is connected to several backgrounds. One is ideas about naturally occurring organized systems and how they function (Ford, 1987; von Bertalanffy, 1968). Another is ideas from robotics (Brooks, 2002; Dawson, 2004; Fellous & Arbib, 2005). As more is learned about how to get artificial agents to do things, some think that knowledge may help understand how people do things.

The easiest way to begin discussing this approach to personality is to think of it as a viewpoint on aspects of motivation. Much of this chapter focuses on how people adopt, prioritize, and attain goals. These functions resemble ideas discussed in Chapter 5 as *motives*. It will also be useful to keep in mind the cognitive view of personality discussed in Chapter 12, because the view that people have an organized network of memories is assumed here, too. Now, though, the focus is on how the cognitions and memories result in behavior.

From Cognition to Behavior

As noted in Chapter 12, the schemas people use to understand events often include information about behavior. People use this information to recognize what others are doing, and they also use it to guide the making of behavior. This information helps people know what to do in the kind of situation the schema represents (Burroughs & Drews, 1991; Dodge, 1986). For example, your *dining out* script lets you understand someone else's evening, and it also reminds you what to do if *you* are dining out— order before you're served and pay the bill before you leave.

What's the relation between the information used to recognize acts and the information used to do acts? It's not clear whether one schema serves both purposes or whether there are two parallel forms—one for understanding and one for doing (Petri & Mishkin, 1994). However, there seems to be at least some overlap. As noted in Chapter 12, what are called *mirror neurons* are active both when an action is being watched and when the same action is being done (Gallese, 2001; Rizzolatti, Fogassi, & Gallese, 2002). This suggests a very strong link between thinking and doing.

INTENTIONS

Sometimes, a situation evokes a schema with guidelines for action. Often, though, actions follow from prior intentions. How are intentions formed? Icek Ajzen and Martin Fishbein (Ajzen, 1985, 1988; Ajzen & Fishbein, 1980) suggested the process uses a kind of mental algebra to create an action probability. If the probability is high enough, an intention forms to do the act.

According to Ajzen and Fishbein, when people decide whether to do something, they weigh several kinds of information (see Figure 13.1). They think about the action's likely outcome and how much they want it. For example, you might think that spending money on a Caribbean trip over spring break would result in a lot of fun, and you really want to have that fun. The outcome and its desirability merge to form an **attitude** about the behavior. Because it stems from your own wants, your attitude is your *personal* orientation to the act.

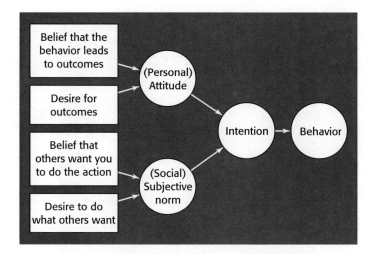

FIGURE 13.1
Foundations of intentions. The belief that an act will produce a particular outcome and the personal desirability of the outcome merge to form an *attitude* (a personal orientation to the act).
The belief that other people want you to do the act and the desire to go along with their wishes
merge to form a *subjective norm* (a social orientation to the act). The attitude and the subjective
norm are weighted in forming the *intention*. The intention then influences the *behavior*.
Source: Based on Ajzen, 1988.

Two other kinds of information pertain to the act's *social* meaning to you. First is
whether people who matter to you want you to do the action. You might think about
your parents, who want you to come home instead. Or you might think about your
friends, who think the trip is a great idea. The other element here is how much you
want to please the people you're thinking about. How much do you want to please
your parents—or at least stay on their good side? How much do you want to please
your friends? What other people want you to do and how much that matters merge
to form a **subjective norm** about the action.

The intention derives from both the attitude and the subjective norm. If both
favor the behavior, you'll form a strong intention to do it. If both oppose the behavior,
you'll form a strong intention *not* to do it. Things are more complex when the attitude
and subjective norm conflict. Sometimes you want to do something, but you know
others want you not to. In those cases, the intention you form depends on which matters more: satisfying yourself or satisfying the others.

GOALS

Behind what we've said so far is the idea that behavior is directed toward *goals*.
Schemas suggest actions to take. Forming an intention means setting up a goal to
reach. The idea that experience is organized around goals has been discussed a lot in
the past two decades (e.g., Austin & Vancouver, 1996; Elliott & Dweck, 1988; Freund
& Baltes, 2002; Johnson, Chang, & Lord, 2006; Pervin, 1983, 1989). Diverse terms
have been used—including *personal strivings* (Emmons, 1986), *current concerns* (Klinger,
1987), and *personal projects* (Little, 1989)—but the core theme runs through all of them.
That theme is that people's goals energize their activities, direct their movements—
even provide meaning for their lives (Baumeister, 1989).

All these constructs assume both overall goals and subgoals. The path you choose
to the overall goal depends on other aspects of your life. Different people use different

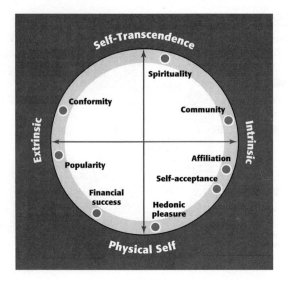

FIGURE 13.2

Circumplex formed by relationships among diverse goals, across 15 cultures. Goals vary along the dimension of intrinsic versus extrinsic and separately along the dimension of concerning the physical self versus transcending the self. *Source:* Based on Grouzet et al., 2005.

strategies to pursue the same life goals (Langston & Cantor, 1989). For example, someone who's relatively shy will have different strategies for making friends than someone who's more outgoing.

In this view, the self is made up partly of goals and the organizations among them. Indeed, there's evidence that traits derive their meaning from the goals to which they relate (Read, Jones, & Miller, 1990; Roberts & Robins, 2000). Goals and aspirations vary from person to person. Yet there's evidence that goals have a coherent relationship among persons from diverse cultures. That is, goals form a two-dimensional space, in which some are compatible and some conflict (Grouzet et al., 2005). For example, *spirituality* is compatible with *community* but in conflict with *hedonic pleasure* (see Figure 13.2). As a person's values shift in importance over time, an increase in the importance of one value (e.g., community) is accompanied by slight increases in the importance of other compatible values (e.g., *spirituality* and *affiliation*) (Bardi, Lee, Hormann-Towfigh, & Soutar, 2009).

GOAL SETTING

Many goals specify actions but don't imply any standard of excellence. The goal of going water skiing on a hot afternoon, for instance, doesn't necessarily imply a goal of excellence (though it might). Forming an intention to go to the grocery store creates a guide for behavior, but it's not really very challenging.

On the other hand, performance level is clearly an issue in some areas. In many activities, the goal isn't just to perform; it's to do *well*. For example, in taking a college course, the goal for many people isn't just to complete the course but to do well in it. Another example is business performance. The goal isn't just to survive but to thrive. One question that arises in such contexts is this: Does setting a particular level of goal influence how well you do?

Yes. Setting specific high goals leads to higher performance (Locke & Latham, 1990). This is true when specific high goals are compared to specific easy goals, and it's also true when specific high goals are compared to the goal of "Do your best." Apparently, most people don't really hear "Do your best." Rather, they hear "Try to do reasonably well." Thus, setting this goal leads to poorer performance than setting a specific high goal.

Why do higher goals lead to better performance? Three reasons. First, setting a higher goal causes you to try harder. For example, you know you won't solve 50 problems in 10 minutes unless you push yourself. So you start out pushing yourself. Second, you're more *persistent*. A brief spurt of effort won't do; you'll have to push yourself the entire time. Third, high goals make you *concentrate* more, making you less susceptible to distractions. In all these respects, setting a lower goal causes people to ease back a little.

The effect of setting high goals is well documented, but it has a very important limitation. In particular, if you're presented with a goal that's totally unrealistic, you won't adopt it and you won't try for it. If you don't adopt it, it's as if the goal doesn't exist. The key, then, is to take up a goal that's high enough to sustain strong effort but not so high that it's rejected instead of adopted.

IMPLEMENTATION INTENTIONS AND THE IMPORTANCE OF STRATEGIES

In describing goals, we noted that there typically are *subgoals*, or strategies related to the goals. Peter Gollwitzer and his colleagues (Brandstätter, Lengfelder, & Gollwitzer, 2001; Gollwitzer, 1999; Gollwitzer & Brandstätter, 1997) have made a similar distinction between two kinds of intentions. A **goal intention** is the intent to reach a particular outcome. An **implementation intention** concerns the how, when, and where of the process. It's the intention to take specific actions when encountering specific circumstances. This linking of context to action is what was described as an *if . . . then* link in Chapter 12 (Mischel & Shoda, 1995). Some *if . . . then* links are habitual and well learned (Brandstätter & Frank, 2002), whereas others need to be formed consciously for specific intended paths of behavior.

Implementation intentions are more concrete than goal intentions. They serve the goal intentions. They're important because they preempt problems that arise in getting the behavior done. They can help people get started in doing the behavior, and they can also help prevent goal striving from straying off course (Achtziger, Gollwitzer, & Sheeran, 2008).

Sometimes people fail to fulfill goal intentions because they haven't decided *how* to do so. Having an implementation intention, which is concrete and specific, takes care of that. Sometimes people fail to act because they're distracted and opportunities pass by. Having an implementation intention helps them recognize the opportunity and act on it (Brandstätter et al., 2001): "*If* I see a chance to spend 10 minutes on this assignment, *then* I will focus extra hard and do so." Sometimes, people fail to act because they're tired. Having an implementation intention helps them overcome that (Webb & Sheeran, 2003). "*If* I feel tired, *then* I will take three deep breaths and renew my focus." Forming an implementation intention to do something hard (e.g., writing an assigned paper over Christmas break) greatly increases the likelihood of actually doing it (Gollwitzer & Brandstätter, 1997). Forming implementation intentions has even been shown to help people eat a healthier diet (Stadler, Oettingen, & Gollwitzer, 2010).

Implementation intentions act both by making the situational cue more easily recognized and by establishing a link from cue to action (Webb & Sheeran, 2007). Even so, implementation intentions by themselves don't seem to be enough. You also have to have a strong and active goal intention (Sheeran, Webb, & Gollwitzer, 2005). In fact, having an implementation intention helps more if the goal fits with your broad sense of self than if it doesn't (Koestner, Lekes, Powers, & Chicoine, 2002).

Implementation intentions create a link between a situational cue and a strategy for moving toward the goal. Other work also shows the importance of having such links. It derives from the concept of *possible self*. As described in Chapter 12, possible selves are images of the person you think you might become. They can serve as reference points for self-regulation (Hoyle & Sherrill, 2006). For a desired possible self to influence behavior, however, you also have to have strategies to attain it (Oyserman, Bybee, & Terry, 2006; Oyserman, Bybee, Terry, & Hart-Johnson, 2004). If the strategies aren't already there to be used, you need to put some effort into creating them.

DELIBERATIVE AND IMPLEMENTAL MINDSETS

Having intentions matters, but forming intentions and executing them are different things. People form and execute with different mindsets (Heckhausen & Gollwitzer, 1987). Forming a goal intention requires weighing possibilities, thinking of pros and cons, and juggling options. This is called a **deliberative mindset**, because the person is deliberating the decision to act. This mindset is relatively open minded, careful, and cautious, in the service of making the best choice (Fujita, Gollwitzer, & Oettingen, 2007; Taylor & Gollwitzer, 1995).

Once the intention has been formed, actually doing the behavior entails a different mindset. People no longer deliberate. Now, it's all about doing. This is called an **implemental mindset**, because it focuses on implementing the intention to act. This mindset is optimistic. It minimizes potential problems, in the service of trying as hard as possible to carry out the action (Taylor & Gollwitzer, 1995). Generally, this mindset fosters persistence (Brandstätter & Frank, 2002).

There's evidence that these two mindsets may use different areas of the brain. Lengfelder and Gollwitzer (2001) studied patients with frontal lobe damage and patients with damage in other areas of the brain. Those people with frontal damage were impaired in deliberating. However, if they were provided with *if . . . then* implementation intentions, they weren't impaired in acting. This finding suggests that the planning is done in the frontal cortex, and the handling of the action is done somewhere else.

Self-Regulation and Feedback Control

We've discussed behavioral schemas, intentions, goals, the impact of lofty goals, and the importance of having strategies. But once a goal has been set—an intention formed—what makes sure the behavior you *actually do* is the one you *set out to do*? This question brings us to the concept of *feedback control* (Carver & Scheier, 1981, 1998; MacKay, 1963, 1966; Miller, Galanter, & Pribram, 1960; Powers, 1973; Scheier & Carver, 1988; Wiener, 1948).

FEEDBACK CONTROL

A **negative feedback loop** has four parts (see Figure 13.3). The first is a value for self-regulation: a goal, standard of comparison, or reference value for behavior (all of these mean the same thing here). These values can come from many places and can exist at many levels of abstraction. For example, plans, intentions, possible selves, and strategies all are values to use in self-regulation.

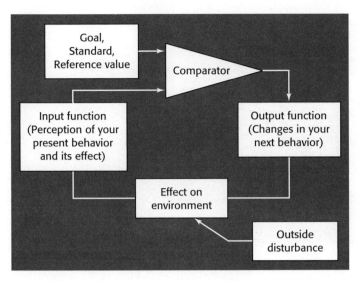

FIGURE 13.3
Diagram of a discrepancy-reducing feedback loop, which shows the basic processes presumed to underlie self-corrective behavioral self-regulation in both artificial and living systems.

The second element, input, is a perception of your present behavior and its effects. This just means noting what you're doing and the effect it's having. Often this is just a flicker of awareness, sensing in a vague way what you're doing. Other times it means thinking carefully about what you've been doing over a longer period. Sometimes, people literally watch what they're doing (e.g., at dance studios). Although it's easiest to talk about input in terms of *thinking*, this function (as a function) doesn't require con-sciousness (Bargh & Ferguson, 2000).

Box 13.1 Theoretical Issue: Feedback versus Reinforcement

It's long been known that people doing tasks benefit from knowing the result of their last effort (Locke & Latham, 1990; Schmidt, 1988). However, this evidence is interpreted differently by different people. According to the view under discussion, knowledge of results is *feedback*, which people use to adjust their behavior. It's some-times argued, however, that feedback is a *reinforcer* (Kulhavy & Stock, 1989). This is a rather different view.

What's the role of reward and punishment in self-regulation? The researchers whose work is discussed in this chapter don't entirely agree. Some see reward—particularly self-reward—as important. For example,

Bandura (1986) holds that self-reward or self-praise a person engages in after attaining a desired goal is a cru-cial aspect of self-regulation. On the other side of the disagreement, we've argued that this concept isn't needed (Carver & Scheier, 1981, 1990), that it doesn't add anything to say the person engages in self-praise after goal attainment. Although self-praise may occur, it's only a reaction to an event; the *event* is what matters. The crucial events, in this view, are the goal attain-ment and the person's realization of how it happened.

The concept of reinforcement comes from learning theory. In thinking about this issue, it's of interest that learn-ing theorists have long argued about the role of reinforcement in learning. Tolman (1932) believed that reward—

even to a laboratory rat—doesn't stamp anything in but just provides information the animal can learn from. Specifically, the animal learns what leads to what, by experiencing the events in association with one another. Tolman said rewards and punishments aren't necessary for learning, but they draw attention to aspects of the learning situation that are particularly relevant.

It's also been found that a simple social reinforcer, such as saying "Good," has more impact if you've been led to believe that the person saying "Good" does so only rarely (Babad, 1973). Presumably, this is because rare events provide more information than common events. This finding supports Tolman's suggestion that it may be the informational value of the reinforcer that matters, not the reinforcer itself.

For feedback control to occur, people need to monitor what they're currently doing.

Input perceptions are compared against the goal by something termed a **comparator**. If you're doing what you intended, there's no discrepancy between the two, and you continue as before. If your behavior *differs* from what you intended, though, a final process kicks in. This process changes the behavior, adjusts it to bring it more in line with your intention. (For a subtle theoretical issue pertaining to this viewpoint, see Box 13.1.)

The word *feedback* is used because when you adjust the action, the result is "fed back" in the form of a new perception, which is rechecked against the reference value. This loop is also called a *control system*, because each event in the loop depends on the result of a previous one. Thus, each prior event controls what goes on in the next one. It's called a *negative* loop because its component processes negate, or eliminate, discrepancies between the behavior and the goal.

This concept has several implications. For one, it assumes that behavior is purposeful (as do the goal concepts discussed earlier). In this view, the structure of most behavior involves trying to conform to some reference value. (We'll return to an exception later.) Life is a process of forming goals and intentions (broad and narrow, short term and long term) and adjusting behavior to match them, using feedback to tell you whether you're doing as you intended.

According to this logic, self-regulation is continuous and never ending. Every change in output changes current conditions. The new condition has to be checked against the goal. In addition, goals are often dynamic—evolving over time. For example, think of the goal of doing well in school, or making a particular impression on someone (and maintaining it), or taking a vacation trip. You do well in school not by going to a particular end point but by doing well at many tasks over time. You take a vacation trip not by leaving and coming back but by doing activities that constitute vacationing. There's a continuous interplay between adjusting your action and moving forward to the next phase of an evolving goal.

As we said about goals, referring to something as a *standard* here means only that it's the value being used as a guide. It doesn't necessarily mean a standard of excellence (though it can). Think of a student who's regulating behavior around the goal of making a C in a course by looking over class notes the night before the exam but not doing much more. The structure of this behavior (setting a goal, checking, and adjusting as needed) is exactly the same as that of a student who's trying to make an A. The two students are just using two different comparison values.

SELF-DIRECTED ATTENTION AND THE ACTION OF THE COMPARATOR

Does human behavior follow the pattern of feedback control? It appears to. One source of evidence is studies of the effects of self-directed attention. It's been argued that when you have a goal or intention in mind, directing your attention inward engages the comparator of the loop that's managing your behavior (Carver & Scheier, 1981, 1998).

Some research on self-directed attention exposes participants to things that remind them of themselves (e.g., an audience, a TV camera, or a mirror). Other studies measure the strength of people's natural tendency to be self-reflective (Fenigstein, Scheier, & Buss, 1975; Trapnell & Campbell, 1999).

The idea that self-directed attention engages a comparator leads to two kinds of predictions. First, self-focus should increase the tendency to compare goals with current behavior. It's hard to study that, but here's an indirect way: Create a situation in which people can't make a mental comparison between a goal and behavior without getting some concrete information. Put people in that situation, then measure how much they seek the information. Presumably, more seeking of the information implies more comparison. In studies based on this reasoning, self-focused persons sought comparison-relevant information more than less self-focused persons (Scheier & Carver, 1983).

If self-directed attention engages a comparator, behavior should be regulated more closely to the goal, and it is. As an illustration, people in one project (Carver, 1975) said they either opposed or favored using punishment as a teaching tool. Later, all had to punish someone for errors in learning. All were told to use their own judgment about how much punishment to use, but only those who were self-aware actually relied on their own opinions. Many other studies also show that self-focus leads to goal matching, ranging quite widely in the salient standards of comparison.

MENTAL CONTRASTING AND GOAL MATCHING

Another set of studies that support the feedback principle has focused more specifically on mental contrasting of present states with desired end states (Oettingen & Kappes, 2009). This research might be viewed as using the mental contrast as engaging the comparator function. Thinking only about a future goal, or only about your present state, doesn't have the same effect as thinking about both together. Given that people are relatively confident about being able to reach the desired goal, mental contrasting energizes their behavior (Oettingen et al., 2009). The result is that people are more successful in attaining their goals.

HIERARCHICAL ORGANIZATION

These studies suggest that feedback processes might be involved in behavior. But how do you actually get physical action out of it? An answer suggested by William Powers (1973) is that feedback loops exist in layers. He argued that this type of organization is what makes physical action possible. Others have made related arguments (e.g., Broadbent, 1977; Gallistel, 1980; Rosenbaum, 1987, 1990; Toates, 2006; Vallacher & Wegner, 1987).

The notion of a **feedback hierarchy** assumes there are both high-level and low-level goals that relate to each other. You have the goal of attaining a particular possible self, but you may also have the goal of having clean clothes to wear and the goal of making it to your psychology class on time. How do these things fit together? Recall the structure of the feedback loop from Figure 13.3. Powers says that in a hierarchy, the *output* of a high-level loop consists of setting a goal for a lower-level loop (see Figure 13.4). High-level loops don't "behave" by creating physical actions but by providing guides to the loops below them. Only the very lowest loops actually create

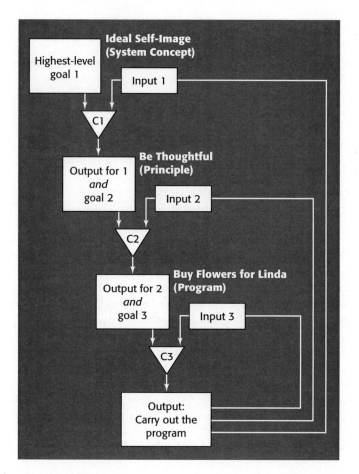

Figure 13.4
Diagram of a three-level hierarchy of feedback systems. This diagram shows the "cascade" of control that flows from higher-level loops to lower-level ones. High-level loops set the goals for the loops directly below them. The levels of control illustrated here are those at the top of the hierarchy proposed by Powers (1973). The diagram shows a cross-section of the behavior of a man who is actively attempting to (1) match his self-perceptions to his idealized self, by (2) following the principle of *thoughtfulness*, which is being manifested (3) in the programmatic activity of buying flowers for his wife.

physical acts, by controlling muscle groups (Rosenbaum, 1987, 1990, 2005). Each layer receives feedback appropriate to its level of abstraction.

The levels proposed by Powers that are most relevant to personality are shown in Figure 13.4. At the top are very abstract qualities he called **system concepts**. An example is the broad sense of ideal self. Richard, the person whose behavior is portrayed in Figure 13.4, is trying to live up to his desired self-image. Doing this resembles the experience of self–actualization (see Chapter 11). It promotes the sense of personal wholeness and integration.

You don't just go out and *be* your ideal self, though. Trying to attain that ideal self means trying to live in accord with the **principles** it incorporates. Thus, Powers called the next level *principle control*. Principles are broad guidelines. They specify broad qualities, which can be displayed in many ways. When they're active, principles help you decide what activities to start and what choices to make as you do them (Verplanken & Holland, 2002). Principles tend to correspond to traits, or values. When people think about their behavior in these relatively abstract terms, they tend to express those values in their actions (Torelli & Kaikati, 2009).

As shown in Figure 13.4, Richard's ideal self includes a principle of *thoughtfulness*. This principle can be used as a guide for many kinds of action, including taking this opportunity to buy flowers. As another example, the principle of *honesty* would lead a person to ignore an opportunity to cheat on an exam. The principle of *frugality* would lead a person to choose a moderately priced restaurant over an expensive one.

What defines something as a *principle* is its abstractness and broad applicability, not its social appropriateness. Thus, expedience is a principle, even though it's not socially desirable (see the cartoon). Knowing only that something is a principle doesn't even tell what direction it pulls behavior. For example, different principles lead people either to support affirmative action or to oppose it (Reyna, Henry, Korfmacher, & Tucker, 2005).

Much of what we do in our day-to-day lives, such as grocery shopping, has a programlike or scriptlike character.

Just as you don't go out and *be* your ideal self, you don't just go out and *do* principles. Principles act by specifying **programs** (or by specifying decisions within programs; see Figure 13.4). A program resembles what we called a script in Chapter 12. It specifies a general course of action but with many details left out. Enacting a program (or script) thus requires you to make choices within a larger set of possibilities. Programs, in effect, are strategies.

The principle of *thoughtfulness* led Richard to enter the program of buying flowers. This program is partly specified: Stop at the florist, pick out flowers, and pay for them. But which flowers he gets will depend on what's available; he can pay with cash or a credit card; and he may or may not have to put money into a parking meter.

Two more things are worth noting about this example: Both stem from the fact that there are several ways to conform to this principle. First, Richard might have chosen another program—perhaps making Linda a special dinner or washing her car. Entering either of these programs would have conformed to the same principle. Second, matching the principle of *thoughtfulness* didn't require *entering* a program; the principle might

Calvin and Hobbes   by Bill Watterson

Although principles often have overtones of goodness and morality, that need not be the case. Principles can also be self-serving. What's necessary is that a principle must be abstract enough to apply to many kinds of behavior.

have come into play *during* a program. For example, if Linda had told Richard to buy flowers on his way home, he'd be buying flowers anyway. The *thoughtfulness* principle might have become salient in the midst of the buying-flowers program, leading Richard to buy Linda's favorite flower, even though it's out of season and therefore expensive.

Much of what people do in their day-to-day lives seems programlike, or scriptlike. Most of the intentions you form in an average day involve programs. Doing the laundry, going to a store or to the movies, studying for an exam, fixing lunch, trying to get noticed by that person in class—all these are programs. They all have general courses of predictable acts and subgoals, but exactly what you do at a given point can vary, depending on the situation.

Very likely there are well-learned links between many principles and the programs to which they pertain. Connections between programs and lower levels of control are probably even stronger. For example, if you have a goal in mind concerning travel, it automatically activates information about a plausible and common way to get where you are thinking about going (Aarts & Dijksterhuis, 2000).

ISSUES CONCERNING HIERARCHICAL ORGANIZATION

Several questions come up when you think about hierarchies. For example, are all the levels active all the time? Not necessarily. People can go for a very long time without thinking about their ideal selves. Behavior often is guided for long periods by programs. To put it differently, lower levels may sometimes be *functionally superordinate*.

That's probably what happens when people do the routine "maintenance" activities of life: buying groceries, washing dishes, driving to school. At such times, people may often lose all sight of their higher-order goals. Note also that programs inherently require decisions. That in itself may cause them to be attended to more often than other levels. It's interesting that when people describe themselves, they tend to describe things they *do*, rather than what they *are* (McGuire & McGuire, 1986). This suggests that the program level may be especially salient to people.

When lower levels are functionally superordinate, it's almost as though the higher layers have been disconnected. But the disconnect isn't permanent. Goals at higher levels can be affected by things that happen while lower levels are in charge. The effect can be either good or bad. A program (buying shoes on sale) can help you match a principle (frugality), even if that's not why you're doing it (you just liked the shoes). A program can also create a problem, if it violates the principle. For example, many health-conscious people have a principle of eating low-fat foods. But if they get caught up in the action at a party (with lower levels in charge), they may eat lots of greasy junk food, which they will later regret.

We said earlier that goals can be achieved in diverse ways. Any specific act can also be done in the service of diverse principles. For example, Richard in Figure 13.4 could have been buying flowers not to be thoughtful but to be manipulative—to get on Linda's good side. The same actions would occur, but they would be aimed at a very different higher-order goal.

Another point is that people often try to match several values at once—at the *same level*. In some cases, the values are compatible (being frugal while being conscientious). In other cases, they're less so (being frugal while dressing well; getting good grades while having a very active social life). In these cases, matching one value creates a problem for the other (Emmons & King, 1988; Emmons, King, & Sheldon, 1993).

EVIDENCE OF HIERARCHICAL ORGANIZATION

Is behavior organized hierarchically? Work by Robin Vallacher and Dan Wegner suggests that it is (Vallacher & Wegner, 1985, 1987). They began by asking how people view their actions, a process called **action identification**. Any action can be identified in many ways. For example, taking notes in class can be seen as "sitting in a room and making marks on paper with a pen," "taking notes in a class," "trying to do well in a course," or "getting an education." Some identities are concrete, others more abstract. How you think about your actions presumably says something about the goals you're using in acting.

Vallacher and Wegner (1985, 1987) suggest that people generally tend to see their actions in as high level a way as they can. Thus, you're more likely to see your student behavior as "attending classes," "getting an education," or "listening to a lecture" than as "walking into a building, sitting down, and listening to someone talk." But if people start to struggle in regulating an act at that high level, they retreat to a lower-level identity for the action. In terms of the last section, difficulty at a high level causes a lower level to become functionally superordinate. Using that lower-level identity, the person irons out the problem. As the problem is resolved, the person tends to drift again to a higher-level identification.

For example, if you're in class taking notes and having trouble understanding the lecture, you may stop thinking of your behavior as "taking helpful notes" and start thinking of it as "writing down as much as I possibly can so I can try to figure it out later." If the lecture gets easier to follow after a while, you may once again be able to start thinking of your behavior in more abstract terms.

CONSTRUAL LEVELS

An interesting twist on the idea of different levels of abstraction was developed by Yaacov Trope and Nira Liberman (2003, 2010). They suggested that how people construe their activities depends partly on how distant those activities are from the present moment. The farther in the future the activities are, the more abstractly they are viewed. When the action comes closer to the present, it becomes more concrete and less abstract.

This reasoning is consistent with the idea that when you actually have to do something, you need to pay attention to the concrete actions involved in doing it. Essentially, the idea is this: When you have a paper due for your psych class at the end of the semester, you think "I'm going to write a paper;" but when the end of the semester is a week and a half away, you think "I'm going to locate those articles and try to fit ideas from one of them together with ideas from the other one and compose it into paragraphs that have a logical flow."

More recently, Trope and Liberman (2010) expanded on this idea. They now view time-based construals as a special case of a more general principle of psychological distance. The greater the psychological distance, the more abstract the mental representation becomes. The closer the psychological distance, the more concrete and detailed the mental representation becomes. Psychological distance can be created in many ways: time, space, social distance, likelihood of occurrence, and even third-person versus first-person viewpoints (Libby, Shaeffer, & Eibach, 2009). Furthermore, the different kinds of distance are interchangeable to some degree. If you think of something as unlikely, it also seems farther away in time and space. Since how people construe their behavior (abstractly or concretely) influences the level at which they try to regulate it, these construal differences can be quite important.

EMOTIONS

How does the self-regulation approach to personality view emotions? Early in the history of this way of thinking, Herb Simon (1967) argued that emotions are crucial. People often have several goals at the same time, but they often have to pursue them sequentially (e.g., you go to a gas station, then stop for lunch, then drive to the beach, where you study for an exam while getting some sun, and then you go home and do some laundry if there's time). The order in which you do things is partly a matter of priorities—how important each goal is to you at the time.

Priorities are subject to rearrangement. Simon (1967) argued that emotions are an internal call to rearrange. *Anxiety* is a signal that you're not paying enough attention to personal well-being (an important goal) and you need to do so. *Anger* may be a signal that your autonomy (another goal that people value) needs to have a higher priority.

Implicit in this analysis is that progress toward many goals is monitored outside awareness, as you focus on one goal at a time. If a problem arises for some goal, emotion pertaining to it arises. If the problem gets big enough, the emotion becomes intense enough to interrupt what you're doing. For example, look back at the goals described two paragraphs earlier. If you had decided to put off buying gas until after doing the other things, you might start to feel anxious about maybe being stranded at the beach with an empty gas tank. If the anxiety got strong enough, you'd change your mind (reprioritize) and stop for the gas after all.

Simon's theory fits the idea that emotions are produced by a system that monitors "how well things are going" toward attaining goals (Carver & Scheier, 1990, 1998). When things are going well, you feel good. When things are going *really* well, you feel joy, even ecstasy. When things are going poorly, on the other hand, negative feelings arise: frustration, anxiety, sadness. If you're actually losing ground, the negative feelings intensify. In all these cases, the emotion is a subjective readout of how well you're doing regarding that goal.

Evidence fitting this view comes from several studies. As an example, Hsee and Abelson (1991, Experiment 2) put people in hypothetical situations where they would bet money on sports events. Each person viewed a display showing progress toward winning—at different rates—and indicated how satisfied he or she would be with each event. Of special interest are events in which the starting and ending points were identical but the rate of change differed. Participants liked the faster change better than the slower one.

Feelings have implications for actions. As suggested by Simon (1967), when something is going badly and negative feelings arise, you engage more effort toward the goal the feeling relates to. If you're behind at something and feeling frustrated, you try harder. If you're scared of something, you try harder to get away from it.

How do positive feelings affect actions? It's been argued that they also affect priorities (Carver, 2003). When you feel good about your progress toward some goal, you can "coast" a little on it and check to see if anything else needs your attention. There's evidence from several sources that this sort of coasting sometimes happens (Fulford, Johnson, Llabre, & Carver, 2010; Louro, Pieters, & Zeelenberg, 2007). Coasting also helps in the process of juggling many goals at once. If you're ahead on one goal, you can ease up on it to attend to other goals you're pursuing.

EFFECTS OF EXPECTANCIES: EFFORT VERSUS DISENGAGEMENT

Until the last section, this chapter focused mostly on behavior when no major difficulties arise. However, things don't always work so smoothly. People often encounter obstacles when they try to carry out their intentions and attain their goals. What happens then?

As indicated just earlier, obstacles cause negative feelings. If the obstacles are serious, they also tend to disrupt effort—sometimes briefly, sometimes longer. This can occur before you start (if you anticipate trouble) or while you're acting (if snags arise along the way). The interruptions remove you temporarily from the action and lead you to assess how likely you are to reach your goal, given the situation you're in.

Box 13.2 Confidence about Life: Effects of Generalized Optimism

Expectancies are important determinants of people's behavior. The expectancies considered in the main text are mostly specific ones: confidence about making a desired impression, achieving an academic goal, or carrying out a specific strategy. However, just as people have both specific and general goals, people also have both specific and generalized expectancies. What's been known for centuries as *optimism* is generalized confidence; what's known as *pessimism* is generalized doubt—not about a specific outcome but about life in general (Carver, Scheier, & Segerstrom, 2010; Scheier & Carver, 1992; Scheier, Carver, & Bridges, 2001). This generalized confidence is very traitlike. It's quite stable over time and seems genetically influenced (Plomin et al., 1992).

Optimism, as a dimension of personality, has been studied for a long while, and a lot is known about

it (Carver et al., 2010; Scheier et al., 2001). People who are optimistic about life are liked better than pessimists (Carver, Kus, & Scheier, 1994). Probably for that reason, they're better at forming social networks when they go to a new environment (Brissette, Scheier, & Carver, 2002). They are also better in relationships, because they are more supportive of their partners in resolving conflicts (Srivastava, McGonigal, Richards, Butler, & Gross, 2006).

A lot of the research on optimism concerns its impact on how people deal with stressful situations. Optimists deal better with adversity than pessimists, whether experiencing a missile attack (Zeidner & Hammer, 1992) or confronting cancer or heart disease (Carver, Pozo et al., 1993; Scheier, Matthews et al., 1989). Optimists have less distress, are more focused on moving forward, and are less likely to withdraw from their usual activities (Carver, Lehman, & Antoni, 2003). In addition, they seem more prepared

to accept the situation as real (Carver, Pozo et al., 1993). They don't stick their heads in the sand and ignore threats to their well-being.

Most of what's known about optimism concerns people's actions and subjective emotional experiences. Increasingly, however, research has gone beyond these topics to look at people's physical responses to adversity. For example, after having major heart surgery, pessimists were more likely than optimists to require rehospitalization (Scheier, Matthews et al., 1999). Optimists literally healed better. Other recent studies have related optimism to a lower risk of cancer death (Allison, Guichard, Fung, & Gilain, 2003), cardiovascular death (Giltay, Kamphuis, Kalmijn, Zitman, & Kromhout, 2006), and mortality in general (Tindle et al., 2009; see also Rasmussen, Scheier, & Greenhouse, 2009). The idea that this personality trait may have pervasive health benefits is increasingly being investigated (Scheier, Carver, & Armstrong, in press).

Expectancy of success is a concept idea that's come up in other chapters. We discussed it in the motive viewpoint (Chapter 5), in social learning theory (Chapter 10), and in the cognitive view (Chapter 12). The way expectancies function in self-regulation models is essentially the same as in the others. Having confidence in overcoming obstacles leads people back to self-regulatory effort. When people feel enough doubt, however, they are more likely to **disengage**, or reduce their effort toward goal attainment. They may even abandon the goal altogether—temporarily or permanently (Klinger, 1975; Kukla, 1972; Wright, 1996).

Levels of effort fall along a continuum. It can be useful, though, to think of variations in effort as forming a rough dichotomy. Think of it as the question of whether you keep trying or quit. In many cases, people have only those two options. This view on what happens lets the person who's "walked into a corner" stop, back out of it, and take up another goal (Wrosch, Dunne, Scheier, & Schulz, 2006; Wrosch, Scheier, Carver, & Schulz, 2003).

Different people emphasize different facets of expectancies. We've focused on confidence versus doubt about attaining outcomes, rather than *reasons* for the confidence or doubt (Carver & Scheier, 1998). Bandura, in contrast (see Chapter 10), stresses *efficacy expectancy*: the belief that one has the personal capability of doing the action that needs to be done. Regardless of which variation you prefer, there's evidence that expectancies play an important role in how hard people try and how well they do. People who are confident about reaching their goals (or who hold perceptions of high efficacy) are more persistent and perform better than people who are doubtful. Confident individuals do better in many ways (see Box 13.2).

For example, consider a study of women learning to protect themselves against sexual assault (Ozer & Bandura, 1990). They learned skills for self-defense and verbal tactics to deal with dangerous situations. At several points, they rated their confidence that they could do both the physical maneuvers and the verbal tactics. They also rated their confidence that they could turn off thoughts about sexual assault. The most important outcome was ratings of the extent to which they took part in (or avoided) activities outside the home.

The results were complex, but a broad theme runs through them. The sense of confidence was very important. The women's confidence that they could use their new coping skills related to perceptions of less vulnerability and ultimately to behavior. In sum, having confidence in diverse areas helped the women cope more effectively with their social world.

PARTIAL DISENGAGEMENT

We've distinguished sharply here between effort and giving up. Sometimes, though, the line blurs. Sometimes a goal can't be attained, but another one can be substituted for it (Freund & Baltes, 2002; Wrosch et al., 2003). For example, suppose that a man who enjoys sports becomes wheelchair bound. He can't play football any longer, but he can turn to sports that don't require using his legs.

Sometimes disengagement involves only scaling back from a lofty goal in a given domain to a less demanding one. That's disengagement, in the sense that the person is giving up the first goal. It's more limited, in the sense that it doesn't mean leaving the domain entirely. Partial disengagement keeps you engaged in the domain you had wanted to quit. By scaling back—giving up in a small way—you keep trying to move ahead—thus *not* giving up in a larger way.

We stress that whether giving up is bad or good depends on the context (Wrosch et al., 2003, 2006). In some cases, it's bad. It's a poor way of coping with the ordinary difficulties of life. Sometimes being persistent would pay off in success. In such cases, the goal shouldn't be abandoned easily. On the other hand, it's necessary to give up or defer goals when circumstances make it hard or impossible to reach them. It's senseless to hold onto a lost love who will never return. Giving up sometimes is the right response, but when it is it sometimes doesn't happen. In these cases, the failure to disengage leads to continuing distress. We return to this point later on, when we consider problems in behavior.

Further Themes in Self-Regulation

The chapter thus far has presented a picture in which people form intentions, then shift to a mode of implementing the intentions, which may go well or poorly. We've talked a little about the fact that people have goals at various levels of abstraction and the fact that people have many goals at once (and thus many semi-autonomous feedback loops going at the same time). Now we bring up three complications to this picture.

APPROACH AND AVOIDANCE

We've focused on the idea that self-regulation involves moving toward goals. An issue that came up in other chapters also comes up here: Not all actions are about *approach*. Some are about *avoidance*. By this, we don't mean disengaging from a desired goal. We mean actively trying to get away (or stay away) from a threat.

Discussion of the motivation view on personality (Chapter 5) noted that two opposite motives can underlie the same overt action. You can try to perform well at a task either to approach success or to avoid failure. The motives aren't the same (and sometimes the behavior isn't quite the same either). Virtually anything you think about doing can be viewed in terms of either *making* one thing happen or *preventing* something else from happening (Higgins, 1997). The same issue arises in this chapter.

As it happens, there's another category of feedback loops that enlarges discrepancies, rather than reducing them. This seems to provide a basis for a model of avoidance. It's clear, as well, that emotions are involved both when trying to approach and when trying to avoid. In either case, you can be doing well or doing poorly. Thus, the self-regulatory model definitely has a place for both approach and avoidance. In the interest of minimizing confusion, though, we will not talk more about the avoidance function here (see Carver & Scheier, 2007).

INTENTION-BASED AND STIMULUS-BASED ACTION

Thus far, the chapter has also focused mostly on behavior that's intentional: behavior that starts with the setting of goals. However, not all behavior happens that way. Some behavior—maybe a lot of it—is cued by stimulus qualities that the person encounters that activate schemas.

Early hints of this phenomenon came from studies intended to show that interpretive schemas were closely linked to specifications for action. These studies used priming techniques to activate schemas and found influences on behavior. In one case, people had to form sentences from scrambled sets of words (Carver, Ganellen, Froming, & Chambers, 1983). For some people but not others, the word sets had hostile content. Later, all the people had to punish someone else while teaching a concept. Those who had read the words with hostile content gave stronger punishments than did the others (see Figure 13.5, A).

Another study used a similar task to prime the stereotype of the elderly (Bargh, Chen, & Burrows, 1996). Some people read many words pertaining to the stereotype; some did not. All then received credit for participation. The outcome of interest was how long it took people to walk down the corridor on their way out. Those exposed to the stereotype of the elderly walked more slowly, as though they were old themselves (see Figure 13.5, B).

The interpretation of these effects goes like this: To form sentences from the words, you have to understand the words. Understanding the words requires activating nodes of meaning in memory. This activation spreads to nodes bearing on *behavior*. This quality then emerges in the person's own behavior (Bargh, 1997). In fact, the link goes both ways: Acting in a way that fits a stereotype brings that stereotype to mind for use in later perception (Mussweiler, 2006).

Findings such as these are part of a large and growing literature on automaticity (some of which was mentioned in Chapter 12; see also Moors & De Houwer, 2006). Much of this work has been done by John Bargh and his colleagues (Bargh, 1997; Bargh & Chartrand, 1999; Bargh & Ferguson, 2000; Dijksterhuis & Bargh, 2001). Many studies now show clearly that goals can be activated (and people pursue them) with no knowledge that it's happening (for review, see Bargh & Williams, 2006). Indeed, some of the studies show that goals can be activated by **subliminal stimuli**: stimuli that are out of one's awareness.

Although it's impressive to see how people's minds can be tricked by various sorts of priming, the more important message here is that automaticity is important. Indeed, it's been argued that habitual actions occur in much the same way as priming

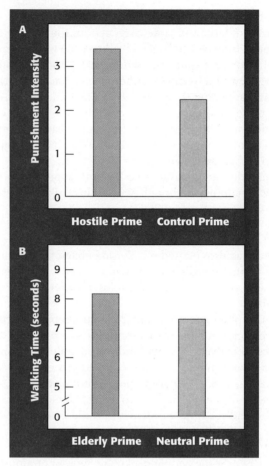

FIGURE 13.5
Effects of priming an interpretive schema on behavior related to that schema. (A) People who had been exposed to hostile content in a sentence-formation task gave punishments of greater intensity in a later task than people exposed to less hostile content. (B) People who had been exposed to elements of the elderly stereotype in a sentence-formation task took longer to walk to the elevator when leaving the experiment than people exposed to neutral words. *Sources:* Panel A is based on data from Carver et al., 1983, Study 2; Panel B is based on data from Bargh et al., 1996, Experiment 2.

effects: Situations activate goals that are associated with them, and behavior follows the goals automatically (Aarts & Dijksterhuis, 2000). Similarly, categories of people activate specific responses that are well learned to that group, and behavior follows automatically (Jonas & Sassenberg, 2006).

Nonetheless, the idea that behavioral qualities can be activated and slide into the ongoing flow of behavior without your awareness is a little startling. Your actions can be affected by things you hear on the radio or read in the paper, by conversations you have, by random stimuli you encounter—and *you don't even know it.* This idea provides an interpretation of modeling effects (see Chapter 10), in which people repeat things they observe others do (Carver et al., 1983). People mimic, without realizing it, the postures and gestures of their partners in interactions (Chartrand & Bargh, 1999). The pervasiveness of such effects leads some people to ask whether behavior is best seen as *directed* or as *self-organizing* (Carver & Scheier, 2002; Vallacher & Nowak, 1997; Vallacher, Read, & Nowak, 2002).

Can both be right? We think so. In Chapter 12, we described dual-process models of cognition. One mode is said to use connectionist, associationist processes, the other mode symbolic processes. The first mode is characterized as *intuitive*, whereas the second is characterized as *rational*. It seems reasonable to suggest that dual-process models can also help reconcile how intentions and automaticity both influence action (Bargh & Williams, 2006; Kuhl, 2000; Rothbart, Ellis, Rueda, & Posner, 2003; Strack & Deutsch, 2004).

The interpretation goes like this. The intuitive system functions automatically. When a stimulus happens to cue an action quality, that action quality slips into the behavioral stream. It seems likely that the action quality has to be either simple or well learned for this to happen. That is, the intuitive system is capable of handling fairly complicated events (Kuhl, 2000), but its capacities derive from associations. It's good at being impulsive and quickly responsive, but it's not good at thinking things through.

The rational system, in contrast, is brought into play when you form an intention, or set a goal purposefully. When this system is in charge, behavior is self-regulated in an effortful, top-down manner. It is planful (Eisenberg et al., 2004). Its purpose is to handle situations that *have* to be thought through, because no automatic, cue-driven response is ready to go. Thinking things through, however, means some delay in action (Keller et al., 2006).

In talking about the cognitive view in Chapter 12, we noted that people have a natural tendency to conserve mental resources, because they have many things on their minds at once. The same principle is true here. Being able to do something with little thought is extremely useful, because it lets you think about other things at the same time as you're doing whatever you're doing (Wood, Quinn, & Kashy, 2002).

SELF-REGULATION AS SELF-CONTROL

Another issue that should receive attention is that acts of *self-regulation* sometimes (though not always) entail *self-control*. That is, sometimes people act to restrain behavior aimed at one goal, in order to make it possible to attain another goal. Self-control always concerns conflicts, because the goals are incompatible.

Situations entailing self-control arise in a great many circumstances, and the conflicts in question apply to very important practical problems (see Part VI in Baumeister & Vohs, 2004). This situation exists, for example, in the context of dieting. Dieters are motivated to eat by their feelings of hunger, and they are motivated to restrain eating by their desire to lose weight. Similar conflicts arise in circumstances surrounding substance abuse and domestic violence. People who are effective at self-control employ a variety of strategies to counteract temptations that keep them from gaining the long-term goal (Friese & Hofmann, 2009; Trope & Fishbach, 2000, 2005).

Discussions of self-control failure (Baumeister & Heatherton, 1996) tend to portray the situations as involving a relatively automatic tendency to act in one way that's opposed by a planful and effortful tendency to restrain the act. The act being restrained is often characterized as an *impulse*: a desire that would automatically be translated into action unless it is controlled (perhaps in part because this action is habitual, perhaps in part because it is more primal).

Once again, this viewpoint seems to have overtones of the dual-process models. Self-control is related both to the strength of underlying impulsive tendencies and to the strength of constraining self-control tendencies (Edmonds, Bogg, & Roberts, 2009). There's also evidence that identifying an action in higher-level terms makes it easier to disregard immediate outcomes in favor of delayed outcomes (Fujita, Trope, Liberman, & Levin-Sagi, 2006).

Box 13.3 Reduction of Self-Regulation: Deindividuation and Alcohol

Elsewhere in the chapter, we described how self-focus causes better self-regulation toward salient standards. If self-focus makes behavior *better* regulated, it follows that reduced self-focus makes behavior *more poorly* regulated. But what does this mean? It doesn't mean the person stops behaving altogether. It means the behavior is more likely to fluctuate—to become less carefully thought out and more responsive to cues of the moment.

Deindividuation occurs when people become immersed in a group. It involves a reduction in self-focus (Diener, 1979; Prentice-Dunn & Rogers, 1982, 1989). The result is aggressive and uninhibited behavior. It's easy to see these effects as reflecting poor self-regulation regarding programs and principles that normally guide action. Thus, there's a tendency to act impulsively—to respond to cues of the moment, rather than to use a well-thought-out plan.

These effects are remarkably similar to some of the effects of alcohol. People who've been drinking are often inappropriately aggressive and overly responsive to cues of the moment. Alcohol is widely regarded as a releaser of inhibitions, and it's sometimes used intentionally for that purpose. Alcohol also appears to act (at least partly) by reducing self-awareness (Hull, 1981; Hull & Rielly, 1986) and

executive function (Giancola, 2004). As this happens, you stop monitoring your values and intentions. Your behavior becomes more disorganized, impulsive, and fragmented.

Another way of looking at both of these phenomena is through the lens of the dual-process view. Deindividuation and alcohol both seem to lessen the influence of the deliberative and planful mode of functioning and increase the influence of the reflexive, impulsive mode. In either view, two distinct sets of phenomena—deindividuation and alcohol intoxication—can be interpreted by the same principles. Both seem to involve interference with a process that underlies the normal self-regulation of behavior.

Assessment

The self-regulation view on personality is fairly new. It's been far more theoretical than applied. Nevertheless, it offers a few suggestions concerning personality assessment.

Assessment of Self-Regulatory Qualities

The view described in this chapter emphasizes the existence of several processes in human experience. This emphasis suggests it may be useful to measure individual differences in those self-regulatory processes (Williams, Moore, Pettibone, & Thomas, 1992).

For example, *private self-consciousness* (Fenigstein et al., 1975) is a tendency to be self-reflective—to think about your feelings, motives, actions, and so on. (The term *self-consciousness* doesn't mean "embarrassment" here, just "self-focus.") People high in self-consciousness are careful and thorough self-regulators (maybe even obsessive–compulsive ones). They notice it if their actions don't match their intentions, and they adjust accordingly. People lower in self-consciousness are more random and less guided in their behavior (see also Box 13.3). Consistent with this characterization, self-consciousness relates to conscientiousness from the five-factor model (Trapnell & Campbell, 1999). There's even evidence that people high in self-consciousness are more prone to engage in self-regulation that's automatic and nonconscious (Hull, Slone, Meteyer, & Matthews, 2002).

Keep in mind that self-focus in itself is relatively content free. That is, its self-regulatory effect is largely unrelated to what goal is being used. Thus, an athlete who's self-conscious should be sure to work out. A self-conscious biology major should be sure to be caught up on the assigned biology reading. A self-conscious musician should focus closely on practicing to move toward his or her music-related goals.

Trapnell and Campbell (1999) distinguished two aspects of self-consciousness. They suggested that two motives underlie it: curiosity (a growth-oriented motive) and the desire to probe negative feeling states (which is ultimately a safety-seeking motive, if the source of the feelings can be isolated). They created a measure called the Rumination–Reflection Questionnaire to focus separately on these motives. *Rumination* items refer to being unable to put something behind you. *Reflection* items refer to being fascinated and inquisitive. Not surprisingly, reflection relates to openness to experience, and rumination relates to neuroticism.

Another self-regulatory function that might be useful to assess is whether people tend to view their behavior in high-level or lower-level terms. Vallacher and Wegner (1989) developed a measure called the Behavior Identification Form for that purpose. They argued that people with similar traits can differ greatly if they think of their goals at different levels. People who identify their actions at high levels tend to look at the "big picture," whether they're socializing, studying, or making music. People who identify their actions at lower levels tend to focus more on the "nuts and bolts" of what's going on.

Yet another aspect of self-regulatory function to assess is self-control tendencies. Several measures of impulsiveness are available (e.g., Cyders et al., 2007; Patton, Stanford, & Barratt, 1995; Whiteside & Lynam, 2001). A Self-Control scale has also been developed (Tangney, Baumeister, & Boone, 2004). It's a measure of overall self-control, although the items tend to focus on persistence (or lack thereof) in completing activities. Self-control turns out to be important: It predicts grade-point average, adjustment, alcohol abuse, and interpersonal skills (Tangney et al., 2004).

ASSESSMENT OF GOALS

Although self-regulatory tendencies are largely independent of the goal toward which self-regulation is taking place, we don't mean to imply that the content of behavior doesn't matter. As we said earlier, the self-regulation view emphasizes *goals*. It would seem useful, from this view, to assess people's goals and how they're organized (Emmons, 1986; Pervin, 1983). One might even want to assess what sort of "possible selves" the person has in mind (Markus & Nurius, 1986). Knowing what goals are salient to a person might be more informative than knowing other aspects of what the person is "like."

An example of this approach is the technique Emmons (1986) used to assess personal strivings. He asked people to describe their recurring personal goals in four areas: work/school, home/family, social relationships, and leisure/recreation. People were to think about their own intentions and goals and not to compare themselves with other people. Within these guidelines, they were free to write down any striving that seemed important to them. This produced an individualized picture of the goal values that occupied the person's mind over a given span of time.

Problems in Behavior, and Behavior Change

Given how new the self-regulation point of view is, one might expect it to have had little or no impact on understanding either problems or therapy. This isn't the case, however (see Hamilton, Greenberg, Pyszczynski, & Cather, 1993; Ingram, 1986; Merluzzi, Rudy, & Glass, 1981). Self-regulation models have made a number of suggestions about those topics.

PROBLEMS AS CONFLICTS AMONG GOALS AND LACK OF STRATEGY SPECIFICATIONS

The hierarchical model suggests several ways for problems to arise (Carver & Scheier, 1990, 1998). The simplest stems from the idea of a deeply rooted conflict between goals. Conflict occurs when a person is committed to two goals that can't be attained easily at the same time (e.g., being a successful attorney while being a good wife and mother; having a close relationship while being emotionally independent). You may alternate between the goals, but that can be exhausting and distressing (Emmons & King, 1988). It takes a lot of effort to keep the conflict from re-emerging. Another solution is to decide that one goal contributes more to your higher-order values than the other and cut back investment in the other one.

A second idea suggested by the hierarchical model is that people sometimes want abstract goals but lack the know-how to reach them. If specifications from level to level are missing, self-regulation falls apart. Thus, many people want to be "fulfilled," "successful," or "well liked" but don't know the strategies to attain these goals. Many people even have more specific goals, such as "not arguing with my wife" or "being more assertive," but can't specify the concrete behaviors that would move them in the right direction. Lacking this knowledge, they can't make progress and are distressed. For things to be better, the strategies need to be built in (Oyserman et al., 2006).

PROBLEMS FROM AN INABILITY TO DISENGAGE

A third source of problems stems from the idea that people who expect failure quit trying. As noted earlier, sometimes quitting is the right response. (If you realize you've forgotten your money and credit card, quit shopping.) Sometimes, though, quitting can't be done easily. Some goals are very hard to give up, even if you have grave doubts about reaching them—for example, doing well in your chosen work and having a fulfilling relationship with another person. Why is it so hard to give up these goals? The hierarchical view says it's because they are high in your hierarchy (thus, central to your self) or represent paths to those higher goals. Sometimes abandoning a concrete goal means giving up on the person you want to be.

When people have serious doubts about attaining goals they can't let go of, they show a predictable pattern. They stop trying but soon confront the goal again. For example, having decided to give up on having a fulfilling relationship, you see a movie about relationships, which reminds you that you want one. Having given up trying to get along with a co-worker, you find you're assigned to work on a project together. Having given up on your calculus assignment, you see it's time for calculus class. Deep doubt about reaching an important goal can lead to a repeated cycle of sporadic effort, doubt, distress, disengagement, and confronting the goal again.

It's not always bad to keep thinking about a failure. It can motivate you to try harder next time (if there is a next time). Sometimes it leads to ideas about how to do things differently next time (Martin & Tesser, 1996). But it's dangerous to dwell on a failure when it can't be undone (Pyszczynski & Greenberg, 1985, 1987; Wrosch et al., 2003). When people lose a big source of self-worth and focus too long on trying to regain it, they experience major distress results. Doing this too often turns it into a habit. Focusing on failure and ignoring success not only maintains depressive symptoms, but it also creates a self-perpetuating pattern.

A similar point was made by Susan Nolen-Hoeksema and her colleagues (Nolen-Hoeksema, Morrow, & Frederickson, 1993; Nolen-Hoeksema, Parker, & Larson, 1994), who argued that people who are prone to depression focus much of their attention on their sad feelings. This rumination acts to prolong the depressed state.

SELF-REGULATION AND THE PROCESS OF THERAPY

Control-process ideas have also been used by several theorists in addressing therapy issues. Fred Kanfer and his colleagues (e.g., Kanfer & Busemeyer, 1982; Kanfer & Hagerman, 1985; Kanfer & Schefft, 1988; see also Semmer & Frese, 1985) depicted therapy in a way that's quite compatible with the self-regulatory ideas presented throughout this chapter.

One point these theorists have made is that much of human behavior isn't monitored consciously but is cued automatically and habitually. This is a point made early in this chapter and has been made by many cognitive theorists as well (e.g., Beck, 1972, 1976; Dodge, 1986; Semmer & Frese, 1985). Therapy is partly an effort to break down the automaticity. The person must engage in more controlled or monitored processing of what's going on. Doing this should yield responses that are more carefully thought out.

Does this mean that people dealing with problems must spend the rest of their lives carefully monitoring their actions? Maybe. To help people avoid lifelong monitoring, therapy must provide them with a way to make the desired responses automatic in place of the problem responses. How do you do that? Presumably, it's an issue of how thoroughly the links are encoded in memory. New responses become automatic by building them into memory very redundantly. This makes them more likely to be used later, when the person is on "automatic pilot." Many therapeutic techniques that are in widespread use probably do exactly this.

Another point made by Kanfer and Busemeyer (1982) is that the process of therapy is itself a dynamic feedback system. It's a series of stages in which clients repeatedly use feedback—both from therapy sessions and from actions outside therapy—to guide their movements through a long-term plan of change. The goals and issues that guide the process of changing behavior also keep changing. As you proceed, you must keep checking to make sure the concrete goals you're working toward support your higher-order goals.

THERAPY IS TRAINING IN PROBLEM SOLVING

A point that's been made by many people is that therapy isn't just for the present. It should make the person a better problem solver, more equipped to deal with problems in the future (Nezu, 1987; Schefft & Lehr, 1985). Being able to generate choices and select the best ones are important skills, whether you get them through therapy or on your own.

A useful way to create choices is called **means–end analysis** (Newell & Simon, 1972). You start by noting the difference between your present state and your desired state (the *end*). Then you think of an action that would reduce the difference (a *means*). At first, the things that come to mind are abstract, involving large-scale goals. You then examine each large step and break it into subgoals. If you keep breaking things down long enough, the means–end paths become complete and concrete enough to get you from here to there. You've created a strategy.

This line of thought was used in a program designed to help low-income, African American middle school students develop an academic identity (Oyserman, Terry, & Bybee, 2002). Students in this program had trouble creating possible selves that involved school as a pathway to adulthood. Oyserman et al. developed a small-group intervention to do that. They gave students the experience of developing academic possible selves. Moreover, the program tied those possible selves to strategies for achieving desired short-term goals and extended them to adult self-images. The program emphasized the solving of everyday problems, breaking them down by means–end analysis. The result was that the students bonded more strongly to school.

Finally, it's important to seek accurate feedback about the effects of your actions. If you get accurate feedback, you don't have to make perfect choices. If you make continual adjustments from the feedback you get, you keep moving in the right direction. This principle, which is basic to the self-regulation approach, yields an important kind of freedom—the freedom from having to be right the first time.

The Self-Regulation Perspective: Problems and Prospects

As is true of the cognitive view of personality, the self-regulation view has received mixed responses. It shares loose ends and unanswered questions with the cognitive view, and it has some of its own. It remains unclear whether these are fatal problems or just gaps to be filled.

One criticism of the self-regulation view derives from the *robotics* metaphor it sometimes employs. Critics say that artificial systems can't possibly be good models for human behavior. Humans have free will and make their own decisions. Robots have to rely on the programs they've been given to run them.

One response to this criticism is that the behavior of so-called intelligent artificial systems moves farther every year in the direction of what looks suspiciously like self-determination (Brooks, 2002). It seems clear that how humans and artificial systems resemble and differ from each other will continue to be debated well into the future. But as the behavior of artifacts becomes more and more humanlike, the debate likely will focus on increasingly subtle points.

Another response is that the robotics metaphor isn't the only one used for this line of thought. Electronic examples are often used to illustrate the principle of feedback control, but the feedback concept wasn't invented by engineers. It was devised to account for functions of the body (Cannon, 1932). The robotics metaphor may not always feel appropriate to living systems, but the feedback principle itself was devised precisely *for* living systems.

Another criticism sometimes made of this approach (even within the physiological metaphor) is that a model based on feedback principles is merely a model of **homeostasis** (literally, "steady state"). Homeostatic mechanisms exist to control body temperature, the levels of various elements in the blood, and many other physical parameters of the body. But how much sense does it make to think this way about something we know is always *changing*? Human behavior isn't about steady states. Doesn't the self-regulation view imply that people should be immobile and stable—or just do the same thing over and over?

Actually, no. People do regulate some things in a recurrently homeostatic way—for example, the amount of affiliation they engage in across time (O'Connor & Rosenblood, 1996)—but not always. As we noted earlier, many goals are dynamic (e.g., going on a vacation trip, having an interesting conversation with someone). Being dynamic doesn't make them any less goal-like. It just means that the whole process of matching the behavior to the goal must be dynamic as well. If the goal is to create a flow of experiences, rather than a state, then the qualities of behavior being monitored will also have this changing quality. So there's no contradiction between the fact that humans keep changing what they're doing and the idea that behavior occurs within a system of feedback control.

Greater difficulty is posed by another criticism aimed at the hierarchical model: that it fails to deal effectively with the homunculus problem. *Homunculus* is a term once used to explain how people act. It refers to a hypothetical tiny man who sits inside your head and tells you what to do. That explains *your* behavior. But who tells the little man what to tell you? If people have hierarchies of goals, where do the highest goals come from—the ones that specify all the lower goals?

One response is that self-regulatory models typically assume an executive system that coordinates other activities, makes decisions, and so on. The executive is manifest in subjective experience as consciousness. The executive presumably has control over many other systems and thus, in some ways, is the analogue of the homunculus. This reasoning is plausible, but it isn't altogether satisfying.

Another response is that people have built-in goals of survival, personal coherence, and so on. These goals are vague enough that they rarely appear in consciousness, but they're pervasive enough that they constantly influence in subtle ways people's decisions about what goals to take up. Thus, behavior is being guided by values that are built into the organism, but which aren't always apparent to the person. This line of reasoning is plausible, too, but it's also less than fully satisfying. The homunculus problem thus remains a real one.

Another criticism of the self-regulation view (as well as the cognitive view of Chapter 12) is similar to a criticism made of the learning perspective: All this seems too much a description from the outside looking in. There's too little feel of what it means to *have* a personality. This view describes the "self-regulation of behavior," but what does it really say about personality? This approach emphasizes structure and process, rather than content. For this reason, some see the ideas as dealing with an empty shell, programmed in ways that aren't well specified, for purposes and goals that are largely arbitrary (e.g., Deci & Ryan, 2000).

There is some merit to this criticism. Note, however, that these ideas weren't really devised to focus directly on *personality*. Rather, they were intended to focus on issues that stand at a slight tangent from personality. Although the ideas aren't a theory of personality, they provide a window on the nature of human experience that seems to have implications for personality: the nature of the pursuit of goals and values in life. Will these ideas evolve into a more complete picture of personality? It's too early to know.

Despite these criticisms, the self-regulation view on personality has proven to have merit. It's had heuristic value, suggesting new places to look for information about how things work. Indeed, it has made some predictions that aren't intuitively suggested by other views. This value alone makes it likely that the self-regulation view will be around for a while. Only the tests of time and further study will tell whether this approach will continue to emerge as a viable perspective on personality.

• SUMMARY •

In self-regulation models, behavior is sometimes specified by interpretive schemas, if an interpretation is closely tied to an action quality. Sometimes, actions follow from intentions: products of a mental algebra in which personally desired outcomes and social considerations are weighed to yield an intent to act or not act.

Theory concerning self-regulation emphasizes goals. The goals underlying behavior have a variety of labels, including life tasks, personal strivings, personal projects, and current concerns. This view treats the structure of the self as an organization among goals. Some goals are fairly neutral, but others imply a standard of excellence. In the latter case, setting higher goals results in higher performances. This is because committing oneself to a more demanding goal focuses one's efforts more fully. If the goal is too high, though, people don't adopt it.

Some intentions concern attaining end goals; others are about implementing action plans to reach those end goals. The latter are important for ensuring that behavior actually gets done. Implementation intentions constitute the linking of strategies to the contexts in which the person wants to engage them. Intentions are formed in a deliberative mindset, but once the person starts to pursue them, he or she is in an implementational mindset.

Once a goal for behavior has been evoked, self-regulation reflects a process of feedback control. A reference value (or goal) is compared against present behavior. If the two differ, behavior is adjusted, leading to a new perception and comparison. Given that many goals are dynamic and evolving, this view emphasizes that self-regulation is a never-ending process. A single feedback loop is too simple to account for the diversity in people's actions alone, but complexity is provided by the fact that feedback systems can be organized in a hierarchy, in which one system acts by providing reference values to the system directly below it. The concept of hierarchy accounts for the fact that a goal can be attained by many kinds of actions, along with the fact that the same action can occur in service to diverse goals.

Within this framework, emotions have been viewed as calls for reprioritizing one's goals. Emotions are viewed as giving a subjective reading of how well you're progressing toward a goal. Emotions thus convey important information that has a strong influence on behavior.

When people encounter obstacles in their efforts, self-regulation is interrupted and they consider whether success or failure is likely. If their expectancies are positive enough, they will keep trying; if not, they may disengage effort and give up. Disengagement is sometimes the adaptive response, but people sometimes give up too quickly. In some cases, disengagement is only partial—goal substitution or scaling back. This keeps the person engaged, in one way, while disengaging in another.

Although much of this chapter concerns conformity to goals, self-regulation models also include discussions of avoidance. *Avoidance* means creating distance instead of conformity. Another issue is that some behavior occurs via intentions, but some actions are triggered fairly automatically, even without the person's awareness. This difference between sources of influence is sometimes dealt with by dual-process models resembling those discussed in Chapter 12. An intuitive system promotes behaviors that are triggered by cues of the moment; a rational system promotes behaviors that are thought out and intentional. Self-regulation sometimes entails self-control: the prevention of pursuing one goal, in service of another more important goal.

Assessment, from this view, is partly a matter of assessing individual differences in self-regulatory functions, such as self-reflectiveness, self-control, and the level of abstraction at which people view their goals. This view also suggests the value of assessing goals themselves. There are several ways to conceptualize problems from this view. One possibility focuses on conflict between incompatible goals. Another points to a lack of specification of midlevel behavioral reference values to guide behavior. Yet another emphasizes that people sometimes are unable to disengage from behaviors that are necessary for the attainment of higher-order goals. There's evidence that people who are depressed display an exaggerated inability to disengage.

Just as behavior can be construed in terms of self-regulatory systems, so can the process of behavior change induced by therapy. People in therapy use feedback from decisions they've put into practice to make further decisions. They monitor the effects of changes in behavior to determine whether the changes have produced the desired effects. One long-term goal of therapy is to make people better problem solvers through techniques such as means–end analysis, so that they can make their own adjustments when confronting new problems.

• GLOSSARY •

Action identification   The way you think of or label whatever action you are performing.

Attitude   A personal evaluation of the likely outcome of an action and the desirability of that outcome.

Comparator   A mechanism that compares two values to each other.

Deliberative mindset   A careful mindset used while deciding whether to take an action.

Disengage   To cease and put aside self-regulation with regard to some goal.

Feedback hierarchy   An organization of feedback loops, in which superordinate loops act by providing reference values to subordinate loops.

Goal intention   The intention to attain some particular outcome.

Homeostasis   Regulation around a constant, steady state.

Implemental mindset   A positively biased mindset that's used while implementing an intention to act.

Implementation intention   The intention to take specific actions in specific contexts.

Means–end analysis   The process of creating a plan to attain an overall goal (end) by breaking it into successively more concrete goals (means).

Negative feedback loop   A self-regulating system that maintains conformity to some comparison value.

Principle   A broad, abstract action quality that could be displayed in any of several programs.

Program   A guideline for the actions that take place in some category of events (as a script).

Subjective norm   Your impression of how relevant others value an action and your interest in pleasing them.

Subliminal stimuli   Stimuli presented too quickly to be consciously recognized.

System concept   A very abstract guide for behavior, such as an ideal sense of self.

CHAPTER 14

Personality in Perspective: Overlap and Integration

Six blind men from Indostan heard of a creature called an *elephant*. They went to determine its nature. One of them bumped into the elephant's side and concluded that elephants resemble walls. The second encountered a tusk and decided that elephants are like spears. The third, grasping the wriggling trunk, decided that elephants are similar to snakes. Wrapping his arms around one of its legs, the fourth concluded that elephants are like trees. The fifth felt a floppy ear and surmised that an elephant is a type of fan. Coming upon the animal's tail, the sixth decided that elephants are like ropes.

Each of these men was sure his investigation had led him to the truth. And, indeed, each of them was partly right. But all were partly wrong.

—Hindu fable

In PREVIOUS chapters, you encountered a series of viewpoints on the nature of personality. Each was rooted in its own assumptions about how best to view human nature. Each had its own way of conceptualizing how people function, and each addressed the importance of individual differences. Each approach had merits and each had drawbacks, places where things were left unexplained or even unexamined.

In writing about these perspectives on personality, we tried to give you a sense of what each was like from inside that perspective. In so doing, we tended to emphasize what makes each approach distinct from the other ones. The views do differ in important ways, and some points of conflict are hard to resolve. For example, how can the belief that people have free will (from the self-actualization perspective) be reconciled with the belief that behavior is determined by patterns of prior outcomes (from the learning perspective) or the belief that behavior is determined by internal forces (from the psychoanalytic perspective)?

Our emphasis on the uniqueness of each theory may have created the impression that the theories are quite different from one another. The diversity may even have led you to wonder whether the theorists were even describing the same *creature* (much like someone listening to the blind men describe the elephant). The diversity of ideas in earlier chapters certainly raises questions: Do the various perspectives have anything in common? Is one perspective right, or better than the others? If so, which one? This chapter considers these questions.

Do the theories you've read about have anything in common? Yes. The first part of this chapter describes several commonalities we think are interesting. You certainly noticed some of them, but others are more subtle and harder to spot. We also consider a couple of key issues that many different theories address, albeit from different angles.

The question of which view is best or right is harder to answer. One answer is that even big differences among perspectives may not mean that one is right and the others are wrong. It often happens that some issue, or some element of personality, seems very important from the view of one theory but is less important or even irrelevant from the view of another theory. Like the blind men, one theory grapples closely with an issue, but another doesn't even touch on it.

Perhaps, then, various perspectives on personality are facets of a bigger picture. From this point of view, the perspectives would complement, rather than contradict, each other. Each may have some truth, but none by itself has the whole truth. The idea that the perspectives are facets of a broader picture is developed more fully in the last part of the chapter.

Similarities among Perspectives

Let's first consider some specific similarities among the views described earlier in the book. We won't point to every one possible. Rather, we'll try to give you a general sense of some of the connections that can be made.

We begin with commonalities between psychoanalysis and other views. Psychoanalysis is a natural starting point. It's been around for a very long time. Some regard it as the only really comprehensive theory of personality ever devised. For both of these reasons, it's a natural comparison point for every other approach.

On the other hand, psychoanalysis is also a particularly *unusual* theory. This suggests it may be hard to find similarities between it and other approaches. As we noted in Chapter 9, even theories that *derive* from psychoanalysis don't seem to share a lot with it. Nonetheless, several similarities are worth noting. In fact, parallels have been suggested between psychoanalysis and at least three other perspectives: the evolutionary, self-regulation, and cognitive perspectives.

PSYCHOANALYSIS AND EVOLUTIONARY PSYCHOLOGY: THE STRUCTURAL MODEL

Often overlooked is the fact that Freud was strongly influenced by Darwin's view of evolution. Psychoanalytic theory is about beings that are deeply preoccupied by biological necessities: survival and reproduction. Attaining these goals is critical, because that's what biological life is all about. It should be no surprise, then, that the core of personality focuses on them. Even so, because humans live in a dangerous world, it's necessary to deal with the complexities imposed by reality. And because we live in groups, it's eventually important to deal with another issue, as well: the fact that people other than us also have needs.

This is the general line of thought that underlies an attempt by Leak and Christopher (1982) to interpret some of Freud's ideas from the framework of evolutionary psychology. They noted that the evolutionary view sees behavior as self-serving (with one exception, to which we turn momentarily). This self-serving quality resembles the selfish nature of Freud's concept of the id. The id is primitive and single minded about its desires. It represents the self-interested animal that our genes make us, as those genes try to continue their existence.

The id isn't rational, and neither are the genes. Freud tied rationality to the ego, a mechanism that mediates between the id and reality. Leak and Christopher (1982) argued that genes also need help in dealing with the complexities of reality and that the cerebral cortex evolved to serve this purpose. Evolution of the cortex in humans would parallel evolution of the ego in the person. Both structures—cortex and ego—permit greater planfulness and care in decision making. Both are adaptations that foster survival.

What about the superego? This is the trickiest part of Leak and Christopher's (1982) argument. To view the superego in evolutionary terms requires one more idea. Specifically, survival isn't only an individual matter. Humans evolved as highly social beings, living and surviving in groups. Because we're so interdependent, we sometimes do better in the long run by letting group needs override personal needs in the short run. As noted in Chapter 6, it's been argued that people in groups evolved mechanisms for inducing—even forcing—reciprocal altruism (Trivers, 1971). Having a genetic mechanism to do this would increase the adaptive success of the group.

In psychological terms, evolving such a mechanism looks like developing a capacity to have a superego. Thus, having a superego confers an evolutionary advantage. People who adopt and conform to the values of their social group will be accepted as members of the group. They will be more likely to get the benefits that follow from group membership (for example, having other members take care of you if you're sick). Clearly, these benefits have survival value.

In sum, Leak and Christopher (1982) suggested that the ego (conscious rationality) is a behavioral management system, for which the id and the superego provide motivation. There are two types of motivation—selfish and group-related—with adaptive value. The id adapts to the physical environment, where competition for resources is intense and selfish. The superego comprises the tendencies that evolved in response to pressures from group living.

PSYCHOANALYSIS AND EVOLUTIONARY PSYCHOLOGY: FIXATIONS AND MATING PATTERNS

We see one more similarity between psychoanalytic and evolutionary views—one that's quite different from the points made by Leak and Christopher. Think back to the Oedipal conflict and the fixations that can emerge from it. For a male, fixation in the phallic stage is said to cause an exaggerated attempt to show that he hasn't been castrated. He does this by having sex with as many women as possible and by seeking power and status. Female fixation in this stage involves a seductiveness that doesn't necessarily lead to sex.

These effects look remarkably similar to the mating strategies that evolutionary psychologists argue are part of our species. Recall from Chapter 6 the idea that men and women have different reproductive strategies, due to differing investment in offspring (Trivers, 1972). The male mating tactic is to create the appearance of power and status and to mate as frequently as possible. The female tactic is to appear highly desirable but to hold out for the best mate available. These tactics have strong echoes in the fixations just described. We can't help but wonder whether Freud noticed a phenomenon that's biologically based, and ascribed psychodynamic properties to it in order to fit it better into his theory.

PSYCHOANALYSIS AND SELF-REGULATION: HIERARCHY AND THE STRUCTURAL MODEL

The psychoanalytic approach to personality also has certain similarities to the self-regulation view. One similarity derives from the notion of a self-regulatory hierarchy. The behavioral qualities range from very limited movements through organized sequences to abstract higher-level qualities. As pointed out in Chapter 13, when attention is diverted from the higher levels, behavior is more spontaneous and responsive to cues of the moment. It's as though low-level action sequences, once triggered, run off by themselves. In contrast to this impulsive style of behavior, actions being regulated according to higher-order values (programs or principles) have a more carefully managed character.

Aspects of this description hint at similarities to Freud's three-part view of personality. Consider the spontaneity and responsiveness to situational cues in the self-regulation model when high-level control isn't being exerted. This resembles aspects of id functioning. An obvious difference is Freud's assumption that id impulses are primarily sexual or aggressive. The self-regulation model, in contrast, makes no such assumption. It's worth noting, though, that alcohol intoxication and deindividuation, which seem to reduce control at high levels (see Chapter 13), often lead to sexual or destructive activity.

The link between id processes and low-level control is a bit tenuous. In contrast, there's quite a strong resemblance between program control in the self-regulation approach and ego functioning in the psychoanalytic approach. Program control involves planning, decision making, and behavior that's pragmatic, as opposed to either impulsive or principled. These qualities also characterize the ego's functioning.

Levels higher than program control resemble, in some ways, the functioning of the superego. Principle control, in at least some cases, induces people to conform to moral principles. Control at the highest level involves an effort to conform to your idealized sense of self. These efforts resemble, in some respects, the attempt to fit your behavior to the principles of the ego ideal and to avoid a guilty conscience for violating these principles.

The fit between models at this high level isn't perfect, partly because not all principles are moralistic. Yet here's a question: Why did Freud focus on morality and ignore other kinds of ideals? Was it because morality was so prominent an issue in his society at that time? Maybe the superego is really the capacity to follow social rules *in general*, rather than just moral rules. If this were so—if the superego actually pushed behavior toward *other* principles as well as moral ones—the similarity between models would be even greater.

PSYCHOANALYSIS AND COGNITIVE PROCESSES

Several links also exist between psychoanalytic themes and ideas from cognitive psychology (e.g., Westen, 1998). Matthew Erdelyi (1985) even suggested that Freud's theory was largely a theory of cognition. Indeed, he said that Freud was straining toward an analogy between mind and computer but never got there because the computer didn't exist yet.

Erdelyi (1985) argued that cognitive psychologists essentially reinvented many psychodynamic concepts. For example, Freud assumed a process that keeps threats out of awareness. This is similar to the filtering process by which the mind preattentively selects information to process more fully. Freud's concept of ego becomes executive control processes. The topography of the mind becomes a matter of levels of processing, and distortions become biases in processing.

As an example of Erdelyi's (1985) approach, consider repression and denial (see also Paulhus & Suedfeld, 1988). When ideas, desires, or perceptions arise that are threatening, repression and denial prevent them from reaching consciousness. This reaction can occur before a threatening stimulus is even experienced, a phenomenon termed **perceptual defense**, or it can involve forgetting an event after it's been experienced. Erdelyi argued that these reflect a sequence of information-processing decisions (see Figure 14.1).

Information is partially analyzed preattentively. This may yield an implicit estimate of how much anxiety would arise if the information reached consciousness. If the estimate exceeds a threshold, processing stops and the information goes no farther. If the estimate is lower, the information goes to a memory area corresponding to the preconscious. Similar decisions are made at other stages, with lower and lower criteria for moving to the next level of processing. This model treats repression, response suppression, and self-deception more generally as reflecting checks at several stages of information processing.

As implied by this description, today's cognitive view assumes that much of the mind's functioning is unconscious. Indeed, the study of unconscious processes is a very active area of work (Hassin, Uleman, & Bargh, 2005). Today's cognitive view tends to equate *consciousness* with *attention*. Events that are unconscious are those that get little or no attention.

There are several reasons an event might get little attention. It may be tagged preattentively as having too much potential for anxiety. Or it might occur in a part of the nervous system that attentional processes can't reach. Many cognitive scientists think of the nervous system as a set of special-purpose components, only some of which can be examined consciously (Gardner, 1985). Thus, the basic "wiring" of the system renders some aspects of experience inaccessible.

Sometimes events are unconscious because some behaviors are highly automatic. Acts that are automatic require little or no monitoring. Highly automated sequences can be triggered by stimuli that are noted by the nervous system at some level but never

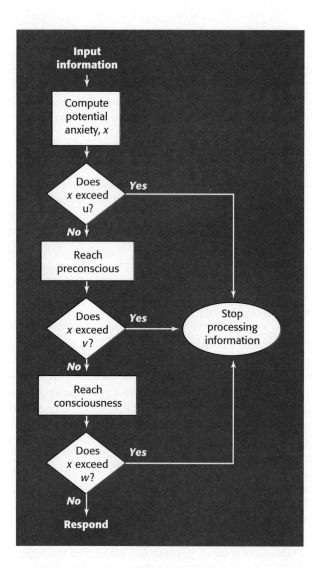

FIGURE 14.1
An information-processing picture of repression and denial. Input information (top)—whether perceptual or from a suppressed memory—is judged preattentively for its anxiety-inducing value. Then come a series of implicit decisions. First, does the anxiety the information would create (x) exceed a criterion of *unbearability* (u)? If so, processing stops; if not, the material goes to a memory area corresponding to the preconscious. Next, does the predicted anxiety exceed a *serious discomfort* criterion (v)? If so, processing ceases and the information stays in memory; if not, the information moves to consciousness. The final decision is whether to acknowledge openly the information that's now conscious, depending on whether the anxiety from doing so will exceed a final criterion (w). This sequence provides for information never to be stored in memory, to be stored but not reach consciousness, to reach consciousness but be suppressed, or to be acknowledged openly. *Source:* Based on Erdelyi, 1985.

reach consciousness (Bargh, 1997; Norman, 1981). Even elaborate actions drop mostly out of awareness as they become routine (which all experienced drivers discover at one time or other, as they arrive at home with no memory of how they got there).

These descriptions obviously differ in important ways from Freud's treatment of the unconscious. Only Erdelyi's (1985) example involving preattentive estimates of anxiety implies the sort of conflict-avoidance process that Freud assumed. All these

Highly programmed acts, such as walking, can occur with little awareness. This suggests a possible point of contact between cognitive and self-regulation ideas and psychodynamic theory.

ideas, however, suggest ways in which information can fail to reach consciousness.

Another body of work has linked cognitive processes to the psychoanalytic concept of *transference*. Transference occurs when a person in therapy displaces emotional reactions onto the therapist. Presumably, these reactions were initially stimulated by significant others in the person's earlier life. Several studies have provided a cognitive explanation for such a turn of events (Andersen, Glassman, Chen, & Cole, 1995; Glassman & Andersen, 1999).

Specifically, the schemas people have of significant others seem chronically to be partially active (and thus accessible). As with other instances of partial activation, this makes it easier for the schema to emerge and be used in perceiving and interpreting other stimuli. As a result, you may view many people through the lens of that schema and not even realize it. If someone does something that reminds you vaguely of your mother's way of inducing guilt, it may evoke your *mother* schema and make you perceive that person as being like your mother.

Indeed, when such schemas pop up, self-aspects relating to those significant others emerge, as well (Hinkley & Andersen, 1996). Thus, if someone tends to induce guilt as your mother did, you may react just as you did to your mother (e.g., by becoming irrationally angry), even if the reaction isn't appropriate to the present situation. All this can happen in therapy—or anywhere.

SOCIAL LEARNING, COGNITIVE, AND SELF-REGULATION VIEWS

As new theories were created over the years, personality psychologists were often influenced by ideas that were being used in other areas of psychology. Indeed, this cross-fertilization has been very common. Among the sources of ideas for personality psychologists during the past several decades were learning psychology and cognitive psychology. To a considerable extent, people who sampled from these sources sampled from both, rather than just one.

One result of this pattern is a set of similarities between social–cognitive learning ideas (Chapter 10) and cognitive and self-regulation approaches (Chapters 12 and 13). These approaches have diverse histories, but their central concepts resemble one another more than just a little. Indeed, as you may have noticed, the work of several people pertains not just to one of these views but to two or more of them.

One area of overlap concerns the importance these approaches ascribe to cognitive processes in creating representations of the world and the self. Differences among perspectives on this issue stem from the fact that each has different *reasons* for emphasizing cognition. In discussing cognition from the social learning approach, Mischel (1973) said that if we want to understand learning, we have to look at people's mental representations of stimuli, not the stimuli themselves. People learn from what *they* think is there, not what an outsider sees. The way the stimuli are mentally represented and transformed determines how people will respond to them (see also Bandura, 1977a, 1986).

From the learning perspective, these statements emphasize that human learning is more complicated than it seems. An event doesn't lead automatically to conditioning that's the same for everyone. From the learning perspective, such statements are qualifications on theories of learning. They say to other learning theorists that the *person* has to be considered in analyzing learning. That's the point of such statements— *when they're made from the learning perspective.*

When embedded in the cognitive view on personality, however, ideas about the role of cognition take on a broader life. From this view, cognitive processes are central to *everything* about personality. From the cognitive view on personality, Mischel (1973) focused not on the subtleties of learning but on how people organize their understanding. Note the difference of emphasis. In the cognitive view, the idea that people *organize* their experience is a key principle regarding the essence of personality. Learning per se is more peripheral. Cognitive processes are also critical to the self-regulation view on personality, although once again there's a difference of emphasis. The focus in the self-regulation approach is mostly on the role cognitions play in *creating behavior.*

Another similarity among the social learning, cognitive, and self-regulation views concerns expectancies. Indeed, expectancies also appear in the motive approach. All these approaches see expectancies as determinants of how hard people try to do things. Many people (e.g., Bandura, 1977a, 1986; Carver & Scheier, 1981, 1998; Kanfer, 1977; Kirsch, 1985, 1990; Mischel, 1973, 1979; Rotter, 1966) have argued that people hold expectancies about the effects their actions are likely to have and whether they can do things they want to do. These expectancies can influence how hard a person tries and what the person learns from an event.

The social learning, cognitive, and self-regulation approaches also resemble each other in the structure they assume underlies behavior. The social learning view says people have *incentives*, which draw them forward into action. Incentives function the same as *goals*, a concept that plays a key role in the self-regulation perspective. Indeed, other perspectives also have constructs that serve a comparable role.

There is, however, one important difference of emphasis here between the learning and self-regulation views. It concerns the concept of reinforcement. The learning view uses this concept explicitly. It's basic to the principle of instrumental learning. As we noted in Chapter 10, however, one social learning theorist—Bandura— consistently used the concept differently than did others. To him, reinforcers create mental representations of future incentives. They cause people to learn expectancies about what actions are useful in what situations. But they don't directly increase the tendency to do the acts that preceded them. The way Bandura used the reinforcement concept raises questions about whether its meaning is compatible with that assumed by other learning theorists.

Keep in mind, though, that Bandura stands with one foot in the learning perspective and one in the self-regulation perspective. His view on reinforcement may reflect Bandura the self-regulation theorist more than Bandura the learning theorist. As we noted in Chapter 13, self-regulation theorists are divided on reinforcement as a concept. Some say that people self-reinforce after success. Others see the concept of self-reinforcement as less useful.

On this issue, the personal histories of the theorists probably influenced how their ideas were constructed. Most self-regulation theorists who assume a role for self-reinforcement began their work in the learning perspective. Only gradually did they identify with the newer self-regulation view. Perhaps they retained a role for self-reinforcement partly because it was a comfortable tie to the past. Of particular interest is the fact that those theorists are more likely to talk about *self-reinforcement* than *external reinforcement* (e.g., Kanfer, 1977). It's the person's own goal representations that matter, after all. Only *you* can decide whether your goal has been met. Thus, self-reinforcement, rather than external reinforcement, is at the heart of these discussions.

To others, introducing self-reinforcement as a concept simply raises questions. Certainly, people often feel pride after success and sadness after failure. But do these reactions create the learning, or are they just emotional reactions to informational events, with the latter being what really matters? This is an issue that hasn't been settled in the self-regulation perspective (or, to some extent, even in the learning perspective).

MASLOW'S HIERARCHY AND HIERARCHIES OF SELF-REGULATION

There are also similarities between elements of the self-actualization perspective and the self-regulation perspective. Consider Maslow's hierarchy of motives (Chapter 11). There are two similarities between that hierarchy and the self-regulation hierarchy.

First, Maslow conceived of the motive qualities at the top of the hierarchy not only as more abstract and subtle, but also as more integrative, than those at lower levels. The levels of the hierarchy of control discussed in Chapter 13 also have this character. Second, Maslow saw the lower motives as more demanding than the higher ones, in the sense that a deficit or a problem lower in the hierarchy draws the person's attention to it and forces him or her to deal with it. Similarly, in at least one version of the self-regulatory hierarchy, if a problem develops at a low level, attention is brought to that level in an attempt to resolve the problem.

There are, however, clear differences between these views, as well. The biggest difference concerns the *content* of the hierarchies. Maslow's analysis was explicitly an analysis of *motives* intended to incorporate both biological needs and psychological motives. The control hierarchy, in contrast, focuses on the structure of *action* with goals that relate to qualities of behavior. This difference means that the two hierarchies are very different at their low levels. Maslow's hierarchy points to survival needs; the other hierarchy points to muscle movements.

At higher levels, though, the two hierarchies are more similar. The highest level of control in the self-regulation view seems roughly equivalent to the concept of self-actualization used by Maslow and Rogers. The nature of the goal at the highest level—an ideal self that relates to the many principles in force at the next lower level—is quite diffuse. It's so diffuse, in fact, that it isn't too hard to imagine that self-regulation toward it might also feel diffuse. In some ways, this echoes the idea that self-actualization has a very quiet voice.

SELF-ACTUALIZATION AND SELF-REGULATION

Two other similarities between the self-actualization view and the self-regulation view of personality go beyond Maslow's hierarchy. One similarity is that both viewpoints use concepts corresponding to idealized and experienced qualities of self. The labels *real self* and *ideal self* are explicit in the view of Rogers. The sense of an idealized self is also one value at the top of the control hierarchy, as is the experienced actual self that's compared with it.

The comparison process itself is also similar between the approaches. Rogers emphasized that people compare their current selves with their ideal selves and that they experience anxiety when there's incongruity between them. The comparison between a sensed condition and a standard, or reference point, is also intimately involved in the self-regulation perspective, not only with respect to an ideal self but at all levels of the hierarchy.

TRAITS AND THEIR EQUIVALENTS IN OTHER MODELS

Another resemblance among theories brings us full circle to an idea with which we began this book. We started with the concept of traits. We now return to it.

As noted in Chapter 1, a major theme of personality psychology is how people differ from one another, not just temporarily but in enduring ways. This theme is the basis for the trait perspective on personality. Other theories also hold assumptions about people's dispositions. The motive perspective assumes enduring motive dispositions. The genetic perspective assumes inherited temperaments, which are the bedrock for traits.

The essence of dispositions, if not the concept itself, is also prominent in at least two more views on personality. The psychoanalytic view assumes that people derive stable personality qualities from childhood psychosexual crises. In the social perspective, Erikson assumed that childhood psychosocial crises shape adult personality, and object relations and attachment theories make similar assumptions.

Although these theories differ regarding the sources of dispositions, they share two assumptions: that something is stamped onto or etched into the individual early in life and that this characteristic continues to influence the person from then on. The disposition has been viewed as a biological temperament, a transformation of sexual drives, a reflection of a psychosocial crisis, a learned motive quality, and simply a trait. Yet all the theories involved treat dispositions as having enduring influences on the person's experiences. This similarity among approaches, which is often overlooked, is not a trivial one.

Indeed, the disposition concept also has a place in other views. For example, one version of the learning approach assumes that people differ in self-efficacy, which helps determine how much effort they expend. One aspect of the self-regulation approach assumes that people vary in the disposition to be self-reflective and thus how carefully self-regulated they are. In both of these cases (and many others, as well), individual differences are seen as stable dispositions that influence a broad range of the person's experiences.

Recurrent Themes, Viewed from Different Angles

Emphasis in the preceding section was on the notion that certain ideas in one theoretical perspective resemble ideas from another perspective. We also want to note another kind of similarity across perspectives: a similarity in the issues the theories consider. We said earlier that different theories often address different issues. That's true. But at least a couple of issues recur across a surprisingly wide range of perspectives.

IMPULSE AND RESTRAINT

One of these issues concerns what seems to be a basic distinction between *impulse* and *restraint*. This issue has been part of personality psychology for a long time, but it has become even more prominent in recent years. It is often introduced in the context of delay of gratification, where a choice must be made between receiving a small reward now or a larger reward later. We've discussed that phenomenon from several viewpoints: psychoanalysis (where we said the ego restrains the id's impulses), social learning theory (where we considered effects of models), and the cognitive perspective (where the focus was on mental images that can foster restraint).

The issue of impulse versus restraint is far broader than delay of gratification, however. In some ways, it's fundamental to personality. As a result, its broader manifestations emerge in many views of personality:

- It's there in trait psychology, in which a trait of conscientiousness is assumed to be defined partly by self-discipline and deliberation (McCrae & Costa, 1987). Indeed, another trait theory treats constraint as a basic dimension of personality (Tellegen, 1985).
- It comes up in temperament theories, where some argue that constraint is, in fact, a basic temperament (Clark & Watson, 1999) and others argue for a similar temperament that's been called *effortful control* (Rothbart et al., 2003).
- It's found in biological process models, where an argument is made that approach and avoidance systems are joined by a system that concerns restraint versus impulsiveness (Carver & Miller, 2006; Depue & Spoont, 1986; Eysenck & Eysenck, 1976; Zuckerman, 2005).
- It's a core issue in psychoanalysis, concerning the balance between the id's desires in many domains and the ego's restraint over how and when those desires are met.
- It's there in cognitive theories, in the form of a contrast between rational and experiential systems (Epstein, 1994) and in a contrast between "hot," incentive-related cognition and "cool," restrained cognition (Metcalfe & Mischel, 1999).
- It also appears in self-regulation theories, in the distinction between deliberative and implemental mindsets (Heckhausen & Gollwitzer, 1987).

Impulse versus restraint has emerged in the past decade as a key issue in several areas of personality psychology (Carver, 2005; Carver, Johnson, & Joormann, 2009). Indeed, this issue is one that's led a number of people to think seriously about cognitive processing occurring in two modes (as described in Chapter 12). In those theories, the management of behavior is seen as subject to two layers of influence, which rely on two different parts of the brain. One system provides an automatic, intuitive, superficial, and fast way of interacting with the world. It's believed to have evolved earlier. The other system provides a rational, deliberative, but slower way of interacting with the world. It's believed to be of more recent origin.

The question of how and why a person chooses to act quickly versus hold back from acting is basic. It's no wonder that many theories say something or other about this question. This issue undoubtedly will remain a focus of interest for many people in the years ahead.

INDIVIDUAL VERSUS GROUP NEEDS

Another fundamental issue concerns the competing pressure of individualistic self-interest versus the needs arising from being involved in groups (or couples). In many cases, this issue is tangled up with the issue of action versus restraint. This is because recognizing other people's needs is often what urges restraining one's own impulses. Conceptually, however, it's a separate issue.

Earlier in this chapter, we noted that psychoanalytic theory and evolutionary psychology both confront the contrast between these pressures. In psychoanalysis, the ego deals with the immediate demands of both social and physical reality and the super-ego deals with other more complex aspects of social needs. In evolutionary psychology, people have individualistic needs—survival, competition for mates. But they also have group-based needs—cooperation with one's mate and with the larger society.

This distinction between individualistic and social goals also appears in other approaches. In trait psychology, it emerges in two places. One is the trait of *agreeableness*, which concerns maintaining positive relations with others. People high on this dimension are attuned to mutual well-being; those lower on the dimension are unconcerned with others' interests. The distinction also emerges in the trait of *extraversion*. Extraverts want to have social impact, whereas introverts are less concerned with group involvement and follow more individualistic paths.

In the motive approach, this issue shows up in the motives to achieve and exert power versus affiliate and attain intimacy. In the biological process approach, this issue appears in unsocialized sensation seeking, with its disregard of others' needs. It's in the psychosocial approach, in the issue of separation–individuation versus merger. It's in the self-actualization approach, in the balance between the self-actualizing tendency and the need for positive regard from other people.

In all these cases, people confront the need to balance the two competing pressures. Both pressures are important but in different ways. Given all this attention from theorists of so many different perspectives, this issue appears to be critically important in human experience.

Combining Perspectives

As should now be apparent, similarities do exist between seemingly unrelated approaches to personality. These similarities may, in time, allow integration of the approaches. As we noted in Chapter 1, several people are trying to move in that direction (e.g., McAdams & Olson, 2010; McAdams & Pals, 2006; Roberts & Wood, 2006). It's probably safe to say, though, that most personality psychologists view that as a desirable but still distant goal. One reason is the sheer size and complexity of the job.

Theorists have sometimes integrated across boundaries, even in the past. Examples include Eysenck and Zuckerman. In describing Eysenck's work in earlier chapters, we treated it as two sets of ideas with separate focuses. One is a hierarchical model of relations among acts, habits, traits, and supertraits. Another is biological, dealing with brain function (and heritability of differences). Even though we presented the ideas as separate, Eysenck viewed them as an integrated model with multiple facets. Zuckerman (1991, 1994, 2005) has made similar statements, binding together—in a single model—trait, inheritance, and biological process views.

A more recent example of integration is the suggestion that different perspectives have different things to offer at different times in human development. For example, McAdams and Olson (2010) noted that infant temperaments (with their biological roots) are the bedrock for traits, which are in place early in life. As the child develops and acquires a sense of self as an agent in the world, issues surrounding motives and goals become more salient. Perspectives on personality that focus on motives and goals have a good deal to say about this part of life.

During adolescence and young adulthood, the narratives emerge that people construct about their lives to help provide meaning and identity. These narratives don't take the place of traits or goals but are layered over them (see also Lodi-Smith, Geise, Roberts, & Robins, 2009). This position suggests an integration across viewpoints that's different from what Eysenck and Zuckerman offered, and one that is potentially quite useful.

ECLECTICISM

Another option, exercised by many psychologists, is to take an eclectic approach to personality. This involves drawing useful ideas from many theories, rather than being tied to just one or two. Essentially, it means saying that different ideas are useful for different purposes and that there may be no approach that's best for all purposes. To understand a phenomenon, you may need to look at it from the angle of a theory that focuses on it, rather than a theory that doesn't. As Scarr (1985) put it, "There is no need to choose a single lens for psychology when we can enjoy a kaleidoscope of perspectives" (p. 511).

This sort of approach suggests that views of personality from the various perspectives may be mutually supportive. It may not be necessary to integrate them into a single set of constructs or principles. As noted earlier, the focus of one theory differs from that of any other theory. By taking bits of theory across several focuses, perhaps we can obtain a more well rounded picture of what personality really is.

For example, most personality psychologists today accept the idea that personality was shaped by evolutionary pressures. Most assume that there are inherited temperaments and that the processes by which personality is reflected are biological. Several ideas from psychoanalytic theory are also widely accepted—for example, that determinants of behavior are sometimes outside awareness and that mechanisms exist within the mind that protect us from things we don't want to think about. Many personality psychologists accept that early experiences have a big impact on what people are like. Obviously, learning has an influence on personality, yet people seem to organize records of the experiences of their lives in idiosyncratic ways. We may well have an inner voice of self-actualization. Behavior may even reflect the operation of feedback loops.

All of these ideas may be true or only some of them. All of them may be useful or only some of them. Many psychologists pick and choose bits from various perspectives and use them wherever they seem reasonable. The choice among the available elements is an individual one.

AN EXAMPLE: BIOLOGY AND LEARNING AS COMPLEMENTARY INFLUENCES ON PERSONALITY

Perhaps the simplest illustration of an eclectic approach is that psychologists almost universally acknowledge the importance to personality of both biology and learning. Almost everyone does: people who focus on biology, people who focus on learning, and people who take some other view of personality. Early learning theorists claimed the mind is a "blank slate," on which any kind of personality can be sketched. It's clear, though, that this isn't true. There are biological constraints on learning.

A key point is that some associations are learned more easily than others. The term used to describe this is **preparedness**. This term implies that organisms are prepared to learn certain connections more easily than others (Öhman & Mineka, 2001; Seligman & Hager, 1972). Preparedness isn't all or nothing. It's a continuum of ease versus difficulty in learning connections. Presumably, this is biologically influenced.

Both biological and learning principles are needed to understand fully the phenomenon of preparedness—such as the biological readiness that chimps and people show in learning to use tools.

For example, if you get sick to your stomach, you could, in theory, develop a conditioned aversive response toward any number of stimuli. If conditioning depended only on associations between stimuli, you should condition aversions to *all* neutral stimuli that are present. However, you're much more likely to develop an aversion to a flavor experienced just before getting sick than to anything else (Garcia & Koelling, 1966). Apparently, the links are just easier to create in the nervous system for some pairs of events than others.

Preparedness also seems to be involved in instrumental learning. That is, some kinds of actions are easier for animals to learn than others, even if the same reward follows both. Rats learn more quickly to avoid a foot shock by jumping than by pressing a bar (Wickelgren, 1977). Pigeons easily learn to peck a spot to obtain food, but it's hard to get them to learn to refrain from pecking to get food.

Just as it's clear the mind isn't a blank slate, it's also clear that the expression of most biological tendencies depends on experience. Earlier in the book, we talked about *diathesis–stress models*, in which a particular kind of stress produces a problem only if the person also has a particular vulnerability (which might be biological, though it doesn't have to be). Such models are widely accepted. One reason is that twin studies of disorders show two things at once: that disorders are genetically influenced and that genes aren't everything. If you are the monozygotic twin of someone with schizophrenia, your chance of being schizophrenic is elevated but still less than 100%. If genes were all that mattered, the figure would be 100%.

Thus, an eclectic acceptance of both biology and learning as important influences on personality seems well founded. Perhaps other combinations will someday prove to be similarly well founded.

Which Theory Is Best?

As we said earlier, one answer to the question of which theory is best is that *no* theory is perfect and you may benefit from using bits and pieces of many theories. We should point out, though, that this question is sometimes answered another way. This answer returns us to a point we made in the book's opening chapter. We think it provides a fitting way to end, as well.

As we said in Chapter 1, over a century ago William James wrote that a theory must account reasonably well for the phenomena that people experience as real; to be successful, however, a theory must do more than that. James (1890) wrote that people will believe those theories which "are most interesting, those which appeal most urgently to our æsthetic, emotional, and active needs" (p. 312). Put more simply, the theory that's best is the one you *like* best. The one that's best—for you—is the one that appeals most to you, the one you find most interesting and engaging.

Edward Tolman (1959) also put it pretty simply: "I have liked to think about psychology in ways that have proved congenial to me. . . . In the end, the only sure criterion is to have fun. And I have had fun" (p. 152).

• SUMMARY •

Although various perspectives on personality differ from one another in important ways, they also resemble one another in important ways. The psychoanalytic perspective is similar to at least three alternative views. First, ideas about evolution in the species parallel Freud's ideas about the evolution of personality in the individual. That is, in each case, a primitive force (the genes, the id) needs another force to help it deal with reality (the cortex, the ego), and eventually it also needs a force to keep it in contact with the social world (inherited sensitivity to social influence, the superego). There are also similarities between Freud's picture of fixations from the Oedipal crisis and the mating tactics that evolutionary theorists posit for males and females. Second, the psychoanalytic view and the self-regulation view resemble each other in that the notion of a hierarchy of control echoes psychoanalytic theory's three components of personality. Third, work from the cognitive viewpoint on unconscious influences has resulted in concepts that resemble, in some ways, those postulated years earlier by Freud.

A substantial overlap exists among the social learning, the cognitive, and the self-regulation viewpoints. They share an emphasis on mental representations of the world, although they have somewhat different rationales for the emphasis. They also have similar views of the importance of people's expectancies and similar views on the basic structure of behavior.

A similarity also exists between the notion of a hierarchy in self-regulation and Maslow's ideas about motives. Although the lower levels of Maslow's motive hierarchy deal with motives that are ignored in the control hierarchy, at their upper levels, the models resemble each other more closely. The principle of self-actualization also resembles the self-regulation model in the concepts of ideal and actual self and the desire for congruity between them.

Another similarity among approaches concerns the notion of disposition. This construct is central to the trait perspective, and it's also important in the psychoanalytic and social views. In all these cases (and by implication in others, as well), the assumption is made that people have qualities that endure over time and circumstances and that influence their behaviors, thoughts, and feelings.

Although the various theories differ in their focus, certain issues do seem to recur across many of them. This represents another kind of similarity among the theories. One issue that many different theories address is the polarity between impulse versus restraint. Indeed, this issue has become increasingly prominent in recent years. Another is the competing pressures of individual self-interest and communal interest.

Thus, there are areas of overlap among theories. Yet the theories also differ. Which theory, then, is right? One answer is that *all* the perspectives seem to have something of value to offer. Maybe the value of each viewpoint depends on what part of the person's life you are focusing on. Many psychologists prefer an eclectic position, taking elements and ideas from several views, rather than just one.

At a minimum, people who operate within the framework of a given theory must take into account the limitations imposed by evidence generated by other views. For example, temperament theorists believe much of personality is determined by genetics, but they also understand that temperaments are modified by learning. Learning theorists believe that personality is a product of a learning history, but it's clear that some kinds of learning are easier than others. Perhaps the future will see greater emphasis on this eclecticism—the sharing of ideas from one perspective to another.

• GLOSSARY •

Perceptual defense   Screening out a threatening stimulus before it enters awareness.

Preparedness   The idea that some conditioning is easy, because the animal is biologically prepared for it to happen.

Aarts, H., & Dijksterhuis, A. (2000). Habits as knowledge structures: Automaticity in goal-directed behavior. *Journal of Personality and Social Psychology, 78,* 53–63.

Aarts, H., & Dijksterhuis, A. (2003). The silence of the library: Environment, situational norm, and social behavior. *Journal of Personality and Social Psychology, 84,* 18–28.

Abramson, L. Y., Alloy, L. B., & Metalsky, G. I. (1995). Hopelessness depression. In G. M. Buchanan & M. E. P. Seligman (Eds.), *Explanatory style* (pp. 113–134). Hillsdale, NJ: Erlbaum.

Abramson, L. Y., Metalsky, G. I., & Alloy, L. B. (1989). Hopelessness depression: A theory-based subtype of depression. *Psychological Review, 96,* 358–372.

Abramson, L. Y., Seligman, M. E. P., & Teasdale, J. D. (1978). Learned helplessness in humans: Critique and reformulation. *Journal of Abnormal Psychology, 87,* 49–74.

Achtziger, A., Gollwitzer, P. M., & Sheeran, P. (2008). Implementation intentions and shielding goal striving from unwanted thoughts and feelings. *Personality and Social Psychology Bulletin, 34,* 381–383.

Adams, G. D., & Fastnow, C. (2000, November 10). A note on the voting irregularities in Palm Beach, Florida. Retrieved January 1, 2011, from http://madison.hss.cmu.edu

Adler, A. (1927). *Practice and theory of individual psychology.* New York, NY: Harcourt, Brace, & World.

Adler, A. (1929). *The science of living.* New York, NY: Greenberg.

Adler, A. (1931). *What life should mean to you.* Boston, MA: Little, Brown.

Agostinelli, G., Sherman, S. J., Presson, C. C., & Chassin, L. (1992). Self-protection and self-enhancement biases in estimates of population prevalence. *Personality and Social Psychology Bulletin, 18,* 631–642.

Ahadi, S., & Diener, E. (1989). Multiple determinants and effect size. *Journal of Personality and Social Psychology, 56,* 398–406.

Ainsworth, M. D. S. (1983). Patterns of infant–mother attachment as related to maternal care. In D. Magnusson & V. Allen (Eds.), *Human development: An interactional perspective.* New York, NY: Academic Press.

Ainsworth, M. D. S., Blehar, M. C., Waters, E., & Wall, T. (1978). *Patterns of attachment.* Hillsdale, NJ: Erlbaum.

Ajzen, I. (1985). From intentions to actions: A theory of planned behavior. In J. Kuhl & J. Beckmann (Eds.), *Action control: From cognition to behavior.* New York, NY: Springer-Verlag.

Ajzen, I. (1988). *Attitudes, personality, and behavior.* Chicago, IL: Dorsey.

Ajzen, I., & Fishbein, M. (1980). *Understanding attitudes and predicting social behavior.* Englewood Cliffs, NJ: Prentice-Hall.

Alexander, R. (1979). *Darwinism and human affairs.* Seattle, WA: University of Washington Press.

Alicke, M. D. (1985). Global self-evaluation as determined by the desirability and controllability of trait adjectives. *Journal of Personality and Social Psychology, 49,* 1621–1630.

Alicke, M. D., & Sedikides, C. (Eds.). (2010). *Handbook of self-enhancement and self-protection.* New York, NY: Guilford Press.

Allen, J. J., Iacono, W. G., Depue, R. A., & Arbisi, P. (1993). Regional electroencephalographic asymmetries in bipolar seasonal affective disorder before and after exposure to bright light. *Biological Psychiatry, 33,* 642–646.

Allen, L. S., & Gorski, R. A. (1992). Sexual orientation and the size of the anterior commissure in the human brain. *Proceedings of the National Academy of Sciences of the U.S.A., 89,* 7199–7202.

Allison, P. J., Guichard, C., Fung, K., & Gilain, L. (2003). Dispositional optimism predicts survival status 1 year after diagnosis in head and neck cancer patients. *Journal of Clinical Oncology, 21*(3), 543–548.

Allport, G. W. (1937). *Personality: A psychological interpretation.* New York, NY: Holt.

Allport, G. W. (1961). *Pattern and growth in personality.* New York, NY: Holt, Rinehart, & Winston.

Amabile, T. M. (1985). Motivation and creativity: Effects of motivational orientation on creative writers. *Journal of Personality and Social Psychology, 48,* 393–399.

Amsel, A. (1967). Partial reinforcement effects on vigor and persistence: Advances in frustration theory derived from a variety of within-subject experiments. In K. W. Spence & J. T. Spence (Eds.), *The psychology of learning and motivation* (Vol. 1). New York, NY: Academic Press.

Andersen, S. M., & Chen, S. (2002). The relational self: An interpersonal social-cognitive theory. *Psychological Review, 109,* 619–645.

Andersen, S. M., Glassman, N. S., Chen, S., & Cole, S. W. (1995). Transference in social perception: The role of chronic accessibility in significant-other representations. *Journal of Personality and Social Psychology, 69,* 41–57.

Anderson, C., John, O. P., Keltner, D., & Kring, A. M. (2001). Who attains social status? Effects of personality and physical attractiveness in social groups. *Journal of Personality and Social Psychology, 81,* 116–132.

Anderson, C. A., Berkowitz, L., Donnerstein, E., Huesmann, L. R., Johnson, J. D., Linz, D., Malamuth, N. M., & Wartella, E. (2003). The influence of media violence on youth. *Psychological Science in the Public Interest, 4,* 81–110.

Anderson, J. A. (1995). *An introduction to neural networks.* Cambridge, MA: MIT Press.

Anderson, J. R. (1976). *Language, memory and thought.* Hillsdale, NJ: Erlbaum.

Anderson, J. R. (1985). *Cognitive psychology and its implications* (2nd ed.). New York, NY: Freeman.

Anderson, J. R. (1991). The adaptive nature of human categorization. *Psychological Review, 98,* 409–429.

Anderson, R. C., & Pichert, J. W. (1978). Recall of previously unrecallable information following a shift in perspective. *Journal of Verbal Learning and Verbal Behavior, 17,* 1–12.

Archer, J. (2006). Testosterone and human aggression: An evaluation of the challenge hypothesis. *Neuroscience and Biobehavioral Reviews, 30,* 319–345.

Archer, J., & Coyne, S. M. (2005). An integrated review of indirect, relational, and social aggression. *Personality and Social Psychology Review, 9,* 212–230.

Arkin, R. M., & Baumgardner, A. H. (1985). Self-handicapping. In J. H. Harvey & G. Weary (Eds.), *Attribution: Basic issues and applications.* New York, NY: Academic Press.

Arndt, J., Schimel, J., Greenberg, J., & Pyszczynski, T. (2002). The intrinsic self and defensiveness: Evidence that activating the intrinsic self reduces self-handicapping and conformity. *Personality and Social Psychology Bulletin, 28,* 671–685.

Arnett, P. A., Smith, S. S., & Newman, J. P. (1997). Approach and avoidance motivation in psychopathic criminal offenders during passive avoidance. *Journal of Personality and Social Psychology, 72,* 1413–1428.

Asendorpf, J. B., Banse, R., & Mücke, D. (2002). Double dissociation between implicit and explicit personality self-concept: The case of shy behavior. *Journal of Personality and Social Psychology, 83,* 380–393.

Asendorpf, J. B., & Wilpers, S. (1998). Personality effects on social relationships. *Journal of Personality and Social Psychology, 74,* 1531–1544.

Ashton, M. C., & Lee, K. (2007). Empirical, theoretical, and practical advantages of the HEXACO model of personality structure. *Personality and Social Psychology Review, 11,* 150–166.

Ashton, M. C., & Lee, K. (2008). The prediction of honesty–humility-related criteria by the HEXACO and five-factor models of personality. *Journal of Research in Personality, 42,* 1216–1228.

Ashton, M. C., Lee, K., & Goldberg, L. R. (2004). A hierarchical analysis of 1,710 English personality-descriptive adjectives. *Journal of Personality and Social Psychology, 87,* 707–721.

Ashton, M. C., Lee, K., Perugini, M., Szarota, P., de Vries, R. E., Di Blas, L., Boies, K., & De Raad, B. (2004). A six-factor structure of personality-descriptive adjectives: Solutions from psycholexical studies in seven languages. *Journal of Personality and Social Psychology, 86,* 356–366.

Assor, A., Roth, G., & Deci, E. L. (2004). The emotional costs of parents' conditional regard: A self-determination theory analysis. *Journal of Personality, 72,* 47–88.

Atkinson, J. W. (1957). Motivational determinants of risk-taking behavior. *Psychological Review, 64,* 359–372.

Atkinson, J. W., & Birch, D. (1970). *The dynamics of action.* New York, NY: Wiley.

Atkinson, J. W., & McClelland, D. C. (1948). The projective expression of needs II. The effect of different intensities of the hunger drive on thematic apperception. *Journal of Experimental Psychology, 38,* 643–658.

Atkinson, J. W., & Raynor, J. O. (Eds.). (1974). *Motivation and achievement.* Washington, DC: V. H. Winston.

Austin, J. T., & Vancouver, J. B. (1996). Goal constructs in psychology: Structure, process, and content. *Psychological Bulletin, 120,* 338–375.

Avia, M. D., & Kanfer, F. H. (1980). Coping with aversive stimulation: The effects of training in a self-management context. *Cognitive Therapy and Research, 4,* 73–81.

Avila, C. (2001). Distinguishing BIS-mediated and BAS-mediated disinhibition mechanisms: A comparison of disinhibition models of Gray (1981, 1987) and of Patterson and Newman (1993). *Journal of Personality and Social Psychology, 80,* 311–324.

Axelrod, R., & Hamilton, W. D. (1981). The evolution of cooperation. *Science, 211*, 1390–1396.

Axline, V. M. (1947). *Play therapy.* Boston, MA: Houghton Mifflin.

Axline, V. M. (1964). *Dibs: In search of self.* Boston, MA: Houghton Mifflin.

Babad, E. Y. (1973). Effects of informational input on the "social deprivation-satisfaction effect." *Journal of Personality and Social Psychology, 27*, 1–5.

Back, M. D., Schmukle, S. C., & Egloff, B. (2009). Predicting actual behavior from the explicit and implicit self-concept of personality. *Journal of Personality and Social Psychology, 97,* 533–548.

Badner, J. A., & Gershon, E. S. (2002). Meta-analysis of whole-genome linkage scans of bipolar disorder and schizophrenia. *Molecular Psychiatry, 7*, 405–411.

Bailey, J. E., Argyropoulos, S. V., Lightman, S. L., & Nutt, D. J. (2003). Does the brain noradrenaline network mediate the effects of the CO2 challenge? *Journal of Psychopharmacology, 17*, 252–259.

Bailey, J. M., Gaulin, S., Agyei, Y., & Gladue, B. A. (1994). Effects of gender and sexual orientation on evolutionarily relevant aspects of human mating psychology. *Journal of Personality and Social Psychology, 66*, 1081–1093.

Baker, L. A., Jacobson, K. C., Raine, A., Lozano, D. I., & Bezdjian, S. (2007). Genetic and environmental bases of childhood antisocial behavior: A multi-informant twin study. *Journal of Abnormal Psychology, 116,* 219–235.

Baldwin, M. W., Keelan, J. P. R., Fehr, B., Enns, V., & Koh-Rangarajoo, E. (1996). Social-cognitive conceptualization of attachment working models: Availability and accessibility effects. *Journal of Personality and Social Psychology, 71*, 94–109.

Balmary, M. (1979). *Psychoanalyzing psychoanalysis: Freud and the hidden fault of his father.* Baltimore, MD: Johns Hopkins University Press.

Baltes, P. B., & Staudinger, U. M. (1993). The search for a psychology of wisdom. *Current Directions in Psychological Science, 2*, 75–80.

Bandura, A. (1965). Influence of models' reinforcement contingencies on the acquisition of imitative response. *Journal of Personality and Social Psychology, 1*, 589–595.

Bandura, A. (1969). *Principles of behavior modification.* New York, NY: Holt, Rinehart, & Winston.

Bandura, A. (1971). Vicarious and self-reinforcement processes. In R. Glaser (Ed.), *The nature of reinforcement.* New York, NY: Academic Press.

Bandura, A. (1973). *Aggression: A social learning analysis.* Englewood Cliffs, NJ: Prentice-Hall.

Bandura, A. (1976). Self-reinforcement: Theoretical and methodological considerations. *Behaviorism, 4*, 135–155.

Bandura, A. (1977a). Self-efficacy: Toward a unifying theory of behavioral change. *Psychological Review, 84*, 191–215.

Bandura, A. (1977b). *Social learning theory.* Englewood Cliffs, NJ: Prentice-Hall.

Bandura, A. (1978). The self system in reciprocal determinism. *American Psychologist, 33*, 344–358.

Bandura, A. (1982). Self-efficacy mechanism in human agency. *American Psychologist, 37*, 122–147.

Bandura, A. (1986). *Social foundations of thought and action: A social cognitive theory.* Englewood Cliffs, NJ: Prentice-Hall.

Bandura, A. (1997). *Self-efficacy: The exercise of control.* New York, NY: Freeman.

Bandura, A. (2006). Toward a psychology of human agency. *Perspectives on Psychological Science, 1*, 164–180.

Bandura, A., Adams, N. E., & Beyer, J. (1977). Cognitive processes mediating behavioral change. *Journal of Personality and Social Psychology, 35*, 125–139.

Bandura, A., Adams, N. E., Hardy, A. B., & Howells, G. N. (1980). Tests of the generality of self-efficacy theory. *Cognitive Therapy and Research, 4*, 39–66.

Bandura, A., Grusec, J. E., & Menlove, F. L. (1967). Vicarious extinction of avoidance behavior. *Journal of Personality and Social Psychology, 5*, 16–23.

Bandura, A., & Jeffery, R. W. (1973). Role of symbolic coding and rehearsal processes in observational learning. *Journal of Personality and Social Psychology, 26*, 122–130.

Bandura, A., Jeffery, R., & Bachicha, D. L. (1974). Analysis of memory codes and cumulative rehearsal in observational learning. *Journal of Research in Personality, 7*, 295–305.

Bandura, A., & Menlove, F. L. (1968). Factors determining vicarious extinction of avoidance behavior through symbolic modeling. *Journal of Personality and Social Psychology, 8*, 99–108.

Bandura, A., & Mischel, W. (1965). Modification of self-imposed delay of reward through exposure to live and symbolic models. *Journal of Personality and Social Psychology, 2*, 698–705.

Bandura, A., & Schunk, D. H. (1981). Cultivating competence, self-efficacy, and intrinsic interest through proximal self-motivation. *Journal of Personality and Social Psychology, 41*, 586–598.

Bandura, A., & Walters, R. (1963). *Social learning and personality development.* New York, NY: Holt, Rinehart, & Winston.

Barash, D. P. (1986). *The hare and the tortoise: Culture, biology, and human nature.* New York, NY: Penguin Press.

Barash, D. P. (2001). *Revolutionary biology: The new, gene-centered view of life.* London, England: Transaction.

Barber, J. P., & DeRubeis, R. J. (1989). On second thought: Where the action is in cognitive therapy for depression. *Cognitive Therapy and Research, 13,* 441–457.

Bardi, A., Lee, J. A., Hofmann-Towfigh, N., & Soutar, G. (2009). The structure of intraindividual value change. *Journal of Personality and Social Psychology, 97,* 913–929.

Bargh, J. A. (1997). The automaticity of everyday life. In R. S. Wyer, Jr. (Ed.), *Advances in social cognition* (Vol. 10, pp. 1–61). Mahwah, NJ: Erlbaum.

Bargh, J. A., & Chartrand, T. L. (1999). The unbearable automaticity of being. *American Psychologist, 54,* 462–479.

Bargh, J. A., Chen, M., & Burrows, L. (1996). Automaticity of social behavior: Direct effects of trait construct and stereotype activation on action. *Journal of Personality and Social Psychology, 71,* 230–244.

Bargh, J. A., & Ferguson, M. J. (2000). Beyond behaviorism: On the automaticity of higher mental processes. *Psychological Bulletin, 126,* 925–945.

Bargh, J. A., Lombardi, W. J., & Higgins, E. T. (1988). Automaticity of chronically accessible constructs in person X situation effects on person perception: It's just a matter of time. *Journal of Personality and Social Psychology, 55,* 599–605.

Bargh, J. A., & Pratto, F. (1986). Individual construct accessibility and perceptual selection. *Journal of Experimental Social Psychology, 22,* 293–311.

Bargh, J. A., & Williams, E. L. (2006). The automaticity of social life. *Current Directions in Psychological Science, 15,* 1–4.

Barkow, J. H., Cosmides, L., & Tooby, J. (1992). *The adapted mind: Evolutionary psychology and the generation of culture.* New York, NY: Oxford University Press.

Barlow, D. H. (Ed.). (1981). *Behavioral assessment of adult disorders.* New York, NY: Guilford Press.

Baron, A. S., & Banaji, M. R. (2006). The development of implicit attitudes: Evidence of race evaluations from ages 6 and 10 and adulthood. *Psychological Science, 17,* 53–58.

Baron, R. A., & Kempner, C. R. (1970). Model's behavior and attraction toward the model as determinants of adult aggressive behavior. *Journal of Personality and Social Psychology, 14,* 335–344.

Baron, R. A., & Richardson, D. R. (1994). *Human aggression* (2nd ed.). New York, NY: Plenum Press.

Barrett, L. F., Williams, N. L., & Fong, G. T. (2002). Defensive verbal behavior assessment. *Personality and Social Psychology Bulletin, 28,* 776–788.

Barron, F. (1953). An ego-strength scale which predicts response to psychotherapy. *Journal of Consulting Psychology, 17,* 327–333.

Bartholomew, K., & Horowitz, L. M. (1991). Attachment styles among young adults: A test of a four-category model. *Journal of Personality and Social Psychology, 61,* 226–244.

Bartholow, B. D., Bushman, B. J., & Sestir, M. A. (2006). Chronic violent video game exposure and desensitization to violence: Behavioral and event-related brain potential data. *Journal of Experimental Social Psychology, 42,* 532–539.

Bartholow, B. D., Sestir, M. A., & Davis, E. B. (2005). Correlates and consequences of exposure to video game violence: Hostile personality, empathy, and aggressive behavior. *Personality and Social Psychology Bulletin, 31,* 1573–1586.

Bauer, J. J., & Bonanno, G. A. (2001). I can, I do, I am: The narrative differentiation of self-efficacy and other self-evaluations while adapting to bereavement. *Journal of Research in Personality, 35,* 424–448.

Bauer, J. J., McAdams, D. P., & Sakaeda, A. R. (2005). Interpreting the good life: Growth memories in the lives of mature, happy people. *Journal of Personality and Social Psychology, 88,* 203–217.

Baumann, N., Kaschel, R., & Kuhl, J. (2005). Striving for unwanted goals: Stress-dependent discrepancies between explicit and implicit achievement motives reduce subjective well-being and increase psychosomatic symptoms. *Journal of Personality and Social Psychology, 89,* 781–799.

Baumeister, R. F. (1989). The problem of life's meaning. In D. M. Buss & N. Cantor (Eds.), *Personality psychology: Recent trends and emerging directions* (pp. 138–148). New York, NY: Springer-Verlag.

Baumeister, R. F. (2002). Ego depletion and self-control failure: An energy model of the self's executive function. *Self and Identity, 1,* 129–136.

Baumeister, R. F., & Campbell, W. K. (1999). The intrinsic appeal of evil: Sadism, sensational thrills, and threatened egotism. *Personality and Social Psychology Review, 3,* 210–221.

Baumeister, R. F., & Heatherton, T. F. (1996). Self-regulation failure: An overview. *Psychological Inquiry, 7,* 1–15.

Baumeister, R. F., & Leary, M. R. (1995). The need to belong: Desire for interpersonal attachments as a fundamental human motivation. *Psychological Bulletin, 117,* 497–529.

Baumeister, R. F., & Vohs, K. D. (Eds.). (2004). *Handbook of self-regulation: Research, theory, and applications.* New York, NY: Guilford Press.

Beck, A. T. (1972). *Depression: Causes and treatments*. Philadelphia, PA: University of Pennsylvania Press.

Beck, A. T. (1976). *Cognitive therapy and the emotional disorders*. New York, NY: International Universities Press.

Beck, A. T. (1991). Cognitive therapy: A 30-year retrospective. *American Psychologist, 46,* 368–375.

Beck, A. T., Rush, A. J., Shaw, B. F., & Emery, G. (1979). *Cognitive therapy of depression: A treatment manual*. New York, NY: Guilford Press.

Becker, E. (1973). *The denial of death*. New York, NY: Free Press.

Beer, J. S. (2002). Implicit self-theories of shyness. *Journal of Personality and Social Psychology, 83,* 1009–1024.

Beevers, C. G. (2005). Cognitive vulnerability to depression: A dual process model. *Clinical Psychology Review, 25,* 975–1002.

Beiswenger, K. L., & Grolnick, W. S. (2010). Interpersonal and intrapersonal factors associated with autonomous motivation in adolescents' after-school activities. *Journal of Early Adolescence, 30,* 369–394.

Bell, M., Billington, R., & Becker, B. (1986). A scale for the assessment of object relations: Reliability, validity, and factorial invariance. *Journal of Clinical Psychology, 42,* 733–741.

Benet, V., & Waller, N. G. (1995). The Big Seven factor model of personality description: Evidence for its cross-cultural generality in a Spanish sample. *Journal of Personality and Social Psychology, 69,* 701–718.

Benet-Martínez, V., & John, O. P. (1998). Los Cinco Grandes across cultures and ethnic groups: Multitrait multimethod analyses of the Big Five in Spanish and English. *Journal of Personality and Social Psychology, 75,* 729–750.

Benjamin, J., Li, L., Patterson, C., Greenberg, B. D., Murphy, D. L., & Hamer, D. H. (1996). Population and familial association between the D4 dopamine receptor gene and measures of novelty seeking. *Nature Genetics, 12,* 81–84.

Bentler, P. M. (1990). Comparative fit indexes in structural models. *Psychological Bulletin, 107,* 238–246.

Berant, E., Mikulincer, M., & Florian, V. (2001). Attachment style and mental health: A 1-year follow-up study of mothers of infants with congenital heart disease. *Personality and Social Psychology Bulletin, 27,* 956–968.

Berenbaum, S. A., & Hines, M. (1992). Early androgens are related to childhood sex-typed toy preferences. *Psychological Science, 3,* 203–206.

Bergeman, C. S., Chipuer, H. M., Plomin, R., Pedersen, N. L., McClearn, G. E., Nesselrode, J. R., Costa, P. T., Jr., & McCrae, R. R. (1993). Genetic and environmental effects on openness to experience, agreeableness, and conscientiousness: An adoption/twin study. *Journal of Personality, 61,* 159–179.

Bergeron, D. M., Block, C. J., & Echtenkamp, B. A. (2006). Disabling the able: Stereotype threat and women's work performance. *Human Performance, 19,* 133–158.

Berghout, C., Zevalkink, J., & Hakkaart-Van Roijen, L. (2010). The effects of long-term psychoanalytic treatment on healthcare utilization and work impairment. *Journal of Psychiatric Practice, 16,* 209–216.

Bergmann, M. S. (1980). Symposium on object relations theory and love: On the intrapsychic function of falling in love. *Psychoanalytic Quarterly, 49,* 56–77.

Bernhardt, P. C., Dabbs, J. M., Jr., Fielden, J., & Lutter, C. (1998). Testosterone changes during vicarious experiences of winning and losing among fans at sporting events. *Physiology and Behavior, 65,* 59–62.

Bernstein, A., Newman, J. P., Wallace, J. F., & Luh, K. E. (2000). Left-hemisphere activation and deficient response modulation in psychopaths. *Psychological Science, 11,* 414–418.

Bernstein, I. L. (1985). Learning food aversions in the progression of cancer and its treatment. *Annals of the New York Academy of Sciences, 443,* 365–380.

Berridge, K. C. (2007). The debate over dopamine's role in reward: The case for incentive salience. *Psychopharmacology, 191,* 391–431.

Berry, D. S., & Miller, K. M. (2001). When boy meets girl: Attractiveness and the five-factor model in opposite-sex interactions. *Journal of Research in Personality, 35,* 62–77.

Bertrand, S., & Masling, J. M. (1969). Oral imagery and alcoholism. *Journal of Abnormal Psychology, 74,* 50–53.

Besser, A., & Priel, B. (2005). The apple does not fall far from the tree: Attachment styles and personality vulnerabilities to depression in three generations of women. *Personality and Social Psychology Bulletin, 31,* 1052–1073.

Bettelheim, B. (1982, March 1). Reflections: Freud and the soul. *New Yorker, 58,* 52–93.

Bettencourt, B. A., & Sheldon, K. (2001). Social roles as mechanisms for psychological need satisfaction within social groups. *Journal of Personality and Social Psychology, 81,* 1131–1143.

Beyers, W., & Seiffge-Krenke, I. (2010). Does identity precede intimacy? Testing Erikson's theory on romantic development in emerging adults of the 21st century. *Journal of Adolescent Research, 25,* 387–415.

Binswanger, L. (1963). *Being-in-the-world: Selected papers of Ludwig Binswanger*. New York, NY: Basic Books.

Birnbaum, G. E., Reis, H. T., Mikulincer, M., Gillath, O., & Orpaz, A. (2006). When sex is more than just sex: Attachment orientations, sexual experience, and relationship quality. *Journal of Personality and Social Psychology, 91,* 929–943.

Bjork, J. M., Dougherty, D. M., Moeller, F. G., & Swann, A. C. (2000). Differential behavioral effects of plasma tryptophan depletion and loading in aggressive and nonaggressive men. *Neuropsychopharmacology, 22,* 357–369.

Bjorklund, D. F., & Pellegrini, A. D. (2002). *Origins of human nature: Evolutionary developmental psychology.* Washington, DC: American Psychological Association.

Bjorner, J. B., Chang, C. , Thissen, D., & Reeve, B. B. (2007). Developing tailored instruments: Item banking and computerized adaptive assessment. *Quality of Life Research, 16,* 95–108.

Black, A. E., & Deci, E. L. (2000). The effects of instructors' autonomy support and students' autonomous motivation on learning organic chemistry: A self-determination theory perspective. *Science Education, 84,* 740–756.

Blackford, J. U., Avery, S. N., Cowan, R. L., Shelton, R. C., & Zald, D. H. (2010). Sustained amygdala response to both novel and newly familiar faces characterizes inhibited temperament. *Social Cognitive and Affective Neuroscience.* First published online July 26, 2010.

Blanck, R., & Blanck, G. (1986). *Beyond ego psychology: Developmental object relations theory.* New York, NY: Columbia University Press.

Blatt, S. J., Wein, S. J., Chevron, E., & Quinlan, D. M. (1979). Parental representations and depression in normal young adults. *Journal of Abnormal Psychology, 88,* 388–397.

Blatt, S. J., & Zuroff, D. C. (1992). Interpersonal relatedness and self-definition: Two prototypes for depression. *Clinical Psychology Review, 12,* 527–562.

Block, J. (1977). Advancing the science of personality: Paradigmatic shift or improving the quality of research? In D. Magnusson & N. S. Endler (Eds.), *Personality at the crossroads: Current issues in interactional psychology* (pp. 37–63). Hillsdale, NJ: Erlbaum.

Block, J. (1995). A contrarian view of the five-factor approach to personality assessment. *Psychological Bulletin, 117,* 187–215.

Block, J. (2001). Millennial contrarianism: The five-factor approach to personality description 5 years later. *Journal of Research in Personality, 35,* 98–107.

Block, J. (2002). *Personality as an affect-processing system: Toward an integrative theory.* Mahwah, NJ: Erlbaum.

Block, J. (2010). The five-factor framing of personality and beyond: Some ruminations. *Psychological Inquiry, 21,* 2–25.

Block, J., & Block, J. H. (2006). Venturing a 30-year longitudinal study. *American Psychologist, 61,* 315–327.

Block, J. H. (1961). *The Q-sort method in personality assessment and psychiatric research.* Springfield, IL: Charles C Thomas.

Block, J. H., & Block, J. (1980). The role of ego-control and ego-resiliency in the organization of behavior. In W. A. Collins (Ed.), *Development of cognition, affect, and social relations* (Minnesota Symposia on Child Psychology, Vol. 13, pp. 39–101). Hillsdale, NJ: Erlbaum.

Bogg, T., & Roberts, B. W. (2004). Conscientiousness and health-related behaviors: A meta-analysis of the leading behavioral contributors to mortality. *Psychological Bulletin, 130,* 887–919.

Bolger, N., & Zuckerman, A. (1995). A framework for studying personality in the stress process. *Journal of Personality and Social Psychology, 69,* 890–902.

Bolles, R. C. (1972). Reinforcement, expectancy, and learning. *Psychological Review, 79,* 394–409.

Booth, A., & Dabbs, J. M., Jr. (1993). Testosterone and men's marriages. *Social Forces, 72,* 463–477.

Borgatta, E. F. (1964). The structure of personality characteristics. *Behavioral Science, 12,* 8–17.

Boring, E. G. (1930). A new ambiguous figure. *American Journal of Psychology, 42,* 444–445.

Borkenau, P., Riemann, R., Angleitner, A., & Spinath, F. M. (2001). Genetic and environmental influences on observed personality: Evidence from the German observational study of adult twins. *Journal of Personality and Social Psychology, 80,* 655–668.

Borkenau, P., Riemann, R., Angleitner, A., & Spinath, F. M. (2002). Similarity of childhood experiences and personality resemblance in monozygotic and dizygotic twins: A test of the equal environments assumption. *Personality and Individual Differences, 33,* 261–269.

Bornstein, R. F., & Masling, J. (1985). Orality and latency of volunteering to serve as experimental subjects: A replication. *Journal of Personality Assessment, 49,* 306–310.

Borsboom, D., Mellenbergh, G. J., & van Heerden, J. (2004). The concept of validity. *Psychological Review, 111,* 1061–1071.

Boss, M. (1963). *Psychoanalysis and Daseinsanalysis.* New York, NY: Basic Books.

Botwin, M. D., & Buss, D. M. (1989). Structure of act-report data: Is the five-factor model of personality recaptured? *Journal of Personality and Social Psychology, 56,* 988–1001.

Bouchard, T. J. (2004). Genetic influence on human psychological traits. *Current Directions in Psychological Science, 13,* 148–151.

Bouchard, T. J., Jr., Lykken, D. T., McGue, M., Segal, N. L., & Tellegen, A. (1990). Sources of human psychological differences: The Minnesota study of twins reared apart. *Science, 250,* 223–228.

Bouton, M. E. (1994). Context, ambiguity, and classical conditioning. *Current Directions in Psychological Science, 3,* 49–53.

Bouton, M. E. (2000). A learning theory perspective on lapse, relapse, and the maintenance of behavior change. *Health Psychology, 19,* 57–63.

Bowlby, J. (1969). *Attachment and loss: Vol. 1, Attachment.* New York, NY: Basic Books.

Bowlby, J. (1988). *A secure base: Parent–child attachment and healthy human development.* New York, NY: Basic Books.

Boyatzis, R. E. (1973). Affiliation motivation. In D. C. McClelland & R. S. Steele (Eds.), *Human motivation: A book of readings.* Morristown, NJ: General Learning Press.

Bradburn, N. M., & Berlew, D. E. (1961). Need for achievement and English industrial growth. *Economic Development and Cultural Change, 10,* 8–20.

Bradley, G. W. (1978). Self-serving biases in the attribution process: A reexamination of the fact or fiction question. *Journal of Personality and Social Psychology, 36,* 56–71.

Brady, J. P. (1972). Systematic desensitization. In W. S. Agras (Ed.), *Behavior modification: Principles and clinical applications.* Boston, MA: Little, Brown.

Brady, S. S., & Matthews, K. A. (2006). Effects of media violence on health-related outcomes among young men. *Archives of Pediatric Adolescent Medicine, 160,* 341–347.

Brandon, T. H., Tiffany, S. T., Obremski, K. M., & Baker, T. B. (1990). Postcessation cigarette use: The process of relapse. *Addictive Behaviors, 15,* 105–114.

Brandstätter, H. (1983). Emotional responses to other persons in everyday life situations. *Journal of Personality and Social Psychology, 45,* 871–883.

Brandstätter, V., & Frank, E. (2002). Effects of deliberative and implemental mindsets on persistence in goal-directed behavior. *Personality and Social Psychology Bulletin, 28,* 1366–1378.

Brandstätter, V., Lengfelder, A., & Gollwitzer, P. M. (2001). Implementation intentions and efficient action initiation. *Journal of Personality and Social Psychology, 81,* 946–960.

Branje, S. J. T., van Lieshout, C. F. M., & van Aken, M. A. G. (2004). Relations between big five personality characteristics and perceived support in adolescents' families. *Journal of Personality and Social Psychology, 86,* 615–628.

Breedlove, S. M. (1992). Sexual dimorphism in the vertebrate nervous system. *Journal of Neuroscience, 12,* 4133–4142.

Breedlove, S. M. (1994). Sexual differentiation of the human nervous system. *Annual Review of Psychology, 45,* 389–418.

Brehm, J. W. (1966). *A theory of psychological reactance.* New York, NY: Academic Press.

Brehm, S. S., & Brehm, J. W. (1981). *Psychological reactance: A theory of freedom and control.* New York, NY: Academic Press.

Brennan, K. A., Clark, C. L., & Shaver, P. R. (1998). Self-report measurement of adult attachment: An integrative overview. In J. A. Simpson & W. S. Rholes (Eds.), *Attachment theory and close relationships* (pp. 46–76). New York, NY: Guilford Press.

Brewer, W. F. (1974). There is no convincing evidence for operant or classical conditioning in adult humans. In W. B. Weimer & D. S. Palermo (Eds.), *Cognition and the symbolic processes.* Hillsdale, NJ: Erlbaum.

Bridger, W. H., & Mandel, I. J. (1964). A comparison of GSR fear responses produced by threat and electric shock. *Journal of Psychiatric Research, 2,* 31–40.

Briggs, S. R. (1989). The optimal level of measurement for personality constructs. In D. M. Buss & N. Cantor (Eds.), *Personality psychology: Recent trends and emerging directions* (pp. 246–260). New York, NY: Springer-Verlag.

Brissette, I., Scheier, M. F., & Carver, C. S. (2002). The role of optimism in social network development, coping, and psychological adjustment during a life transition. *Journal of Personality and Social Psychology, 82,* 102–111.

Britt, T. W., & Shepperd, J. A. (1999). Trait relevance and trait assessment. *Personality and Social Psychology Review, 3,* 108–122.

Broadbent, D. E. (1977). Levels, hierarchies, and the locus of control. *Quarterly Journal of Experimental Psychology, 29,* 181–201.

Brokaw, D. W., & McLemore, C. W. (1983). Toward a more rigorous definition of social reinforcement: Some interpersonal clarifications. *Journal of Personality and Social Psychology, 44,* 1014–1020.

Brooks, R. A. (2002). *Flesh and machines: How robots will change us.* New York, NY: Pantheon.

Bruner, J. S. (1957). On perceptual readiness. *Psychological Review, 64,* 123–152.

Brunstein, J. C., & Maier, G. W. (2005). Implicit and self-attributed motives to achieve: Two separate but interacting needs. *Journal of Personality and Social Psychology, 89,* 205–222.

Brunstein, J. C., Schultheiss, O. C., & Grässmann, R. (1998). Personal goals and emotional well-being: The moderating role of motive dispositions. *Journal of Personality and Social Psychology, 75,* 494–508.

Brunswik, E. (1951). The probability point of view. In M. H. Marx (Ed.), *Psychological theory.* New York, NY: Macmillan.

Buccino, G., Binkofski, F., Fink, G. R., Fadiga, L., Fogassi, L., Gallese, V., Seitz, R. J., Zilles, K., Rizzolatti, G., & Freund, H.-J. (2001). Action observation activates premotor and parietal areas in somatotopic manner: An fMRI study. *European Journal of Neuroscience, 13,* 400–404.

Buchanan, A., Brock, D. W., Daniels, N., & Wikler, D. (2000). *From chance to choice: Genetics and justice.* New York, NY: Cambridge University Press.

Buchanan, G. M. (1995). Explanatory style and coronary heart disease. In G. M. Buchanan & M. E. P. Seligman (Eds.), *Explanatory style* (pp. 225–232). Hillsdale, NJ: Erlbaum.

Buller, D. J. (2005a). *Adapting minds: Evolutionary psychology and the persistent quest for human nature.* Cambridge, MA: MIT Press.

Buller, D. J. (2005b). Evolutionary psychology: The emperor's new paradigm. *Trends in Cognitive Sciences, 9,* 277–283.

Burnstein, E., Crandall, C., & Kitayama, S. (1994). Some neo-Darwinian decision rules for altruism: Weighing cues for inclusive fitness as a function of the biological importance of the decision. *Journal of Personality and Social Psychology, 67,* 773–789.

Burroughs, W. J., & Drews, D. R. (1991). Rule structure in the psychological representation of physical settings. *Journal of Experimental Social Psychology, 27,* 217–238.

Bushman, B. J., & Baumeister, R. F. (1998). Threatened egotism, narcissism, self-esteem, and direct and displaced aggression: Does self-love or self-hate lead to violence? *Journal of Personality and Social Psychology, 75,* 219–229.

Bushman, B. J., Baumeister, R. F., & Phillips, C. M. (2001). Do people aggress to improve their mood? Catharsis beliefs, affect regulation opportunity, and aggressive responding. *Journal of Personality and Social Psychology, 81,* 17–32.

Buss, A. H. (1983). Social rewards and personality. *Journal of Personality and Social Psychology, 44,* 553–563.

Buss, A. H., & Plomin, R. (1975). *A temperament theory of personality development.* New York, NY: Wiley-Interscience.

Buss, A. H., & Plomin, R. (1984). *Temperament: Early developing personality traits.* Hillsdale, NJ: Erlbaum.

Buss, D. M. (1984). Toward a psychology of person-environment correlation: The role of spouse selection. *Journal of Personality and Social Psychology, 47,* 361–377.

Buss, D. M. (1985). Human mate selection. *American Scientist, 73,* 47–51.

Buss, D. M. (1988). The evolution of human intrasexual competition: Tactics of mate attraction. *Journal of Personality and Social Psychology, 54,* 616–628.

Buss, D. M. (1989). Sex differences in human mate preferences: Evolutionary hypotheses tested in 37 cultures. *Behavioral and Brain Sciences, 12,* 1–49.

Buss, D. M. (1991). Evolutionary personality psychology. *Annual Review of Psychology, 42,* 459–491.

Buss, D. M. (1994a). *The evolution of desire: Strategies of human mating.* New York, NY: Basic Books.

Buss, D. M. (1994b). The strategies of human mating. *American Scientist, 82,* 238–249.

Buss, D. M. (1995). Evolutionary psychology: A new paradigm for psychological science. *Psychological Inquiry, 6,* 1–30.

Buss, D. M. (2001). Cognitive biases and emotional wisdom in the evolution of conflict between the sexes. *Current Directions in Psychological Science, 10,* 219–223.

Buss, D. M. (2005). *The murderer next door: Why the mind is designed to kill.* New York, NY: Penguin Press.

Buss, D. M., Gomes, M., Higgins, D. S., & Lauterbach, K. (1987). Tactics of manipulation. *Journal of Personality and Social Psychology, 52,* 1219–1229.

Buss, D. M., Larsen, R. J., Westen, D., & Semmelroth, J. (1992). Sex differences in jealousy: Evolution, physiology, and psychology. *Psychological Science, 3,* 251–255.

Buss, D. M., & Schmitt, D. P. (1993). Sexual strategies theory: An evolutionary perspective on human mating. *Psychological Review, 100,* 204–232.

Buss, D. M., & Shackelford, T. K. (1997). From vigilance to violence: Mate retention tactics in married couples. *Journal of Personality and Social Psychology, 72,* 346–361.

Butcher, J. N. (Ed.). (1996). *International adaptations of the MMPI-2: Research and clinical applications.* Minneapolis, MN: University of Minnesota Press.

Butcher, J. N., Dahlstrom, W., Graham, J., Tellegen, A., & Kaemmer, B. (1989). *Manual for administering and scoring the MMPI-2.* Minneapolis, MN: University of Minnesota Press.

Butzer, B., & Campbell, L. (2008). Adult attachment, sexual satisfaction, and relationship satisfaction: A study of married couples. *Personal Relationships, 15,* 141–154.

Byrne, D., McDonald, R. D., & Mikawa, J. (1963). Approach and avoidance affiliation motives. *Journal of Personality, 31,* 21–37.

Cacioppo, J. T., & Petty, R. E. (1980). The effects of orienting task on differential hemispheric EEG activation. *Neuropsychologia, 18,* 675–683.

Cadinu, M., Maass, A., Rosabianca, A., & Kiesner, J. (2005). Why do women underperform under stereotype threat? Evidence for the role of negative thinking. *Psychological Science, 16,* 572–578.

Cain, D. J., & Seeman, J. (Eds.). (2002). *Humanistic psychotherapies: Handbook of research and practice.* Washington, DC: American Psychological Association.

Cambron, M. J., & Acitelli, L. K. (2010). Examining the link between friendship contingent self-esteem and the self-propagating cycle of depression. *Journal of Social and Clinical Psychology, 29,* 701–726.

Cambron, M. J., Acitelli, L. K., & Steinburg, L. (2010). When friends make you blue: The role of friendship contingent self-esteem in predicting self-esteem and depressive symptoms. *Personality and Social Psychology Bulletin, 36,* 384–397.

Cameron, O. G., Abelson, J. L., & Young, E. A. (2004). Anxious and depressive disorders and their comorbidity: Effect on central nervous system noradrenergic function. *Biological Psychiatry, 56,* 875–883.

Campbell, D. T. (1960). Recommendations for the APA test standards regarding construct, trait, and discriminant validity. *American Psychologist, 15,* 546–553.

Campbell, D. T., & Fiske, D. W. (1959). Convergent and discriminant validation by the multitrait-multimethod matrix. *Psychological Bulletin, 56,* 81–105.

Campbell, W. K. (1999). Narcissism and romantic attraction. *Journal of Personality and Social Psychology, 77,* 1254–1270.

Campbell, W. K., & Foster, C. A. (2002). Narcissism and commitment in romantic relationships: An investment model analysis. *Personality and Social Psychology Bulletin, 28,* 484–495.

Cannon, W. B. (1932). *The wisdom of the body.* New York, NY: Norton.

Cantor, N., & Mischel, W. (1977). Traits as prototypes: Effects on recognition memory. *Journal of Personality and Social Psychology, 35,* 38–48.

Caporael, L. R. (2001). Evolutionary psychology: Toward a unifying theory and a hybrid science. *Annual Review of Psychology, 52,* 607–628.

Carey, G. (2003). *Human genetics for the social sciences.* Thousand Oaks, CA: Sage.

Carlston, D. E., & Skowronski, J. J. (1994). Savings in the relearning of trait information as evidence for spontaneous inference generation. *Journal of Personality and Social Psychology, 66,* 840–856.

Carnagey, N. L., & Anderson, C. A. (2005). The effects of reward and punishment in violent video games on aggressive affect, cognition, and behavior. *Psychological Science, 16,* 882–889.

Carnagey, N. L., Anderson, C. A., & Bushman, B. J. (2007). The effect of video game violence on physiological desensitization to real life violence. *Journal of Experimental Social Psychology, 43,* 489–496.

Carnelley, K. B., Pietromonaco, P. R., & Jaffe, K. (1994). Depression, working models of others, and relationship functioning. *Journal of Personality and Social Psychology, 66,* 127–140.

Carroll, L. (1987). A study of narcissism, affiliation, intimacy, and power motives among students in business administration. *Psychological Reports, 61,* 355–358.

Carter, B. L., & Tiffany, S. T. (1999). Meta-analysis of cue reactivity in addiction research. *Addiction, 94,* 327–340.

Carter, C. S. (1998). Neuroendocrine perspectives on social attachment and love. *Psychoneuroimmunology, 23,* 779–818.

Carver, C. S. (1975). Physical aggression as a function of objective self-awareness and attitudes toward punishment. *Journal of Experimental Social Psychology, 11,* 510–519.

Carver, C. S. (1997). Adult attachment and personality: Converging evidence and a new measure. *Personality and Social Psychology Bulletin, 23,* 865–883.

Carver, C. S. (1998). Generalization, adverse events, and development of depressive symptoms. *Journal of Personality, 66,* 609–620.

Carver, C. S. (2003). Pleasure as a sign you can attend to something else: Placing positive feelings within a general model of affect. *Cognition and Emotion, 17,* 241-261.

Carver, C. S. (2004). Negative affects deriving from the behavioral approach system. *Emotion, 4,* 3–22.

Carver, C. S. (2005). Impulse and constraint: Perspectives from personality psychology, convergence with theory in other areas, and potential for integration. *Personality and Social Psychology Review, 9,* 312–333.

Carver, C. S., & Baird, E. (1998). The American dream revisited: Is it *what* you want or *why* you want it that matters? *Psychological Science, 9,* 289–292.

Carver, C. S., Ganellen, R. J., Froming, W. J., & Chambers, W. (1983). Modeling: An analysis in terms of category accessibility. *Journal of Experimental Social Psychology, 19,* 403–421.

Carver, C. S., & Harmon-Jones, E. (2009). Anger is an approach-related affect: Evidence and implications. *Psychological Bulletin, 135,* 183–204.

Carver, C. S., Johnson, S. L., & Joormann, J. (2008). Serotonergic function, two-mode models of self-regulation, and vulnerability to depression: What depression has in common with impulsive aggression. *Psychological Bulletin, 134*, 912–943.

Carver, C. S., Johnson, S. L., & Joormann, J. (2009). Two-mode models of self-regulation as a tool for conceptualizing effects of the serotonergic system in normal behavior and diverse disorders. *Current Directions in Psychological Science, 18*, 195–199.

Carver, C. S., Johnson, S. L., Joormann, J., Kim, Y., & Nam, J. Y. (2011). Serotonin transporter polymorphism interacts with childhood adversity to predict aspects of impulsivity. *Psychological Science, 22*, in press.

Carver, C. S., Kus, L. A., & Scheier, M. F. (1994). Effects of good versus bad mood and optimistic versus pessimistic outlook on social acceptance versus rejection. *Journal of Social and Clinical Psychology, 13*, 138–151.

Carver, C. S., LaVoie, L., Kuhl, J., & Ganellen, R. J. (1988). Cognitive concomitants of depression: A further examination of the roles of generalization, high standards, and self-criticism. *Journal of Social and Clinical Psychology, 7*, 350–365.

Carver, C. S., Lawrence, J. W., & Scheier, M. F. (1999). Self-discrepancies and affect: Incorporating the role of feared selves. *Personality and Social Psychology Bulletin, 25*, 783–792.

Carver, C. S., Lehman, J. M., & Antoni, M. H. (2003). Dispositional pessimism predicts illness-related disruption of social and recreational activities among breast cancer patients. *Journal of Personality and Social Psychology, 84*, 813–821.

Carver, C. S., & Miller, C. J. (2006). Relations of serotonin function to personality: Current views and a key methodological issue. *Psychiatry Research, 144*, 1–15.

Carver, C. S., Pozo, C., Harris, S. D., Noriega, V., Scheier, M. F., Robinson, D. S., Ketcham, A. S., Moffat, F. L., & Clark, K. C. (1993). How coping mediates the effect of optimism on distress: A study of women with early stage breast cancer. *Journal of Personality and Social Psychology, 65*, 375–390.

Carver, C. S., & Scheier, M. F. (1981). *Attention and self-regulation: A control-theory approach to human behavior.* New York, NY: Springer-Verlag.

Carver, C. S., & Scheier, M. F. (1990). Principles of self-regulation: Action and emotion. In E. T. Higgins & R. M. Sorrentino (Eds.), *Handbook of motivation and cognition: Foundations of social behavior* (Vol. 2, pp. 3–52). New York, NY: Guilford Press.

Carver, C. S., & Scheier, M. F. (1998). *On the self-regulation of behavior.* New York, NY: Cambridge University Press.

Carver, C. S., & Scheier, M. F. (2002). Control processes and self-organization as complementary principles underlying behavior. *Personality and Social Psychology Review, 6*, 304–315.

Carver, C. S., & Scheier, M. F. (2007). Feedback processes in the simultaneous regulation of action and affect. In J. Y. Shah & W. L. Gardner (Eds.), *Handbook of motivation science.* New York, NY: Guilford Press.

Carver, C. S., Scheier, M. F., & Segerstrom, S. C. (2010). Optimism. *Clinical Psychology Review, 30,* 879–889.

Carver, C. S., & White, T. L. (1994). Behavioral inhibition, behavioral activation, and affective responses to impending reward and punishment: The BIS/BAS scales. *Journal of Personality and Social Psychology, 67*, 319–333.

Casey, B. J., Giedd, J. N., & Thomas, K. M. (2000). Structural and functional brain development and its relation to cognitive development. *Biological Psychology, 54*, 241–257.

Caspar, F., Rothenfluh, T., & Segal, Z. (1992). The appeal of connectionism to clinical psychology. *Clinical Psychology Review, 12*, 719–762.

Caspi, A., Hariri, A. R., Holmes, A., Uher, R., & Moffitt, T. E. (2010). Genetic sensitivity to the environment: The case of the serotonin transporter gene and its implications for studying complex diseases and traits. *American Journal of Psychiatry, 167*, 509–527.

Caspi, A., & Herbener, E. S. (1990). Continuity and change: Assortative marriage and the consistency of personality in adulthood. *Journal of Personality and Social Psychology, 58*, 250–258.

Caspi, A., McClay, J., Moffitt, T. E., Mill, J., Martin, J., Craig, I. W., Taylor, A., & Poulton, R. (2002). Role of genotype in the cycle of violence in maltreated children. *Science, 297*, 851–854.

Caspi, A., Roberts, B. W., & Shiner, R. L. (2005). Personality development: Stability and change. *Annual Review of Psychology, 56*, 453–484.

Cassidy, J., & Shaver, P. R. (Eds.). (1999). *Handbook of attachment: Theory, research, and clinical applications.* New York, NY: Guilford Press.

Cattell, H. E. P. (1993). Comment on Goldberg. *American Psychologist, 48*, 1302–1303.

Cattell, R. B. (1947). Confirmation and clarification of primary personality factors. *Psychometrica, 12*, 197–220.

Cattell, R. B. (1965). *The scientific analysis of personality.* Baltimore, MD: Penguin Press.

Cattell, R. B. (1978). *The scientific use of factor analysis.* New York, NY: Plenum Press.

Cattell, R. B. (1979). *Personality and learning theory, Volume 1. The structure of personality in its environment.* New York, NY: Springer.

Cattell, R. B., Eber, H. W., & Tatsuoka, M. M. (1977). *Handbook for the 16 personality factor questionnaire.* Champaign, IL: IPAT.

Cattell, R. B., & Kline, P. (1977). *The scientific analysis of personality and motivation.* New York, NY: Academic Press.

Cervone, D. (1997). Social-cognitive mechanisms and personality coherence: Self-knowledge, situational beliefs, and cross-situational coherence in perceived self-efficacy. *Psychological Science, 8,* 43–50.

Cervone, D. (2004). The architecture of personality. *Psychological Review, 111,* 183–204.

Chamorro-Premuzic, T., & Furnham, A. (2003). Personality predicts academic performance: Evidence from two longitudinal university samples. *Journal of Research in Personality, 37,* 319–338.

Champagne, F. A., & Mashoodh, R. (2009). Genes in context: Gene-environment interplay and the origins of individual differences in behavior. *Current Directions in Psychological Science, 18,* 127–131.

Chance, S. E., Brown, R. T., Dabbs, J. M., Jr., & Casey, R. (2000). Testosterone, intelligence and behavior disorders in young boys. *Personality and Individual Differences, 28,* 437–445.

Chaplin, W. F., Phillips, J. B., Brown, J. D., Clanton, N. R., & Stein, J. L. (2000). Handshaking, gender, personality, and first impressions. *Journal of Personality and Social Psychology, 79,* 110–117.

Chapman, L. J. (1967). Illusory correlations in observational report. *Journal of Verbal Learning and Verbal Behavior, 6,* 151–155.

Chartrand, T. L., & Bargh, J. A. (1996). Automatic activation of impression formation and memorization goals: Nonconscious goal priming reproduces effects of explicit task instructions. *Journal of Personality and Social Psychology, 71,* 464–478.

Chartrand, T. L., & Bargh, J. A. (1999). The chameleon effect: The perception–behavior link and social interaction. *Journal of Personality and Social Psychology, 76,* 893–910.

Chassin, L., Flora, D. B., & King, K. M. (2004). Trajectories of alcohol and drug use and dependence from adolescence to adulthood: The effects of familial alcoholism and personality. *Journal of Abnormal Psychology, 113,* 483–498.

Chatterjee, B. B., & Eriksen, C. W. (1962). Cognitive factors in heart rate conditioning. *Journal of Experimental Psychology, 64,* 272–279.

Chen, E., & Matthews, K. A. (2001). Cognitive appraisal biases: An approach to understanding the relation between socioeconomic status and cardiovascular reactivity in children. *Annals of Behavioral Medicine, 23,* 101–111.

Chen, S. (2003). Psychological-state theories about significant others: Implications for the content and structure of significant-other representations. *Personality and Social Psychology Bulletin, 29,* 1285–1302.

Cheung, R. M., & Hardin, C. D. (2010). Costs and benefits of political ideology: The case of economic self-stereotyping and stereotype threat. *Journal of Experimental Social Psychology, 46,* 761–766.

Christensen, A. J., Ehlers, S. L., Wiebe, J. S., Moran, P. J., Raichle, K., Ferneyhough, K., & Lawton, W. J. (2002). Patient personality and mortality: A 4-year prospective examination of chronic renal insufficiency. *Health Psychology, 21,* 315–320.

Chung, B. G., Ehrhart, M. G., Ehrhart, K. H., Hattrup, K., & Solamon, J. (2010). Stereotype threat, state anxiety, and specific self-efficacy as predictors of promotion exam performance. *Group & Organization Management, 35,* 77–107.

Church, A. T. (Ed.). (2001). Introduction: Culture and personality [Special issue]. *Journal of Personality, 69,* 787–801.

Church, A. T., & Burke, P. J. (1994). Exploratory and confirmatory tests of the big five and Tellegen's three- and four-dimensional models. *Journal of Personality and Social Psychology, 66,* 93–114.

Ciminero, A. R., Calhoun, K. S., & Adams, H. E. (Eds.). (1977). *Handbook of behavioral assessment.* New York, NY: Wiley.

Claridge, G. S. (1967). *Personality and arousal.* New York, NY: Pergamon Press.

Clark, L. A. (2007). Assessment and diagnosis of personality disorder: Perennial issues and an emerging reconceptualization. *Annual Review of Psychology, 58,* 227–257.

Clark, L. A., Kochanska, G., & Ready, R. (2000). Mothers' personality and its interaction with child temperament as predictors of parenting behavior. *Journal of Personality and Social Psychology, 79,* 274–285.

Clark, L. A., & Watson, D. (1999). Temperament: A new paradigm for trait psychology. In L. A. Pervin & O. P. John (Eds.), *Handbook of personality: Theory and research* (2nd ed., pp. 399–423). New York, NY: Guilford Press.

Clark, R. A., & McClelland, D. C. (1956). A factor-analytic integration of imaginative and performance measures of the need for achievement. *Journal of General Psychology, 55,* 73–83.

Clark, R. D., & Hatfield, E. (1989). Gender differences in receptivity to sexual offers. *Journal of Psychology and Human Sexuality, 2,* 39–55.

Clark, W. R. (1996). *Sex and the origins of death*. New York, NY: Oxford University Press.

Cleare, A. J., & Bond, A. J. (1995). The effect of tryptophan depletion and enhancement on subjective and behavioural aggression in normal male subjects. *Psychopharmacology, 118,* 72–81.

Cleare, A. J., & Bond, A. J. (1997). Does central serotonergic function correlate inversely with aggression? A study using D-fenfluramine in healthy subjects. *Psychiatry Research, 69,* 89–95.

Cloninger, C. R. (1987). A systematic method of clinical description and classification of personality variants: A proposal. *Archives of General Psychiatry, 44,* 573–588.

Cloninger, C. R. (1988). A unified biosocial theory of personality and its role in the development of anxiety states: A reply to commentaries. *Psychiatric Developments, 2,* 83–120.

Clower, C. E., & Bothwell, R. K. (2001). An exploratory study of the relationship between the Big Five and inmate recidivism. *Journal of Research in Personality, 35,* 231–237.

Coccaro, E. F., Kavoussi, R. J., Cooper, T. B., & Hauger, R. L. (1997). Central serotonin activity and aggression: Inverse relationship with prolactin response to *d*-fenfluramine, but not CSF 5-HIAA concentration, in human subjects. *American Journal of Psychiatry, 154,* 1430–1435.

Cohen, D., Nisbett, R. E., Bowdle, B. F., & Schwarz, N. (1996). Insult, aggression, and the Southern culture of honor: An "experimental ethnology." *Journal of Personality and Social Psychology, 70,* 945–960.

Cohen-Bendahan, C. C. C., van de Beek, C., & Berenbaum, S. A. (2005). Prenatal sex hormone effects on child and adult sex-typed behavior: Methods and findings. *Neuroscience and Biobehavioral Reviews, 29,* 353–384.

Cole, S. W. (2009). Social regulation of human gene expression. *Current Directions in Psychological Science, 18,* 132–137.

Collins, N. L., Ford, M. B., Guichard, A. C., & Feeney, B. C. (2006). Responding to need in intimate relationships: Normative processes and individual differences. In M. Mikulincer & G. Goodman (Eds.), *The dynamics of love: Attachment, caregiving, and sex* (pp. 149–189). New York, NY: Guilford Press.

Collins, N. L., & Read, S. J. (1990). Adult attachment, working models, and relationship quality in dating couples. *Journal of Personality and Social Psychology, 58,* 644–663.

Conklin, C. A. (2006). Environments as cues to smoke: Implications for human extinction-based research and treatment. *Experimental and Clinical Psychopharmacology, 14,* 12–19.

Conklin, C. A., Perkins, K. A., Robin, N., McClernon, F. J., & Salkeld, R. P. (2010). Bringing the real world into the laboratory: Personal smoking and nonsmoking environments. *Drug and Alcohol Dependence, 111,* 58–63.

Conklin, C. A., Robin, N., Perkins, K. A., Salkeld, R. P., & McClernon, F. J. (2008). Proximal versus distal cues to smoke: The effects of environments on smokers' cue-reactivity. *Experimental and Clinical Psychopharmacology, 16,* 207–214.

Conklin, C. A., & Tiffany, S. T. (2001). The impact of imagining personalized versus standardized urge scenarios on cigarette craving and autonomic reactivity. *Experimental and Clinical Psychopharmacology, 9,* 399–408.

Conklin, C. A., & Tiffany, S. T. (2002). Applying extinction research and theory to cue-exposure addiction treatments. *Addiction, 97,* 155–167.

Conley, J. J. (1985). Longitudinal stability of personality traits: A multitrait-multimethod-multioccasion analysis. *Journal of Personality and Social Psychology, 49,* 1266–1282.

Conner, T., & Barrett, L. F. (2005). Implicit self-attitudes predict spontaneous affect in daily life. *Emotion, 5,* 476–488.

Conner, T. S., Tennen, H., Fleeson, W., & Barrett, L. F. (2009). Experience sampling methods: A modern idiographic approach to personality research. *Social and Psychology Compass, 3,* 292–313.

Constantian, C. A. (1981). Attitudes, beliefs, and behavior in regard to spending time alone. Unpublished doctoral dissertation, Harvard University, Cambridge, MA.

Converse, J., & Presser, S. (1986). *Survey questions: Handcrafting the standardized questionnaire*. Newbury Park, CA: Sage.

Conway, M., & Giannopoulos, C. (1993). Dysphoria and decision making: Limited information use for evaluations of multiattribute targets. *Journal of Personality and Social Psychology, 64,* 613–623.

Cook, K. F., O'Malley, K. J., & Roddey, T. S. (2005). Dynamic assessment of health outcomes: Time to let the CAT out of the bag? *Health Services Research, 40,* 1694–1711.

Cook, M. L., & Peterson, C. (1986). Depressive irrationality. *Cognitive Therapy and Research, 10,* 293–298.

Cook, W. L. (2000). Understanding attachment security in a family context. *Journal of Personality and Social Psychology, 78,* 285–294.

Cooley, E. J., & Spiegler, M. D. (1980). Cognitive versus emotional coping responses as alternatives to test anxiety. *Cognitive Therapy and Research, 4*, 159–166.

Corr, P. J., Pickering, A. D., & Gray, J. A. (1997). Personality, punishment, and procedural learning: A test of J. A. Gray's anxiety theory. *Journal of Personality and Social Psychology, 73*, 337–344.

Costa, P. T., Jr., & McCrae, R. R. (1985). *The NEO Personality Inventory manual.* Odessa, FL: Psychological Assessment Resources.

Costa, P. T., Jr., & McCrae, R. R. (1988a). From catalog to classification: Murray's needs and the five-factor model. *Journal of Personality and Social Psychology, 55*, 258–265.

Costa, P. T., Jr., & McCrae, R. R. (1988b). Personality in adulthood: A six-year longitudinal study of self-reports and spouse ratings on the NEO personality inventory. *Journal of Personality and Social Psychology, 54*, 853–863.

Costa, P. T., Jr., & McCrae, R. R. (1989). Personality continuity and the changes of adult life. In M. Storandt & G. R. VandenBos (Eds.), *The adult years: Continuity and change* (pp. 45–77). Washington, DC: American Psychological Association.

Costa, P. T., Jr., & McCrae, R. R. (1992). *Revised NEO Personality Inventory (NEO-PI-R) and NEO Five-Factor Inventory (NEO-FFI) professional manual.* Odessa, FL: Psychological Assessment Resources.

Costa, P. T., Jr., & McCrae, R. R. (1995). Domains and facets: Hierarchical personality assessment using the revised NEO Pesonality Inventory. *Journal of Personality Assessment, 64*, 21–50.

Costa, P. T., Jr., & Widiger, T. A. (Eds.). (2002). *Personality disorders and the five-factor model of personality* (2nd ed.). Washington, DC: American Psychological Association.

Couch, A., & Keniston, K. (1960). Yeasayers and naysayers: Agreeing response set as a personality variable. *Journal of Abnormal and Social Psychology, 60*, 151–174.

Craighead, W. E., Kazdin, A. E., & Mahoney, M. J. (1981). *Behavior modification: Principles, issues, and applications.* Boston, MA: Houghton Mifflin.

Cramer, P. (2000). Defense mechanisms in psychology today: Further processes for adaptation. *American Psychologist, 55*, 637–646.

Crawford, C. B. (1989). The theory of evolution: Of what value to psychology? *Journal of Comparative Psychology, 103*, 4–22.

Crawford, C. B., Smith, M. S., & Krebs, D. (Eds.). (1987). *Sociobiology and psychology: Ideas, issues and applications.* Hillsdale, NJ: Erlbaum.

Crawford, L. E., & Cacioppo, J. T. (2002). Learning where to look for danger: Integrating affective and spatial information. *Psychological Science, 13*, 449–453.

Crews, F. (1996). The verdict on Freud. *Psychological Science, 7*, 63.

Crick, N. R., & Dodge, K. A. (1994). A review and reformulation of social information-processing mechanisms in children's social adjustment. *Psychological Bulletin, 115*, 74–101.

Cristóbal-Azkarate, J., Chavira, R., Boeck, L., Rodríguez-Luna, E., & Veàl, J. J. (2006). Testosterone levels of free-ranging resident mantled howler monkey males in relation to the number and density of solitary males: A test of the challenge hypothesis. *Hormones and Behavior, 49*, 261–267.

Crittenden, P. M. (1990). Internal representational models of attachment relationships. *Infant Mental Health Journal, 11*, 259–277.

Crocker, J. (1981). Judgment of covariation by social perceivers. *Psychological Bulletin, 90*, 272–292.

Crocker, J., & Knight, K. M. (2005). Contingencies of self-worth. *Current Directions in Psychological Science. 14*, 200–203.

Crocker, J., Luhtanen, R. K., Cooper, M. L., & Bouvrette, A. (2003). Contingencies of self-worth in college students: Theory and measurement. *Journal of Personality and Social Psychology, 85*, 894–908.

Crocker, J., & Park, L. E. (2004). The costly pursuit of self-esteem. *Psychological Bulletin, 130*, 392–414.

Crocker, J., & Wolfe, C. T. (2001). Contingencies of self-worth. *Psychological Review, 108*, 593–623.

Cronbach, L. J., & Meehl, P. E. (1955). Construct validity in psychological tests. *Psychological Bulletin, 52*, 281–302.

Crouse, B. B., & Mehrabian, A. (1977). Affiliation of opposite-sexed strangers. *Journal of Research in Personality, 11*, 38–47.

Crowne, D. P., & Marlowe, D. (1964). *The approval motive: Studies in evaluative dependence.* New York, NY: Wiley.

Csikszentmihalyi, M. (1975). *Beyond boredom and anxiety.* San Francisco, CA: Jossey-Bass.

Csikszentmihalyi, M. (1978). Attention and the holistic approach to behavior. In K. S. Pope & J. L. Singer (Eds.), *The stream of consciousness: Scientific investigations into the flow of human experience.* New York, NY: Plenum Press.

Csikszentmihalyi, M. (1990). *Flow: The psychology of optimal experience.* New York, NY: Harper & Row.

Csikszentmihalyi, M., & Csikszentmihalyi, I. S. (Eds.). (1988). *Optimal experience: Psychological studies of flow in consciousness.* New York, NY: Cambridge University Press.

Csikszentimihalyi, M., & LeFevre, J. (1989). Optimal experience in work and leisure. *Journal of Personality and Social Psychology, 56,* 815–822.

Cunningham, M. R., Barbee, A. P., & Pike, C. L. (1990). What do women want? Facialmetric assessment of multiple motives in the perception of male facial physical attractiveness. *Journal of Personality and Social Psychology, 59,* 61–72.

Custers, R, & Aarts, H. (2007). Goal-discrepant situations prime goal-directed actions if goals are temporarily or chronically accessible. *Personality and Social Psychology Bulletin, 33,* 623–633.

Cutter, H. S. G., Boyatzis, R. E., & Clancy, D. D. (1977). The effectiveness of power motivation training in rehabilitating alcoholics. *Journal of Studies on Alcohol, 38,* 131–141.

Cyders, M. A., Smith, G. T., Spillane, N. S., Fischer, S., Annus, A. M., & Peterson, C. (2007). Integration of impulsivity and positive mood to predict risky behavior: Development and validation of a measure of positive urgency. *Psychological Assessment, 19,* 107–118.

Dabbs, J. M., Jr. (1992a). Testosterone and occupational achievement. *Social Forces, 70,* 813–824.

Dabbs, J. M., Jr. (1992b). Testosterone measurements in social and clinical psychology. *Journal of Social and Clinical Psychology, 11,* 302–321.

Dabbs, J. M., Jr. (1997). Testosterone, smiling, and facial appearance. *Journal of Nonverbal Behavior, 21,* 45–55.

Dabbs, J. M., Jr. (1998). Testosterone and the concept of dominance. *Behavioral and Brain Sciences, 21,* 370–371.

Dabbs, J. M., Jr., Alford, E. C., & Fielden, J. A. (1998). Trial lawyers: Blue collar talent in a white collar world. *Journal of Applied Social Psychology, 28,* 84–94.

Dabbs, J. M., Jr., Bernieri, F. J., Strong, R. K., Campo, R., & Milun, R. (2001). Going on stage: Testosterone in greetings and meetings. *Journal of Research in Personality, 35,* 27–40.

Dabbs, J. M., Jr., & Dabbs, M. G. (2000). *Heroes, rogues and lovers: Testosterone and behavior.* New York, NY: McGraw-Hill.

Dabbs, J. M., Jr., de La Rue, D., & Williams, P. M. (1990). Testosterone and occupational choice: Actors, ministers, and other men. *Journal of Personality and Social Psychology, 59,* 1261–1265.

Dabbs, J. M., Jr., Frady, R. L., Carr, T. S., & Besch, N. F. (1987). Saliva testosterone and criminal violence in young adult prison inmates. *Psychosomatic Medicine, 49,* 174–182.

Dabbs, J. M., Jr., Hargrove, M. F., & Heusel, C. (1996). Testosterone differences among college fraternities:

Well-behaved vs. rambunctious. *Personality and Individual Differences, 290,* 157–161.

Dabbs, J. M., Jr., & Mallinger, A. (1999). High testosterone levels predict low voice pitch among men. *Personality and Individual Differences, 27,* 801–804.

Dabbs, J. M., Jr., & Mohammed, S. (1992). Male and female salivary testosterone concentrations before and after sexual activity. *Physiology and Behavior, 52,* 195–197.

Dabbs, J. M., Jr., & Morris, R. (1990). Testosterone, social class, and antisocial behavior in a sample of 4,462 men. *Psychological Science, 1,* 209–211.

Dabbs, J. M., Jr., Riad, J. K., & Chance, S. E. (2001). Testosterone and ruthless homicide. *Personality and Individual Differences, 31,* 599–603.

Dabbs, J. M., Jr., Ruback, R. B., Frady, R. L., Hopper, C. H., & Sgoutas, D. S. (1988). Saliva testosterone and criminal violence among women. *Personality and Individual Differences, 9,* 269–275.

Daitzman, R., & Zuckerman, M. (1980). Disinhibitory sensation seeking, personality and gonadal hormones. *Personality and Individual Differences, 1,* 103–110.

Daly, M., & Wilson, M. I. (1988). *Homicide.* New York, NY: Aldine de Gruyter.

Daly, M., & Wilson, M. I. (1990). Killing the competition: Female/female and male/male homicide. *Human Nature, 1,* 81–107.

Daly, M., & Wilson, M. I. (1996). Violence agianst stepchildren. *Current Directions in Psychological Science, 5,* 77–81.

Daniels, D. (1986). Differential experiences of siblings in the same family as predictors of adolescent sibling personality differences. *Journal of Personality and Social Psychology, 51,* 339–346.

Daniels, D., & Plomin, R. (1985). Differential experience of siblings in the same family. *Developmental Psychology, 21,* 747–760.

Davidson, R. J. (1988). EEG measures of cerebral asymmetry: Conceptual and methodological issues. *International Journal of Neuroscience, 39,* 71–89.

Davidson, R. J. (1992). Prolegomenon to the structure of emotion: Gleanings from neuropsychology. *Cognition and Emotion, 6,* 245–268.

Davidson, R. J. (1995). Cerebral asymmetry, emotion, and affective style. In R. J. Davidson & K. Hugdahl (Eds.), *Brain asymmetry* (pp. 361–387). Cambridge, MA: MIT Press.

Davidson, R. J., Ekman, P., Saron, C. D., Senulis, J. A., & Friesen, W. V. (1990). Approach–withdrawal and cerebral asymmetry: Emotional expression and brain physiology I. *Journal of Personality and Social Psychology, 58,* 330–341.

Davidson, R. J., Jackson, D. C., & Kalin, N. H. (2000). Emotion, plasticity, context, and regulation: Perspectives from affective neuroscience. *Psychological Bulletin, 126,* 890–909.

Davidson, R. J., Pizzagalli, D., Nitschke, J. B., & Putnam, K. (2002). Depression: Perspectives from affective neuroscience. *Annual Review of Psychology, 53,* 545–574.

Davidson, R. J., & Sutton, S. K. (1995). Affective neuroscience: The emergence of a discipline. *Current Opinion in Neurobiology, 5,* 217–224.

Davila, J., Burge, D., & Hammen, C. (1997). Why does attachment style change? *Journal of Personality and Social Psychology, 73,* 826–838.

Davis, D., Shaver, P. R., & Vernon, M. L. (2003). Physical, emotional, and behavioral reactions to breaking up: The roles of gender, age, emotional involvement, and attachment style. *Personality and Social Psychology Bulletin, 29,* 871–884.

Davis, T. E., Ollendick, T. H., & Öst, L. (2009). Intensive treatment of specific phobias in children and adolescents. *Cognitive and Behavioral Practice, 16,* 294–303.

Davison, G. C., & Wilson, G. T. (1973). Processes of fear reduction in systematic desensitization: Cognitive and social reinforcement factors in humans. *Behavior Therapy, 4,* 1–21.

Daw, N. D., Niv, Y., & Dayan, P. (2005). Uncertainty-based competition between prefrontal and dorsolateral striatal systems for behavioral control. *Nature Neuroscience, 8,* 1704–1711.

Dawkins, R. (1976). *The selfish gene.* New York, NY: Oxford University Press.

Dawson, M. E., & Furedy, J. J. (1976). The role of awareness in human differential autonomic classical conditioning: The necessary-gate hypothesis. *Psychophysiology, 13,* 50–53.

Dawson, M. E., Rissling, A. J., Schell, A. M., & Wilcox, R. (2007). Under what conditions can human affective conditioning occur without contingency awareness? Test of the evaluative conditioning paradigm. *Emotion, 7,* 755–766.

Dawson, M. R. W. (2004). *Minds and machines.* Walden, MA: Blackwell.

Dawson, M. R. W. (2005). *Connectionism: A hands-on approach.* Malden, MA: Blackwell.

De Houwer, J., Thomas, S., & Baeyens, F. (2001). Associative learning of likes and dislikes: A review of 25 years of research on human evaluative conditioning. *Psychological Bulletin, 127,* 853–869.

de Maat, S., Philipszoon, F., Schoevers, R., Dekker, J., & De Jonghe, F. (2007). Costs and benefits of long-term psychoanalytic therapy: Changes in health care use and work impairment. *Harvard Review of Psychiatry, 15,* 289–300.

De Neys, W. (2006). Dual processing in reasoning: Two systems but one reasoner. *Psychological Science, 17,* 428–433.

de St. Aubin, E., McAdams, D. P., & Kim, T. (2004). *The generative society: Caring for future generations.* Washington, DC: American Psychological Association.

Deci, E. L. (1975). *Intrinsic motivation.* New York, NY: Plenum Press.

Deci, E. L., Koestner, R., & Ryan, R. M. (1999). A meta-analytic review of experiments examining the effects of extrinsic rewards on intrinsic motivation. *Psychological Bulletin, 125,* 627–668.

Deci, E. L., La Guardia, J. G., Moller, A. C., Scheiner, M. J., & Ryan, R. M. (2006). On the benefits of giving as well as receiving autonomy support: Mutuality in close friendships. *Personality and Social Psychology Bulletin, 32,* 313–327.

Deci, E. L., & Ryan, R. M. (1980). The empirical exploration of intrinsic motivational processes. In L. Berkowitz (Ed.), *Advances in experimental social psychology* (Vol. 13). New York, NY: Academic Press.

Deci, E. L., & Ryan, R. M. (1985). *Intrinsic motivation and self-determination in human behavior.* New York, NY: Plenum Press.

Deci, E. L., & Ryan, R. M. (1991). A motivational approach to self: Integration in personality. In R. Dienstbier (Ed.), *Nebraska symposium on motivation: Perspectives on motivation* (Vol. 38, pp. 237–288). Lincoln, NE: University of Nebraska Press.

Deci, E. L., & Ryan, R. M. (2000). The "what" and "why" of goal pursuits: Human needs and the self-determination of behavior. *Psychological Inquiry, 11,* 227–268.

DeHart, T., Pelham, B. W., & Tennen, H. (2006). What lies beneath: Parenting style and implicit self-esteem. *Journal of Experimental Social Psychology, 42,* 1–17.

DeLisi, L. E., Shaw, S. H., Crow, T. J., et al. (2002). A genome-wide scan for linkage to chromosomal regions in 382 sibling pairs with schizophrenia or schizoaffective disorder. *American Journal of Psychiatry, 159,* 803–812.

Deluty, R. H. (1985). Consistency of assertive, aggressive, and submissive behavior for children. *Journal of Personality and Social Psychology, 49,* 1054–1065.

Depue, R. A. (1979). *The psychobiology of the depressive disorders: Implications for the effect of stress.* New York, NY: Academic Press.

Depue, R. A. (1995). Neurobiological factors in personality and depression. *European Journal of Personality, 9,* 413–439.

Depue, R. A., & Collins, P. F. (1999). Neurobiology of the structure of personality: Dopamine, facilitation of incentive motivation, and extraversion. *Behavioral and Brain Sciences, 22*, 491–517.

Depue, R. A., & Iacono, W. G. (1989). Neurobehavioral aspects of affective disorders. *Annual Review of Psychology, 40*, 457–492.

Depue, R. A., Krauss, S. P., & Spoont, M. R. (1987). A two-dimensional threshold model of seasonal bipolar affective disorder. In D. Magnusson & A. Öhman (Eds.), *Psychopathology: An interactional perspective* (pp. 95–123). Orlando, FL: Academic Press.

Depue, R. A., Luciana, M., Arbisi, P., Collins, P., & Leon, A. (1994). Dopamine and the structure of personality: Relation of agonist-induced dopamine cativity to positive emotionality. *Journal of Personality and Social Psychology, 67*, 485–498.

Depue, R. A., & Morrone-Strupinsky, J. V. (2005). A neurobehavioral model of affiliative bonding: Implications for conceptualizing a human trait of affiliation. *Behavioral and Brain Sciences, 28*, 313–395.

Depue, R. A., & Spoont, M. R. (1986). Conceptualizing a serotonin trait: A behavioral dimension of constraint. *Annals of the New York Academy of Sciences, 487*, 47–62.

Derryberry, D., & Rothbart, M. K. (1997). Reactive and effortful processes in the organization of temperament. *Development and Psychopathology, 9*, 633–652.

DeRubeis, R. J., Tang, T. Z., & Beck, A. T. (2001). Cognitive therapy. In Dobson, K. S. (Ed.), *Handbook of cognitive-behavioral therapies* (2nd ed., pp. 349–392). New York, NY: Guilford Press.

DeSteno, D., Bartlett, M. Y., Braverman, J., & Salovey, P. (2002). Sex differences in jealousy: Evolutionary mechanism or artifact of measurement? *Journal of Personality and Social Psychology, 83*, 1103–1116.

Detera-Wadleigh, S. D., Berrettini, W. H., Goldin, L. R., Boorman, D., Anderson, S., & Gershon, E. S. (1987). Close linkage of c-harvey-ras-1 and the insulin gene to affective disorder is ruled out in three North American pedigrees. *Nature, 325*, 806–808.

DeWall, C. N., Twenge, J. M., Gitter, S. A., & Baumeister, R. F. (2009). It's the thought that counts: The role of hostile cognition in shaping aggressive responses to social exclusion. *Journal of Personality and Social Psychology, 96*, 45–59.

DeYoung, C. G. (2006). Higher-order factors of the big five in a multi-informant sample. *Journal of Personality and Social Psychology, 91*, 1138–1151.

DeYoung, C. G., Shamosh, N. A., Green, A. E., Braver, T. S., & Gray, J. R. (2009). Intellect as distinct from openness: Differences revealed by fMRI of working memory. *Journal of Personality and Social Psychology, 97*, 883–892.

DeYoung, C. G., Quilty, L. C., & Peterson, J. B. (2007). Between facets and domains: 10 aspects of the big five. *Journal of Personality and Social Psychology, 93*, 880–896.

Di Blas, L., & Forzi, M. (1999). Refining a descriptive structure of personality attibutes in the Italian language: The abridged big three circumplex structure. *Journal of Personality and Social Psychology, 76*, 451–481.

Dick, D. M., & Rose, R. J. (2002). Behavior genetics: What's new? What's next? *Current Directions in Psychological Science, 11*, 70–74.

Dickens, W. T., & Flynn, J. R. (2001). Heritability estimates versus large environmental effects: The IQ paradox resolved. *Psychological Review, 108*, 346–369.

DiClemente, C. C. (1981). Self-efficacy and smoking cessation. *Cognitive Therapy and Research, 5*, 175–187.

Diener, E. (1979). Deindividuation, self-awareness, and disinhibition. *Journal of Personality and Social Psychology, 37*, 1160–1171.

Digman, J. M. (1990). Personality structure: Emergence of the five-factor model. *Annual Review of Psychology, 41*, 417–440.

Digman, J. M. (1997). Higher-order factors of the Big Five. *Journal of Personality and Social Psychology, 73*, 1246–1256.

Digman, J. M., & Inouye, J. (1986). Further specification of the five robust factors of personality. *Journal of Personality and Social Psychology, 50*, 116–123.

Digman, J. M., & Shmelyov, A. G. (1996). The structure of temperament and personality in Russian children. *Journal of Personality and Social Psychology, 71*, 341–351.

Dijksterhuis, A., & Bargh, J. A. (2001). The perception–behavior expressway. In M. P. Zanna (Ed.), *Advances in experimental social psychology* (Vol. 33, pp. 1–40). San Diego, CA: Academic Press.

Dijkstra, P., & Buunk, B. P. (1998). Jealousy as a function of rival characteristics: An evolutionary perspective. *Personality and Social Psychology Bulletin, 24*, 1158–1166.

DiLalla, L. F., & Gottesman, I. I. (1991). Biological and genetic contributors to violence—Widom's untold tale. *Psychological Bulletin, 109*, 125–129.

Dodge, K. A. (1986). A social information-processing model of social competence in children. In M. Perlmutter (Ed.), *Minnesota symposium on child psychology* (Vol. 18). Hillsdale, NJ: Erlbaum.

Dodge, K. A., & Crick, N. R. (1990). Social information-processing bases of aggressive behavior in children. *Personality and Social Psychology Bulletin, 16*, 8–22.

Domes, G., Heinrichs, M., Michel, A., Berger, C., & Herpertz, S. C. (2007). Oxytocin improves "mind reading" in humans. *Biological Psychiatry, 61*, 731–733.

Donnellan, M. B., Burt, S. A., Levendosky, A. A., & Klump, K. L. (2008). Genes, personality, and attachment in adults: A multivariate behavioral genetic analysis. *Personality and Social Psychology Bulletin, 34*, 3–16.

Donnellan, M. B., Conger, R. D., & Bryant, C. M. (2004). The big five and enduring marriages. *Journal of Research in Personality, 38*, 481–504.

Drabman, R. S., & Spitalnik, R. (1973). Training a retarded child as a behavioral teaching assistant. *Journal of Behavior Therapy and Experimental Psychiatry, 4*, 269–272.

Dreisbach, G., & Goschke, T. (2004). How positive affect modulates cognitive control: Reduced perseveration at the cost of increased distractibility. *Journal of Experimental Psychology: Learning, Memory, and Cognition, 30*, 343–353.

Dulany, D. E. (1968). Awareness, rules and propositional control: A confrontation with S-R behavior theory. In T. R. Dixon & D. L. Horton (Eds.), *Verbal behavior and general behavior theory*. Englewood Cliffs, NJ: Prentice-Hall.

Duncan, L. E., & Peterson, B. E. (2010). Gender and motivation for achievement, affiliation-intimacy, and power. In J. C. Duncan & D. R. McCreary (Eds.), *Handbook of gender research in psychology* (2nd ed., pp. 41–62). New York, NY: Springer.

Dunn, J., & Plomin, R. (1990). *Separate lives: Why siblings are so different*. New York, NY: Basic Books.

Dunning, D., & McElwee, R. O. (1995). Idiosyncratic trait definitions: Implications for self-description and social judgment. *Journal of Personality and Social Psychology, 68*, 936–946.

Dweck, C. S., & Leggett, E. L. (1988). A social-cognitive approach to motivation and personality. *Psychological Review, 95*, 256–273.

Eagle, M. N. (1984). *Recent developments in psychoanalysis: A critical evaluation*. New York, NY: McGraw-Hill.

Eaves, L. J., Eysenck, H. J., & Martin, N. G. (1989). *Genes, culture, and personality: An empirical approach*. San Diego, CA: Academic Press.

Eberhart, N. K., & Hammen, C. L. (2009). Interpersonal predictors of stress generation. *Personality and Social Psychology Bulletin, 35*, 544–556.

Ebstein, R. P., Novick, O., Umansky, R., Priel, B., Osher, Y., Blaine, D., Bennett, E. R., Nemanov, L., Katz, M., & Belmaker, R. H. (1996). Dopamine D4 receptor (D4DR) exon III polymorphism associated with the human personality trait of novelty seeking. *Nature Genetics, 12*, 78–80.

Edmonds, G. W., Bogg, T., & Roberts, B. W. (2009). Are personality and behavioral measures of impulse control convergent or distinct predictors of health behaviors? *Journal of Research in Personality, 43*, 806–814.

Edwards, A. L. (1957). *The social desirability variable in personality assessment and research*. New York, NY: Dryden.

Egeland, J. A., Gerhard, D. S., Pauls, D. L., Sussex, J. N., & Kidd, K. K. (1987). Bipolar affective disorders linked to DNA markers on chromosome 11. *Nature, 325*, 783–787.

Ein-Dor, T., Doron, G., Solomon, Z., Mikulincer, M., & Shaver, P. R. (2010). Together in pain: Attachment-related dyadic processes and posttraumatic stress disorder. *Journal of Counseling Psychology, 57*, 317–327.

Eisenberg, N. (2002). Emotion-related regulation and its relation to quality of social functioning. In W. W. Hartup & R. A. Weinberg (Eds.), *Child psychology in retrospect and prospect: The Minnesota symposium on child psychology* (Vol. 32, pp. 133–171). Mahwah, NJ: Erlbaum.

Eisenberg, N., Fabes, R. A., Murphy, B., Karbon, M., Maszk, P., Smith, M., O'Boyle, C., & Suh, K. (1994). The relations of emotionality and regulation to dispositional and situational empathy-related responding. *Journal of Personality and Social Psychology, 66*, 776–797.

Eisenberg, N., Spinrad, T. L., Fabes, R. A., Reiser, M., Cumberland, A., Shepard, S. A., Valiente, C., Losoya, S. H., Guthrie, I. K., & Thompson, M. (2004). The relations of effortful control and impulsivity to children's resiliency and adjustment. *Child Development, 75*, 25–46.

Eisenberger, R., Armeli, S., & Pretz, J. (1998). Can the promise of reward increase creativity? *Journal of Personality and Social Psychology, 74*, 704–714.

Eisenberger, R., & Rhoades, L. (2001). Incremental effects of reward on creativity. *Journal of Personality and Social Psychology, 81*, 728–741.

Eisenberger, R., & Selbst, M. (1994). Does reward increase or decrease creativity? *Journal of Personality and Social Psychology, 66*, 1116–1127.

Ekehammar, B. (1974). Interactionism in personality from a historical perspective. *Psychological Bulletin, 81*, 1026–1048.

Elder, G. H., Jr., & MacInnis, D. J. (1983). Achievement imagery in women's lives from adolescence to adulthood. *Journal of Personality and Social Psychology, 45*, 394–404.

Elder, G. H., Jr., Caspi, A., & Downey, G. (1986). Problem behavior and family relationships: Life course and intergenerational themes. In A. B. Sorenson, F. Weinert, & L. R. Sherrod (Eds.), *Human development and the life course: Multidisciplinary perspectives* (pp. 293–340). Hillsdale, NJ: Erlbaum.

Elliot, A. J. (2005). A conceptual history of the achievement goal construct. In A. J. Elliot & C. S. Dweck (Eds.), *Handbook of competence and motivation* (pp. 52–72). New York, NY: Guilford Press.

Elliot, A. J., & Harackiewicz, J. M. (1994). Goal setting, achievement orientation, and intrinsic motivation: A mediational analysis. *Journal of Personality and Social Psychology, 66,* 968–980.

Elliot, A. J., & Harackiewicz, J. M. (1996). Approach and avoidance achievement goals and intrinsic motivation: A mediational analysis. *Journal of Personality and Social Psychology, 70,* 461–475.

Elliot, A. J., & Maier, M. A. (2007). Color and psychological functioning. *Current Directions in Psychological Science, 16,* 250–254.

Elliot, A. J., Maier, M. A., Binser, M. J., Friedman, R., & Pekrun, R. (2009). The effect of red on avoidance behavior in achievement contexts. *Personality and Social Psychology Bulletin, 35,* 365–375.

Elliot, A. J., Maier, M. A., Moller, A. C., Friedman, R., & Meinhardt, J. (2007). Color and psychological functioning: The effect of red on performance attainment. *Journal of Experimental Psychology: General, 136,* 154–168.

Elliot, A. J., & McGregor, H. A. (2001). A 2 x 2 achievement goal framework. *Journal of Personality and Social Psychology, 80,* 501–519.

Elliot, A. J., & Sheldon, K. M. (1997). Avoidance achievement motivation: A personal goals analysis. *Journal of Personality and Social Psychology, 73,* 171–185.

Elliot, A. J., & Thrash, T. M. (2002). Approach–avoidance motivation in personality: Approach and avoidance temperaments and goals. *Journal of Personality and Social Psychology, 82,* 804–818.

Elliott, E. S., & Dweck, C. S. (1988). Goals: An approach to motivation and achievement. *Journal of Personality and Social Psychology, 54,* 5–12.

Ellis, A. E. (1987). The impossibility of achieving consistently good mental health. *American Psychologist, 42,* 364–375.

Elman, J. L. (2005). Connectionist models of cognitive development: Where next? *Trends in Cognitive Sciences, 9,* 112–117.

Emmons, R. A. (1986). Personal strivings: An approach to personality and subjective well-being. *Journal of Personality and Social Psychology, 51,* 1058–1068.

Emmons, R. A., & Diener, E. (1986). Situation selection as a moderator of response consistency and stability. *Journal of Personality and Social Psychology, 51,* 1013–1019.

Emmons, R. A., Diener, E., & Larsen, R. J. (1986). Choice and avoidance of everyday situations and affect congruence: Two models of reciprocal interactionism. *Journal of Personality and Social Psychology, 51,* 815–826.

Emmons, R. A., & King, L. A. (1988). Conflict among personal strivings: Immediate and long-term implications for psychological and physical well-being. *Journal of Personality and Social Psychology, 54,* 1040–1048.

Emmons, R. A., King, L. A., & Sheldon, K. (1993). Goal conflict and the self-regulation of action. In D. M. Wegner & J. W. Pennebaker (Eds.), *Handbook of mental control* (pp. 528–551). Englewood Cliffs, NJ: Prentice-Hall.

Endler, N. S., & Magnusson, D. (1976). *Interactional psychology and personality.* Washington, DC: Hemisphere.

Entwisle, D. R. (1972). To dispel fantasies about fantasy-based measures of achievement motivation. *Psychological Bulletin, 77,* 377–391.

Epstein, L. H., Saelens, B. E., Myers, M. D., & Vito, D. (1997). Effects of decreasing sedentary behaviors on activity choice in obese children. *Health Psychology, 16,* 107–113.

Epstein, S. (1985). The implications of cognitive–experiential self theory for research in social psychology and personality. *Journal for the Theory of Social Behavior, 15,* 283–310.

Epstein, S. (1990). Cognitive–experiential self-theory. In L. Pervin (Ed.), *Handbook of personality: Theory and research* (pp. 165–192). New York, NY: Guilford Press.

Epstein, S. (1994). Integration of the cognitive and the psychodynamic unconscious. *American Psychologist, 49,* 709–724.

Epstein, S., Lipson, A., Holstein, C., & Huh, E. (1992). Irrational reactions to negative outcomes: Evidence for two conceptual systems. *Journal of Personality and Social Psychology, 62,* 328–339.

Erdelyi, M. H. (1985). *Psychoanalysis: Freud's cognitive psychology.* New York, NY: Freeman.

Erdelyi, M. H. (2006). The unified theory of repression. *Behavioral and Brain Sciences, 29,* 499–551.

Ericsson, K. A., & Simon, H. A. (1993). *Protocol analysis: Verbal reports as data* (Rev. ed.). Cambridge, MA: MIT Press.

Erikson, E. H. (1950). *Childhood and society* (1st ed.). New York, NY: Norton.

Erikson, E. H. (1963). *Childhood and society* (2nd ed.). New York, NY: Norton.

Erikson, E. H. (1964). *Insight and responsibility.* New York, NY: Norton.

Erikson, E. H. (1968). *Identity: Youth and crisis.* New York, NY: Norton.

Erikson, E. H. (1974). *Dimensions of a new identity.* New York, NY: Norton.

Erikson, E. H. (1982). *The life cycle completed: A review.* New York, NY: Norton.

Ernst, C., & Angst, J. (1983). *Birth order: Its influence on personality.* Berlin, Germany: Springer-Verlag.

Esterson, A. (1993). *Seductive mirage: An exploration of the work of Sigmund Freud.* Chicago, IL: Open Court.

Esterson, A. (1998). Jeffrey Masson and Freud's seduction theory: A new fable based on old myths. *History of the Human Sciences, 11,* 1–21.

Ewart, C. K. (1978). Self-observation in natural environments: Reactive effects of behavior desirability and goal-setting. *Cognitive Therapy and Research, 2,* 39–56.

Exner, J. E., Jr. (1974). *The Rorschach systems.* New York, NY: Grune & Stratton.

Exner, J. E., Jr. (1993). *The Rorschach: A comprehensive system: Vol. 1. Basic foundations* (3rd ed.). New York, NY: Wiley.

Eysenck, H. J. (1952). *The scientific study of personality.* New York, NY: Macmillan.

Eysenck, H. J. (1961). The effects of psychotherapy. In H. J. Eysenck (Ed.), *Handbook of abnormal psychology.* New York, NY: Basic Books.

Eysenck, H. J. (1964a). *Crime and personality.* Boston, MA: Houghton Mifflin.

Eysenck, H. J. (1964b). Involuntary rest pauses in tapping as a function of drive and personality. *Perceptual and Motor Skills, 18,* 173–174.

Eysenck, H. J. (1967). *The biological basis of personality.* Springfield, IL: Charles C Thomas.

Eysenck, H. J. (1970). *The structure of human personality* (3rd ed.). London, England: Methuen.

Eysenck, H. J. (1975). *The inequality of man.* San Diego, CA: EdITS.

Eysenck, H. J. (1983). Psychopharmacology and personality. In W. Janke (Ed.), *Response variability to psychotropic drugs.* London, England: Pergamon Press.

Eysenck, H. J. (1986). Models and paradigms in personality research. In A. Angleitner, A. Furnham, & G. Van Heck (Eds.), *Personality psychology in Europe, Vol. 2: Current trends and controversies* (pp. 213–223). Lisse, Holland: Swets & Zeitlinger.

Eysenck, H. J. (1992). Four ways five factors are *not* basic. *Personality and Individual Differences, 13,* 667–673.

Eysenck, H. J. (1993). Comment on Goldberg. *American Psychologist, 48,* 1299–1300.

Eysenck, H. J. (Ed.). (1981). *A model for personality.* Berlin, Germany: Springer-Verlag.

Eysenck, H. J., & Eysenck, M. W. (1985). *Personality and individual differences: A natural science approach.* New York, NY: Plenum Press.

Eysenck, H. J., & Eysenck, S. B. G. (1975). *Manual of the Eysenck Personality Questionnaire.* San Diego, CA: EdITS.

Eysenck, H. J., & Eysenck, S. B. G. (1976). *Psychoticism as a dimension of personality.* London, England: Hodder & Stoughton.

Fadiga, L., Fogassi, L., Gallese, V., & Rizzolatti, G. (2000). Visuomotor neurons: Ambiguity of the discharge or 'motor' perception? *International Journal of Psychophysiology, 35,* 165–177.

Fairbairn, W. R. D. (1954). *An object relations theory of personality.* New York, NY: Basic Books.

Fairbanks, L. A. (2001). Individual differences in response to a stranger: Social impulsivity as a dimension of temperament in vervet monkeys (*Cercopithecus aethiops sabaeus*). *Journal of Comparative Psychology, 115,* 22–28.

Faraone, S. V., Taylor, L., & Tsuang, M. (2002). The molecular genetics of schizophrenia: An emerging consensus. *Expert Reviews in Molecular Medicine, 23.* Retrieved from www.expertreviews.org/02004751h.htm

Farrar, A. M., Pereira, M., Velasco, F., Hockemeyer, J., Müller, C. E., & Salamone, J. D. (2007). Adenosine A2A receptor antagonism reverses the effects of dopamine receptor antagonism on instrumental output and effort-related choice in the rat: Implications for studies of psychomotor slowing. *Psychopharmacology, 191,* 579–586.

Feather, N. T. (1961). The relationship of persistence at a task to expectations of success and achievement-related motivation. *Journal of Abnormal and Social Psychology, 63,* 552–561.

Feeney, B. C. (2004). A secure base: Responsive support of goal strivings and exploration in adult intimate relationships. *Journal of Personality and Social Psychology, 87,* 631–648.

Feeney, B. C. (2006). An attachment theory perspective on the interplay between intrapersonal and interpersonal processes. In K. D. Vohs & E. J. Finkel (Eds.), *Self and relationships* (pp. 133–159). New York, NY: Guilford Press.

Feeney, B. C. (2007). The dependency paradox in close relationships: Accepting dependence promotes independence. *Journal of Personality and Social Psychology, 92,* 268–285.

Feeney, B. C., & Cassidy, J. A. (2003). Reconstructive memory related to adolescent-parent conflict interactions: The influence of attachment-related representations on immediate perceptions and changes in perceptions over time. *Journal of Personality and Social Psychology, 85,* 945–955.

Feeney, B. C., Cassidy, J., & Ramos-Marcuse, F. (2008). The generalization of attachment representations to new social situations: Predicting behavior during initial interactions with strangers. *Journal of Personality and Social Psychology, 95,* 1481–1498.

Feeney, B. C., & Collins, N. L. (2001). Predictors of caregiving in adult intimate relationships: An attachment theoretical perspective. *Journal of Personality and Social Psychology, 80,* 972–994.

Feeney, B. C., & Collins, N. L. (2003). Motivations for caregiving in adult intimate relationships: Influences on caregiving behavior and relationship functioning. *Personality and Social Psychology Bulletin, 29,* 950–968.

Feeney, B. C., & Thrush R. L. (2010). Relationship influences on exploration in adulthood: The characteristics and function of a secure base. *Journal of Personality and Social Psychology, 98,* 57–76.

Feeney, J. A., & Noller, P. (1990). Attachment style as a predictor of adult romantic relationships. *Journal of Personality and Social Psychology, 58,* 281–291.

Fehr, E., & Gächter, S. (2002). Altruistic punishment in humans. *Nature, 415,* 137–140.

Feingold, A. (1992). Gender differences in mate selection preferences: A test of the parental investment model. *Psychological Bulletin, 112,* 125–139.

Fekken, G. C., & Holden, R. R. (1992). Response latency evidence for viewing personality traits as schema indicators. *Journal of Research in Personality, 26,* 103–120.

Feldman, F. (1968). Results of psychoanalysis in clinic case assignments. *Journal of the American Psychoanalytic Association, 16,* 274–300.

Feldman, R., Weller, A., Zagoory-Sharon, O., & Levine, A. (2007). Evidence for a neuroendocrinological foundation of human affiliation: Plasma oxytocin levels across pregnancy and the postpartum period predict mother-infant bonding. *Psychological Science, 18,* 965–970.

Fellous, J-M., & Arbib, M. A. (Eds.). (2005). *Who needs emotions? The brain meets the robot.* New York, NY: Oxford University Press.

Fenigstein, A., Scheier, M. F., & Buss, A. H. (1975). Public and private self-consciousness: Assessment and theory. *Journal of Consulting and Clinical Psychology, 43,* 522–527.

Ferguson, M. J. (2008). On becoming ready to pursue a goal you don't know you have: Effects of nonconscious goals on evaluative readiness. *Journal of Personality and Social Psychology, 95,* 1268–1294.

Ferguson, M. J., Bargh, J. A., & Nayak, D. A. (2005). After-affects: How automatic evaluations influence the interpretation of subsequent, unrelated stimuli. *Journal of Experimental Social Psychology, 41,* 182–191.

Finkel, E. J., & Campbell, W. K. (2001). Self-control and accommodation in close relationships: An interdependence analysis. *Journal of Personality and Social Psychology, 81,* 263–277.

Fischer, M. J. (2010). A longitudinal examination of the role of stereotype threat and racial climate on college outcomes for minorities at elite institutions. *Social Psychology of Education, 13,* 19–40.

Fisher, S. (1973). *The female orgasm.* New York, NY: Basic Books.

Fisher, S., & Greenberg, R. P. (1977). *The scientific credibility of Freud's theories and therapy.* New York, NY: Basic Books.

Fiske, D. W. (1949). Consistency of the factorial structures of personality ratings from different sources. *Journal of Abnormal and Social Psychology, 44,* 329–344.

Fiske, S. T., & Taylor, S. E. (1984). *Social cognition.* Reading, MA: Addison-Wesley.

Fitzsimons, G. M., & Bargh, J. A. (2003). Thinking of you: Nonconscious pursuit of interpersonal goals associated with relationship partners. *Journal of Personality and Social Psychology, 84,* 148–164.

Fitzsimons, G. M., & Bargh, J. A. (2004). Automatic self-regulation. In R. F. Baumeister & K. D. Vohs (Eds.), *Handbook of self-regulation: Research, theory, and applications* (pp. 151–170. New York, NY: Guilford Press.

Flanders, J. P. (1968). A review of research on imitative behavior. *Psychological Bulletin, 69,* 316–337.

Fleeson, W. (2001). Toward a structure- and process-integrated view of personality: Traits as density distributions of states. *Journal of Personality and Social Psychology, 80,* 1011–1027.

Fleeson, W. (2004). Moving personality beyond the person-situation debate. *Current Directions in Psychological Science, 13,* 83–87.

Fleeson, W., Leicht, C. (2006). On delineating and integrating the study of variability and stability in personality psychology: Interpersonal trust as illustration. *Journal of Research in Personality, 40,* 5–20.

Fleeson, W., Malanos, A. B., & Achille, N. M. (2002). An intraindividual process approach to the relationship between extraversion and positive affect: Is acting extraverted as "good" as being extraverted? *Journal of Personality and Social Psychology, 83,* 1409–1422.

Flink, C., Boggiano, A. K., & Barrett, M. (1990). Controlling teaching strategies: Undermining children's self-determination and performance. *Journal of Personality and Social Psychology, 59,* 916–924.

Florian, V., Mikulincer, M., & Hirschberger, G. (2002). The anxiety-buffering function of close relationships:

Evidence that relationship commitment acts as a terror management mechanism. *Journal of Personality and Social Psychology, 82,* 527–542.

Flynn, F. J. (2005). Having an open mind: The impact of openness to experience on interracial attitudes and impression formation. *Journal of Personality and Social Psychology, 88,* 816–826.

Foa, E. B., & Meadows, E. A. (1997). Psychosocial treatments for posttraumatic stress disorder: A critical review. *Annual Review of Psychology, 48,* 449–480.

Fodor, E. M., & Wick, D. P. (2009). Need for power and affective response to negative audience reaction to an extemporaneous speech. *Journal of Research in Personality, 43,* 721–726.

Ford, D. H. (1987). *Humans as self-constructing living systems: A developmental perspective on behavior and personality.* Hillsdale, NJ: Erlbaum.

Fowles, D. C. (1980). The three arousal model: Implications of Gray's two-factor learning theory for heart rate, electrodermal activity, and psychopathy. *Psychophysiology, 17,* 87–104.

Fox, N. A., & Davidson, R. J. (1988). Patterns of brain electrical activity during facial signs of emotion in 10-month-old infants. *Developmental Psychology, 24,* 230–236.

Fraley, R. C. (2002). Attachment stability from infancy to adulthood: Meta-analysis and dynamic modeling of developmental mechanisms. *Personality and Social Psychology Review, 6,* 123–151.

Fraley, R. C., Garner, J. P., & Shaver, P. R. (2000). Adult attachment and the defensive regulation of attention and memory: Examining the role of preemptive and postemptive defensive processes. *Journal of Personality and Social Psychology, 79,* 816–826.

Fraley, R. C., & Shaver, P. R. (1998). Airport separations: A naturalistic study of adult attachment dynamics in separating couples. *Journal of Personality and Social Psychology, 75,* 1198–1212.

Frank, E., & Brandstätter, V. (2002). Approach versus avoidance: Different types of commitment in intimate relationships. *Journal of Personality and Social Psychology, 82,* 208–221.

Frank, M. J., & Claus, E. D. (2006). Anatomy of a decision: Striato-orbitofrontal interactions in reinforcement learning, decision making, and reversal. *Psychological Review, 113,* 300–326.

Frank, M. J., & O'Reilly, R. C. (2006). A mechanistic account of striatal dopamine function in human cognition: Psychopharmacological studies with cabergoline and haloperidol. *Behavioral Neuroscience, 120,* 497–517.

Frank, M. J., Seeberger, L. C., & O'Reilly, R. C. (2004). By carrot or by stick: Cognitive reinforcement learning in Parkinsonism. *Science, 306,* 1940–1943.

Frankl, V. E. (1969). *The doctor and the soul.* New York, NY: Bantam.

French, E. G. (1955). Some characteristics of achievement motivation. *Journal of Experimental Psychology, 50,* 232–236.

Freud, A. (1966). *The ego and the mechanisms of defense* (Rev. ed.). New York, NY: International Universities Press.

Freud, S. (1933). *New introductory lectures on psychoanalysis* (W. J. H. Sprott, Trans.). New York, NY: Norton.

Freud, S. (1936). *The problem of anxiety* (H. A. Bunker, Trans.). New York, NY: Norton. (Original work published 1926)

Freud, S. (1949). *An outline of psychoanalysis* (J. Strachey, Trans.). New York, NY: Norton. (Original work published 1940)

Freud, S. (1953). The interpretation of dreams. In J. Strachey (Ed.), *The standard edition of the complete psychological works of Sigmund Freud* (Vols. 4 and 5). London, England: Hogarth Press. (Original work published 1900)

Freud, S. (1955). Beyond the pleasure principle. In J. Strachey (Ed.), *The standard edition of the complete psychological works of Sigmund Freud* (Vol. 18). London, England: Hogarth Press. (Original work published 1920)

Freud, S. (1959). Inhibitions, symptoms and anxiety. In J. Strachey (Ed.), *The standard edition of the complete psychological works of Sigmund Freud* (Vol. 20). London, England: Hogarth Press. (Original work published 1926)

Freud, S. (1960). Psychopathology of everyday life. In J. Strachey (Ed.), *The standard edition of the complete psychological works of Sigmund Freud* (Vol. 6). London, England: Hogarth Press. (Original work published 1901)

Freud, S. (1962). *The ego and the id.* New York, NY: Norton. (Original work published 1923)

Freund, A. M., & Baltes, P. B. (2002). Life-management strategies of selection, optimization, and compensation. Measurement by self-report and construct validity. *Journal of Personality and Social Psychology, 82,* 642–662.

Freyd, J. J. (1987). Dynamic mental representations. *Psychological Review, 94,* 427–438.

Freyd, J. J. (1996). *Betrayal trauma: The logic of forgetting childhood abuse.* Cambridge, MA: Harvard University Press.

Friedman, L. J. (1999). *Identity's architect: A biography of Erik H. Erikson.* New York, NY: Scribner.

Friese, M., & Hofmann, W. (2009). Control me or I will control you: Impulses, trait self-control, and the guidance of behavior. *Journal of Research in Personality, 43,* 795–805.

Fujita, K., Gollwitzer, P. M., & Oettingen, G. (2007). Mindsets and pre-conscious open-mindedness to incidental information. *Journal of Experimental Social Psychology, 43,* 48–61.

Fujita, K., Trope, Y., Liberman, N., & Leven-Sagi, M. (2006). Construal levels and self-control. *Journal of Personality and Social Psychology, 90,* 351–567.

Fukuyama, F. (2002). *Our posthuman future: Consequences of the biotechnology revolution.* New York, NY: Farrar, Straus, & Giroux.

Fulford, D., Johnson, S. L., Llabre, M. M., & Carver, C. S. (2010). Pushing and coasting in dynamic goal pursuit: Coasting is attenuated in bipolar disorder. *Psychological Science, 21,* 1021–1027.

Funder, D. C. (1991). Global traits: A neo-Allportian approach to personality. *Psychological Science, 2,* 31–39.

Funder, D. C. (2001). Personality. *Annual Review of Psychology, 52,* 197–221.

Funder, D. C., & Block, J. (1989). The role of ego-control, ego-resiliency, and IQ in delay of gratification in adolescence. *Journal of Personality and Social Psychology, 57,* 1041–1050.

Funder, D. C., Block, J. H., & Block, J. (1983). Delay of gratification: Some longitudinal personality correlates. *Journal of Personality and Social Psychology, 44,* 1198–1213.

Funder, D. C., & Colvin, C. R. (1991). Explorations in behavioral consistency: Properties of persons, situations, and behaviors. *Journal of Personality and Social Psychology, 60,* 773–794.

Funder, D. C., & Ozer, D. J. (1983). Behavior as a function of the situation. *Journal of Personality and Social Psychology, 44,* 107–112.

Furr, R. M., & Funder, D. C. (2004). Situational similarity and behavioral consistency: Subjective, objective, variable-centered, and person-centered approaches. *Journal of Research in Personality, 38,* 421–447.

Gable, S. L., Reis, H. T., & Elliot, A. J. (2000). Behavioral activation and inhibition in everyday life. *Journal of Personality and Social Psychology, 78,* 1135–1149.

Gacsaly, S. A., & Borges, C. A. (1979). The male physique and behavioral expectancies. *Journal of Psychology, 101,* 97–102.

Gallese, V. (2001). The "shared manifold" hypothesis: From mirror neurons to empathy. *Journal of Consciousness Studies, 8,* 33–50.

Gallistel, C. R. (1980). *The organization of action: A new synthesis.* Hillsdale, NJ: Erlbaum.

Ganellen, R. J. (1996). Comparing the diagnostic efficiency of the MMPMI, MCMI-II, and Rorschach: A review. *Journal of Personality Assessment, 67,* 219–243.

Gangestad, S. W., & Simpson, J. A. (2000). The evolution of human mating: Trade-offs and strategic pluralism. *Behavioral and Brain Sciences, 23,* 573–587.

Gangestad, S. W., & Snyder, M. (1985). "To carve nature at its joints": On the existence of discrete classes in personality. *Psychological Review, 92,* 317–349.

Garcia, J., & Koelling, R. A. (1966). Relation of cue to consequence in avoidance learning. *Psychonomic Science, 4,* 123–124.

Gardner, H. (1985). *The mind's new science: A history of the cognitive revolution.* New York, NY: Basic Books.

Garver-Apgar, C. E., Gangestad, S. W., Thornhill, R., Miller, R. D., & Olp, J. J. (2006). Major histocompatibility complex alleles, sexual responsivity, and unfaithfulness in romantic couples. *Psychological Science, 17,* 830–835.

Gauthier, J., & Ladouceur, R. (1981). The influence of self-efficacy reports on performance. *Behavior Therapy, 12,* 436–439.

Geen, R. G. (1998). Aggression and antisocial behavior. In D. T. Gilbert, S. T. Fiske, & G. Lindzey (Eds.), *The handbook of social psychology* (Vol. 2, 4th ed., pp. 317–356). Boston, MA: McGraw-Hill.

Geen, R. G., Stonner, D., & Shope, G. L. (1975). The facilitation of aggression by aggression: Evidence against the catharsis hypothesis. *Journal of Personality and Social Psychology, 31,* 721–726.

Gelhorn, H., Hartman, C., Sakai, J., Mikulich-Gilbertson, S., Stallings, M., Young, S., et al. (2009). An item response theory analysis of DSM-IV conduct disorder. *Journal of the American Academy of Child and Adolescent Psychiatry, 48,* 42–50.

Gentile, D. A., Anderson, C. A., Yukawa, S., Ihori, N., Saleem, M., Ming, L. K., et al. (2009). The effects of prosocial video games on prosocial behaviors: International evidence from correlational, longitudinal, and experimental studies. *Personality and Social Psychology Bulletin, 35,* 752–763.

George, D. T., Umhau, J. C., Phillips, M. J., Emmela, D., Ragan, P. W., Shoaf, S. E., & Rawlings, R. R. (2001). Serotonin, testosterone, and alcohol in the etiology of domestic violence. *Psychiatry Research, 104,* 27–37.

Gerst, M. S. (1971). Symbolic coding processes in observational learning. *Journal of Personality and Social Psychology, 19,* 7–27.

Giancola, P. R. (2004). Executive functioning and alcohol-related aggression. *Journal of Abnormal Psychology, 113,* 541–555.

Gigerenzer, G., & Goldstein, D. G. (1996). Reasoning the fast and frugal way: Models of bounded rationality. *Psychological Review, 103*, 650–669.

Gilbert, S. F., & Epel, D. (2009). *Ecological developmental biology: Integrating epigenetics, medicine, and evolution.* Sunderland, MA: Sinauer Associates.

Giltay, E. J., Kamphuis, M. H., Kalmijn, S., Zitman, F. G., & Kromhout, D. (2006). Dispositional optimism and the risk of cardiovascular death: The Zutphen elderly study. *Archives of Internal Medicine, 166*, 431–436.

Glassman, N. S., & Andersen, S. M. (1999). Activating transference without consciousness: Using significant-other representations to go beyond what is subliminally given. *Journal of Personality and Social Psychology, 77*, 1146–1162.

Glue, P., Wilson, S., Coupland, N., Ball, D., & Nutt, D. (1995). The relationship between benzodiazepine receptor sensitivity and neuroticism. *Journal of Anxiety Disorders, 9*, 33–45.

Goddard, A. W., Mason, G. F., Almai, A., Rothman, D. L., Behar, K. L., Petroff, O. A. C., Charney, D. S., & Krystal, J. H. (2001). Reductions in occipital cortex GABA levels in panic disorder detected with H-Magnetic resonance spectroscopy. *Archives of General Psychiatry, 58*, 556–561.

Goldberg, A. (Ed.). (1985). *Progress in self psychology* (Vol. 1). New York, NY: Guilford Press.

Goldberg, L. R. (1981). Language and individual differences: The search for universals in personality lexicons. In L. Wheeler (Ed.), *Review of personality and social psychology* (Vol. 2, pp. 141–165). Beverly Hills, CA: Sage.

Goldberg, L. R. (1982). From ace to zombie: Some explorations in the language of personality. In C. D. Spielberger & J. N. Butcher (Eds.), *Advances in personality assessment* (Vol. 1). Hillsdale, NJ: Erlbaum.

Goldberg, L. R. (1993a). The structure of personality traits: Vertical and horizontal aspects. In D. C. Funder, R. Parke, C. Tomlinson-Keasey, & K. Widaman (Eds.), *Studying lives through time: Approaches to personality and development* (pp. 169–188). Washington, DC: American Psychological Association.

Goldberg, L. R. (1993b). The structure of phenotypic personality traits. *American Psychologist, 48*, 26–34.

Goldenberg, J. L., Pyszczynski, T., Greenberg, J., & Solomon, S. (2000). Fleeing the body: A terror management perspective on the problem of human corporeality. *Personality and Social Psychology Review, 4*, 200–218.

Goldenberg, J. L., Pyszczynski, T., Greenberg, J., Solomon, S., Kluck, B., & Cornwell, R. (2001). I am *not* an animal: Mortality salience, disgust, and the denial of human creatureliness. *Journal of Experimental Psychology: General, 130*, 427–435.

Goldfield, G. S., & Epstein, L. H. (2002). Can fruits and vegetables and activities substitute for snack foods? *Health Psychology, 21*, 299–303.

Goldfried, M. R., & Davison, G. C. (1976). *Clinical behavior therapy.* New York, NY: Holt, Rinehart, & Winston.

Goldiamond, I. (1976). Self-reinforcement. *Journal of Applied Behavior Analysis, 9*, 509–514.

Goldstein, S. E., Chesir-Teran, D., & McFaul, A. (2008). Profiles and correlates of relational aggression in young adults' romantic relationships. *Journal of Youth and Adolescents, 37*, 251–265.

Gollwitzer, P. M. (1999). Implementation intentions: Strong effects of simple plans. *American Psychologist, 54*, 493–503.

Gollwitzer, P. M, & Brandstätter, V. (1997). Implementation intentions and effective goal pursuit. *Journal of Personality and Social Psychology, 73*, 186–199.

Gosling, S. D. (2001). From mice to men: What can we learn about personality from animal research? *Psychological Bulletin, 127*, 45–86.

Gosling, S. D. (2008). *Snoop: What your stuff says about you.* New York, NY: Basic Books.

Gotlib, I. H. (1983). Perception and recall of interpersonal feedback: Negative bias in depression. *Cognitive Therapy and Research, 7*, 399–412.

Gottesman, I. I., & Shields, J. (1972). *Schizophrenia and genetics.* New York, NY: Academic Press.

Govorun, O., Fuegen, K., & Payne, B. K. (2006). Stereotypes focus defensive projection. *Personality and Social Psychology Bulletin, 32*, 781–793.

Grace, A. A. (2010). Animal models of schizophrenia: Focus on hippocampal disruption of dopamine system regulation. In W. F. Gattaz, & G. Busatto (Eds.), *Advances in Schizophrenia Research 2009* (pp. 175–191). New York, NY: Springer.

Grammer, K., & Thornhill, R. (1994). Human facial attractiveness and sexual selection: The role of symmetry and averageness. *Journal of Comparative Psychology, 108*, 233–242.

Gray, J. (1992). *Men are from Mars, women are from Venus: A practical guide for improving communication and getting what you want in your relationships.* New York, NY: HarperCollins.

Gray, J. A. (1982). *The neuropsychology of anxiety: An enquiry into the functions of the septo-hippocampal system.* New York, NY: Oxford University Press.

Gray, J. A. (1987). Perspectives on anxiety and impulsivity: A commentary. *Journal of Research in Personality, 21*, 493–509.

Gray, J. A. (1990). Brain systems that mediate both emotion and cognition. *Cognition and Emotion, 4,* 269–288.

Gray, J. A. (1991). The neuropsychology of temperament. In J. Strelau & A. Angleitner (Eds.), *Explorations in temperament: International perspectives on theory and measurement* (pp. 105–128). New York, NY: Plenum Press.

Gray, J. A. (1994a). Personality dimensions and emotion systems. In P. Ekman & R. J. Davidson (Eds.), *The nature of emotion: Fundamental questions* (pp. 329–331). New York, NY: Oxford University Press.

Gray, J. A. (1994b). Three fundamental emotion systems. In P. Ekman & R. J. Davidson (Eds.), *The nature of emotion: Fundamental questions* (pp. 243–247). New York, NY: Oxford University Press.

Gray, J. D., & Silver, R. C. (1990). Opposite sides of the same coin: Former spouses' divergent perspectives in coping with their divorce. *Journal of Personality and Social Psychology, 59,* 1180–1191.

Graziano, W. G., & Eisenberg, N. H. (1999). Agreeableness as a dimension of personality. In R. Hogan, J. Johnson, & S. Briggs (Eds.), *Handbook of personality* (pp. 795–825). San Diego, CA: Academic Press.

Graziano, W. G., Jensen-Campbell, L. A., & Hair, E. C. (1996). Perceiving interpersonal conflict and reacting to it: The case for agreeableness. *Journal of Personality and Social Psychology, 70,* 820–835.

Green, J. D., & Campbell, W. K. (2000). Attachment and exploration in adults: Chronic and contextual accessibility. *Personality and Social Psychology Bulletin, 26,* 452–461.

Greenberg, B. D., Li, Q., Lucas, F. R., Hu, S., Sirota, L. A., Benjamin, J., Lesch, K-P., Hamer, D., & Murphy, D. L. (2000). Association between the serotonin transporter promoter polymorphism and personality traits in a primarily female population sample. *American Journal of Medical Genetics (Neuropsychiatric Genetics), 96,* 202–216.

Greenberg, J., Pyszczynski, T., & Solomon, S. (1982). The self-serving attributional bias: Beyond self-presentation. *Journal of Experimental Social Psychology, 18,* 56–67.

Greenberg, J., Pyszczynski, T., & Solomon, S. (1986). The causes and consequences of a need for self-esteem: A terror management theory. In R. F. Baumeister (Ed.), *Public self and private self* (pp. 189–212). New York, NY: Springer-Verlag.

Greenberg, J., Solomon, S., & Pyszczynski, T. (1997). Terror management theory of self-esteem and social behavior: Empirical assessments and conceptual refinements. In M. P. Zanna (Ed.), *Advances in experimental social psychology* (Vol. 29, pp. 61–139). New York, NY: Academic Press.

Greene, D. L., & Winter, D. G. (1971). Motives, involvements, and leadership among Black college students. *Journal of Personality, 39,* 319–332.

Greenwald, A. G., & Banaji, M. R. (1989). The self as a memory system: Powerful, but ordinary. *Journal of Personality and Social Psychology, 57,* 41–54.

Greenwald, A. G., Banaji, M. R., Rudman, L. A., Farnham, S. D., Nosek, B. A., & Mellott, D. S. (2002). A unified theory of implicit attitudes, stereotypes, self-esteem, and self-concept. *Psychological Review, 109,* 3–25.

Greenwald, A. G., McGhee, D. E., & Schwartz, J. L. K. (1998). Measuring individual differences in implicit cognition: The implicit association test. *Journal of Personality and Social Psychology, 74,* 1464–1480.

Greenwald, A. G., McGhee, D. E., & Schwartz, J. L. K. (2008). Measuring individual differences in implicit cognition: The Implicit Association Test. In R. H. Fazio & R. E. Petty (Eds.), *Attitudes: Their structure, function, and consequences* (pp. 109–131). New York, NY: Psychology Press.

Greenwald, A. G., & Pratkanis, R. A. (1984). The self. In R. S. Wyer, Jr., & T. K. Srull (Eds.), *Handbook of social cognition* (Vol. 3). Hillsdale, NJ: Erlbaum.

Greer, S., & Morris, T. (1975). Psychological attributes of women who develop breast cancer: A controlled study. *Journal of Psychosomatic Research, 19,* 147–153.

Greguras, G. J., & Diefendorff, J. M. (2010). Why does proactive personality predict employee life satisfaction and work behaviors? A field investigation of the mediating role of the self-concordance model. *Personality Psychology, 63,* 539–560.

Grewen, K. M., Girdler, S. S., Amico, J., & Light, K. C. (2005). Effects of partner support on resting oxytocin, cortisol, norepinephrine, and blood pressure before and after warm partner contact. *Psychosomatic Medicine, 67,* 531–538.

Griffin, D., & Bartholomew, K. (1994). Models of the self and other: Fundamental dimensions underlying measures of adult attachment. *Journal of Personality and Social Psychology, 67,* 430–445.

Grigsby, J., & Stevens, D. (2000). *Neurodynamics of personality.* New York, NY: Guilford Press.

Grimes, J. M., Ricci, L. A., & Melloni, R. H., Jr. (2006). Plasticity in anterior hypothalamic vasopressin correlates with aggression during anabolic-androgenic steroid withdrawal in hamsters. *Behavioral Neuroscience, 120,* 115–124.

Grings, W. W. (1973). The role of consciousness and cognition in autonomic behavior change. In F. J. McGuigan & R. Schoonover (Eds.), *The psychophysiology of thinking.* New York, NY: Academic Press.

Griskevicius, V., Tybur, J. M., Gangestad, S. W., Perea, E. F., Shapiro, J. R., & Kenrick, D. T. (2009). Aggress to impress: Hostility as an evolved context-dependent strategy. *Journal of Personality and Social Psychology, 96,* 980–994.

Grolnick, W. S., & Ryan, R. M. (1989). Parent styles associated with children's self-regulation and competence in school. *Journal of Educational Psychology, 81,* 143–154.

Grossmann, K. E., Grossmann, K., & Waters, E. (2005). *Attachment from infancy to adulthood: The major longitudinal studies.* New York, NY: Guilford Press.

Grouzet, F. M. E., Kasser, T., Ahuvia, A., Fernández Dols, J. M., Kim, Y., Lau, S., Ryan, R. M., Saunders, S., Schmuck, P., & Sheldon, K. M. (2005). The structure of goal contents across 15 cultures. *Journal of Personality and Social Psychology, 89,* 800–816.

Gruber, A. J., & Pope, H. G., Jr. (2000). Psychiatric and medical effects of anabolic-androgenic steroid use in women. *Psychotherapy and Psychosomatics, 69,* 19–26.

Gruen, R. J., & Mendelsohn, G. (1986). Emotional responses to affective displays in others: The distinction between empathy and sympathy. *Journal of Personality and Social Psychology, 51,* 609–614.

Guisinger, S., & Blatt, S. J. (1994). Individuality and relatedness: Evolution of a fundamental dialectic. *American Psychologist, 49,* 104–111.

Gutierres, S. E., Kenrick, D. T., & Partch, J. J. (1999). Beauty, dominance, and the mating game: Contrast effects in self-assessment reflect gender differences in mate selection. *Personality and Social Psychology Bulletin, 25,* 1126–1134.

Haaga, D. A. F., Dyck, M. J., & Ernst, D. (1991). Empirical status of cognitive theory of depression. *Psychological Bulletin, 110,* 215–236.

Haas, B. W., Omura, K., Constable, R. T., & Canli, T. (2007). Emotional conflict and neuroticism: Personality-dependent activation in the amygdala and subgenual anterior cingulate. *Behavioral Neuroscience, 121,* 249–256.

Haas, B. W., Omura, K., Constable, R. T., & Canli, T. (2007). Is automatic emotion regulation associated with agreeableness? A perspective using a social neuroscience approach. *Psychological Science, 18,* 130–132.

Haas, H. A. (2002). Extending the search for folk personality constructs: The dimensionality of the personality-relevant proverb domain. *Journal of Personality and Social Psychology, 82,* 594–609.

Haemmerlie, F. M., & Montgomery, R. L. (1984). Purposefully biased interactions: Reducing heterosocial anxiety through self-perception theory. *Journal of Personality and Social Psychology, 47,* 900–908.

Halpern, J. (1977). Projection: A test of the psychoanalytic hypothesis. *Journal of Abnormal Psychology, 86,* 536–542.

Halverson, C. F., Jr., Kohnstamm, G. A., & Martin, R. P. (Eds.). (1994). *The developing structure of temperament and personality from infancy to adulthood.* Hillsdale, NJ: Erlbaum.

Hamilton, J. C., Greenberg, J., Pyszczynski, T., & Cather, C. (1993). A self-regulatory perspective on psychopathology and psychotherapy. *Journal of Psychotherapy Integration, 3,* 205–248.

Hamilton, W. D. (1964). The genetical evolution of social behavior. *Journal of Theoretical Biology, 7,* 1–52.

Hampson, S. E., & Friedman, H. S. (2008). Personality and health: A life span perspective. In O. P. John, R. Robins, & L. Pervins (Eds.), *Handbook of personality* (3rd ed., pp. 770–794). New York, NY: Guilford Press.

Hampson, S. E., Andrews, J. A., Barckley, M., Lichtenstein, E., & Lee, M. E. (2000). Conscientiousness, perceived risk, and risk-reduction behaviors: A preliminary study. *Health Psychology, 19,* 496–500.

Hampson, S. E., Goldberg, L. R., Vogt, T. M., & Dubanoski, J. P. (2006). Forty years on: Teachers' assessments of children's personality traits predict self-reported health behaviors and outcomes at midlife. *Health Psychology, 25,* 57–64.

Handley, S. L. (1995). 5-Hydroxytryptamine pathways in anxiety and its treatment. *Pharmacology and Therapeutics, 66,* 103–148.

Hankin, B. L., Kassel, J. D., & Abela, J. R. Z. (2005). Adult attachment dimensions and specificity of emotional distress symptoms: Prospective investigations of cognitive risk and interpersonal stress generation as mediating mechanisms. *Personality and Social Psychology Bulletin, 31,* 136–151.

Hansenne, M., Pinto, E., Pitchot, W., Reggers, J., Scantamburlo, G., Moor, M., & Ansseau, M. (2002). Further evidence on the relationship between dopamine and novelty seeking: A neuroendocrine study. *Personality and Individual Differences, 33,* 967–977.

Harackiewicz, J. M. (1979). The effects of reward contingency and performance feedback on intrinsic motivation. *Journal of Personality and Social Psychology, 37,* 1352–1363.

Hardy, K. R. (1957). Determinants of conformity and attitude change. *Journal of Abnormal and Social Psychology, 54,* 289–294.

Harmon-Jones, E., & Allen, J. J. (1997). Behavioral activation sensitivity and resting frontal EEG asymmetry: Covariation of putative indicators related to risk for mood disorders. *Journal of Abnormal Psychology, 106,* 159–163.

Harmon-Jones, E., Lueck, L., Fearn, M., & Harmon-Jones, C. (2006). The effect of personal relevance and approach-related action expectation on relative left frontal cortical activity. *Psychological Science, 17,* 434–440.

Harms, P. D., Roberts, B. W., & Wood, D. (2007). Who shall lead? An integrative personality approach to the study of the antecedents of status in informal social organizations. *Journal of Research in Personality, 41,* 689–699.

Harris, C. R. (2002). Sexual and romantic jealousy in heterosexual and homosexual adults. *Psychological Science, 13,* 7–12.

Harris, C. R. (2003). A review of sex differences in sexual jealousy, including self-report data, psychophysiological responses, interpersonal violence, and morbid jealousy. *Personality and Social Psychology Review, 7,* 102–128.

Harris, J. L., Bargh, J. A., & Brownell, K. D. (2009). Priming effects of television food advertising on eating behavior. *Health Psychology, 28,* 404–413.

Harrison, R. J., Connor, D. F., Nowak, C., Nash, K., & Melloni, R. H., Jr. (2000). Chronic anabolic-androgenic steroid treatment during adolescence increases anterior hypothalamic vasopressin and aggression in intact hamsters. *Psychoneuroendocrinology, 25,* 317–338.

Hart, H. M., McAdams, D. P., Hirsch, B. J., & Bauer, J. J. (2001). Generativity and social involvement among African Americans and white adults. *Journal of Research in Personality, 35,* 208–230.

Hassin, R. R., Bargh, J. A., & Uleman, J. S. (2002). Spontaneous causal inferences. *Journal of Experimental Social Psychology, 38,* 515–522.

Hassin, R. R., Uleman, J. S., & Bargh, J. A. (Eds.). (2005). *The new unconscious.* New York, NY: Oxford University Press.

Hathaway, S. R., & McKinley, J. C. (1943). *MMPI manual.* New York, NY: Psychological Corporation.

Hayes, A. M., Harris, M. S., & Carver, C. S. (2004). Predictors of self-esteem variability. *Cognitive Therapy and Research, 28,* 369–385.

Hayne, H., Garry, M., & Loftus, E. F. (2006). On the continuing lack of science evidence for repression. *Behavioral and Brain Science, 29,* 521–522.

Haynes, S. N., & O'Brien, W. H. (2000). *Principles and practice of behavioral assessment.* Amsterdam, The Netherlands: Kluwer.

Hazan, C., & Shaver, P. R. (1987). Romantic love conceptualized as an attachment process. *Journal of Personality and Social Psychology, 52,* 511–524.

Hazan, C., & Shaver, P. R. (1990). Love and work: An attachment-theoretical perspective. *Journal of Personality and Social Psychology, 59,* 270–280.

Hazan, C., & Shaver, P. R. (1994). Attachment as an organizational framework for research on close relationships. *Psychological Inquiry, 5,* 1–22.

Hazen, N. L., & Durrett, M. E. (1982). Relationship of security of attachment to exploration and cognitive mapping abilities in 2-year-olds. *Developmental Psychology, 18,* 751–759.

Heath, A. C., Neale, M. C., Kessler, R. C., Eaves, L. J., & Kendler, K. S. (1992). Evidence for genetic influences on personality from self-reports and informant ratings. *Journal of Personality and Social Psychology, 63,* 85–96.

Heckhausen, H. (1967). *The anatomy of achievement motivation.* New York, NY: Academic Press.

Heckhausen, H., & Gollwitzer, P. M. (1987). Thought contents and cognitive functioning in motivational versus volitional states of mind. *Motivation and Emotion, 11,* 101–120.

Heckhausen, H., Schmalt, H. D., & Schneider, K. (1985). *Achievement motivation in perspective.* New York, NY: Academic Press.

Heiby, E. M. (1982). A self-reinforcement questionnaire. *Behaviour Research and Therapy, 20,* 397–401.

Heider, F. (1944). Social perception and phenomenal causation. *Psychological Review, 51,* 358–374.

Heider, F. (1958). *The psychology of interpersonal relations.* New York, NY: Wiley.

Heilbrun, K. S. (1980). Silverman's psychodynamic activation: A failure to replicate. *Journal of Abnormal Psychology, 89,* 560–566.

Helgeson, V. S. (1994). Relation of agency and communion to well-being: Evidence and potential explanations. *Psychological Bulletin, 116,* 412–428.

Helgeson, V. S. (2003). Gender-related traits and health. In J. Suls & K. A. Wallston (Eds.), *Social psychological foundations of health and illness* (pp. 367–394). Oxford, England: Blackwell.

Helgeson, V. S. (in press). Gender and health: A social psychological perspective. In A. Baum, T. Revenson, & J. Singer (Eds.), *Handbook of health psychology* (2nd ed.). New York, NY: Psychology Press.

Helgeson, V. S., & Fritz, H. L. (1998). A theory of unmitigated communion. *Personality and Social Psychology Review, 2,* 173–183.

Helgeson, V. S., & Fritz, H. L. (1999). Unmitigated agency and unmitigated communion: Distinctions from agency and communion. *Journal of Research in Personality, 33,* 131–158.

Heller, M. S., & Polsky, S. (1975). *Studies in violence and television*. New York, NY: American Broadcasting Companies.

Helson, R., Kwan, V. S. Y., John, O. P., & Jones, C. (2002). The growing evidence for personality change in adulthood: Findings from research with personality inventories. *Journal of Research in Personality, 36,* 287–306.

Helson, R., & Srivastava, S. (2002). Creative and wise people: Similarities, differences, and how they develop. *Personality and Social Psychology Bulletin, 28,* 1430–1440.

Henderlong, J., & Lepper, M. R. (2002). The effects of praise on children's intrinsic motivation: A review and synthesis. *Psychological Bulletin, 128,* 774–795.

Hennig, J., Reuter, M., Netter, P., Burk, C., & Landt, O. (2005). Two types of aggression are differentially related to serotonergic activity and the A779C TPH polymorphism. *Behavioral Neuroscience, 119,* 16–25.

Henriques, J. B., & Davidson, R. J. (1990). Asymmetrical brain electrical activity discriminates between previously depressed subjects and healthy controls. *Journal of Abnormal Psychology, 99,* 22–31.

Henriques, J. B., & Davidson, R. J. (1991). Left frontal hypoactivation in depression. *Journal of Abnormal Psychology, 100,* 535–545.

Hermans, E. J., Putman, P., & van Honk, J. (2006). Testosterone administration reduces empathetic behavior: A facial mimicry study. *Psychoneuroendocrinology, 31,* 859–866.

Hersen, M., & Bellack, A. (Eds.). (1976). *Behavioral assessment*. New York, NY: Pergamon Press.

Heschl, A. (2002). *The intelligent genome: On the origin of the human mind by mutation and selection*. New York, NY: Springer.

Hewitt, P. L., & Genest, M. (1990). The ideal self: Schematic processing of perfectionistic content in dysphoric university students. *Journal of Personality and Social Psychology, 59,* 802–808.

Higgins, E. T. (1987). Self-discrepancy: A theory relating self and affect. *Psychological Review, 94,* 319–340.

Higgins, E. T. (1990). Personality, social psychology, and person–situation relations: Standards and knowledge activation as a common language. In L. A. Pervin (Ed.), *Handbook of personality: Theory and research* (pp. 301–338). New York, NY: Guilford Press.

Higgins, E. T. (1997). Beyond pleasure and pain. *American Psychologist, 52,* 1280–1300.

Higgins, E. T., & Bargh, J. A. (1987). Social cognition and social perception. *Annual Review of Psychology, 38,* 369–425.

Higgins, E. T., & Brendl, C. M. (1995). Accessibility and applicability: Some "activation rules" influencing judgment. *Journal of Experimental Social Psychology, 31,* 218–243.

Higgins, E. T., King, G. A., & Mavin, G. H. (1982). Individual construct accessibility and subjective impressions and recall. *Journal of Personality and Social Psychology, 43,* 35–47.

Higgins, R. L., Snyder, C. R., & Berglas, S. (Eds.). (1990). *Self-handicapping: The paradox that isn't*. New York, NY: Plenum Press.

Higgins, S. T., Wong, C. J., Badger, G. J., Ogden, D. E. H., & Dantona, R. L. (2000). Contingent reinforcement increases cocaine abstinence during outpatient treatment and 1 year of follow-up. *Journal of Consulting and Clinical Psychology, 68,* 64–72.

Hill, C. A. (1991). Seeking emotional support: The influence of affiliative need and partner warmth. *Journal of Personality and Social Psychology, 60,* 112–121.

Hill, T., Lewicki, P., Czyzewska, M., & Boss, A. (1989). Self-perpetuating development of encoding biases in person perception. *Journal of Personality and Social Psychology, 57,* 373–387.

Hilton, N. Z., Harris, G. T., & Rice, M. E. (2000). The functions of aggression by male teenagers. *Journal of Personality and Social Psychology, 79,* 988–994.

Hinkley, K., & Andersen, S. M. (1996). The working self-concept in transference: Significant-other activation and self change. *Journal of Personality and Social Psychology, 71,* 1279–1295.

Hirt, E. R., McCrea, S. M., & Boris, H. I. (2003). "I know you self-handicapped last exam": Gender differences in reactions to self-handicapping. *Journal of Personality and Social Psychology, 84,* 177–193.

Hobfoll, S. E., Rom, T., & Segal, B. (1989). Sensation seeking, anxiety, and risk taking in the Israeli context. In S. Einstein (Ed.), *Drugs and alcohol use: Issues and factors* (pp. 53–59). New York, NY: Plenum Press.

Hodgins, H. S., Koestner, R., & Duncan, N. (1996). On the compatibility of autonomy and relatedness. *Personality and Social Psychology Bulletin, 22,* 227–237.

Hodgkinson, S., Sherrington, R., Gurling, H., Marchbanks, R., & Reeders, S. (1987). Molecular genetic evidence for heterogeneity in manic depression. *Nature, 325,* 805–806.

Hoffman, E. (1988). *The right to be human: A biography of Abraham Maslow*. Los Angeles, CA: Jeremy P. Tarcher.

Hoffman, L. W. (1991). The influence of the family environment on personality: Accounting for sibling differences. *Psychological Bulletin, 110,* 187–203.

Hofstee, W. K. B., de Raad, B., & Goldberg, L. R. (1992). Integration of the big five and circumplex approaches to trait structure. *Journal of Personality and Social Psychology, 63,* 146–163.

Hogan, R., & Nicholson, R. A. (1988). The meaning of personality test scores. *American Psychologist, 43,* 621–626.

Hogan, R., DeSoto, C. B., & Solano, C. (1977). Traits, tests, and personality research. *American Psychologist, 32,* 255–264.

Hokanson, J. E., & Burgess, M. (1962a). The effects of status, type of frustration, and aggression on vascular processes. *Journal of Abnormal and Social Psychology, 65,* 232–237.

Hokanson, J. E., & Burgess, M. (1962b). The effects of three types of aggression on vascular processes. *Journal of Abnormal and Social Psychology, 64,* 446–449.

Hokanson, J. E., Burgess, M., & Cohen, M. F. (1963). Effects of displaced aggression on systolic blood pressure. *Journal of Abnormal and Social Psychology, 67,* 214–218.

Holmes, D. S. (1981). Existence of classical projection and the stress-reducing function of attribution projection: A reply to Sherwood. *Psychological Bulletin, 90,* 460–466.

Holroyd, C. B., & Coles, M. G. H. (2002). The neural basis of human error processing: Reinforcement learning, dopamine, and the error-related negativity. *Psychological Review, 109,* 679–709.

Holt, R. (1966). Measuring libidinal and aggressive motives and their controls by means of the Rorschach test. In D. Levine (Ed.), *Nebraska symposium on motivation.* Lincoln, NE: University of Nebraska Press.

Holtzworth-Munroe, A. (1992). Social skill deficits in maritally violent men: Interpreting the data using a social information processing model. *Clinical Psychology Review, 12,* 605–617.

Holyoak, K. J., & Spellman, B. A. (1993). Thinking. *Annual Review of Psychology, 44,* 265–315.

Hopkin, K. (1995). Programmed cell death: A switch to the cytoplasm? *Journal of NIH Research, 7,* 39–41.

Hormuth, S. E. (1990). *The ecology of the self: Relocation and self-concept change.* Cambridge, England: Cambridge University Press.

Horvath, P., & Zuckerman, M. (1993). Sensation seeking, risk appraisal, and risky behavior. *Personality and Individual Differences, 14,* 41–52.

Howard, G. S. (1990). On the construct validity of self-reports: What do the data say? *American Psychologist, 45,* 292–294.

Howard, G. S., Maxwell, S. E., Weiner, R. L., Boynton, K. S., & Rooney, W. M. (1980). Is a behavioral measure the best estimate of behavioral parameters? Perhaps not. *Applied Psychological Measurement, 4,* 293–311.

Hoyle, R. H., & Sherrill, M. R. (2006). Future orientation in the self-system: Possible selves, self-regulation, and behavior. *Journal of Personality, 74,* 1673–1696.

Hsee, C. K., & Abelson, R. P. (1991). The velocity relation: Satisfaction as a function of the first derivative of outcome over time. *Journal of Personality and Social Psychology, 60,* 341–347.

Hubbard, J. A., Dodge, K. A., Cillessen, A. H. N., Coie, J. D., & Schwartz, D. (2001). The dyadic nature of social information processing in boys' reactive and proactive aggression. *Journal of Personality and Social Psychology, 80,* 268–280.

Hull, J. G. (1981). A self-awareness model of the causes and effects of alcohol consumption. *Journal of Abnormal Psychology, 90,* 586–600.

Hull, J. G., & Rielly, N. P. (1986). An information-processing approach to alcohol use and its consequences. In R. E. Ingram (Ed.), *Information processing approaches to clinical psychology.* New York, NY: Academic Press.

Hull, J. G., Slone, L. B., Meteyer, K. B., & Matthews, A. R. (2002) The nonconsciousness of self-consciousness. *Journal of Personality and Social Psychology, 83,* 406–424.

Humphreys, L. G. (1939). The effect of random alteration of reinforcement on the acquisition and extinction of conditioned eyelid reactions. *Journal of Experimental Psychology, 15,* 141–158.

Hustinx, P. W. J., Kuyper, H., van der Werf, M. P. C., & Dijkstra, P. (2009). Achievement motivation revisited: New longitudinal data to demonstrate its predictive power. *Educational Psychology, 29,* 561–582.

Hutchison, K. E., McGeary, J., Smolen, A., Bryan, A., & Swift, R. M. (2002). The DRD4 VNTR polymorphism moderates craving after alcohol consumption. *Health Psychology, 21,* 139–146.

Hymbaugh, K., & Garrett, J. (1974). Sensation seeking among skydivers. *Perceptual and Motor Skills, 38,* 118.

Ilgen, M., McKellar, J., & Tiet, Q. (2005). Abstinence self-efficacy and abstinence 1 year after substance use disorder treatment. *Journal of Consulting and Clinical Psychology, 73,* 1175–1180.

Ingram, R. E. (Ed.). (1986). *Information-processing approaches to clinical psychology.* New York, NY: Academic Press.

Isabella, R. A., Belsky, J., & von Eye, A. (1989). Origins of infant–mother attachment: An examination of interactional synchrony during the infant's first year. *Developmental Psychology, 25,* 12–21.

Jackson, D. N. (1984). *Personality Research Form manual* (3rd ed.). Port Huron, MI: Research Psychologists Press.

Jackson, D. N., & Messick, S. (Eds.). (1967). *Problems in assessment*. New York, NY: McGraw-Hill.

Jacob, S., McClintock, M. K., Zelano, B., & Ober, C. (2002). Paternally inherited HLA alleles are associated with women's choice of male odor. *Nature Genetics, 30*, 175–179.

James, W. (1890). *The principles of psychology* (Vol. 2). New York, NY: Holt.

Janel, D., & Pennebaker, J. W. (2009). The healing powers of expressive writing. In S. B. Kaufman & J. C. Kaufman (Eds.), *The psychology of creative writing* (pp. 264–273). New York, NY: Cambridge University Press.

Jang, K. L., Livesley, W. J., Angleitner, A., Riemann, R., & Vernon, P. A. (2002). Genetic and environmental influences on the covariance of facets defining the domains of the five-factor model of personality. *Personality and Individual Differences, 33*, 83–101.

Jang, K. L., Livesley, W. J., & Vernon, P. A. (1996). Heritability of the big five personality dimensions and their facets: A twin study. *Journal of Personality, 64*, 577–591.

Jang, K. L., McCrae, R. R., Angleitner, A., Riemann, R., & Livesley, W. J. (1998). Heritability of facet-level traits in a cross-cultural twin sample: Support for a hierarchical model of personality. *Journal of Personality and Social Psychology, 74*, 1556–1565.

Janoff-Bulman, R., & Leggatt, H. K. (2002). Culture and social obligation: When "shoulds" are perceived as "wants." *Journal of Research in Personality, 36*, 260–270.

Janoff-Bulman, R., Sheikh, S., & Hepp, S. (2009). Proscriptive versus prescriptive morality: Two faces of moral regulation. *Journal of Personality and Social Psychology, 96*, 521–537.

Jenkins, S. R. (1987). Need for achievement and women's careers over 14 years: Evidence for occupational structure effects. *Journal of Personality and Social Psychology, 53*, 922–932.

Jenkins, S. R. (1994). Need for power and women's careers over 14 years: Structural power, job satisfaction, and motive change. *Journal of Personality and Social Psychology, 66*, 155–165.

Jensen, M. B. (1987). Psychobiological factors predicting the course of breast cancer. *Journal of Personality, 55*, 317–342.

Jensen-Campbell, L. A., Adams, R., Perry, D. G., Workman, K. A., Furdella, J. Q., & Egan, S. K. (2002). Agreeableness, extraversion, and peer relations in early adolescence: Winning friends and deflecting aggression. *Journal of Research in Personality, 36*, 224–251.

Jensen-Campbell, L. A., Gleason, K. A., Adams, R., & Malcolm, K. T. (2003). Interpersonal conflict, agreeableness, and personality development. *Journal of Personality, 71*, 1059–1086.

Jensen-Campbell, L. A., & Graziano, W. G. (2001). Agreeableness as a moderator of interpersonal conflict. *Journal of Personality, 69*, 323–362.

Jensen-Campbell, L. A., Graziano, W. G., & West, S. G. (1995). Dominance, prosocial orientation, and female preferences: Do nice guys really finish last? *Journal of Personality and Social Psychology, 68*, 427–440.

Jensen-Campbell, L. A., & Malcolm, K. T. (2007). The importance of conscientiousness in adolescent interpersonal relationships. *Personality and Social Psychology Bulletin, 33*, 368–383.

Job, V., Oertig, D., Brandstätter, & Allemand, M. (2010). Discrepancies between implicit and explicit motivation and unhealthy eating behavior. *Journal of Personality, 78*, 1209–1238.

Jockin, V., McGue, M., & Lykken, D. T. (1996). Personality and divorce: A genetic analysis. *Journal of Personality and Social Psychology, 71*, 288–299.

John, O. P. (1990). The big-five factor taxonomy: Dimensions of personality in the natural language and in questionnaires. In L. Pervin (Ed.), *Handbook of personality theory and research* (pp. 66–100). New York, NY: Guilford Press.

John, O. P., & Robins, R. W. (1994). Accuracy and bias in self-perception: Individual differences in self-enhancement and the role of narcissism. *Journal of Personality and Social Psychology, 66*, 206–219.

Johnson, A. M., Vernon, P. A., & Feiler, A. R. (2008). Behavior genetic studies of personality: An introduction and review of the results of 50+ years of research. In G. J. Boyle, G. Matthews, & D. H. Saklofske (Eds.), *Handbook of personality theory and assessment* (Vol. 1, pp. 145–173). Los Angeles, CA: Sage.

Johnson, J. A., Germer, C. K., Efran, J. S., & Overton, W. F. (1988). Personality as the basis for theoretical predilections. *Journal of Personality and Social Psychology, 55*, 824–835.

Johnson, J. A., & Ostendorf, F. (1993). Clarification of the five-factor model with the abridged big five dimensional circumplex. *Journal of Personality and Social Psychology, 65*, 563–576.

Johnson, R. E., Chang, C. H., & Lord, R. G (2006). Moving from cognition to behavior: What the research says. *Psychological Bulletin, 132*, 381–415.

Johnson, S. L. (2005). Mania and goal regulation: A review. *Clinical Psychology Review, 25*, 241–262.

Johnson, S. L., & Leahy, R. L. (Eds.). (2003). *Psychological treatment of bipolar disorder*. New York, NY: Guilford Press.

Johnson, S. L., Sandrow, D., Meyer, B., Winters, R., Miller, I., Solomon, D., & Keitner, G. (2000). Increases in manic symptoms after life events involving goal attainment. *Journal of Abnormal Psychology, 109,* 721–727.

Johnson, W., & Kieras, D. (1983). Representation-saving effects of prior knowledge in memory for simple technical prose. *Memory and Cognition, 11,* 456–466.

Johnson, W., Turkheimer, E., Gottesman, I. I., & Bouchard, T. J., Jr. (2009). Beyond heritability: Twin studies in behavioral research. *Current Directions in Psychological Science, 18,* 217–220.

Johnson-Laird, P. N., Mancini, F., & Gangemi, A. (2006). A hyper-emotion theory of psychological illnesses. *Psychological Review, 113,* 822–841.

Joireman, J., Anderson, J., & Strathman, A. (2003). The aggression paradox: Understanding links among aggression, sensation seeking, and the consideration of future consequences. *Journal of Personality and Social Psychology, 84,* 1287–1302.

Jonas, E., Schimel, J., Greenberg, J., & Pyszczynski, T. (2002). The Scrooge effect: Evidence that mortality salience increases prosocial attitudes and behavior. *Personality and Social Psychology Bulletin, 28,* 1342–1353.

Jonas, K. J., & Sassenberg, K. (2006). Knowing how to react: Automatic response priming from social categories. *Journal of Personality and Social Psychology, 90,* 709–721.

Jones, E. E., & Berglas, S. (1978). Control of attributions about the self through self-handicapping strategies: The appeal of alcohol and the role of underachievement. *Personality and Social Psychology Bulletin, 4,* 200–206.

Jones, E. E., & Pittman, T. S. (1982). Toward a general theory of strategic self-presentation. In J. Suls (Ed.), *Psychological perspectives on the self* (Vol. 1). Hillsdale, NJ: Erlbaum.

Jones, J. T., Pelham, B. W., Carvallo, M., & Mirenberg, M. C. (2004). How do I love thee? Let me count the Js: Implicit egotism and interpersonal attraction. *Journal of Personality and Social Psychology, 87,* 665–683.

Jones, S. S. (2007). Imitation in infancy: The development of mimicry. *Psychological Science, 18,* 593–599.

Jones, W. H., Hobbes, S. A., & Hockenberg, D. (1982). Loneliness and social skills deficits. *Journal of Personality and Social Psychology, 42,* 682–689.

Jöreskog, K. G., & Sörbom, D. (1979). *Advances in factor analysis and structural equations.* Cambridge, MA: Abt Associates.

Joseph, J. E., Liu, X., Jiang, Y., Lynam, D., & Kelly, T. H. (2009). Neural correlates of emotional reactivity in sensation seeking. *Psychological Science, 20,* 215–223.

Josephs, R. A., Sellers, J. G., Newman, M. L., & Mehta, P. H. (2006). The mismatch effect: When testosterone and status are at odds. *Journal of Personality and Social Psychology, 90,* 999–1013.

Jung, C. G. (1933). *Psychological types.* New York, NY: Harcourt, Brace, & World.

Juni, S. (1981). Maintaining anonymity vs. requesting feedback as a function of oral dependency. *Perceptual and Motor Skills, 52,* 239–242.

Juni, S., & Fischer, R. E. (1985). Religiosity and preoedipal fixation. *Journal of Genetic Psychology, 146,* 27–35.

Juni, S., & Lo Cascio, R. (1985). Preference for counseling and psychotherapy as related to preoedipal fixation. *Psychological Reports, 56,* 431–438.

Juni, S., Masling, J., & Brannon, R. (1979). Interpersonal touching and orality. *Journal of Personality Assessment, 43,* 235–237.

Jussim, L. (1991). Social perception and social reality: A reflection–construction model. *Psychology Review, 98,* 54–73.

Kahn, M. (2002). *Basic Freud: Psychoanalytic thought for the 21st century.* New York, NY: Basic Books.

Kahn, S., Zimmerman, G., Csikszentmihalyi, M., & Getzels, J. W. (1985). Relations between identity in young adulthood and intimacy at midlife. *Journal of Personality and Social Psychology, 49,* 1316–1322.

Kamarck, T. W., Muldoon, M. F., Shiffman, S. S., & Sutton-Tyrrell, K. (2007). Experiences of demand and control during daily life are predictors of carotid atherosclerotic progression among healthy men. *Health Psychology, 26,* 324–332.

Kamarck, T. W., Shiffman, S. S., & Wethington, E. (2011). Measurement of daily psychosocial stress: Use of real-time methods. In R. Contrada & A. Baum (Eds.), *The handbook of stress science: Biology, psychology, and health* (pp. 597–617). New York, NY: Springer.

Kanayama, G., Gruber, A. J., Pope, H. G., Jr., Borowiecki, J. J., & Hudson, J. I. (2001). Over-the-counter drug use in gymnasiums: An underrecognized substance abuse problem? *Psychotherapy and Psychosomatics, 70,* 137–140.

Kanfer, F. H. (1977). The many faces of self-control, or behavior modification changes its focus. In R. B. Stuart (Ed.), *Behavioral self-management: Strategies, techniques, and outcomes.* New York, NY: Brunner/Mazel.

Kanfer, F. H., & Busemeyer, J. R. (1982). The use of problem-solving and decision-making in behavior therapy. *Clinical Psychology Review, 2,* 239–266.

Kanfer, F. H., & Hagerman, S. M. (1981). The role of self-regulation. In L. P. Rehm (Ed.), *Behavior therapy for depression: Present status and future directions.* New York, NY: Academic Press.

Kanfer, F. H., & Hagerman, S. M. (1985). Behavior therapy and the information-processing paradigm. In S. Reiss & R. R. Bootzin (Eds.), *Theoretical issues in behavior therapy.* New York, NY: Academic Press.

Kanfer, F. H., Karoly, P., & Newman, A. (1975). Reduction of children's fear of the dark by competence-related and situational threat-related verbal cues. *Journal of Consulting and Clinical Psychology, 43,* 251–258.

Kanfer, F. H., & Marston, A. R. (1963). Human reinforcement: Vicarious and direct. *Journal of Experimental Psychology, 65,* 292–296.

Kanfer, F. H., & Schefft, B. K. (1988). *Guiding the process of therapeutic change.* Champaign, IL: Research Press.

Kaplan, J. R., Manuck, S. B., Fontenot, M. B., & Mann, J. J. (2002). Central nervous system monoamine correlates of social dominance in cynomolgus monkeys (*Macaca fascicularis*). *Neuropsychopharmacology, 26,* 431–443.

Karylowski, J. J. (1990). Social reference points and accessibility of trait-related information in self–other similarity judgments. *Journal of Personality and Social Psychology, 58,* 975–983.

Kasser, T. (2002). *The high price of materialism.* Cambridge, MA: Bradford Books.

Kasser, T., Koestner, R., & Lekes, N. (2002). Early family experiences and adult values: A 26-year, prospective longitudinal study. *Personality and Social Psychology Bulletin, 28,* 826–835.

Kasser, T., & Ryan, R. M. (1993). A dark side of the American dream: Correlates of financial success as a central life aspiration. *Journal of Personality and Social Psychology, 65,* 410–422.

Katigbak, M. S., Church, A. T., Guanzon-Lapeña, Ma. A., Carlota, A. J., & del Pilar, G. H. (2002). Are indigenous personality dimensions culture specific? Philippine inventories and the five-factor model. *Journal of Personality and Social Psychology, 82,* 89–101.

Kawada, C. L. K., Oettingen, G., Gollwitzer, P. M., & Bargh, J. A. (2004). The projection of implicit and explicit goals. *Journal of Personality and Social Psychology, 86,* 545–559.

Kazdin, A. E. (1974). Effects of covert modeling and reinforcement on assertive behavior. *Journal of Abnormal Psychology, 83,* 240–252.

Kazdin, A. E. (1975). Covert modeling, imagery assessment, and assertive behavior. *Journal of Consulting and Clinical Psychology, 43,* 716–724.

Keane, T. M., Kolb, L. C., Kaloupek, D. G., Orr, S. P., Blanchard, E. B., Thomas, R. G., Hsieh, F. Y., & Lavori, P. W. (1998). Utility of psychophysiological measurement in the diagnosis of posttraumatic stress disorder: Results from a Department of Veteran Affairs cooperative study. *Journal of Consulting and Clinical Psychology, 66,* 914–923.

Keller, J., & Bless, H. (2008). Flow and regularity compatibility: An experimental approach to the flow model of intrinsic motivation. *Personality and Social Psychology Bulletin, 34,* 196–209.

Keller, P. E., Wascher, E., Prinz, W., Waszak, F., Koch, I., & Rosenbaum, D. A. (2006). Differences between intention-based and stimulus-based actions. *Journal of Psychophysiology, 20,* 9–20.

Kelly, A. E., Klusas, J. A., von Weiss, R. T., & Kenny, C. (2001). What is it about revealing secrets that is beneficial? *Personality and Social Psychology Bulletin, 27,* 651–665.

Kelly, G. A. (1955). *The psychology of personal constructs* (Vols. 1 and 2). New York, NY: Norton.

Kendler, K. S. (1997). Social support: A genetic–epidemiological analysis. *American Journal of Psychiatry, 154,* 1398–1404.

Kendler, K. S. (2005). "A gene for …": The nature of gene action in psychiatric disorders. *American Journal of Psychiatry, 162,* 1243–1252.

Kenford, S. L., Fiore, M. C., Jorenby, D. E., & Smith, S. S. (1994). Predicting smoking cessation: Who will quit with and without the nicotine patch. *Journal of the American Medical Association, 217,* 589–594.

Kenrick, D. T., Groth, G. E., Trost, M. R., & Sadalla, E. K. (1993). Integrating evolutionary and social exchange perspectives on relationships: Effects of gender, self-appraisal, and involvement level on mate selection criteria. *Journal of Personality and Social Psychology, 64,* 951–969.

Kenrick, D. T., & Keefe, R. C. (1992). Age preferences in mates reflect sex differences in human reproductive strategies. *Behavioral and Brain Sciences, 15,* 75–91.

Kenrick, D. T., Neuberg, S. L., Zierk, K. L., & Krones, J. M. (1994). Evolution and social cognition: Contrast effects as a function of sex, dominance, and physical attractiveness. *Personality and Social Psychology Bulletin, 20,* 210–217.

Kenrick, D. T., Sadalla, E. K., Groth, G., & Trost, M. R. (1990). Evolution, traits, and the stages of human courtship: Qualifying the parental investment model. *Journal of Personality, 58,* 97–116.

Kenrick, D. T., Sundie, J. M., Nicastle, L. D, & Stone, G. O. (2001). Can one ever be too wealthy or too chaste? Searching for nonlinearities in mate judgment. *Journal of Personality and Social Psychology, 80,* 462–471.

Kern, M. L., & Friedman, H. S. (2008). Do conscientious individuals live longer? A quantitative review. *Health Psychology, 27,* 505–512.

Kernberg, O. (1976). *Borderline conditions and pathological narcissism*. New York, NY: Jason Aronson.

Kernberg, O. (1980). *Internal world and external reality*. New York, NY: Jason Aronson.

Kessler, R. C., Kendler, K. S., Heath, A., Neale, M. C., & Eaves, L. J. (1992). Social support, depressed mood, and adjustment to stress: A genetic epidemiologic investigation. *Journal of Personality and Social Psychology, 62*, 257–272.

Keyes, C. L. M., Shmotkin, D., & Ryff, C. D. (2002). Optimizing well-being: The empirical encounter of two traditions. *Journal of Personality and Social Psychology, 82*, 1007–1022.

Kieras, J. E., Tobin, R. M., Graziano, W. G., & Rothbart, M. K. (2005). You can't always get what you want: Effortful control and children's responses to undesirable gifts. *Psychological Science, 16*, 391–396.

Kim, Y., Carver, C. S., Deci, E. L., & Kasser, T. (2008). Adult attachment and psychological well-being in cancer caregivers: The meditational role of spouses' motives for caregiving. *Health Psychology, 27*, S144–S154.

Kimura, D. (1999). *Sex and cognition*. Cambridge, MA: MIT Press.

Kirkpatrick, L. A. (1998). God as a substitute attachment figure: A longitudinal study of adult attachment style and religious change in college students. *Personality and Social Psychology Bulletin, 24*, 961–973.

Kirkpatrick, L. A., & Davis, K. E. (1994). Attachment style, gender, and relationship stability: A longitudinal analysis. *Journal of Personality and Social Psychology, 66*, 502–512.

Kirsch, I. (1985). Response expectancy as a determinant of experience and behavior. *American Psychologist, 40*, 1189–1202.

Kirsch, I. (1990). *Changing expectations: A key to effective psychotherapy*. Pacific Grove, CA: Brooks/Cole.

Kirsch, I., Mearns, J., & Catanzaro, S. J. (1990). Mood-regulation expectancies as determinants of dysphoria in college students. *Journal of Counseling Psychology, 37*, 306–312.

Kitcher, P. (1987). Précis of *Vaulting ambition: Sociobiology and the quest for human nature*. *Behavioral and Brain Sciences, 10*, 61–100.

Klein, J. (1987). *Our need for others and its roots in infancy*. London, England: Tavistock.

Klein, M. (1935). *The psychoanalysis of children*. New York, NY: Norton.

Klein, M. (1955a). The psychoanalytic play technique. *American Journal of Orthopsychiatry, 112*, 418–422.

Klein, M. (1955b). The psychoanalytic play technique, its history and significance. In M. Klein, P. Heiman, &

R. Money-Kyrle (Eds.), *New directions in psychoanalysis: The significance of infant conflict in the pattern of adult behavior*. New York, NY: Basic Books.

Klimstra, T. A., Hale, W. W. III, Raaijmakers, Q. A. W., Branje, S. J. T., & Meeus, A. W. (2009). Maturation of personality in adolescence. *Journal of Personality and Social Psychology, 96*, 898–912.

Klinesmith, J., Kasser, T., & McAndrew, F. T. (2006). Guns, testosterone, and aggression: An experimental test of a mediational hypothesis. *Psychological Science, 17*, 568–571.

Klinger, E. (1975). Consequences of commitment to and disengagement from incentives. *Psychological Review, 82*, 1–25.

Klinger, E. (1987). Current concerns and disengagement from incentives. In F. Halisch & J. Kuhl (Eds.), *Motivation, intention, and volition* (pp. 337–347). Berlin, Germany: Springer-Verlag.

Knapp, R. R. (1976). *Handbook for the Personal Orientation Inventory*. San Diego, CA: EdITS.

Knee, C. R., Lonsbary, C., Canevello, A., & Patrick, H. (2005). Self-determination and conflict in romantic relationships. *Journal of Personality and Social Psychology, 89*, 997–1009.

Knee, C. R., Patrick, H., Vietor, N. A., Nanayakkara, A., & Neighbors, C. (2002). Self-determination as growth motivation in romantic relationships. *Personality and Social Psychology Bulletin, 28*, 609–619.

Knickmeyer, R., Baron-Cohen, S., Raggatt, P., Taylor, K., & Hackett, G. (2006). Fetal testosterone and empathy. *Hormones and Behavior, 49*, 282–292.

Knutson, B., Wolkowitz, O. M., Cole, S. W., Chan, T., Moore, E. A., Johnson, R. C., Terpstra, J., Turner, R. A., & Reus, V. I. (1998). Selective alteration of personality and social behavior by serotonergic intervention. *American Journal of Psychiatry, 155*, 373–379.

Kobak, R. R., & Hazan, C. (1991). Attachment in marriage: Effects of security and accuracy of working models. *Journal of Personality and Social Psychology, 60*, 861–869.

Kochanska, G., Friesenborg, A. E., Lange, L. A., & Martel, M. M. (2004). Parents' personality and infants' temperament as contributors to their emerging relationship. *Journal of Personality and Social Psychology, 86*, 744–759.

Kochanska, G., & Knaack, A. (2003). Effortful control as a personality characteristic of young children: Antecedents, correlates, and consequences. *Journal of Personality, 71*, 1087–1112.

Koestner, R., Lekes, N., Powers, T. A., & Chicoine, E. (2002). Attaining personal goals: Self-concordance plus implementation intentions equals success. *Journal of Personality and Social Psychology, 83*, 231–244.

Koestner, R., Zuckerman, M., & Koestner, J. (1987). Praise, involvement, and intrinsic motivation. *Journal of Personality and Social Psychology, 53*, 383–390.

Koffka, K. (1935). *Principles of Gestalt psychology*. New York, NY: Harcourt, Brace.

Kohler, E., Keysers, C., Umiltà, M. A., Fogassi, L., Gallese, V., & Rizzolatti, G. (2002). Hearing sounds, understanding actions: Action representation in mirror neurons. *Science, 297*, 846–848.

Köhler, W. (1947). *Gestalt psychology*. New York, NY: Liveright.

Kohut, H. (1977). *The restoration of the self*. New York, NY: International Universities Press.

Koole, S. L., Greenberg, J., & Pyszczynski, T. (2006). Introducing science to the psychology of the soul: Experimental existential psychology. *Current Directions in Psychological Science, 15,* 212–216.

Koole, S. L., Jager, W., van den Berg, A. E., Vlek, C. A. J., & Hofstee, W. K. B. (2001). On the social nature of personality: Effects of extraversion, agreeableness, and feedback about collective resource use on cooperation in a resource dilemma. *Personality and Social Psychology Bulletin, 27*, 289–301.

Korchmaros, J. D., & Kenny, D. A. (2001). Emotional closeness as a mediator of the effect of genetic relatedness on altruism. *Psychological Science, 12*, 262–265.

Kornhaber, R. C., & Schroeder, H. E. (1975). Importance of model similarity on extinction of avoidance behavior in children. *Journal of Consulting and Clinical Psychology, 43*, 601–607.

Kosfeld, M., Heinrichs, M., Zack, P. J., Fischbacher, U., & Fehr, E. (2005). Oxytocin increases trust in humans. *Nature, 435*, 673–676.

Kotler, M., Cohen, H., Segman, R., Gritsenko, L., Nemanov, L., Lerer, B., Kramer, I., Zer-Zion, M., Kletz, I., & Ebstein, R. P. (1997). Excess dopamine D4 receptor (D4DR) exon III seven repeat allele in opioid-dependent subjects. *Molecular Psychiatry, 2*, 251–254.

Kotre, J. (1984). *Outliving the self: Generativity and the interpretation of lives*. Baltimore, MD: Johns Hopkins University Press.

Kowaz, A. M., & Marcia, J. E. (1991). Development and validation of a measure of Eriksonian industry. *Journal of Personality and Social Psychology, 60*, 390–396.

Krach, S., Paulus, F. M., Bodden, M., & Kircher, T. (2010, May 28). The rewarding nature of social interactions. *Frontiers in Behavioral Neuroscience*. Retrieved October 13, 2010, from www.frontiersin.org

Kramer, P. D. (1993). *Listening to Prozac: A psychiatrist explores anti-depressant drugs and the remaking of the self*. New York, NY: Viking.

Kraus, M. W., & Chen, S. (2009). Striving to be known by significant others: Automatic activation of self-verification goals in relationship contexts. *Journal of Personality and Social Psychology, 97,* 58–73.

Kretschmer, E. (1925). *Physique and character*. New York, NY: Harcourt, Brace.

Kriegman, D., & Knight, C. (1988). Social evolution, psychoanalysis, and human nature. *Social Policy, 19*, 49–55.

Krueger, R. F. (2002). Personality from a realist's perspective: Personality traits, criminal behaviors, and the externalizing spectrum. *Journal of Research in Personality, 36*, 564–572.

Krueger, R. F., Schmutte, P. S., Caspi, A., Moffitt, T. E., Campbell, K., & Silva, P. A. (1994). Personality traits are linked to crime among men and women: Evidence from a birth cohort. *Journal of Abnormal Psychology, 103*, 328–338.

Krueger, R. F., Watson, D., & Barlow, D. H. (Eds.). (2005). Toward a dimensionally based taxonomy of psychopathology [Special section]. *Journal of Abnormal Psychology, 114,* 491–569.

Krusemark, E. A., Campbell, W. K., & Clementz, B. A. (2008). Attributions, deception, and event related potentials: An investigation of the self-serving bias. *Psychophysiology, 45*, 511–515.

Kuhl, J. (2000). The volitional basis of Personality Systems Interaction Theory: Applications in learning and treatment contexts. *International Journal of Educational Research, 33*, 665–703.

Kuhl, J., & Helle, P. (1986). Motivational and volitional determinants of depression: The degenerated-intention hypothesis. *Journal of Abnormal Psychology, 95*, 247–251.

Kuiper, N. A., & Derry, P. A. (1981). The self as a cognitive prototype: An application to person perception and depression. In N. Cantor & J. Kihlstrom (Eds.), *Cognition, social interaction, and personality*. Hillsdale, NJ: Erlbaum.

Kukla, A. (1972). Foundations of an attributional theory of performance. *Psychological Review, 79*, 454–470.

Kulhavy, R. W., & Stock, W. A. (1989). Feedback in written instruction: The place of response certitude. *Educational Psychology Review, 1*, 279–308.

Kunda, Z. (1999). *Social cognition: Making sense of people*. Cambridge, MA: MIT Press.

Kunda, Z., & Thagard, P. (1996). Forming impressions from stereotypes, traits, and behaviors: A parallel-constraint-satisfaction theory. *Psychological Review, 103*, 284–308.

Kunzmann, U., & Baltes, P. B. (2003). Wisdom-related knowledge: Affective, motivational, and interpersonal correlates. *Personality and Social Psychology Bulletin, 29,* 1104–1119.

La Greca, A. M., & Santogrossi, D. A. (1980). Social skills training with elementary school students: A behavioral group approach. *Journal of Consulting and Clinical Psychology, 48,* 220–227.

La Greca, A. M., Stone, W. L., & Bell, C. R., III (1983). Facilitating the vocational–interpersonal skills of mentally retarded individuals. *American Journal of Mental Deficiency, 88,* 270–278.

La Guardia, J. G., Ryan, R. M., Couchman, C. E., & Deci, E. L. (2000). Within-person variation in security of attachment: A self-determination theory perspective on attachment, need fulfillment, and well-being. *Journal of Personality and Social Psychology, 79,* 367–384.

Lakoff, G. (1987). *Women, fire, and dangerous things: What categories reveal about the mind.* Chicago, IL: University of Chicago Press.

Landreth, G. L. (1991). *Play therapy: The art of the relationship.* Muncie, IN: Accelerated Development.

Landy, F. J. (1986). Stamp collecting versus science: Validation as hypothesis testing. *American Psychologist, 41,* 1183–1192.

Lane, R. D., & Nadel, L. (Eds.). (2000). *Cognitive neuroscience of emotion.* New York, NY: Oxford University Press.

Lang, P. J., & Lazovik, A. D. (1963). Experimental desensitization of a phobic. *Journal of Abnormal and Social Psychology, 66,* 519–525.

Langens, T. A., & Schmalt, H-D. (2002). Emotional consequences of positive daydreaming: The moderating role of fear of failure. *Personality and Social Psychology Bulletin, 28,* 1725–1735.

Langner, C. A., & Winter, D. G. (2001). The motivational basis of concessions and compromise: Archival and laboratory studies. *Journal of Personality and Social Psychology, 81,* 711–727.

Langston, C., & Cantor, N. (1989). Social anxiety and social constraint: When "making friends" is hard. *Journal of Personality and Social Psychology, 56,* 649–661.

Lanning, K. (1994). Dimensionality of observer ratings on the California Adult Q-set. *Journal of Personality and Social Psychology, 67,* 151–160.

Lansdale, M., & Baguley, T. (2008). Dilution as a model of long-term forgetting. *Psychological Review, 115,* 864–892.

Lansing, J. B., & Heyns, R. W. (1959). Need affiliation and frequency of four types of communication. *Journal of Abnormal and Social Psychology, 58,* 365–372.

Larsen, R. J., & Ketelaar, T. (1991). Personality and susceptibility to positive and negative emotional states. *Journal of Personality and Social Psychology, 61,* 132–140.

Larstone, R. M., Jang, K. L., Livesley, W. J., Vernon, P. A., & Wolf, H. (2002). The relationship between Eysenck's P-E-N model of personality, the five-factor model of personality, and traits delineating personality dysfunction. *Personality and Individual Differences, 33,* 25–37.

Lau, R. R. (1989). Construct accessibility and electoral choice. *Political Behavior, 11,* 5–32.

Laurenceau, J.-P., Barrett, L. F., & Pietromonaco, P. R. (1998). Intimacy as an interpersonal process: The importance of self-disclosure, and perceived partner responsiveness in interpersonal exchanges. *Journal of Personality and Social Psychology, 74,* 1238–1251.

Laurenceau, J-P., & Bolger, N. (2005). Using diary methods to study marital and family processes. *Journal of Family Psychology, 19,* 86–97.

Laurenceau, J-P., Kleinman, B. M., Kaczynski, K. J., & Carver, C. S. (2010). Assessment of relationship-specific incentive and threat sensitivities: Predicting satisfaction and affect in adult intimate relationships. *Psychological Assessment, 22,* 407–419.

Le Vay, S. (1991). A difference in hypothalamic structure between heterosexual and homosexual men. *Science, 253,* 1034–1037.

Le Vay, S. (1993). *The sexual brain.* Cambridge, MA: MIT Press.

Leak, G. K., & Christopher, S. B. (1982). Freudian psychoanalysis and sociobiology: A synthesis. *American Psychologist, 37,* 313–322.

Leary, M. R., & Baumeister, R. F. (2000). The nature and function of self-esteem: Sociometer theory. In M. P. Zanna (Ed.), *Advances in experimental social psychology* (Vol. 32, pp. 1–62). San Diego, CA: Academic Press.

Lee, A., & Hankin, B. L. (2009). Insecure attachment, dysfunctional attitudes, and low self-esteem predicting prospective symptoms of depression and anxiety among adolescents. *Journal of Clinical Child & Adolescent Psychology, 38,* 219–231.

Lee, R., Ferris, C., Van de Kar, L. D., & Coccaro, E. F. (2009). Cerebrospinal fluid oxytocin, life history of aggression, and personality disorder. *Psychoneuroendocrinology, 34,* 1567–1573.

Leit, R. A., Pope, H. G., Jr., & Gray, J. J. (2001). Cultural expectations of muscularity in men: The evolution of playgirl centerfolds. *International Journal of Eating Disorders, 29,* 90–93.

Lemann, N. (1994, February). Is there a science of success? *Atlantic Monthly, 273,* 83–98.

Lengfelder, A., & Gollwitzer, P. M. (2001). Reflective and reflexive action control in patients with frontal brain lesions. *Neuropsychology, 15,* 80–100.

Lepper, M. R., & Greene, D. (1975). Turning play into work: Effects of adult surveillance and extrinsic rewards on children's intrinsic motivation. *Journal of Personality and Social Psychology, 31,* 479–486.

Lepper, M. R., & Greene, D. (1978). *The hidden costs of reward.* Hillsdale, NJ: Erlbaum.

Lesch, K-P., & Mössner, R. (1998). Genetically driven variation in serotonin uptake: Is there a link to affective spectrum, neurodevelopmental, and neurodegenerative disorders? *Biological Psychiatry, 44,* 179–192.

Lesch, K-P., Bengel, D., Heils, A., Sabol, S. Z., Greenberg, B. D., Petri, S., et al. (1996). Association of anxiety-related traits with a polymorphism in the serotonin transporter gene regulatory region. *Science, 274,* 1527–1531.

Levenson, R. W., & Ruef, A. M. (1992). Empathy: A physiological substrate. *Journal of Personality and Social Psychology, 63,* 234–246.

Levine, D. S., & Leven, S. J. (Eds.). (1992). *Motivation, emotion, and goal direction in neural networks.* Hillsdale, NJ: Erlbaum.

Lewin, D. I. (1990). Gene therapy nears starting gate. *Journal of NIH Research, 2,* 36–38.

Lewin, K. (1951a). *Field theory in social science.* New York, NY: Harper.

Lewin, K. (1951b). The nature of field theory. In M. H. Marx (Ed.), *Psychological theory.* New York, NY: Macmillan.

Lewis, D. J., & Duncan, C. P. (1956). Effect of different percentages of money reward on extinction of a lever pulling response. *Journal of Experimental Psychology, 52,* 23–27.

Lewontin, R. C., Rose, S., & Kamin, L. J. (1984). *Not in our genes: Biology, ideology, and human nature.* New York, NY: Penguin Press.

Li, N. P., Bailey, J. M., Kenrick, D. T., & Linsenmeier, J. A. W. (2002). The necessities and luxuries of mate preferences: Testing the tradeoffs. *Journal of Personality and Social Psychology, 82,* 947–955.

Li, T., Xu, K., Deng, H., Cai, G., Liu, J., Liu, X., Wang, R., Xiang, X., Zhao, J., Murray, R. M., Sham, P. C., & Collier, D. A. (1997). Association analysis of the dopamine D4 gene exon III VNTR and heroin abuse in Chinese subjects. *Molecular Psychiatry, 2,* 413–416.

Libby, L. K., Shaeffer, E. M., & Eibach, R. P. (2009). Seeing meaning in action: A bidirectional link between visual perspective and action identification level. *Journal of Experimental Psychology, 4,* 503–516.

Libera, C. D., & Chelazzi, L. (2006). Visual selective attention and the effects of monetary rewards. *Psychological Science, 17,* 222–227.

Libera, C. D., & Chelazzi, L. (2009). Learning to attend and to ignore is a matter of gains and losses. *Psychological Science, 20,* 778–785.

Lichtenfeld, S., Maier, M. A., Elliot, A. J., & Pekrun, R. (2009). The semantic red effect: Processing the word red undermines intellectual performance. *Journal of Experimental Social Psychology, 45,* 1273–1276.

Lieberman, M. D., Gaunt, R., Gilbert, D. T., & Trope, Y. (2002). Reflection and reflexion: A social cognitive neuroscience approach to attributional inference. In M. Zanna (Ed.), *Advances in experimental social psychology* (pp. 199–249). San Diego, CA: Academic Press.

Liebert, R. M., & Baron, R. A. (1972). Some immediate effects of televised violence on children's behavior. *Developmental Psychology, 6,* 469–475.

Liebert, R. M., & Fernandez, L. E. (1970). Effects of vicarious consequences on imitative performance. *Child Development, 41,* 841–852.

Light, K. C., Smith, T. E., Johns, J. M., Brownley, K. A., Hofheimer, J. A., & Amico, J. A. (2000). Oxytocin responsivity in mothers of infants: A preliminary study of relationships with blood pressure during laboratory stress and normal ambulatory activity. *Health Psychology, 19,* 560–567.

Lilienfeld, S. O., Wood, J. M., & Garb, H. N. (2000). The scientific status of projective techniques. *Psychological Science in the Public Interest, 1,* 27–66.

Linville, P. W. (1987). Self-complexity as a cognitive buffer against stress-related illness and depression. *Journal of Personality and Social Psychology, 52,* 663–676.

Little, B. R. (1989). Personal projects analysis: Trivial pursuits, magnificent obsessions, and the search for coherence. In D. M. Buss & N. Cantor (Eds.), *Personality psychology: Recent trends and emerging directions* (pp. 15–31). New York, NY: Springer-Verlag.

Locke, E. A., & Latham, G. P. (1990). *A theory of goal setting and task performance.* Englewood Cliffs, NJ: Prentice-Hall.

Locurto, C. M., Terrace, H. S., & Gibbon, J. (Eds.). (1980). *Autoshaping and conditioning theory.* New York, NY: Academic Press.

Lodi-Smith, J., Geise, A. C., Roberts, B. W., & Robins, R. W. (2009). Narrating personality change. *Journal of Personality and Social Psychology, 96,* 679–689.

Loehlin, J. C. (1992). *Genes and environment in personality development.* Newbury Park, CA: Sage.

Loehlin, J. C., & Nichols, R. C. (1976). *Heredity, environment, and personality.* Austin, TX: University of Texas Press.

Loehlin, J. C., Willerman, L., & Horn, J. M. (1985). Personality resemblances in adoptive families when the children are late-adolescent or adult. *Journal of Personality and Social Psychology, 48*, 376–392.

Louro, M. J., Pieters, R., & Zeelenberg, M. (2007). Dynamics of multiple-goal pursuit. *Journal of Personality and Social Psychology, 93*, 174–193.

Lovejoy, C. M., & Durik, A. M. (2010). Self-handicapping: The interplay between self-set and assigned achievement goals. *Motivation and Emotion, 34*, 242–252.

Lowell, E. L. (1952). The effect of need for achievement on learning and speed of performance. *Journal of Psychology, 33*, 31–40.

Lucas, R. E., & Diener, E. (2001). Understanding extraverts' enjoyment of social situations: The importance of pleasantness. *Journal of Personality and Social Psychology, 81*, 343–356.

Lucas, R. E., Diener, E., Grob, A., Suh, E. M., & Shao, L. (2000). Cross-cultural evidence for the fundamental features of extraversion. *Journal of Personality and Social Psychology, 79*, 452–468.

Lumsden, C., & Wilson, E. O. (1981). *Genes, mind, and culture.* Cambridge, MA: Harvard University Press.

Lundy, A. C. (1985). The reliability of the Thematic Apperception Test. *Journal of Personality Assessment, 49*, 141–145.

Lütkenhaus, P., Grossmann, K. E., & Grossmann, K. (1985). Infant-mother attachment at twelve months and style of interaction with a stranger at the age of three years. *Child Development, 56*, 1538–1542.

Lykken, D. T., & Tellegen, A. (1993). Is human mating adventitious or the result of lawful choice? A twin study of mate selection. *Journal of Personality and Social Psychology, 65*, 56–68.

Lynam, D. R., Leukefeld, C., & Clayton, R. R. (2003). The contribution of personality to the overlap between antisocial behavior and substance use/misuse. *Aggressive Behavior, 29*, 316–331.

Lynn, R. (2001). *Eugenics: A reassessment.* Westport, CT: Praeger.

MacKay, D. M. (1963). Mindlike behavior in artefacts. In K. M. Sayre & F. J. Crosson (Eds.), *The modeling of mind: Computers and intelligence.* Notre Dame, IN: University of Notre Dame Press.

MacKay, D. M. (1966). Cerebral organization and the conscious control of action. In J. C. Eccles (Ed.), *Brain and conscious experience.* Berlin, Germany: Springer-Verlag.

Macrae, C. N., & Boderhausen, G. V. (2000). Social cognition: Thinking categorically. *Annual Review of Psychology, 51*, 93–120.

Macrae, C. N., Milne, A. B., & Bodenhausen, G. V. (1994). Stereotypes as energy-saving devices: A peek inside the cognitive toolbox. *Journal of Personality and Social Psychology, 66*, 37–47.

Magee, J. C., & Langner, C. A. (2008). How personalized and socialized power motivation facilitate antisocial and prosocial decision-making. *Journal of Research in Personality, 42*, 1547–1559.

Magnus, K., Diener, E., Fujita, F., & Pavot, W. (1993). Extraversion and neuroticism as predictors of objective life events: A longitudinal analysis. *Journal of Personality and Social Psychology, 65*, 1046–1053.

Magnusson, D., & Endler, N. S. (Eds.). (1977). *Personality at the crossroads: Current issues in interactional psychology.* Hillsdale, NJ: Erlbaum.

Mahler, M. S. (1968). *On human symbiosis and the vicissitudes of individuation: Infantile psychosis.* New York, NY: International Universities Press.

Mahler, M. S., Pine, F., & Bergman, A. (1975). *The psychological birth of the human infant: Symbiosis and individuation.* New York, NY: Basic Books.

Mahoney, M. J. (1977). Some applied issues in self-monitoring. In J. D. Cone & R. P. Hawkins (Eds.), *Behavioral assessment: New directions in clinical psychology.* New York, NY: Brunner/Mazel.

Main, M., & Cassidy, J. (1988). Categories of response to reunion with the parent at age 6: Predictable from infant attachment classifications and stable over a 1-month period. *Developmental Psychology, 24*, 415–426.

Main, M., Kaplan, N., & Cassidy, J. (1985). Security in infancy, childhood, and adulthood: A move to the level of representation. In I. Bretherton & E. Waters (Eds.), *Growing points of attachment theory and research. Monographs of the Society for Research in Child Development 50* (1–2, Serial No. 209), 66–104.

Maio, G. R., Pakizeh, A., Cheung, W. Y., & Rees, K. J. (2009). Changing, priming, and acting on values: Effects via motivational relations in a circular model. *Journal of Personality and Social Psychology, 97*, 699–715.

Major, B., Cozzarelli, C., Sciacchitano, A. M., Cooper, M. L., Testa, M., & Mueller, P. M. (1990). Perceived social support, self-efficacy, and adjustment to abortion. *Journal of Personality and Social Psychology, 59*, 452–463.

Major, B., Richards, C., Cooper, M. L., Cozzarelli, C., & Zubek, J. (1998). Personal resilience, cognitive appraisals, and coping: An integrative model of adjustment to abortion. *Journal of Personality and Social Psychology, 74*, 735–752.

Malec, J., Park, T., & Watkins, J. T. (1976). Modeling with role playing as a treatment for test anxiety. *Journal of Consulting and Clinical Psychology, 44,* 679.

Maner, J. K., DeWall, C. N., & Gailliot, M. T. (2008). Selective attention to signs of success: Social dominance and early stage interpersonal perception. *Personality and Social Psychology Bulletin, 34,* 488–501.

Mansfield, E. D., & McAdams, D. P. (1996). Generativity and themes of agency and communion in adult autobiography. *Personality and Social Psychology Bulletin, 22,* 721–731.

Manuck, S. B., Flory, J. D., Ferrell, R. E., Mann, J. J., & Muldoon, M. F. (2000). A regulatory polymorphism of the monoamine oxidase-A gene may be associated with variability in aggression, impulsivity, and central nervous system serotonergic responsivity. *Psychiatry Research, 95,* 9–23.

Manuck, S. B., Flory, J. D., McCaffery, J. M., Matthews, K. A., Mann, J. J., & Muldoon, M. F. (1998). Aggression, impulsivity, and central nervous system serotonergic responsivity in a nonpatient sample. *Neuropsychopharmacology, 19,* 287–299.

Manuck, S. B., Flory, J. D., Muldoon, M. F., & Ferrell, R. E. (2003). A neurobiology of intertemporal choice. In G. Loewenstein, D. Read, & R. F. Baumeister (Eds.), *Time and decision: Economic and psychological perspectives on intertemporal choice* (pp. 139–172). New York, NY: Russell Sage Foundation.

Marangoni, C., Garcia, S., Ickes, W., & Teng, G. (1995). Empathic accuracy in a clinically relevant setting. *Journal of Personality and Social Psychology, 68,* 854–869.

Markey, C. N., Markey, P. M., & Tinsley, B. J. (2003). Personality, puberty, and preadolescent girls' risky behaviors: Examining the predictive value of the five-factor model of personality. *Journal of Research in Personality, 37,* 405–419.

Markon, K. E., Krueger, R. F., & Watson, D. (2005). Delineating the structure of normal and abnormal personality: An integrative hierarchical approach. *Journal of Personality and Social Psychology, 88,* 139–157.

Markus, H. (1977). Self-schemata and processing information about the self. *Journal of Personality and Social Psychology, 35,* 63–78.

Markus, H., & Nurius, P. (1986). Possible selves. *American Psychologist, 41,* 954–969.

Markus, H., & Sentis, K. (1982). The self and social information processing. In J. Suls (Ed.), *Psychological perspectives on the self* (Vol. 1, pp. 41–70). Hillsdale, NJ: Erlbaum.

Markus, H., & Wurf, E. (1987). The dynamic self-concept: A social psychological perspective. *Annual Review of Psychology, 38,* 299–337.

Martin, L. L., & Tesser, A. (1996). Some ruminative thoughts. In R. S. Wyer, Jr. (Ed.), *Advances in social cognition* (Vol. 9, pp. 1–47). Mahwah, NJ: Erlbaum.

Martin, L. R., Friedman, H. S., & Schwartz, J. E. (2007). Personality and mortality risk across the life span: The importance of conscientiousness as a biopsychosocial attribute. *Health Psychology, 26,* 428–436.

Masling, J. M., & Bornstein, R. F. (Eds.). (1994). *Empirical perspectives on object relations theory.* Washington, DC: American Psychological Association.

Masling, J. M., Johnson, C., & Saturansky, C. (1974). Oral imagery, accuracy of perceiving others, and performance in Peace Corps training. *Journal of Personality and Social Psychology, 30,* 414–419.

Masling, J. M., O'Neill, R., & Jayne, C. (1981). Orality and latency of volunteering to serve as experimental subjects. *Journal of Personality Assessment, 45,* 20–22.

Masling, J. M., O'Neill, R., & Katkin, E. S. (1982). Autonomic arousal, interpersonal climate, and orality. *Journal of Personality and Social Psychology, 42,* 529–534.

Masling, J. M., Price, J., Goldband, S., & Katkin, E. S. (1981). Oral imagery and autonomic arousal in social isolation. *Journal of Personality and Social Psychology, 40,* 395–400.

Masling, J. M., Rabie, L., & Blondheim, S. H. (1967). Obesity, level of aspiration, and Rorschach and TAT measures of oral dependence. *Journal of Consulting Psychology, 31,* 233–239.

Masling, J. M., Weiss, L., & Rothschild, B. (1968). Relationships of oral imagery to yielding behavior and birth order. *Journal of Consulting and Clinical Psychology, 32,* 38–81.

Maslow, A. H. (1955). Deficiency motivation and growth motivation. In M. R. Jones (Ed.), *Nebraska symposium on motivation.* Lincoln, NE: University of Nebraska Press.

Maslow, A. H. (1962). *Toward a psychology of being.* Princeton, NJ: Van Nostrand.

Maslow, A. H. (1968). *Toward a psychology of being* (2nd ed.). New York, NY: Van Nostrand.

Maslow, A. H. (1970). *Motivation and personality* (Rev. ed.). New York, NY: Harper & Row.

Maslow, A. H. (1971). *The farther reaches of human nature.* New York, NY: Viking.

Maslow, A. H. (1979). *The journals of A. H. Maslow* (R. J. Lowry, Ed., 2 vols.). Monterey, CA: Brooks/Cole.

Mason, A., & Blankenship, V. (1987). Power and affiliation motivation, stress, and abuse in intimate relationships. *Journal of Personality and Social Psychology, 52,* 203–210.

Matas, L., Arend, R. A., & Sroufe, L. A. (1978). Continuity of adaptation in the second year: The relationship between quality of attachment and later competence. *Child Development, 49,* 547–556.

Matthews, K. A., Batson, C. D., Horn, J., & Rosenman, R. (1981). "Principles in his nature which interest him in the fortune of others . . .": The heritability of empathic concern for others. *Journal of Personality, 49,* 237–247.

Matthews, K. A., & Gallo, L. C. (2011). Psychological perspectives on pathways linking socioeconomic status to physical health. *Annual Review of Psychology, 62,* 501–530.

Matthews, K. A., Owens, J. F., Kuller, L. H., Sutton-Tyrrell, K., & Jansen-McWilliams, L. (1998). Are hostility and anxiety associated with carotid atherosclerosis in healthy postmenopausal women? *Psychosomatic Medicine, 60,* 633–638.

Matthiesen, A-S., Ransjö-Arvidson, A-B., Nissen, E., & Uvnäs-Moberg, K. (2001). Postpartum maternal oxytocin release by newborns: Effects of infant hand massage and sucking. *Birth, 28,* 13–19.

May, R. (1953). *Man's search for himself.* New York, NY: Norton.

May, R. (1958). The origins and significance of the existential movement in psychology. In R. May, E. Angel, & H. F. Ellenberger (Eds.), *Existence: A new dimension in psychiatry and psychology.* New York, NY: Basic Books.

May, R. (Ed.). (1969). *Existential psychology* (2nd ed.). New York, NY: Random House.

Mazur, A. (1985). A biosocial model of status in face-to-face primate groups. *Social Forces, 64,* 377–402.

Mazur, A., & Booth, A. (1998). Testosterone and dominance in men. *Behavior and Brain Sciences, 21,* 353–397.

Mazur, A., Booth, A., & Dabbs, J. M., Jr. (1992). Testosterone and chess competition. *Social Psychology Quarterly, 55,* 70–77.

McAdams, D. P. (1982). Experiences of intimacy and power: Relationships between social motives and autobiographical memory. *Journal of Personality and Social Psychology, 42,* 292–302.

McAdams, D. P. (1984). Human motives and personal relationships. In V. J. Derlaga (Ed.), *Communication, intimacy, and close relationships.* New York, NY: Academic Press.

McAdams, D. P. (1985). *Power, intimacy, and the life story: Personological inquiries into identity.* New York, NY: Guilford Press.

McAdams, D. P. (1989). *Intimacy: The need to be close.* New York, NY: Doubleday.

McAdams, D. P. (1992). The five-factor model *in* personality: A critical appraisal. *Journal of Personality, 60,* 329–361.

McAdams, D. P. (1993). *The stories we live by: Personal myths and the making of the self.* New York, NY: Morrow.

McAdams, D. P. (2001). The psychology of life stories. *Review of General Psychology, 5,* 100–122.

McAdams, D. P. (2006). *The redemptive self: Stories Americans live by.* New York, NY: Oxford University Press.

McAdams, D. P., Anyidoho, N. A., Brown, C., Huang, Y. T., Kaplan, B., & Machado, M. A. (2004). Traits and stories: Links between dispositional and narrative features of personality. *Journal of Personality, 72,* 761–784.

McAdams, D. P., & Bryant, F. B. (1987). Intimacy motivation and subjective mental health in a nationwide sample. *Journal of Personality, 55,* 395–413.

McAdams, D. P., & Constantian, C. A. (1983). Intimacy and affiliation motives in daily living: An experience sampling analysis. *Journal of Personality and Social Psychology, 45,* 851–861.

McAdams, D. P., & de St. Aubin, E. (1992). A theory of generativity and its assessment through self-report, behavioral acts, and narrative themes in autobiography. *Journal of Personality and Social Psychology, 62,* 1003–1015.

McAdams, D. P., Diamond, A., de St. Aubin, E., & Mansfield, E. (1997). Stories of commitment: The psychosocial construction of generative lives. *Journal of Personality and Social Psychology, 72,* 678–694.

McAdams, D. P., Healy, S., & Krause, S. (1984). Social motives and patterns of friendship. *Journal of Personality and Social Psychology, 47,* 828–838.

McAdams, D. P., Jackson, R. J., & Kirshnit, C. (1984). Looking, laughing, and smiling in dyads as a function of intimacy motivation and reciprocity. *Journal of Personality, 52,* 261–273.

McAdams, D. P., & Olson, B. D. (2010). Personality development: Continuity and change over the life course. *Annual Review of Psychology, 61,* 517–542.

McAdams, D. P., & Pals, J. L. (2006). A new big five: Fundamental principles for an integrative science of personality. *American Psychologist, 3,* 204–217.

McAdams, D. P., & Powers, J. (1981). Themes of intimacy in behavior and thought. *Journal of Personality and Social Psychology, 40,* 573–587.

McAdams, D. P., Reynolds, J., Lewis, M., Patten, A. H., & Bowman, P. J. (2001). When bad things turn good and good things turn bad: Sequences of redemption and contamination in life narrative and their relation to psychosocial adaptation in midlife adults and in students. *Personality and Social Psychology Bulletin, 27,* 474–485.

McAdams, D. P., & Vaillant, G. E. (1982). Intimacy motivation and psychosocial adjustment: A longitudinal study. *Journal of Personality Assessment, 46*, 586–593.

McAdams, D. P., & Walden, K. (2010). Jack Block, the Big Five, and personality from the standpoints of actor, agent, and author. *Psychological Inquiry, 21,* 50–56.

McArthur, L. Z. (1981). The role of attention in impression formation and causal attribution. In E. T. Higgins, C. P. Herman, & M. P. Zanna (Eds.), *Social cognition: The Ontario Symposium* (Vol. 1). Hillsdale, NJ: Erlbaum.

McClelland, D. C. (1961). *The achieving society*. Princeton, NJ: Van Nostrand.

McClelland, D. C. (1965). Toward a theory of motive acquisition. *American Psychologist, 20*, 321–333.

McClelland, D. C. (1979). Inhibited power motivation and high blood pressure in men. *Journal of Abnormal Psychology, 88*, 182–190.

McClelland, D. C. (1984). *Human motivation*. Glenview, IL: Scott, Foresman.

McClelland, D. C. (1985). How motives, skills, and values determine what people do. *American Psychologist, 40*, 812–825.

McClelland, D. C. (1989). Motivational factors in health and disease. *American Psychologist, 44*, 675–683.

McClelland, D. C., Atkinson, J. W., Clark, R. A., & Lowell, E. L. (1953). *The achievement motive*. New York, NY: Appleton-Century-Crofts.

McClelland, D. C., & Boyatzis, R. E. (1982). Leadership motive pattern and long-term success in management. *Journal of Applied Psychology, 67*, 737–743.

McClelland, D. C., Davis, W. N., Kalin, R., & Wanner, E. (Eds.). (1972). *The drinking man*. New York, NY: Free Press.

McClelland, D. C., Koestner, R., & Weinberger, J. (1989). How do self-attributed and implicit motives differ? *Psychological Review, 96*, 690–702.

McClelland, D. C., & Winter, D. G. (1969). *Motivating economic achievement*. New York, NY: Free Press.

McClelland, J. L. (1999). Cognitive modeling, connectionist. In R. W. Wilson & F. C. Keil (Eds.), *The MIT encyclopedia of the cognitive sciences* (pp. 137–139). Cambridge, MA: MIT Press.

McClelland, J. L., Rumelhart, D. E., & PDP Research Group (Eds.). (1986). *Parallel distributed processing: Explorations in the microstructure of cognition: Vol. 2. Psychological and biological models*. Cambridge, MA: MIT Press.

McCrae, R. R. (1993). Moderated analyses of longitudinal personality stability. *Journal of Personality and Social Psychology, 65*, 577–585.

McCrae, R. R. (1996). Social consequences of experiential openness. *Psychological Bulletin, 120*, 323–337.

McCrae, R. R. (2010). The place of the FFM in personality psychology. *Psychological Inquiry, 21*, 57–64.

McCrae, R. R., & Costa, P. T., Jr. (1987). Validation of the five-factor model of personality across instruments and observers. *Journal of Personality and Social Psychology, 52*, 81–90.

McCrae, R. R., & Costa, P. T., Jr. (1989). The structure of interpersonal traits: Wiggins's circumplex and the five-factor model. *Journal of Personality and Social Psychology, 56*, 586–595.

McCrae, R. R., & Costa, P. T., Jr. (1997). Personality trait structure as a human universal. *American Psychologist, 52*, 509–516.

McCrae, R. R., & Costa, P. T., Jr. (2003). *Personality in adulthood: A five-factor theory perspective* (2nd ed.). New York, NY: Guilford Press.

McCrae, R. R., Costa, P. T., Jr., Martin, T. A., Oryol, V. E., Senin, I. G., & O'Cleirigh, C. (2007). Personality correlates of HIV stigmatization in Russia and the United States. *Journal of Research in Personality, 41*, 190–196.

McCrae, R. R., & John, O. P. (1992). An introduction to the five-factor model and its implications. *Journal of Personality, 60*, 175–215.

McCrae, R. R., Terracciano, A., et al. (2005). Universal features of personality traits from the observer's perspective: Data from 50 cultures. *Journal of Personality and Social Psychology, 88*, 547–561.

McCrae, R. R., Zonderman, A. B., Costa, P. J., Jr., Bond, M. H., & Paunonen, S. V. (1996). Evaluating replicability of factors in the Revised NEO Personality Inventory: Confirmatory factor analysis versus procrustes rotation. *Journal of Personality and Social Psychology, 70*, 552–566.

McCullough, M. E. (2008). *Beyond revenge: The evolution of the forgiveness instinct*. San Francisco, CA: Jossey-Bass.

McCullough, M. E., Emmons, R. A., Kilpatrick, S. D., & Mooney, C. N. (2003). Narcissists as "victims": The role of narcissism in the perception of transgressions. *Personality and Social Psychology Bulletin, 29*, 885–893.

McCullough, M. E., & Hoyt, W. T. (2002). Transgression-related motivational dispositions: Personality substrates of forgiveness and their links to the big five. *Personality and Social Psychology Bulletin, 28*, 1556–1573.

McCullough, M. E., Tsang, J., & Brion, S. (2003). Personality traits in adolescence as predictors of religiousness in early adulthood: Findings from the Terman longitudinal study. *Personality and Social Psychology Bulletin, 29*, 980–991.

McFall, R., & Twentyman, C. T. (1973). Four experiments on relative contributions of rehearsal, modeling and coaching to assertion training. *Journal of Abnormal Psychology, 81,* 199–218.

McGregor, H. A., & Elliot, A. J. (2005). The shame of failure: Examining the link between fear of failure and shame. *Personality and Social Psychology Bulletin, 31,* 218–231.

McGregor, I., Zanna, M. P., Holmes, J. G., & Spencer, S. J. (2001). Compensatory conviction in the face of personal uncertainty: Going to extremes and being oneself. *Journal of Personality and Social Psychology, 80,* 472–488.

McGue, M., & Lykken, D. T. (1992). Genetic influence on risk of divorce. *Psychological Science, 3,* 368–373.

McGuffin, P., Rijsdijk, F., Andrew, M., Sham, P., Katz, R., & Cardno, A. (2003). The heritability of bipolar affective disorder and the genetic relationship to unipolar depression. *Archives of General Psychiatry, 60,* 497–502.

McGuire, W. J., & McGuire, C. V. (1986). Differences in conceptualizing self versus conceptualizing other people as manifested in contrasting verb types used in natural speech. *Journal of Personality and Social Psychology, 51,* 1135–1143.

Medin, D. L. (1989). Concepts and conceptual structure. *American Psychologist, 44,* 1469–1481.

Meehl, P. E. (1962). Schizotaxia, schizotypy, schizophrenia. *American Psychologist, 17,* 827–838.

Meehl, P. E. (1992). Factors and taxa, traits and types, differences of degree and differences in kind. *Journal of Personality, 60,* 117–174.

Megargee, E. I. (1966). Undercontrolled and overcontrolled personality types in extreme antisocial aggression. In E. I. Megargee & J. E. Moranson (Eds.), *Psychological Monographs.* New York, NY: Harper & Row.

Megargee, E. I. (1971). The role of inhibition in the assessment and understanding of violence. In J. L. Singer (Ed.), *The control of aggression and violence.* New York, NY: Academic Press.

Megargee, E. I., Cook, P. E., & Mendelsohn, G. A. (1967). Development and evaluation of an MMPI scale of assaultiveness in overcontrolled individuals. *Journal of Abnormal Psychology, 72,* 519–528.

Meichenbaum, D. (1971). Examination of model characteristics in reducing avoidance behavior. *Journal of Personality and Social Psychology, 17,* 298–307.

Meichenbaum, D. (1977). *Cognitve-behavior modification: An integrative approach.* New York, NY: Plenum Press.

Meier, B. P., & Robinson, M. D. (2004). Does quick to blame mean quick to anger? The role of agreeableness in dissociating blame and anger. *Personality and Social Psychology Bulletin, 30,* 856–867.

Meier, B. P., Robinson, M. D., & Wilkowski, B. M. (2006). Turning the other cheek: Agreeableness and the regulation of aggression-related primes. *Psychological Science, 17,* 136–142.

Melamed, B. G., & Siegel, L. J. (1975). Reduction of anxiety in children facing hospitalization and surgery by use of filmed modeling. *Journal of Consulting and Clinical Psychology, 43,* 511–521.

Melamed, B. G., Weinstein, D., Hawes, R., & Katin-Borland, M. (1975). Reduction of fear-related dental management problems using filmed modeling. *Journal of the American Dental Association, 90,* 822–826.

Meltzoff, A. N. (1985). Immediate and deferred imitation in fourteen- and twenty-four-month-old infants. *Child Development, 56,* 62–72.

Mendoza-Denton, R., Ayduk, O., Mischel, W., Shoda, Y., & Testa, A. (2001). Person x situation interactionism in self-encoding (*I am . . . when . . .*): Implications for affect regulation and social information processing. *Journal of Personality and Social Psychology, 80,* 533–544.

Merluzzi, T. V., Glass, C. R., & Genest, M. (Eds.). (1981). *Cognitive assessment.* New York, NY: Guilford Press.

Merluzzi, T. V., Rudy, T. E., & Glass, C. R. (1981). The information-processing paradigm: Implications for clinical science. In T. V. Merluzzi, C. R. Glass, & M. Genest (Eds.), *Cognitive assessment.* New York, NY: Guilford Press.

Mershon, B., & Gorsuch, R. L. (1988). Number of factors in the personality sphere: Does increase in factors increase predictability of real-life criteria? *Journal of Personality and Social Psychology, 55,* 675–680.

Metcalfe, J., & Mischel, W. (1999). A hot/cool-system analysis of delay of gratification: Dynamics of willpower. *Psychological Review, 106,* 3–19.

Meyer, J. P., & Pepper, S. (1977). Need compatibility and marital adjustment in young married couples. *Journal of Personality and Social Psychology, 35,* 331–342.

Mickelson, K. D., Kessler, R. C., & Shaver, P. R. (1997). Adult attachment in a nationally representative sample. *Journal of Personality and Social Psychology, 73,* 1092–1106.

Mikulincer, M. (1998). Adult attachment style and individual differences in functional versus dysfunctional experiences of anger. *Journal of Personality and Social Psychology, 74,* 513–524.

Mikulincer, M., Florian, V., & Hirschberger, G. (2003). The existential function of close relationships: Introducing death into the science of love. *Personality and Social Psychology Review, 7,* 20–40.

Mikulincer, M., Florian, V., & Weller, A. (1993). Attachment styles, coping strategies, and posttraumatic psychological distress: The impact of the Gulf War in

Israel. *Journal of Personality and Social Psychology, 64,* 817–826.

Mikulincer, M., & Goodman, G. S. (2006). *Dynamics of romantic love: Attachment, caregiving, and sex.* New York, NY: Guilford Press.

Mikulincer, M., Hirschberger, G., Nachmias, O., & Gillath, O. (2001). The affective component of the secure base schema: Affective priming with representations of attachment security. *Journal of Personality and Social Psychology, 81,* 305–321.

Mikulincer, M., & Horesh, N. (1999). Adult attachment style and the perception of others: The role of projective mechanisms. *Journal of Personality and Social Psychology, 76,* 1022–1034.

Mikulincer, M., & Nachshon, O. (1991). Attachment styles and patterns of self-disclosure. *Journal of Personality and Social Psychology, 61,* 321–331.

Mikulincer, M., & Shaver, P. R. (2001). Attachment theory and intergroup bias: Evidence that priming the secure base schema attenuates negative reactions to out-groups. *Journal of Personality and Social Psychology, 81,* 97–115.

Mikulincer, M., & Shaver, P. R. (2005). Attachment security, compassion, and altruism. *Current Directions in Psychological Science, 14,* 34–38.

Mikulincer, M., & Shaver, P. R. (2007). *Attachment in adulthood: Structure, dynamics, and change.* New York, NY: Guilford Press.

Mikulincer, M., Shaver, P. R., Gillath, O., & Nitzberg, R. A. (2005). Attachment, caregiving, and altruism: Boosting attachment security increases compassion and helping. *Journal of Personality and Social Psychology, 89,* 817–839.

Miller, G. (2010). The seductive allure of behavioral epigenetics. *Science, 329,* 24–27.

Miller, G. A., Galanter, E., & Pribram, K. H. (1960). *Plans and the structure of behavior.* New York, NY: Holt, Rinehart, & Winston.

Miller, J. D., Lynam, D., & Leukefeld, C. (2003). Examining antisocial behavior through the lens of the five factor model of personality. *Aggressive Behavior, 29,* 497–514.

Miller, L. C., Putcha-Bhagavatula, A., & Pedersen, W. C. (2002). Men's and women's mating preferences: Distinct evolutionary mechanisms? *Current Directions in Psychological Science, 11,* 88–93.

Miller, N. E., & Dollard, J. (1941). *Social learning and imitation.* New Haven, CT: Yale University Press.

Miller, N., Pedersen, W. C., Earleywine, M., & Pollock, V. E. (2003). A theoretical model of triggered displaced aggression. *Personality and Social Psychology Review, 7,* 75–97.

Miller, R. S. (1987). Empathic embarrassment: Situational and personal determinants of reactions to the embarrassment of another. *Journal of Personality and Social Psychology, 53,* 1061–1069.

Miller, S., Saccuzzo, D., & Braff, D. (1979). Information-processing deficits in remitted schizophrenics. *Journal of Abnormal Psychology, 88,* 446–449.

Mineka, S., & Zinbarg, R. (2006). A contemporary learning theory perspective on the etiology of anxiety disorders. *American Psychologist, 61,* 10–26.

Mischel, W. (1961). Delay of gratification, need for achievement, and acquiescence in another culture. *Journal of Abnormal and Social Psychology, 62,* 543–552.

Mischel, W. (1966). Theory and research on the antecedents of self-imposed delay of reward. In B. A. Maher (Ed.), *Progress in experimental personality research* (Vol. 3). New York, NY: Academic Press.

Mischel, W. (1968). *Personality and assessment.* New York, NY: Wiley.

Mischel, W. (1973). Toward a cognitive social learning reconceptualization of personality. *Psychological Review, 80,* 252–283.

Mischel, W. (1974). Processes in delay of gratification. In L. Berkowitz (Ed.), *Advances in experimental social psychology* (Vol. 7). New York, NY: Academic Press.

Mischel, W. (1977). The interaction of person and situation. In D. Magnusson & N. S. Endler (Eds.), *Personality at the crossroads: Current issues in interactional psychology.* Hillsdale, NJ: Erlbaum.

Mischel, W. (1979). On the interface of cognition and personality: Beyond the person–situation debate. *American Psychologist, 34,* 740–754.

Mischel, W. (1990). Personality dispositions revisited and revised: A view after three decades. In L. A. Pervin (Ed.), *Handbook of personality: Theory and research* (pp. 111–134). New York, NY: Guilford Press.

Mischel, W., & Baker, N. (1975). Cognitive transformations of reward objects through instructions. *Journal of Personality and Social Psychology, 31,* 254–261.

Mischel, W., & Ebbesen, E. (1970). Attention in delay of gratification. *Journal of Personality and Social Psychology, 16,* 329–337.

Mischel, W., Ebbesen, E., & Zeiss, A. (1973). Selective attention to the self: Situational and dispositional determinants. *Journal of Personality and Social Psychology, 27,* 129–142.

Mischel, W., & Liebert, R. M. (1966). Effects of discrepancies between observed and imposed reward criteria on their acquisition and transmission. *Journal of Personality and Social Psychology, 3,* 45–53.

Mischel, W., & Shoda, Y. (1995). A cognitive–affective system theory of personality: Reconceptualizing situations, dispositions, and invariance in personality structure. *Psychological Review, 102,* 246–268.

Mischel, W., Shoda, Y., & Mendoza-Denton, R. (2002). Situation–behavior profiles as a locus of consistency in personality. *Current Directions in Psychological Science, 11,* 50–54.

Moffitt, T. E. (2005a). Genetic and environmental influences on antisocial behaviours: Evidence from behavioral-genetic research. *Advances in Genetics, 55,* 41–104.

Moffitt, T. E. (2005b). The new look of behavioral genetics in developmental psychopathology: Gene-environment interplay in antisocial behaviors. *Psychological Bulletin, 131,* 533–554.

Moffitt, T. E., Caspi, A., & Rutter, M. (2006). Measured gene-environment interactions in psychopathology: Concepts, research strategies, and implications for research, intervention, and public understanding of genetics. *Perspectives on Psychological Science, 1,* 5–27.

Moffitt, T. E., Caspi, A., & Rutter, M. (2006). Measured gene-environment interactions in psychopathology: Concepts, research strategies, and implications for research, intervention, and public understanding of genetics. *Perspectives on Psychological Science, 1,* 5–27.

Molenaar, P. C. M., & Campbell, C. G. (2009). The new person-specific paradigm in psychology. *Current Directions in Psychological Science, 18,* 112–116.

Moller, A. C., Elliot, A. J., & Maier, M. A. (2009). Basic hue-meaning associations, *Emotion, 9,* 898–902.

Monson, T., Hesley, J., & Chernick, L. (1982). Specifying when personality traits can and cannot predict behavior: An alternative to abandoning the attempt to predict single-act criteria. *Journal of Personality and Social Psychology, 43,* 385–399.

Moore, B., Mischel, W., & Zeiss, A. (1976). Comparative effects of the reward stimulus and its cognitive representation in voluntary delay. *Journal of Personality and Social Psychology, 34,* 419–424.

Moors, A., & De Houwer, J. (2006). Automaticity: A theoretical and conceptual analysis. *Psychological Bulletin, 132,* 297–326.

Morf, C. C., & Rhodewalt, F. (1993). Narcissism and self-evaluation maintenance: Explorations in object relations. *Personality and Social Psychology Bulletin, 19,* 668–676.

Morgan, C. D., & Murray, H. A. (1935). A method for investigating fantasies. *Archives of Neurology and Psychiatry, 34,* 289–306.

Morilak, D. A., Barrera, G., Echevarria, D. J., Garcia, A. S., Hernandez, A., Ma, S., & Petre, C. O. (2005). Role of brain norepinephrine in the behavioral response to stress. *Biological Psychiatry, 29,* 1214–1224.

Morrison, K. R., Wheeler, S. C., & Smeesters, D. (2007). Significant other primes and behavior: Motivation to respond to social cues moderates pursuit of prime-induced goals. *Personality and Social Psychology Bulletin, 33,* 1661–1674.

Morrone, J. V., Depue, R. A., Scherer, A. J., & White, T. L. (2000). Film-induced incentive motivation and positive activation in relation to agentic and affiliative components of extraversion. *Personality and Individual Differences, 29,* 199–216.

Moskowitz, D. S. (1994). Cross-situational generality and the interpersonal circumplex. *Journal of Personality and Social Psychology, 66,* 921–933.

Moskowitz, G. B. (1993). Individual differences in social categorization: The influence of personal need for structure on spontaneous trait inferences. *Journal of Personality and Social Psychology, 65,* 132–142.

Motley, M. T. (1985). Slips of the tongue. *Scientific American, 253,* 116–127.

Mowrer, R. R., & Klein, S. B. (Eds.). (2001). *Handbook of contemporary learning theories.* Mahwah, NJ: Erlbaum.

Mroczek, D. K., & Spiro, A., III. (2007). Personality change influences mortality in older men. *Psychological Science, 18,* 371–376.

Mroczek, D. K., Spiro, A., III, & Turiano, N. A. (2009). Do health behaviors explain the effect of neuroticism on mortality? Longitudinal findings from the VA normative aging study. *Journal of Research in Personality, 43,* 653–659.

Mueller, C. M., & Dweck, C. S. (1998). Praise for intelligence can undermine children's motivation and performance. *Journal of Personality and Social Psychology, 75,* 33–52.

Muraven, M., & Baumeister, R. F. (2000). Self-regulation and depletion of limited resources: Does self-control resemble a muscle? *Psychological Bulletin, 126,* 247–259.

Murray, H. A. (1938). *Explorations in personality.* New York, NY: Oxford University Press.

Murray, S. L., Holmes, J. G., & Griffin, D. W. (2000). Self-esteem and the quest for felt security: How perceived regard regulates attachment processes. *Journal of Personality and Social Psychology, 78,* 478–498.

Murray, S. L., Holmes, J. G., Griffin, D. W., Bellavia, G., & Rose, P. (2001). The mismeasure of love: How self-doubt contaminates relationship beliefs. *Personality and Social Psychology Bulletin, 27,* 423–436.

Mussweiler, T. (2006). Doing is for thinking! Stereotype activation by stereotypic movements. *Psychological Science, 17,* 17–21.

Nasby, W. (1985). Private self-consciousness, articulation of the self-schema, and the recognition memory of trait adjectives. *Journal of Personality and Social Psychology, 49,* 704–709.

Neimeyer, G. J., & Neimeyer, R. A. (1981). Personal construct perspectives on cognitive assessment. In T. V. Merluzzi, C. R. Glass, & M. Genest (Eds.), *Cognitive assessment.* New York, NY: Guilford Press.

Nell, V. (2002). Why young men drive dangerously: Implications for injury prevention. *Current Directions in Psychological Science, 11,* 75–79.

Nelson, R. O. (1977). Methodological issues in assessment via self-monitoring. In J. D. Cone & R. P. Hawkins (Eds.), *Behavioral assessment: New directions in clinical psychology.* New York, NY: Brunner/Mazel.

Netter, P., Hennig, J., & Rohrmann, S. (1999). Psychobiological differences between the aggression and psychoticism dimension. *Pharmacopsychiatry, 32,* 5–12.

Neuberg, S. L., & Newsom, J. T. (1993). Personal need for structure: Individual differences in the desire for simple structure. *Journal of Personality and Social Psychology, 65,* 113–131.

Neuringer, A. (2004). Reinforced variability in animals and people: Implications for adaptive action. *American Psychologist, 59,* 891–906.

Newcomb, M. D., & McGee, L. (1991). Influence of sensation seeking on general deviance and specific problem behaviors from adolescence to young adulthood. *Journal of Personality and Social Psychology, 61,* 614–628.

Newell, A., & Simon, H. A. (1972). *Human problem solving.* Englewood Cliffs, NJ: Prentice-Hall.

Newman, J. P., Wallace, J. F., Strauman, T. J., Skolaski, R. L., Oreland, K. M., Mattek, P. W., Elder, K. A., & McNeeley, J. (1993). Effects of motivationally significant stimuli on the regulation of dominant responses. *Journal of Personality and Social Psychology, 65,* 165–175.

Newman, L. S., Duff, K. J., & Baumeister, R. F. (1997). A new look at defensive projection: Thought suppression, accessibility, and biased person perception. *Journal of Personality and Social Psychology, 72,* 980–1001.

Nezu, A. M. (1987). A problem-solving formulation of depression: A literature review and proposal of a pluralistic model. *Clinical Psychology Review, 7,* 121–144.

Niedenthal, P. M., Halberstadt, J. B., & Innes-Ker, A. H. (1999). Emotional response categorization. *Psychological Review, 106,* 337–361.

Niedenthal, P. M., Setterlund, M. B., & Wherry, M. B. (1992). Possible self-complexity and affective reactions to goal-relevant evaluation. *Journal of Personality and Social Psychology, 63,* 5–16.

Nigg, J. T. (2000). On inhibition/disinhibition in developmental pychopathology: Views from cognitive and personality psychology as a working inhibition taxonomy. *Psychological Bulletin, 126,* 220–246.

Nigg, J. T., John, O. P., Blaskey, L. G., Huang-Pollock, C. L., Willcutt, E. G., Hinshaw, S. P., & Pennington, B. (2002). Big five dimensions and ADHD symptoms: Links between personality traits and clinical symptoms. *Journal of Personality and Social Psychology, 83,* 451–469.

Nisbett, R. E., & Cohen, D. (1996). *Culture of honor.* Boulder, CO: Westview Press.

Nisbett, R. E., & Ross, L. (1980). *Human inference: Strategies and shortcomings of social judgment.* Englewood Cliffs, NJ: Prentice-Hall.

Noftle, E. E., & Robins, R. W. (2007). Personality predictors of academic outcomes: Big five correlates of GPA and SAT scores. *Journal of Personality and Social Psychology, 93,* 116–130.

Noftle, E. E., & Shaver, P. R. (2006). Attachment dimensions and the big five personality traits: Associations and comparative ability to predict relationship quality. *Journal of Research in Personality, 40,* 179–208.

Nolen-Hoeksema, S., Morrow, J., & Frederickson, B. L. (1993). Response styles and the duration of episodes of depressed mood. *Journal of Abnormal Psychology, 102,* 20–28.

Nolen-Hoeksema, S., Parker, L., & Larson, J. (1994). Ruminative coping with depressed mood following loss. *Journal of Personality and Social Psychology, 67,* 92–104.

Norman, D. A. (1981). Categorization of action slips. *Psychological Review, 88,* 1–15.

Norman, W. T. (1963). Toward an adequate taxonomy of personality attributes: Replicated factor structure in peer nomination personality ratings. *Journal of Abnormal and Social Psychology, 66,* 574–583.

Nowak, A., Vallacher, R. R., Tesser, A., & Borkowski, W. (2000). Society of self: The emergence of collective properties in self-structure. *Psychological Review, 107,* 39–61.

O'Connor, B. P. (2002). The search for dimensional structure differences between normality and abnormality: A statistical review of published data on personality and psychopathology. *Journal of Personality and Social Psychology, 83,* 962–982.

O'Connor, B. P., & Dyce, J. A. (2001). Rigid and extreme: A geometric representation of personality disorders in five-factor model space. *Journal of Personality and Social Psychology, 81,* 1119–1130.

O'Connor, S. C., & Rosenblood, L. K. (1996). Affiliation motivation in everyday experience: A theoretical comparison. *Journal of Personality and Social Psychology, 70,* 513–522.

O'Donnell, M. C., Fisher, R., Rickard, M., & McConaghy, N. (2000). Emotional suppression: Can it predict cancer outcome in women with suspicious screening mammograms? *Psychological Medicine, 30,* 1079–1088.

O'Leary, K. D., & Becker, W. C. (1967). Behavior modification of an adjustment class: A token reinforcement program. *Exceptional Children, 33,* 637–642.

Oettingen, G., & Kappes, A. (2009). Mental contrasting of the future and reality to master negative feedback. In K. D. Mark, W. M. Klein, & J. A. Suhr, *Handbook of imagination and mental simulation* (pp. 395–412). New York, NY: Psychology Press.

Oettingen, G., Mayer, D., Sevincer, A. T., Stephens, E. J., Pak, H-j., & Hagenah, M. (2009). Mental contrasting and goal commitment: The mediating role of energization. *Personality and Social Psychology Bulletin, 35,* 608–622.

Ogilvie, D. M. (1987). The undesired self: A neglected variable in personality research. *Journal of Personality and Social Psychology, 52,* 379–385.

Öhman, A., & Mineka, S. (2001). Fears, phobias, and preparedness: Toward an evolved module of fear and fear learning. *Psychological Review, 108,* 483–522.

Oliver, M. B., & Hyde, J. S. (1993). Gender differences in sexuality: A meta-analysis. *Psychological Bulletin, 114,* 29–51.

Olson, J. M., Vernon, P. A., Harris, J. A., & Jang, K. L. (2001). The heritability of attitudes: A study of twins. *Journal of Personality and Social Psychology, 80,* 845–860.

Olsson, A., Nearing, K. I., & Phelps, E. A. (2007). Learning fears by observing others: The neural system of social fear transmission. *Social Cognitive and Affective Neuroscience, 2,* 3–11.

Oreland, L. (2004). Platelet monoamine oxidase, personality and alcoholism: The rise, fall and resurrection. *Neurotoxicology, 25,* 79–89.

Orlofsky, J. L., Marcia, J. E., & Lesser, I. M. (1973). Ego identity states and the intimacy versus isolation crisis of young adulthood. *Journal of Youth and Adolescence, 27,* 211–219.

Orr, S. P., Lasko, N. B., Metzger, L. J., Berry, N. J., Ahern, C. E., & Pitman, R. K. (1998). Psychophysiologic assessment of women with posttraumatic stress disorder resulting from childhood sexual abuse. *Journal of Consulting and Clinical Psychology, 66,* 906–913.

Öst, L. G., Ferebee, I., & Furmark, T. (1997). One-session group therapy of spider phobia: Direct versus indirect treatments. *Behavior Research and Therapy, 35,* 721–732.

Over, H., & Carpenter, M. (2009). Eighteen-month-old infants show increased helping following priming with affiliation. *Psychological Science, 20,* 1189–1193.

Overall, N. C., Fletcher, G. J. O., & Friesen, M. D. (2003). Mapping the intimate relationship mind: Comparisons between three models of attachment representations. *Personality and Social Psychology Bulletin, 29,* 1479–1493.

Overwalle, F. V., & Siebler, F. (2005). A connectionist model of attitude formation and change. *Personality and Social Psychology Review, 9,* 231–274.

Owen, M. J., Williams, N. M., & O'Donovan, M. C. (2004). The molecular genetics of schizophrenia: New findings promise new insights. *Molecular Psychiatry, 9,* 14–27.

Oyserman, D., Bybee, D., & Terry, K. (2006). Possible selves and academic outcomes: How and when possible selves impel action. *Journal of Personality and Social Psychology, 91,* 188–204.

Oyserman, D., Bybee, D., Terry, K., & Hart-Johnson, T. (2004) Possible selves as roadmaps. *Journal of Research in Personality, 38,* 130–149.

Oyserman, D., Terry, K., & Bybee, D. (2002). A possible selves intervention to enhance school involvement. *Journal of Adolescence, 25,* 313–326.

Ozer, D. J. (1986). *Consistency in personality: A methodological framework.* New York, NY: Springer-Verlag.

Ozer, D. J., & Benet-Martínez, V. (2006). Personality and the prediction of consequential outcomes. *Annual Review of Psychology, 57,* 401–421.

Ozer, D. J., & Reise, S. P. (1994). Personality assessment. *Annual Review of Psychology, 45,* 357–388.

Ozer, E. M., & Bandura, A. (1990). Mechanisms governing empowerment effects: A self-efficacy analysis. *Journal of Personality and Social Psychology, 58,* 472–486.

Paaver, M., Eensoo, D., Pulver, A., & Harro, J. (2006). Adaptive and maladaptive impulsivity, platelet monoamine oxidase (MAO) activity and risk-admitting in different types of risky drivers. *Psychopharmacology, 186,* 32–40.

Pang, J. S., & Schultheiss, O. C. (2005). Assessing implicit motives in U. S. college students: Effects of picture type and position, gender and ethnicity, and cross-cultural comparisons. *Journal of Personality Assessment, 85,* 280–294.

Panksepp, J. (1998). *Affective neuroscience: The foundations of human and animal emotions.* New York, NY: Oxford University Press.

Panksepp, J., & Cox, J. (1986). An overdue burial for the serotonin theory of anxiety. *Behavioral and Brain Sciences, 9,* 340–341.

Park, J-W., Yoon, S-O., Kim, K-H., & Wyer, R. S., Jr. (2001). Effects of priming a bipolar attribute concept on dimension versus concept-specific accessibility of semantic memory. *Journal of Personality and Social Psychology, 81*, 405–420.

Park, L. E., & Crocker, J. (2008). Contingencies of self-worth and responses to negative interpersonal feedback. *Self and Identity, 7*, 184–203.

Parke, R. D. (1969). Effectiveness of punishment as an interaction of intensity, timing, agent nurturance, and cognitive structuring. *Child Development, 40*, 211–235.

Patterson, C. M., & Newman, J. P. (1993). Reflectivity and learning from aversive events: Toward a psychological mechanism for the syndromes of disinhibition. *Psychological Review, 100*, 716–736.

Patton, J. H., Stanford, M. S., & Barratt, E. (1995). Factor structure of the Barratt Impulsiveness Scale. *Journal of Clinical Psychology, 51*, 768–774.

Paul, G. L. (1966). *Insight vs. desensitization in psychotherapy: An experiment in anxiety reduction.* Stanford, CA: Stanford University Press.

Paulhus, D. L. (1998). Interpersonal and intrapsychic adaptiveness of trait self-enhancement: A mixed blessing? *Journal of Personality and Social Psychology, 74*, 1197–1208.

Paulhus, D. L., & Suedfeld, P. (1988). A dynamic complexity model of self-deception. In J. S. Lockard & D. L. Paulhus (Eds.), *Self-deception: An adaptive mechanism?* Englewood Cliffs, NJ: Prentice-Hall.

Paunonen, S. V. (1989). Consensus in personality judgments: Moderating effects of target–rater acquaintanceship and behavior observability. *Journal of Personality and Social Psychology, 56*, 823–833.

Paunonen, S. V. (1998). Hierarchical organization of personality and prediction of behavior. *Journal of Personality and Social Psychology, 74*, 538–556.

Paunonen, S. V., & Ashton, M. C. (2001a). Big Five factors and facets and the prediction of behavior. *Journal of Personality and Social Psychology, 81*, 524–539.

Paunonen, S. V., & Ashton, M. C. (2001b). Big Five predictors of academic achievement. *Journal of Research in Personality, 35*, 78–90.

Paunonen, S. V., Jackson, D. N., Trzebinski, J., & Forsterling, F. (1992). Personality structure across cultures: A multimethod evaluation. *Journal of Personality and Social Psychology, 62*, 447–456.

Pavlov, I. P. (1927). *Conditioned reflexes.* Oxford, England: Oxford University Press.

Pavlov, I. P. (1955). *Selected works.* New York, NY: Foreign Languages.

Payne, B. K. (2005). Conceptualizing control in social cognition: How executive functioning modulates the expression of automatic stereotyping. *Journal of Personality and Social Psychology, 89*, 488–503.

Peabody, D. (1984). Personality dimensions through trait inferences. *Journal of Personality and Social Psychology, 46*, 384–403.

Peabody, D., & De Raad, B. (2002). The substantive nature of psycholexical personality factors: A comparison across languages. *Journal of Personality and Social Psychology, 83*, 983–997.

Peabody, D., & Goldberg, L. R. (1989). Some determinants of factor structures from personality-trait descriptors. *Journal of Personality and Social Psychology, 57*, 552–567.

Pedersen, N. L., Plomin, R., McClearn, G. E., & Friberg, L. (1988). Neuroticism, extraversion, and related traits in adult twins reared apart and reared together. *Journal of Personality and Social Psychology, 55*, 950–957.

Pelham, B. W., Mirenberg, M. C., & Jones, J. T. (2002). Why Susie sells seashells by the seashore: Implicit egotism and major life decisions. *Journal of Personality and Social Psychology, 82*, 469–487.

Pennebaker, J. W. (1989). Confession, inhibition, and disease. In L. Berkowitz (Ed.), *Advances in experimental social psychology* (Vol. 22, pp. 211–244). San Diego, CA: Academic Press.

Pennebaker, J. W. (1993). Putting stress into words: Health, linguistic, and therapeutic implications. *Behaviour Research and Therapy, 31*, 539–548.

Pennebaker, J. W., & Beall, S. K. (1986). Confronting a traumatic event: Toward an understanding of inhibition and disease. *Journal of Abnormal Psychology, 95*, 274–281.

Pennebaker, J. W., & Chung, C. K. (2007). Expressive writing, emotional upheavals, and health. In H. S. Friedman & R. C. Silver (Eds.), *Foundations of health psychology* (pp. 263–284). New York, NY: Oxford University Press.

Pennebaker, J. W., & Graybeal, A. (2001). Patterns of natural language use: Disclosure, personality, and social integration. *Current Directions in Psychological Science, 10*, 90–93.

Pennebaker, J. W., Kiecolt-Glaser, J. K., & Glaser, R. (1988). Disclosure of traumas and immune function: Health implications for psychotherapy. *Journal of Consulting and Clinical Psychology, 56*, 239–245.

Peplau, L. A., & Perlman, D. (Eds.). (1982). *Loneliness: A sourcebook of current theory, research, and therapy.* New York, NY: Wiley.

Perkins, K. A. (1999). Nicotine self-administration. *Nicotine and Tobacco Research, 1* (Suppl.), 133–137.

Pervin, L. A. (1983). The stasis and flow of behavior: Toward a theory of goals. In M. M. Page & R.

Dienstbier (Eds.), *Nebraska symposium on motivation* (Vol. 31). Lincoln, NE: University of Nebraska Press.

Pervin, L. A. (1985). Personality: Current controversies, issues, and directions. *Annual Review of Psychology, 36,* 83–114.

Pervin, L. A. (Ed.). (1989). *Goal concepts in personality and social psychology.* Hillsdale, NJ: Erlbaum.

Peterson, C. (1995). Explanatory style and health. In G. M. Buchanan & M. E. P. Seligman (Eds.), *Explanatory style* (pp. 233–246). Hillsdale, NJ: Erlbaum.

Petri, H. L., & Mishkin, M. (1994). Behaviorism, cognitivism, and the neuropsychology of memory. *American Scientist, 82,* 30–37.

Petry, N. M., Martin, B., Cooney, J. L., & Kranzler, H. R. (2000). Give them prizes, and they will come: Contingency management for treatment of alcohol dependence. *Journal of Consulting and Clinical Psychology, 68,* 250–257.

Piedmont, R. L., McCrae, R. R., & Costa, P. T., Jr. (1992). An assessment of the Edwards Personal Preference Schedule from the perspective of the five-factor model. *Journal of Personality Assessment, 58,* 67–78.

Pierce, T., & Lydon, J. E. (2001). Global and specific relational models in the experience of social interactions. *Journal of Personality and Social Psychology, 80,* 613–631.

Pietromonaco, P. R., & Barrett, L. F. (1997). Working models of attachment and daily social interactions. *Journal of Personality and Social Psychology, 73,* 1409–1423.

Pietromonaco, P. R., & Carnelley, K. B. (1994). Gender and working models of attachment: Consequences for perception of self and romantic relationships. *Personal Relationships, 1,* 3–26.

Plaks, J. E., Stroessner, S. J., Dweck, C. S., & Sherman, J. W. (2001). Person theories and attention allocation: Preferences for stereotypic versus counterstereotypic information. *Journal of Personality and Social Psychology, 80,* 876–893.

Plomin, R. (1974). *A temperament theory of personality development: Parent–child interactions.* Unpublished doctoral dissertation, University of Texas at Austin.

Plomin, R. (1981). Ethnological behavioral genetics and development. In K. Immelmann, G. W. Barlow, L. Petrinovich, & M. Main (Eds.), *Behavioral development: The Bielefeld interdisciplinary project.* Cambridge, England: Cambridge University Press.

Plomin, R. (1989). Environment and genes: Determinants of behavior. *American Psychologist, 44,* 105–111.

Plomin, R. (1995). Molecular genetics and psychology. *Current Directions in Psychological Science, 4,* 114–117.

Plomin, R. (1997). *Behavioral genetics.* New York, NY: Freeman.

Plomin, R., & Crabbe, J. (2000). DNA. *Psychological Bulletin, 126,* 806–828.

Plomin, R., & Daniels, D. (1987). Why are children in the same family so different from one another? *Behavioral and Brain Sciences, 10,* 1–60.

Plomin, R., DeFries, J. C., Craig, I. W., & McGuffin, P. (Eds.). (2003). *Behavioral genetics in the postgenomic era.* Washington, DC: American Psychological Association.

Plomin, R., DeFries, J. C., & McClearn, G. E. (1990). *Behavioral genetics: A primer* (2nd ed.). New York, NY: Freeman.

Plomin, R., & Rende, R. (1991). Human behavioral genetics. *Annual Review of Psychology, 42,* 161–190.

Plomin, R., & Rowe, D. C. (1977). A twin study of temperament in young children. *Journal of Psychology, 97,* 107–113.

Plomin, R., Scheier, M. F., Bergeman, C. S., Pedersen, N. L., Nesselroade, J. R., & McClearn, G. E. (1992). Optimism, pessimism, and mental health: A twin/adoption analysis. *Personality and Individual Differences, 13,* 921–930.

Pollak, S., & Gilligan, C. (1982). Images of violence in Thematic Apperception Test stories. *Journal of Personality and Social Psychology, 42,* 159–167.

Poropat, A. E. (2009). A meta-analysis of the five-factor model of personality and academic performance. *Psychological Bulletin, 135,* 322–338.

Posner, M. I., & DiGirolamo, G. J. (2000). Cognitive neuroscience: Origins and promise. *Psychological Bulletin, 126,* 873–889.

Postman, L. (1951). Toward a general theory of cognition. In J. H. Rohrer & M. Sherif (Eds.), *Social psychology at the crossroads.* New York, NY: Harper.

Powell, R. A., & Boer, D. P. (1994). Did Freud mislead patients to confabulate memories of abuse? *Psychological Reports, 74,* 1283–1298.

Powers, M. B., Halpern, J. M., Ferenschak, M. P., Gillihan, S. J., & Foa, E. B. (2010). A meta-analytic review of prolonged exposure for posttraumatic stress disorder. *Clinical Psychology Review, 30,* 635–641.

Powers, S. I., Pietromonaco, P. R., Gunlicks, M., & Sayer, A. (2006). Dating couples' attachment styles and patterns of cortisol reactivity and recovery in response to a relationship conflict. *Journal of Personality and Social Psychology, 90,* 613–628.

Powers, W. T. (1973). *Behavior: The control of perception.* Chicago, IL: Aldine.

Pratt, M. W., Danso, H. A., Arnold, M. L., Norris, J. E., & Filyer, R. (2001). Adult generativity and the socialization of adolescents: Relations to mothers' and fathers' parenting beliefs, styles, and practices. *Journal of Personality, 69*, 89–120.

Pratto, F., & Hegarty, P. (2000). The political psychology of reproductive strategies. *Psychological Science, 11*, 57–62.

Prentice-Dunn, S., & Rogers, R. W. (1982). Effects of public and private self-awareness on deindividuation and aggression. *Journal of Personality and Social Psychology, 43*, 503–513.

Prentice-Dunn, S., & Rogers, R. W. (1989). Deindividuation and the self-regulation of behavior. In P. B. Paulus (Ed.), *Psychology of group influence* (2nd ed., pp. 87–109). Hillsdale, NJ: Erlbaum.

Preston, K. L., Umbricht, A., Wong, C. J., & Epstein, D. H. (2001). Shaping cocaine abstinence by successive approximation. *Journal of Consulting and Clinical Psychology, 69*, 643–654.

Price, M. A., Tennant, C. C., Smith, R. C., Butow, P. N., Kennedy, S. J., Kossoff, M. B., & Dunn, S. M. (2001). The role of psychosocial factors in the development of breast carcinoma: Part I. The cancer-prone personality. *Cancer, 91*, 679–685.

Privette, G., & Landsman, T. (1983). Factor analysis of peak performance: The full use of potential. *Journal of Personality and Social Psychology, 44*, 195–200.

Pronin, E., Steele, C. M., & Ross, L. (2004). Identity bifurcation in response to stereotype threat: Women and mathematics. *Journal of Experimental Social Psychology, 40,* 152–168.

Pryor, J. B., Reeder, G. D., Yeadon, C., & Hesson-McInnis, M. (2004). A dual-process model of reactions to perceived stigma. *Journal of Personality and Social Psychology, 87,* 436–452.

Purpura, D. J., Wilson, S. B., & Lonigon, C. J. (2010). Attention-deficit/hyperactivity disorder symptoms in preschool children: Examining psychometric properties using item response theory. *Psychological Assessment, 22,* 546–558.

Pyszczynski, T., & Greenberg, J. (1985). Depression and preference for self-focusing stimuli after success and failure. *Journal of Personality and Social Psychology, 49*, 1066–1075.

Pyszczynski, T., & Greenberg, J. (1987). Self-regulatory perseveration and the depressive self-focusing style: A self-awareness theory of reactive depression. *Psychological Bulletin, 102*, 122–138.

Pyszczynski, T., Greenberg, J., & Solomon, S. (2000). Proximal and distal defense: A new perspective on unconscious motivation. *Current Directions in Psychological Science, 9*, 156–160.

Pyszczynski, T., Greenberg, J., Solomon, S., Arndt, J., & Schimel, J. (2004). Why do people need self-esteem? A theoretical and empirical review. *Psychological Bulletin, 130*, 435–468.

Pyszczynski, T., Solomon, S., & Greenberg, J. (2002). *In the wake of 9/11: The psychology of terror.* Washington, DC: American Psychological Association.

Pytlik Zillig, L. M., Hemenover, S. H., & Dienstbier, R. A. (2002). What do we assess when we assess a Big 5 trait? A content analysis of the affective, behavioral, and cognitive processes represented in Big 5 personality inventories. *Personality and Social Psychology Bulletin, 28*, 847–858.

Rabin, A. I., Zucker, R. A., Emmons, R. A., & Frank, S. (Eds.). (1990). *Studying persons and lives.* New York, NY: Springer.

Rachman, J., & Teasdale, J. (1969). *Aversion therapy and behaviour disorders: An analysis.* Coral Gables, FL: University of Miami Press.

Rachman, S. (Ed.). (1978). *Advances in behaviour research and therapy* (Vol. 1). Oxford, England: Pergamon Press.

Raine, A. (2008). From genes to brain to antisocial behavior. *Current Directions in Psychological Science, 17,* 323–328.

Rash, C. J., Alessi, S. M., & Petry, N. M. (2008). Contingency management is efficacious for cocaine abusers with prior treatment attempts. *Experimental and Clinical Psychopharmacology, 16,* 547–554.

Rasmussen, H. N., Scheier, M. F., & Greenhouse, J. B. (2009). Optimism and physical health: A meta-analytic review. *Annals of Behavioral Medicine, 37,* 239–256.

Razran, G. H. S. (1940). Conditioned response changes in rating and appraising sociopolitical slogans. *Psychological Bulletin, 37,* 481.

Read, S. J. (1987). Constructing causal scenarios: A knowledge structure approach to causal reasoning. *Journal of Personality and Social Psychology, 52,* 288–302.

Read, S. J., Jones, D. K., & Miller, L. C. (1990). Traits as goal-based categories: The importance of goals in the coherence of dispositional categories. *Journal of Personality and Social Psychology, 58,* 1048–1061.

Read, S. J., & Miller, L. C. (Eds.). (1998). *Connectionist models of social reasoning and social behavior.* Mahwah, NJ: Erlbaum.

Read, S. J., & Miller, L. C. (2002). Virtual personalities: A neural network model of personality. *Personality and Social Psychology Review, 6,* 357–369.

Read, S. J., Vanman, E. J., & Miller, L. C. (1997). Connectionism, parallel constraint satisfaction processes, and Gestalt principles: (Re)introducing cognitive dynamics to social psychology. *Review of Personality and Social Psychology, 1,* 26–53.

Reason, J., & Mycielska, K. (1982). *Absent-minded? The psychology of mental lapses and everyday errors.* Englewood Cliffs, NJ: Prentice-Hall.

Reback, C. J., Peck, J. A., Dierst-Davies, R., Nuno, M., Kamien, J. B., & Amass, L. (2010). Contingency management among homeless, out-of-treatment men who have sex with men. *Journal of Substance Abuse Treatment, 39,* 255–263.

Reeve, B. B., Hays, R. D., Chang, C., & Perfetto, E. M. (2007). Applying item response theory to enhance health outcomes assessment. *Quality of Life Research, 16,* 1–3.

Reichow, B., & Volkmar, F. R. (2010). Social skills interventions for individuals with autism: Evaluation for evidence-based practices within a best evidence synthesis framework. *Journal of Autism and Developmental Disorders, 40,* 149–166.

Reinisch, J. M. (1981). Prenatal exposure to synthetic progestins increases potential for aggression in humans. *Science, 211,* 1171–1173.

Repetti, R. L. (1989). Effects of daily workload on subsequent behavior during marital interactions: The role of social withdrawal and spouse support. *Journal of Personality and Social Psychology, 57,* 651–659.

Rescorla, R. A. (1987). A Pavlovian analysis of goal-directed behavior. *American Psychologist, 42,* 119–129.

Rescorla, R. A. (1988). Pavlovian conditioning: It's not what you think it is. *American Psychologist, 43,* 151–160.

Rescorla, R. A. (1997). Response-inhibition in extinction. *Quarterly Journal of Experimental Psychology: Comparative and Physiological Psychology, 50B,* 238–252.

Rescorla, R. A. (1998). Instrumental learning: Nature and persistence. In M. Sabourin, F. Craik, et al. (Eds.), *Advances in psychological science, Vol. 2: Biological and cognitive aspects* (pp. 239–257). Hove, England: Psychology Press.

Reuter, M., Schmitz, A., Corr, P., & Hennig, J. (2006). Molecular genetics support Gray's personality theory: The interaction of COMT and DRD2 polymorphisms predicts the behavioural approach system. *International Journal of Neuropsychopharmacology, 9,* 155–166.

Reyna, C., Henry, P. J., Korfmacher, W., & Tucker, A. (2005). Examining the principles in principled conservatism: The role of responsibility stereotypes as cues for deservingness in racial policy decisions. *Journal of Personality and Social Psychology, 90,* 109–128.

Reynolds, S. K., & Clark, L. A. (2001). Predicting dimensions of personality disorder from domains and facets of the five-factor model. *Journal of Personality, 69,* 199–222.

Rhawn, J. (1980). Awareness, the origin of thought, and the role of conscious self-deception in resistance and repression. *Psychological Reports, 46,* 767–781.

Rhee, S. H., & Waldman, I. D. (2002). Genetic and environmental influences on antisocial behavior: A meta-analysis of twin and adoption studies. *Psychological Bulletin, 128,* 490–529.

Rhodewalt, F., & Morf, C. C. (1998). On self-aggrandizement and anger: A temporal analysis of narcissism and affective reactions to success and failure. *Journal of Personality and Social Psychology, 74,* 672–685.

Rholes, W. S., & Simpson, J. A. (2004). *Adult attachment: Theory, research, and clinical implications.* New York, NY: Guilford Press.

Rholes, W. S., Simpson, J. A., & Friedman, M. (2006). Avoidant attachment and the experience of parenting. *Personality and Social Psychology Bulletin, 32,* 275–285.

Rholes, W. S., Simpson, J. A., Tran, S., Martin, A. M., III, & Friedman, M. (2007). Attachment and information seeking in romantic relationships. *Personality and Social Psychology Bulletin, 33,* 422–439.

Rholes, W. S., Simpson, J. A., & Oriña, M. M. (1999). Attachment and anger in an anxiety-provoking situation. *Journal of Personality and Social Psychology, 76,* 940–957.

Richardson, R. C. (2007). *Evolutionary psychology as maladapted psychology.* Cambridge, MA: MIT Press.

Risley, T. R. (1968). The effects and side effects of punishing the autistic behaviors of a deviant child. *Journal of Applied Behavior Analysis, 1,* 21–34.

Ritter, M., Bucci, W., Beebe, B., Jaffe, J., & Maskit, B. (2007). Do mothers of secure infants speak differently than mothers of avoidant infants in natural conversations? An interpersonal exploration of language differences. *Journal of the American Psychoanalytic Association, 55,* 269–274.

Ritvo, L. B. (1990). *Darwin's influence on Freud: A tale of two sciences.* New Haven, CT: Yale University Press.

Rizzolatti, G., Fogassi, L., & Gallese, V. (2002). Motor and cognitive functions of the ventral premotor cortex. *Current Opinion in Neurobiology, 12,* 149–154.

Roberts, B. W., & Bogg, T. (2004). A longitudinal study of the relationships between conscientiousness and the social-environmental factors and substance-use behaviors that influence health. *Journal of Personality, 72,* 325–354.

Roberts, B. W., & Del Vecchio, W. F. (2000). The rank-order consistency of personality traits from childhood to old age: A quantitative review of longitudinal studies. *Psychological Bulletin, 126,* 3–25.

Roberts, B. W., Kuncel, N. R., Shiner, R., Caspi, A., & Goldberg, L. R. (2007). The power of personality:

The comparative validity of personality traits, socio-economic status, and cognitive ability for predicting important life outcomes. *Perspectives on Psychological Science, 2,* 313–345.

Roberts, B. W., & Robins, R. W. (2000). Broad dispositions, broad aspirations: The intersection of personality traits and major life goals. *Personality and Social Psychology Bulletin, 26,* 1284–1296.

Roberts, B. W., Walton, K. E., & Bogg, T. (2005). Conscientiousness and health across the life course. *Review of General Psychology, 9,* 156–168.

Roberts, B. W., Walton, K. E., & Viechtbauer, W. (2006). Patterns of mean-level change in personality traits across the life course: A meta-analysis of longitudinal studies. *Psychological Bulletin, 132,* 1–25.

Roberts, B. W., & Wood, D. (2006). Personality development in the context of the neo-socioanalytic model of personality. In D. K. Mroczek & T. D. Little (Eds.), *Handbook of personality development* (pp. 11–39). Mahwah, NJ: Erlbaum.

Roberts, J. E., Gotlib, I. H., & Kassel, J. D. (1996). Adult attachment security and symptoms of depression: The mediating roles of dysfunctional attitudes and low self-esteem. *Journal of Personality and Social Psychology, 70,* 310–320.

Roberts, J. E., & Monroe, S. M. (1994). A multidimensional model of self-esteem in depression. *Clinical Psychology Review, 14,* 161–181.

Robins, R. W., John, O. P., Caspi, A., Moffitt, T. E., & Stouthamer-Loeber, M. (1996). Resilient, overcontrolled, and undercontrolled boys: Three replicable personality types. *Journal of Personality and Social Psychology, 70,* 157–171.

Robins, R. W., & Pals, J. L. (2002). Implicit self-theories in the academic domain: Implications for goal orientation, attributions, affect, and self-esteem change. *Self and Identity, 1,* 313–336.

Robinson, S., Sandstrom, S. M., Denenberg, V. H., & Palmiter, R. D. (2005). Distinguishing whether dopamine regulates liking, wanting, and/or learning about rewards. *Behavioral Neuroscience, 119,* 5–15.

Roccas, S., Sagiv, L., Schwartz, S. H., & Knafo, A. (2002). The Big Five personality factors and personal values. *Personality and Social Psychology Bulletin, 28,* 789–801.

Rogers, C. R. (1951). *Client-centered therapy: Its current practice, implications and theory.* Boston, MA: Houghton Mifflin.

Rogers, C. R. (1959). A theory of therapy, personality and interpersonal relationships, as developed in the client-centered framework. In S. Koch (Ed.), *Psychology: A study of a science* (Vol. 3). New York, NY: McGraw-Hill.

Rogers, C. R. (1961). *On becoming a person.* Boston, MA: Houghton Mifflin.

Rogers, C. R. (1965). *Client-centered therapy: Its current practice, implication, and theory.* Boston, MA: Houghton Mifflin.

Rogers, C. R., & Dymond, R. F. (Eds.). (1954). *Psychotherapy and personality change: Co-ordinated research studies in the client-centered approach.* Chicago, IL: University of Chicago Press.

Rogers, C. R., & Stevens, B. (1967). *Person to person: The problem of being human.* New York, NY: Simon & Schuster.

Rogers, T. B. (1981). A model of the self as an aspect of the human information-processing system. In N. Cantor & J. F. Kihlstrom (Eds.), *Personality, cognition and social interaction.* Hillsdale, NJ: Erlbaum.

Rogers, T. B., Kuiper, N. A., & Kirker, W. S. (1977). Self-reference and the encoding of personal information. *Journal of Personality and Social Psychology, 35,* 677–688.

Roisman, G. I. (2009). Adult attachment: Toward a rapprochement of methodological cultures. *Current Directions in Psychological Science, 18,* 122–126.

Roisman, G. I., Holland, A., Fortuna, K., Fraley, R. C., Clausell, E., & Clarke, A. (2007). The Adult Attachment Interview and self-reports of attachment style: An empirical rapprochement. *Journal of Personality and Social Psychology, 92,* 678–697.

Ronay, R., & von Hippel, W. (2010). The presence of an attractive woman elevates testosterone and physical risk taking in young men. *Social Psychological and Personality Science, 1,* 57–64.

Roney, J. R. (2003). Effects of visual exposure to the opposite sex: Cognitive aspects of mate attraction in human males. *Personality and Social Psychology Bulletin, 29,* 393–404.

Rorschach, H. (1942). *Psychodiagnostics.* Berne, Switzerland: Huber.

Rosch, E., & Mervis, C. (1975). Family resemblances: Studies in the internal structure of categories. *Cognitive Psychology, 7,* 573–605.

Rosekrans, M. A. (1967). Imitation in children as a function of perceived similarity and vicarious reinforcement. *Journal of Personality and Social Psychology, 7,* 307–315.

Rosenbaum, D. A. (1987). Hierarchical organization of motor programs. In S. Wise (Ed.), *Neural and behaviorial approaches to higher brain function* (pp. 45–66). New York, NY: Wiley.

Rosenbaum, D. A. (1990). *Human motor control.* San Diego, CA: Academic Press.

Rosenbaum, D. A. (2005). The Cinderella of psychology: The neglect of motor control in the science of mental life and behavior. *American Psychologist, 60,* 308–317.

Rosenthal, T. L., & Reese, S. L. (1976). The effects of covert and overt modeling on assertive behavior. *Behavior Research and Therapy, 14,* 463–469.

Rosenwald, G. C. (1972). Effectiveness of defenses against anal impulse arousal. *Journal of Consulting and Clinical Psychology, 39,* 292–298.

Ross, D. M., Ross, S. A., & Evans, T. A. (1971). The modification of extreme social withdrawal by modeling with guided participation. *Journal of Behavior Therapy and Experimental Psychiatry, 2,* 273–279.

Ross, M. (1989). Relation of implicit theories to the construction of personal histories. *Psychological Review, 96,* 341–357.

Ross, M., & Fletcher, G. J. O. (1985). Attribution and social perception. In G. Lindzey & E. Aronson (Eds.), *The handbook of social psychology* (3rd ed., pp. 73–122). Reading, MA: Addison-Wesley.

Rothbart, M. K., Ahadi, S. A., & Evans, D. E. (2000). Temperament and personality: Origins and outcomes. *Journal of Personality and Social Psychology, 78,* 122–135.

Rothbart, M. K., Ahadi, S. A., Hershey, K., & Fisher, P. (2001). Investigations of temperament at three to seven years: The Children's Behavior Questionnaire. *Child Development, 72,* 1394–1408.

Rothbart, M. K., & Bates, J. E. (1998). Temperament. In W. Damon (Series Ed.) & N. Eisenberg (Vol. Ed.), *Handbook of child psychology: Vol 3. Social, emotional and personality development* (5th ed., pp. 105–176). New York, NY: Wiley.

Rothbart, M. K., Ellis, L. K., Rueda M. R., & Posner, M. I. (2003). Developing mechanisms of temperamental effortful control. *Journal of Personality, 71,* 1113–1143.

Rothbart, M. K., & Posner, M. (1985). Temperament and the development of self-regulation. In L. C. Hartlage & C. F. Telzrow, (Eds.), *The neuropsychology of individual differences: A developmental perspective* (pp. 93–123). New York, NY: Plenum Press.

Rotter, J. B. (1954). *Social learning and clinical psychology.* New York, NY: Prentice-Hall.

Rotter, J. B. (1966). Generalized expectancies for internal versus external control of reinforcement. *Psychological Monographs, 80* (1, Whole No. 609).

Rotter, J. B. (1982). *The development and applications of social learning theory: Selected papers.* New York, NY: Praeger.

Rowe, D. C. (1994). *The limits of family influence: Genes, experience, and behavior.* New York, NY: Guilford Press.

Rowe, D. C. (2001). *Biology and crime.* Los Angeles, CA: Roxbury.

Rowe, D. C., Jacobson, K. C., & Van den Oord, E. J. C. G. (1999). Genetic and environmental influences on vocabulary IQ: Parental education level as moderator. *Child Development, 70,* 1151–1162.

Roy-Byrne, P. (2005). The GABA-benzodiazepine receptor complex: Structure, function, and role in anxiety. *Journal of Clinical Psychiatry, 66,* 14–20.

Ruchkin, V., Koposov, R. A., af Klinteberg, B., Oreland, L., & Grigorenko, E. L. (2005). Platelet MAO-B, personality, and psychopathology. *Journal of Abnormal Psychology, 114,* 477–482.

Rudman, L. A., Phelan, J. E., & Heppen, J. B. (2007). Developmental sources of implicit attitudes. *Personality and Social Psychology Bulletin, 33,* 1700–1713.

Rushton, J. P. (1988). Genetic similarity, mate choice, and fecundity in humans. *Ethology and Sociobiology, 9,* 329–335.

Rushton, J. P. (1989a). Genetic similarity, human altruism, and group selection. *Behavioral and Brain Sciences, 12,* 503–559.

Rushton, J. P. (1989b). Genetic similarity in male friendships. *Ethology and Sociobiology, 10,* 361–373.

Rushton, J. P., & Bons, T. A. (2005). Mate choice and friendship in twins. *Psychological Science, 16,* 555–559.

Rushton, J. P., Fulker, D. W., Neale, M. C., Nias, D. K. B., & Eysenck, H. J. (1986). Altruism and aggression: The heritability of individual differences. *Journal of Personality and Social Psychology, 50,* 1192–1198.

Rushton, J. P., Russell, R. J. H., & Wells, P. A. (1984). Genetic similarity theory: Beyond kin selection. *Behavior Genetics, 14,* 179–193.

Rutter, M. (2006). *Genes and behavior: Nature-nurture interplay explained.* Oxford, England: Blackwell.

Ryan, R. M. (1982). Control and information in the intrapersonal sphere: An extension of cognitive evaluation theory. *Journal of Personality and Social Psychology, 43,* 450–461.

Ryan, R. M. (1993). Agency and organization: Intrinsic motivation, autonomy, and the self in psychological development. In J. Jacobs (Ed.), *Nebraska symposium on motivation: Developmental perspectives on motivation* (Vol. 40, pp. 1–56). Lincoln, NE: University of Nebraska Press.

Ryan, R. M., & Connell, J. P. (1989). Perceived locus of causality and internalization: Examining reasons for acting in two domains. *Journal of Personality and Social Psychology, 57,* 749–761.

Ryan, R. M., & Deci, E. L. (2000). Self-determination theory and the facilitation of intrinsic motivation, social development, and well-being. *American Psychologist, 55,* 68–78.

Ryan, R. M., & Deci, E. L. (2001). On happiness and human potentials: A review of research on hedonic and eudaimonic well-being. *Annual Review of Psychology, 52,* 141–166.

Ryan, R. M., Rigby, S., & King, K. (1993). Two types of religious internalization and their relations to religious orientations and mental health. *Journal of Personality and Social Psychology, 65,* 586–596.

Ryan, R. M., Sheldon, K. M., Kasser, T., & Deci, E. L. (1996). All goals are not created equal: An organismic perspective on the nature of goals and their regulation. In P. M. Gollwitzer & J. A. Bargh (Eds.), *The psychology of action: Linking cognition and motivation to behavior* (pp. 7–26). New York, NY: Guilford Press.

Rydell, R. J., Shiffrin, R. M., Boucher, K. L., Van Loo, K., & Rydell, M. T. (2010). Stereotype threat prevents perceptual learning. *Proceedings of the National Academy of Sciences, 107,* 14042–14047.

Sabini, J., & Green, M. C. (2004). Emotional responses to sexual and emotional infidelity: Constants and differences across genders, samples, and methods. *Personality and Social Psychology Bulletin, 30,* 1375–1388.

Sadalla, E. K., Kenrick, D. T., & Vershure, B. (1987). Dominance and heterosexual attraction. *Journal of Personality and Social Psychology, 52,* 730–738.

Salamone, J. D., Correa, M., Farrar, A., & Mingote, S. M. (2007). Effort-related functions of nucleus accumbens dopamine and associated forebrain circuits. *Psychopharmacology, 191,* 461–482.

Samuel, D. B., Simms, L. J., Clark, L. A., Livesley, W. J., & Widiger, T. A. (2010). An item response theory integration of normal and abnormal personality scales. *Personality Disorders: Theory, Research, and Treatment, 1,* 5–21.

Samuel, D. B., & Widiger, T. A. (2006). Clinicians' judgments of clinical utility: A comparison of the DSM-IV and five-factor models. *Journal of Abnormal Psychology, 115,* 298–308.

Sarason, I. G. (1975). Test anxiety and the self-disclosing coping model. *Journal of Consulting and Clinical Psychology, 43,* 148–153.

Saucier, G. (1992). Benchmarks: Integrating affective and interpersonal circles with the big-five personality factors. *Journal of Personality and Social Psychology, 62,* 1025–1035.

Saucier, G., & Goldberg, L. R. (2001). Lexical studies of indigenous personality factors: Premises, products, and prospects. *Journal of Personality, 69,* 847–879.

Saucier, G., & Ostendorf, F. (1999). Hierarchical subcomponents of the Big Five personality factors: A cross-language replication. *Journal of Personality and Social Psychology, 76,* 613–627.

Saucier, G., & Simonds, J. (2006). The structure of personality and temperament. In D. K. Mroczek & T. D. Little (Eds.), *Handbook of personality development* (pp. 109–128). Mahwah, NJ: Erlbaum.

Saudino, K. J., Pedersen, N. L., Lichtenstein, P., McClearn, G. E., & Plomin, R. (1997). Can personality explain genetic influences on life events? *Journal of Personality and Social Psychology, 72,* 196–206.

Scarr, S. (1985). Constructing psychology: Making facts and fables for our time. *American Psychologist, 40,* 499–512.

Scarr, S., & Carter-Saltzman, L. (1979). Twin method: Defense of a critical assumption. *Behavior Genetics, 9,* 527–542.

Scarr, S., & McCartney, K. (1983). How people make their own environments: A theory of genotype environment effects. *Child Development, 54,* 424–435.

Schaller, M., & Murray, D. R. (2008). Pathogen, personality, and culture: Disease prevalence predicts worldwide variability in sociosexuality, extraversion, and openness to experience. *Journal of Personality and Social Psychology, 95,* 212–221.

Schank, R. C., & Abelson, R. P. (1977). *Scripts, plans, goals, and understanding.* Hillsdale, NJ: Erlbaum.

Schefft, B. K., & Lehr, B. K. (1985). A self-regulatory model of adjunctive behavior change. *Behavior Modification, 9,* 458–476.

Scheier, M. F., & Carver, C. S. (1983). Self-directed attention and the comparison of self with standards. *Journal of Experimental Social Psychology, 19,* 205–222.

Scheier, M. F., & Carver, C. S. (1988). A model of behavioral self-regulation: Translating intention into action. In L. Berkowitz (Ed.), *Advances in experimental social psychology* (Vol. 21, pp. 303–346). New York, NY: Academic Press.

Scheier, M. F., & Carver, C. S. (1992). Effects of optimism on psychological and physical well-being: Theoretical overview and empirical update. *Cognitive Therapy and Research, 16,* 201–228.

Scheier, M. F., Carver, C. S., & Armstrong, G. H. (in press). Behavioral self-regulation, health, and illness. In A. S. Baum, T. A. Revenson, & J. E. Singer (Eds.), *Handbook of health psychology* (2nd ed.). New York, NY: Psychology Press.

Scheier, M. F., Carver, C. S., & Bridges, M. W. (2001). Optimism, pessimism, and psychological well-being. In E. C. Chang (Ed.), *Optimism and pessimism: Implications for theory, research, and practice* (pp. 189–216). Washington, DC: American Psychological Association.

Scheier, M. F., Matthews, K. A., Owens, J. F., Magovern, G. J., Lefebvre, R. C., Abbott, R. A., & Carver, C. S. (1989). Dispositional optimism and recovery from coronary artery bypass surgery: The beneficial effects on physical and psychological well-being. *Journal of Personality and Social Psychology, 57,* 1024–1040.

Scheier, M. F., Matthews, K. A., Owens, J. F., Schulz, R., Bridges, M. W., Magovern, G. J., Sr., & Carver, C. S. (1999). Optimism and rehospitalization following coronary artery bypass graft surgery. *Archives of Internal Medicine, 159,* 829–835.

Schell, T. L., Klein, S. B., & Babey, S. H. (1996). Testing a hierarchical model of self-knowledge. *Psychological Science, 7,* 170–173.

Schiedel, D. G., & Marcia, J. E. (1985). Ego identity, intimacy, sex-role orientation, and gender. *Journal of Personality and Social Psychology, 21,* 149–160.

Schimel, J., Arndt, J., Pyszczynski, T., & Greenberg, J. (2001). Being accepted for who we are: Evidence that social validation of the intrinsic self reduces general defensiveness. *Journal of Personality and Social Psychology, 80,* 35–52.

Schimel, J., Greenberg, J., & Martens, A. (2003). Evidence that projection of a feared trait can serve a defensive function. *Personality and Social Psychology Bulletin, 29,* 969–979.

Schimel, J., Hayes, J., Williams, T., & Jahrig, J. (2007). Is death really the worm at the core? Converging evidence that worldview threat increases death-thought accessibility. *Journal of Personality and Social Psychology, 92,* 789–803.

Schimmack, U., Oishi, S., Furr, R. M., & Funder, D. C. (2004). Personality and life satisfaction: A facet-level analysis. *Personality and Social Psychology Bulletin, 30,* 1062–1075.

Schmidt, L. A. (1999). Frontal brain electrical activity in shyness and sociability. *Psychological Science, 10,* 316–320.

Schmidt, R. A. (1988). *Motor control and learning: A behavioral emphasis* (2nd ed.). Champaign, IL: Human Kinetics.

Schmitt, D. P. (2003). Universal sex differences in the desire for sexual variety: Tests from 52 nations, 6 continents, and 13 islands. *Journal of Personality and Social Psychology, 85,* 85–104.

Schmitt, D. P. (2004). Patterns and universals of mate poaching across 53 nations: The effects of sex, culture and personality on romantically attracting another person's partner. *Journal of Personality and Social Psychology, 86,* 560–584.

Schmitt, D. P., & Buss, D. M. (1996). Strategic self-promotion and competitor derogation: Sex and context effects on the perceived effectiveness of mate attraction tactics. *Journal of Personality and Social Psychology, 70,* 1185–1204.

Schmitt, D. P., & Buss, D. M. (2001). Human mate poaching: Tactics and temptations for infiltrating existing mateships. *Journal of Personality and Social Psychology, 80,* 894–917.

Schmitt, W. A., Brinkley, C. A., & Newman, J. P. (1999). Testing Damasio's somatic marker hypothesis with psychopathic individuals: Risk takers or risk averse? *Journal of Abnormal Psychology, 108,* 538–543.

Schneider, D. J. (1991). Social cognition. *Annual Review of Psychology, 42,* 527–561.

Schneider, K. J., Bugental, J. F. T., & Pierson, J. F. (Eds.). (2001). *The handbook of humanistic psychology: Leading edges in theory, research, and practice.* Thousand Oaks, CA: Sage.

Schriesheim, C. A., & Hill, K. D. (1981). Controlling acquiescence response bias by item reversals: The effect on questionnaire validity. *Educational and Psychological Measurement, 41,* 1101–1114.

Schuckit, M. A., & Rayses, V. (1979). Ethanol ingestion: Differences in blood acetaldehyde concentrations in relatives of alcoholics and controls. *Science, 203,* 54–55.

Schüler, J., Job, V., Fröhlich, S. M., & Brandstätter, V. (2008). A high implicit affiliation motive does not always make you happy: A corresponding explicit motive and corresponding behavior are further needed. *Motivation and Emotion, 32,* 231–242.

Schultheiss, O. C. (2002). An information-processing account of implicit motive arousal. In P. R. Pintrich & M. L. Maehr (Eds.), *Advances in motivation and achievement: New directions in measures and methods* (Vol. 12, pp. 1–41). Amsterdam, The Netherlands: Elsevier.

Schultheiss, O. C., & Brunstein, J. C. (2001). Assessment of implicit motives with a research version of the TAT: Picture profiles, gender differences, and relations to other personality measures. *Journal of Personality Assessment, 77,* 71–86.

Schultheiss, O. C., & Brunstein, J. C. (2002). Inhibited power motivation and persuasive communication: A lens model analysis. *Journal of Personality, 70,* 553–582.

Schultheiss, O. C., & Brunstein, J. C. (2010). *Implicit motives.* Oxford, England: Oxford University Press.

Schultheiss, O. C., Campbell, K. L., & McClelland, D. C. (1999). Implicit power motivation moderates men's testosterone responses to imagined and real dominance success. *Hormones and Behavior, 36,* 234–241.

Schultheiss, O. C., Dargel, A., & Rohde, W. (2003). Implicit motives and sexual motivation and behavior. *Journal of Research in Personality, 37,* 224–230.

Schultheiss, O. C., & Hale, J. A. (2007). Implicit motives modulate attentional orienting to facial expressions of emotion. *Motivation and Emotion, 31,* 13–24.

Schultheiss, O. C., Liening, S. H., & Schad, D. (2008). The reliability of a picture story exercise measure of implicit motives: Estimates of internal consistency, retest reliability, and ipsative stability. *Journal of Research in Personality, 42,* 1560–1571.

Schultheiss, O. C., & Pang, J. S. (2007). Measuring implicit motives. In R. W. Robins, R. C. Fraley, & R. F. Krueger (Eds.), *Handbook of research methods in personality psychology* (pp. 322–344). New York, NY: Guilford Press.

Schultheiss, O. C., Pang, J. S., Torges, C. M., Wirth, M. M., & Treynor, W. (2005). Perceived facial expressions of emotion as motivational incentives: Evidence from a differential implicit learning paradigm. *Emotion, 5,* 41–54.

Schultheiss, O. C., & Rohde, W. (2002). Implicit power motivation predicts men's testosterone changes and implicit learning in a contest situation. *Hormones and Behavior, 41,* 195–202.

Schultheiss, O. C., Wirth, M. M., Torges, C. M., Pang, J. S., Villacorta, M. A., & Welsh, K. M. (2005). Effects of implicit power motivation on men's and women's implicit learning and testosterone changes after social victory or defeat. *Journal of Personality and Social Psychology, 88,* 174–188.

Schultz, C. B., & Pomerantz, M. (1976). Achievement motivation, locus of control, and academic achievement behavior. *Journal of Personality, 44,* 38–51.

Schultz, T. R., & Lepper, M. R. (1996). Cognitive dissonance reduction as constraint satisfaction. *Psychological Review, 103,* 219–240.

Schultz, W. (2000). Multiple reward signals in the brain. *Nature Reviews, 1,* 199–207.

Schultz, W. (2006). Behavioral theories and the neurophysiology of reward. *Annual Reviews of Psychology, 57,* 87–115.

Schutte, N. S., Kenrick, D. T., & Sadalla, E. K. (1985). The search for predictable settings: Situational prototypes, constraint, and behavioral variation. *Journal of Personality and Social Psychology, 49,* 121–128.

Schwarz, N. (1990). Feelings as information: Informational and motivational functions of affective states. In E. T. Higgins & R. M. Sorrentino (Eds.), *Handbook of motivation and cognition: Foundations of social behavior* (Vol. 2, pp. 527–561). New York, NY: Guilford Press.

Sederer, L., & Seidenberg, R. (1976). Heiress to an empty throne: Ego-ideal problems of contemporary women. *Contemporary Psychoanalysis, 12,* 240–251.

Segal, N. L. (1993). Twin, sibling, and adoption methods: Tests of evolutionary hypotheses. *American Psychologist, 48,* 943–956.

Segal, Z. V. (1988). Appraisal of the self-schema construct in cognitive models of depression. *Psychological Bulletin, 103,* 147–162.

Seidenberg, M. S. (2005). Connectionist models of word reading. *Current Directions in Psychological Science, 14,* 238–242.

Seligman, M. E. P., & Hager, J. L. (Eds.). (1972). *Biological boundaries of learning.* New York, NY: Appleton-Century-Crofts.

Seltzer, R. A. (1973). Simulation of the dynamics of action. *Psychological Reports, 32,* 859–872.

Semmer, N., & Frese, M. (1985). Action theory in clinical psychology. In M. Frese & J. Sabini (Eds.), *Goal directed behavior: The concept of action in psychology.* Hillsdale, NJ: Erlbaum.

Sen, S., Villafuerte, S., Nesse, R., Stoltenberg, S. F., Hopcian, J., Gleiberman, L., Weder, A., & Burmeister, M. (2004). Serotonin transporter and GABA(A) alpha 6 receptor variants are associated with neuroticism. *Biological Psychiatry, 55,* 244–249.

Sexton, J. D., & Pennebaker, J. W. (2009). The healing powers of expressive writing. In S. B. Kaufman & J. C. Kaufman (Eds.), *The psychology of creative writing* (pp. 264–273). New York, NY: Cambridge University Press.

Shane, M. S., & Peterson, J. B. (2004). Self-induced memory distortions and the allocation of processing resources at encoding and retrieval. *Cognition and Emotion, 18,* 533–558.

Shao, C., Li, Y., Jiang, K., Zhang, D., Xu, Y., Lin, L., Wang, Q., Zhao, M., & Jin, L. (2006). Dopamine D4 receptor polymorphism modulates cue-elicited heroin craving in Chinese. *Psychopharmacology, 186,* 185–190.

Shaver, P. R., & Brennan, K. A. (1992). Attachment styles and the "big five" personality traits: Their connections with each other and with romantic relationship outcomes. *Personality and Social Psychology Bulletin, 18,* 536–545.

Shaver, P. R., & Mikulincer, M. (2002). Dialogue on adult attachment: Diversity and integration. *Attachment & Human Development, 4,* 243–257.

Shaver, P. R., & Rubenstein, C. (1980). *Childhood attachment experience and adult loneliness.* In L. Wheeler (Ed.), *Review of personality and social psychology* (Vol. 1, pp. 42–73). Beverly Hills, CA: Sage.

Sheeran, P., Webb, T. L., & Gollwitzer, P. M. (2005). The interplay between goal intentions and implementation intentions. *Personality and Social Psychology Bulletin, 31,* 87–98.

Sheldon, K. M. (2005). Positive value change during college: Normative trends and individual differences. *Journal of Research in Personality, 39,* 209–223.

Sheldon, K. M., & Elliot, A. J. (1998). Not all personal goals are personal: Comparing autonomous and controlled reasons for goals as predictors of effort and attainment. *Personality and Social Psychology Bulletin, 24,* 546–557.

Sheldon, K. M., & Elliot, A. J. (1999). Goal striving, need satisfaction, and longitudinal well-being: The self-concordance model. *Journal of Personality and Social Psychology, 76,* 482–497.

Sheldon, K. M., Elliot, A. J., Kim, Y., & Kasser, T. (2001). What is satisfying about satisfying events? Testing 10 candidate psychological needs. *Journal of Personality and Social Psychology, 80,* 325–339.

Sheldon, K. M., & Gunz, A. (2009). Psychological need as basic motives, not just experimental requirements. *Journal of Personality, 77,* 1467–1492.

Sheldon, K. M., & Houser-Marko, L. (2001). Self-concordance, goal attainment, and the pursuit of happiness: Can there be an upward spiral? *Journal of Personality and Social Psychology, 80,* 152–165.

Sheldon, K. M., & Kasser, T. (1998). Pursuing personal goals: Skills enable progress but not all progress is beneficial. *Personality and Social Psychology Bulletin, 24,* 1319–1331.

Sheldon, K. M., King, L. A., Houser-Marko, L., Osbaldiston, R., & Gunz, A. (2007). Comparing IAT and TAT measures of power versus intimacy motivation. *European Journal of Personality, 21,* 263–280.

Sheldon, K. M., Ryan, R. M., & Reis, H. (1996). What makes for a good day? Competence and autonomy in the day and in the person. *Personality and Social Psychology Bulletin, 22,* 1270–1279.

Sheldon, W. H. (with the collaboration of S. S. Stevens). (1942). *The varieties of temperament: A psychology of constitutional differences.* New York, NY: Harper.

Sher, K. J., Bartholow, B. D., & Wood, M. D. (2000). Personality and substance use disorders: A prospective study. *Journal of Consulting and Clinical Psychology, 68,* 818–829.

Sherwood, G. G. (1981). Self-serving biases in person perception: An examination of projection as a mechanism of defense. *Psychological Bulletin, 90,* 445–459.

Shiner, R. L., Masten, A. S., & Tellegen, A. (2002). A developmental perspective on personality in emerging adulthood: Childhood antecedents and concurrent adaptation. *Journal of Personality and Social Psychology, 83,* 1165–1177.

Shoal, G. D., & Giancola, P. R. (2003). Negative affectivity and drug use in adolescent boys: Moderating and mediating mechanisms. *Journal of Personality and Social Psychology, 84,* 221–233.

Shoda, Y., Mischel, W., & Wright, J. C. (1989). Intuitive interactionism in person perception: Effects of situation–behavior relations on dispositional judgments. *Journal of Personality and Social Psychology, 56,* 41–53.

Shoda, Y., Mischel, W., & Wright, J. C. (1993). The role of situational demands and cognitive competencies in behavior organization and personality coherence. *Journal of Personality and Social Psychology, 65,* 1023–1035.

Shoda, Y., Mischel, W., & Wright, J. C. (1994). Intraindividual stability in the organization and patterning of behavior: Incorporating psychological situations into the idiographic analysis of personality. *Journal of Personality and Social Psychology, 67,* 674–687.

Shostrom, E. L. (1964). An inventory for the measurement of self-actualization. *Educational and Psychological Measurement, 24,* 207–218.

Shostrom, E. L. (1974). *Manual for the Personal Orientation Inventory.* San Diego, CA: EdITS.

Showers, C. J., & Ryff, C. D. (1996). Self-differentiation and well-being in a life transition. *Personality and Social Psychology Bulletin, 22,* 448–460.

Sidanius, J., Pratto, F., & Bobo, L. (1994). Social dominance orientation and the political psychology of gender: A case of invariance? *Journal of Personality and Social Psychology, 67,* 998–1011.

Silverman, L. H. (1976). Psychoanalytic theory: "The reports of my death are greatly exaggerated." *American Psychologist, 31,* 621–637.

Simon, D. P., & Simon, H. A. (1978). Individual differences in solving physics problems. In R. S. Siegler (Ed.), *Children's thinking: What develops?* (pp. 325–348). Hillsdale, NJ: Erlbaum.

Simon, D., Snow, C. J., & Read, S. J. (2004). The redux of cognitive consistency theories: Evidence judgments by constraint satisfaction. *Journal of Personality and Social Psychology, 86,* 814–837.

Simon, H. A. (1967). Motivational and emotional controls of cognition. *Psychological Review, 74,* 29–39.

Simpson, J. A. (1990). Influence of attachment styles on romantic relationships. *Journal of Personality and Social Psychology, 59,* 971–980.

Simpson, J. A., Collins, A., Tran, S., & Haydon, K. C. (2007). Attachment and the experience and expression of emotions in romantic relationships: A developmental perspective. *Journal of Personality and Social Psychology, 92,* 355–367.

Simpson, J. A., Rholes, W. S., & Nelligan, J. S. (1992). Support seeking and support giving within couples in an anxiety-provoking situation: The role of attachment styles. *Journal of Personality and Social Psychology, 62,* 434–446.

Simpson, J. A., Rholes, W. S., Oriña, M. M., & Grich, J. (2002). Working models of attachment, support giving, and support seeking in a stressful situation. *Personality and Social Psychology Bulletin, 28,* 598–608.

Singer, J. A. (2004). Narrative identity and meaning making across the adult lifespan: An introduction. *Journal of Personality, 72,* 437–459.

Singer, J. A. (2005). *Personality and psychotherapy: Treating the whole person.* New York, NY: Guilford Press.

Singh, D. (1995). Female judgment of male attractiveness and desirability for relationships: Role of waist-to-hip ratio and financial status. *Journal of Personality and Social Psychology, 69,* 1089–1101.

Skinner, B. F. (1938). *The behavior of organisms.* New York, NY: Appleton-Century-Crofts.

Skowronski, J. J., Carlston, D. E., Mae, L., & Crawford, M. T. (1998). Spontaneous trait transference: Communicators take on the qualities they describe in others. *Journal of Personality and Social Psychology, 74,* 837–848.

Sloman, S. A. (1996). The empirical case for two forms of reasoning. *Psychological Bulletin, 119,* 3–22.

Small, M. F. (1993). *Female choices: Sexual behavior of female primates.* Ithaca, NY: Cornell University Press.

Smith, C. P. (Ed.). (1992). *Motivation and personality: Handbook of thematic content analysis.* New York, NY: Cambridge University Press.

Smith, E. E., Shoben, E. J., & Rips, L. J. (1974). Structure and process in semantic memory: A featural model for semantic decisions. *Psychological Review, 81,* 214–241.

Smith, E. R. (1996). What do connectionism and social psychology offer each other? *Journal of Personality and Social Psychology, 70,* 893–912.

Smith, E. R., Murphy, J., & Coats, S. (1999). Attachment to groups: Theory and measurement. *Journal of Personality and Social Psychology, 77,* 94–110.

Smith, G. M. (1967). Usefulness of peer ratings of personality in educational resarch. *Educational and Psychological Measurement, 27,* 967–984.

Smith, M. L., & Glass, G. V. (1977). Meta-analysis of psychotherapy outcome studies. *American Psychologist, 32,* 752–760.

Smith, M. L., Glass, G. V., & Miller, T. I. (1980). *The benefits of psychotherapy.* Baltimore, MD: Johns Hopkins Press.

Smolensky, P. (1988). On the proper treatment of connectionism. *Behavioral and Brain Sciences, 11,* 1–23.

Smolensky, P., Mozer, M. C., & Rumelhart, D. E. (Eds.). (1996). *Mathematical perspectives on neural networks.* Mahwah, NJ: Erlbaum.

Smyth, J. M. (1998). Written emotional expression: Effect sizes, outcome types, and moderating variables. *Journal of Consulting and Clinical Psychology, 66,* 174–184.

Sneed, J. R., Whitbourne, S. K., & Culang, M. E. (2006). Trust, identity, and ego integrity: Modeling Erikson's core stages over 34 years. *Journal of Adult Development, 13,* 148–157.

Snyder, C. R., & Higgins, R. L. (1988). Excuses: Their effective role in the negotiation of reality. *Psychological Bulletin, 104,* 23–35.

Snyder, M. L., Stephan, W. G., & Rosenfield, D. (1976). Egotism and attribution. *Journal of Personality and Social Psychology, 33,* 435–441.

Snyder, M. L., Stephan, W. G., & Rosenfield, D. (1978). Attributional egotism. In J. H. Harvey, W. Ickes, & R. F. Kidd (Eds.), *New directions in attributional research* (Vol. 2). Hillsdale, NJ: Erlbaum.

Sobotka, S. S., Davidson, R. J., & Senulis, J. A. (1992). Anterior brain electrical asymmetries in response to reward and punishment. *Electroencephalography and Clinical Neurophysiology, 83,* 236–247.

Sokolowski, K. (2008). Social bonding: Affiliation motivation and intimacy motivation. In J. Heckhausen & H. Heckhausen (Eds.) *Motivation and action* (pp. 184–201). Cambridge, England: Cambridge University Press.

Solomon, R. L. (1964). Punishment. *American Psychologist, 19,* 239–253.

Somer, O., & Goldberg, L. R. (1999). The structure of Turkish trait-descriptive adjectives. *Journal of Personality and Social Psychology, 76,* 431–450.

Sorg, B. A., & Whitney, P. (1992). The effect of trait anxiety and situational stress on working memory capacity. *Journal of Research in Personality, 26,* 235–241.

Sorrentino, R. M., & Field, N. (1986). Emergent leadership over time: The functional value of positive motivation. *Journal of Personality and Social Psychology, 50,* 1091–1099.

Soubrié, P. (1986). Reconciling the role of central serotonin neurons in human and animal behavior. *Behavioral and Brain Sciences, 9,* 319–364.

Spacapan, S., & Cohen, S. (1983). Effects and aftereffects of stressor expectations. *Journal of Personality and Social Psychology, 45,* 1243–1254.

Spangler, W. D., & House, R. J. (1991). Presidential effectiveness and the leadership motive profile. *Journal of Personality and Social Psychology, 60,* 439–455.

Speer, N. K., Reynolds, J. R., Swallow, K, M., & Zacks, J. M. (2009). Reading stories activates neural representations of visual and motor experiences. *Psychological Science, 20,* 989–999.

Spielberger, C. D., & DeNike, L. D. (1966). Descriptive behaviorism versus cognitive theory in verbal operant conditioning. *Psychological Review, 73,* 309–326.

Spoont, M. R. (1992). Modulatory role of serotonin in neural information processing: Implications for human psychopathology. *Psychological Bulletin, 112,* 330–350.

Sprecher, S., Sullivan, Q., & Hatfield, E. (1994). Mate selection preferences: Gender differences examined in a national sample. *Journal of Personality and Social Psychology, 66,* 1074–1080.

Srivastava, S., Angelo, K. M., & Vallereux, S. R. (2008). Extraversion and positive affect: A day reconstruction study of person-environment transactions. *Journal of Research in Personality, 42,* 1613–1618.

Srivastava, S., McGonigal, K. M., Richards, J. M., Butler, E. A., & Gross, J. J. (2006). Optimism in close relationships: How seeing things in a positive light makes them so. *Journal of Personality and Social Psychology, 91,* 143–153.

Sroufe, L. A., & Fleeson, J. (1986). Attachment and the construction of relationships. In W. W. Hartup & Z. Rubin (Eds.), *Relationships and development* (pp. 51–71). Hillsdale, NJ: Erlbaum.

Srull, T. K., & Wyer, R. S., Jr. (1979). The role of category accessibility in the interpretation of information about persons: Some determinants and implications. *Journal of Personality and Social Psychology, 37,* 1660–1672.

St. Clair, M. (1986). *Object relations and self psychology: An introduction.* Monterey, CA: Brooks/Cole.

Staats, A. W. (1996). *Behavior and personality: Psychological behaviorism.* New York, NY: Springer.

Staats, A. W., & Burns, G. L. (1982). Emotional personality repertoire as cause of behavior. *Journal of Personality and Social Psychology, 43,* 873–881.

Staats, A. W., & Staats, C. K. (1958). Attitudes established by classical conditioning. *Journal of Abnormal and Social Psychology, 57,* 37–40.

Staats, C. K., & Staats, A. W. (1957). Meaning established by classical conditioning. *Journal of Experimental Psychology, 54,* 74–80.

Stadler, G., Oettingen, G., & Gollwitzer, P. M. (2010) Intervention effects of information and self-regulation on eating fruit and vegetables over two years. *Health Psychology, 29,* 274–283.

Stahl, C., Unkelbach, C., & Corneille, O. (2009). On the respective contributions of awareness of unconditioned stimulus valence and unconditioned stimulus identity in attitude formation through evaluative conditioning. *Journal of Personality and Social Psychology, 97,* 404–420.

Stanton, S. J., & Edelstein, R. S. (2009). The physiology of women's power motive: Implicit power motivation is positively associated with estradiol levels in women. *Journal of Research in Personality, 43,* 1109–1113.

Stanton, S. J., & Schultheiss, O. C. (2007). Basal and dynamic relationships between implicit power motivation and estradiol in women. *Hormones and Behavior, 52,* 571–580.

Steele, C. M. (1997). A threat in the air: How stereotypes shape intellectual identity and performance. *American Psychologist, 52,* 613–629.

Steele, C. M., & Aronson, J. (1995). Stereotype threat and the intellectual test performance of African Americans. *Journal of Personality and Social Psychology, 69,* 797–811.

Steronko, R. J., & Woods, D. J. (1978). Impairment in early stages of visual information processing in nonpsychotic schizotypic individuals. *Journal of Abnormal Psychology, 87,* 481–490.

Stevens, R. (1983). *Erik Erikson: An introduction.* New York, NY: St. Martin's Press.

Stock, G. (2002). *Redesigning humans: Our inevitable genetic future.* Boston, MA: Houghton Mifflin.

Stolberg, S. (1994, March 27). Genetic bias: Held hostage by heredity. *Los Angeles Times,* p. 1A.

Stone, A. A., Kennedy-Moore, E., & Neale, J. M. (1995). Association between daily coping and end-of-day mood. *Health Psychology, 14,* 341–349.

Strack, F., & Deutsch, R. (2004). Reflective and impulsive determinants of social behavior. *Personality and Social Psychology Review, 8,* 220–247.

Straub, R. E., Jiang, Y., MacLean, C. J., Ma, Y., Webb, B. T., et al. (2002). Genetic variation in the 6p22.3 gene *DTNBP1,* the human ortholog of the mouse dysbindin gene, is associated with schizophrenia. *American Journal of Human Genetics, 71,* 337–348.

Strauss, M. E., & Smith, G. T. (2009). Construct validity: Advances in theory and methodology. *Annual Review of Clinical Psychology, 5,* 1–25.

Streiner, D. L. (2010). Measure for measure: New developments in measurement and item response theory. *Canadian Journal of Psychiatry, 55,* 180–186.

Strong, R. K., & Dabbs, J. M., Jr. (2000). Testosterone and behavior in normal young children. *Personality and Individual Differences, 28,* 909–915.

Strube, M. J. (1989). Evidence for the *type* in Type A behavior: A taxometric analysis. *Journal of Personality and Social Psychology, 56,* 972–987.

Stucke, T. S., & Sporer, S. L. (2002). When a grandiose self-image is threatened: Narcissism and self-concept clarity as predictors of negative emotions and aggression following ego-threat. *Journal of Personality, 70,* 509–532.

Stumpf, H. (1993). The factor structure of the Personality Research Form: A cross-national evaluation. *Journal of Personality, 61,* 27–48.

Sutton, S. K., & Davidson, R. J. (1997). Prefrontal brain asymmetry: A biological substrate of the behavioral approach and inhibition systems. *Psychological Science, 8,* 204–210.

Swann, W. B., Jr. (1987). Identity negotiation: Where two roads meet. *Journal of Personality and Social Psychology, 53,* 1038–1051.

Swann, W. B., Jr. (1990). To be adored or to be known: The interplay of self-enhancement and self-verification. In E. T. Higgins & R. M. Sorrentino (Eds.), *Handbook of motivation and cognition* (Vol. 2, pp. 408–448). New York, NY: Guilford Press.

Swann, W. B., Jr., Bosson, J. K., & Pelham, B. W. (2002). Different partners, different selves: Strategic verification of circumscribed identities. *Personality and Social Psychology Bulletin, 28,* 1215–1228.

Swann, W. B., Jr., Pelham, B. W., & Krull, D. S. (1989). Agreeable fancy or disagreeable truth? Reconciling self-enhancement and self-verification. *Journal of Personality and Social Psychology, 57,* 782–791.

Swann, W. B., Jr., Wenzlaff, R. M., & Tafarodi, R. W. (1992). Depression and the search for negative evaluations: More evidence of the role of self-verification strivings. *Journal of Abnormal Psychology, 101,* 314–317.

Tangney, J. P., Baumeister, R. F., & Boone, A. L. (2004). High self-control predicts good adjustment, less pathology, better grades, and interpersonal success. *Journal of Personality, 72,* 271–324.

Tannen, D. (1990). *You just don't understand: Women and men in conversation.* New York, NY: Ballantine Books.

Tavris, C., & Wade, C. (1984). *The longest war: Sex differences in perspective* (2nd ed.). New York, NY: Harcourt Brace Jovanovich.

Taylor, S. E. (2002). *The tending instinct: How nurturing is essential to who we are and how we live.* New York, NY: Henry Holt.

Taylor, S. E. (2006). Tend and befriend: Biobehavioral bases of affiliation under stress. *Current Directions in Psychological Science, 15,* 273–277.

Taylor, S. E., & Brown, J. D. (1988). Illusion and well-being: A social psychological perspective on mental health. *Psychological Bulletin, 103,* 193–210.

Taylor, S. E., & Fiske, S. T. (1978). Salience, attention, and attribution: Top of the head phenomena. In L. Berkowitz (Ed.), *Advances in experimental social psychology* (Vol. 11). New York, NY: Academic Press.

Taylor, S. E., & Gollwitzer, P. M. (1995). Effects of mindset on positive illusions. *Journal of Personality and Social Psychology, 69,* 213–226.

Taylor, S. E., Klein, L. C., Lewis, B. P., Gruenewald, T. L., Gurung, R. A. R., & Updegraff, J. A. (2000). Biobehavioral responses to stress in females: Tend-and-befriend, not fight-or-flight. *Psychological Review, 107,* 411–429.

Tellegen, A. (1985). Structure of mood and personality and their relevance to assessing anxiety, with an emphasis on self-report. In A. H. Tuma & J. D. Maser (Eds.), *Anxiety and the anxiety disorders* (pp. 681–706). Hillsdale, NJ: Erlbaum.

Tellegen, A., Lykken, D. T., Bouchard, T. J., Jr., Wilcox, K. J., Segal N. L., & Rich, S. (1988). Personality similarity in twins reared apart and together. *Journal of Personality and Social Psychology, 54,* 1031–1039.

Tesch, S. A., & Whitbourne, S. K. (1982). Intimacy status and identity status in young adults. *Journal of Personality and Social Psychology, 43,* 1041–1051.

Tesser, A. (1991). Social vs. clinical approaches to self psychology: The self-evaluation maintenance model and Kohutian object relations theory. In R. Curtis (Ed.), *The relational self: Theoretical convergences in psychoanalysis and social psychology* (pp. 257–281). New York, NY: Guilford Press.

Tesser, A. (1993). The importance of heritability in psychological research: The case of attitudes. *Psychological Review, 100,* 129–142.

Thagard, P. (1989). Explanatory coherence. *Behavioral and Brain Sciences, 12,* 435–467.

Thagard, P., & Millgram, E. (1995). Inference to the best plan: A coherence theory of decision. In A. Ram & D. B. Leake (Eds.), *Goal-driven learning* (pp. 439–454). Cambridge, MA: MIT Press.

Thelen, M. H., & Rennie, D. L. (1972). The effect of vicarious reinforcement on imitation: A review of the literature. In B. Maher (Ed.), *Progress in experimental personality research* (Vol. 6). New York, NY: Academic Press.

Thiessen, D., & Gregg, B. (1980). Human assortative mating and genetic equilibrium: An evolutionary perspective. *Ethology and Sociobiology, 1,* 111–140.

Thomason-Schill, S. L., Ramscar, M., & Chrysikou, E. G. (2009). Cognition without control: When a little frontal lobe goes a long way. *Current Directions in Psychological Science, 18,* 259–263.

Thorndike, E. L. (1898). Animal intelligence: An experimental study of the associative processes in animals. *Psychological Monographs, 2* (Whole No. 8).

Thorndike, E. L. (1905). *The elements of psychology.* New York, NY: A. G. Seiler.

Thorndike, E. L. (1933). *An experimental study of rewards.* New York, NY: Columbia University Teachers College Press.

Thorne, A. (1987). The press of personality: A study of conversations between introverts and extraverts. *Journal of Personality and Social Psychology, 53,* 718–726.

Thorne, A., Korobov, N., & Morgan, E. M. (2007). Channeling identity: A study of storytelling in conversations between introverted and extraverted friends. *Journal of Research in Personality, 41,* 1008–1031.

Thrash, T. M., & Elliot, A. J. (2002). Implicit and self-attributed achievement motives: Concordance and predictive validity. *Journal of Personality, 70,* 729–755.

Thronquist, M. H., Zuckerman, M., & Exline, R. V. (1991). Loving, liking, looking, and sensation seeking in unmarried college couples. *Personality and Individual Differences, 12,* 1283–1292.

Tindle, H. A., Chang, Y., Kuller, L. H., Manson, J. E., Robinson, J. G., Rosal, M. C., Siegle, G. J., & Matthews, K. A. (2009). Optimism, cynical hostility, and incident coronary heart disease and mortality in the Women's Health Initiative. *Circulation, 120,* 656–662.

Toates, F. (2006). A model of the hierarchy of behaviour, cognition, and consciousness. *Consciousness and Cognition, 15,* 75–118.

Tolman, E. C. (1932). *Purposive behavior in animals and men.* New York, NY: Appleton-Century-Crofts.

Tolman, E. C. (1959). Principles of purposive behavior. In S. Koch (Ed.), *Psychology: A study of a science* (Vol. 2, pp. 92–157). New York, NY: McGraw-Hill.

Toner, I. J., & Smith, R. A. (1977). Age and overt verbalization in delay-maintenance behavior in children. *Journal of Experimental Child Psychology, 24,* 123–128.

Tooby, J., & Cosmides, L. (1989). Evolutionary psychology and the generation of culture, Part I. *Ethology and Sociobiology, 10,* 29–49.

Tooby, J., & Cosmides, L. (1990). On the universality of human nature and the uniqueness of the individual. *Journal of Personality, 58,* 17–67.

Torelli, C. J., & Kaikati, A. M. (2009). Values as predictors of judgments and behaviors: The role of abstract and concrete mindsets. *Journal of Personality and Social Psychology, 96,* 231–247.

Torges, C. M., Stewart, A. J., & Duncan, L. E. (2008). Achieving ego integrity: Personality development in late midlife. *Journal of Research in Personality, 42,* 1004–1019.

Trapnell, P. D., & Campbell, J. D. (1999). Private self-consciousness and the five-factor model of personality: Distinguishing rumination from reflection. *Journal of Personality and Social Psychology, 76,* 284–304.

Trapnell, P. D., & Wiggins, J. S. (1990). Extension of the interpersonal adjective scales to include the big five dimensions of personality. *Journal of Personality and Social Psychology, 59,* 781–790.

Trivers, R. L. (1971). The evolution of reciprocal altruism. *Quarterly Review of Biology, 46,* 35–57.

Trivers, R. L. (1972). Parental investment and sexual selection. In B. Campbell (Ed.), *Sexual selection and the descent of man: 1871–1971* (pp. 136–179). Chicago, IL: Aldine.

Trobst, K. K., Herbst, J. H., Masters, H. L., III, & Costa, P. T., Jr. (2002). Personality pathways to unsafe sex: Personality, condom use, and HIV risk behaviors. *Journal of Research in Personality, 36,* 117–133.

Trope, Y. (1975). Seeking information about one's own ability as a determinant of choice among tasks. *Journal of Personality and Social Psychology, 32,* 1004–1013.

Trope, Y. (1979). Uncertainty-reducing properties of achievement tasks. *Journal of Personality and Social Psychology, 37,* 1505–1518.

Trope, Y. (1980). Self-assessment, self-enhancement, and task preference. *Journal of Experimental Social Psychology, 16,* 116–129.

Trope, Y., & Fishbach, A. (2000). Counteractive self-control in overcoming temptation. *Journal of Personality and Social Psychology, 79,* 493–506.

Trope, Y., & Fishbach, A. (2005). Going beyond the motivation given: Self-control and situational control over behavior. In R. R. Hassin, J. S. Uleman, & J. A. Bargh (Eds.), *The new unconscious* (pp. 537–563). New York, NY: Oxford University Press.

Trope, Y., & Liberman, N. (2003). Temporal construal. *Psychological Review, 110,* 403–421.

Trope, Y., & Liberman, N. (2010). Construal-level theory of psychological distance. *Psychological Review, 117,* 440–463.

Tse, W. S., & Bond, A. J. (2001). Serotonergic involvement in the psychosocial dimension of personality. *Journal of Psychopharmacology, 15,* 195–198.

Tulving, E. (1972). Episodic and semantic memory. In E. Tulving & W. Donaldson (Eds.), *Organization of memory.* New York, NY: Academic Press.

Tulving, E. (1993). What is episodic memory? *Current Directions in Psychological Science, 2,* 67–70.

Turkheimer, E. (1998). Heritability and biological explanation. *Psychological Review, 105,* 782–791.

Turner, J. L., Foa, E. B., & Foa, U. G. (1971). Interpersonal reinforcers: Classification, interrelationship, and some differential properties. *Journal of Personality and Social Psychology, 19,* 168–170.

Turner, R. A., Altemus, M., Enos, T., Cooper, B., & McGuinness, T. (1999). Preliminary research on plasma oxytocin in normal cycling women: Investigating emotion and interpersonal distress. *Psychiatry, 62,* 97–113.

Twenge, J. M., & Campbell, W. K. (2003). "Isn't it fun to get the respect that we're going to deserve?" Narcissism, social rejection, and aggression. *Personality and Social Psychology Bulletin, 29,* 261–272.

Tyner, S. D., Venkatachalam, S., Choi, J., Jones, S., Ghebranious, N., Igelmann, H., Lu, X., Soron, G., Cooper, B., Brayton, C., Park, S. H., Thompson, T., Karsenty, G., Bradley, A., & Donehower, L. A. (2002). p53 mutant mice that display early ageing-associated phenotypes. *Nature, 415,* 45–53.

Udry, J. R., & Talbert, L. M. (1988). Sex hormone effects on personality at puberty. *Journal of Personality and Social Psychology, 54,* 291–295.

Uebelacker, L. A., Strong, D., Weinstock, L. M., & Miller, I. W. (2009). Use of item response theory to understand differential functioning of DSM-IV major depression symptoms by race, ethnicity and gender. *Psychological Medicine, 39,* 591–601.

Underwood, B. J. (1975). Individual differences as a crucible in theory construction. *American Psychologist, 30,* 128–134.

Vallacher, R. R., & Nowak, A. (1997). The emergence of dynamical social psychology. *Psychological Inquiry, 8,* 73–99.

Vallacher, R. R., & Wegner, D. M. (1985). *A theory of action identification.* Hillsdale, NJ: Erlbaum.

Vallacher, R. R., & Wegner, D. M. (1987). Action identification theory: The representation and control of behavior. *Psychological Review, 94,* 3–15.

Vallacher, R. R., & Wegner, D. M. (1989). Levels of personal agency: Individual variation in action identification. *Journal of Personality and Social Psychology, 57,* 660–671.

Vallacher, R. R., Read, S. J., & Nowak, A. (Eds.). (2002). The dynamical perspective in personality and social psychology [Special issue]. *Personality and Social Psychology Review, 6(4).*

Vallerand, R. J. (1997). Toward a hierarchical model of intrinsic and extrinsic motivation. In M. P. Zanna (Ed.), *Advances in experimental social psychology* (Vol. 29, pp. 271–360). San Diego, CA: Academic Press.

van Honk, J., & Schutter, D. J. L. G. (2007). Testosterone reduces conscious detection of signals serving social correction: Implications for antisocial behavior. *Psychological Science, 18,* 663–667.

van Honk, J., Schutter, D. J. L. G., Hermans, E. J., Putman, P., Tuiten, A., & Koppeschaar, H. (2004). Testosterone shifts the balance between sensitivity for

punishment and reward in healthy young women. *Psychoneuroendocrinology, 29,* 937–943.

Vandenberg, S. G., Singer, S. M., & Pauls, D. L. (1986). *The heredity of behavior disorders in adults and children.* New York, NY: Plenum Press.

Vandewater, E. A., Ostrove, J. M., & Stewart, A. J. (1997). Predicting women's well-being in midlife: The importance of personality development and social role involvements. *Journal of Personality and Social Psychology, 72,* 1147–1160.

Vernon, D. T. A. (1974). Modeling and birth order in responses to painful stimuli. *Journal of Personality and Social Psychology, 29,* 794–799.

Vernon, P. E. (1964). *Personality assessment: A critical survey.* New York, NY: Wiley.

Verplanken, B., & Holland, R. W. (2002). Motivated decision making: Effects of activation and self-centrality of values on choices and behavior. *Journal of Personality and Social Psychology, 82,* 434–447.

Viken, R. J., Rose, R. J., Kaprio, J., & Koskenvuo, M. (1994). A developmental genetic analysis of adult personality: Extraversion and neuroticism from 18 to 59 years of age. *Journal of Personality and Social Psychology, 66,* 722–730.

von Bertalanffy, L. (1968). *General systems theory.* New York, NY: Braziller.

Wagerman, S. A., & Funder, D. C. (2007). Acquaintance reports of personality and academic achievement: A case for conscientiousness. *Journal of Research in Personality, 41,* 221–229.

Wagner, A. R., Siegel, S., Thomas, E., & Ellison, G. D. (1964). Reinforcement history and the extinction of a conditioned salivary response. *Journal of Comparative and Physiological Psychology, 58,* 354–358.

Walker, E. F., & Diforio, D. (1997). Schizophrenia: A neural diathesis-stress model. *Psychological Review, 104,* 667–685.

Wallace, H. M., & Baumeister, R. F. (2002). The performance of narcissists rises and falls with perceived opportunity for glory. *Journal of Personality and Social Psychology, 82,* 819–834.

Walters, R. H., & Parke, R. D. (1964). Influence of response consequences to a social model on resistance to deviation. *Journal of Experimental Child Psychology, 1,* 269–280.

Walther, E. (2002). Guilty by mere association: Evaluative conditioning and the spreading attitude effect. *Journal of Personality and Social Psychology, 82,* 919–934.

Walton, K. E., & Roberts, B. W. (2004). On the relationship between substance use and personality traits: Abstainers are not maladjusted. *Journal of Research in Personality, 38,* 515–535.

Walton, K. E., Roberts, B. W., Krueger, R. F., Blonigen, D. M., & Hicks, B. M. (2008). Capturing abnormal personality with normal personality inventories: An item response theory approach. *Journal of Personality, 76*, 1623–1647.

Watson, D., Clark, L. A., McIntyre, C. W., & Hamaker, S. (1992). Affect, personality, and social activity. *Journal of Personality and Social Psychology, 63*, 1011–1025.

Webb, T. L., & Sheeran, P. (2003) Can implementation intentions help to overcome ego-depletion? *Journal of Experimental Social Psychology, 39*, 279–286.

Webb, T. L., & Sheeran, P. (2007). How do implementation intentions promote goal attainment? A test of component processes. *Journal of Experimental Social Psychology, 43*, 295–302.

Wegner, D. M. (1989). *White bears and other unwanted thoughts: Suppression, obsession, and the psychology of mental control.* New York, NY: Viking Penguin.

Wegner, D. M. (1994). Ironic processes of mental control. *Psychological Review, 101*, 34–52.

Wegner, D. M. (2002). *The illusion of conscious will.* Cambridge, MA: MIT Press.

Wegner, D. M., Shortt, J. W., Blake, A. W., & Page, M. S. (1990). The suppression of exciting thoughts. *Journal of Personality and Social Psychology, 58*, 409–418.

Wegner, D. M., Wenzlaff, R. M., & Kozak, M. (2004). Dream rebound: The return of suppressed thoughts in dreams. *Psychological Science, 15*, 232–236.

Wegner, D. M., & Wheatley, T. (1999). Apparent mental causation: Sources of the experience of will. *American Psychologist, 54*, 480–492.

Weiner, B. (1979). A theory of motivation for some classroom experiences. *Journal of Educational Psychology, 71*, 3–25.

Weiner, B. (1986). *An attributional theory of motivation and emotion.* New York, NY: Springer-Verlag.

Weiner, B. (1990). Attribution in personality psychology. In L. A. Pervin (Ed.), *Handbook of personality: Theory and research* (pp. 465–485). New York, NY: Guilford Press.

Weiner, B., & Litman-Adizes, T. (1980). An attributional, expectancy–value analysis of learned helplessness and depression. In J. Garber & M. E. P. Seligman (Eds.), *Human helplessness: Theory and applications.* New York, NY: Academic Press.

Weiss, A., Bates, T. C., & Luciano, M. (2008). Happiness is a personal(ity) thing: The genetics of personality and well-being in a representative sample. *Psychological Science, 19,* 205–210.

Weiss, L., & Masling, J. (1970). Further validation of a Rorschach measure of oral imagery: A study of six clinical groups. *Journal of Abnormal Psychology, 76*, 83–87.

Weiss, R. S. (Ed.). (1973). *Loneliness: The experience of emotional and social isolation.* Cambridge, MA: MIT Press.

Wendelken, C., & Shastri, L. (2005). Connectionist mechanisms for cognitive control. *Neurocomputing: An International Journal, 65–66,* 663–672.

Wenzlaff, R. M., & Wegner, D. M. (2000). Thought suppression. *Annual Review of Psychology, 51*, 59–91.

Wenzlaff, R. M., Wegner, D. M., & Roper, D. W. (1988). Depression and mental control: The resurgence of unwanted negative thoughts. *Journal of Personality and Social Psychology, 55*, 1–11.

Westen, D. (1998). The scientific legacy of Sigmund Freud: Toward a psychodynamically informed psychological science. *Psychological Bulletin, 124*, 333–371.

Westmaas, J. L., & Silver, R. C. (2001). The role of attachment in responses to victims of life crises. *Journal of Personality and Social Psychology, 80*, 425–438.

Wheeler, R. E., Davidson, R. J., & Tomarken, A. J. (1993). Frontal brain asymmetry and emotional reactivity: A biological substrate of affective style. *Psychophysiology, 30*, 82–89.

Whitbeck, L. B., Hoyt, D. R., Simons, R. L., Conger, R. D., Elder, G. H., Jr., Lorenz, F. O., & Huck, S. (1992). Intergenerational continuity of parental rejection and depressed affect. *Journal of Personality and Social Psychology, 63*, 1036–1045.

Whitbourne, S. K., Sneed, J. R., & Sayer, A. (2009). Psychosocial development from college through midlife: A 34-year sequential study. *Developmental Psychology, 45*, 1328–1340.

White, R. W. (1959). Motivation reconsidered: The concept of competence. *Psychological Review, 66*, 297–333.

White, R. W. (1963). *Ego and reality in psychoanalytic theory: A proposal regarding independent ego energies* (Psychological Issues Monograph 11). New York, NY: International Universities Press.

Whiteside, S. P., & Lynam, D. R. (2001). The Five Factor Model and impulsivity: Using a structural model of personality to understand impulsivity. *Personality and Individual Differences, 30*, 669–689.

Wickelgren, W. A. (1977). *Learning and memory.* Englewood Cliffs, NJ: Prentice-Hall.

Wicker, F. W., Brown, G., Wiehe, J. A., Hagen, A. S., & Reed, J. L. (1993). On reconsidering Maslow: An examination of the deprivation/domination proposition. *Journal of Research in Personality, 27*, 118–133.

Widiger, T. A., & Mullins-Sweatt, S. N. (2009). Five-factor model of personality disorder: A proposal for DSM-V. *Annual Review of Clinical Psychology, 5,* 197–220.

Widiger, T. A., & Trull, T. J. (2007). Plate tectonics in the classification of personality disorder. Shifting to a dimensional model. *American Psychologist, 62,* 71–83.

Widiger, T. A., Trull, T. J., Clarkin, J. F., Sanderson, C., & Costa, P. T., Jr. (2002). A description of the DSM-IV personality disorders with the five-factor model. In P. T. Costa, Jr., & T. A. Widiger (Eds.), *Personality disorders and the five-factor model of personality* (2nd ed., pp. 89–99). Washington, DC: American Psychological Association.

Wiedenfeld, S. A., O'Leary, A., Bandura, A., Brown, S., Levine, S., & Raska, K. (1990). Impact of perceived self-efficacy in coping with stressors on components of the immune system. *Journal of Personality and Social Psychology, 59,* 1082–1094.

Wiener, N. (1948). *Cybernetics: Control and communication in the animal and the machine.* Cambridge, MA: MIT Press.

Wiggins, J. S. (1973). *Personality and prediction: Principles of personality assessment.* Reading, MA: Addison-Wesley.

Wiggins, J. S. (1979). A psychological taxonomy of trait-descriptive terms: The interpersonal domain. *Journal of Personality and Social Psychology, 37,* 395–412.

Wiggins, J. S. (Ed.). (1996). *The five-factor model of personality: Theoretical perspectives.* New York, NY: Guilford Press.

Wiggins, J. S., Phillips, N., & Trapnell, P. (1989). Circular reasoning about interpersonal behavior: Evidence concerning some untested assumptions underlying diagnostic classification. *Journal of Personality and Social Psychology, 56,* 296–305.

Wijngaards-de Meij, L., Stroebe, M., Schut, H., Stroebe, W., van den Bout, J., van der Heijden, P., & Dijkstra, I. (2007). Neuroticism and attachment insecurity as predictors of bereavement outcome. *Journal of Research in Personality, 41,* 498–505.

Wijngaards-de Meij, L., Stroebe, M., Schut, H., Stroebe, W., van den Bout, J., van der Heijden, P. G. M., & Dijkstra, I. (2007). Patterns of attachment and parents' adjustment to the death of their child. *Personality and Social Psychology Bulletin, 33,* 537–548.

Willerman, L., Loehlin, J. C., & Horn, J. M. (1992). An adoption and a cross-fostering study of the Minnesota Multiphasic Personality Inventory (MMPI) Psychopathic Deviate scale. *Behavior Genetics, 22,* 515–529.

Williams, G. C., & Deci, E. L. (1996). Internalization of biopsychosocial values by medical students: A test of self-determination theory. *Journal of Personality and Social Psychology, 70,* 767–779.

Williams, G. C., Grow, V. M., Freedman, Z. R., Ryan, R. M., & Deci, E. L. (1996). Motivational predictors of weight loss and weight-loss maintenance. *Journal of Personality and Social Psychology, 70,* 115–126.

Williams, P. G., Rau, H. K., Cribbet, M. R., & Gunn, H. E. (2009). Openness to experience and stress regulation. *Journal of Research in Personality, 43,* 777–784.

Williams, R. L., Moore, C. A., Pettibone, T. J., & Thomas, S. P. (1992). Construction and validation of a brief self-report scale of self-management practices. *Journal of Research in Personality, 26,* 216–234.

Wilson, A. E., Smith, M. D., Ross, H. S., & Ross, M. (2004). Young children's personal accounts of their sibling disputes. *Merrill-Palmer Quarterly, 50,* 39–66.

Wilson, D. S., & Wilson, E. O. (2008). Evolution "for the good of the group." *American Scientist, 96,* 380–389.

Wilson, E. O. (1975). *Sociobiology: The new synthesis.* Cambridge, MA: Harvard University Press.

Wilson, J. Q., & Herrnstein, R. J. (1985). *Crime and human nature.* New York, NY: Simon & Schuster.

Wilson, M. I., & Daly, M. (1985). Competitiveness, risk-taking, and violence: The young male syndrome. *Ethology and Sociobiology, 6,* 59–73.

Wilson, M. I., & Daly, M. (1996). Male sexual proprietariness and violence against wives. *Current Directions in Psychological Science, 5,* 2–7.

Winter, D. G. (1972). The need for power in college men: Action correlates and relationship to drinking. In D. C. McClelland, W. N. Davis, R. Kalin, & E. Wanner (Eds.), *The drinking man.* New York, NY: Free Press.

Winter, D. G. (1973). *The power motive.* New York, NY: Free Press.

Winter, D. G. (1988). The power motive in women—and men. *Journal of Personality and Social Psychology, 54,* 510–519.

Winter, D. G. (1993). Power, affiliation, and war: Three tests of a motivational model. *Journal of Personality and Social Psychology, 65,* 532–545.

Winter, D. G. (1994). *Manual for scoring motive imagery in running text.* Ann Arbor, MI: University of Michigan.

Winter, D. G. (1996). *Personality: Analysis and interpretation of lives.* New York, NY: McGraw-Hill.

Winter, D. G. (1998). "Toward a science of personality psychology": David McClelland's development of empirically derived TAT measures. *History of Psychology, 1,* 130–153.

Winter, D. G. (2007). The role of motivation, responsibility, and integrative complexity in crisis escalation: Comparative studies of war and peace crises. *Journal of Personality and Social Psychology, 92,* 920–937.

Winter, D. G. (2010). Why achievement motivation predicts success in business but failure in politics: The importance of personal control. *Journal of Personality, 78,* 1637–1688.

Winter, D. G., & Barenbaum, N. B. (1985). Responsibility and the power motive in women and men. *Journal of Personality, 53,* 335–355.

Winter, D. G., John, O. P., Stewart, A. J., Klohnen, E. C., & Duncan, L. E. (1998). Traits and motives: Toward an integration of two traditions in personality research. *Psychological Review, 105,* 230–250.

Winter, D. G., Stewart, A. J., & McClelland, D. C. (1977). Husband's motives and wife's career level. *Journal of Personality and Social Psychology, 35,* 159–166.

Wirth, M. M., Welsh, K., & Schultheiss, O. C. (2006). Salivary cortisol changes in humans after winning or losing a dominance contest depend on implicit power motivation. *Hormones and Behavior, 49,* 346–352.

Wise, R. A. (2004). Dopamine, learning and motivation. *Nature Reviews Neuroscience, 5,* 1–10.

Wisman, A., & Koole, S. L. (2003). Hiding in the crowd: Can mortality salience promote affiliation with others who oppose one's worldviews? *Journal of Personality and Social Psychology, 84,* 511–526.

Wispé, L. (1986). The distinction between sympathy and empathy: To call forth a concept, a word is needed. *Journal of Personality and Social Psychology, 50,* 314–321.

Woike, B. A. (1995). Most-memorable experiences: Evidence for a link between implicit and explicit motives and social cognitive processes in everyday life. *Journal of Personality and Social Psychology, 68,* 1081–1091.

Woike, B., Mcleod, S., & Goggin, M. (2003). Implicit and explicit motives influence accessibility to different autobiographical knowledge. *Personality and Social Psychology Bulletin, 29,* 1046–1055.

Wolfe, J. B. (1936). Effectiveness of token-rewards for chimpanzees. *Comparative Psychology Monographs, 12* (Whole No. 60).

Wolfe, R. N., & Kasmer, J. A. (1988). Type versus trait: Extraversion, impulsivity, sociability, and preferences for cooperative and competitive activities. *Journal of Personality and Social Psychology, 54,* 864–871.

Wolpe, J. (1981). Behavior therapy versus psychoanalysis: Therapeutic and social implications. *American Psychologist, 36,* 159–164.

Wong, M. M., & Csikszentmihalyi, M. (1991). Affiliation motivation and daily experience: Some issues on gender differences. *Journal of Personality and Social Psychology, 60,* 154–164.

Wood, J. M., Nezworski, M. T., & Stejskal, W. J. (1996a). The comprehensive system for the Rorschach: A critical examination. *Psychological Science, 7,* 3–10.

Wood, J. M., Nezworski, M. T., & Stejskal, W. J. (1996b). Thinking critically about the comprehensive system for the Rorschach: A reply to Exner. *Psychological Science, 7,* 14–17.

Wood, R., & Bandura, A. (1989). Impact of conceptions of ability on self-regulatory mechanisms and complex decision making. *Journal of Personality and Social Psychology, 56,* 407–415.

Wood, W., Quinn, F. M., & Kashy, D. A. (2002) Habits in everyday life: Thought, emotion, and action. *Journal of Personality and Social Psychology, 83,* 1281–1297.

Wood, W., Tam, L., & Witt, M. G. (2005). Changing circumstances, disrupting habits. *Journal of Personality and Social Psychology, 88,* 918–933.

Wright, J. C., Lindgren, K. P., & Zakriski, A. L. (2001). Syndromal versus contextualized personality assessment: Differentiating environmental and dispositional determinants of boys' aggression. *Journal of Personality and Social Psychology, 81,* 1176–1189.

Wright, J. C., & Mischel, W. (1988). Conditional hedges and the intuitive psychology of traits. *Journal of Personality and Social Psychology, 55,* 454–469.

Wright, J. C., & Zakriski, A. L. (2003). When syndromal similarity obscures functional dissimilarity: Distinctive evoked environments of externalizing and mixed syndrome boys. *Journal of Consulting and Clinical Psychology, 71,* 516–527.

Wright, J. C., Zakriski, A. L., & Drinkwater, M. (1999). Developmental psychopathology and the reciprocal patterning of behavior and environment: Distinctive situational and behavioral signatures of internalizing, externalizing, and mixed-syndrome children. *Journal of Consulting and Clinical Psychology, 67,* 95–107.

Wright, R. A. (1996). Brehm's theory of motivation as a model of effort and cardiovascular response. In P. M. Gollwitzer & J. A. Bargh (Eds.), *The psychology of action: Linking cognition and motivation to behavior* (pp. 424–453). New York, NY: Guilford Press.

Wrosch, C., Dunne, E., Scheier, M. F., & Schulz, R. (2006). Self-regulation of common age-related challenges: Benefits for older adults' psychological and physical health. *Journal of Behavioral Medicine, 29,* 299–306.

Wrosch, C., Scheier, M. F., Carver, C. S., & Schulz, R. (2003). The importance of goal disengagement in adaptive self-regulation: When giving up is beneficial. *Self and Identity, 2,* 1–20.

Wulfert, E., Block, J. A., Santa Ana, E., Rodriguez, M. L., & Colsman, M. (2002). Delay of gratification: Impulsive choices and problem behaviors in early and late adolescence. *Journal of Personality, 70,* 533–552.

Wyer, R. S., Jr., & Srull, T. K. (1986). Human cognition in its social context. *Psychology Review, 93,* 322–359.

Xu, A. J., & Wyer, R. S., Jr. (2008). The comparative mind-set: From animal comparisons to increased purchase intentions. *Psychological Science, 19,* 859–864.

Yamagata, S., Suzuki, A., Ando, J., Ono, Y., Kijima, N., Yoshimura, K., et al. (2006). Is the genetic structure of human personality universal? A cross-cultural twin study from North American, Europe, and Asia. *Journal of Personality and Social Psychology, 90,* 987–998.

Yates, B. T., & Mischel, W. (1979). Young children's preferred attentional strategies for delaying gratification. *Journal of Personality and Social Psychology, 37,* 286–300.

York, K. L., & John, O. P. (1992). The four faces of Eve: A typological analysis of women's personality at midlife. *Journal of Personality and Social Psychology, 63,* 494–508.

Young, J. E., & Klosko, J. S. (1993). *Reinventing your life.* New York, NY: Plume.

Zald, D. H., & Depue, R. A. (2001). Serotonergic functioning correlates with positive and negative affect in psychiatrically healthy males. *Personality and Individual Differences, 30,* 71–86.

Zeidner, M., & Hammer, A. L. (1992). Coping with missile attack: Resources, strategies, and outcomes. *Journal of Personality, 60,* 709–746.

Zeldow, P. B., Daugherty, S. R., & McAdams, D. P. (1988). Intimacy, power, and psychological well-being in medical students. *Journal of Nervous and Mental Disease, 176,* 182–187.

Zelenski, J. M., & Larsen, R. J. (1999). Susceptibility to affect: A comparison of three personality taxonomies. *Journal of Personality, 67,* 761–791.

Zimmerman, D. W. (1957). Durable secondary reinforcement: Method and theory. *Psychological Review, 14,* 373–383.

Zinbarg, R. E., & Mohlman, J. (1998). Individual differences in the acquisition of affectively valenced associations. *Journal of Personality and Social Psychology, 74,* 1024–1040.

Zucker, A. N., Ostrove, J. M., & Stewart, A. J. (2002). College-educated women's personality development in adulthood: Perceptions and age differences. *Psychology and Aging, 17,* 236–244.

Zuckerman, M. (1979). *Sensation seeking: Beyond the optimal level of arousal.* Hillsdale, NJ: Erlbaum.

Zuckerman, M. (1985). Biological foundations of the sensation-seeking temperament. In J. Strelau, F. H. Farley, & A. Gale (Eds.), *The biological bases of personality and behavior. Vol. 1. Theories, measurement techniques, and development.* Washington, DC: Hemisphere.

Zuckerman, M. (1991). *The psychobiology of personality.* New York, NY: Cambridge University Press.

Zuckerman, M. (1992). What is a basic factor and which factors are basic? Turtles all the way down. *Personality and Individual Differences, 13,* 675–681.

Zuckerman, M. (1993). P-impulsive sensation seeking and its behavioral, psychophysiological and biochemical correlates. *Neuropsychobiology, 28,* 30–36.

Zuckerman, M. (1994). *Behavioral expression and biosocial bases of sensation seeking.* New York, NY: Cambridge University Press.

Zuckerman, M. (1995). Good and bad humors: Biochemical bases of personality and its disorders. *Psychological Science, 6,* 325–332.

Zuckerman, M. (1996). The psychobiological model for impulsive unsocialized sensation seeking: A comparative approach. *Neuropsychobiology, 34,* 125–129.

Zuckerman, M. (2005). *Psychobiology of personality.* New York, NY: Cambridge University Press.

Zuckerman, M., Kieffer, S. C., & Knee, C. R. (1998). Consequences of self-handicapping: Effects on coping, academic performance, and adjustment. *Journal of Personality and Social Psychology, 74,* 1619–1628.

Zuckerman, M., Kuhlman, D. M., Joireman, J., Teta, P., & Kraft, M. (1993). A comparison of three structural models for personality: The big three, the big five, and the alternative five. *Journal of Personality and Social Psychology, 65,* 757–768.

Zuckerman, M., & Neeb, M. (1980). Demographic influences in sensation seeking and expressions of sensation seeking in religion, smoking, and driving habits. *Personality and Individual Differences, 1,* 197–206.

Zuckerman, M., & Tsai, F. (2005). Costs of self-handicapping. *Journal of Personality, 73,* 411–442.

Zuroff, D. C. (1986). Was Gordon Allport a trait theorist? *Journal of Personality and Social Psychology, 51,* 993–1000.

Zwanzger, P., & Rupprecht, R. (2005). Selective GABAergic treatment for panic? Investigations in experimental panic induction and panic disorder. *Journal of Psychiatry and Neuroscience, 30,* 167–175.